NATURAL LAW AND THE TWO KINGDOMS

EMORY UNIVERSITY STUDIES IN LAW AND RELIGION

John Witte Jr., General Editor

BOOKS IN THE SERIES

Faith and Order: The Reconciliation of Law and Religion
Harold J. Berman

Rediscovering the Natural Law in Reformed Theological Ethics
Stephen J. Grabill

The Ten Commandments in History:
Mosaic Paradigms for a Well-Ordered Society
Paul Grimley Kuntz

Theology of Law and Authority in the English Reformation
Joan Lockwood O'Donovan

Suing for America's Soul: John Whitehead, The Rutherford Institute,
and Conservative Christians in the Courts
R. Jonathan Moore

Political Order and the Plural Structure of Society
James W. Skillen and Rockne M. McCarthy

The Idea of Natural Rights:
Studies on Natural Rights, Natural Law, and Church Law, 1150-1625
Brian Tierney

The Fabric of Hope: An Essay
Glenn Tinder

Religious Human Rights in Global Perspective: Legal Perspectives
Johan D. van der Vyver and John Witte Jr.

Natural Law and the Two Kingdoms:
A Study in the Development of Reformed Social Thought
David VanDrunen

Early New England: A Covenanted Society
David A. Weir

God's Joust, God's Justice
John Witte Jr.

Religious Human Rights in Global Perspective: Religious Perspectives
John Witte Jr. and Johan D. van der Vyver

Natural Law and the Two Kingdoms

*A Study in the Development
of Reformed Social Thought*

David VanDrunen

WILLIAM B. EERDMANS PUBLISHING COMPANY

GRAND RAPIDS, MICHIGAN / CAMBRIDGE, U.K.

Published 2010 by

Wm. B. Eerdmans Publishing Co.

2140 Oak Industrial Drive N.E., Grand Rapids, Michigan 49505 /

P.O. Box 163, Cambridge CB3 9PU U.K.

Printed in the United States of America

15 14 13 12 11 10   7 6 5 4 3 2 1

ISBN 978-0-8028-6443-7

www.eerdmans.com

Contents

Preface   ix

1. Natural Law, the Two Kingdoms, and the
   Untold Story of Reformed Social Thought   1

2. Precursors of the Reformed Tradition   21

3. Reforming Natural Law and the Two Kingdoms:
   John Calvin and His Contemporaries   67

4. Natural Law in Early Reformed Resistance Theory   119

5. The Age of Orthodoxy: Natural Law and the
   Two Kingdoms in Reformed Doctrine and Practice   149

6. Theocratic New England, Disestablished Virginia,
   and the Spirituality of the Church   212

7. An Ambiguous Transition: Abraham Kuyper on
   Natural Law and the Two Kingdoms   276

8. The Christological Critique: The Thought of Karl Barth   316

9. The Kuyperian Legacy (I): Herman Dooyeweerd and
   North American Neo-Calvinism   348

10. The Kuyperian Legacy (II): Cornelius Van Til and
the Van Tillians   386

Conclusion: The Survival and Revival of Reformed
Natural Law and Two Kingdoms Doctrine   423

Bibliography   435

Index   463

Preface

As a law student and then a doctoral student in ethics, I often wished that I could read a book explaining the fate of natural law in my own Reformed theological tradition. As far as I could tell that book did not exist, and I was left to my own resources, with the vague sense that the rhetoric of many recent Reformed theologians did not match that of Reformation and post-Reformation Reformed writers that I was running across. After I finished my studies and got settled in my teaching position I decided to try to write the book that I had wished to read.

When I was a good way through my research, the appearance of Stephen Grabill's *Rediscovering the Natural Law in Reformed Theological Ethics* made an excellent contribution to this area of study. It seemed to me, however, that there was still more of the story to tell. For one thing, Grabill focused upon sixteenth- and seventeenth-century Reformed writers, while I hoped, perhaps too ambitiously, to follow the story into the present. But I was also coming to the conviction that the two kingdoms theme could provide very helpful insight into Reformed thinking on natural law. The fates of natural law and the two kingdoms have been interconnected in the Reformed tradition, and examining these two ideas simultaneously provides a useful window into broader questions about evolving Reformed perspectives on Christianity, culture, and social ethics.

I am very grateful to John Witte for expressing interest in my project while it was still in its early stages and for his encouragement to submit it to the Emory University Studies in Law and Religion. It is a privilege to participate in this fine series, and I thank Amy Wheeler for her kind assistance through the review process and thereafter. My thanks also to the staff at Eerdmans for their support of the Emory series and for guiding my book to publication.

I am profoundly thankful for the whole community at Westminster Seminary California — faculty, students, staff, and board — which has provided such a supportive environment for pursuing this project. Special thanks to colleagues who took time to read and comment on chapters: Bob Godfrey, Mike Horton, Scott Clark, and Elizabeth Park — and especially to Bryan Estelle and John Fesko, not only for reading the whole manuscript but also for the camaraderie and encouragement along the way. Thank you to student assistants Casey Carmichael and Matt Tuininga, who provided valuable help in later stages of the project. I am also grateful to those in other places and institutions who read sections of drafts and offered feedback, including John Bolt, Aaron Denlinger, Richard Gaffin, Ryan Glomsrud, Darryl Hart, Paul Helm, Jody Morris, and Scott Oliphint.

As always, thanks to Katherine and Jack for their love and support. Thinking about our family's circumstances when I began the reading that would lead to this volume, from an extended-stay hotel in Minneapolis, is a reminder of how much we have to be thankful for.

Several sections of this book are modifications and adaptations of previously published journal articles. I would like to thank the editors of these journals for their permission to reuse material found in the following pieces: "Medieval Natural Law and the Reformation: A Comparison of Aquinas and Calvin," *American Catholic Philosophical Quarterly* 80, no. 1 (2006): 77-98; "The Two Kingdoms: A Reassessment of the Transformationist Calvin," *Calvin Theological Journal* 40 (2005): 248-66; "Abraham Kuyper and the Reformed Natural Law and Two Kingdoms Traditions," *Calvin Theological Journal* 42 (2007): 283-307; "The Context of Natural Law: John Calvin's Doctrine of the Two Kingdoms," *Journal of Church and State* 46 (Summer 2004): 503-25; "The Two Kingdoms Doctrine and the Relationship of Church and State in the Early Reformed Tradition," *Journal of Church and State* 49 (Autumn 2007): 743-63; "Natural Law in Early Calvinist Resistance Theory," *Journal of Law and Religion* 21, no. 1 (2005-2006): 143-67; and "The Importance of the Penultimate: Reformed Social Thought and the Contemporary Critiques of the Liberal Society," *Journal of Markets and Morality* 9 (Fall 2006): 219-49.

CHAPTER 1

Natural Law, the Two Kingdoms, and the Untold Story of Reformed Social Thought

Reformed Christianity is widely respected for having a vibrant tradition of social thought. Whether the examples be taken from John Calvin's Geneva, Puritan New England, or Abraham Kuyper in the Netherlands, friend and foe alike often admire Reformed Christianity for inspiring its adherents to think not only about ecclesiastical piety but also about the wide spectrum of political and cultural affairs. Many people, accordingly, have written about the tradition of Reformed social thought from a variety of angles. Yet there are important aspects of this tradition that are largely unknown and frequently overlooked in such studies. The place of the natural law and the two kingdoms doctrines in the development of Reformed social thought is one of these aspects.

For the better part of four centuries Reformed thinkers widely affirmed doctrines of natural law and the two kingdoms and treated them as foundational concepts for their social thought. In affirming natural law they professed belief that God had inscribed his moral law on the heart of every person, such that through the testimony of conscience all human beings have knowledge of their basic moral obligations and, in particular, have a universally accessible standard for the development of civil law. In affirming the two kingdoms doctrine, they portrayed God as ruling all human institutions and activities, but as ruling them in two fundamentally different ways. According to this doctrine, God rules the church (the spiritual kingdom) as redeemer in Jesus Christ and rules the state and all other social institutions (the civil kingdom) as creator and sustainer, and thus these two kingdoms have significantly different ends, functions, and modes of operation. Furthermore, classic Reformed theology interconnected the natural law and two kingdoms doctrines, particularly in looking to natural law as the primary moral standard for life in the civil kingdom. Through these two doctrines, therefore, the older Reformed writers rooted political and cultural life in God's work of creation and providence, not in his work of redemption and eschatological restoration through Jesus Christ.

In the present day, however, at least in North America, most adherents of Reformed Christianity look with suspicion upon or expressly reject the doctrines of natural law and the two kingdoms. And most outside observers of Reformed social thought would not think to identify these two ideas with the Reformed tradition. For many contemporary Reformed people, natural law is at best a sub-theological Roman Catholic idea wedded to Rome's unduly optimistic view of human moral and epistemological capabilities and unduly low view of the importance of Scripture. At worst it is an Enlightenment idea designed to foster social dialogue without reference to religion or apart from God altogether.[1] Contemporary Reformed people also typically dismiss the two kingdoms doctrine as a Lutheran construct that creates an unwarranted dualism between the church and the world, which in turn tends to confine religion to private life and to encourage uncritical conservatism and passivity in public life.[2] In other words, recent Reformed writers have not simply set aside the previously common categories of natural law and the two kingdoms but have rejected them as inherently foreign to Reformed theology. Yet, with some exceptions, they have done so without dem-

1. For an extensive survey of negative Reformed attitudes toward natural law in the past century, see Stephen J. Grabill, *Rediscovering the Natural Law in Reformed Theological Ethics* (Grand Rapids: Eerdmans, 2006), 3-11, 21-53. More briefly, see also Thomas K. Johnson, *Natural Law Ethics: An Evangelical Proposal* (Bonn: Verlag für Kultur und Wissenschaft, 2005), 15-31; and Daniel Westburg, "The Reformed Tradition and Natural Law," in *A Preserving Grace: Protestants, Catholics, and Natural Law*, ed. Michael Cromartie (Grand Rapids: Eerdmans, 1997), 103-4. Though they came into my hands too late to permit me to interact with them in the present volume, two recent books also contain discussion of this matter. See J. Daryl Charles, *Retrieving the Natural Law: A Return to Moral First Things* (Grand Rapids: Eerdmans, 2008); and Craig A. Boyd, *A Shared Morality: A Narrative Defense of Natural Law Ethics* (Grand Rapids: Brazos, 2007).

2. For a couple of recent examples explicitly contrasting the Reformed tradition with the Lutheran two kingdoms tradition, see Mark A. Noll, *America's God: From Jonathan Edwards to Abraham Lincoln* (New York: Oxford University Press, 2002), 33-36; and David M. Smolin, "A House Divided? Anabaptist and Lutheran Perspectives on the Sword," in *Christian Perspectives on Legal Thought*, ed. Michael W. McConnell, Robert F. Cochran, Jr., and Angela C. Carmella (New Haven: Yale University Press, 2001), 374-81. Two relevant books that were published too late to permit me to interact with them in the present volume are D. A. Carson, *Christ & Culture Revisited* (Grand Rapids: Eerdmans, 2008) and John M. Frame, *The Christian Life* (Phillipsburg, NJ: P&R, 2008). Carson treats the two kingdoms doctrine as solely a Lutheran idea and Frame treats it as primarily a Lutheran idea.

onstrating significant acquaintance with how the earlier Reformed tradition actually defended and used these categories.[3] It is this often forgotten story of the place of natural law and the two kingdoms in the Reformed tradition that this book seeks to tell and to interpret.

Before I proceed, a few comments about my use of potentially slippery terms such as "social" and "culture" in this book are appropriate. By "social" or "society" I generally refer to the common life that people live together in their various economic, political, and legal (etc.) relations. By "culture" I generally refer to that vast range of activities that constitute human life, including but not limited to our commercial, scientific, artistic, academic, familial, and recreational endeavors. These terms do not mean the same thing, but they are largely overlapping (though some cultural activities are not strictly social) and sometimes I use them virtually interchangeably. In both cases I use such terms to refer to activities and institutions *outside of the church and other religious bodies.* This is not to say, of course, that religious bodies are not social and do not have their own cultures which may influence and be influenced by the world at large. As will be evident to readers, however, this book is very much concerned with how ecclesiastical society and culture relates to the society and culture of the world more broadly, and hence my use of terms such as "social" and "cultural" in a non-ecclesiastical sense.

Contemporary Reformed Social Thought

A number of writers, from both mainline and smaller, conservative Reformed circles, have offered various alternatives in place of the older natural law and two kingdoms categories. For the introductory purposes of this chapter, I will take one popular perspective among many self-consciously Reformed writers

---

3. One recent writer who has critiqued the historic Reformed two kingdoms doctrine, but as one well acquainted with what it teaches, is an exception who illustrates the rule. David McKay, a minister of the Reformed Presbyterian Church of Ireland, representing a small stream of the Reformed tradition that teaches the doctrine of Jesus Christ's mediatorial kingship over all the nations, has explained that his own church largely does not realize that this doctrine is different from seventeenth-century teaching about the kingship of Christ and the two kingdoms by some of the Reformed theologians it most admires. See David McKay, "From Popery to Principle: Covenanters and the Kingship of Christ," in *The Faith Once Delivered: Essays in Honor of Dr. Wayne Spear*, ed. Anthony T. Selvaggio (Phillipsburg, NJ: P&R, 2007), 135-69; and W. D. J. McKay, *An Ecclesiastical Republic: Church Government in the Writings of George Gillespie* (Carlisle: Paternoster, 1997), ch. 2.

today in North America as representative of a contemporary Reformed approach, namely, the school of thought often referred to as neo-Calvinism. Those taking this perspective continue to commend a high view of God's work of creation and many other themes clearly reflective of historic Reformed theology. But for them the foundation for cultural activity is not so much the creation order as it is being *preserved* as it is God's *redeeming* the creation order and moving it toward its eschatological goal of a new heavens and new earth. A common motif of Reformed neo-Calvinist thought is that of creation-fall-redemption: God created all things, all things fell, and now God is redeeming all things. Rather than two kingdoms, these writers affirm one kingdom of God. This kingdom, encompassing all human activities and institutions, was originally created by God in perfect righteousness (with potentialities that were to be actuated in history), was corrupted through the fall into sin, and is now being redeemed from corruption and advanced toward its eschatological goal. Christians are not to dismiss any area of life as outside of God's redemptive concern, and thus are to seek to transform all activities and institutions in ways that reflect the kingdom of God and its final destiny. Proponents of this vision often attempt to develop biblical models for what a redeemed, transformed society would look like, to construct a Christian account of all of reality through a Reformed world and life view, and to subject non-Christian thought and action to radical critique.[4] Though they may cite Dutch polymaths Abraham Kuyper or Herman Dooyeweerd as more immediate inspiration for their vision, they also hail it as "Reformational" and as drawn from the thought of Calvin in particular. The differences between Calvin and his neo-Calvinist followers today, however, are often striking, yet largely unobserved. For instance, Calvin identified only the church with the redemptive kingdom of Christ and denounced the claim that civil government was a part of Christ's kingdom. But today Reformed intellectuals frequently assert that Christ's kingdom penetrates every legitimate social institution, and ordinary Reformed people found goat-breeding societies on a "Reformed basis" and wrestle with how to develop college football programs in accordance with a Reformed world and life view.[5] Whatever the points of

4. Writers associated with this line of thought who are discussed in Chapter 9 are Henry Stob, Cornelius Plantinga, Albert Wolters, Craig Bartholomew, and Michael Goheen. Most of these were influenced by the writings of Herman Dooyeweerd, who is also often regarded as a neo-Calvinist and whose thought is also explored at some length in Chapter 9.

5. On the Christian goat breeders' society in the Netherlands, see M. Eugene Oosterhaven, *The Spirit of the Reformed Tradition* (Grand Rapids: Eerdmans, 1971), 164, n. 9. On the attempt to build a football program consistent with the "Reformed Christian worldview" of Dordt College

continuity with the earlier tradition, surely some significant things have changed in Reformed social thought.

The larger context within which these theological changes have occurred makes these shifts puzzling in certain ways. The first couple of centuries of Reformed Christianity existed within the confines of Christendom, the long Western project dating back to Constantine and marked by the ideal of a unified Christian society with church and state in close partnership. Though the early Reformed theologians taught the two kingdoms doctrine and advanced natural law as the standard for civil law, they held on to this Christendom ideal and regularly advocated state repression of unorthodox religious practice. The Reformed social thought of the past century, however, has taken place within a context in which only the remnants of Christendom survive after a long process of deterioration. In its place the Western world has almost universally embraced freedom of religion, accepted the idea of a religiously pluralistic civil society, and ended or significantly weakened ecclesiastical establishments, a situation to which most Reformed people, including those of neo-Calvinist persuasion, have given their assent. Yet even as they have given their assent to a tolerant, politically liberal, religiously pluralistic society, they have sought to construct specifically Christian world views, bring Christ's kingdom to expression in every area of life, and level radical critiques of non-Christian thought. In short, earlier Reformed writers affirmed a natural law and two kingdoms perspective, which seems to have offered theological reasons for positing a common social life among all people of whatever religion, yet simultaneously supported religious repression in their Christendom-inspired societies; but recent Reformed writers have affirmed a different perspective, which encourages recognition of the sharp antithesis between Christian and non-Christian thought and the Christianization of all things, even while supporting the free exercise of religion. Certainly the development of Reformed social thought presents some puzzling historical questions.

Reformed Social Thought and Contemporary Christian Discussions

How this puzzling history and current state of affairs came to be may be an interesting enough story as it is. But a couple of other things make it all the

in Sioux Center, Iowa, see Sally Jongsma, "Football Is Coming," *The Voice* 52, no. 4 (Summer 2007): 10.

more intriguing. The first is that in very recent years a fledgling renaissance of interest in the natural law and two kingdoms doctrines has emerged in some Reformed circles. Throughout the twentieth century writers here and there voiced dissent concerning the reigning Reformed paradigm of social thought. In some cases they preserved awareness of older Reformed ideas through historical studies and in others sought to refine older doctrines (sometimes even unwittingly) through their own constructive projects.[6] But a number of books and articles from Reformed sources in the past several years have displayed a self-conscious desire to retrieve and revitalize older patterns of Reformed social thought. In 2006 alone three Reformed writers published books advancing various versions of the natural law and/or two kingdoms doctrines.[7] Even outside of Reformed circles, several competent scholars recently have attempted to recapture similar ideas, at least through the medium of Augustine, whose work is an important precursor to early Reformed social thought.[8]

A second thing that adds interest to the story of Reformed social thought, viewed from the lens of the natural law and two kingdoms doctrines, is its potential to contribute to broader contemporary discussions about Christian participation in cultural and political life. Reformed social thought ought not to be evaluated simply as a parochial affair. Other Christian traditions, particularly Protestant, have often looked to Reformed Christianity as a leader in articulating Christian social thought. Today that reputation for leadership seems rather well-deserved, as many pieces of evidence suggest that ideas animating contemporary Reformed social thought have gained wide acceptance in many Protestant circles, in a number of Christian ecumenical discussions beyond mere Protestantism, and even in

6. Among examples are the following writers noted in the Conclusion: J. Gresham Machen, John T. McNeill, Susan Schreiner, John Bolt, Paul Helm, and Meredith G. Kline.

7. Grabill, *Rediscovering the Natural Law;* Darryl Hart, *A Secular Faith: Why Christianity Favors the Separation of Church and State* (Chicago: Ivan R. Dee, 2006); and David VanDrunen, *A Biblical Case for Natural Law* (Grand Rapids: Acton Institute, 2006).

8. E.g., see Robert A. Markus, *Christianity and the Secular* (Notre Dame: University of Notre Dame Press, 2006), who argues that Christianity has a place for affirming a secular realm that is religiously neutral but not amoral, a sphere of common interest among Christians and others; also Robert P. Kraynak, *Christian Faith and Modern Democracy: God and Politics in the Fallen World* (Notre Dame: University of Notre Dame Press, 2001), who argues that there is no particular social arrangement or political ideology that should be identified with Christianity; and H. Jefferson Powell, "The Earthly Peace of the Liberal Republic," in *Christian Perspectives on Legal Thought,* 73-92, who uses Augustine's thought as a model for developing a Christian critique of modern liberal, secular American society while at the same time being a genuine participant in that society.

central concepts widely favored in the mainstream Western intellectual world. In Protestant circles relatively close to home, one can see the significant influence of twentieth-century Reformed social thought in the calls for cultural transformation and for development of a Christian world and life view in the rhetoric of many historically non-Reformed evangelical colleges. In broader, ecumenical Christian discussions many have advanced the case that religious arguments have an important and even necessary place in the public square.[9] In the mainstream Western intellectual world perhaps furthest from home, the very prevalence of postmodern philosophy, with its insistence that theories are never neutral nor void of worldview-driven assumptions, makes twentieth-century Reformed figures such as Dooyeweerd and Cornelius Van Til, though no postmoderns themselves, look like prophets.

Most profitable for present purposes, however, may be a somewhat lengthier consideration of some influential recent trends and movements in broader, ecumenical Christian thought which seem remarkably friendly, and in some cases perhaps indebted, to the last century of Reformed social thought. The so-called New Perspective on Paul, a major player in contemporary biblical studies, offers a case in point. While scholars associated with this school of thought, such as N. T. Wright, are better known for critiquing historic "Lutheran" (but also Reformed) views of Paul on the doctrine of justification which have allegedly skewed New Testament scholarship for centuries, they have also disputed the historic "Lutheran" (and Reformed) two kingdoms doctrine that has allegedly dichotomized religion and politics and thereby obscured important aspects of Paul's thought.[10] The echoes of many decades of recent Reformed social thought is evident in this latter concern about an unwarranted division between religion and politics, and it is perhaps of little surprise that some contemporary Reformed neo-Calvinists have expressed their own appreciation of and debt to Wright.[11]

Another example comes from the recent revival in interest in the social

9. Most importantly, see Richard John Neuhaus, *The Naked Public Square: Religion and Democracy in America*, 2d ed. (Grand Rapids: Eerdmans, 1986); and more recently, e.g., Brendan Sweetman, *Why Politics Needs Religion: The Place of Religious Arguments in the Public Square* (Downers Grove: InterVarsity, 2006).

10. E.g., see N. T. Wright, *Paul: In Fresh Perspective* (Minneapolis: Fortress, 2005), 49, 60-61. For a critique of a recent foray into politics by Bishop Wright, see Gilbert Meilaender, "Wrong from Wright," *First Things*, no. 170 (February 2007): 9-11.

11. E.g., see Craig G. Bartholomew and Michael W. Goheen, *The Drama of Scripture: Finding Our Place in the Biblical Story* (Grand Rapids: Baker, 2004), 12-13.

tenets of the radical reformation, historically associated with the Anabaptists and Mennonites. The most influential voice here is surely that of Stanley Hauerwas, though himself a Methodist. A perspective grounded in the radical reformation would not ordinarily be associated with a perspective looking to Calvin and the magisterial reformation for inspiration, but they in fact share remarkable similarities. Hauerwas was influenced not only by Mennonite theologian John Howard Yoder but also by the eminent philosopher Alasdair MacIntyre, whose *tour de force, After Virtue,* subjected modern, post-Enlightenment, liberal, secular, value-free Western society to a withering critique. MacIntyre concluded that the autonomous individuals within it share no common story or *telos* and therefore have no resources from which to draw in order to have genuine moral discussions about anything.[12] Not only has Hauerwas picked up on such analysis in condemning the quest for freedom and autonomy in a morally fragmented world scarred by capitalism and materialism, but he has also rejected, as inimical to Christian faith, the idea of a universal ethic or common morality grounded in natural law. Nevertheless, he has called for Christian activism in the world, but in a way peculiar to Christianity. The church, he says, is to live out its existence as a community of faith and hence display to the world how the peaceful kingdom of Christ provides an alternative to a politics built upon violence and falsehood.[13] Hence Hauerwas voices familiar contemporary Reformed themes in rejecting a natural law social ethic, sharply critiquing modern thought and practice, promoting social activism, and calling on Christians to have the ways of the kingdom of Christ shape all of their activity in the church and in the world. Hauerwas has many admirers that have picked up and developed such themes, including those associated with the New Perspective on Paul[14] and scholars in American evangelical circles

12. Alasdair MacIntyre, *After Virtue,* 2d ed. (1981; Notre Dame: University of Notre Dame Press, 1984). Among John Howard Yoder's important works is *The Politics of Jesus: Vicit Agnus Noster* (Grand Rapids: Eerdmans, 1972).

13. Among his influential works, see, e.g., Stanley Hauerwas, *The Peaceable Kingdom: A Primer in Christian Ethics* (Notre Dame: University of Notre Dame Press, 1983); and Stanley Hauerwas and William H. Willimon, *Resident Aliens: Life in the Christian Colony* (Nashville: Abingdon, 1989). Also see Glen H. Stassen, D. M. Yeager, and John Howard Yoder, *Authentic Transformation: A New Vision of Christ and Culture* (Nashville: Abingdon, 1996) for several essays from a radical reformation perspective that defend and redefine the transformation of culture according to the norms of the kingdom of Christ.

14. E.g., see Richard B. Hays, *The Moral Vision of the New Testament: Community, Cross, New Creation; A Contemporary Introduction to New Testament Ethics* (New York: HarperSanFrancisco, 1996), especially 317-46.

without historic connection to Mennonite theology.[15] The work of Brian McLaren, a chief spokesperson for the so-called emerging church movement, is also similar in many important respects.[16]

A third example of an influential contemporary movement in broader ecumenical Christian discussions that bears significant resemblances to recent Reformed social thought is that of Radical Orthodoxy. The best-known proponent of this school of thought is John Milbank, whose massive *Theology and Social Theory* gave Radical Orthodoxy its initial impetus. Milbank professed common cause with MacIntyre's critique of modern, liberal, secular society, but has also sought to extend his critique even to the ancient Western traditions of virtue, which MacIntyre has viewed favorably. In his *magnum opus*, Milbank sought to expose modern secular society and social theory, which are based on autonomous reason and an atomistic, individualistic view of society, as a Christian heresy parasitic off orthodox theology. He argued that Christian orthodoxy is the only thing able to overcome secular nihilism and he held up a Christian Platonism as the necessary ontological basis for cultural life.[17] Again, the similarities of Milbank and colleagues within Radical Orthodoxy to central neo-Calvinist themes are remarkable. Like many recent Reformed writers, the proponents of Radical Orthodoxy have developed radical critiques of non-Christian thought in all sorts of different fields and have sought to give a thick, Christian account of all of reality. And they too have a strong presuppositional bent, denying that either Christian orthodoxy or modern secularism is more rationally justifiable than the other, there being no neutral, universal human reason upon which both could be judged.[18] Again, it is not surpris-

---

15. E.g., see Craig A. Carter, *Rethinking Christ and Culture: A Post-Christendom Perspective* (Grand Rapids: Brazos, 2006); and Gregory A. Boyd, *The Myth of a Christian Nation* (Grand Rapids: Zondervan, 2005).

16. For his recent views on the kingdom of God and Christian social activism, see, e.g., Brian D. McLaren, *Everything Must Change: Jesus, Global Crises, and a Revolution of Hope* (Nashville: Thomas Nelson, 2007).

17. John Milbank, *Theology and Social Theory: Beyond Secular Reason* (Oxford: Blackwell, 1990).

18. One area to which a number of proponents of Radical Orthodoxy have applied such analysis is economics; e.g., see Daniel M. Bell, Jr., *Liberation Theology After the End of History: The Refusal to Cease Suffering* (New York: Routledge, 2001); D. Stephen Long, *Divine Economy: Theology and the Market* (New York: Routledge, 2000); Graham Ward, "Radical Orthodoxy and/as Cultural Politics," in *Radical Orthodoxy? — A Catholic Enquiry*, ed. Laurence Paul Hemming (Burlington, VT: Ashgate, 2000), 103-4; and John Milbank, "Socialism of the Gift, Socialism by Grace," *New Blackfriars* 77 (1996): 532-48. An example of Radical Orthodox critique applied to pol-

ing that some writers in neo-Calvinist circles have expressed great appreciation for Radical Orthodoxy.[19]

Several of the most significant schools of thought in broader Christian intellectual discourse, therefore, promulgate perspectives suggesting great affinity with the contemporary project of Reformed social thought. The claim of Reformed Christianity to leadership in the Christian world on such issues therefore has a degree of plausibility and Reformed Christianity seems at least pleasantly situated in the midst of cutting-edge discussions about these important issues. The apparent relevance of contemporary Reformed social thought for these broader discussions, however, deserves some critical scrutiny. I suggest that the considerable comfort that it may feel within these broader discussions may in fact betray significant internal tensions that it experiences just below the surface and challenge it to reckon with its present claims in light of the claims of the earlier Reformed tradition. Pressing this matter in turn opens up the question whether a recovery of the older Reformed natural law and two kingdoms categories may in fact provide the larger Christian community with a more challenging and helpful perspective as well as one with greater integrity with respect to historic Reformed patterns of thought.

Perhaps the best way to pursue this point is by turning to the critique of the violent, coercive state proffered by the retrievers of the radical reformation.[20] As discussed above, those retrieving the radical reformation seem to be on the same page as contemporary Reformed transformationists in making sharp critiques of the modern world and in desiring to bring the witness of the kingdom of Christ into every aspect of social life. But these writers typically press these points more consistently than many recent Reformed writers. For they have observed that Scripture portrays the kingdom of Christ as a non-violent, peaceful kingdom which does not wield the sword.

---

itics is William T. Cavanaugh, *Theopolitical Imagination: Discovering the Liturgy as a Political Act in an Age of Global Consumerism* (New York: T&T Clark, 2002). For an example of a Radical Orthodox study of a theological doctrine (Christology), with the goal of cultural transformation, see Graham Ward, *Christ and Culture* (Oxford: Blackwell, 2005).

19. E.g., see James K. A. Smith, *Introducing Radical Orthodoxy: Mapping a Post-Secular Theology* (Grand Rapids: Baker, 2004). See also John Milbank's Foreword to this volume for his own reflections on Radical Orthodoxy's relation to the Reformed tradition.

20. Many proponents of Radical Orthodoxy have also critiqued the state as an institution based upon violence, often in philosophically sophisticated ways. They have tended to offer practical responses to this reality different from those of the retrievers of the radical reformation, however, and in this introductory chapter I simply use the latter for purposes of comparison.

Therefore Christians, in witnessing for this kingdom and expressing its way of life in all of their activities, ought to pursue non-violent means of acting in the world. In the face of societies filled with violence and of civil governments that use coercion for their own purposes, the Christian's non-violent way of life is powerful testimony. For some of these writers, the violent, sword-bearing state plays some necessary purpose in a sinful world. But most of them reject any Christian participation in the coercive activity of the state, such as assuming combat roles in the military. Even if someone must bear the sword, therefore, such is not the way of Christ's kingdom and Christians should not be the ones to do so. Christians exist as the church and for the world not as a community complementary to the state, but as an alternative to the state.[21]

The writers making such claims seem to have a strong case to make from a biblical perspective. Jesus said that his kingdom is not of this world and instructed his disciples to turn the other cheek. Paul taught that the weapons that Christians wield are not the weapons of this world. These facts indicate that the coercive state, whatever it is, cannot be the kingdom of Christ. To refuse to participate in its coercive activity seems a consistent application of the conviction that Christians are to strive to make all of their work the work of Christ's kingdom.

Yet if this is the case then why have so many contemporary Reformed writers comfortably identified the state as a good part of God's creation, as another area of life subject to redemption, as an arena in which Christians do well to participate? If the coercive power of the sword lies at some level behind all state activity, which indeed it does, then participating in its activities in the name of the kingdom of Christ is to associate this kingdom with the sword. Those reviving the peace traditions of the radical reformation therefore challenge contemporary Reformed social thought to carry through more consistently one of its own most basic premises (the need for Christians to express the way of Christ's kingdom in all of their activities) and join them in a thoroughly non-violent lifestyle. But for Reformed Christians to do so would in fact be no small step in ironing out a minor inconsistency. To do so would constitute a major break with their heritage and a *de facto* admission that Calvin and the magisterial Reformation were mistaken at a fun-

---

21. In addition to many works of Hauerwas, see also articulate expressions of this perspective in Hays, *The Moral Vision*, 317-46; Carter, *Rethinking Christ and Culture;* Boyd, *The Myth of a Christian Nation;* and Glen H. Stassen and David P. Gushee, *Kingdom Ethics: Following Jesus in Contemporary Context* (Downers Grove: InterVarsity, 2003).

damental point of their polemics against the Anabaptists and other representatives of the radical reformation. For if Calvin's most systematic treatment of civil government (written very explicitly against the backdrop of Anabaptist claims) meant to communicate anything at all, it meant to defend the full *legitimacy* of the sword-bearing state, the God-ordained character of the office of civil magistrate, the moral goodness of Christian participation in the institution of the state, and the requirement that Christians submit gratefully to its authority.[22] In the specter of the radical reformation Calvin and his Reformed colleagues (not to mention Lutherans and Roman Catholics) perceived the threat of anarchy and the insolence of spurning that which God had established.

The Reformed neo-Calvinists of the past century have certainly appreciated this part of their tradition, for they have stressed the divinely-ordained character of the state (and many other social institutions), the goodness of Christian participation in the state, and the fundamentally complementary rather than competitive relationship of state and church. But as the preceding comparison with contemporary heirs of the radical reformation has suggested, in retaining this aspect of their tradition alongside the conviction that the work of the state and all other institutions is the work of the kingdom, much contemporary Reformed social thought has encountered a serious difficulty from a biblical perspective: associating the peaceful kingdom of Christ with the sword-wielding state. But it is worth noting here that Calvin and the early Reformed tradition did not encounter this same difficulty, at least at a theoretical, theological level. Because the early Reformed tradition affirmed *two* kingdoms of God, the civil and the spiritual, it could posit the full legitimacy of the coercive state as a God-ordained institution without running afoul of biblical teaching about the peaceful nature of Christ's spiritual kingdom. Whatever practical inconsistencies the earlier Reformed tradition undoubtedly displayed, it could assert both the God-ordained legitimacy of the sword-bearing state (per Romans 13:1-7) and the noncoercive nature of the church whose weapons are not those of this world (per 2 Corinthians 10:3-6).

Here, I suggest, we find how the fledgling renaissance of natural law and two kingdoms thinking among some Reformed writers today may provide a fresh and coherent contribution to wider discussions about Christianity and culture. The historic Reformed natural law and two kingdoms doctrines provide theological categories for affirming some of the most compelling as-

---

22. See John Calvin, *Institutes of the Christian Religion*, 4.20.

pects of the vision of those retrieving the radical reformation. Namely, these historic Reformed doctrines affirm a sharp distinction between the church as the non-violent kingdom of Christ and the sword-bearing, coercive state. Hence, the state is not and cannot be the kingdom of Christ and, as Hauerwas and others have said, the demise of Christendom can be celebrated rather than mourned. Yet, over against those drawing upon the radical reformation, these historic Reformed categories allow one also to affirm the God-ordained legitimacy of the state and the possibility of righteous Christian participation in its work. The state, as an institution of the civil kingdom, is radically different from the redeemed, spiritual kingdom of Christ expressed in the church, but it too is under God's authority and is good and legitimate in itself. And though not operating according to the same governing rules as the church, the state is not at all an amoral institution, thanks to the universal testimony of God-given natural law.

Therefore, the classic Reformed theological paradigm suggests that Christians are citizens of two distinct kingdoms, both of which are ordained of God and under his law, yet exist for different purposes, have different functions, and operate according to different rules. In their capacity as citizens of the spiritual kingdom of Christ, Christians insist upon non-violence and the ways of peace, refusing to bear arms on behalf of his kingdom; in their capacity as citizens of the civil kingdom, they participate as necessary in the coercive work of the state, bearing arms on its behalf when occasion warrants. As citizens of the spiritual kingdom they have no patriotic allegiance to any earthly nation; but as citizens of the civil kingdom a healthy patriotism is certainly possible.[23] As citizens of the spiritual kingdom they can make radical critiques of all theories, practices, and institutions that are not submissive to the redemptive lordship of Christ; but as citizens of the civil kingdom they can acknowledge the significant benefits that the state brings for earthly life, enjoy the amazing products of human culture, and seek common cause with non-Christians on a variety of social projects. As citizens of the spiritual kingdom they submit to the redemptive ethic of

---

23. This seems to be a point of difference with the proposal presented by Stephen H. Webb in *American Providence: A Nation with a Mission* (New York: Continuum, 2004), who offers his own alternative to the likes of Hauerwas. Similarly to what I suggest here from the perspective of natural law and the two kingdoms, Webb advocates a healthy but not unqualified patriotism and the legitimacy of the state as state. Yet Webb's proposal differs from my suggestion in that he explicitly connects people's identity as citizens to their identity as Christians, through his interpretation of how God brings about his kingdom historically through his special providence over the affairs of nations.

Scripture; yet as citizens of the civil kingdom they can engage in genuine moral conversation with those of other faiths through the universally accessible law of nature, without making adherence to Scripture a test for participating in cultural affairs. As citizens of the spiritual kingdom they can view the state and other social institutions as temporal and destined to pass away; but as citizens of the civil kingdom they can have keen interest in promoting the welfare of human society here and now.

This paradigm is certainly not identical at every point to the concrete practice of the early Reformed social ethic, but does represent, I believe, a plausible and coherent application of its basic theological categories. Though it certainly generates difficult questions of its own, it can affirm on the one hand the radical nature of the church and Christians' ability to make radical critiques of the modern world, and on the other hand the full legitimacy of the state and other social institutions without collapsing them into the kingdom of Christ. It suggests that a secular realm can serve great temporal good though it can never be one's ultimate hope. With these credentials, it is a perspective well worth consideration in broader conversations about the relation of Christians to their cultures. At the very least, the Reformed natural law and two kingdoms doctrines represent a perspective worthy of a contemporary defense.

The Task of the Present Study

I hope in the relatively near future to offer a detailed biblical, theological, and ethical defense of the Reformed natural law and two kingdoms doctrines, revised in certain respects and applied to important concrete social issues. Before such a defense is presented, however — by me or someone else — it makes sense that these doctrines long neglected by the heirs of the Reformed tradition undergo a historical examination. Such an examination would do well to explore what exactly these doctrines meant to the earlier tradition, how they related to each other, what role they played in its broader theology and particularly in its social thought, and how consistently they were applied. It might also identify how these doctrines fell out of favor and what exactly has taken their place. This sort of historical study is what the present book undertakes. If successful, it will lay some parameters and give helpful suggestions for those wishing to make a constructive defense of the Reformed natural law and two kingdoms doctrines, but this book itself will not make that defense. I also hope that the material uncovered in this study will prove useful for a range of other people whose constructive purposes may be much different from mine and even unanticipated by me.

My argument in the present volume is that the early Reformed tradition, drawing from and building upon important strands of patristic and medieval theology, developed clear and interconnected categories of natural law and the two kingdoms that played a foundational role in its social thought. In this early tradition, Reformed thinkers grounded social life in God's work of creation and providence, not in his work of redemption, though they often did not apply their theological categories with complete coherence. As ideas about religious liberty took hold in Western society in the late eighteenth century and through the nineteenth century, some significant Reformed theologians continued to use the historic categories and, with some greater degree of coherence than their predecessors, sought to apply them in the context of a free and tolerant society. Finally, in the twentieth century, under the influence of several important though diverse thinkers, Reformed theology largely neglected and often rejected the natural law and two kingdoms doctrines and sought to give a redemptive and eschatological grounding to culture and Christians' participation in it.

This study is, therefore, largely a tracing of the development of two doctrines through the history of a particular theological tradition, with special reference to the relationship of these doctrines to its social thought. This means that there are a great many things that this study is not. It is not a comprehensive examination of Reformed social thought; instead, it examines Reformed social thought through the lens of two particular doctrines, even while recognizing that it could be examined through other lenses as well. Neither is this book a study of natural theology. Natural theology (which concerns knowledge of God's existence and attributes obtained through nature) and natural law (which concerns knowledge of God's moral requirements obtained through nature) are certainly related topics. Stephen Grabill's recent work, *Rediscovering the Natural Law for Reformed Theological Ethics*, explores their connection in the early Reformed tradition in some depth. It is not natural theology but natural law, particularly in its relevance for political and cultural life, that is of interest here. This book is also not a study of the influence of Calvinism on the development of the Western legal and political traditions, though it does deal with issues important for those engaging in such a study.[24] Furthermore, the present book does not offer a

---

24. Hence this volume does not comment upon the famous theories of Max Weber about Calvinism and capitalism, as expressed, e.g., in his *The Protestant Ethic and the Spirit of Capitalism*

thorough study of the philosophical background that influenced Reformed thinkers in their articulation of the natural law and two kingdoms doctrines. Certainly I have tried to be attentive to the intellectual and social contexts within which these doctrines developed, but my focus is upon the doctrines themselves and their practical outworking.

Even without extensive exploration of these interesting and related issues, this study covers a large topic. Some five hundred years and hundreds of writers and thousands of volumes are potentially within its scope. In order to make this project manageable for both author and reader, some significant selection of sources is necessary. First, as already made clear, I have focused my efforts on the *Reformed* tradition. But this designation itself is somewhat vague and it will not be immediately obvious to all readers which writers or movements are properly considered Reformed. Such a difficulty faces everybody hoping to examine any of the various Christian traditions, but the problem may be exacerbated in the case of Protestant traditions consisting of many ecclesiastical denominations which have no common magisterial body with the authority to arbitrate conflicting claims. But unlike some other Protestant traditions, Reformed Christianity is a confessional Christianity — or at least that is how I am taking it. Important documents such as the Heidelberg Catechism and the Westminster Confession of Faith have served as secondary standards for Reformed churches around the world, whether of continental Reformed or British Presbyterian origin. For purposes of giving the term "Reformed" some greater clarity, therefore, I focus in this study largely on figures who were self-consciously committed theologically and ecclesiastically to the historic Reformed creedal standards, in something like their original meaning. Some readers may have lingering reservations about the Reformed identity of certain writers examined in the chapters below, and this attempt to narrow the scope is admittedly less than fully precise. But it will, I hope, help the reader to understand why I have not

---

(1904-1905; London: Allen and Unwin, 1978). Among the many studies of the relationship between Reformed Christianity and the broader Western legal and political traditions, see, e.g., Philip S. Gorski, *The Disciplinary Revolution: Calvinism and the Rise of the State in Early Modern Europe* (Chicago: University of Chicago Press, 2003); Harold J. Berman, *Law and Revolution, II: The Impact of the Protestant Reformations on the Western Legal Tradition* (Cambridge: Belknap/Harvard University Press, 2003), Part II; Philip Benedict, *Christ's Churches Purely Reformed: A Social History of Calvinism* (New Haven: Yale University Press, 2002); Ralph C. Hancock, *Calvin and the Foundation of Modern Politics* (Ithaca: Cornell University Press, 1989); and Quentin Skinner, *The Foundations of Modern Political Thought*, vol. 2, *The Age of Reformation* (Cambridge: Cambridge University Press, 1978).

considered a number of significant theologians who either regard themselves or are regarded by others as working in the Reformed tradition. I
think, for example, of the immensely important Friedrich Schleiermacher
(1768-1834) or, more recently, the theological ethicist James Gustafson. Such
figures indeed show the influence of the Reformed theological tradition, but
they certainly did not stake their theological identities on adherence to historic Reformed confessions.[25]

Among the still large pool of confessionally Reformed writers, my
choice to focus upon certain figures will be obvious and upon others not. I
will offer some reasons for my choice of particular figures along the way, but
in general I have attempted to deal with enough different writers, and from a
variety of Reformed communities, in order to give this study a broad (if not
comprehensive) feel. Yet to keep this study within manageable bounds and
to deal as fairly as possible with the figures who are considered, I have not
dealt with a number of relevant and interesting Reformed thinkers. As the
author, I hope that my choice of figures for consideration will not bring undue criticism, but I do invite competent scholars to take up for themselves
the present topic and extend the examination to relevant writers that I have
passed by.[26] For that matter, I invite others to press further the analysis of
particular figures that I do discuss. Many of them are worthy of more than
the chapter or part of a chapter that I give them. Finally, I acknowledge, as
readers will quickly note, that this study focuses entirely on developments
among Reformed writers in Europe and North America. The great bulk of

25. James M. Gustafson says as much about himself in *Ethics from a Theocentric Perspective*,
vol. 1, *Theology and Ethics* (Chicago: University of Chicago Press, 1981), 163-64: "That I choose to
develop my work out of the Reformed tradition is a matter of religious and theological conviction. That my work takes such revisionist turns that many of the adherents of that tradition will
find the work an inadequate representation, or even a dissembling, of the tradition, stems also
from convictions. . . . One which has not been acknowledged, and which is important, is that I am
a 'Free Church' theologian despite the perils of fragmentation that such a conviction brings; I do
not believe that a theologian ought to be limited by commitments to historic creedal formula-
tions. . . . I shall subsequently indicate a number of points on which I deviate, in some instances
radically, from that [Reformed] tradition."

26. To offer but one example, this study might be fruitfully extended to a number of contemporary scholars writing from various Reformed backgrounds who have presented theological and
legal studies of human rights. Among theologians, see, e.g., J. M. Vorster, *Ethical Perspectives on
Human Rights* (Potchefstroom: Potchefstroom Theological Publications, 2004); and Max L.
Stackhouse, *Creeds, Society, and Human Rights* (Grand Rapids: Eerdmans, 1984). Among legal
scholars, see, e.g., Johan D. van der Vyver, *Seven Lectures on Human Rights* (Cape Town: Juta,
1976); and John Witte, Jr., *The Reformation of Rights: Law, Religion, and Human Rights in Early
Modern Calvinism* (Cambridge: Cambridge University Press, 2007).

Reformed theology has been written in European and North American contexts, of course, though the long Reformed experience in South Africa and more newly-established Reformed communities in Africa and Asia, for example, provide other interesting contexts in which the development of Reformed social thought in relation to natural law and the two kingdoms might be observed. Again, I invite other scholars to take up such projects.

Before providing a brief summary of the subsequent chapters, I might also say a word about the intended audience of this book. The book is primarily theological, but its subject matter is inter-disciplinary and thus I hope that it will reach an inter-disciplinary audience. My own training is in theology, law, and ethics, and I suspect that the pertinence of this study for those fields is rather obvious. But historians, political theorists, and a wide variety of others interested in the much-discussed relationship of Christianity and culture should also find much relevant material here. In writing this book I have kept an inter-disciplinary audience before my mind. I have thus quoted and cited English translations of originally foreign language texts and have attempted to write in as accessible a manner as possible without compromising responsible scholarship or avoiding necessary technical discussions.

The subsequent chapters proceed in a fairly strict chronological order, and readers will best profit by taking them in sequence rather than turning first to their favorite theologian. Chapter 2 considers some important patristic and medieval precursors to the development of Reformed natural law and two kingdoms doctrine. Early Reformed theologians did not invent these ideas, and this chapter reflects on their provenance in figures such as Augustine, Aquinas, Scotus, Ockham, and Luther, among others. Chapter 3 then turns to the origins of the Reformed tradition itself. Without meaning to suggest the untrue notion that he is *the* origin of the Reformed tradition, this chapter focuses primarily, though not exclusively, on Calvin and his interrelated doctrines of natural law and the two kingdoms. Next, Chapter 4 constitutes a sort of case study, examining how some important early Reformed social thinkers, the so-called resistance theorists, utilized natural law in their intellectual wrestling with civil authority and the right of rebellion. Chapter 5 explores the teaching on natural law and the two kingdoms in the development of Reformed orthodoxy in the later sixteenth and seventeenth centuries. Theologians Samuel Rutherford and Francis Turretin and legal/political theorist Johannes Althusius, along with a few others, will come under special scrutiny in this chapter. In general, these initial chapters will conclude that early Reformed theology set forth clear doctrines of natural law and the two kingdoms which were foundational for Reformed social thought, but that these doctrines were not always applied coherently, particularly with regard to the civil magistrate's responsibilities in religious matters.

Chapter 6 marks a significant transition in the book. In turning to the North American Reformed experience, it begins in the same time period in which the previous chapter ends, with John Cotton, an older contemporary of Rutherford and Turretin. Yet after exploring the natural law and two kingdoms doctrines in Cotton as a representative of the Puritan experiment in New England, this chapter turns its attention to the first extended encounter of Reformed Christianity with modern ideas about religious freedom. It examines the American Presbyterians' eventual embrace of the American view of religious liberty in the late eighteenth century and then explores the nineteenth-century American Presbyterian debate over the spirituality of the church and its relation to the two kingdoms doctrine. The encounter of Reformed theology with modern ideas about politics and social life continues to be of concern in Chapter 7. Here attention turns back across the Atlantic to Abraham Kuyper's appropriation of the Reformed tradition in his grand attempt to construct a Christian account of political and cultural life. Chapters 6 and 7 will conclude that significant Reformed theologians in the nineteenth and early twentieth centuries, such as Stuart Robinson and James Henley Thornwell in America and Kuyper in the Netherlands, continued to utilize classic Reformed natural law and two kingdoms categories and developed these categories in some creative ways generally more coherent than their predecessors — though not without some lingering difficulties of their own.

Chapters 8 through 10 explore twentieth-century Reformed thought, which in large part meant the abandonment and even rejection of the natural law and two kingdoms doctrines. Chapter 8 explores the groundbreaking theological project of Karl Barth, who, though seeking to work in the Reformed tradition, self-consciously rejected its older ideas about natural law and the two kingdoms and sought instead to ground his social and cultural thought (along with everything else) on a reworked Christological basis. Chapter 9, then, turns to Herman Dooyeweerd and a number of contemporary North American neo-Calvinists influenced by his thought, all of whom have helped to shape the contours of contemporary Reformed social thought. This chapter concludes that though they are obviously indebted to Kuyper's project, they have dismissed key aspects of Kuyper's thought that rooted him in the earlier natural law and two kingdoms traditions. Instead, they resemble Barth in seeking a redemptively Christological basis for the transformation of social and cultural life (despite very important theological differences that many of them have with Barth). Chapter 10 discusses the thought of Cornelius Van Til and finds it ambiguous in regard to the Reformed natural law and two kingdoms doctrines, such that subsequent projects of those influenced by his thought have gone in significantly different directions with respect to the earlier tradition.

Finally, the Conclusion mentions some twentieth-century and contemporary figures who have kept alive aspects of the Reformed natural law and two kingdoms traditions even while so many Reformed figures looked in other directions. This study then ends by reflecting on the prospects for the future relevance of Reformed natural law and two kingdoms doctrine and by identifying difficult issues that will have to be faced by those wishing to take up their defense for the sake of faithful Christian life in a sinful world.

CHAPTER 2

Precursors of the Reformed Tradition

The doctrines of natural law and the two kingdoms in the Reformed tradition did not spring from nowhere at the time of the Reformation. They were rooted, in different ways, in nearly a millennium and a half of Christian reflection upon the natural knowledge of God's law possessed by every human being and the relation of Christians individually and the church as a corporate body to civil society, and especially to the state. The purpose of this chapter is to set the stage for the specific consideration of Reformed teaching on natural law and the two kingdoms in the chapters that follow. Of course, nothing remotely resembling a comprehensive survey of pre-Reformation teaching is possible here. What might be profitably achieved, however, is the identification of major themes from significant theologians concerning the doctrines of natural law and the two kingdoms (or precursors to these doctrines), themes that had shaped the state of Western theology at the time of the Reformation and impacted the articulation of early Reformed thought.

To achieve this goal, I first examine some of the most significant pre-Reformation teaching on the various twofold visions of the Christian's life in the present world, including the at times complementary and at times competing ideas of two cities, two powers, and two swords. The second main section considers the teaching of Christian theology on natural law in the Middle Ages and the status of this doctrine leading up to the Reformation. Finally, I consider Martin Luther's compelling presentation of the two kingdoms idea and the role of natural law within this two kingdoms scheme.

Pre-Reformation Predecessors of the Two Kingdoms Doctrine

In this first major section, I discuss a series of twofold visions of Christian life in the world developed in patristic and medieval theology. These important visions — Augustine's two cities, the two powers or swords, and William of Ockham's alternative to a prevailing two swords theory of his day — intimately shaped the theological environment in which the Reformers operated. By understanding these visions and their distinctive views of the relationship of the church to the world, we will be better equipped to identify and penetrate the contribution of the Reformation to this perennial question.

Augustine's Two Cities

Certainly the most important of these pre-Reformation twofold visions is the two cities doctrine of Augustine. It remains unmatched in its complexity, grandeur, sweep, and influence. All of the subsequent visions to be examined below derive their inspiration, however tenuously, from Augustine's two cities framework. Augustine identified these two cities as the City of God and the City of Man. The City of God, according to Augustine, is ultimately an eschatological city, the heavenly Jerusalem, comprising all true worshipers of God through history. Yet Christians here on earth constitute the City of God on pilgrimage, sojourning in this world as foreigners on the way to their eternal home. The City of Man, on the other hand, consists of all evildoers, those who have rejected the true God. Augustine describes this city too as ultimately eschatological, doomed to everlasting perdition in hell, but this city also is present on earth in the society of the wicked. Each individual is a member of one city, and one city only. Christians belong to the City of God and unbelievers to the City of Man, and these two cities exist in stark antithesis, marked by two different kinds of love. Augustine loosely identifies the church as the City of God on earth and the civil government as the earthly manifestation of the City of Man. Nevertheless, these institutional identifications are not firm. In fact, the two cities are intermingled in the present age, unbelievers often participating in the life of the church and believers in the life of the broader society. In this dynamic, Christians, though members only of the City of God, may participate in the state and the broader society, seeking a relative, earthly peace in its midst and using its goods for their own ends.

This brief summary of Augustine's two cities doctrine is elucidated below. Before getting there, it is worth noting that several of the important themes that intertwine through his *De Civitate Dei* had already appeared in earlier Christian theology — and that Augustine's great work presented an approach to the Christian's life in the world sharply different from a very prevalent vision of his own day.

One of the important themes of Augustine's two cities doctrine, the stark *antithesis* between Christianity and its opposite, was foreshadowed already in the late first or early second century by the *Didache*, a short but influential document perhaps used as an instruction manual for new converts.[1] The *Didache* sets forth "two ways," of life and death, between which stands an unbridgeable divide: "There are two ways, one of life and one of death; and between the two ways there is a great difference."[2] These two ways are characterized by opposing traits and contrasting lifestyles, and they must remain separate from each other. The way of life is summarized by the command to love God and neighbor, while the way of death is "wicked and thoroughly blasphemous: murders, adulteries, lusts, fornications, thefts, idolatries, magic arts, sorceries, robberies, false witness, hypocrisies, duplicity, deceit, arrogance, malice, stubbornness, greediness, filthy talk, jealousy, audacity, haughtiness, boastfulness."[3] From this perspective, the early Christians viewed themselves as called to live radically different lives from those of their neighbors and to exist in a fundamental antithesis to those who rejected Christianity.

Another theme animating Augustine's *City of God* is one not opposed to the theme of antithesis, but one certainly sounding a quite different note and adding an enormously important nuance to it. This theme might be described as *commonality*, and is perhaps most vividly exemplified in another second-century document, the *Epistle to Diognetus*. This anonymous letter certainly does not stand in contradiction to the *Didache*. It too presumes a

---

1. Among recent discussions of the background and content of the *Didache*, see William Varner, *The Way of the Didache: The First Christian Handbook* (Lanham: University Press of America, 2007); *The Didache: Its Jewish Sources and Its Place in Early Judaism and Christianity*, ed. Huub van de Sandt and David Flusser (Minneapolis: Fortress, 2002); Kurt Niederwimmer, *The Didache* (Minneapolis: Fortress, 1998); *The Didache in Modern Research*, ed. Jonathan A. Draper (Leiden: Brill, 1996); *The Didache in Context: Essays on Its Text, History, and Transmission*, ed. Clayton Jefford (Leiden: Brill, 1995).

2. "The Teaching of the Twelve Apostles, Commonly Called the Didache," in *Early Christian Fathers*, trans. and ed. Cyril C. Richardson (New York: Collier, 1970), 171.

3. "Didache," 171-73.

vast difference between the life of believers and the life of unbelievers. Sounding a heightened note of beleaguerment and suffering at the hands of the world, the *Epistle to Diognetus* describes Christians as being persecuted, condemned, put to death, poor, destitute, dishonored, defamed, reviled, affronted, and punished as evildoers even when doing good. Christians are different from the world in shunning infanticide and marital infidelity.[4] There is antithesis with the world, to be sure. Nevertheless, the Christian's antithetical relationship with the world is tempered by a broad sense of commonality with it. In a remarkable passage early in the letter, the author describes Christians as rightly sharing a host of things with their non-Christian neighbors: "For Christians cannot be distinguished from the rest of the human race by country or language or customs. They do not live in cities of their own; they do not use a peculiar form of speech; they do not follow an eccentric manner of life." He adds shortly thereafter that Christians "follow the customs of the country in clothing and food and other matters of daily living. . . . They have a share in everything as citizens. . . . They marry, like everyone else, and they beget children. . . ." This never means their absorption into the world, for they share these commonalities only as "aliens" and "foreigners" whose "citizenship is in heaven." They obey the established laws of their city, yet never if it means falling into sin, and they distinguish themselves especially by going "far beyond what the laws require."[5]

Augustine's *City of God*, we will see, says much more about these things than does the *Epistle to Diognetus*. Arguably, however, it says nothing fundamentally different. The anonymous author of this early letter writes in the context of a generally hostile culture to which Christians stand in basic antithesis. Yet he states that Christians recognize a broad sphere of life marked by commonality with the world and characterized by things (such as language, clothing, food, and marriage) that are religiously indifferent *per se.* The Christian character of society is certainly not presumed or even imagined as a goal to be achieved. Nevertheless, the author asserts a wide realm of commonness amidst the fundamental hostility between two distinct sets of people, Christians and the rest.[6]

4. "So-called Letter to Diognetus," in *Early Christian Fathers,* 217.

5. "Letter to Diognetus," 216-217.

6. More than eighteen hundred years after its composition, contemporary thinkers still occasionally appeal to this letter as a model for Christian social activity. For example, a prominent Roman Catholic figure such as George Weigel not long ago used the epistle as starting-point for a constructive proposal for contemporary Christian involvement in political life; see "The Church's

The theme of the *Epistle to Diognetus,* adopting and qualifying that of the *Didache,* is therefore characterized by commonality amidst antithesis to a hostile world. Before this theme found embodiment and elaboration in Augustine, a rather different sort of perspective would arise and loom large in the Christian thought of the fourth century. This perspective, following close upon the heels of Emperor Constantine's conversion to Christianity and the toleration and even embrace of the Christian religion by the Roman Empire, left behind the earlier view of the world as a fundamentally hostile place, toward which Christians had to live in basic antithesis. In contrast, this perspective portrayed the Roman Empire as a Christianized entity and, as such, part of the eschatological realization of the kingdom of God in history. Perhaps no better illustration of this perspective is that offered by the eminent fourth-century church historian, Eusebius, in the tenth book of his *Ecclesiastical History.* Eusebius interprets the events of Constantine's conversion and its aftermath as the restoration of the church after long hardship, even as the fulfillment of Old Testament prophecies.[7] In his rather one-sided description of the conflict between Constantine and his co-emperor Licinius, Eusebius makes God Constantine's friend and protector and portrays Licinius as fighting against God by virtue of his struggle against Constantine. Constantine's ultimate victory over Licinius, Eusebius proclaims, was granted as the fruit of piety.[8] Thus comes a shift whose significance seems difficult to overestimate: the fundamentally hostile character of the world assumed in documents such as the *Didache* and the *Epistle to Diognetus* yields to a perspective which sees the world (or at least the Roman Empire) as fundamentally allied to the church and even bringing Christianity to its fullest realization. The posture of hostility and tension — of commonality only amidst antithesis — dissipates before a fundamental friendship between Christians and the world, church and empire.

Political Hopes for the World; or, Diognetus Revisited," in *The Two Cities of God: The Church's Responsibility for the Earthly City,* ed. Carl E. Braaten and Robert W. Jenson (Grand Rapids: Eerdmans, 1997), 59-77. From a different perspective, neo-Calvinist philosopher Nicholas Wolterstorff also appeals to this epistle as a guide for a contemporary Christian approach to politics in "Christian Political Reflection: Diognetian or Augustinian," *Princeton Seminary Bulletin* 20, no. 2 (1999): 150-68.

7. Eusebius, *Ecclesiastical History,* trans. Roy J. Deferrari, *The Fathers of the Church,* vol. 29 (New York: Fathers of the Church, 1955), 10.1; see also 10.3-4. Among Old Testament prophecies that he sees fulfilled are Psalm 46:8-9 (Vulgate).

8. Eusebius, *Ecclesiastical History,* 10.8-9. For a comparison of Eusebius's perspective on Christianity and the world with that of Augustine, see, for example, Johannes van Oort, *Jerusalem and Babylon: A Study into Augustine's* City of God *and the Sources of His Doctrine of the Two Cities* (Leiden: Brill, 1991), 154-58.

As many scholars have explored, the younger Augustine shared this basic perspective of Eusebius. But by the time he was writing the *City of God* in the early fifth century, Augustine had abandoned this view and the optimism that it entailed. Rome had suffered serious setbacks and enemies of Christianity had found this new religion at fault for it. Augustine, therefore, was offered concrete circumstances in which to reconsider his earlier positions.[9] In response, Augustine articulated a perspective like that of the *Epistle to Diognetus,* though greatly layered and elaborated. Making general claims such as this about Augustine's work is certainly dangerous. Not only is his work complex, which heightens the temptation to focus upon one aspect of his thought to the exclusion of other relevant and qualifying aspects, but also his historical context is of course significantly different from that of contemporary Western social-cultural life, which makes modern readers susceptible to importing invalid assumptions and implications into Augustine's work.[10] Through the centuries, Christian thinkers have read Augustine in a variety of ways, as a theocrat on one extreme and as a proto-liberal on the other.[11] My own reading seeks to avoid overly simplistic and radicalized interpretations. I believe, however, that a reading of the *City of God* as a whole, and especially of Book 19, surely one of the most discussed and most important sections of the book on issues relevant to the present discussion, suggests what I might call a Diognetian approach to the Christian's role in the broader world.[12]

The first element of the Diognetian perspective that I described above is

9. Already in Book 1 of the *City of God,* Augustine addresses specifically the claims of those who blamed Christianity for Rome's ills. For discussion of Augustine's shift away from a Eusebian sort of perspective, see, e.g., van Oort, *Jerusalem and Babylon,* 154-64; R. A. Markus, *Saeculum: History and Society in the Theology of St. Augustine* (1970; Cambridge: Cambridge University Press, 1988), ch. 2; and Eugene TeSelle, *Living in Two Cities: Augustinian Trajectories in Political Thought* (Scranton: University of Scranton Press, 1998), 19-20. For a comprehensive study of the sources of the two cities view that emerged from this shift, see van Oort, *Jerusalem and Babylon,* ch. 5.

10. Jean Bethke Elshtain offers helpful comments along these lines in *Augustine and the Limits of Politics* (Notre Dame: University of Notre Dame Press, 1995), 23-24.

11. Among surveys of interpretation of the *City of God* through history, see especially Miika Ruokanen, *Theology of Social Life in Augustine's* De civitate Dei (Göttingen: Vandenhoeck & Ruprecht, 1993), Introduction. See also van Oort, *Jerusalem and Babylon,* 123-24.

12. As is evident in what follows, I see much more continuity between the *Epistle to Diognetus* and Augustine than does Wolterstorff in "Christian Political Reflection," who sets these two against each other as offering alternative approaches. As should also be evident later in this chapter, however, I agree generally with Wolterstorff's claim that Augustine lacks a robustly positive view of the state, certainly in comparison with many later theologians, whatever his relationship to the *Epistle to Diognetus.*

that a fundamental hostility and antithesis exists between Christians and unbelievers. Such an antithesis lies at the heart of Augustine's two cities doctrine. For Augustine, the City of God and City of Man lie in basic, eschatological tension with each other. Christians belong to the former and unbelievers to the latter, and there is no overlapping or dual membership. The citizens of the city of God look to the true God as its founder while the "citizens of the earthly city prefer their own gods, not knowing that He is the God of gods. . . ."[13] The two cities are marked by two different kinds of lifestyles, the one "after the flesh" and the other "after the spirit." Thus, though there are many nations on earth, "yet there are no more than two kinds of human society, which we may justly call two cities. . . ."[14] Perhaps most poignantly, Augustine sets the two cities in antithesis by claiming that they are characterized by contrasting loves: "Two cities have been formed by two loves: the earthly by the love of self, even to the contempt of God; the heavenly by the love of God, even to the contempt of self."[15] These two cities are marked not only by this ethical antithesis, but by an antithesis of end. The City of God distinguishes itself from the world and its philosophies by recognizing that life eternal is the supreme good and eternal death the supreme evil.[16] In all of this, Augustine sets forth no middle ground. Each person belongs to one city and to one city only.[17]

As considered below, Augustine attributed some relative good to unbelievers and their relations in the world. Nevertheless, even in the relative good the ultimate futility of their endeavors and their starkly contrasting existence to that of the City of God is manifest. Unbelievers' judicial judgments may maintain an outward peace, but in fact they serve to display the misery of human life, for example, through their frequent condemnation of the innocent. Some wars are justly fought, yet even these are lamentable. Human friendship provides some solace in life, but friendships also provoke misunderstanding and anxiety.[18] Augustine admits that unbelievers long for peace and try to attain it, and even that there is a certain blessedness that accompanies peace in this life. But he says that such a blessedness is misery compared

---

13. Augustine, *City of God*, 11.1. English translations of this work are taken from Saint Augustine, *The City of God*, trans. Markus Dods (New York: The Modern Library, 1950).

14. Augustine, *City of God*, 14.1.

15. Augustine, *City of God*, 14.28.

16. Augustine, *City of God*, 19.4.

17. For a similar interpretation of this antithesis between the two cities, see, e.g., van Oort, *Jerusalem and Babylon*, 92, 115-16.

18. Augustine, *City of God*, 19.6-8.

with the final felicity of God's people. Unbelievers, even in attaining a measure of peace, are still wretched.[19] In a famous passage, Augustine says that Rome and all other nations constitute a people, in the sense that they are bound by common agreement as to their objects of love. Nevertheless, he comments that if Cicero was right in saying that where there is no justice there is no republic, then Rome was never a true republic, because it deserted the true God.[20] Even at its best, then, the earthly city is destitute and shorn of true goodness and hope, in direct contrast to the City of God.

Augustine's perspective is Diognetian not only because of this strong antithesis between the two cities, however. As in the *Epistle to Diognetus*, Augustine asserts a strong measure of commonality between the cities amidst their antithesis. As he explains, the two cities, though eschatologically separate, are in this present world "commingled, and as it were entangled together."[21] Though Augustine certainly associates the City of God with the church, even calling it the City of God on pilgrimage, the church is not identical to the City of God,[22] and in fact there are many unbelievers in its midst. And though he also associates the City of Man with civil society (and especially the Roman Empire), neither are the state or other civil institutions identical to the City of Man. Christians work within them, and a Christian may even rightly serve as emperor. Thus, the sharp antithesis between the cities is not always easy to see in this world, and certainly not institutionally. How to define this area of commingling has not been an easy one for Augustine scholars. Perhaps the most influential proposal in recent years is that of R. A. Markus, who saw in Augustine the positing of the "saeculum." For Markus, Augustine viewed all social institutions as radically ambiguous. He emphasized that the state is the City of Man only in a secondary or derivative sense. Membership in the two cities is mutually incompatible, but membership in either one is compatible with membership in the church or in the

---

19. Augustine, *City of God*, 19.10-13.

20. Augustine, *City of God*, 19.21, 24. For a detailed study of Augustine's use of Cicero here, see Robert Dodaro, *Christ and the Just Society in the Thought of Augustine* (Cambridge: Cambridge University Press, 2004). Augustine's comments here regarding Rome perhaps helpfully illustrate the truth of Eugene TeSelle's claim that he had room for "comparative judgments within the earthly city." See *Living in Two Cities*, 61.

21. Augustine, *City of God*, 11.1; see also 19.26.

22. See, e.g., *City of God*, 19.17, on the church as the City of God on pilgrimage. The claim that the City of God and the church are not identical or interchangeable is contested in the literature. For example, van Oort (*Jerusalem and Babylon*, 127) claims that they are while Ruokanen (*Theology of Social Life*, 88) asserts that they are not.

state.[23] According to Markus, Augustine saw the Roman Empire as hovering between the two cities, in the region where they overlap. Augustine, therefore, defined a secular sphere that gave a new positive focus to Christians' political activity, yet which did not have ultimate significance, as it did in the Platonic tradition.[24] Markus's interpretation has not gone unchallenged. Perhaps it is most vulnerable in portraying the state, in particular the Roman Empire, as a sort of neutral, third city.[25] Augustine, rather, seems to associate the Empire with the earthly city, though not in an absolute way nor in a way that prohibits intermingling with the citizens of the City of God.

However one describes the area in which the two cities intermingle, what does this mean practically for Christians? Augustine explains that though Christians seek eternal blessings by faith, they use, as pilgrims, the advantages of time and earth that do not divert them from God. The earthly city seeks an earthly peace for things beneficial to this life, and the citizens of the heavenly city must make use of this peace while it lasts. "Thus the things necessary for this mortal life are used by both kinds of men and families alike, but each has its own peculiar and widely different aim in using them." In light of this, Augustine offers a number of exhortations that sound distinctly Diognetian in their description of commonality. The heavenly city "makes no scruple to obey the laws of the earthly city, whereby the things necessary for the maintenance of this mortal life are administered; and thus, as this life is common to both cities, so there is a harmony between them in regard to what belong to it." It does not scruple "about diversities in the manners, laws, and institutions whereby earthly peace is secured and maintained. . . ." Yet this commonality can only go so far. There can be no "common laws of religion" between the cities, and thus Christians may accede to the diverse practices of society "so long only as no hindrance to the worship

---

23. Markus, *Saeculum,* ch. 3.

24. Markus, *Saeculum,* 98, 102-4. He has revisited these claims about Augustine and appropriated his insights for contemporary issues in Robert A. Markus, *Christianity and the Secular* (Notre Dame: University of Notre Dame Press, 2006).

25. This is the particular critique of van Oort, *Jerusalem and Babylon,* 139, 151-53. Ruokanen, *Theology of Social Life,* 110-11, offers a view similar to Markus's on this issue. A somewhat distinct interpretation of Augustine on these points is offered in Peter S. Hawkins, "Polemical Counterpoint in *De Civitate Dei,*" *Augustinian Studies* 6 (1975): 97-106. Another prominent critic of Markus (though an appreciative one) is Oliver O'Donovan, who cites as the single weakness of *Saeculum* that he obscures the fact that the earthly city has a common end and not just a common use of goods, meaning that members of the heavenly city are never *bona fide* members of the earthly city; see "Augustine's *City of God* XIX and Western Political Thought," *Dionysius* 11 (Dec 1987): 98.

of the one supreme and true God is thus introduced." Therefore, the heavenly city on pilgrimage "avails itself of the peace of earth, and, so far as it can without injuring faith and godliness, desires and maintains a common agreement among men regarding the acquisition of the necessaries of life, and makes this earthly peace bear upon the peace of heaven."[26] Again echoing the *Epistle to Diognetus*, Augustine writes that those who convert to Christianity must live in conformity to the "commandments of God," but are not called to change "their dress and mode of living, which are no obstacle to religion."[27] In fact, it is in Christians' interest that the City of Man enjoy peace in this life, since during the time of the two cities' commingling they also enjoy the peace of Babylon.[28]

In Augustine, therefore, there is a strong strand of commonality between Christians and the world alongside of the fundamental antithesis dividing them. As will be explored later in this book, this dual emphasis on antithesis and commonality would seem to make room for Christians both to make radical critiques of the world and to develop a theologically-informed social ethics designed for common life in a religiously plural world. It is significant to mention, however, for purposes of later chapters and in order not to leave a distorted impression, that Augustine's promotion of the idea of commonality between the cities did not mean his rejection of the use of civil power against schismatics. Augustine faced a situation that the author of the *Epistle to Diognetus* and other early Christians did not face and perhaps did not concretely contemplate, that of Christians serving as civil magistrates, even as Roman emperors. In this context, he was willing to call for civil action against those separating themselves from the catholic church, such as the North African Christian sect, the Donatists. From the contemporary Western liberal perspective it may be difficult not to see this as a contradiction in his thought. Indeed, some of Augustine's most notable recent interpreters, such as Markus and John Milbank, have taken this view, though they have not always agreed in identifying where exactly the contradiction lies.[29]

---

26. Augustine, *City of God*, 19.17. The pilgrimage theme in Augustine is explored extensively in van Oort, *Jerusalem and Babylon*, 93-163.

27. Augustine, *City of God*, 19.19.

28. Augustine, *City of God*, 19.26. When mentioning "Babylon" here, Augustine refers to Jeremiah 29:7, in which the prophet commands the Israelite exiles to seek the peace of the city in which they lived.

29. Markus speaks of Augustine's assent to religious persecution as something that had tragically survived his later repudiation of the ideas that had justified it, particularly those involving the Christianization of the Roman Empire. Thus a tension in his thought was created. Markus ex-

Others, such as Robert Dodaro, have approached the issue of religious persecution in Augustine not so much as a contradiction in his broader thought as instead a direct implication of aspects of his theology.[30] The final explanation for the relation of Augustine's advocacy of religious persecution with the rest of his thought is not a matter to be pursued further here. In subsequent chapters, I will attempt an explanation for a somewhat similar question in the case of Calvin and Reformed orthodoxy. For now, whether we have here an inconsistency in his thinking (which is possible) or a sensible application of his theology that tends to escape the perception of those steeped in a Western liberal context, a full description of Augustine's combination of antithesis and commonality must include a place for the use of the sword against some who have separated themselves from the catholic church.

In spite of questions that may linger regarding Augustine's call for civil coercion against the Donatists, his basic perspective is not obscure. Over against the background that provoked Eusebius and others to associate the Roman Empire with the breaking in of the eschaton, Augustine returned to a basic Diognetian approach: commonality amidst antithesis. Augustine's vision was, however, a more mature expression of this basic, general way of looking at Christians' relation to their surrounding culture. With the idea of a Christianized society a very real and plausible option before him, as it was not for the author of the *Epistle to Diognetus,* Augustine rejected it anyway.

---

plained that the later Augustine looked at the Christian magistrate as acting not institutionally but individually, not on behalf of the state but of the church. See especially *Saeculum,* ch. 6. John Milbank, on the other hand, critiques Augustine for this consent to Christian use of violence in spite of his assertion of the ontological priority of peace over violence; see *Theology and Social Theory: Beyond Secular Reason* (Oxford: Blackwell, 1990), ch. 12. For comparison of Milbank and Markus on Augustine's advocacy of coercion, see Michael J. Hollerich, "John Milbank, Augustine, and the 'Secular,'" in *History, Apocalypse, and the Secular Imagination: New Essays on Augustine's City of God,* ed. Mark Vessey, Karla Pollmann, and Alan D. Fitzgerald, O.S.A. (Bowling Green: Philosophy Documentation Center, 1999), 312-26.

30. According to Dodaro, Augustine saw the Christian statesman's primary objective as assisting his subjects to love God in the truest way possible, by which the statesman himself loves God and neighbor (there being no greater good he can seek for his neighbor). See *Christ and the Just Society,* 210-11. Robert L. Wilken offers a somewhat theocratic interpretation of Augustine that also seems to eliminate the need to see tension in his thought regarding religious persecution. According to Wilken, Augustine's statement that the City of God does not abolish earthly institutions "provided that" they offer no hindrance to religion means that "the earthly city must honor and venerate the one true God." See "Augustine's City of God Today," in *The Two Cities of God,* 36-40. Wilken, it seems to me, illegitimately turns a negative condition (the state should not hinder true religion) into a positive requirement (the state should promote true religion).

He refused to embrace an idyllic, theocratic, or Christianized view of the world.[31] Christians here on earth are a people on pilgrimage, their citizenship and their hope lying in an everlasting, heavenly city. Civil society (the Roman Empire), roughly associated with the City of Man, is ultimately vain and condemned, but serves limited, yet good, earthly and temporal purposes of which Christians ought to make use. Thus, on a certain level civil society is characterized by things that are religiously indifferent *per se,* though at a more ultimate level — concerning what one loves and what one's supreme good is — there is no commonality at all with the City of God. What is worth keeping in mind, however, in light of discussion below, is that Augustine does not emphasize the legitimate and God-ordained status of civil government as a positive matter.[32]

The Two Swords Doctrines

The two cities idea, clearly, became something of a standard for subsequent Christian reflection on the relation of Christianity to the broader world. Another major paradigm for approaching this issue, and particularly the narrower matter of the relation of church and state, emerged with special importance toward the end of the fifth century. This paradigm may be called generally the "two swords" doctrine. There is no single two swords doctrine, however, as is evident from a comparison of two of its most significant expressions, that of Pope Gelasius I in the 490s and that of Pope Boniface VIII around the year 1300. The doctrine of Gelasius, though certainly not entirely incompatible with Augustine's two cities idea, nevertheless worked with certain assumptions and made certain prescriptions absent in Augustine. The doctrine of Boniface, enunciated at the height of the medieval struggles between the papacy and the European crowns, made at least one major adjustment to Gelasius's two swords model. This adjustment would seem to distinguish the two swords doctrine even further from Augustine's two cities doctrine, and it had significant impact upon later Christian thought, as will be evident in discussion below. I now examine the ideas of Gelasius and Boniface in turn.

---

31. For relevant discussion supporting this claim, see, e.g., O'Donovan, "Augustine's *City of God* XIX," 103-6; Ruokanen, *Theology of Social Life,* 117, 152, 158-59; and van Oort, *Jerusalem and Babylon,* 92.

32. O'Donovan, making a similar point, claims that Augustine had no conception of the state as an institution, but only of the earthly peace as a condition of order; see "Augustine's *City of God* XIX," 99. Also see Ruokanen, *Theology of Social Life,* 137, for related discussion.

Pope Gelasius I set forth the "original 'two swords' doctrine," particularly in his famous letter to Emperor Anastasius in 494.[33] In this letter, Gelasius propounded a clear institutional distinction between the civil and ecclesiastical powers. The world, he claimed, is ruled by two, "the sacred authority of the priesthood and the royal power." For Gelasius, both are from God and have distinct purposes. As Gelasius explained in a treatise two years later, *On the Bond of Anathema,* Christ himself "distinguished between the offices of both powers according to their own proper activities and separate dignities. . . ." This distinction in activities entailed the prohibition of either authority from encroaching upon the work of the other (though clearly Gelasius's primary concern when writing to the emperor was to protect the church's jurisdiction from that of state usurpation). In the later treatise, Gelasius spoke of each having its "appropriate functions." How then did he differentiate these appropriate functions? In the letter to the emperor and the subsequent treatise, he referred to the state's concerns variously as "public order," "mundane matters," and "temporal affairs." The church, on the other hand, was to concern itself with "divine affairs," "heavenly sacraments," "the sacred mysteries," and "attaining eternal life." He explicitly contrasted "spiritual activities" and "secular affairs," which were the exclusive domains of clergy and magistrates respectively. In divine affairs, emperors were to "submit" to bishops, while in "the sphere of public order" bishops were to "obey" the emperors' laws.[34]

This two swords doctrine does not, of course, deal with exactly the same issue as does the two cities model of Augustine. Augustine's two cities are first and foremost eschatological concepts, with present institutional expression in church and empire only a secondary matter. Here, in contrast, Gelasius's two swords doctrine is specifically institutional in its focus. This fact cautions interpreters not to be hasty in setting these two models in opposition to one

33. Thus claims Harold Berman in *Law and Revolution: The Formation of the Western Legal Tradition* (Cambridge: Harvard University Press, 1983), 92. John Witte, Jr. refers to this letter as the "locus classicus for many later theories of a basic separation between pope and emperor, clergy and laity, regnum and sacerdotium." See "Facts and Fictions About the History of Separation of Church and State," *Journal of Church and State* 48 (Winter 2006): 19. For extensive discussion of the pre-Gelasian Christian development of the idea that power on earth is divided between two bodies, the church and monarchy, see Lester L. Field, Jr., *Liberty, Dominion, and the Two Swords: On the Origins of Western Political Theology (180-398)* (Notre Dame: University of Notre Dame Press, 1998).

34. For English translations of the letter to Anastasius and of *On the Bond of Anathema,* see Brian Tierney, *The Crisis of Church & State: 1050-1300* (Englewood Cliffs, NJ: Prentice-Hall, 1964), 13-15.

another, for the "two cities" and the "two swords" had slightly different referents. With this caveat in mind, a few points of comparison may be offered. First, Gelasius's two swords doctrine seems to envision a fundamental harmony and cooperation between church and state that distinguishes it from Augustine's model. For Augustine, Christians could coexist with the world, the church with the Empire. With some exceptions, however (such as the church's calling upon the state to suppress ecclesiastical dissension with the sword in certain circumstances), Augustine portrayed this coexistence as an uneasy cooperation in temporal things and, lying behind this uneasy cooperation, as presupposing a more basic opposition and antithesis between them. Gelasius's doctrine describes no two realms or two peoples, coexisting yet in fundamental antithesis. Instead, he envisions but one body of people, which has two authorities governing them (and each other) in distinct but complementary ways. The Augustinian (and Diognetian) perspective of Christians as pilgrims sojourning through a foreign land is certainly not prominent here. There is no equivalent to the Augustinian idea of a sphere of commonality between Christians and unbelievers, since the place of unbelievers is not explicitly contemplated. Second, Gelasius's model is distinguishable from Augustine's in its granting the state specific institutional legitimacy. Gelasius told the emperor that "the imperial office was conferred on you by divine disposition."[35] In Augustine's writings, the work of the state and its bearing of the physical sword seem always to exist under a cloud of suspicion. Not exactly illegitimate, but not precisely unproblematic either, magistrates do their work as an unfortunate necessity in the present evil age. The very existence of the state bespeaks the tragedy of this *saeculum* for Augustine, a perspective that does not seem to qualify Gelasius's doctrine.

The later two swords doctrine of Boniface VIII sounds at many points similar to that of Gelasius, but has at least one very important modification. Boniface's ideas were certainly not brand new to him, though he gave them famous expression. By the turn of the fourteenth century, what Harold Berman has termed the "Papal Revolution" had been already in place for some two centuries. According to Berman, the Papal Revolution had not only embodied the work of the spiritual sword in a system of canon law for the first time, but had also expanded the range of things entrusted to the jurisdiction of the spiritual sword, including matters of marriage, inheritance, and business ethics.[36] Fur-

---

35. See Tierney, *Crisis of Church & State*, 14.

36. See generally Berman, *Law and Revolution*, and page 521 particularly for a helpful summary of this point.

thermore, Boniface's expression of the two swords doctrine, particularly in his famous bull *Unam Sanctam* of 1302, was forged out of a protracted series of conflicts with French king Philip IV. Clashing with Philip on issues of the relative authority of church and state, such as a king's right to tax and to put on trial the clergy living in his realm, Boniface rearticulated, but also reformulated, the two swords theory.[37]

After beginning with an affirmation of the unity of the "holy, Catholic and apostolic church," outside of which there is no salvation, *Unam Sanctam* proceeds to identify, reminiscent of Gelasius, the existence of "two swords, a spiritual one and a temporal one." In introducing the two swords idea, however, Boniface places them not in the hands of the church and the state respectively, but instead proclaims that both of them belong "in this church and in her power." Both, he says, "are in the power of the church, the material sword and the spiritual." The church, however, has delegated the material sword to the state, though not at all absolutely or irrevocably: "The one is exercised for the church, the other by the church, the one by the hand of the priest, the other by the hand of kings and soldiers, though at the will and sufferance of the priest. One sword ought to be under the other and the temporal authority subject to the spiritual power." Boniface offers several lines of defense for his doctrine, both biblical and metaphysical. From the biblical angle, he appeals first to Luke 22:38, in which the disciples told Christ that they had "two swords." Boniface does not elaborate his interpretation of this verse except to say that this expressed a truth about the church, "since it was the apostles who spoke," and Christ "did not reply that it was too many but enough." The only other biblical support he offers is Matthew 26:52, in which Christ ordered Peter to put his sword back in its sheath, demonstrating that "the temporal sword is in the hands of Peter. . . ." Boniface then turns to a metaphysical rationale, citing the work of (Pseudo) Dionysius. He states: "it is the law of divinity for the lowest to be led to the highest through intermediaries," and thus in the order of the universe "the lowest are ordered by the intermediate and inferiors by superiors." In light of the fact, then, that spiritual power excels earthly power and spiritual things temporal things, the spiritual sword is to rule the temporal sword. Boniface states the practical implications clearly: "Therefore, if the earthly power errs, it shall be judged by the spiritual power, if a lesser spiritual power errs it shall be judged by its superior, but if the supreme spiritual power errs it can be

---

37. For historical background on these conflicts, see Tierney, *Crisis of Church & State*, 172-75, 180-85.

judged only by God. . . ." At the end of the bull, Boniface concludes that resisting the sole supremacy of the church and its spiritual power is akin to Manichaeism, which "imagines that there are two beginnings."[38]

There are, of course, evident similarities between the two swords doctrines of Boniface and Gelasius. Like his predecessor, and unlike Augustine, Boniface's doctrine envisioned no fundamental hostility (nor coexisting commonality) between two realms or peoples. Instead, Boniface envisioned but one body of Christian people, with both temporal and spiritual authorities governing them. But whereas Gelasius described the two swords as entrusted to church and state directly by God, Boniface asserted that Christ entrusted both swords to the church and that the church, then, delegated the temporal sword to the state, with strings attached. Thus, while Gelasius set forth a simple division of jurisdiction in which the emperor answered to the bishop on one side and the bishop to the emperor on the other, Boniface made the church supreme over all things, even if it was not ordinarily to be the direct executor of temporal functions.

The Anti-Papalist Doctrine of Church and State in William of Ockham

The next, and last, important thinker to consider in this larger section is William of Ockham (1280–ca. 1349). Ockham presented a forceful counter-position to the sort of papalist view represented by Boniface VIII. In rejecting the pope's claim to temporal authority, Ockham returned to a perspective on the Christian's life in the world bearing significant similarities to the older views of Gelasius, Augustine, and even the *Epistle to Diognetus,* though not identical to any of them. His renewing of older themes in the face of papalist claims and the reappearance of some of these themes in the Reformation make Ockham an interesting figure to consider in the larger story of Christian theological reflection on life in the world.

Ockham is best known as a nominalist philosopher and theologian, but he spent the last twenty years of his life writing little theology *per se* and much on a variety of political topics. The relationship of his nominalism to his political thought is a disputed issue, and one that I discuss in the next section of this chapter. For now, I explore some of the major lines of Ockham's approach to the Christian's place in the world, and specifically the

---

38. For English translation of *Unam Sanctam,* see Tierney, *Crisis of Church & State,* 188-89.

relationship of church and state, without reference to their possible nominalist underpinnings. What may be noted here, however, are some significant concrete ecclesiastical and political circumstances in which Ockham wrote his political treatises. Ockham, a Franciscan, became involved in political debates through various controversies with the popes in Avignon over the Franciscan vows of poverty and papal authority. In the midst of these controversies he even called the pope a heretic. As a result, he spent the last part of his life living in an exile of sorts, in Munich, under the protection of monarch Louis of Bavaria. Also in exile in Munich at this time, interestingly, was another famous dissident political thinker, Marsilius of Padua. Ockham wrote most of his political writings in Munich and died there, excommunicated.[39] Thus, as Boniface VIII composed his rousing defense of papal authority in the light of his power struggles with Philip of France, so Ockham penned his polemics against such papal claims in the light of his personal conflicts with the popes of his time. Despite his personal stake in these debates, Ockham defended his claims with extensive biblical and theological argumentation, and he sounded themes that would continue to reverberate in the Reformation and beyond.

One of his significant political works, "A Short Discourse on Tyrannical Government," lays out with particular force Ockham's case against the sort of papal power enunciated by Boniface VIII. After defending in Book 1 the very inquiry itself, Ockham turns in Book 2 to address specifically the view "that the pope has fullness of power from Christ in such a way that in matters both temporal and spiritual he can do by right all things not against natural or divine law. . . ."[40] After noting various arguments in favor of such fullness of power, he states: "In my opinion that assertion is not only false, and dangerous to the whole community of the faithful, but even heretical."[41] Throughout Book 2 Ockham provides a wide range of arguments for his

39. For discussion of Ockham's thought in the light of these historical circumstances, see, e.g., Arthur Stephen McGrade, *The Political Thought of William of Ockham: Personal and Institutional Principles* (Cambridge: Cambridge University Press, 1974), ch. 1; as well as Paul Vincent Spade, "Introduction," in *The Cambridge Companion to Ockham,* ed. Paul Vincent Spade (Cambridge: Cambridge University Press, 1999), 1-16; and William J. Courtenay, "The Academic and Intellectual Worlds of Ockham," in *Cambridge Companion to Ockham,* 17-30; and John Kilcullen, "The Political Writings," in *Cambridge Companion to Ockham,* 305-25.

40. Ockham, *A Short Discourse on Tyrannical Government,* 2.1. English translations are taken from William of Ockham, *A Short Discourse on Tyrannical Government,* ed. Arthur Stephen McGrade, trans. John Kilcullen (Cambridge: Cambridge University Press, 1992).

41. Ockham, *Short Discourse,* 2.3.

conclusion, biblical as well as historical. His particular concern is that the pope should not use the power that Christ has given him in "temporal matters" and "secular business."[42] Against the argument that Christ possessed fullness of temporal power, Ockham counters by denying that the pope has power equal to Christ, even in his human nature, and by asserting that Christ, in any case, did not himself possess fullness of power in temporal matters "as passible and mortal man."[43] He adds, "Christ absolutely rejected, not only unjust and tyrannical, but also legitimate and just, secular rule. . . . Secular rulership, in reality and in name, Christ therefore excepted by word and example from the power promised to Peter."[44] On this point, Marsilius expressed similar sentiments, writing: "Christ came into the world to dispose not about carnal or temporal rule or coercive judgment, but about the spiritual or heavenly kingdom; for almost always it was only about this latter that he spoke and preached. . . ."[45]

In Book 3, Ockham turns to consider the claim that there is no true emperor or temporal jurisdiction apart from the pope and the church. As he says, "There are indeed some who say that the Empire is from the pope in such a way that no one can be true emperor unless he has been confirmed or chosen by the pope."[46] To refute this assertion, Ockham gathers arguments from the Old Testament, New Testament, and patristic literature.[47] He explains that "true lordship of temporal things" and "true temporal jurisdiction" exist among unbelievers. In fact, he argues that it is "to the prejudice of all mortals" to deny this. Just as unbelievers are capable of receiving all sorts of material and spiritual gifts from the divine kindness, such as food and drink, courage and beauty, so they "are likewise capable, while their unbelief remains, of receiving lordship of temporal things, temporal jurisdiction, and other worldly rights and honors."[48] Such lordship is "common" to the human race and was brought about by divine law, God having given such power "without intermediary not only to believers but also to unbelievers,"

---

42. Ockham, *Short Discourse*, 2.7.

43. Ockham, *Short Discourse*, 2.22.

44. Ockham, *Short Discourse*, 2.19.

45. See *The Defender of Peace*, vol. 2, *The* Defensor Pacis, trans. Alan Gewirth (New York: Columbia University Press, 1956), 117 (Disc. 2, 4.6). Marsilius also placed Christ and the apostles, and all whom they taught, "in property and in person" under "the coercive jurisdiction of secular rulers. . . ." See *The Defender of Peace*, vol. 2, 114 (Disc. 2, 4.3).

46. Ockham, *Short Discourse*, 3.1.

47. Ockham, *Short Discourse*, 3.2-4.

48. Ockham, *Short Discourse*, 3.5-6.

such that it "obliges everyone, believer and unbeliever alike."[49] Human beings, Ockham explains, were given power to establish judges and rulers over themselves by both divine law and natural law, though it is by human laws that they appoint particular people to these offices.[50] When condemning Pope John XXII on such matters, he states an ascending theory of political authority: the power of making human laws belonged first to the people and then they transferred it to the emperor.[51]

As will be evident in a later chapter, some of the Reformed orthodox theologians were adamant that civil authority was divinely ordained and legitimate even in those places where Christianity had never reached. A similar conviction is clearly evident in this material just surveyed from Book 3 of Ockham's treatise, and he augments his case in Books 4 and 5 by considering a concrete historical issue, the legitimacy of the Roman Empire. Ockham summarizes his basic case at the opening of Book 4: "The Empire existed before the papacy, as is plainly certain from sacred literature, because it existed before the birth of Christ. . . . Further, the Empire existed among unbelievers before it existed among believers, as the Scriptures . . . make clear. . . ."[52] Related to such a position was the conviction that God alone established the Empire, a fact that Ockham sees taught in Romans 13:1 and by many respected figures through the history of the church. And thus, he claims, "in temporal matters the emperor is subject to God alone. . . ."[53] Through much of the rest of Book 4 he harmonizes this claim with the concurrent assertion that the Roman Empire is also from the people.[54] But he is unwilling to grant that the Empire is from the pope in any sense. In Book 5, Ockham continues discussing these issues and particularly seeks to answer arguments used to defend papal origins of the Roman Empire. A few of the ways by which Ockham refutes his opponents are of some interest here in the light of future Protestant hermeneutics. One example is his dismissal of the mystical interpretation of the famous two swords passage, Luke 22:38. Because the idea that these two swords signify the temporal and spiritual powers is not "explicit in any part of Scripture whatever," Ockham argued, this verse cannot be used to prove that the Empire is from the pope or that both temporal and spiritual power belong to the pope.[55] A second

49. Ockham, *Short Discourse*, 3.7-8.

50. Ockham, *Short Discourse*, 3.11.

51. Ockham, *Short Discourse*, 3.14.

52. Ockham, *Short Discourse*, 4.1.

53. Ockham, *Short Discourse*, 4.2.

54. See Ockham, *Short Discourse*, 4.3-9.

55. Ockham, *Short Discourse*, 5.5; see also 5.3-4 for the more general hermeneutical discussion.

example is his denial that submission of monarch to pope can be founded upon the fact that Old Testament priests such as Samuel anointed kings. Ockham rejects such things as "empty and frivolous" and smacking of "manifest heresy." He appeals to the fact that the church "by no means imitates many of the deeds and works of the Old Testament," and he proceeds to claim that the church therefore is "not bound to imitate the deeds and works of the Old Law except on points of morality, to which all Christians are bound; in ceremonial, judicial, and sacramental matters it is not bound, and in some of them imitation is forbidden."[56] In other words, Ockham points to discontinuity alongside continuity when considering the relationship of Old and New Testaments and the consequences for understanding temporal authority.

This important example of Ockham's political thought places him in clear and direct opposition to the version of the two swords doctrine articulated by Boniface VIII. Temporal authority, for Ockham, most emphatically is not entrusted to the pope for qualified delegation to the civil magistrate. Where ought Ockham to be placed, then, in comparison to previous figures examined in this chapter on the various issues under consideration? Certain aspects of Ockham's thought suggest an affinity with Gelasius's earlier two swords doctrine. Ockham shared with Gelasius a belief in the existence of two authorities, temporal and spiritual, that have distinct roles and functions. Like Gelasius, but unlike Boniface, Ockham affirmed that God bestowed the temporal authority directly upon the civil ruler, and not through the mediation and supervision of the pope. Or, to put it more precisely, he described the people as a whole as the recipient of the temporal authority, which they in turn handed over to the rulers of their choosing. Ockham and Gelasius, to be sure, had different purposes in setting forth their respective doctrines about the dual authorities. Gelasius wrote to the emperor and warned him to respect the church's authority in spiritual matters; Ockham wrote about the pope and spurned his claim to authority in temporal matters. Nevertheless, there is much in Ockham's thought that aligns him with the thrust of Gelasius's doctrine.[57] There is also at least one point at which difference might be perceived. Whereas Gelasius's model seems to presume that there is one body of people being governed by both powers, with both powers mutually submitting to each other, Ockham seems less tied to such a

---

56. Ockham, *Short Discourse*, 5.7.

57. Kilcullen interprets Ockham in a similar direction, noting that, in order to define and limit the pope's power, he defended "the older medieval idea that the world is ruled by *two* powers," and cites Gelasius's letter to Emperor Anastasius. See "The Political Writings," 311.

vision. The idea of a Christian empire, even one not entirely controlled by the pope, seems to play no essential role in Ockham's political thought.

It is at this point, then, that Ockham's thought may be compared to Augustine, and even back to the *Epistle to Diognetus*. Augustine set aside the vision of a Christianized empire, though it was certainly a live option for him. Ockham seems to move in the same direction. The material considered above concurs with the conclusions of A. S. McGrade, one of the leading scholars of Ockham's political thought in recent years, who has written of Ockham's desacralization of temporal power, his elimination of the need for its specifically religious basis. Ockham, indeed, denied that Christ's coming transformed either the basis or nature of the imperial power.[58] One matter of striking similarity between Ockham and Augustine (and the author of the *Epistle to Diognetus* before him), and a point that is absent in both the Gelasian and Bonifacian two swords doctrines, is the idea that temporal matters concern things that are *common* to believers and unbelievers. Whatever their ultimate differences, there are a range of things concerning life in the present world that believers and unbelievers must share. For Ockham, as seen above, this clearly includes even political authority. And perhaps here is an issue where a degree of dissimilarity with Augustine emerges as well. While Augustine affirmed a range of temporal things that believers and unbelievers hold in common and a relative good in the power of the physical sword, Ockham more clearly presents the authority of the temporal sword as a positive good, legitimate and God-ordained (even apart from any particular religious commitment of people or ruler).

Ockham, in short, maintained the strong, legitimate, divinely-ordained institutional dualism of Gelasius, while also recalling the principle of commonality between Christians and non-Christians espoused by Augustine

---

58. See especially McGrade, *Political Thought*, 103. McGrade interprets Ockham as a dualist in a unitary age, an opponent of both descending (papalist) and ascending (ala Marsilius of Padua) theories of the origin of political power, both of which sought to subordinate one power (pope or emperor) to the other. Janet Coleman interprets the difference between Marsilius and Ockham similarly in *A History of Political Thought: From the Middle Ages to the Renaissance* (Oxford: Blackwell, 2000), 171. Kilcullen, "Political Writings," 314, also contrasts Ockham with Marsilius, his fellow Bavarian exile, in regard to the latter's view of the papacy as a purely human invention. Though Marsilius clearly shared some of Ockham's cherished convictions on the church's authority as spiritual and not temporal, as noted above, he did espouse a rather democratic ecclesiology. For example, he places the power of excommunication with the "whole body of the faithful" rather than with bishops or priests alone; see *Defender of Peace*, vol. 2, 147-52 (Disc. 2, 6.1-10). He also gave considerable powers over the church to the civil authorities, such as the appointment of people to ecclesiastical office; see, e.g., *Defender of Peace*, vol. 2, 259 (Disc. 2, 17.9).

over against visions of a Christianized empire. How these various themes are played out in the early Reformation will be observed below in the last section of this chapter. Before that, however, I now turn to the question of natural law and reflect upon its status in Christian theology on the eve of the Reformation.

Pre-Reformation Doctrines of Natural Law

In this section I turn to the subject of natural law and explore its place in medieval Christianity. Beginning in the second century is perhaps not as important here as it was in the previous section. No patristic paradigm is as crucial for understanding medieval and Reformation natural law as are paradigms such as the two cities and two swords doctrines, which were developed in the early centuries of the Christian church, for understanding subsequent Christian reflection on temporal authority and civil life. For present purposes it must suffice to focus attention upon perhaps the three most prominent theologians of the high and late Middle Ages, Thomas Aquinas, Duns Scotus, and William of Ockham.

According to some popular ways of analyzing medieval natural law, Thomas (representing the realist or intellectualist tradition) offered the great defense of natural law, Scotus weakened the theological foundations of natural law, and Ockham (representing the larger projects of nominalism and voluntarism) destroyed the theological foundations of natural law and thereby ushered in modernity, marked as it has been by moral relativism, legal positivism, and all sorts of related ills. This section does not at all dispute the fact that these medieval thinkers articulated different theological explanations of natural law. What this section affirms, however, is that natural law was an important concept for all three theologians, whatever its respective underpinnings, and that for Ockham as well as for Thomas natural law served as a basic foundation for civil law and authority. This idea has important ramifications for an understanding of the Reformation and Reformed tradition on natural law, as will be explored later in this book. Though there were different schools or traditions of medieval theology extant during the Reformation, and though early Protestant theologians had various degrees of exposure and sympathy to these different schools, none of these schools opposed natural law or its importance for civil law. This, we will see, helps to explain why the Reformers and their Reformed successors embraced the concept of natural law and seemed to feel no anguish in doing so.

Natural Law in Thomas Aquinas

Thomas Aquinas presented a compelling view of natural law, set in the context of his larger theological and moral thought. Contemporary readers should beware of assuming that Thomas's thought gained immediate recognition and praise in the medieval church or that it represents the pinnacle of medieval theology, the standard from which all subsequent medieval theology is a deflection. Yet his theology as a whole, and certainly his view of natural law as one aspect of it, have enjoyed a disproportionate influence in the seven centuries that have followed. Thomas's natural law theology, therefore, deserves some discussion, in particular as it bears upon issues that would continue to be important in the development of a Reformed view of natural law.[59]

In his *Summa Theologiae,* Thomas defines law in general as "an ordinance of reason for the common good, made by him who has care of the community, and promulgated."[60] He goes on to identify four particular types of law: eternal, natural, human, and divine. His understanding of natural law certainly cannot be well understood except in relation to the other three. Eternal law is "the type of Divine Wisdom, as directing all actions and movements." In defining it as such, Thomas identifies the eternal law with divine reason, by which God governs the whole universe, imprinting principles of proper action upon all creatures.[61] In this way, eternal law, like all law, is not simply the will of a legislator but is grounded in reason; in this case, of God himself.[62]

---

59. The literature on this topic is immense, though among significant secondary works in recent years are: John Finnis, *Aquinas: Moral, Political, and Legal Theory* (Oxford: Oxford University Press, 1998); Pamela M. Hall, *Narrative and the Natural Law: An Interpretation of Thomistic Ethics* (Notre Dame: University of Notre Dame Press, 1994); Anthony J. Lisska, *Aquinas's Theory of Natural Law: An Analytic Reconstruction* (Oxford: Clarendon, 1996); Daniel Mark Nelson, *The Priority of Prudence: Virtue and Natural Law in Thomas Aquinas and the Implications for Modern Ethics* (University Park: Pennsylvania State University Press, 1992); Jean Porter, *Natural and Divine Law: Reclaiming the Tradition for Christian Ethics* (Grand Rapids: Eerdmans, 1999); and Martin Rhonheimer, *Natural Law and Practical Reason: A Thomist View of Moral Autonomy,* trans. Gerald Malsbury (New York: Fordham University Press, 2000). My own description of Thomas's natural law is found in David VanDrunen, *Law and Custom: The Thought of Thomas Aquinas and the Future of the Common Law* (New York: Peter Lang, 2003), ch. 3.

60. *Summa Theologiae,* 1a2ae 90.4. English translations are taken from *Summa Theologica,* trans. Fathers of the English Dominican Province, rev. ed., vols. 1-3 (1920; reprint, Allen, TX: Christian Classics, 1981). Latin quotations are taken from *Summa Theologica,* vol. 2 (Rome: Ex Typographia Senatus, 1886).

61. *Summa Theologiae,* 1a2ae 91.1; 93.1; 93.5.

62. In *Summa Theologiae,* 1a2ae 90.1, ad. 3, Thomas writes: "But in order that the volition of

All creatures partake of the eternal law in a way appropriate to their natures. In regard to irrational creatures, "God imprints *(imprimit)* on the whole of nature the principles of its proper actions."[63] Human beings, as rational creatures, partake in a special way, and at this point natural law enters the picture: "The light of natural reason, whereby we discern what is good and what is evil, which is the function of the natural law, is nothing else than an imprint *(impressio)* on us of the Divine light." He appeals to Romans 2:14 in support of this general idea.[64] Elsewhere Thomas defines "natural law" *(lex naturalis)* as "the rational creature's participation of the eternal law" and by this a person discerns right and wrong according to the light of natural reason.[65] Natural law consists of several self-evident precepts — the first being "good is to be done and pursued, and evil is to be avoided" — upon which other ethical precepts are based. And thus "whatever the practical reason naturally apprehends as man's good (or evil) belongs to the precepts of the natural law as something to be done or avoided."[66] This power of reason to apprehend the precepts of natural law does remain after the fall into sin, but it is worth noting that Thomas believed that sin has had serious consequences on human existence. For example, he states that man "fell under the influence of his sensual impulses" which involves deviation from the "path of reason" or the "law of reason." God punishes human beings for sin by stripping them of original justice and hence their reason is left "bereft of its vigor."[67]

Though the concept of conscience became a significant part of the doctrine of natural law for many later theologians, it did not play a direct role in Thomas's. Thomas understands both synderesis and conscience as belonging to the intellect. Synderesis is a habit which disposes a person to perceive the first practical principles of the natural law. Conscience, an act rather than a habit, proceeds to make moral judgments about particular acts.[68]

The relationship of natural law to human law is of special importance

---

what is commanded may have the nature of law, it needs to be in accord with some rule of reason. And in this sense is to be understood the saying that the will of the sovereign has the force of law; otherwise the sovereign's will would savor of lawlessness rather than of law."

63. *Summa Theologiae*, 1a2ae 93.5.

64. *Summa Theologiae*, 1a2ae 91.2.

65. *Summa Theologiae*, 1a2ae 91.2.

66. *Summa Theologiae*, 1a2ae 94.2.

67. *Summa Theologiae*, 1a2ae 91.6. Reflections on the effects of sin appear in many other places in Thomas's treatment of law. E.g., see *Summa Theologiae*, 1a2ae 93.6; 94.6; 98.6; 99.2 ad.2.

68. E.g., see *Summa Theologiae*, 1a 79.13; 1a2ae 94.1.

to the present study. Human law, which Thomas divides into the law of nations and civil law, is necessary for the tranquility of the state and the virtue
of its people.[69] He understands human law as "particular determinations,
devised by human reason" proceeding to more concrete matters from the
"indemonstrable principles" of the natural law. This derivation of human
law from natural law takes place in different ways, as "conclusions from
premises" (which bear exactly the same force as natural law) and as "determinations" from general considerations (which are more remotely related
to natural law).[70] Though one must exercise care in drawing practical conclusions from the following statement, Thomas did say of human law that
"if at any point it deflects from the law of nature, it is no longer a law but a
perversion of law." This is because the force of a law depends upon its justice. He explains: "Now in human affairs a thing is said to be just, from being right, according to the rule of reason. But the first rule of reason is the
law of nature. . . ."[71]

Significantly, Thomas asserts that that civil law is derived from natural
law in a flexible manner. He explains that the "general principles of the natural law cannot be applied to all men in the same way on account of the great
variety of human affairs: and hence arises the diversity of positive laws
among various people."[72] He also defends the necessity that law be adapted
to place and time. Later, Thomas says that human law should be proportionate to the common good, which is its end, and since the common good consists of many things, human law should itself take account of many things,
such as persons, matters, and times. In addition, since human laws must be
imposed on people in a way fitting to their condition, human law cannot re-
press all vices. But which vices any particular human legal system should re-
press depends in part on the character of the people it governs. Furthermore,
Thomas also explains that laws can be rightly changed on account of
changed circumstances and allows local custom an important role in shaping law.[73] Thomas, therefore, believed that natural law could be expressed in
a variety of ways and expected civil law to take on significantly different
shape in different situations.

A final issue to mention in regard to Thomas is the relationship between
natural law and divine law. Thomas understands divine law, which he di-

---

69. *Summa Theologiae*, 1a2ae 98.1; 99.3.
70. *Summa Theologiae*, 1a2ae 91.3; 95.2.
71. *Summa Theologiae*, 1a2ae 95.2.
72. *Summa Theologiae*, 1a2ae 95.2 ad.3.
73. See *Summa Theologiae*, 1a2ae 95.3; 96.1; 96.2; 97.1; 97.3.

vides into Old Law and New Law, as supernatural revelation.[74] He identifies four reasons for its necessity. First, only divine law can direct human beings to the end of supernatural happiness, whereas natural law directs them simply to ends proportionate to their natural faculties. The second reason is that human judgment alone is very uncertain, particularly on contingent and particular matters. Third, only divine law makes people capable of judging interior movements (in addition to exterior acts). And, finally, since human law can prohibit only some evil deeds, for the sake of the common good, divine law is necessary for prohibiting all evil deeds.[75]

An important issue pertaining to the relationship of natural and divine law in Thomas is the nature and purpose of the law of Moses. A few aspects of his doctrine of the Mosaic law may be mentioned here. First, Thomas adopts a paradigm already common in his day, that of dividing the Mosaic law into moral, ceremonial, and judicial laws.[76] Second, he views the natural law, the moral law, and the Decalogue as basically identical. In doing so, Thomas defends the claim that all of the moral precepts of the Mosaic law belong to the natural law, though he explains that some are immediately recognized by natural reason while others are recognized only after deliberation by the wise. Shortly thereafter, he answers affirmatively the question whether all the moral precepts are reducible to the ten precepts of the Decalogue.[77] This moral law, summarized in the Decalogue, is permanently binding.[78] Third, the purpose of the Mosaic judicial laws was to preserve justice and order among God's Old Testament people, though Thomas denies that it is binding for contemporary civil law. As to its original purpose, Thomas speaks of the judicial law as "the determination of the general precepts of that justice which is to be observed among men" and as that which "directed the relations between man and man."[79] As to its contemporary use, Thomas asserts, in a very clear and nuanced statement, that the judicial laws were annulled at the coming of Christ, yet in a different sense from the ceremonial

---

74. *Summa Theologiae,* 1a2ae 91.4-5.

75. See *Summa Theologiae,* 1a2ae 91.4.

76. *Summa Theologiae,* 1a2ae 99.4. Stephan J. Casselli offers a recent study of Thomas on this topic and sees continuity with the later Reformed tradition; see "The Threefold Division of the Law in the Thought of Aquinas," *Westminster Theological Journal* 61 (Fall 1999): 175-207. Working in the Franciscan tradition, Aquinas's contemporary Bonaventure also adopted this three-fold division; see *Breviloquium,* 5.9.1.

77. *Summa Theologiae,* 1a2ae 100.1; 100.3.

78. *Summa Theologiae,* 1a2ae 100.8.

79. *Summa Theologiae,* 1a2ae 99.4; 104.2.

laws (which were categorically annulled). He explains that a civil ruler could impose Mosaic judicial laws on his kingdom, but not "as though they derived their binding force through being institutions of the Old Law." A ruler could impose these laws, presumably, by reason of their continuing suitability to his own people as understood from the natural law, but "the intention of observing them, as though one were bound by the Law, is prejudicial to the truth of faith: because it would follow that the former state of the people still lasts, and that Christ has not yet come."[80]

Subsequent Medieval Views on Natural Law

Having presented this summary of Thomas Aquinas's theology of natural law, I now turn to consider briefly the fate of natural law in the subsequent centuries of the Middle Ages and, thus, the status of this doctrine at the dawn of the Reformation. In lumping together the whole post-Thomas medieval natural law tradition, I may appear to be falling into the common temptation to view Thomas as the pinnacle of medieval thought and everything else as a deflection from this supreme standard. This is not my intention. Rather, my goal in this subsection, for purposes of the larger argument of the book, is to show that though later medieval theologians often presented views at variance with Thomas's, some of which did indeed bear upon their understandings of natural law, the conviction that natural law in fact existed and was decidedly important for ethics generally and for civil life in particular remained quite constant through the last centuries of the Middle Ages.[81] As a consequence, this conviction was a commonplace of Christian theology at the time of the Reformation.

According to popular renderings, late medieval nominalism and voluntarism made a radical break with Thomas's realism and intellectualism and thereby gave birth to a host of ills of the modern world, such as moral rela-

---

80. *Summa Theologiae*, 1a2ae 104.3.

81. Scotus scholar Allan Wolter also claims that the content of natural law was the same across the medieval theological traditions: "Given the fact that Scotus, in determining what pertains to natural law, continually falls back on what is naturally good for human nature, it is not surprising that for him, as well as for Ockham, who followed him, that the substantive content of the natural law seems to be roughly the same as it was for the generality of the scholastics. It is only in their interpretation of why and how it binds that we discover a significant difference. . . ." See Allan B. Wolter, O.F.M., *Duns Scotus on the Will and Morality* (Washington, D.C.: Catholic University of America Press, 1986), 27.

tivism and legal positivism. By rejecting metaphysical universals (nominalism) and locating law in the will rather than in reason (voluntarism), this new theology and philosophy enervated natural law and thus stripped much subsequent Western thought of a universal foundation for morality and reduced civil law to the arbitrary will of the legislator. As this story is often told, Duns Scotus (1266-1308) was something of a transitional figure, weakening if not entirely breaking with the Thomistic way of thought. Subsequently, William of Ockham's full-fledged nominalism and voluntarism represented a clear rejection of Thomas on natural law and a host of other things. Though it has been effectively challenged of late, variations of this interpretation have circulated for a long time. The great historian of Christian social ethics, Ernst Troeltsch, told a version of this story nearly a century ago,[82] as have subsequent Roman Catholic chroniclers of the development of natural law in Western thought.[83] Eminent medieval scholars,[84] conservative critics of modernity,[85] and even proponents of Radical Orthodoxy[86] have also presented their own distinctive versions of the story.

Since Scotus and Ockham are often portrayed as the two main protagonists, some observations about their views of natural law should at least display their continuing belief in its existence and high regard for its importance for ethics and civil law, despite some undeniable differences with Thomas's theology more broadly. A number of general aspects of Scotus's natural law doctrine display its importance for him and, in fact, a fair degree of continuity with Thomas. Scotus, for example, states quite clearly that the

82. See Ernst Troeltsch, *The Social Teaching of the Christian Churches,* vol. 1, trans. Olive Wyon (New York: Macmillan, 1931), ch. 2.

83. E.g., see Heinrich A. Rommen, *The Natural Law: A Study in Legal and Social History and Philosophy,* trans. Thomas R. Hanley (St. Louis: Herder, 1949), 39-40, 57-58; and Yves Simon, *The Tradition of Natural Law: A Philosopher's Reflections* (1965; reprinted New York: Fordham University Press, 1992).

84. E.g., see Francis Oakley, "Medieval Theories of Natural Law: William of Ockham and the Significance of the Voluntarist Tradition," *Natural Law Forum* 6 (1961): 72-73, 83; Michel Bastit, *Naissance de la loi moderne* (Paris: Presses Universitaires de France, 1990); and the many studies of Michel Villey.

85. E.g., Richard M. Weaver, *Ideas Have Consequences* (Chicago: University of Chicago Press, 1948); and George Weigel, *The Cube and the Cathedral: Europe, America, and Politics Without God* (New York: Basic Books, 2005), 78-86.

86. E.g., see Milbank, *Theology and Social Theory,* 12-17, 302-3, where Duns Scotus is the key transitional figure; also see James K. A. Smith, *Introducing Radical Orthodoxy: Mapping a Postsecular Theology* (Grand Rapids: Baker, 2004), 95-103. It should be noted that natural law is not the category that Radical Orthodoxy tends to find particularly attractive in Aquinas over against Scotus.

moral good of an action consists in its conformity to right reason.[87] Elsewhere, he makes a distinction similar to that of Thomas in saying that things can belong to natural law in two ways, either "as first practical principles known from their terms or as conclusions necessarily entailed by them."[88] In light of such evidence, many contemporary scholars have refuted simplistic dismissals of Scotus as a voluntarist or divine-command ethicist and highlighted the role in ethics that he ascribed to right reason and natural law.[89] As one has commented: "The theory of natural law is the heart of the ethics of John Duns Scotus."[90] Another point of continuity with Thomas is his understanding of synderesis and conscience, both in their roles and in their location in the intellect rather than will.[91]

Scotus is sometimes suspected of breaking crucially from Thomas on a few matters, however. Thomas, as seen above, rooted law ultimately not only in the divine will but especially in God's intellect, in divine reason. Did Scotus, in contrast, root law in the divine will in such a way that what God has commanded is rather arbitrary, that is, that God could have commanded precepts contrary to the natural law had he so willed? There are some differences with Thomas here, but, arguably, they are not as radical as might be suspected. He placed certain bounds on God's freedom, while giving it generally wide scope, and offered a qualified answer to the question of whether the natural law could have been other than what God in fact made it.

Scotus identified two definitions of justice, the rectitude of the will served for its own sake and uprightness toward others. God cannot operate against or beyond the first, but can act contrary to the second, for he can do whatever does not include a contradiction. God's rectitude always inclines him to render to his own goodness what is his due.[92] Thus, God is a debtor

---

87. See Duns Scotus, *Ordinatio* I, dist. 17; for Latin text and English translation, see *Duns Scotus on the Will and Morality*, trans. Allan B. Wolter, O.F.M. (Washington, D.C.: Catholic University of America Press, 1986), 206-7.

88. Duns Scotus, *Ordinatio* III, suppl. dist. 37; *Duns Scotus on the Will and Morality*, 276-77. See also *Ordinatio* IV, dist. 17; *Duns Scotus on the Will and Morality*, 262-63.

89. E.g., see Allan B. Wolter's general introduction in *Duns Scotus on the Will and Morality*, especially 3-5; and Richard Cross, *Duns Scotus* (Oxford: Oxford University Press, 1999), 90-91.

90. Hannes Mohle, "Scotus's Theory of Natural Law," in *The Cambridge Companion to Duns Scotus*, ed. Thomas Williams (Cambridge: Cambridge University Press, 2003), 312.

91. See Duns Scotus, *Ordinatio* II, dist. 39; *Duns Scotus on the Will and Morality*, 198-203. For discussion of Scotus's views of synderesis and conscience in relation to earlier thinkers such as Aquinas and Bonaventure, see Douglas C. Langston, *Conscience and Other Virtues: From Bonaventure to MacIntyre* (University Park: Pennsylvania State University Press, 2001), 53-61.

92. Duns Scotus, *Ordinatio* IV, dist. 46; *Duns Scotus on the Will and Morality*, 240-47.

unqualifiedly only in respect to loving his own goodness. In regard to creatures, he is a debtor in a sense to his own generosity, in light of the fact that he gives creatures what their nature demands. Hence, Scotus explains, God is just in an unqualified sense only in relationship to his first justice, since creatures are willed by the divine will.[93] Related to these ideas is Scotus's understanding of the classic distinction between ordained and absolute power. He writes that there are some general laws, which order things rightly, that are established "beforehand by the divine will and by the divine intellect, as something antecedent to any act of the divine will." Insofar as God acts according to these laws set up previously, he acts according to his ordained power, and insofar as he does things not in accord with, but beyond, these preestablished laws, he acts according to his absolute power.[94]

This plays out concretely in how he describes the relationship between natural law and the Decalogue and the question of whether they could have been otherwise. Scotus, as noted above, explains that things can belong to the natural law in two ways, "as first practical principles known from their terms or as conclusions necessarily entailed by them." He goes on to say, crucially, that "These things belong to the natural law in the strictest sense, and there can be no dispensation in their regard." Hence, what belongs strictly to natural law cannot and could not be otherwise. Do the precepts of the Decalogue belong to natural law in this way, as Thomas basically asserted? Scotus provides a nuanced answer. The precepts of the second table do not, because "they contain no goodness such as is necessarily prescribed for attaining the goodness of the ultimate end, nor in what is forbidden is there such malice as would turn one away necessarily from the last end. . . ." The first two commands of the Decalogue (the first three according to the later Reformed numeration), however, belong to the natural law strictly, as does the third command (regarding the Sabbath) insofar as it commands that some worship be rendered to God but not insofar as it specifies a particular time for it. Nevertheless, Scotus also identifies another way in which things can belong to the natural law, by being "exceedingly in harmony with that law, even though they do not follow necessarily from those first practical principles known from their terms." The precepts of the second table do in fact belong to natural law in this way. Thus, institutions such as private property are not absolute necessities of natural law, but are consonant with it.[95]

93. Duns Scotus, *Ordinatio* IV, dist. 46; *Duns Scotus on the Will and Morality*, 252-55.

94. Duns Scotus, *Ordinatio* I, dist. 44; *Duns Scotus on the Will and Morality*, 256-57.

95. Duns Scotus, *Ordinatio* III, suppl. dist. 44; *Duns Scotus on the Will and Morality*, 268-81.

Scotus offers his own summary of his position on this issue: "First, we deny that all the commandments of the second table pertain strictly to the law of nature; second, we admit that the first two commandments belong strictly to the law of nature; third, there is some doubt about the third commandment of the first table; fourth, we concede that all the commandments fall under the law of nature, speaking broadly."[96] Scotus, therefore, makes a significant attempt to be nuanced and precise in his treatment. He sees natural law itself as immutable and exceptionless, and he associates every one of the precepts of the Decalogue with it, either by necessity or consonance. For Scotus, therefore, there is nothing arbitrary about natural law nor is morality in any genuine sense relative.

One final point to mention in regard to Scotus concerns a matter of particular relevance for the present study, that of the relationship of natural law and civil law. He wrote relatively little on the issue. As Allan Wolters notes, Scotus did not produce a body of political writings nor write a commentary on Aristotle's *Politics*, and hence those looking for political material from him will not find much.[97] One comment by Scotus is worth noting here, however. For a positive law to be just, the legislator must establish it "according to practical right reason," which requires prudence. Furthermore, the legislator must operate with proper authority.[98] These two particular requirements echo two of Thomas's four requirements for what constitutes just law: an ordinance of reason by one with care for the community.

I now turn back to Ockham. As discussed above, Ockham's nominalism and especially his voluntarism have been blamed for the dissolution of natural law theory and the elevation of moral relativism and legal positivism, that is, the idea that law is simply the command of the sovereign. Though Ockham certainly did hold nominalist and voluntarist views[99] (which may or may not be theologically problematic, depending on one's proclivities), he also acknowledged the existence of natural law and ascribed it impor-

---

96. Duns Scotus, *Ordinatio* III, suppl. dist. 44; *Duns Scotus on the Will and Morality*, 280-81. For further discussion of this issue in Scotus, see, e.g., Wolter, *Duns Scotus on the Will and Morality*, 23-24; and Mohle, "Scotus's Theory," 315-16.

97. Wolter, *Duns Scotus on the Will and Morality*, 73-74.

98. Duns Scotus, *Ordinatio* IV, dist. 15, q. 2; *Duns Scotus on the Will and Morality*, 314-15.

99. For general discussion of Ockham's nominalism, see, e.g., Paul Vincent Spade, "Ockham's Nominalist Metaphysics: Some Main Themes," in *Cambridge Companion to Ockham*, 100-117. On the relation of Ockham's nominalism to the thought of Scotus, in a broader discussion of Ockham's ethics, see Rega Wood, *Ockham on the Virtues* (West Lafayette: Purdue University Press, 1997), 12-13.

tance particularly for political life. Whatever the ultimate effects of Ockham's thought on Western civilization, he and later medieval nominalist theologians continued a broad tradition of seeing natural law as foundational for understanding individual and social morality.

Without going into Ockham's thought on morality and law in detail, I note first that much recent scholarship, while not denying his voluntarism, has affirmed the integral role of reason and natural law in it. A wide range of Ockham scholars relate that Ockham viewed God as free and a debtor to no one but his own goodness, with no limits upon his will but the law of contradiction, able to command the opposite of what he has commanded. This means that God could even command us to hate him.[100] It is not that God could command evil, but that what might otherwise be evil would not be evil if he so willed it.[101] Yet Ockham, viewing acts as morally neutral in themselves and intentions as determining the goodness or badness of an act, held to a twofold norm of morality, one subjective or proximate (right reason) and the other objective and ultimate (the will of God).[102] A number of these scholars who have studied Ockham's ethics closely note that he claims repeatedly that conformity to right reason is required for an act to be morally good.[103] Potential contradictions (e.g., right reason indicating that God is worthy of love over against a divine command ordering people to hate him) do not become actual in practice, where in fact right reason and divine commands yield the same results.[104]

Also necessary for a balanced view of Ockham is consideration of recent challenges to the idea, typically advanced by those who demonize him, that his political thought can be deduced from his speculative philosophy and

100. E.g., see Marilyn McCord Adams, "William Ockham: Voluntarist or Naturalist?" in *Studies in Medieval Philosophy,* ed. John F. Wippel (Washington, D.C.: Catholic University of American Press, 1987), 241; Marilyn McCord Adams, "Ockham on Will, Nature, and Morality," in *Cambridge Companion to Ockham,* 263-65; A. S. McGrade, "Natural Law and Moral Omnipotence," in *Cambridge Companion to Ockham,* 279; Lucan Freppert, O.F.M., *The Basis of Morality According to William Ockham* (Chicago: Franciscan Herald Press, 1988), 103-9, 121-25 (Freppert, however, thinks that the idea of God commanding us to hate him is a contradiction in his thought, since elsewhere Ockham teaches the equivalence of love for God and obedience to him).

101. E.g., see McGrade, "Natural Law," 281-82; Freppert, *Basis of Morality,* 112.

102. See especially Freppert, *Basis of Morality,* 13; and also Peter King, "Ockham's Ethical Theory, in *Cambridge Companion to Ockham,* 227-28, 235-37.

103. E.g., see Adams, "William Ockham," 242; Freppert, *Basis of Morality,* 50-51; and Takashi Shogimen, "From Disobedience to Toleration: William of Ockham and the Medieval Discourse on Fraternal Correction," *Journal of Ecclesiastical History* 52 (Oct 2001): 615.

104. See Adams, "Ockham on Will," 265-66.

theology. According to McGrade, for example, the relation of God's will to natural law has little bearing upon Ockham's concrete political thought.[105] Other scholars, such as Brian Tierney and Annabel Brett, contest the claim that his voluntarism effected a major shift in Western legal thought by developing ideas of subjective or natural right.[106] McGrade argues, in fact, that natural law was crucial for Ockham's view of practical politics and that his political thought shows that he believed that right reason should always be followed, and for its own sake.[107] McGrade sees Ockham's rather secular, non-theological view of politics not as a rejection of a Christian anthropology but as based on the fact that God gave few political directions in the New Testament and had left human beings to their own reasonable devices.[108]

Discussing all of these issues in Ockham's philosophical, theological, and political work is not necessary for the particular purposes of the present study. A few examples from the work of Ockham considered in the previous section, however, *A Short Discourse on Tyrannical Government,* give very clear indication of the importance that natural law did indeed play in his political thought. In this sense at least, Ockham carried on a catholic Christian tradition.

One example of Ockham's use of natural law in the *Short Discourse* is his wielding it as a weapon to limit the power of the pope. He calls a "heretical absurdity" the claim that the pope can "universally do all things contrary to divine and natural law in which God can do something by way of dispensation. . . ."[109] Shortly thereafter, he insists that papal power does not exclude either the rights of emperors or "the liberties granted to mortals by God and nature."[110] Later, when offering the first of his two definitions of "natural equity," which is "natural law" or "conformity with right reason," Ockham speaks of it as exceptionless, such that any act of the pope contrary to it is

105. McGrade, *Political Thought,* ch. 1; see also 175-76. See also Arthur Stephen McGrade, "Ockham and the Birth of Individual Rights," in *Authority and Power: Studies on Medieval Laws and Government Presented to Walter Ullmann on His Seventieth Birthday,* ed. Brian Tierney and Peter Linehan (Cambridge: Cambridge University Press, 1980), 149-65.

106. See Brian Tierney, *The Idea of Natural Rights: Studies on Natural Rights, Natural Law and Church Law 1150-1625* (Atlanta: Scholars Press, 1997), ch. 1; and Annabel S. Brett, *Liberty, Right and Nature: Individual Rights in Later Scholastic Thought* (Cambridge: Cambridge University Press, 1997).

107. McGrade, *Political Thought,* ch. 4.

108. McGrade, *Political Thought,* 200-202. See also McGrade, *Political Thought,* 168-69; and McGrade, "Natural Law and Moral Omnipotence," 291-92.

109. Ockham, *Short Discourse,* 2.14.

110. Ockham, *Short Discourse,* 2.17; see also 5.2.

null "by the law itself."[111] Along another line of thought, Ockham appeals to natural law in his discussions of the authority of the people to set up civil leaders over themselves. Just as unbelievers, he writes, are bound by "God's precept and by natural law" to honor their parents, so also they are bound at times to appoint secular rulers over themselves. "By divine and natural law men were given power to set up a judge and ruler with power to coerce those subject to him. . . ."[112] In addition to the role of natural law within these very important elements of Ockham's political thought, he makes passing references to natural law and its authority throughout this work, such as defending claims by appealing to what "natural reason . . . dictates" and claiming that "nature made all men equals and peers. . . ."[113] Also worth noting is that Ockham makes the common threefold distinction between the moral, civil, and ceremonial laws in the law of Moses, making the moral law alone binding and indicating that some of the others are absolutely forbidden to the New Testament Christian.[114]

There were, of course, many other medieval nominalist theologians after Ockham. A number of studies have demonstrated that they continued to affirm natural law, even as immutable, and never intended by their use of the absolute/ordained power distinction to call into question the way in which God works in this world.[115] One question that has emerged in debates about the place of natural law in the Reformation is the influence of the different medieval theological schools on various early Protestant theologians. In some cases, it is easy to identify influences and the impact of one of these schools. In other cases, it is not easy at all, as will be seen in the case of John Calvin in the next chapter. What seems necessary to say, however, as we move into the era of Reformation is that natural law was affirmed and utilized in both Thomistic circles and nominalist circles. Whatever medieval school or schools may have influenced particular Re-

---

111. Ockham, *Short Discourse*, 2.24.

112. Ockham, *Short Discourse*, 3.8, 3.11; see also 4.10.

113. See Ockham, *Short Discourse*, 4.4, 4.9.

114. Ockham, *Short Discourse*, 5.7.

115. See especially Heiko Oberman, *The Harvest of Medieval Theology: Gabriel Biel and Late Medieval Nominalism* (1963; reprint Grand Rapids: Baker, 2000), especially ch. 4; and Francis Oakley, *The Political Thought of Pierre d'Ailly: The Voluntarist Tradition* (New Haven: Yale University Press, 1964), 27-29, ch. 6 (though Oakley exhibits here many of the standard biases against nominalism). More generally on the richness, complexity, and variety of late medieval nominalism, see also William J. Courtenay, "Nominalism and Late Medieval Religion," in *The Pursuit of Holiness*, ed. Charles Trinkhaus and Heiko A. Oberman (Leiden: Brill, 1974), 26-59.

formers, therefore, natural law was part of a common, catholic theological inheritance.

Martin Luther's Doctrines of Natural Law and the Two Kingdoms

Following these brief studies of pre-Reformation Christian thought on issues related to natural law and the two kingdoms, we come now to Martin Luther. Luther had significant things to say about both doctrines and he saw the two as related to one another. In his exposition of these issues, he displayed both continuity and discontinuity with previous Christian articulations and, as explored in following chapters, the Reformed wing of the Reformation followed many of Luther's ideas on natural law and the two kingdoms, while also differing from him at some points. In order to see Luther in the light of previous Christian reflection and also to set the stage for subsequent discussion of Reformed thought, I first discuss Luther's view of the two kingdoms and then turn to his treatment of natural law.

Luther on the Two Kingdoms

Like the figures considered above in regard to the various twofold understandings of the Christian's life in the world, Luther wrote in light of and in response to concrete circumstances. Among the many facets of Luther's complex life, perhaps most significant for understanding the context of his two kingdoms doctrine is the fact that he stood situated at the crossroads of great struggles involving not merely theologians but also civil and ecclesiastical authorities. Hence the political and ecclesiastical milieu in which Luther worked ought to be seen as another chapter in the ongoing and developing saga of the interaction between the temporal and spiritual powers. And certainly he did not sit detached as a disinterested spectator. As Bernhard Lohse notes, the University of Wittenberg was founded by Frederick the Wise and was not a papal university. In fact, as a professor at this institution, Luther was an official of his elector and, as such, bore a particular legal standing. Furthermore, during his time in Wittenberg, when the general shape of his two kingdoms doctrine took something close to its final shape, Luther continually received help from his elector.[116] In this context, it

---

116. Bernhard Lohse, *Martin Luther's Theology: Its Historical and Systematic Development,* trans. and ed. Roy A. Harrisville (Minneapolis: Fortress, 1999), 152, 314.

is perhaps not surprising that he produced a two kingdoms doctrine with a robust view of temporal authority. Yet, Luther defended his position with profound theological reflection and did not hesitate to challenge abuses that he perceived in the conduct of civil magistrates and to set quite sharp bounds to their own authority.

Luther wrote voluminously, but his most well-known and significant articulation of the two kingdoms doctrine is surely his treatise "Temporal Authority," of October 1522. Though there is some dispute in the literature, most scholars agree that the general lines of his doctrine had been formulated by this point and that his subsequent writings on political themes do not evidence any fundamental differences from "Temporal Authority," though he developed and nuanced certain themes in response to new situations.[117] In light of this, it seems fair to focus upon this treatise for the present analysis of Luther on the two kingdoms. Though it is perhaps too much to expect pure systematic consistency from it,[118] it is a remarkable and coherent expression of an approach to the Christian's relation to the broader world that drew on many common ideas of the Christian tradition and yet was certainly as a whole unprecedented.

Early in this treatise, Luther asserts that temporal authority, with its law and sword, exist by God's ordinance. Citing Genesis 4:14-15 and 9:6, he says that they have thus existed since the beginning of the world and have been confirmed by the law of Moses, John the Baptist, and Christ.[119] Luther then divides the human race into two classes, those belonging to the kingdom of

---

117. Among those seeing a relatively mature expression of the two kingdoms doctrine in "Temporal Authority" are Heinrich Bornkamm, *Luther's Doctrine of the Two Kingdoms*, trans. Karl H. Hertz (Philadelphia: Fortress, 1966), 12; William Lazareth, *Christians in Society: Luther, the Bible, and Social Ethics* (Minneapolis: Fortress, 2001), 139; and Lohse, *Martin Luther's Theology*, 153, 157. John Witte, Jr. takes a slightly different view, arguing that by the late 1520s Luther had moved away from his earlier, Augustinian view of the earthly kingdom as the kingdom of the devil and had developed a more positive and nuanced view of it; see *Law and Protestantism: The Legal Teachings of the Lutheran Reformation* (Cambridge: Cambridge University Press, 2002), 92. A helpful general defense of the continuity of Luther's thought across the years on issues such as the two kingdoms, secular authority, and religious freedom is offered by David M. Whitford, "*Cura Religionis* or Two Kingdoms: The Late Luther on Religion and the State in the Lectures on Genesis," *Church History* 73, no. 1 (2004): 41-62. Whitford argues particularly with James Estes, who presents a contrasting view in "The Role of Godly Magistrates in the Church: Melanchthon as Luther's Interpreter and Collaborator," *Church History* 67, no. 3 (1998): 463-84.

118. On this point, note the comments of Lohse, *Martin Luther's Theology*, 154-55.

119. Martin Luther, "Temporal Authority: To What Extent It Should be Obeyed," in *Luther's Works*, vol. 45, ed. Walther I. Brandt (Philadelphia: Muhlenberg, 1962), 85-88.

God (true believers) and those belonging to the kingdom of the world. The former, he explains, need neither law nor sword, but the latter do and are under their authority.[120] In light of this, God has established two governments in order to complement these two kingdoms. The purpose of the spiritual government is for the Holy Spirit to produce righteous Christians under the rule of Christ and the purpose of the temporal government is for restraining the wicked and non-Christians by the temporal sword. The world cannot be ruled in a "Christian and evangelical manner" since most people are not real Christians and a common Christian government is therefore impossible. Thus, Luther states that "one must carefully distinguish between these two governments" and yet affirm the existence of both, one to produce righteousness and the other to secure "external peace and prevent evil deeds." In fact, Luther says, "Christ's government does not extend over all men; Christians are always a minority in the midst of non-Christians."[121]

With these ideas in hand, Luther propounded a novel reading of the Sermon on the Mount's exhortations to shun violence and retaliation. In opposition especially to those who proposed that Christ commanded these things not to all Christians but only as counsel to those who wished to be perfect,[122] Luther urges that these commands apply to all Christians, though only to Christians. Christ commands Christians to refrain from violence because the sword has no place in Christ's kingdom. Non-Christians, on the other hand, are "under another government" and by external constraint are "compelled to keep the peace and do what is good." Christ sanctioned the sword, but he made no use of it and rules by his Spirit alone, the sword serving "no purpose in his kingdom. . . ."[123] Thus, Christians are under a spiritual government that does not bear the sword — hence the commands of the Sermon on the Mount — and non-Christians are under a temporal government that indeed uses the sword to keep order among the wicked. For Luther, the Sermon on the Mount was not intended for some Christians who wished to attain a higher righteousness, but was the norm for all Christians, all of whom are under Christ's spiritual government.

Luther's interpretation of the Sermon on the Mount through the two governments paradigm, however, did not separate Christians entirely from use of the sword or make political life irrelevant to them. He goes on to ex-

120. Luther, "Temporal Authority," 85-88.
121. Luther, "Temporal Authority," 91-92.
122. See Luther's initial introduction to this question and his statement of disagreement with the "sophists in the universities" in "Temporal Authority," 81-83.
123. Luther, "Temporal Authority," 92-93.

plain that though Christians have no use of the law or sword among themselves, they submit to its rule and even do all that they can to help the civil authorities, in order to be of service and benefit to others. In fact, he explains, "If he did not so serve he would be acting not as a Christian but even contrary to love. . . ."[124] This counter-intuitive conclusion leads Luther to encourage Christians to seek out temporal occupations, even those that require using the sword: "If you see that there is a lack of hangmen, constables, judges, lords, or princes, and you find that you are qualified, you should offer your services and seek the position. . . ." Luther reconciles these seemingly contrary injunctions by emphasizing that Christians should never take up these tasks for the purpose of their own vengeance, but only for the safety and peace of their neighbors. And so, when a matter arises concerning themselves, Christians live according to Christ's spiritual government, "gladly turning the other cheek and letting the cloak go with the coat when the matter concerned you and your cause." This, claims Luther, brings harmony to the Christian's life in both kingdoms: "at one and the same time you satisfy God's kingdom inwardly and the kingdom of the world outwardly."[125] Shortly thereafter, Luther announces the final reconciliation of life in the two kingdoms: "No Christian shall wield or invoke the sword for himself and his cause. In behalf of another, however, he may and should wield it and invoke it to restrain wickedness and to defend godliness."[126]

In the second part of this treatise, which he calls the main part, Luther explores how far temporal authority extends, "lest it extend too far and encroach upon God's kingdom and government." Luther's principal claim here is that temporal authority can enact laws only that "extend no further than to life and property and external affairs on earth, for God cannot and will not permit anyone but himself to rule over the soul."[127] In a move quite understandable to inhabitants of contemporary Western society, but nevertheless striking in the light of Augustine's conclusions discussed above and the conclusions of Calvin and the Reformed orthodox theologians discussed below, Luther forbad civil magistrates to exercise coercion in religious matters. "Heresy can never be restrained by force." Rather than the sword, Luther states, "God's word must do the fighting."[128] (Later in his life Luther did ac-

124. Luther, "Temporal Authority," 94.
125. Luther, "Temporal Authority," 95-96.
126. Luther, "Temporal Authority," 103.
127. Luther, "Temporal Authority," 104-5.
128. Luther, "Temporal Authority," 114.

quiesce to civil persecution of some Anabaptists[129] and he assigned care for all external church government to the state, since he considered this a temporal rather than a spiritual concern.)[130]

Where does Luther's doctrine of the two kingdoms and two governments fit within the broader stream of theological reflection on the Christian's relation to the broader world? Perhaps the first thing to note is the very strong Augustinian (and Diognetian) strain expressed in "Temporal Authority," more so than in the later Gelasian and Ockhamist doctrines, to which Luther's thought also bears certain similarities. In particular, Luther's description of the two kingdoms in the opening sections of "Temporal Authority" closely resembles key features of Augustine's two cities. The two kingdoms are inhabited by two distinct peoples, Christians and non-Christians, and, strictly speaking, there is no overlapping membership between them. Reminiscent of Augustine, Luther draws a stark antithesis between these two peoples in their two kingdoms, the one marked by righteousness, the Spirit, and the lack of any need for law and the physical sword and the other marked by wickedness and the dire need for law and the sword if any outward peace is to be maintained. Between the two kingdoms there is not only an absolute eschatological antithesis, the one destined for eternal blessedness and the other for eternal condemnation, but also a striking ethical antithesis, the one governed by the non-coercive love displayed in the Sermon on the Mount and the other ruled by a law of external constraint under threat of the sword.

Yet this antithesis between the kingdoms is not the only feature of Luther's doctrine. His doctrine also resembles the perspectives set forth in Augustine's *City of God* and the *Epistle to Diognetus* in propounding a strong conception of commonness amidst fundamental hostility. As such, Luther's thought also seems to leave room for both radical critique of the world and

---

129. Lohse, *Martin Luther's Theology*, 319, proposes that Luther could not keep strictly to his principles in concrete political life, due to his concern for the maintenance of public order and to the strength of the enduring tradition of suppressing heresy through the temporal sword.

130. Harold Berman claims that Luther completely withdrew the sword from the church, a move that Berman attributes to Luther's way of relating the law-gospel and two kingdoms distinctions: law governs the earthly kingdom and gospel governs the heavenly kingdom. This point is then related to the differences between the early Reformed and Lutheran traditions on the respective jurisdictions of church and state, a point to be noted again in subsequent chapters. See Harold J. Berman, *Law and Revolution, II: The Impact of the Protestant Reformations on the Western Legal Tradition* (Cambridge: Belknap/Harvard University Press, 2003), 40-41, 58. On this matter see also Witte, *Law and Protestantism*, 110.

theologically-informed social ethics designed for common life in a religiously plural world. As he articulates the idea of the two governments that rule these two kingdoms, Luther makes clear that the temporal authority, which executes the legal and coercive government of the earthly kingdom, brings both Christians and non-Christians under its sway. Christians and non-Christians alike can hold civil office and bear the physical sword. Christians and non-Christians alike ought to submit to the civil laws in matters of "life and property and external affairs," to which temporal authority extends. Yet, also echoing the Augustinian and Diognetian perspectives, this commonness has its limits, even within these temporal affairs. Luther, exploring aspects of this issue not clearly discussed by Augustine and the author of the *Epistle to Diognetus,* warned Christians against using the sword for their own benefit or even pursuing coercive civil remedies to protect their own interests. Furthermore, though the temporal authority operates in a realm of commonality between Christians and non-Christians, Luther does not treat it as a morally neutral realm, but gives civil rulers strong exhortations to exercise their sword with justice and within the limits of their authority.

At other points, Luther's doctrine clearly must be distinguished from a straightforward Augustinian two cities doctrine, not so much in contradicting it as in supplementing it with certain significant ideas. To some degree, Luther's adding the nuance of two governments to the two kingdoms template accounts for this constructive development of Augustinian thought.[131] For example, Luther's two governments framework gives the two kingdoms an institutional expression — in church and state — that lurks just below the surface in the *City of God* but is never unambiguously expressed. Furthermore, and connected with this previous point, Luther articulates through the two governments idea a view of temporal authority that is wholly legitimate and divinely-ordained. Whereas Augustine never condemned civil rule as illegitimate, it did exist under a cloud of reservation and suspicion for him. For Luther, on the other hand, the temporal government of the earthly kingdom is truly God's own government, his way of ruling the present affairs of a sinful world, however different from his way of ruling his spiritual kingdom. Finally, Luther's distinction from Augustine may be seen in the genuine dual membership of Christians in the administration of the

---

131. Among commentators exploring this dynamic, Lazareth helpfully notes that Luther's more particular two kingdoms doctrine emulates Augustine's cosmic dualism, while his two governments idea complements this inaugurated eschatology with a dialectical historical corollary. See *Christians in Society,* 110.

two governments. Luther's initial description of the two kingdoms in "Temporal Authority," like Augustine's portrayal of the two cities, made their membership exclusive and non-overlapping, Christians belonging to one and one only, non-Christians to the other and that only. Yet Luther presses beyond Augustine and makes the picture more complex as he adds the two governments to the equation, for in this supplemental paradigm he makes clear that Christians ought heartily to embrace their roles in the civil realm as an unambiguous expression of their Christian love, seeing themselves genuinely as citizens of an earthly domain. Christians in some sense truly have dual citizenship, different as their two homelands are.[132]

In Luther's more explicitly positive view of temporal authority, with its institutional divine legitimacy and its being a forum for the unambiguous expression of Christian love and duty, the Reformer may resemble more closely the post-Augustine theories of Gelasius and Ockham. Both of these men had positive accounts of the divine establishment of the temporal sword and of the goodness of the work of the civil authorities. As discussed in a previous section of this chapter, both of these men moved beyond Augustine in these matters. But neither was Luther simply following a Gelasian or Ockhamist paradigm. In regard to Gelasius, Luther differed from any of the major two swords views particularly in creating a space for commonality between believers and unbelievers. And though Luther's two kingdoms and two governments doctrine resembles Ockham's thought in many significant ways, Luther articulates a twofold ethic for Christians corresponding to life under the two governments — both of whose prongs are rooted in love yet find sharply different expressions — that forges beyond the discussions developed by Ockham or by any of his theological predecessors.[133]

As will be explored in following chapters, the early Reformed tradition embraced a two kingdoms doctrine closely resembling that of Luther, yet also with its own distinctives. Among the issues on which the Reformed spoke with somewhat different accent from Luther are the relationship between the law-gospel distinction and the two kingdoms distinction, the things placed under the jurisdiction of the two kingdoms, and the use of the physical sword for matters of religious concern. Nevertheless, even as Luther

---

132. A number of writers make similar points in regard to Luther's relationship to Augustine's two cities doctrine; e.g., see David C. Steinmetz, *Luther in Context*, 2nd ed. (Grand Rapids: Baker, 2002), 115; Lazareth, *Christians in Society*, 162; Lohse, *Martin Luther's Theology*, 318-20; and Bornkamm, *Luther's Doctrine*, 21-26.

133. For comments on Luther's relation to medieval debates and to Ockham (and Marsilius) in particular, see Lohse, *Martin Luther's Theology*, 317.

continued and developed a line of discussion on Christian life in the broader world that had been ongoing for more than a millennium, so the Reformed would continue and develop it further, though in a way that clearly bore the marks of Luther.

Luther on Natural Law

In this final subsection of the chapter, I now turn to Luther's view of natural law. Though Luther certainly could speak harshly about reason and though some older scholarship was dismissive of the significance of natural law for his theology, a number of more recent writers agree that natural law did in fact have an integral place in his thought, especially in regard to social and political matters, and that on this issue he stood in substantial continuity with much of the medieval tradition.[134] Though there is no space in this overview for a comprehensive examination of such claims, I identify here several key features of Luther's natural law thought which in fact do place him firmly within the broader Christian tradition, though I also note a few aspects that distinguish him from his theological predecessors. As later chapters will explore, Reformed treatment of natural law reflects Luther's doctrine in its many points of continuity and discontinuity with the medieval traditions.

A first feature of Luther's understanding of natural law that places him in continuity with the broader tradition is his affirmation of natural law as the basis for civil law. Luther makes this point in "Temporal Authority." Toward the end of this treatise he addresses a specific question, the restitution of debts. He argues in part that natural law is a higher standard than human civil law, such that one might be in violation of the former even if not of the latter. Hence he counsels that people abide by "love and natural law" and warns that judicial decisions derived from "lawbooks" may be un-

---

134. For some general affirmations about Luther on natural law, see, e.g., Lohse, *Martin Luther's Theology*, 273-74; and Lazareth, *Christians in Society*, 15-16. Among those arguing a strong case for the continuity of Luther's natural law with the medieval traditions despite certain differences, see W. D. J. Cargill Thompson, *The Political Thought of Martin Luther* (Sussex: Harvester Press, 1984), ch. 5; and especially John T. McNeill, "Natural Law in the Thought of Luther," *Church History* 10 (Sept 1941): 211-27, countering the claims of scholars such as August Lang, Karl Holl, and Emil Doumergue. Whitford notes: "Luther uses the phrases, 'natural law,' 'laws of nature,' and 'command of God' 583 times in the American Edition of his works. Their occurrences stretch from the very earliest writings to the very last." See *"Cura Religionis,"* 57.

just.[135] Luther is clearly not advocating the elimination of the judicial system, however, and in fact he concludes shortly thereafter: "we should keep written laws subject to reason, from which they originally welled forth as from the spring of justice."[136] This twin conviction, that civil law should be grounded in natural law and that civil law in fact so often is not, is part of the dynamic that leads many writers to speak helpfully of natural law, for Luther, as providing for a "relative" or "remedial" justice in civil society.[137] It should also be noted, however, that Luther did not view civil government and civil law as wholly a natural phenomenon. For example, he ascribed an important role to God's supernatural appointment of the state and the authority of its laws in the Noahic covenant in Genesis 9.[138]

A second aspect of Luther's natural law thought that places him in continuity with the prior tradition is his pointing to Romans 2:14-15 as biblical basis for the doctrine. He took a natural law interpretation of this text already early in his career, in his 1515 commentary on Romans,[139] and subsequently made references to it in order to demonstrate natural law's existence.[140] Third, Luther placed himself within the prior tradition by perceiving the Decalogue as a summary of the natural law. For example, when commenting on the Decalogue he states that "the natural laws were never so orderly and well written as by Moses" and when appealing to natural law asserts that "the Ten Commandments are a mirror of our life. . . ."[141]

A fourth and final feature of Luther's natural law thought that places him in continuity with prior medieval traditions is his use of natural law to

135. Luther, "Temporal Authority," 127-28.

136. Luther, "Temporal Authority," 129. Many scholars have made similar observations; see, e.g., Lazareth, *Christians in Society,* 152. For a fairly recent argument against the idea that Luther saw natural law as foundational for an orderly society and that natural law was an underlying premise of his political thought, see Harvey Owen Brown, "Martin Luther: A Natural Law Theorist?" in *The Medieval Tradition of Natural Law,* ed. Harold J. Johnson (Kalamazoo: Medieval Institute, 1987), 13-25.

137. E.g., see Steinmetz, *Luther in Context,* 114, 123-24; Lazareth, *Christians in Society,* 146; and McNeill, "Natural Law in the Thought of Luther," 120.

138. E.g., see Luther's discussion (from 1536) in "Lectures on Genesis," in *Luther's Works,* vol. 2, ed. Jaroslav Pelikan (St. Louis: Concordia, 1960), 140-42.

139. See Luther, "Lectures on Romans," in *Luther's Works,* vol. 25, ed. Hilton C. Oswald (St. Louis: Concordia, 1972), 186-87.

140. E.g., see Luther, "Against the Heavenly Prophets in the Matter of Images and Sacraments," in *Luther's Works,* vol. 40, ed. Conrad Bergendoff (Philadelphia: Fortress, 1958), 97.

141. See Luther, "Against the Heavenly Prophets," 98; and "How Christians Should Regard Moses," in *Luther's Works,* vol. 35, ed. E. Theodore Bachmann (Philadelphia: Fortress, 1960), 172-73.

explain the current applicability of the Mosaic law. Luther's basic position is that the law of Moses was given to and binding upon Old Testament Israel alone, and hence that Moses was lawgiver for neither Old Testament Gentiles nor New Testament Christians. Nevertheless, he acknowledges that Christians continue to obey many things that Moses commanded. This is not because Moses is binding *per se,* but because many of the same laws that Moses promulgated are also promulgated to all people through natural law. Natural law, then, becomes an important criterion for the continuing applicability of Mosaic precepts: "We will regard Moses as a teacher, but we will not regard him as our lawgiver — unless he agrees with both the New Testament and the natural law."[142] This is another point of Luther's natural law thought that he came to express quite early in his life.[143] In a later treatment of the issue, Luther states clearly: "To be sure, the Gentiles have certain laws in common with the Jews, such as these: there is one God, no one is to do wrong to another, no one is to commit adultery or murder or steal, and others like them. This is written by nature into their hearts; they did not hear it straight from heaven as the Jews did. This is why this entire text does not pertain to the Gentiles." Later in this same treatise he adds: "What God has given the Jews from heaven, he has also written in the hearts of all men. Thus I keep the commandments which Moses has given, not because Moses gave commandments, but because they have been implanted in me by nature. . . . Now this is the first thing that I ought to see in Moses, namely, the commandments to which I am not bound except insofar as they are [implanted in everyone] by nature [and written in everyone's heart]."[144]

In addition to these features of Luther's natural law thought that place him in continuity with the medieval traditions, there are also several aspects of his theology that serve to distinguish him from his predecessors. I cannot here develop these matters at any length, but they are worth referring to briefly because many similar things will be explored in subsequent chapters concerning the Reformed tradition's relation to medieval natural law. First, Luther sets forth the relationship of natural law and civil law in the context of his distinctive two kingdoms doctrine.[145] Second, Luther's serious cri-

---

142. Luther, "How Christians Should Regard Moses," 165.

143. E.g., see Luther, "Lectures on Romans," 180.

144. Luther, "How Christians Should Regard Moses," 164, 168.

145. This is evident, for example, in his treatise considered above, "Temporal Authority," 127-29. Among scholars seeing natural law as particularly important for the earthly kingdom in Luther, see Steinmetz, *Luther in Context,* 114, 123-24; Thompson, *Political Thought,* ch. 5; and McNeill, "Natural Law in the Thought of Luther," 220. For a recent argument against a strict connection be-

tique of the pretensions of reason in fallen humanity distance him, in degree if not absolutely, from many of his medieval predecessors on issues related to natural law.[146] Third, Luther developed views on conscience that differed from Thomas, Scotus, and other medieval theologians, rejecting, for example, use of the concept of synderesis.[147] Fourth, Luther did not ground natural law in eternal law in any explicit way, as did many medieval thinkers.[148] Fifth, and finally, Luther often identifies natural law with love, a move that distinguishes him from medieval theologians who posited love as a higher, supernatural virtue.[149]

Conclusion

A long line of thinking about natural law and the Christian's role in the broader world existed before the Reformation, and Luther (with some of his colleagues) offered profound reflections on these same issues before the development of a distinctively Reformed Protestant tradition. This chapter has identified some of the prevalent themes that the Christian tradition has produced relating to these matters and presented a picture of both continuity and discontinuity among the various theologians and eras considered. In the

---

tween natural law and the earthly kingdom in Luther, which is critiqued as "dualistic," see Antti Raunio, "Natural Law and Faith: The Forgotten Foundations of Ethics in Luther's Theology," in *Union with Christ: The New Finnish Interpretation of Luther*, ed. Carl E. Braaten and Robert W. Jenson (Grand Rapids: Eerdmans, 1998), 96-124.

146. This point is explored helpfully in Lohse, *Martin Luther's Theology*, 196-99, 204-5. Brown identifies this point as one of two in which Luther's natural law thought must be distinguished from the medieval traditions; see "Martin Luther," 19. See also Thompson, *Political Thought*, 81-84, 86.

147. For extensive treatment of this issue, see Michael G. Baylor, *Action and Person: Conscience in Late Scholasticism and the Young Luther* (Leiden: Brill, 1977), ch. 5-6. Baylor also mentions that, for Luther, conscience did not focus upon individual acts so much as upon the person as a whole, and that he drew a parallel between the judgment of God concerning a person and the judgment of conscience. For further discussion of the relation between Luther and his medieval predecessors, see also Langston, *Conscience and Other Virtues*, ch. 5.

148. Ernst Wolf views this as the decisive point of difference between Luther and medieval scholastic natural law theory; see "The Law of Nature in Thomas Aquinas and Luther," in *Faith & Action: Basic Problems in Christian Ethics: A Selection of Contemporary Discussions*, ed. H.-H. Schrey (Edinburgh: Oliver & Boyd, 1970), 247-49.

149. See discussion in Lazareth, *Christians in Society*, 148-49; Raunio, "Natural Law and Faith" 96-124; and Antti Raunio, "Divine and Natural Law in Luther and Melanchthon," in *Lutheran Reformation and the Law*, ed. Virpi Mäkinen (Leiden: Brill, 2006), 21-61.

next chapters I will return often to these earlier themes in order to place Reformed thinking on natural law and the two kingdoms in relation to the medieval and patristic traditions. Reformed theologians continued many of the prominent themes of these earlier traditions, even as they developed them in often distinctive ways. I now turn to explain and defend this claim.

CHAPTER 3

Reforming Natural Law and the Two Kingdoms: John Calvin and His Contemporaries

In this chapter attention turns to the ideas of natural law and the two kingdoms at the origins of the Reformed tradition. As the last chapter has argued, these ideas and the issues surrounding them were hardly new to Christian theology. Many of the most significant theologians of patristic and medieval vintage wrestled with them and articulated various versions of natural law and the twofold authority or jurisdiction in the world. At the dawn of the Protestant Reformation, Martin Luther propounded doctrines of natural law and the two kingdoms as crucial aspects of his social thought. Early Reformed theologians also took up these ideas and articulated them in ways evidencing much continuity with the past traditions yet also distinctive in important respects.

The primary, though not exclusive, focus of this chapter is the thought of John Calvin (1509-64). Too much scholarship on the early centuries of Protestantism has looked at Calvin as practically the exclusive standard by which to judge subsequent Reformed theology. The present chapter does not wish to make this mistake. As some recent writers have argued, Calvin was but one of a number of Reformed theologians of his generation that had a profound impact upon later Reformed thought. Propping up Calvin as the one measure by which later Reformed theology must be assessed is troublesome in many respects, not least of which is the theological variety evident already in the earliest years of the formation of a Reformed tradition distinct from Lutheranism within the broader Protestant orbit.[1] Nevertheless, in a

---

1. See, e.g., the discussion in Richard A. Muller, *Post-Reformation Reformed Dogmatics: The Rise and Development of Reformed Orthodoxy, ca. 1520 to ca. 1725*, vol. 1, *Prolegomena to Theology*, 2d ed. (Grand Rapids: Baker, 2003), 38, 52-59.

67

study such as this, which must of necessity be selective, granting Calvin the spotlight seems well justified.[2] Though his influence on the later Reformed tradition was not exclusive, it was certainly not surpassed by any of his contemporaries. Furthermore, Calvin did address the topics of natural law and the two kingdoms quite explicitly and, as is argued below, in ways dependent upon each other. Finally, Calvin's legal training as a youth and his key role in the fascinating social experiment in Geneva during the height of his ministry make his theological reflections on these subjects all the more intriguing.

In this chapter, I argue that Calvin articulated doctrines of natural law and the two kingdoms that place him in definite continuity with earlier Christian traditions, most especially with the thought of Luther, his older contemporary. Within this continuity, however, Calvin expressed himself in tones distinctive from the medieval traditions and even from Luther himself. Contrary to those who find the genius of Calvin's theology hostile to natural law, Calvin unambiguously affirmed the existence of natural law and even accorded it positive roles. Contrary to those who find Calvin a precursor to popular contemporary Reformed views of culture and the kingdom of God, Calvin clearly distinguished the two kingdoms and affirmed their continuing dual roles in this world (despite alleged tensions between his two kingdoms theology and the relation of church and state in Geneva). And certainly of significance for the present study, Calvin's views of natural law and the two kingdoms were dependent upon each other in significant respects.

In addition, this chapter (particularly when read alongside Chapter 5) adds further evidence to the extensive critique that has already been mounted against the so-called Calvin vs. the Calvinists thesis. According to this thesis, in its various permutations, the later sixteenth- and seventeenth-century Calvinists practiced a rationalistic and scholastic theology that corrupted the more biblical and humanist theology of Calvin. The present chapter, by examining Calvin on natural law and the two kingdoms, shows significant elements of continuity between Calvin and his medieval predecessors and sets the stage for the argument in Chapter 5 that a great deal of continuity also exists between Calvin and his Reformed scholastic successors. Since the natural knowledge of God is one of the matters particularly highlighted by some as a point of significant discontinuity between Calvin

2. Perhaps pertinent here are the words of Philip Benedict, who, while acknowledging the importance of figures such as Heinrich Bullinger and John à Lasco, states that Calvin "unquestionably merits the leading role traditionally assigned him in the history of the Reformed tradition." See *Christ's Churches Purely Reformed: A Social History of Calvinism* (New Haven: Yale University Press, 2002), 77.

and the Reformed scholastics, the ongoing argument of this book contributes additional evidence against the Calvin vs. the Calvinists claim.[3]

This chapter begins by examining Calvin's understanding of the two kingdoms, especially in his theological writings but also against the background of his experience in Geneva. Subsequently, I examine his doctrine of natural law and, as with his two kingdoms doctrine, attempt to place it in the context of the broader Christian tradition. Finally, I consider briefly how the ideas of natural law and the two kingdoms fared with several of Calvin's contemporaries, in order to provide at least some sense of the unity and diversity on such matters within the earliest Reformed theology.

Calvin on the Two Kingdoms

Though John Calvin is not often associated with the two kingdoms doctrine,[4] he affirmed it from the beginning to the end of his theological career and put it to work when addressing various topics, perhaps most notably Christian liberty and the respective authority of church and state. This first

3. Among important works generally advocating a Calvin vs. the Calvinists approach, see Brian G. Armstrong, *Calvinism and the Amyraut Heresy: Protestant Scholasticism and Humanism in Seventeenth-Century France* (Madison: University of Wisconsin Press, 1969); and R. T. Kendall, *Calvin and English Calvinism to 1649* (Oxford: Oxford University Press, 1979). Utilizing this approach in order to portray Calvin as a social emancipator and transformer, see Paul Chung, *Spirituality and Social Ethics in John Calvin: A Pneumatological Perspective* (Lanham: University Press of America, 2000). Among particularly important works critiquing this approach and arguing for development within continuity from the Reformation into later sixteenth- and seventeenth-century Reformed scholasticism (or, Reformed orthodoxy), see Richard A. Muller, *After Calvin: Studies in the Development of a Theological Tradition* (Oxford: Oxford University Press, 2003); Richard A. Muller, *Post-Reformation Reformed Dogmatics: The Rise and Development of Reformed Orthodoxy, ca. 1520 to ca. 1725,* 4 vols. (Grand Rapids: Baker, 2003); *Reformation and Scholasticism: An Ecumenical Enterprise,* ed. Willem J. van Asselt and Eef Dekker (Grand Rapids: Baker, 2001); *Protestant Scholasticism: Essays in Reassessment,* ed. Carl Trueman and R. Scott Clark (Carlisle: Paternoster, 1999); and Paul Helm, *Calvin and the Calvinists* (Edinburgh: Banner of Truth, 1982).

4. In his influential taxonomy of Christian views on the relationship of Christianity and culture, H. Richard Niebuhr placed Calvin in a different category from that of Luther and his two kingdoms position (though without offering any textual support for his interpretation of Calvin as a transformer of culture); see *Christ and Culture* (New York: Harper & Brothers, 1951), 217-18. More recently, one can find statements such as the following: "Is the use of the term 'Calvin's Two Kingdom Theory' perhaps problematic? I am not convinced that Calvin operated with any concept of two kingdoms." See Frank C. Roberts, "Response," in *Calvin and the State,* ed. Peter De Klerk (Grand Rapids: Calvin Studies Society, 1993), 104.

major section of the chapter addresses Calvin's understanding of the two kingdoms. As we will see, Calvin's theological articulation of the doctrine, particularly in his *Institutes of the Christian Religion* (both early and late editions), exhibits a position similar to that of Luther. Nevertheless, any evaluation of Calvin's doctrine is complicated by other aspects of his theology and by consideration of the concrete social situation of Geneva, in which Calvin actively participated and which he in part molded. This practical outworking of Calvin's social thought indicates that he indeed took the two kingdoms idea in some different directions from that envisioned by Luther and, in fact, that Calvin merged a two kingdoms doctrine with an institutional arrangement of church and state that hearkened back in certain ways to a Gelasian two swords paradigm. I will argue, therefore, that Calvin's thought on these matters reflects significant points of continuity with the earlier Christian traditions, yet took a unique shape, both theologically and practically.

Calvin's Theological Articulation of the Two Kingdoms Doctrine

I begin this consideration of Calvin on the two kingdoms with a description of his theological articulation of the doctrine, especially in the *Institutes*. His theology of the two kingdoms remained remarkably constant during his career. This point is evident simply by comparing what he wrote in the first edition of the *Institutes* (1536), composed as a young man shortly after his conversion to Protestantism and before his first arrival in Geneva, with what he wrote in the last edition (1559), only a few years before his death. Many of the sections dealing directly with the two kingdoms remained nearly identical.[5]

---

5. E.g., compare sections 3.19.15 and 4.20.1-2 in the 1559 edition with sections 6.13, 35-36 in the 1536 edition. Subsequently, English translations of these works will be taken respectively from *Institutes of the Christian Religion*, 2 vols., trans. Henry Beveridge (Grand Rapids: Eerdmans, 1953) and *Institutes of the Christian Religion*, trans. Ford Lewis Battles (Grand Rapids: Eerdmans, 1986). References to the *Institutes* will be to the 1559 edition unless otherwise noted. A critical edition of the 1559 edition is published as *Institutes of the Christian Religion*, ed. John T. McNeill, trans. Ford Lewis Battles (Philadelphia: Westminster, 1960). I have chosen to use the Beveridge translation for several reasons, including what I take to be its somewhat more literal rendering of the Latin text. For positive comments on the Beveridge translation, see Richard A. Muller, *The Unaccommodated Calvin: Studies in the Foundation of a Theological Tradition* (New York: Oxford University Press, 2000), 68, 218 n26. Latin quotations from the *Institutes* and from his biblical commentaries are taken from *Ioannis Calvini opera quae supersunt omnia*, ed. Guilielmus Baum, Eduardus Cunitz, and Eduardus Reuss, vols. 29-87 of *Corpus Reformatorum* (Brunswick: C. A. Schwetschke, 1863-1900).

Calvin affirmed a clear distinction between a heavenly, spiritual kingdom that finds present expression in the church and a civil, earthly kingdom whose most notable institutional expression is the civil government. From his earliest Protestant days to the end of his life, therefore, Calvin displayed the influence of Luther's teaching on the two kingdoms and two governments.[6]

Lying behind Calvin's discussions of the two kingdoms is an Augustinian two cities paradigm, though never to my knowledge explicitly expressed as such. Calvin, in other words, believed that a fundamental antithesis divided Christians from non-Christians, both in regard to eternal destiny and to knowledge and conduct in the present world.[7] But, as with Luther, Calvin moved beyond this antithetical paradigm and expressed additionally another twofold conception. Contrary to what some recent Reformed writers have suggested,[8] Calvin's two kingdoms were not the kingdoms of God and Satan, or even of God and man. Hence, Calvin's doctrine of the two kingdoms was not Augustine's doctrine of the two cities. Both of Calvin's two kingdoms are God's, but are ruled by him in distinctive ways. Each has significantly positive roles to play for life in the world. Christians are members of both kingdoms during their earthly lives. Calvin perceived a clear difference between these kingdoms but not a fundamental antithesis. The antithesis lay elsewhere.

Calvin offered perhaps no better basic summary of his two kingdoms doctrine than the following explanation:

6. I am more optimistic about the usefulness of comparing Calvin and Luther on the two kingdoms than is Willem van't Spijker, who writes: "Luther's idea of the two kingdoms has a different scope than that of Calvin, which is not very congenial for a comparison." See "The Kingdom of Christ according to Bucer and Calvin," in *Calvin and the State,* 121-22. Helpful comparison of Calvin with Luther on the two kingdoms doctrine appears in John Witte, Jr., "Moderate Religious Liberty in the Theology of John Calvin," *Calvin Theological Journal* 31 (1996): 359-403.

7. Numerous sections of Calvin's writings could illustrate this point. Notable examples include the lengthy section *Institutes* 2.2, where he focuses upon the status of fallen human reason, and then section 2.6.1, where he turns to focus upon the redemption that God provides in Christ.

8. E.g., see Klaas Runia, "The Kingdom of God in the Bible, in History, and Today," *European Journal of Theology* 1, no. 1 (1992): 40: "The one is the kingdom of Christ, who reigns from on high; the other is the kingdom of Satan, who constantly opposes Christ and his kingdom." See also Cornelius Plantinga Jr., *Engaging God's World: A Christian Vision of Faith, Learning, and Living* (Grand Rapids: Eerdmans, 2002), 111; and Henry R. Van Til, *The Calvinistic Concept of Culture* (1959; Grand Rapids: Baker, 2001), 81-83. Runia and others are correct that Calvin highlights the conflict between Christ and Satan, but his two kingdoms doctrine considered here is something distinct from this. Correctly differentiating Calvin's two kingdoms from Augustine's two cities, on the other hand, is van't Spijker, who writes that the ideas "are totally different" ("The Kingdom of Christ," 121-22).

Let us observe that in man government is twofold: the one spiritual, by which the conscience is trained to piety and divine worship; the other civil, by which the individual is instructed in those duties which, as men and citizens, we are bound to perform. . . . To these two forms are commonly given the not inappropriate names of spiritual and temporal jurisdiction, intimating that the former species has reference to the life of the soul, while the latter relates to matters of the present life, not only to food and clothing, but to the enacting of laws which require a man to live among his fellows purely, honourably, and modestly. The former has its seat within the soul, the latter only regulates the external conduct. We may call the one the spiritual, the other the civil kingdom.[9]

Many of the points that he touches upon here are discussed in the following paragraphs. What might be noted first of all is the clarity and starkness with which Calvin distinguishes these two kingdoms. In the same section as the quotation above, for example, Calvin writes: "Now, these two, as we have divided them, are always to be viewed apart from each other. When the one is considered, we should call off our minds, and not allow them to think of the other. For there exists in man a kind of two worlds, over which different kings and different laws can preside."[10] When discussing the authority of the church in Book 4 of the *Institutes,* Calvin echoes himself, calling the "spiritual government" of the church something "altogether distinct from civil government" and noting "the distinction and dissimilarity between ecclesiastical and civil power."[11] When turning his attention to civil government, he recalls his previous discussion of the two kingdoms and warns against those who "imprudently confound these two things, the nature of which is altogether different," and then adds that "the spiritual kingdom of Christ and civil government are things very widely separated." To "seek and include the kingdom of Christ under the elements of this world," he explains, is a "Jewish vanity."[12] Clearly such strong statements, peppered through a variety of contexts, leave no doubt that any complete description of Calvin's theology must account for this contrast between the kingdoms. I turn now to describe Calvin's view of the nature of these kingdoms and thereby to explain why he drew this contrast so sharply.

In order to do this, I identify three important attributes of each kingdom

9. Calvin, *Institutes,* 3.19.15.
10. Calvin, *Institutes,* 3.19.15.
11. Calvin, *Institutes,* 4.11.1, 3.
12. Calvin, *Institutes,* 4.20.1.

that display the contrast of one with the other. The three attributes of the kingdom of Christ are its redemptive character, its spiritual or heavenly identity, and its present institutional expression in the church. The three attributes of the civil kingdom are its non-redemptive character, its external or earthly identity, and its present (though not exclusive) expression in civil government.

First, then, I consider the redemptive character of the spiritual kingdom in contrast to the non-redemptive character of the civil kingdom. One helpful place for seeing this is *Institutes* 3.19, concerning Christian liberty. Calvin makes plain that Christian liberty lies at the heart of the salvation granted to believers in Christ. It is, he explains, "a proper appendix to Justification, and is of no little service in understanding its force,"[13] and is foundational for understanding and living in godliness. Calvin identifies three parts in which Christian liberty consists: having one's conscience assured of justification and no longer seeking justification by the law, being obedient to the law voluntarily rather than under legal compulsion, and being freed from obligation to do or not to do external things that are in themselves morally indifferent.[14] Immediately after explaining this last point, however, Calvin becomes attentive to potential misuses of the doctrine. He notes that "Christian liberty is in all its parts a spiritual matter" and warns against those "who use it as a cloak for their lusts, and they may licentiously abuse the good gifts of God. . . ."[15] Christian liberty does not entail libertine behavior or a rejection of all authority on earth. And thus when Calvin states that the believer's conscience is "exempted from all human authority," he notes that "the moment the abolition of human constitutions is mentioned, the greatest disturbances are excited. . . ."[16]

It is precisely at this point, to extricate himself from misunderstanding, that Calvin turns to the two kingdoms doctrine. He refers to the "spiritual and temporal jurisdiction" or, alternatively, to "the spiritual" and "the civil kingdom." The former pertains to the soul and the latter to external things, and different kings and laws pertain to each. Here Calvin expands upon his claim that Christian liberty is spiritual: "By attending to this distinction, we will not erroneously transfer the doctrine of the gospel concerning spiritual liberty to civil order, as if in regard to external government Christians were less subject to human laws, because their consciences are unbound before

13. Calvin, *Institutes*, 3.19.1.
14. Calvin, *Institutes*, 3.19.2-8.
15. Calvin, *Institutes*, 3.19.9.
16. Calvin, *Institutes*, 3.19.14.

God. . . ." The unpacking of this point is somewhat complex, and Calvin in fact refers his readers to subsequent sections of the *Institutes* for further elaboration. But one of his basic claims is of great relevance for the present study: the redemptive doctrine of Christian liberty applies to life in the spiritual kingdom but not to life in the civil kingdom. No human authority can bind the believer's conscience in regard to participation in the spiritual kingdom of Christ. Over against Roman Catholic claims, Calvin teaches that Scripture is the *only* authority in this realm. Hence, as he explains in *Institutes* 4.10-11, the church can minister the word of God alone and never its own opinions, and it can prescribe for worship only those things that Scripture prescribes (though it ought to do so in appropriate ways that promote decency and order, to which Christians should willingly submit). In the external things of the civil kingdom, in contrast, salvation in Christ does not at all diminish Christians' obligation to obey magistrates. The "doctrine of the gospel" does not apply to "civil order" with its "external government." As Calvin explains in *Institutes* 4.20, this means that civil magistrates are to be obeyed in all things, except if this would mean direct violation of Scripture. In other words, the officers of the church have authority to do and command only those things prescribed in Scripture, and Christians in the spiritual kingdom are thus free in conscience from anything *beyond* this; but civil magistrates have a broader discretion to promote justice and order in the civil kingdom, and Christians are bound to obey them except if their commands *contradict* their biblical obligations. This will prove to be an important issue in subsequent chapters.

In short, the reality of Christian liberty gained through redemption in Christ has profound impact on Christians' life in the spiritual kingdom (and thus in the church) but does not change their basic obligations in the civil kingdom (and thus under the civil government).[17] God rules the spiritual kingdom as its redeemer and the civil kingdom as its creator and sustainer but not as its redeemer.

To describe Calvin's theology in this way is to risk objection on several fronts from those influenced by Barthian or neo-Calvinist schools of thought considered in Chapters 8 and 9 below. Does my description of Calvin imply that Christ has nothing at all to do with the civil kingdom?[18] Does

---

17. Calvin, *Institutes*, 3.19.15.

18. E.g., see an article written in response to my claims about Calvin and the two kingdoms: Timothy P. Palmer, "Calvin the Transformationist and the Kingship of Christ," *Pro Rege* 35, no. 3 (March 2007): 32-39.

it insert an unwarranted "dualism" or "dichotomy" or "bifurcation" in Calvin's thought that fails to account for his religiously unified view of life?[19] These sorts of objections unnecessarily create dilemmas. Calvin did in fact provide a holistic theological and even Christological account of the world and its history. But he did so only while working with fundamental distinctions between God's non-redemptive work of creation and providence through his Eternal Son and his redemptive work through the incarnate Lord Jesus Christ. God created human beings in his image through his Son, the Word who had not yet become incarnate, and if these human beings had obeyed his law they would have attained heaven without need of redemption through an incarnate Mediator.[20] Even after the fall into sin and the Son's incarnation, according to Calvin, Christ does not exist and operate in the world solely through his human nature in his capacity as redeemer. For over against the Lutheran doctrine of ubiquity (i.e., that after his incarnation the human nature of Christ is present everywhere, wherever his divine nature is), Calvin teaches that Christ's divine nature is present *etiam extra carnem* ("even outside of his flesh"). This gives Calvin categories for affirming that the Son of God rules one kingdom in a redemptive manner and the other kingdom in a non-redemptive manner. In his description of Calvin's social thought, John Bolt helpfully explains: "As mediator, the divine *Logos* is not limited to his incarnate form even after the incarnation. He was mediator of creation prior to his incarnation and as mediator continues to *sustain* creation independent of his mediatorial work as *reconciler* of creation in the incarnation, death, resurrection, and ascension of Jesus of Nazareth."[21] The

---

19. E.g., Gordon J. Spykman struggles with this issue in his analysis of Calvin in "Sphere-Sovereignty in Calvin and the Calvinist Tradition," in *Exploring the Heritage of John Calvin*, ed. David E. Holwerda (Grand Rapids: Baker, 1976), 189-94. Spykman deserves credit at least for acknowledging and wrestling honestly with Calvin's two kingdoms doctrine from a neo-Calvinist perspective, though he too operates with a view of the two kingdoms doctrine as inherently problematic to Reformed theology.

20. On the Son's role in creation as the *logos asarkos*, the non-incarnate Word, see, e.g., Calvin, *Institutes of the Christian Religion*, 1.13.7; 2.12.6. On Adam and Eve being given a law before the fall into sin that would have brought them to heaven had they been obedient, see, e.g., Calvin's *Commentary on Genesis* 2:16-17; for English translation, see John Calvin, *Commentaries on the First Book of Moses Called Genesis,* trans. John King, *Calvin's Commentaries,* vol. 1 (Grand Rapids: Baker, 2003).

21. John Bolt, "Church and World: A Trinitarian Perspective," *Calvin Theological Journal* 18, no. 1 (April 1983): 30. Similar points are developed in Heiko Augustinus Oberman, *The Dawn of the Reformation: Essays in Late Medieval and Early Reformation Thought* (Edinburgh: T&T Clark, 1986), ch. 10; see also Byung-Ho Moon, *Christ the Mediator of the Law: Calvin's Christological Un-*

doctrine that Bolt alludes to here, that of the two mediatorships of the Son of God, over creation and redemption respectively, was developed by later generations of Reformed theologians and came to serve as crucial foundation for their two kingdoms doctrine. Subsequent chapters of this book will explore this issue at much greater length, but the fact that Calvin laid the groundwork is worthy of note.[22] In some sense Calvin certainly did have a religiously unified and even Christological view of life, but he expressed this only by making clear distinctions between God's work of creation and redemption and between the civil and spiritual kingdoms.

A second set of contrasting attributes of the two kingdoms is the spiritual, heavenly character of the kingdom of Christ and the external, earthly character of the civil kingdom. This contrast is evident in the discussion above regarding Christian liberty in *Institutes* 3.19. There the spiritual and civil kingdoms were distinguished by the latter's association with "the life of the soul" and the former's with "matters of the present life" or "external conduct."[23] Lying behind this account, however, are important discussions in Book 2. In a section on human depravity, *Institutes* 2.2, he "draws a distinction" between "inferior objects" and "superior objects." Though Calvin's primary concern here is to begin to describe how and why sinful human beings can make some progress in regard to the former but really none at all in regard to the latter, his comments have a more general import relevant for the present discussion. Calvin states that the distinction between inferior and superior objects may also be described as a distinction between "intelligence of earthly things" and "of heavenly things." He explains: "By earthly things, I mean those which relate not to God and his kingdom, to true righteousness and future blessedness, but have some connection with the present life, and are in a manner confined within its boundaries." On the other hand, "By heavenly things, I mean the pure knowledge of God, the method of true

---

derstanding of the Law as the Rule of Living and Life-Giving (Waynesboro, GA: Paternoster, 2006), 105-11. On Calvin's so-called *extra Calvinisticum* Christology more broadly, see E. David Willis, *Calvin's Catholic Christology: The Function of the So-Called Extra Calvinisticum in Calvin's Theology* (Leiden: Brill, 1966).

22. While I suggest here that Calvin's understanding of the *extra Calvinisticum* is theologically coherent with and in some sense precedent for the later Reformed doctrine of the two mediatorships of Christ, W. D. J. McKay has argued for an element of discontinuity between Calvin's understanding of Christ's kingship over the nations and the understanding of seventeenth-century Reformed thought; see *An Ecclesiastical Republic: Church Government in the Writings of George Gillespie* (Carlisle: Paternoster, 1997), 56-57.

23. Calvin, *Institutes*, 3.19.15.

righteousness, and the mysteries of the heavenly kingdom."[24] Therefore, it is evident that Calvin associates the kingdom of Christ with what is heavenly and the civil kingdom with what is earthly and of the present life. Subsequent sections of the *Institutes* elucidate both of these points.

Calvin expounds the heavenly character of the kingdom of Christ perhaps most clearly in his treatment of Christ's kingship later in Book 2. In a series of rather moving passages, Calvin lifts his readers' eyes away from present earthly existence toward a future, heavenly life. He writes: "I come to the Kingly office [of Christ], of which it were in vain to speak, without previously reminding the reader that its nature is spiritual; because it is from thence we learn its efficacy, the benefits it confers, its whole power and eternity." He proceeds to explain that "we see that everything which is earthly, and of the world, is temporary, and soon fades away. Christ, therefore, to raise our hope to the heavens, declares that his kingdom is not of this world. . . . In fine, let each of us, when he hears that the kingdom of Christ is spiritual, be roused by the thought to entertain the hope of a better life. . . ."[25] Against this background, Calvin frequently uses the image of Christians as "pilgrims" to describe their status in the present world[26] and he portrays their earthly lot as one of suffering and hardship:

> That the strength and utility of the kingdom of Christ cannot, as we have said, be fully perceived, without recognizing it as spiritual, is sufficiently apparent, even from this, that having during the whole course of our lives to war under the cross, our condition here is bitter and wretched. What then would it avail us to be ranged under the government of a heavenly King, if its benefits were not realized beyond the present earthly life? These words [Romans 14:7] briefly teach what the kingdom of Christ bestows upon us. Not being earthly or carnal, and so subject to corruption, but spiritual, it raises us even to eternal life, so that we can patiently live at present under toil, hunger, cold, contempt, disgrace, and other annoyances; contented with this, that our King will never abandon us, but will supply our necessities until our warfare is ended, and we are called to tri-

24. Calvin, *Institutes*, 2.2.13.

25. Calvin, *Institutes*, 2.15.3. On the spiritual nature of Christ's kingdom, see also "Brief Instruction," in John Calvin, *Treatises Against the Anabaptists and Against the Libertines*, trans. and ed. Benjamin Wirt Farley (Grand Rapids: Baker, 1982), 86.

26. See Calvin, *Institutes*, 2.16.14; 3.2.4; 3.7.3; 3.10.1; 3.25.1-2; 4.20.2. Calvin identifies the end of Christians' lives as the end of their pilgrimage, with the hope of resurrection the only thing sustaining them in their present suffering; see *Institutes*, 3.25.1-2.

umph: such being the nature of his kingdom, that he communicates to us whatever he received of his Father.[27]

Despite the common practice of contemporary Reformed theologians to view politics and all sorts of other cultural activities as the work of Christ's kingdom, as later chapters will explore, these quotations demonstrate the other-worldliness of Calvin's kingdom theology. In fact, the emphasis here upon the heavenly and spiritual aspects of Christ's kingdom is reinforced by his later explicit denial that civil matters pertain to it. In *Institutes* 4.20.1, for example, he states that "the spiritual kingdom of Christ and civil government are things very widely separated" and that "it is a Jewish vanity to seek and include the kingdom of Christ under the elements of this world. . . ." He then concludes this section by deriving from the Apostle Paul that "it matters not what your condition is among men, nor under what laws you live, since in them the kingdom of Christ does not at all consist."[28]

As Calvin explicitly describes the heavenly and spiritual character of Christ's kingdom, so he also sets forth the earthly and external character of the civil kingdom. This is surely most evident in *Institutes* 4.20.1. Early in this section, Calvin states that the civil kingdom "pertains only to civil institutions and the external regulation of manners." Though the relation of the civil kingdom to the state and other cultural matters is discussed more explicitly below, at present I wish to highlight merely the sorts of things about

27. Calvin, *Institutes*, 2.15.4. Calvin poignantly speaks of suffering as a mark of the Christian experience in the present age in *Institutes*, 3.8.1.

28. Calvin, *Institutes*, 4.20.1. John Bolt presents a similar interpretation of Calvin on the heavenly nature of Christ's kingdom, also in contrast to much contemporary Reformed thought, in *Christian and Reformed Today* (Jordan Station, Ontario: Paideia, 1984), 135-41. Another helpful treatment of many of the issues addressed here is offered by David E. Holwerda, "Eschatology and History: A Look at Calvin's Eschatological Vision," in *Exploring the Heritage of John Calvin*, ed. David E. Holwerda (Grand Rapids: Baker, 1976), 110-39. Especially relevant is his discussion of the idea of pilgrimage in Calvin (see 118-19) and on Calvin's identification of the kingdom of God with the church (see 134-35). Most of the claims made in Holwerda's essay are consistent with the claims of the present chapter, including his important statement that "the eschatological reordering of the world occurs here and now — at least in its beginnings — in the believer and the church. Hence the destiny of the world becomes visible in the reordering which occurs in the body of Christ" (136). Nevertheless, Holwerda in the end agrees (albeit with some helpful qualifications) with the common judgment, which the present chapter treats more warily, that Calvin was a "social and political revolutionary" (138-39). In the passage asserting the crucial connection between Calvin's view of the church as kingdom and his "political activism," however, Holwerda does not demonstrate textually that Calvin himself made this connection, but cites only secondary literature (see 136-37).

which the civil kingdom, especially though not exclusively through the state, has concern. Specifically, the civil kingdom, in contrast to the heavenly kingdom, deals with earthly and external things. The civil kingdom has to do with "the body" and "the present fleeting life."[29] Among its concerns are "human society . . . civil justice . . . common peace and tranquility."[30] Through civil government it seeks to cultivate "innocent commerce" and "honesty and modesty."[31] The "only study" of those entrusted with civil authority should be "to provide for the common peace and safety."[32] Hence the fact that such authorities "maintain our safety" is "the highest gift of his [the Lord's] beneficence."[33]

A third and final point of contrast between the spiritual and civil kingdoms for Calvin is the former's institutional expression in the church and the latter's expression in a broad range of cultural endeavors, especially (and institutionally) in civil government. As discussed above, Calvin emphasized that the spiritual kingdom of Christ is of heavenly character and does not pertain to civil affairs. Clearly, however, he did not mean to affirm that there is no institutional manifestation of the spiritual kingdom in the present life. Where he located it, and the only place where he located it, was in the church, notwithstanding the perpetuation of claims to the contrary.[34] Calvin writes specifically on a number of occasions about the connection between the church and the spiritual kingdom. In Book 2 of the *Institutes,* for example, he notes that the devil and the whole world cannot destroy the church, because it "is founded on the eternal throne of Christ." Shortly thereafter, Calvin states that God rules and defends his church through the exalted Christ, to whom he has given "the whole power of government." After citing Philippians 2:9-11, he concludes: "In these words, also, he commends an arrangement in the kingdom of Christ, which is necessary for our present infirmity. Thus Paul rightly infers that God will then be the only Head of the Church, because the office of Christ,

---

29. Calvin, *Institutes,* 4.20.1.

30. Calvin, *Institutes,* 4.20.2.

31. Calvin, *Institutes,* 4.20.3.

32. Calvin, *Institutes,* 4.20.9.

33. Calvin, *Institutes,* 4.20.25.

34. E.g., Runia, without a citation of Calvin's own writings, portrays him as if he were a contemporary neo-Calvinist: "The kingdom of Christ (which is the present form of the kingdom of God) is much wider than the church. From the Word that is being preached in the church it extends to and penetrates into family life and into all aspects of society at large." See "The Kingdom of God," 40.

in defending the Church, shall then have been completed."[35] In Book 4 Calvin puts things perhaps most clearly. In one place he writes that "the Church is the kingdom of Christ"[36] and elsewhere he distinctly identifies the church with the "spiritual and internal kingdom of Christ" and says that the church "in some measure begins the heavenly kingdom in us, even now upon earth, and in this mortal and evanescent life commences immortal and incorruptible blessedness. . . ."[37]

In regard to present expression of the civil kingdom, Calvin is certainly more expansive. In his discussion of "inferior" and "superior" objects, considered above, he defines the former as those things that "have some connection with the present life, and are in a manner confined within its boundaries." He includes in this category "matters of policy and economy, all mechanical arts and liberal studies."[38] It would seem fair, therefore, to conclude that Calvin saw the range of (non-ecclesiastical) cultural endeavors as constituting the civil kingdom. But within this broad conception Calvin also accorded a particularly important place to civil government and its laws. This is evident at the beginning of his discussion of civil government in *Institutes* 4.20. After stating that the civil kingdom "pertains only to civil institutions and the external regulation of manners," Calvin turns explicitly to consideration of civil government, which he proceeds to make the focal point of his contrast with the spiritual kingdom.[39] He writes similarly in subsequent sections, contrasting "civil polity" with the "spiritual kingdom of Christ,"[40] for example.

This dissociation of civil government from the spiritual kingdom did not in any way compromise the legitimacy of the former. Calvin, in fact, over against Anabaptists in particular, defended God's ordination and establishment of civil authority at considerable length.[41] As noted above, over against

35. Calvin, *Institutes*, 2.15.3, 5.

36. Calvin, *Institutes*, 4.2.4.

37. Calvin, *Institutes*, 4.20.2. Calvin's identification of the church as the spiritual kingdom of Christ on earth is evident in many places in his biblical commentaries as well. E.g., see his comments on Micah 4:2, 7; for English translation, see John Calvin, *Commentaries on the Twelve Minor Prophets*, vol. 3, trans. John Owen, in *Calvin's Commentaries*, vol. 14 (Grand Rapids: Baker, 2003).

38. Calvin, *Institutes*, 2.2.13.

39. Calvin, *Institutes*, 4.20.1.

40. Calvin, *Institutes*, 4.20.12.

41. E.g., see Calvin, *Institutes*, 4.20.4-7; and his *Commentary on Romans* 13:1-7. For English translation of the latter, see John Calvin, *Commentaries on the Epistle of Paul the Apostle to the Romans*, trans. John Owen, in *Calvin's Commentaries*, vol. 19 (Grand Rapids: Baker, 2003). For a brief summary of Calvin's view of the legitimacy of civil government, see William R. Stevenson,

some popular contemporary interpretations of Calvin, Calvin was a dualist of sorts in making his two kingdoms distinction. But this did not relegate God or religious considerations to just one realm of life, for he also insisted that both kingdoms have been ordained by God and that Christians can offer pleasing service to God in executing the respective responsibilities of each one.

Calvin's basic identification of the spiritual and civil kingdoms with the church and civil government had significant concrete impact upon his understanding of the nature of ecclesiastical and civil authority and their relation to each other. Calvin contrasted ecclesiastical and civil authority in no uncertain terms: "The Church of God . . . needs a kind of spiritual government. This is altogether distinct from civil government."[42] Perhaps most importantly, Calvin perceived their distinction in the fact that God entrusted the sword to the civil magistrate but withheld it from the church. Some, he says, "are led astray, by not observing the distinction and dissimilarity between ecclesiastical and civil power. For the Church has not the right of the sword to punish or restrain, has no power to coerce, nor prison nor other punishments which the magistrate is wont to inflict." The church merely seeks the repentance of sinners. Therefore, these two authorities "are widely different, because neither does the Church assume anything to herself which is proper to the magistrate, nor is the magistrate competent to what is done by the Church."[43] Later in the same discussion, Calvin reasserts these claims, noting that Christ debarred "the ministers of his word from civil domination and worldly power" and that "the church has not, and ought not to wish to have, the power of compulsion (I speak of civil coercion). . . ."[44] In contrast, Calvin defends at some length the legitimacy of the magistrate's use of the sword.[45] Another interesting consequence of the correspondence of the two kingdoms with the church and civil government is the role of Scripture in governing these institutions. Whereas Calvin demanded biblical warrant for everything that the church did, he did not make such a demand for the actions of civil government. After raising the pacifist objection that the New Testament gives no warrant for warfare, Calvin dismisses it by noting: "in the Apostolical writings we are not to look for a distinct exposition of those

---

"Calvin and Political Issues," in *The Cambridge Companion to John Calvin,* ed. Donald K. McKim (Cambridge: Cambridge University Press, 2004), 173-74.

42. Calvin, *Institutes,* 4.11.1.

43. Calvin, *Institutes,* 4.11.3.

44. Calvin, *Institutes,* 4.11.8, 16.

45. E.g., see Calvin, *Institutes,* 4.20.10-12.

matters, their object being not to form a civil polity, but to establish the spiritual kingdom of Christ."[46]

Two other points are worth mentioning briefly in regard to the relation of church and state in light of the two kingdoms doctrine. First, Calvin prohibited the same person from holding the offices of both pastor and civil magistrate, the two differing "so widely that they cannot be united in the same individual."[47] Second, Calvin's sharp distinction between these two authorities did not mean their absolute disjunction. He argues instead, like Gelasius before him, for a sort of mutual submission between them, according to their respective competencies. The pious magistrate, having "civil jurisdiction," seeks not to abolish the church's "spiritual jurisdiction," having "no wish to exempt himself from the common subjection of the children of God."[48] Likewise, pastors were to reject the Roman Catholic clergy's claim to civil immunity and instead follow the example of "the ancient bishops," who "did not think it any injury to themselves and their order to act as subjects."[49] Yet Calvin advocated not only mutual submission according to their rightful jurisdictions, but also that each authority should actually serve to strengthen the other. The church's spiritual government "does much to aid and promote" civil government and the civil government is to assist the church in preventing "offences to religion" such as idolatry and blasphemy from breaking out among the populace.[50] "Thus they ought to combine their efforts, the one being not an impediment but a help to the other."[51] At this point, however, potentially complicating factors emerge and thus it is appropriate to turn to these factors, including the practical outworking of Calvin's ideas in Geneva.

Church and State in Calvin's Theology and Practice

This coordination and mutual support between church and state draw us into the question of how Calvin himself envisioned his theological account of the two kingdoms being put into practice. The focus of this book is theological, yet the question of how Calvin's Geneva compares to Calvin's theology seems unavoidable. Many suspect Calvin of being to at least some degree

---

46. Calvin, *Institutes*, 4.20.12.
47. Calvin, *Institutes*, 4.11.8.
48. Calvin, *Institutes*, 4.11.4.
49. Calvin, *Institutes*, 4.11.15.
50. Calvin, *Institutes*, 4.11.1; 4.20.3.
51. Calvin, *Institutes*, 4.11.3.

inconsistent in moving from theology to practice, or even of being inconsistent in his theology itself. Philip Benedict expresses the judgment of many others in finding "tension" here.[52] In this subsection, therefore, I consider some features of Geneva's social life and also of Calvin's theology that have raised particular questions about the coherence of his thought. In particular, two related alleged difficulties are the seemingly civil roles accorded to the church and the seemingly religious roles accorded to the state. Due to my own lack of expertise in social history, I avoid drawing dogmatic conclusions, but I do offer some suggestions for interpreting Calvin here and placing him within the broader stream of Christian reflection on such matters.

As we explore this issue it is helpful to keep in mind how greatly different the social circumstances of Calvin's day were from our own. The medieval legacy of Christendom, in which church and state were distinguished but viewed as parts of a larger, unified Christian society, continued to hold sway at the time of the Reformation. The widely shared belief throughout Europe was that only one church and one religion should be recognized in a given jurisdiction. Concrete models of orderly, functioning, religiously plural societies were not readily available. All of these things are relevant when considering Geneva and Calvin's relation to it.

Important aspects of Genevan life have been known for some time, particularly through documents such as the *Ecclesiastical Ordinances.* This was promulgated in 1541, shortly after Calvin's return to Geneva following his banishment from the city, and was largely the brainchild of Calvin himself.[53] But the concrete outworking of the legal arrangements has become much better understood in recent years, especially on marriage and family issues, thanks to the detailed work of a number of scholars.[54] There is no need here to recount in detail the institutional structures in Geneva, as other writers have done so competently.[55] To put it briefly, the civil government consisted

52. Benedict, *Christ's Churches,* 89. See also the claims of W. Fred Graham, *The Constructive Revolutionary: John Calvin and His Socio-Economic Impact* (Richmond: John Knox Press, 1971), 158.

53. For English translation, see *The Register of the Company of Pastors of Geneva in the Time of Calvin,* ed. and trans. Philip Edgcumbe Hughes (Grand Rapids: Eerdmans, 1966), 35-49.

54. E.g., see John Witte, Jr. and Robert M. Kingdon, *Sex, Marriage, and Family in John Calvin's Geneva,* vol. 1, *Courtship, Engagement, and Marriage* (Grand Rapids: Eerdmans, 2005); Robert M. Kingdon, *Adultery and Divorce in Calvin's Geneva* (Cambridge: Harvard University Press, 1995); and William G. Naphy, *Calvin and the Consolidation of the Genevan Reformation* (Manchester: Manchester University Press, 1994).

55. E.g., see Kingdon, *Adultery and Divorce,* ch. 1; and Jeannine E. Olson, "Calvin and Social-ethical Issues," in *The Cambridge Companion to John Calvin,* 153-72.

of a number of bodies of various size and frequency of activity. At the largest level was the General Council, consisting of all citizens and bourgeois but meeting just once a year, followed by the Council of Two Hundred, the Council of Sixty, and the Small Council. The Small Council consisted of only 25 members, but met nearly every day and thus played a significant role in Genevan daily life. Ecclesiastical government consisted of four offices: pastors, teachers, elders, and deacons. Particularly important for Genevan society was the Consistory, comprised of some of the pastors and elders in the city. That the civil and ecclesiastical governments stood in a close and intertwined relationship is clear from the *Ecclesiastical Ordinances*. John Witte and Robert Kingdon refer to this relationship as "a creative new alliance" that displayed an "extraordinary interdependence" of theological and legal resources.[56]

The Consistory, as an ecclesiastical body, had serious constraints on its power. As to be expected from Calvin's theological writings, the Consistory lacked the coercive power of the sword: "All this is to be done in such a way that the ministers have no civil jurisdiction and wield only the spiritual sword of the Word of God, as St. Paul commands them. . . ."[57] It could rebuke and exhort, and ultimately ban people from the Lord's Supper through excommunication.[58] But despite this official denial of civil power, a number of features of the ecclesiastical bodies suggest a high degree of civil entanglement. For example, the elders were nominated and approved by the civil government, and in such a way that they would represent the various civil Councils.[59] In addition, the Consistory's range of concerns included general education and medical care and, according to Witte and Kingdon, especially sex, marriage, and family, but also in later years "business practices and disrespect for the leaders of government and church."[60] As many of these matters were of concern to the civil government as well, the Consistory often re-

56. Witte and Kingdon, *Sex, Marriage, and Family*, 1-2.

57. From the *Ecclesiastical Ordinances*, in *Register of the Company*, 49. See also Kingdon, *Adultery and Divorce*, 16-18.

58. See *Ecclesiastical Ordinances*, in *Register of the Company*, 48-49; and Kingdon, *Adultery and Divorce*, 17-18.

59. See *Ecclesiastical Ordinances*, in *Register of the Company*, 42; and Kingdon, *Adultery and Divorce*, 14. It is worth noting that this power of excommunication, particularly in regard to participation in the Lord's Supper, was a right of the church for which Calvin had to fight amidst serious opposition, and never fully received; e.g., see Bernard Cottret, *Calvin: A Biography*, trans. M. Wallace McDonald (Grand Rapids: Eerdmans, 2000), 130-31, 159, 163-68, 197.

60. See *Ecclesiastical Ordinances*, in *Register of the Company*, 41, 43-44; and Witte and Kingdon, *Sex, Marriage, and Family*, 71.

ferred cases to the Small Council when civil penalties were necessary and made recommendations to the Small Council when the Small Council referred cases back to it.[61] The Consistory thus "often acted as a kind of preliminary hearings court, something like a Grand Jury in Anglo-Saxon practice" (as well "as a compulsory counseling service, and as an educational institution").[62] Furthermore, the Consistory had authority in such matters over all people in Geneva, not just over those in good standing in the local congregations.[63] And, as recent writers have noted, a sentence of excommunication by the Consistory not only served as an official ecclesiastical penalty but also had all sorts of adverse civil consequences, such that many of the excommunicated ended up leaving Geneva.[64]

In addition to this involvement of ecclesiastical authorities in seemingly civil affairs and their coordination with civil authorities, questions about the coherence of Calvin's thought also emerge with regard to the practical involvement of the civil authorities in seemingly spiritual, religious affairs. Perhaps but one example is necessary here: the well-known execution by burning of the notorious heretic Michael Servetus when he was recognized while passing through Geneva. Such an extreme measure was not at all ordinary in Geneva, but all sorts of other lesser illustrations might also be given.

Many have found these concrete practices in Geneva to be, to one degree or another, inconsistent with his two kingdoms doctrine, but can support for these practices be found in Calvin's theological writings? Certainly Calvin does say things that indicate both general and specific approbation of such practices. Generally, Calvin offers a brief defense of a coordinated system of ecclesiastical and civil handling of seemingly civil affairs in the *Institutes*. Using the cases of drunkenness and prostitution as examples, Calvin discusses how both the state and church ought to be involved, the state imposing penalties such as imprisonment and the church imposing excommunication if there is no repentance. In this way, Calvin explains, the church may "assist the magistrate in diminishing the number of offenders" and the two can "combine their efforts" so as to be "a help to the other."[65]

---

61. See Witte and Kingdon, *Sex, Marriage, and Family,* 69-71.

62. Witte and Kingdon, *Sex, Marriage, and Family,* 68; Kingdon, *Adultery and Divorce,* 4. See also Witte, "Moderate Religious Liberty," 395.

63. This seems to be suggested in the *Ecclesiastical Ordinances,* in *Register of the Company,* 41, 47, 48; and Kingdon confirms that this was the actual practice in *Adultery and Divorce,* 4.

64. See Kingdon, *Adultery and Divorce,* 18; and Witte and Kingdon, *Sex, Marriage, and Family,* 71.

65. Calvin, *Institutes,* 4.11.3.

There is also clear evidence in Calvin's writings of his support for magisterial involvement in seemingly religious matters. Such appears, in fact, immediately following Calvin's strong reiteration of his two kingdoms doctrine at the beginning of *Institutes* 4.20. Calvin writes that among the duties of civil government are "to foster and maintain the external worship of God, to defend sound doctrine and the condition of the Church," to ensure that "a public form of religion may exist among Christians," and "to prevent the true religion, which is contained in the law of God, from being with impunity openly violated and polluted by public blasphemy."[66] Later he affirms that civil authority extends to both tables of the Decalogue.[67] Calvin even consents to Augustine's use of Luke 14:23 "to prove that godly princes may lawfully issue edicts, for *compelling* obstinate and rebellious persons to worship the true God, and to maintain the unity of the faith." Though acknowledging that faith is voluntary, he states that "such methods are useful for subduing the obstinacy of those who will not yield until they are compelled."[68] One interesting thing to note is that Calvin himself sensed that there was something potentially problematic in saying such things, for he writes: "Let no one be surprised that I now attribute the task of constituting religion aright to human polity, though I seem above to have placed it beyond the will of man. . . ."[69] Thus, one must conclude that although Calvin recognized the potential for taking his theology as inconsistent at this point, he thought about it and dismissed such an objection.

Analysis of Calvin's Two Kingdoms Theology

What is to be made of these potential difficulties? Was Calvin inconsistent on these matters or do these potential difficulties instead suggest that his two kingdoms theology is more complicated than it appears? Perhaps there is some truth to both conclusions. In this final subsection on Calvin's two kingdoms doctrine, I reflect both upon the consistency of Calvin's theology at this point and upon the place of his two kingdoms thought, in its complexity, within the broader development of the Christian tradition.

When considering the question of the consistency and harmony of Cal-

66. Calvin, *Institutes*, 4.20.2-3.

67. Calvin, *Institutes*, 4.20.9.

68. John Calvin, *Commentary on a Harmony of the Evangelists, Matthew, Mark, and Luke*, vol. 2, trans. William Pringle, in *Calvin's Commentaries*, vol. 16 (Grand Rapids: Baker, 2003), 173.

69. Calvin, *Institutes*, 4.20.3.

vin's thought, it is perhaps worth saying first that, whether or not Calvin said things at variance with the practices of Geneva, he said many other things indicating approval of them. This seems to mean that the proper question is not so much whether Calvin's theory and practice were in tension, but whether at the theoretical, theological level there was some inconsistency. I suggest that Calvin can be vindicated of inconsistency at many points, though there are certain remaining issues that understandably continue to defy easy harmonization.

In regard to the church's assumption of seemingly civil affairs, a few points may be raised in defense of its consistency with Calvin's two kingdoms theology. First, Calvin frequently reminds the church, even when assigning such affairs to it, that it does not have civil jurisdiction or the power to coerce through the sword.[70] Second, most of the civil affairs which Calvin made answerable to the Consistory can be said to have a spiritual dimension. Certainly the issues of marriage and family that took up so much of the Consistory's attention are matters that, while clearly civil, also implicate the spiritual condition of people and thus are of rightful concern to their pastors and elders. Broadly, one might say that since people can fall into sin in any area of life, no area of life can be completely slotted as civil and not at all as spiritual.

Nevertheless, in my judgment, Calvin is not so easily acquitted of the charge of inconsistency on other related matters. Given the strong distinction he makes between the civil and spiritual kingdoms and between their institutional authorities in state and church, it is difficult to explain the procedure of entrusting the nomination and appointment of ecclesiastical officers to the civil government. Likewise, the fact that the Consistory, as an ecclesiastical body, was given jurisdiction over *all* residents of Geneva is difficult to reconcile with Calvin's two kingdoms theology, for it gives the church jurisdiction over those who are not members of the church, a spiritual jurisdiction over those outside of the spiritual kingdom. If the Genevan civil government had no jurisdiction over those who did not reside in Geneva, it is difficult to understand how the Genevan church could have jurisdiction over those outside of the church in Geneva. At this point, the Gelasian two swords idea of a unified Christian society seems to clash with a two kingdoms doctrine. Finally, questions can rightfully be raised, in light of Calvin's two kingdoms doctrine, about the city's use of the Consistory as a sort of court of preliminary hearing. However many caveats were offered about the Consistory's lack of civil jurisdiction or coercive power, such a sys-

---

70. E.g., see Calvin, *Institutes*, 4.11.3; *Ecclesiastical Ordinances*, in *Register of the Company*, 49.

tem inevitably made the church's courts a link in the civil judicial processes. The assertion of a lack of civil jurisdiction seems to fall somewhat short of reality when the church in fact played a key role in the accomplishment of civil justice.

Second, in regard to the civil government's assumption of seemingly spiritual, religious affairs, Calvin can again be partially acquitted of the charge of inconsistency. I mention a few items initially that might serve as a defense of Calvin's consistency in regard to his two kingdoms doctrine. First, Calvin defended himself against potential objection to his entrusting religious concerns to the magistrate by reminding readers that he "no more than formerly allow[s] men at pleasure to enact laws concerning religion and the worship of God. . . ."[71] In other words, Calvin refused to allow the state any initiative in doing its own pleasure in religious matters; it had a certain power of execution but not of legislation. Second, Calvin emphasized on a number of occasions that the state had responsibilities only as to outward, external manifestation of religion. His language is clear in entrusting to the state concern for the "external worship of God," a "public form of religion," the "open" violation of God's law, and "public blasphemy."[72] This gives some plausibility to characterizing the magistrate's activities even here as civil rather than spiritual, given Calvin's contrast of the two kingdoms in terms of the external and internal.[73] Finally, Calvin's consistency might be defended in that he does not necessarily need recourse to Scripture in order to support the magistrate's interest in things such as idolatry and blasphemy. This is because Calvin, as will be discussed below, saw natural law as the standard for civil law, and yet he (with much of the broader Christian tradition) identified natural law with the Ten Commandments, the first several of which concern matters of idolatry and blasphemy.

But though all of these points may offer some means of reconciling Calvin's two kingdoms doctrine with his ascription of religious responsibilities to civil magistrates, they seem to fall somewhat short of a full explanation for why he so strongly supported the latter. Nothing mentioned in the previous paragraph *demands* that the hand of the civil magistrate reach this far, not even the idea that idolatry and blasphemy are prohibited by the natural law, for Calvin did not believe that every sin condemned by natural law was necessarily to receive civil punishment. Perhaps more than anything else,

---

71. Calvin, *Institutes,* 4.20.3. On this point, see also Witte, "Moderate Religious Liberty," 387.

72. Calvin, *Institutes,* 4.20.2-3.

73. As, for example, in Calvin, *Institutes,* 3.19.15.

what explains why Calvin went this route was his concern for social order and the responsibility of the civil magistrate to ensure it. Much has been made about the concept of order in Calvin's theology. The evidence is so overwhelming that Calvin did indeed have a passion for order that the question is really not whether he did but what its significance is. Some scholars have used Calvin's passion for order to make him a virtual neurotic, but others have explored profitably its ramifications without the psychological speculation.[74] Calvin was vividly attuned to the dangers of the present life, and he marveled at the order exhibited in the natural world, attributing it solely to God and his providence.[75] In both the cosmic and social realms he feared anarchy and chaos and rejoiced when God's benevolent hand kept order in what would otherwise fall apart. The civil kingdom concerned order in the sense that, for Calvin, its highest priorities were to maintain peace and safety in human society.[76] For example, he says that civil magistrates "are the ordained guardians and vindicators of public innocence, modesty, honour, and tranquillity, so that it should be their only study to provide for the common peace and safety."[77] It is plausible to suggest that Calvin, as a man of his

74. William J. Bouwsma, *John Calvin: A Sixteenth-Century Portrait* (New York: Oxford University Press, 1988), presents a much-discussed psychological portrait of a very neurotic Calvin. Susan E. Schreiner, *The Theater of His Glory: Nature and the Natural Order in the Thought of John Calvin* (Durham: Labyrinth, 1991), lacks the psychological dimension, but explores the ramifications of Calvin's view of order in a number of different areas of his thought, many of which are closely related to the matters discussed in this chapter. Note also the centrality of order ascribed to Calvin in Ralph C. Hancock, *Calvin and the Foundation of Modern Politics* (Ithaca: Cornell University Press, 1989), ch. 8.

75. See, e.g., Calvin, *Institutes*, 1.14.11; 1.14.20-22; 1.16.4; 3.8.11; *Commentary on Romans* 1:18; *Treatises*, 243. Note Bouwsma, *John Calvin*, 72, on Calvin's interest in astronomy and opposition to the ideas of Copernicus; on similar matters, compare Cottret, *Calvin*, 285-86, and Alistair McGrath, *A Life of John Calvin: A Study in the Shaping of Western Culture* (Oxford: Blackwell, 1990), xiv. See Schreiner, *Theater*, ch. 1, on the role of providence in checking the inherent instability of the cosmos.

76. Among numerous examples, see Calvin, *Commentary on Romans* 13:1-3; *Commentary on 1 Peter* 2:13-14; "Prefatory Address," in *Institutes*, 4; *Institutes*, 2.8.46; 3.10.6; 3.19.1; 4.1.3; 4.20.2-3; 4.20.11; 4.20.23; and *Treatises*, 85. For English translation of the second of these, see John Calvin, *Commentaries on the Catholic Epistles*, trans. John Owen, in *Calvin's Commentaries*, vol. 22 (Grand Rapids: Baker, 2003), For helpful discussion of relevant issues, see also I. John Hesselink, *Calvin's Concept of the Law* (Allison Park, PA: Pickwick Publications, 1992), 242, 247; Harro Hopfl, *The Christian Polity of John Calvin* (Cambridge: Cambridge University Press, 1982), 48, 67; and Alexandre Ganoczy, *The Young Calvin*, trans. David Foxgrover and Wade Provo (Philadelphia: Westminster, 1987), 129.

77. Calvin, *Institutes*, 4.20.9.

time, could not imagine a functioning religiously plural society, and the necessities of peace, safety, and, particularly, order demanded that some uniformity in religious practice be maintained, and this work necessarily involved the authority that bore the sword, the civil magistrate. Giving credence to this suggestion is the way in which Calvin on several occasions mentions the religion-protecting and order-keeping functions of the magistrate in the same breath.[78]

The previous paragraphs offer various lines by which Calvin's thought might be harmonized with itself. It is unlikely, however, that such explanations will banish the accusations of inconsistency. Behind Calvin's defenses of civil involvement in religious affairs seems to lie an assumption: that *some* coercion in regard to religion is necessary or at least highly desirable. Certain statements of Calvin in fact only make sense upon this assumption. For example, he writes: "Seeing the church has not, and ought not to wish to have, the power of compulsion (I speak of civil coercion), it is the part of pious kings and princes to maintain religion by laws, edicts, and sentences."[79] In other words, the state has to do it because the church cannot. But why assume that religion needs to be maintained by outward compulsion of some sort, or even that religion (or society) is benefited if such takes place? In hindsight, from the perspective of twenty-first-century America, such an assumption seems dubious or at least eminently debatable, though in Calvin's sixteenth-century context it was surely more plausible. In any case, given the lack of any New Testament warrant for civil magistrates' enforcement of the Christian religion and Calvin's insistence that the civil kingdom (and therefore the state) is a non-redemptive entity whose polity cannot be found in the New Testament anyway, questions about the consistency of Calvin's thought are not likely to go away. How is a non-redemptive institution, whose polity is not governed by the New Testament, to make proper judg-

---

78. For example, magistrates are "to foster and maintain the external worship of God, to defend sound doctrine and the condition of the Church, to adapt our conduct to human society, to form our manners to civil justice, to conciliate us to each other, to cherish common peace and tranquillity" (Calvin, *Institutes*, 4.20.2); similarly, the object of magistrates is that "no idolatry, no blasphemy against the name of God, no calumnies against his truth, nor other offences to religion, break out and be disseminated among the people; that the public quiet be not disturbed, that every man's property be kept secure, that men may carry on innocent commerce with each other, that honesty and modesty be cultivated . . ." (4.20.3). See also *Commentary on 1 Timothy* 2:2; for English translation, see John Calvin, *Commentaries on the Epistles to Timothy, Titus and Philemon*, trans. William Pringle, in *Calvin's Commentaries*, vol. 21 (Grand Rapids: Baker, 2003).

79. Calvin, *Institutes*, 4.11.16.

ments about what kind of religious worship, speech, and doctrine falls within and without the pale? However "external" idolatry or blasphemy may be, they seem to be spiritual matters requiring spiritual judgments that are, on Calvin's two kingdoms premises, rather awkwardly entrusted to a civil institution.

One question that also may be put to Calvin briefly at this point is whether his distinguishing the two kingdoms in terms of things that are "external" and "internal" or that concern the body and the soul accurately captures his intentions in regard to the institutions of church and state. Calvin surely did not mean to suggest that the spiritual kingdom is concerned only about things that are immaterial, since he assigned to the church tasks such as diaconal relief of the poor and administration of sacraments. Witte helpfully notes that Calvin's two kingdoms doctrine was not merely a political theory of institutions.[80] But since it was this in part, one wonders whether this less than precise language contributed to the lack of full consistency between his theology of the two kingdoms and his views on concrete social matters.

I now close this section by attempting to place Calvin's two kingdoms theology within the broader stream of the Christian tradition, particularly in relation to those theologians considered in the previous chapter. As already noted, much of Calvin's two kingdoms theology resembles Luther's theology of the two kingdoms and two governments, as articulated in his "Temporal Authority." Calvin, like Luther, recognized the presence of a fundamental *antithesis* between believers and unbelievers, a conviction prominent in the Diognetian and Augustinian approaches considered in the previous chapter. Calvin too, like Luther and the Diognetian and Augustinian perspectives before him, acknowledged a realm of *commonality* among believers and unbelievers amidst the antithesis. This is true at least in some of the things that Calvin writes, such as his admiring account of the many accomplishments of non-Christians in various cultural endeavors in the civil kingdom,[81] though this issue must be explored a little further below. Calvin also resembles Luther in affirming explicitly the institutional legitimacy of the state, a move that Augustine did not so clearly make but was more firmly propounded by the two swords tradition. Yet Calvin, again like Luther, resembled much more Gelasius's account than Boniface's on this point, for he

---

80. E.g., see John Witte, Jr., *The Reformation of Rights: Law, Religion, and Human Rights in Early Modern Calvinism* (Cambridge: Cambridge University Press, 2007), 44.

81. See Calvin, *Institutes*, 2.2.13-17.

viewed the state as ordained directly by God, not through the mediation of the church.

Calvin, however, is not entirely like Luther in his two kingdoms theology. One point of difference is in regard to coercion in religious matters. Though Calvin and Luther both adamantly deprived the church of the physical sword, Calvin advocated civil use of the sword against certain religious deviations, while Luther, in "Temporal Authority" (though he was not always consistent on this point through his life), permitted no coercion at all against things such as heresy. Another point at which the two Reformers seem to differ is in the relation of the law-gospel distinction (i.e., between what God commands and what God promises) to the two kingdoms distinction. As touched upon in the previous chapter, Luther viewed the earthly kingdom as being governed by the law and the heavenly kingdom as governed by the gospel. Calvin too certainly believed in the importance of distinguishing law and gospel.[82] But he did not therefore see law as the exclusive province of the earthly kingdom. Calvin believed that the church, the present manifestation of the spiritual kingdom, was also to have an established government and system of discipline.[83] Thus, while Luther and the Lutheran tradition tended to associate the visible, institutional aspects of the church's life with the earthly kingdom (and hence entrusted these to the civil magistrate), Calvin defended mightily the independence and jurisdiction of the church on these matters.[84] Thus it might be said that Calvin identified ecclesiastical affairs as a whole with the spiritual kingdom, and not just its work of ministering the gospel, as was the tendency within Lutheranism.

Another way in which Calvin differed from Luther was in entrusting the church with a role in the administration of civil justice. Here we return to questions of Calvin's own consistency. The role of the law in the spiritual kingdom might simply be a matter of intramural dispute among two kingdoms proponents such as Luther and Calvin. But assigning the church a role in the system of civil justice raises the kind of fundamental difficulties

82. For discussion of this point, see Michael S. Horton, "Calvin and the Law-Gospel Hermeneutic," *Pro Ecclesia* 6 (Winter 1997): 27-42.

83. As evident, e.g., in Calvin, *Institutes*, 4.11.1.

84. See, e.g., Harold J. Berman, *Law and Revolution, II: The Impact of the Protestant Reformations on the Western Legal Tradition* (Cambridge: Belknap/Harvard University Press, 2003), 40-41, 58; and John Witte, Jr., *Law and Protestantism: The Legal Teachings of the Lutheran Reformation* (Cambridge: Cambridge University Press, 2002), 110. Also see Ronald S. Wallace, *Calvin, Geneva and the Reformation: A Study of Calvin as Social Reformer, Churchman, Pastor and Theologian* (Grand Rapids: Baker, 1988), 56-57.

explored in the previous subsection. At this point Witte's suggestion may be helpful. He proposes that Calvin in fact superimposed his own version of a two swords theory onto the Lutheran two kingdoms model.[85] The way in which Calvin, unlike Luther, distributed the handling of social matters between institutions of church and state in Geneva would seem to support this proposal. As Gelasius believed that God ruled the world through two powers, so apparently did Calvin. Gelasius assigned church and state their own functions (earthly and spiritual) and urged each to be submissive to the other according to their respective competencies. In a similar way so did Calvin.[86]

And this perhaps is where things must be left with Calvin: a mostly Luther-like two kingdoms theology intersected by a Gelasius-like two swords theory. The point of particular tension here is the matter of commonality. Is the civil realm one that Christians and non-Christians share in common in the present age, as Luther's two kingdoms theology held, following Diognetian and Augustinian lines? Or is the civil realm governed by church and state, albeit in their own ways, according to a vision in which the civil realm is populated, or at least ought properly be populated, by a Christian people, as a Gelasian vision suggests? In other words, is the civil realm ultimately characterized by commonality or Christianity? Though Calvin's two kingdoms doctrine provides theological ground for affirming the former, in practice the latter prevailed.

Calvin on Natural Law

In this section I turn to Calvin's view of natural law. Despite the considerable degree of interest in Calvin's social thought generally, relatively little scholarship has considered his two kingdoms doctrine in great depth. The same cannot be said about Calvin's view of natural law over the past century. That

---

85. Witte, "Moderate Religious Liberty," 375-77; and Witte, *The Reformation of Rights*, 58. I should note that in a previous publication I expressed some skepticism about this proposal. After further study and reflection, I have come to agree with Witte's general idea, though Witte seems to find somewhat more difference between the early and late Calvin on the two kingdoms doctrine *per se* than I do.

86. Witte here comments that by the end of Calvin's life "these disciplinary codes resurrected a good deal of the traditional Catholic canon law and restored to the church consistory courts a good deal of the traditional authority that Calvin and other early Protestants had so hotly criticized three decades before" ("Moderate Religious Liberty," 394).

Calvin appealed to the concept of natural law on numerous occasions is a simple fact, but interpretation of these appeals has long puzzled and divided scholars. As William Klempa helpfully explains in his survey of twentieth-century scholarship on Calvin and natural law, two principal lines of interpretation emerged.[87] One line views Calvin's use of natural law as a peripheral and relatively unimportant aspect of his thought, and perhaps even inconsistent with his broader theology. Proponents of this view typically stress the discontinuity between Calvin's natural law and the natural law of both his (particularly Thomistic) medieval predecessors and Reformed scholastic successors.[88] The other line of interpretation sees natural law as crucial for Calvin's legal and political views and tends to highlight the continuity be-

87. See William Klempa, "John Calvin on Natural Law," in *John Calvin and the Church: A Prism of Reform,* ed. Timothy George (Louisville: Westminster/John Knox, 1990), 73-76. Since the writing of Klempa's article, several books in English have appeared that make substantial contributions to the understanding of Calvin's natural law thought; see especially Schreiner, *The Theater of His Glory;* I. John Hesselink, *Calvin's Concept of the Law* (Allison Park, PA: Pickwick Publications, 1992); Guenther H. Haas, *The Concept of Equity in Calvin's Ethics* (Waterloo: Wilfrid Laurier University Press, 1997); Paul Helm, *John Calvin's Ideas* (Oxford: Oxford University Press, 2004), ch. 12; and Stephen J. Grabill, *Rediscovering the Natural Law in Reformed Theological Ethics* (Grand Rapids: Eerdmans, 2006), ch. 3. Important also is Irena Backus, "Calvin's Concept of Natural and Roman Law," *Calvin Theological Journal* 38 (2003): 7-26.

88. Probably the most well-known articulation of such views is that of Karl Barth, in dispute with Emil Brunner; see Barth, "No!" in *Natural Theology,* trans. Peter Fraenkel (London: Geoffrey Bles: Centenary, 1946), 67-128. Before Barth, German scholar August Lang made a similar case in "The Reformation and Natural Law," trans. J. Gresham Machen, in *Calvin and the Reformation: Four Studies* (New York: Fleming H. Revell, 1909), 56-98. Michael Walzer generally follows this line of interpretation in *The Revolution of the Saints: A Study in the Origins of Radical Politics* (Cambridge: Harvard University Press, 1965; London: Weidenfeld and Nicolson, 1966), 30-31. See also T. H. L. Parker, *The Doctrine of the Knowledge of God: A Study in the Theology of John Calvin* (Edinburgh: Oliver and Boyd, 1952), ch. 2; T. H. L. Parker, *Calvin: An Introduction to His Thought* (Louisville: Westminster John Knox, 1995), Part 1; and Edward A. Dowey, *The Knowledge of God in Calvin's Theology* (New York: Columbia University Press, 1952). Barth's interpretation is followed by James Torrance, "Interpreting the Word by the Light of Christ or the Light of Nature? Calvin, Calvinism, and Barth," in *Calviniana: Ideas and Influence of Jean Calvin,* ed. Robert V. Schnucker (Kirksville, MO: Sixteenth Century Journal Publishers, 1988), 256-57. While disagreeing with Barth at some points, Hesselink concurs with him on the crucial point of seeing all of Calvin's theology, including his view of the law, as centered in Christ (*Calvin's Concept,* 24-36), and he emphasizes the discontinuity between the Reformation and Middle Ages on natural law (*Calvin's Concept,* 67-70). Among Roman Catholic natural law thinkers, Josef Fuchs argues that Romanist-Reformation differences on the nature-grace distinction caused a great chasm in their respective natural law claims; see especially Josef Fuchs, S.J, *Natural Law: A Theological Investigation,* trans. Helmut Reckter, S.J., and John A. Dowling (New York: Sheed and Ward, 1965), 10-11, 46-47, 62-63.

tween the natural law thought of the Reformation and that of the Middle Ages.[89] Some scholars, understandably, have offered somewhat mediating perspectives on this long-simmering debate.[90] Part of the controversy certainly depends upon different understandings of how theology developed from the high and late Middle Ages through the Reformation and on to Protestant scholasticism. But another part of the controversy is textual. Calvin at times spoke negatively of sinful human beings' knowledge of natural revelation and at other times quite positively. How is one to interpret these seemingly contrasting strands of his thought?

This section will traverse this contested ground in interaction with, though not beholden to, these recent scholarly debates. Of particular concern here is to articulate Calvin's understanding of natural law in a way that accounts for the various theological contexts in which he addressed it and that places it in helpful relation to the medieval and Reformation traditions before him, recognizing both similarity and distinctiveness. In order to accomplish this, I first consider the question of Calvin's relation to the different medieval theological schools and then turn to expound his natural law theology in its various aspects. Two conclusions stand out as of particular significance for the present book. One is that Calvin's understanding of natural law indeed stood in considerable continuity to the medieval natural law traditions, including the Thomistic, though its Reformation distinctiveness must also be recognized. Second, correlating Calvin's doctrine of natural law with his doctrine of the two kingdoms is of great help for reconciling the seemingly discordant strains of his statements about natural law and thereby proves to be a key aspect of its distinctiveness in comparison to the medieval traditions.

---

89. Emil Brunner's articulation of this line of thought provoked Barth's essay cited above; see Brunner, "Nature and Grace," in *Natural Theology*, 15-64. A short time after Brunner's essay, John T. McNeill penned a relentless argument supporting the continuity of Calvin with his medieval predecessors on natural law: "Natural Law in the Teaching of the Reformers," *Journal of Religion* 26 (1946): 168-82. McNeill's claims are generally, if more cautiously, supported in Richard A. Muller, *The Unaccommodated Calvin*, 39; Schreiner, *Theater*, 2-3, 77; Susan E. Schreiner, "Calvin's Use of Natural Law," in *A Preserving Grace: Protestants, Catholics, and Natural Law*, ed. Michael Cromartie (Washington, D.C.: Ethics and Public Policy Center; Grand Rapids: Eerdmans, 1997), 54-55, 73; Paul Helm, "Calvin and Natural Law," *Scottish Bulletin of Evangelical Theology* 2 (1984): 9-12; Helm, *John Calvin's Ideas*, ch. 12; Backus, "Calvin's Concept," 11-12; Grabill, *Rediscovering the Natural Law*, ch. 3; and C. Scott Pryor, "God's Bridle: John Calvin's Application of Natural Law," *Journal of Law and Religion* 22, no. 1 (2006-2007): 225-54.

90. This is the approach of Klempa, "John Calvin on Natural Law." See also R. S. Clark, "Calvin and the *Lex Naturalis*," *Stulos* 6 (May-November 1998): 1-22.

Calvin and the Schools of Medieval Theology

The previous chapter noted that some scholars have argued that one school of medieval theology, the *via antiqua* (associated with realism and intellectualism), strongly upheld the natural law tradition while another medieval theological school, the *via moderna* (associated with nominalism and voluntarism), promoted the breakdown of a natural law theology and significantly contributed to the development of moral relativism and legal positivism. Some of the writers who adopt variations of this argument place the Reformers, including Calvin, firmly in the latter, *via moderna,* theological tradition.[91] According to this line of thought, Calvin resided in a theological trajectory fundamentally hostile to natural law. A somewhat different, though related, kind of claim relevant to the present subsection comes from those associated with twentieth-century neo-orthodoxy. Such writers claim that Calvin's admittedly positive references to natural law and the natural knowledge of God are the result of a failure to carry through on his own fundamental insight that all theology — all knowledge of God — must come through Christ.[92] According to this line of thought, then, a positive view of natural law was contrary to the genius of Calvin's theology but snuck in here and there due, presumably, either to a failure to think through this issue closely enough or to historical ignorance of the real threat that natural law posed to a genuine Protestant theology.

These sorts of views run into numerous difficulties. One is that there are clear obstacles to characterizing the nominalist tradition as hostile to natural law, as observed in the previous chapter. Despite certain differences with earlier figures such as Thomas in regard to epistemology and the theological foundations of natural law, leading nominalist figures, including William of Ockham, affirmed the existence of natural law and even accorded it an important role in their consideration of ethics and civil law. Another difficulty

---

91. For example, see Francis Oakley, "Medieval Theories of Natural Law: William of Ockham and the Significance of the Voluntarist Tradition," *Natural Law Forum* 6 (1961): 72-73. Compare also A. P. d'Entreves, *Natural Law: An Introduction to Legal Philosophy* (London: Hutchinson, 1970), 69-71.

92. E.g., see Torrance, "Interpreting the Word," 256-57. Torrance believed that Karl Barth applied Calvin's insight more consistently than Calvin, and hence rightly banished natural law from Reformed theology. Barth himself attributed Calvin's lingering positive use of the natural knowledge of God to an insufficient knowledge of Aquinas among the Reformers. The Reformers, as a consequence, could not see "the superior system" of Thomas in comparison to that of the later nominalists and therefore did not recognize the need to exercise a more thorough and decisive critique of the natural knowledge of God than they did. See Barth, "No!" 99-103.

is that, even if nominalism might properly be characterized as hostile to natural law, it is extremely difficult to place Calvin firmly in one of the medieval *viae*. Not only does it remain unproven that Calvin studied with nominalist figure John Major, but it also seems clear that Calvin did not have any extensive training in medieval scholastic thought as a young student. Though he did gain an acquaintance with medieval scholastic theology later in his career, it is often not clear who his actual sources were.[93]

A final difficulty is with the idea that natural law was somehow peripheral to the genius of Calvin's theology or that he failed to think thoroughly enough about it and thus did not recognize the need to critique it. There is every reason to think, in fact, that Calvin thought a great deal about natural law and recognized it as a standard part of theological orthodoxy. In light of the acknowledgment of natural law by the various medieval schools, Calvin would have confronted natural law as an ordinary aspect of catholic orthodoxy as he grew in his knowledge of medieval thought. But in addition to this consideration, it is important to note that he was trained as a lawyer, under two of the leading legal scholars of his day, in the midst of the Renaissance and Humanist interest in exploring the sources of the Roman law tradition,[94] of which natural law was a part.[95] Indeed, ideas of natural law were intimately woven into the fabric of the European *ius commune* in which Calvin the law student was immersed in his youth.[96] Furthermore, Calvin's first

93. On these issues, see, e.g., Cottret, *Calvin,* 20; Ganoczy, *The Young Calvin,* 60-61, 133, ch. 16; Muller, *The Unaccommodated Calvin,* 12-13, 41, 44-45; Richard A. Muller, "*Fides* and *Cognitio* in Relation to the Problem of Intellect and Will in the Theology of John Calvin," *Calvin Theological Journal* 25 (November 1990): 223; David C. Steinmetz, *Calvin in Context* (New York: Oxford University Press, 1995), 40-41. Many of these writers do recognize nominalist theological themes in Calvin's thought; on this point, see also McGrath, *A Life of John Calvin,* 36-47, 162-63, 168-69.

94. For historical material on Calvin's legal studies, see especially Cottret, *Calvin,* 20-23; McGrath, *A Life,* 58-62; Ganoczy, *The Young Calvin,* ch. 3; and Moon, *Christ the Mediator,* 23-38. On various aspects of the importance of Calvin's legal training for the development of his thought, see Backus, "Calvin's Concept"; Haas, *The Concept of Equity,* ch. 1; Ford Lewis Battles and André Malan Hugo, "Introduction," in *Calvin's Commentary on Seneca's De Clementia* (Leiden: Brill, 1969), 137-138; H. A. Lloyd, "Calvin and the Duty of Guardians to Resist," *Journal of Ecclesiastical History* 32 (1981): 65-67.

95. Significantly, the *Corpus Juris Civilis* acknowledges the importance of natural law. For example, it understands private law to be "composed of three elements, and consists of precepts belonging to natural law, to the law of nations, and to the civil law." *The Institutes of Justinian,* trans. Thomas Collett Sanders (Westport, CN: Greenwood Press, 1970), 6 (1.1.4).

96. On natural law and the European *ius commune,* see generally Kenneth Pennington, *The Prince and the Law, 1200-1600: Sovereignty and Rights in the Western Legal Tradition* (Berkeley: University of California Press, 1993).

book was an examination of Seneca's *De Clementia,* a work permeated with legal themes.[97] From the first to the last edition of the *Institutes* Calvin grounded civil law in natural law, and his biblical commentaries, which reflect his week-by-week preaching labors, teem with references to natural law.[98] Moreover, recent studies of sixteenth-century Geneva show an important role for concrete natural law thinking in the civil life of that city under Calvin's gaze.[99] And it is not as if Calvin never thought polemically about natural law (infrequent as it may have been) — and his polemics are in defense of natural law rather than in criticism of the idea.[100] The conclusion seems warranted that Calvin was broadly exposed to a pervasive natural law tradition, that he accepted it, that he incorporated it into his theology and practical civil life, and that he defended it when necessary.

The study of Calvin's understanding of natural law in the material that follows supports the claim that Calvin incorporated long-standing ideas about natural law into his theology. Natural law was not peripheral, but was connected to his reflections on epistemology, theology proper, anthropology, and various matters related to social life. Furthermore, Calvin's natural law theology exhibits many similarities to that of the medieval traditions, including the realist tradition of Thomas Aquinas[101] (though certainly I do

97. For English translation, see *Calvin's Commentary on Seneca's De Clementia,* trans. Ford Lewis Battles and André Malan Hugo (Leiden: Brill, 1969).

98. See Calvin, *Institutes* (1536), 216-17 (sect. 49); *Institutes* (1559), 4.20.16. On the frequency of Calvin's use of natural law in his commentaries, see Hesselink, *Calvin's Concept,* 52. Hopfl, *The Christian Polity,* 179-80, argues that his appeals to natural law were by no means occasional or peripheral.

99. See the comments of Don S. Browning, "Foreword," in Witte and Kingdon, *Sex, Marriage, and Family,* xxii. The city officials in Geneva actually involved Calvin intimately in the drafting of the city constitutions, a work seemingly out of place for a pastor but one for which he was well suited and apparently highly skilled; see R. M. Kingdon, "Calvin and the Government of Geneva," in *Calvinus Ecclesiae Genevensis Custos,* ed. Wilhelm Neuser (Frankfurt am Main: Peter Lang, 1984), 59-60; and Wallace, *Calvin, Geneva and the Reformation,* 28-29.

100. E.g., in Calvin, *Institutes* 4.20.15-16, when he defends natural law as the basis for civil law over against those who sought to make the law of Moses a permanent standard for civil law.

101. This chapter, then, makes a stronger case for continuity between Calvin and the medieval realist natural law tradition than is ordinarily encountered. A perhaps even stronger case is offered by Helm in *John Calvin's Ideas,* 367-78. As Helm helpfully puts it, in regard to natural law "Calvin was, in general, a contented occupant of a general climate of thought of which Aquinas was a distinguished member," but he also notes that Calvin "did not hesitate to depart from elements in this climate of thought when he judged this to be necessary." See Helm, "Calvin and Natural Law," 10. Another generally favorable account of Calvin's continuity with the realist natural law tradition appears in Grabill, *Rediscovering the Natural Law,* ch. 3.

not argue for a direct impact of Thomas upon Calvin).[102] Yet Calvin spoke about natural law in certain distinctive ways, and ways that we might expect given his broader theology. Calvin, in other words, provided a Reformed account of a catholic doctrine.

General Characteristics of Calvin's Natural Law Theology

Calvin's affirmation of natural law is rooted in his general belief in a natural knowledge of God, a knowledge to be distinguished from a saving knowledge of God. An epistemological question — the relation of the knowledge of God and self — confronts Calvin's readers at the outset of the *Institutes*. Calvin, with some hesitation, begins with a treatment of the knowledge of God. Human beings know God in two ways, as Creator and Redeemer. The first is made known in Scripture, to be sure, but also in nature and the created order. This knowledge proclaimed in nature and therefore accessible to all people reveals much about God, but does not reveal God's saving action in Jesus Christ.[103] Calvin's statements about the manifestation of God in creation abound in both his exegetical and more systematic work. For Calvin, the natural world is a beautiful "theatre" of God's glory and no part of creation, no matter how lowly or corrupted, fails to throw off "some sparks of beauty." Calvin found it inconceivable that one could contemplate this world and fail to be overwhelmed by "the immense weight of glory."[104] Though obviously fascinated and astounded by the glories of the cosmos, Calvin was no less impressed by the intricate structure of the human body and human nature more generally. Though he located the image of God especially in the soul, Calvin, in a remarkable move for his day, granted that the image also resided in the body. The human person, he believed, was a *microcosm*, a world in miniature. The glory of the Creator displayed in the world at large was also revealed in small figures in each person.[105]

102. Compare the analogous claim of Steinmetz when asking, in the context of predestination and Romans 9, whether Calvin was part of a Thomistic school tradition mediated to him by Martin Bucer: "their agreement may be better explained by appealing to a common Augustinian heritage than to a common school tradition" (*Calvin in Context*, 153).

103. Calvin, *Institutes*, 1.2.1.

104. See Calvin, *Institutes*, 1.5.1; 1.14.20; 1.15.3; and Calvin, *Commentary on Romans* 1:20 and 1:21.

105. Calvin, *Institutes*, 1.5.1-2; and Calvin, *Commentary on Genesis* 1:26. On Calvin's view of human beings as "microcosm," see, for example, Bouwsma, *John Calvin*, 78-80; and Mary Potter Engel, *John Calvin's Perspectival Anthropology* (Atlanta: Scholars Press, 1988), appendix 1.

Related to this general knowledge of God in creation was the natural law. In a way similar to many of his theological predecessors, Calvin wrote about God's law written on the heart and turned especially to Romans 2 to demonstrate it. In his commentary on Romans 2:14-15, he speaks of a natural "implanting" *(ingenitas)* and "imprinting" *(inscriptum)* of the law of God on the human heart.[106] Likewise, in the *Institutes* he returns to this theme repeatedly. The knowledge of God, the sense of Deity, that exists in the human mind, by natural instinct, is "indelibly engraven" *(insculptum)* on the heart, "naturally engendered *(ingenitam)* in all," and "fixed *(infixam)* as it were in our bones." Universal reason and intelligence are "naturally implanted" *(inditam)* and the righteousness of the law is "naturally engraven" *(insculptam)* on the mind. The internal law, consisting of the commands of the Decalogue, are "written and stamped *(inscriptam & quasi impressam)* on every heart." The moral law is the testimony of natural law and the conscience, which God has "engraven *(insculpta)* on the minds of men."[107]

As evident in this last quotation, Calvin closely associated this natural law with the idea of conscience. In his commentary on Romans 2:14-15, where he writes explicitly about natural law, Calvin defines conscience as the reasons that come to mind by which we defend what is rightly done and accuse and reprove our vices. In the *Institutes,* Calvin says, in regard to knowledge of spiritual things, that the end of natural law is to render people inexcusable, "the judgment of conscience distinguishing sufficiently between just and unjust, and by convicting men of their own testimony, depriving them of all pretext for ignorance." Later he writes that the internal law dictates to us the precepts of the Decalogue and is written and stamped on the heart: "For conscience . . . acts as an inward witness and monitor . . . points out the distinction between good and evil. . . ." Toward the close of the *Institutes,* Calvin asserts that the moral law is the testimony of natural law and the conscience that has been engraven on the minds of human beings.[108] As Randall Zachman helpfully summarizes, conscience for Calvin is the awareness of divine judgment that continually places us before the judgment seat of God. This recognition or apprehension of conscience, which distinguishes between good and evil and proclaims the basic content of the Decalogue, is the natural law.[109] Along similar lines, David L. Foxgrover has

---

106. Calvin, *Commentary on Romans* 2:14-15.

107. Calvin, *Institutes,* 1.3.1; 1.3.3; 2.2.14; 2.2.22; 2.8.1; 4.20.16.

108. Calvin, *Institutes,* 2.2.22; 2.8.1; 4.20.16.

109. Randall C. Zachman, *The Assurance of Faith: Conscience in the Theology of Martin Luther and John Calvin* (Minneapolis: Fortress, 1993), 99-101.

identified three ways in which Calvin's understanding of conscience unites God and man: as an awareness of the divine judgment, as a natural understanding of God's law, or the natural law, and as a distinction between good and evil.[110]

Though Calvin shared the general conviction of his theological predecessors that God had engraven the natural law on the hearts of all people, as taught in Romans 2:14-15, his convictions about natural law and conscience distinguish him in certain ways from the medieval inheritance. This becomes evident when comparing Calvin to Thomas, for example, but many later medieval figures, even of nominalist persuasion, shared Thomas's basic views on conscience.[111] Whereas Thomas spoke of conscience as reason's application of general precepts to particular moral acts, Calvin (more resembling Luther) speaks of conscience as awareness of God's law and judgment. Though Calvin associates conscience with the intellect, he does not describe it as movement from premises to conclusions, but as bringing an immediate awareness of the requirements of natural law. Thomas, on the other hand, made the connection between natural law and conscience indirect. He viewed conscience in terms of reasoning from premises to conclusions and therefore also thought that human laws and virtues are known not immediately by natural law but by deduction from its first principles.[112] The precepts of the Decalogue themselves are known only after (slight) reflection and other principles are known only by the wise after careful reflection.[113] As Thomas wrote, all people have equal knowledge of natural law as to general precepts, but not as to matters of detail, due to the nature of contingent matters.[114] In other words, when it comes to concrete moral decisions in life, the learned and wise understand better than the ordinary person what is right and wrong.

Calvin also states that the learned may have deeper insight into the natural knowledge of God and the world than do the uneducated. In the same

---

110. David L. Foxgrover, "John Calvin's Understanding of Conscience" (Ph.D. diss., Claremont Graduate School, 1978), ch. IV.

111. The similarity of Scotus's view of conscience to Thomas's was considered briefly in the previous chapter. Michael G. Baylor's account of nominalists Ockham and Gabriel Biel on conscience displays the similarity of their views to Thomas's also, though Ockham did not make use of the concept of synderesis; see *Action and Person: Conscience in Late Scholasticism and the Young Luther* (Leiden: Brill, 1977), ch. 3.

112. E.g., see *Summa Theologiae*, 1a2ae 91.3; 94.3; 95.2.

113. *Summa Theologiae*, 1a2ae 100.3.

114. *Summa Theologiae*, 1a2ae 94.4.

context, however, he also emphasizes that even illiterate peasants can see God's wisdom in the structure of the universe and the frame of the human body.[115] And as to natural *moral* knowledge, Calvin stresses the implanting of the natural law on every heart and the inescapable sense of responsibility before God's judgment.[116] A hierarchy of natural law knowledge among the wise and the unlearned seems not to have a place in Calvin's theology. Harro Hopfl has compiled a list of moral items that Calvin believed were taught by natural law, and their specificity is striking.[117] It is surely ironic that Calvin, whose thought many have portrayed as fundamentally hostile to natural law, seemed to believe that, through conscience, a far greater amount of specific moral knowledge is immediately accessible to all people than did Thomas, recognized as a great champion of natural law.[118]

Calvin, in summary, believed that the natural law was stamped upon the heart and mind and known through conscience. Natural law thus served to define human moral nature. But what did Calvin see as the relationship between the natural law and God's own nature? This question brings us inevitably to consideration of Calvin's relation to the Thomistic strands of the medieval tradition, with its emphasis upon God's character as the source of natural law, and the nominalist or voluntarist strands, with its emphasis

---

115. Calvin, *Institutes*, 1.5.2.

116. E.g., Calvin, *Institutes*, 2.8.1.

117. Hopfl, *The Christian Polity,* 179-180: "Although lists are tiresome, it is necessary to offer some illustration of the range of moral questions on which Calvin took natural law to deliver rules of conduct, and the sometimes surprisingly specific character of those deliverances. Thus Calvin thought that 'nature' or 'natural sense' or 'reason' teaches the authority of fathers over wives and children, the sanctity of monogamous marriage, the duty to care for families, breast-feeding, primogeniture (albeit with qualifications) [sic] the sacrosanctity of envoys and ambassadors, the obligation of promises, degrees of marriage, the need for witnesses in murder trials, the need for a distinction of ranks in society; and natural law prohibits incest, murder, adultery, slavery, and even the rule of one man. And again, nature itself teaches the duty to award honours only to those qualified, respect for the old, equity in commercial dealings, and that religion must be the first concern of governors."

118. Perhaps an interesting corollary to this matter is the relationship of natural law and love in these two theologians. For Thomas, love — at least the highest form of it, Christian charity — is a supernatural virtue. As such, it is a matter not of nature, but of grace, not accessible to natural powers on the basis of reason and natural law (see *Summa Theologiae*, 1a2ae 62.2-3; 2a2ae 23-27). For Calvin, on the other hand, charity is "the true and eternal rule of righteousness prescribed to the men of all nations and of all times." Civil laws, which must be based on natural law, are to be tested by nothing other than the rule of charity (see *Institutes*, 4.20.15). For Calvin, all people know the requirement of charity through the law of nature. Again, it is ironic to note that in some ways Calvin, rather than Thomas, has the richer substantive view of natural law.

upon the will of God as its source. Many scholars have not only claimed Calvin for the nominalist tradition, but have also asserted the importance of this point especially for the question of natural law.[119] It is certainly true that one can find statements by Calvin that sound starkly voluntarist. A commonly cited example is this passage from the *Institutes:*

> It [the divine will] is itself, and justly ought to be, the cause of all that exists. For if his will has any cause, there must be something antecedent to it, and to which it is annexed; this it were impious to imagine. The will of God is the supreme rule of righteousness [*summa . . . iustitiae regula*], so that everything which he wills must be held to be righteous by the mere fact of his willing it. Therefore, when it is asked why the Lord did so, we must answer, Because he pleased. But if you proceed farther to ask why he pleased, you ask for something greater and more sublime than the will of God, and nothing such can be found.[120]

As Calvin continues his discussion (of the doctrines of election and reprobation), however, he adds important clarifications. In particular, he exalts God's will, but also intimately coordinates it with his general moral character:

> We, however, give no countenance to the fiction of absolute power [*absolutae potentiae*], which, as it is heathenish, so it ought justly to be held in detestation by us. We do not imagine God to be lawless [*exlegum*]. He is a law to himself [*sibi ipsi lex*]. . . . The will of God is not only free from all vice, but is the supreme standard of perfection, the law of all laws. But we deny that he is bound to give an account of his procedure; and we moreover deny that we are fit of our own ability to give judgment in such a case.[121]

Calvin did not wish to separate the divine will from the divine character. This point suggests that Calvin in many important respects shared the concern of the Thomistic tradition to find the substantive source of natural law in God's own nature. Such a conclusion is confirmed by noting a couple of other things he has said previously in the *Institutes.* For example, in discussing providence he states:

119. Among those asserting the importance of nominalism or voluntarism for Calvin's natural law thought, see Clark, "Calvin and the *Lex Naturalis*"; and Oakley, "Medieval Theories," 73.

120. Calvin, *Institutes,* 3.23.2.

121. Calvin, *Institutes,* 3.23.2.

Therefore, since God claims to himself the right of governing the world, a right unknown to us, let it be our law of modesty and soberness to acquiesce in his supreme authority, regarding his will as our only rule of justice, and the most perfect cause of all things, — not that absolute will, indeed, of which sophists prate, when by a profane and impious divorce, they separate his justice from his power, but that universal overruling Providence from which nothing flows that is not right, though the reasons thereof may be concealed.[122]

Even closer to the point are Calvin's remarks at the conclusion of his exposition of the Decalogue. Calvin, who identified natural law with the Decalogue, makes clear that the moral content found in these sources is rooted nowhere else but in the divine character:

Such, then, is the Second Table of the Law, in which we are sufficiently instructed in the duties which we owe to man for the sake of God, on a consideration of whose nature the whole system of love is founded. . . . It will now not be difficult to ascertain the general end contemplated by the whole Law — viz. the fulfillment of righteousness [*complementum iustitiae*], that man may form his life on the model of the divine purity. For therein God has so delineated his own character, that any one exhibiting in action what is commanded, would in some measure exhibit a living image of God.[123]

Calvin certainly emphasized the divine will and defended it from challenges to its authority, as one might expect in the voluntarist tradition. However, Calvin also, like Thomas, believed that natural law was in no way a reflection of the arbitrary will of God, but was instead rooted in the perfection of God's own mind and character.[124]

Yet even while Calvin grounds the natural law in God's perfect moral nature, he clearly differs from a thinker such as Thomas in not utilizing the concept of eternal law to explain such a truth. As seen in the previous chapter,

---

122. Calvin, *Institutes*, 1.17.2.

123. Calvin, *Institutes*, 2.8.50-51.

124. Among those interpreting Calvin in similar ways on this point, see Helm, "Calvin and Natural Law," 10-11; Helm, *Calvin's Ideas*, chapters 11-12; Schreiner, *Theatre*, 33-35, 78; Steinmetz, *Calvin in Context*, ch. 3 (though Steinmetz and Helm disagree about Calvin's attitude toward the absolute/ordained power distinction); and Allen Verhey, "Natural Law in Aquinas and Calvin," in *God and the Good: Essays in Honor of Henry Stob*, ed. Clifton Orlebeke and Lewis Smedes (Grand Rapids: Eerdmans, 1975), 81.

Thomas grounded his explanation of natural law in the reality of eternal law, which is the divine reason or plan of the universe existing in God's mind. The natural law is human reason's participation in the divine reason as eternal law. Calvin never writes of natural law in this way. While he thought that natural law reflects the divine character, as seen above, he never explains this in Thomas's neo-Platonic participatory framework that suggests some intersection between the divine and human minds.[125] Clear and significant differences exist here, though they should not completely overshadow certain similarities on related issues. For example, Thomas's discussion of eternal law in terms of God's providence and wisdom and his moving all things to their due end seems to find an echo in Calvin. Calvin writes of God's providence in terms of his "disposing and directing of everything to its proper end by incomprehensible wisdom."[126] Likewise, Thomas's claim that the eternal law is imprinted on all creatures such that they "derive their respective inclinations to their proper acts and ends" bears resemblance to Calvin's assertion that all created species are "moved by a secret instinct of nature [*arcano naturae instinctu*], as if they obeyed the eternal command of God, and spontaneously followed the course which God at first appointed."[127]

To this point I have discussed aspects of Calvin's theology that express a rather positive view of natural law. These aspects are often underappreciated. But of course there is also the better-known side of Calvin that believed that natural law has severe limitations. He shared with Thomas and other medieval figures the conviction that sin had seriously affected human use of reason and also that supernatural revelation was necessary in addition to the knowledge of God in nature. But Calvin also went beyond his medieval predecessors in emphasizing the dire effects of sin and the consequent necessity of supernatural revelation, and in this he followed Luther's lead and expressed common Reformation convictions.

Calvin identified a general perversion of the order of nature produced by the fall into sin.[128] This perversion also reached human nature, defacing the image of God and corrupting even knowledge and the use of reason.[129]

---

125. This is one of two major differences between Thomas and Calvin on natural law identified by Backus, "Calvin's Concept," 11-12. Helm perhaps underestimates the importance of their difference on this matter when he states that there is "considerable agreement" between them on the ontological status of natural law." See *Calvin's Ideas*, 370.

126. *Summa Theologiae*, 1a2ae 93.1; Calvin, *Institutes*, 1.16.4.

127. *Summa Theologiae*, 1a2ae 91.2; Calvin, *Institutes*, 1.16.4.

128. Calvin, *Institutes*, 2.1.5.

129. The primary material in Calvin on this point is vast. Generally, see *Institutes*, 1.4.1-4;

Because of this, Calvin insisted that sin makes the natural knowledge of God insufficient and therefore that moral understanding requires a revealed written law.[130] Specifically in regard to the natural law, he writes vividly: "Therefore, as a necessary remedy, both for our dullness and our contumacy, the Lord has given us his written Law, which, by its sure attestations, removes the obscurity of the law of nature [*lege naturali*], and also, by shaking off our lethargy, makes a more lively and permanent impression on our minds."[131]

One way to observe how Calvin's thoughts on these issues clearly differentiate him from many of his medieval predecessors and align him with Luther is by comparing him to Thomas on the relation of nature and grace. Thomas's notion of the relation of nature and grace helps to explain both his generous use of natural philosophy and the limits that he assigns to it. For example, Thomas follows Aristotle in identifying the four cardinal virtues. He claims that they are attainable by human beings' natural powers alone and that their end is happiness. But he modifies Aristotle's account by positing three supernatural or theological virtues as well: faith, hope, and love. No one can attain these by the powers of nature but only by the infusion of supernatural grace. These virtues also have happiness as their end, but a supreme happiness consisting of the beatific vision, which far surpasses the temporal happiness that the natural virtues can produce.[132] These ideas also govern Thomas's account of the need for divine revelation. Thomas held that natural law, known by reason, can guide people only to an end proportionate to their natural faculties, whereas divine law, supernaturally revealed by grace, is necessary to guide people to a supernatural, heavenly end.[133] This nature-grace structure, therefore, assigns true usefulness as well as considerable limits to natural law.

1.5.11-15; 2.1; 2.2; 2.3; and his *Commentary on Romans* 1:21-22 and *Commentary on I Corinthians* 1.20-21. For English translation of the latter, see John Calvin, *Commentary on the Epistles of Paul the Apostle to the Corinthians*, trans. John Pringle, *Calvin's Commentaries*, vol. 20 (Grand Rapids: Baker, 2003). On the distinction between human beings before and after the fall, see *Institutes*, 1.15.1; 1.15.8; 2.1.1; 2.1.6. On the defacement of the image of God, see *Institutes*, 1.15.4. Schreiner, *Theater*, 66-67, helpfully comments on how, for Calvin, the fall as a confusion of the natural order corresponds to the confusion in the order of knowing. Steinmetz, *Calvin in Context*, ch. 2, argues that Calvin's interpretation of Romans 1, though generally in agreement with the previous exegetical tradition, departed from it in affirming the noetic effects of sin, the damage to reason itself.

130. See Calvin, *Institutes*, 1.5.14; 1.6.1-4; 1.8.1.

131. Calvin, *Institutes*, 2.8.1.

132. Thomas gives an extensive account of the virtues in his *Summa Theologiae*; on the points made here, see especially 1a2ae 62.1.

133. See *Summa Theologiae*, 1a2ae 91.4.

For purposes of comparing to Calvin, the relative absence of the topic of sin in Thomas's discussions mentioned in the preceding paragraph is noteworthy. For Thomas, the fundamental reason why grace is needed in addition to nature is not corruption of nature due to the fall into sin, but the inherent limits of nature itself. While sin aggravates the need for grace in the post-fall world, Thomas's nature-grace structure remains in all essential aspects the same before and after the fall.

Calvin at times adopts similar language to Thomas's in this regard. For example, he approves the traditional distinction between natural and supernatural gifts, the former including reason and the latter associated with heavenly life and everlasting felicity.[134] This is not a way in which Calvin organizes his thought in general or his view of natural law in particular, however. There are several points at which Calvin's thought stands in some tension with Thomas's nature-grace structure. First, while Calvin sometimes praises the learning and achievements of the (non-Christian) philosophers,[135] his assessments of them tend to be negative. He affirms that most theologians have taught that sin has seriously injured reason, but he also warns that they have approached too near to the philosophers and have tried to reconcile the doctrine of Scripture with the teaching of philosophy.[136] Furthermore, in expositing his very stark view of the effects of sin, he asserts that reason, though not entirely taken away, is a corrupted and shapeless ruin.[137] Such affirmations certainly display differences with Thomas's approach. Also different are Calvin's rationales for the necessity of supernatural revelation. Calvin treats the topic not so much in terms of ontological necessity, as Thomas does, but in terms of ethical necessity; in other words, human sin rather than the limits of human nature is the principal reason why supernatural revelation is necessary.[138]

---

134. Calvin, *Institutes*, 2.2.12.

135. For example, see Calvin, *Institutes*, 2.2.15.

136. See Calvin, *Institutes*, 2.2.4. Calvin makes pertinent remarks also in his *Commentary on 1 Corinthians* 1:20.

137. See *Institutes*, 2.2.12.

138. For example, see Calvin, *Institutes*, 1.6.1-4; 2.8.1. On the comparison of Calvin and Thomas on these points generally, see relevant comments in Helm, *Calvin's Ideas*, 371-73; and Verhey, "Natural Law," 82.

Natural Law, Civil Law, and Mosaic Law in Calvin

The previous subsection considered a number of general features of Calvin's natural law theology. In this subsection I turn to some particular matters that are of interest to the present study: the relationship of natural law to both civil law and the Mosaic law. Calvin's convictions on these issues place him in remarkable continuity with the broader Christian tradition. In making natural law the standard for contemporary civil law and a crucial aspect of the Mosaic law, Calvin resembled a variety of medieval thinkers as well as Luther, all of whom, as observed in the previous chapter, made very similar moves.

First, like figures such as Thomas, Scotus, Ockham, and Luther before him, Calvin rooted the justice of human civil law in the law of nature. For example, when commenting on Romans 2:14-15, he calls the law implanted on the heart seeds or ideas of knowledge, justice, and rectitude. These are expressed in part by unbelievers' laws against adultery, theft, murder, and bad faith in commercial transactions.[139] In the last chapter of the *Institutes* Calvin is most clear that natural law is the proper standard for civil law. The moral law of God which is the testimony of the natural law "alone ought to be the aim [*scopus*], the rule [*regula*], and the end [*terminus*] of all laws." In this section, Calvin points particularly to the concept of equity. Equity, which is prescribed in the law of nature, ought to be the aim of all law, the foundation upon which the enactment of all civil law rests.[140]

A second point is that Calvin, also like theologians before him, asserted that civil law is derived from natural law in a flexible manner, with discretion given to human legislators. He explains: "Equity, as it is natural, cannot be the same in all, and therefore ought to be proposed by all laws, according to the nature of the thing enacted. As constitutions have some circumstances on which they partly depend, there is nothing to prevent their diversity, provided they all alike aim at equity as their end." He goes on to emphasize his comfort with this diversity: "Wherever laws are formed after this rule, directed to this aim, and restricted to this end, there is no reason why they should be disapproved by us, however much they may differ from the Jewish law, or from each other." Calvin's discussion then turns concrete. He gives

---

139. Calvin, *Commentary on Romans*, 2:14-15.

140. Calvin, *Institutes*, 4.20.16. On the close connection between equity and natural law in Calvin's thought, see Haas, *The Concept of Equity*, 68-71; Helm, *John Calvin's Ideas*, 363-67; Hancock, *Calvin and the Foundation of Modern Politics*, 86; Hopfl, *The Christian Polity*, 179.

examples of how different punishments are rightly imposed on the same crime in different places and examples of when circumstances dictate different laws or punishments. He dismisses as "most absurd" the objection that the judicial law of Moses is insulted when other laws are adopted instead. He explains: "Others are not preferred when they are more approved, not absolutely, but from regard to time and place, and the condition of the people, or when those things are abrogated which were never enacted for us."[141] As with Thomas, for example, diversity and mutability are characteristics of civil law as derived from natural law.

With regard to the relationship of natural law and Mosaic law, Calvin again sounds quite similar to his Reformation and medieval predecessors. A number of points are worth mentioning. First, Calvin agrees that the Mosaic law is properly distinguished into moral, ceremonial, and judicial laws.[142] Second, Calvin sees a substantive identity of the natural law, moral law, and Decalogue. The moral law, which at one point he calls "the true and eternal rule of righteousness prescribed to the men of all nations and of all times," is later said to be "nothing else than the testimony of natural law."[143] Calvin had already made clear earlier in the *Institutes* that he found the content of this moral or natural law in the Decalogue: "The very things contained in the two tables are, in a manner, dictated to us by that internal law [*lex interior*], which, as has been already said, is in a manner written and stamped on every heart."[144] As evident in a quotation earlier in this paragraph, Calvin viewed this moral law summarized in the Decalogue as permanently binding.

A related point at which Calvin again fell in line with the broader tradition concerns the role and nature of the Mosaic judicial law. Like others before him, he saw the purpose of the judicial laws as that of preserving justice and order among God's Old Testament people. Calvin says that the judicial law, "given them as a kind of polity, delivered certain forms of equity and

---

141. Calvin, *Institutes*, 4.20.16. In light of the similarities on this point between Calvin and Thomas, I incline to think that Backus overstates her case in claiming that the "close link between natural law and political government" is something that distinguishes Calvin's concept of natural law from Aquinas's (and Gratian's); see Backus, "Calvin's Concept," 15.

142. *Summa Theologiae*, 1a2ae 99.4; Calvin, *Institutes*, 4.20.14. Stephan J. Casselli offers a recent study of Thomas on this topic and sees continuity with the later Reformed tradition; see "The Threefold Division of the Law in the Thought of Aquinas," *Westminster Theological Journal* 61:2 (Fall 1999): 175-207.

143. Calvin, *Institutes*, 4.20.15-16.

144. Calvin, *Institutes*, 2.8.1.

justice, by which they might live together innocently and quietly."[145] Furthermore, he insisted that the judicial laws are not to be considered binding today nor obligatory for contemporary civil law. One of the few places where Calvin polemicized about the natural law is at this precise point. Some held that commonwealths had to be governed by the law of Moses rather than the "common law of nations," but Calvin condemned such views as "perilous and seditious," "stupid and false." Instead, as seen above, each nation is free to enact the laws that it deems beneficial, judged by the rule of charity and equity, for the Lord "did not deliver it [the Old Testament law] by the hand of Moses to be promulgated in all countries, and to be everywhere enforced. . . ."[146] With Thomas, Luther, and many others, therefore, Calvin shared strikingly similar views on the Mosaic judicial law and its relation to natural law.

Natural Law and the Two Kingdoms in Calvin

I claimed above that Calvin's doctrines of natural law and the two kingdoms are intimately related. Finally it is time to defend that claim and, with it, to bring this section to a close. Calvin's natural law theology has presented its interpreters with a difficult problem, that of reconciling his quite positive handling of natural law in certain contexts and his rather harsh verdict against the usefulness of natural law in other contexts. This problem has led, as noted above, to very different conclusions about Calvin's basic attitude toward natural law. That Calvin makes both these positive and negative statements cannot be denied. The question is how to account for this without jettisoning one for the other and without judging Calvin to be simply inconsistent. I argue here that Calvin was in fact not inconsistent in speaking as he did. Instead, Calvin ascribed surprisingly positive use for natural law (in the form of various cultural achievements) in his discussions of life in the civil kingdom and consistently negative use for it (in the form of leaving all people inexcusable for their sin) in his discussions of life in the spiritual kingdom. Calvin's different evaluations of the use of natural law were not the result of intellectual inconsistency but of his view that though natural law permits even pagans to form good laws and produce other social goods in the civil kingdom, it is completely incapable of producing true spiritual

145. Calvin, *Institutes*, 4.20.15.
146. Calvin, *Institutes*, 4.20.14-16.

good in people for the attainment of heavenly bliss, the realm of the spiritual kingdom.

This claim is perhaps best illustrated in Book Two, Chapter Two of the *Institutes,* where Calvin's distinction between how sinful people handle "earthly" things and how they handle "heavenly" things is crucial for seeing the connection in Calvin's thought between natural law and the two kingdoms.[147] He begins this chapter by attacking the view of the "philosophers," who held that reason is a sufficient guide in all things, including government of one's self.[148] Calvin's initial concern to debunk overconfidence in fallen reason, however, moves to a consideration of the great gifts and accomplishments that many non-Christians display. How does Calvin reconcile his wariness toward reason with his admiration of those relying on nothing but reason? He begins by expressing his satisfaction with the traditional theological view that fallen humanity's natural gifts were corrupted by sin and their supernatural gifts taken away. According to this view, reason is a natural gift, and was thus weakened and corrupted in part, but not totally destroyed.[149] Following this general claim, Calvin becomes more concrete. He introduces the distinction between earthly and heavenly things (or, inferior and superior things). For purposes of this chapter, it is crucial to recognize that this distinction clearly corresponds to the distinction that he makes elsewhere between the civil and spiritual kingdoms. By earthly things, explains Calvin, he does not refer to things pertaining "to God and his kingdom, to true righteousness and future blessedness," but to things which "have some connection with the present life, and are in a manner confined within its boundaries." By contrast, Calvin speaks of the heavenly things as "the pure knowledge of God, the method of true righteousness, and the mysteries of the heavenly kingdom."[150] The two kingdoms distinction and the distinction between earthly and heavenly things are evidently the same distinction, viewed from two slightly different angles.

Calvin immediately reveals the importance of this distinction. He claims that sinners "have one kind of intelligence of earthly things, and another of heavenly things." In regard to earthly things, sinful human reason continues to operate at a basic level and enables the human race to maintain

---

147. Klempa, "John Calvin on Natural Law," 85, points to the importance of Calvin's distinction between earthly and heavenly things for understanding his natural law thought, though Klempa does not develop this with reference to the two kingdoms doctrine.

148. Calvin, *Institutes*, 2.2.3-4.

149. Calvin, *Institutes*, 2.2.12.

150. Calvin, *Institutes*, 2.2.13.

a degree of civil order and at times to discover and achieve great things. The fact that "no man is devoid of the light of reason" is proven by the continuing natural instinct to be a social animal and the primary ideas of justice that express themselves in all human societies.[151] The accomplishments of sinful human beings in the "manual and liberal arts" display "the fact of an universal reason and intelligence naturally implanted."[152] The works of pagan authors, the enactments of ancient lawgivers, and the various accomplishments of the philosophers, rhetoricians, physicians, and mathematicians all remind "how many gifts the Lord has left in possession of human nature" and warn against rejecting the truth wherever it appears.[153] Calvin concludes that reason is "one of the essential properties of our nature," something that distinguishes human beings as divine image-bearers from the rest of creation.[154]

What then of Calvin's view of human ability to understand the heavenly things, that is, things pertaining to "the kingdom of God, and spiritual discernment"? In regard to knowledge of God and salvation, the first two branches of spiritual knowledge, Calvin believed that "men otherwise the most ingenious are blinder than moles" and that "human reason makes not the least approach" in its understanding. The "natural man," who excels in all of the things listed in the previous paragraph, "has no understanding in the spiritual mysteries of God."[155] In Calvin's mind, therefore, the possibilities of human achievement in the earthly and heavenly things could not differ more greatly.

For Calvin, the sinful human person, by use of reason and natural knowledge, can attain great things in the domain of earthly things, that is, in the civil kingdom. By use of reason and natural knowledge, in contrast, the sinful person cannot even begin to approach knowledge of salvation and eternal life, that is, knowledge of the heavenly kingdom of Christ. Natural law, therefore, has a positive function to play in the life of the earthly, civil kingdom, according to Calvin. But as he explains in a subsequent section, natural law has only a negative function to play in regard to spiritual things and the heavenly kingdom of Christ, where it serves merely to convict peo-

---

151. Calvin, *Institutes*, 2.2.13.

152. Calvin, *Institutes*, 2.2.14.

153. Calvin, *Institutes*, 2.2.15.

154. Calvin, *Institutes*, 2.2.17.

155. Calvin, *Institutes*, 2.2.20. For discussion of related issues pertaining to human learning in Calvin, see also Davis A. Young, *John Calvin and the Natural World* (Lanham: University Press of America, 2007), ch. 1.

plc of their sins and to strip them of all pretexts for ignorance.[156] These conclusions show the practical context in which Calvin put natural law to work. He denied that natural law could ever give knowledge of salvation in the heavenly kingdom, even while he affirmed that it provided true and useful knowledge of mundane things in the civil kingdom.

This connection between Calvin's doctrines of natural law and the two kingdoms is also evident in his discussion of natural law and civil government in Book 4.20 of the *Institutes*. Elsewhere, as explored above, he looked to Scripture as the sole standard for the doctrine and government of the church. Of course, Calvin did not think Scripture irrelevant for civil law in the other kingdom, as his practice of applying the example of Old Testament kings and events to contemporary civil issues illustrates.[157] But Calvin did not believe that the civil kingdom can be governed solely or primarily by the teaching of Scripture. Even the Mosaic law, which contains the only comprehensive body of civil law found in Scripture, was simply a wise application of a more basic law — natural law — that is to underlie all civil enactments.

The material in the preceding two paragraphs may be tied together by recalling a couple of matters. An earlier part of this chapter discussed the distinction between the civil and spiritual kingdoms in terms of the distinction between God's non-redemptive work of creation and preservation and his work of redemption. Another part of this chapter portrayed Calvin's association of natural law with creation and preservation (particularly through God's inscribing the law on the heart and sustaining the testimony of conscience). This meant, for Calvin, that God gave natural law as part of his creating work and not as part of his redeeming work. Hence, Calvin was quite coherent in recognizing natural law as the standard for life in the civil kingdom, where God rules but not in a redemptive manner, but not as the standard for the spiritual kingdom, which is the realm of God's redemptive activity.

This connection between natural law and the two kingdoms thus sheds light upon the above-mentioned dilemma that has often plagued scholarship on Calvin's view of natural law. One of the reasons that Calvin could affirm both a doctrine of the bondage of the will to sin and a positive use of natural law on the part of those under this bondage is that he viewed such issues under the rubric of the two kingdoms. For Calvin, any action performed apart from the saving grace of Christ, arising out of the judgment of

---

156. Calvin, *Institutes*, 2.2.22. Calvin offers a similar analysis in his *Commentary on 1 Corinthians* 1:20-21 and 3:19.

157. Among many examples, see Calvin, *Treatises*, 77-78.

reason alone, is sinful and displeasing in God's sight. No such action can earn any merit before God. This conviction, however, pertained to matters of salvation[158] and thus to the spiritual kingdom of Christ. The same action, having no value for one's standing in the spiritual kingdom of Christ, may be of great value from the perspective of the civil kingdom. The ancient law-givers of whom Calvin wrote accomplished astonishingly great things for life in the civil kingdom, though their achievements were worthless for attaining life in the kingdom of Christ. Calvin, therefore, could attribute both a wholly negative role and a remarkably positive role to natural law not because of internal inconsistency but because the former was true for the kingdom of Christ and the latter for the civil kingdom. Karl Barth's famous claims about Calvin on the natural knowledge of God and his law are thus at best only half true. His appraisal that Calvin viewed the natural knowledge of God and his law as wholly negative and merely a possibility in principle, not in reality,[159] would be basically accurate — if his discussion was limited to matters of the spiritual kingdom of Christ. In fact, Barth overlooked the importance of Calvin's two kingdoms doctrine at this point. His claim that Calvin always viewed the natural knowledge of God and his law in terms of the history of salvation[160] is certainly incorrect and seems rooted in a failure to recognize that much of his treatment of this natural knowledge occurred in the context of the civil kingdom.

Calvin's setting of natural law within the context of the two kingdoms doctrine is, in my judgment, a move that differentiates him from his medieval predecessors and links him strongly to Luther. Though the medieval figures considered in the previous chapter treated the issue in ways that may bear certain resemblances to Calvin on this point, none of them held to a two kingdoms doctrine like that of Calvin, and thus none articulated a theology of natural law in quite the way that he did. Luther, on the other hand, did connect natural law with his two kingdoms doctrine, like Calvin seeing a positive role for natural law primarily in the civil kingdom. Calvin, therefore, following the lead of Luther, developed a distinctive, Reformation theology of natural law that stood in continuity with the past but that also took

---

158. Compare, for example, Calvin, *Institutes* 2.3.3 and 3.15.1-3. Calvin acknowledges that in every age there are some people, living solely by the guidance of nature, who "were all their lives devoted to virtue" and showed that there was some "purity in their nature." Yet he explains that, "in the sight of God," their works, because impure and imperfect, can merit nothing and cannot achieve justification.

159. See Barth, "No!," 105-8.

160. Barth, "No!," 108-9.

its own shape. And this shape was in no small way correlated to the doctrine of the two kingdoms.

Natural Law and the Two Kingdoms in Calvin's Contemporaries

As mentioned at the beginning of this chapter, Calvin was not the lone fount of the Reformed theological tradition. A number of other significant figures also contributed to the development of a distinctively Reformed Protestant theology and had impact upon the following generations. A great deal of space could justly be given to several of these theologians in regard to their treatment of themes related to natural law and the two kingdoms. Due to constraints of space and the necessary selectivity of the present study, I discuss only a few of these figures, and these only briefly. The purpose of this section is to provide a small taste of the broader thought of early Reformed theology and to offer some examples that indicate that others worked with similar themes and along similar lines as Calvin, though with their own differences and distinctives on certain issues.

In regard to the two kingdoms doctrine, perhaps Martin Bucer (1491-1551), reformer and pastor in Strassburg (where Calvin spent some time while exiled from Geneva), is most interesting to consider, in part because of his considerable influence and also because he wrote a long treatise on the kingdom of Christ, *De Regno Christi* (1551). In this treatise, Bucer does not adopt the "two kingdoms" language and does not deal with all of the themes in Calvin addressed above. Nevertheless, his understanding of the kingdom of Christ bears many similarities to Calvin's. From the start, he identifies the kingdom of Christ as an eternal and heavenly reality.[161] As to its earthly expression, Bucer on many occasions explicitly equates the kingdom with the church.[162] Bucer believed that the kingdom would best flourish when supported and purified by the civil magistrate. Indeed, he devoted the entire second book of *De Regno* to explaining how his addressee, King Edward VI of England, ought to be of service to the kingdom. In many respects, one can hear the echoes here of Calvin's correspondence with royalty, particularly with Jeanne d'Albret.[163] Nevertheless, Bucer consistently spoke of Edward's

161. For English translation, see Martin Bucer, *De Regno Christi*, in *Melanchthon and Bucer*, ed. Wilhelm Pauck (Philadelphia: Westminster, 1969), 179.

162. E.g., see Bucer, *De Regno*, 194, 203, 204-5, 216, 217, 227-28.

163. E.g., see *Letters of John Calvin*, vol. 4, ed. Jules Bonnet, trans. Marcus Robert Gilchrist (New York: Burt Franklin, 1972), 290-94.

civil kingdom as something distinct from the kingdom of Christ,[164] even if, as he explicitly says, the kingdoms of the world and the kingdom of Christ are to be in mutual subordination according to their particular roles.[165] Some aspects of Bucer's conception of the kingdom of Christ seem to differ from that of Calvin as I have interpreted it, however. For example, while Bucer clearly differentiates the kingdom of Christ and the kingdoms of the world, he seems rather less clear and adamant than Calvin about the need to keep the two realms separate and unconfused and to make training in piety and divine worship the particular concern of the kingdom of Christ. Furthermore, while Calvin seems to be driven more by negative concerns about keeping order when speaking about magistrates' responsibilities toward religious matters, Bucer tends to sport a more positive and almost utopian tone in commending such responsibilities. Finally, Bucer's concern that the king actively reform and purify the church seems to go beyond Calvin's concern that the magistrate support and defend the church and get rid of idolatry from the land.[166]

It is also worth noting that, while Calvin's two kingdoms doctrine drove him to assert the independence of the church from the state in regard to its particular functions, there were some early Reformed theologians who advocated what came to be known as an "Erastian" position. This is a view of church and state associated with the Heidelberg physician Thomas Erastus (1524-1583) in which most ecclesiastical functions, including discipline, were placed ultimately under the authority of the civil magistrate.[167] Significant figures to mention here are Peter Martyr Vermigli (1499-1562) and Wolfgang Musculus (1497-1563).[168] Despite such differences here with Calvin, one can

164. E.g., see Bucer, *De Regno,* 179-91.

165. Bucer, *De Regno,* 186-87.

166. For reflection on the relationship of Calvin and Bucer on these matters that seeks to account for both similarities and differences, see T. F. Torrance, "Kingdom and Church in the thought of Martin Butzer," *Journal of Ecclesiastical History* 6 (April 1955): 58-59; Willem van't Spijker, "Bucer's Influence on Calvin: Church and Community," in *Martin Bucer: Reforming Church and Community,* ed. D. F. Wright (Cambridge: Cambridge University Press, 1994), 32-44; and van't Spijker, "The Kingdom of Christ," 109-32.

167. On Erastus generally, see Charles Dewey Gunnoe, Jr., "Thomas Erastus in Heidelberg: A Renaissance Physician during the Second Reformation, 1558-1580" (Ph.D. dissertation, University of Virginia, 1998). See Chapter 5 below for further discussion about Erastianism and the early Reformed tradition.

168. In regard to Vermigli, see Torrance Kirby, "Peter Martyr Vermigli and Pope Boniface VIII: The Difference Between Civil and Ecclesiastical Power," in *Peter Martyr Vermigli and the European Reformations: Semper Reformanda,* ed. Frank A. James III (Leiden: Brill, 2004),

still see similar themes to the Genevan's. For example, Vermigli asserted that God is the author of all political power, that civil/political power is distinct from ecclesiastical/spiritual power, that civil power is not subject to ecclesiastical power (contra the two swords theory of Boniface VIII, whom he refutes at some length), and that magistrates should get rid of idolatry, blasphemy, and superstition.[169]

In regard to natural law, I look briefly at Jerome Zanchi (1516-1590). Zanchi seems an important figure here for several reasons, including his later influence and the fact that he composed a massive treatise on law in which he treats natural law at some length.[170] Also of interest is the fact that Zanchi, like Vermigli, had received theological training in the Thomist tradition and continued to reflect that background in his writings.[171] Despite the common association of Calvin with the nominalist tradition, it is certainly significant that a Reformed contemporary like Zanchi, with a Thomistic philosophical background, affirmed so many similar things about natural law. A few points can be mentioned. Like Calvin, Zanchi believed that natural law was "inscribed" or "instilled" by God in human beings and he appealed to Romans 2:14-15 in support of this idea (though he differed with Calvin in claiming that this inscribed natural law was not a remnant of the original image of God but a divine re-inscription made necessary because of sin).[172] Zanchi

---

291-304; and Robert M. Kingdon, "Introduction," in *The Political Thought of Peter Martyr Vermigli: Selected Texts and Commentary* (Geneva: Droz, 1980), xii-xiii. In regard to Musculus, especially his 1560 *Loci Communes*, see James Thomas Ford, "Wolfgang Musculus on the Office of the Christian Magistrate," *Archiv für Reformationsgeschichte* 91 (2000): 149-67; and Benedict, *Christ's Churches*, 62-63.

169. See various translated passages from Vermigli's writings in Kingdon, *Political Thought*, 3-4, 6, 28, 31-33-34, 38-47, 54.

170. For background material on this and on his natural law thought generally, see Stephen J. Grabill, "Introduction," *Journal of Markets and Morality* 6 (Spring 2003): 309-16; and Grabill, *Rediscovering the Natural Law*, 132-42.

171. On the Thomisim of Zanchi and Vermigli, see Harm Goris, "Thomism in Zanchi's Doctrine of God," in *Protestant Scholasticism*, 121-40; John Patrick Donnelly, S.J., "Calvinist Thomism," *Viator* 7 (1976): 441-55; John Patrick Donnelly, *Calvinism and Scholasticism in Vermigli's Doctrine of Man and Grace* (Leiden: Brill, 1976); Frank A. James III, "Peter Martyr Vermigli: At the Crossroads of Late Medieval Scholasticism, Christian Humanism and Resurgent Augustinianism," in *Protestant Scholasticism*, 62-78; and Grabill, *Rediscovering the Natural Law*, 102.

172. For English translation, see Jerome Zanchi, "On the Law in General," trans. Jeffrey J. Veenstra, in *Journal of Markets and Morality* 6 (Spring 2003): 330; this is a translation of D. Hieronymus Zanchius, *Operum theologicorum*, tome 4, *De primi hominis lapsu, de peccato, and* [*sic*] *de legi Dei* (Genevae: Sumptibus Samuelis Crispini, 1617), Cap. X, "De lege in genere," fols. 185-221. Subsequent citations to Zanchi will also be to this translation.

also saw natural law as the proper source and standard for civil law[173] and indicated that it was to be applied flexibly in forming civil law.[174] He resembled Calvin as well on the relationship of natural law to the law of Moses. For instance, he made the common classification of Mosaic law as moral, judicial, and ceremonial and closely associated natural law with the moral law and Decalogue.[175] Furthermore, Zanchi made natural law the test for present application of the judicial law, noting also that the Gentiles were never bound by Moses but only by the natural law.[176] At all of these points Zanchi resembled Calvin and many others in the medieval and Reformation traditions.

Conclusion

This chapter has focused upon the theology of John Calvin on the themes of natural law and the two kingdoms. Calvin made a strong distinction between the civil and spiritual kingdoms and, despite certain tensions or even inconsistencies, drew pointed conclusions from this distinction in his social and ecclesiastical thought. In the end, Calvin stands very much in line with Luther's two kingdoms doctrine, with its Augustinian bent, though modified somewhat by a Gelasian two swords model of church and state. Calvin also affirmed the existence of natural law in numerous places and related it to many things he wrote about anthropology, the Mosaic law, and civil government. Though distinctive in regard to certain matters, such as conscience and the effects of sin, Calvin's natural law theology placed him comfortably within the broader Christian tradition of natural law. In respects similar to Luther, Calvin articulated his natural law and two kingdoms doctrines in ways that made them intimately related to one another. Calvin developed a distinctive Reformed theology of natural law and the two kingdoms, yet one that stood in significant continuity with vast parts of earlier Lutheran and medieval traditions.

173. Zanchi, "On the Law," 323, 338-40.

174. Zanchi, "On the Law," 339, 344-48.

175. Zanchi, "On the Law," 332, 337, 384.

176. Zanchi, "On the Law," 379-80, 394. He writes, for example: "How great is the iniquity, then, if Christians want to subject people today, Gentiles and magistrates, to Judaic law! As long as those laws were handed down to the Israelites, they did not apply to the Gentiles. It is only when they coincide with natural law and were confirmed by Christ himself that they apply to all people."

CHAPTER 4

Natural Law in Early Reformed Resistance Theory

This chapter addresses one of the two themes around which this book is structured and functions as a case study of how early Reformed Christianity put its theological convictions about natural law into concrete practice. As the previous chapter explored at some length, John Calvin as well as his prominent Reformed contemporaries articulated a strong, yet nuanced, theology of natural law and asserted its importance for social life, particularly in its role as the standard for civil law. The rise of the so-called Calvinist resistance theories in the mid to later sixteenth century affords an opportunity to observe just how seriously early Reformed Christians took this understanding of natural law when faced with a very particular, momentously significant socio-political problem, namely, whether and to what extent rebellion was permitted against hostile monarchs persecuting Protestant churches.

Reformed resistance theory has proven to be no parochial issue. It has generated a large amount of literature from scholars exploring the development of Western political thought, many of whom have identified it as a key source for the emergence of revolutionary thinking, constitutional democracy, and modernization more generally. The present chapter is not concerned with the resistance theories *per se* nor their precise role in the history of Western politics. Instead, I focus upon two famous expressions of Reformed resistance theory, the "Marian exiles" who fled Britain for the Continent under the persecution of Bloody Mary Tudor in the 1550s and the French Huguenots who wrote in the aftermath of the St. Bartholomew's Day Massacre of 1572, and examine a topic that has not been considered systematically in the secondary literature: their use of natural law in confronting the question of civil rebellion. Clear differences exist among the six writers addressed here, Marian exiles John Knox, John Ponet, and Christopher

Goodman and Huguenots Theodore Beza, François Hotman, and the pseudonymous author of the *Vindiciae contra Tyrannos*. They came from different backgrounds, displayed different degrees of intellectual sophistication, and arrived at varying conclusions about the nature and limits of political authority. Nevertheless, their treatises exhibit remarkable similarities in their use of natural law.

In the main part of this chapter, I argue three related points. First, these writers coordinate natural law and biblical morality by using natural law arguments to supplement, illustrate, and mold their biblical appeals. Second, they view natural law not only as expressing general principles of morality and justice, but also as circumscribing rulers' authority and prescribing remedies for tyranny. Third, they make natural law types of arguments by invoking a wide variety of analogies from human and animal life, by appeals to non-Christian authors and historical evidence, and by recourse to concepts of experience and expediency. After reflecting upon such themes in the writings of these Marian exiles and Huguenots, I turn briefly to note the perpetuation of many of the themes in a couple of other significant Reformed treatises on political resistance, George Buchanan's *A Dialogue on the Law of Kingship among the Scots* (1579) and Samuel Rutherford's *Lex, Rex* (1644).

This study of natural law in early Reformed resistance theory serves a couple of general purposes for the book as a whole. First, it illustrates the continuity that exists in the understanding of natural law between these later expressions of Reformed social thought and the theology of the Reformation, as well as with the medieval traditions before them both. Second, it displays an expansive rather than minimalistic view of natural law among these Reformed thinkers. These writers put natural law in a prominent place in the development of their resistance theories, saw natural law as a rich source of moral knowledge, and displayed great appreciation for the accomplishments of the non-Christian world. This chapter, therefore, serves as a bridge between the previous chapter, concerning the thought of the Reformers on natural law and the two kingdoms, and the next chapter, concerning natural law and the two kingdoms in Reformed orthodox writers of the later sixteenth and seventeenth centuries.

Background to the Marian and Huguenot Resistance Treatises

Before examination of the place of natural law in the resistance treatises themselves, some background information about them may be helpful. In this first section, therefore, I discuss briefly the teaching on obedience and rebellion in Calvin and a few other early Reformed theologians, the historical context in which these treatises were composed, and the sorts of claims that contemporary scholarship has made about the treatises.

Questions about the obedience required to civil authorities and the possibility of rebelling against them faced Reformed theology and practice from their infancy. Calvin, for example, knew many of the resistance theorists personally, had particular concern for persecuted Huguenots in his native France throughout his years in Geneva, and concluded his *Institutes* with a discussion of obedience and resistance. Calvin's convictions on this subject were, on the whole, strikingly conservative. In an extended series of discussions toward the close of the *Institutes,* he hailed the honor and reverence due to magistrates as a consequence of their appointment by God.[1] Calvin exhorts Christians that they must "with ready minds prove our obedience to them, whether in complying with edicts, or in paying tribute, or in undertaking public offices and burdens, which relate to the common defence, or in executing any other orders."[2] He goes on to make clear that this applies to bad rulers as well as to good: "But if we have respect to the word of God, it will lead us farther, and make us subject not only to the authority of those princes who honestly and faithfully perform their duty toward us, but all princes, by whatever means they have so become, although there is nothing they less perform than the duty of princes."[3] "The only thing remaining for you," Calvin adds shortly thereafter, "will be to receive their commands, and be obedient to their words."[4]

Nevertheless, Calvin did provide one route for overthrowing a tyrannical ruler. In a famous passage following his exhortations to obedience, he reminds his readers once again that theirs is to obey and that it is God's to avenge, yet goes on to add the qualifying phrase: "I speak only of private men." He proceeds to speak of "popular magistrates" that have been appointed for the purpose of reining in the tyranny of monarchs and offers examples of such lesser magistrates among the ancient Spartans, Romans, and Athenians. Such magistrates, he concludes, not only may resist tyrants, but must: "So far am I from forbidding these officially to check the undue license of kings, that if they connive at kings when they tyrannise and insult

---

1. Calvin, *Institutes,* 4.20.22-29.
2. Calvin, *Institutes* 4.20.23.
3. Calvin, *Institutes,* 4.20.25.
4. Calvin, *Institutes,* 4.20.26.

over the humbler of the people, I affirm that their dissimulation is not free from nefarious perfidy, because they fraudulently betray the liberty of the people, while knowing that, by the ordinance of God, they are its appointed guardians."[5] This is, quite clearly, a rather narrow exception to a strict, general rule: only lesser magistrates may curb tyrants and, in fact, only lesser magistrates who have been already appointed for such a task. But it was an exception that, in one form or another, a number of Calvin's fellow early Reformed theologians also embraced. Peter Martyr Vermigli, for one, though judging anarchy a worse evil than tyranny and generally counseling obedience to civil rulers, not only permitted Christians to disobey when commanded to do something contrary to piety but also asserted the idea of resistance through lesser magistrates in his interpretation of Romans 13:1-7 and other biblical passages.[6]

Though Calvin, Vermigli, and others wrestled with these questions, a particular spotlight has shone on the Marian and Huguenot Reformed writers who confronted extreme provocation by hostile monarchs and produced extended, detailed treatises on the subject of rebellion.[7] The three Marian exiles, Knox, Ponet, and Goodman, despite differences, shared some important similarities. Knox, a Scot who was probably educated at the University of St. Andrews, was involved in early rebellious activity on behalf of the Reformation in Scotland. He was captured and imprisoned on a galley ship for nearly two years, after which time he took up pastoral ministry in the Church of England.[8] Ponet, an Englishman, was educated at Cambridge un-

---

5. Calvin, *Institutes*, 4.20.31. For a brief summary of Calvin's view of political resistance, see William R. Stevenson, "Calvin and Political Issues," in *The Cambridge Companion to John Calvin*, ed. Donald K. McKim (Cambridge: Cambridge University Press, 2004), 181-86.

6. E.g., see Vermigli's commentary on Romans 13 and Judges 3:29-30 in Robert M. Kingdon, *The Political Thought of Peter Martyr Vermigli: Selected Texts and Commentary* (Geneva: Droz, 1980), 10-11, 99-100. For discussion of Vermigli on resistance, see, e.g., Kingdon, "Introduction," in *The Political Thought*, xiv-xvii; and Marvin W. Anderson, "Royal Idolatry: Peter Martyr and the Reformed Tradition," *Archiv für Reformationsgeschichte* 69 (1978): 157-201. For a study of another influential early Reformed theologian who also pointed to the duty of lesser magistrates to curb tyrants, Pierre Viret, see Robert D. Linder, "John Calvin, Pierre Viret and the State," in *Calvin and the State*, ed. Peter De Klerk (Grand Rapids: Calvin Studies Society, 1993), 171-88.

7. For some reflections on the line of thought developing in Vermigli and Calvin through the Huguenot writers, see, e.g., Kingdon, "Introduction," in *The Political Thought*, xiv-xxi; and Paul Chung, *Spirituality and Social Ethics in John Calvin: A Pneumatological Perspective* (Lanham: University Press of America, 2000), ch. 6.

8. Among many biographies of Knox, see W. Stanford Reid, *Trumpeter of God: A Biography of John Knox* (New York: Scribner, 1974); and more recently, Rosalind Kay Marshall, *John Knox* (Edinburgh: Birlinn, 2000).

der Protestant and humanist influence. He developed a reputation as a fine scholar, especially in the classics, and also served as a bishop of Rochester and Winchester.[9] Goodman was trained at Oxford and later served there as Lady Margaret Professor of Divinity. Like many English Protestants who went into exile upon the ascension of Mary Tudor, a Roman Catholic, to the throne of England in 1554, Knox, Ponet, and Goodman fled to the Continent. Ponet went to Strasbourg, and there, in 1556, wrote his resistance piece, *A Short Treatise on Politique Power, and of the True Obedience which Subjects Owe to Kings and Other Civil Governors.*[10] Goodman too went to Strasbourg, but later migrated to Basel, Frankfurt, and finally Geneva, where he composed his *How Superior Powers Ought to be Obeyed* in January 1558.[11] Finally, Knox spent time in Frankfurt with Goodman and also migrated to Geneva. After spending some time elsewhere, Knox later returned to Geneva, and it was here that his *The First Blast of the Trumpet against the Monstrous Regiment of Women* was published in the spring of 1558, though he probably wrote it somewhat earlier.[12]

The treatises bear their own distinctive characteristics. Knox's infamous *First Blast* addresses various legal-political issues, but its primary purpose is to argue that female political rule is an abomination. Though he obviously had Mary Tudor in mind, he argued on general principle. Ponet's *A Short Treatise* offers a more systematic and thorough treatment of political authority. He discusses, in an orderly way, the origins of political power, the extent of monarchs' authority, the duties of subjects towards their rulers, and the deposition of tyrants. Goodman's *How Superior Powers* grew out of a sermon he preached on the confrontation between the Jewish authorities and the apos-

9. Winthrop S. Hudson offers rather extensive biographical information on Ponet in *John Ponet (1516?-1556): Advocate of Limited Monarchy* (Chicago: University of Chicago Press, 1942), Part I.

10. The original edition is available on microfilm: (Ann Arbor: University Microfilms, 1967), Early English books, 1641-1700; 252:E.154, no. 36. It is also reproduced in Hudson, *John Ponet*. For helpful commentary on the circumstances of its composition, see, e.g., Dan G. Danner, "Resistance and the Ungodly Magistrate in the Sixteenth Century: The Marian Exiles," *Journal of the American Academy of Religion* 49, no. 3 (1981): 473.

11. Christopher Goodman, *How superior Powers Oght To Be Obeyd* (1558; New York: Columbia University Press, 1931). On the historical background, see Danner, "Resistance and the Ungodly Magistrate," 474.

12. A recent critical edition appears in John Knox, *On Rebellion*, ed. Roger A. Mason (Cambridge: Cambridge University Press, 1994), 3-47. Subsequent citations to this work are to this edition. For helpful commentary on the circumstances of its composition, see, e.g., Roger A. Mason, "Introduction," in *On Rebellion*, xiii-xv.

tles Peter and John in Acts 4. Using Acts 4 as a starting-point, Goodman argues at length that God is to be obeyed over human beings, even to the point of commending the overthrow of tyrants by the people themselves.

The Huguenot resistance theorists shared some of the experiences of their English counterparts, including exposure to humanist education and exile from their homeland. Beza was trained in his native France in law and humanist studies and was gaining a place among the cultured elite. Due to his Protestant religious convictions, however, he fled to Switzerland, first to Lausanne and later to Geneva, where he became Calvin's trusted colleague and remained for the rest of his life. He published his *Concerning the Rights of Rulers* in Lyon in 1573 after Geneva refused.[13] Hotman lived a remarkably complex life as a scholar and political activist. Born into the French nobility, he received a humanist legal education in his native country, but spent most of his life abroad. The peripatetic Hotman found himself, at various times, in Geneva, Lausanne, Strasbourg, Valence, Bourges, and Basel. His *Francogallia* was first published in Geneva in 1573, though there is evidence that he began work on it several years earlier.[14] The author of the *Vindiciae contra Tyrannos* wrote under a pseudonym, though most scholars identify Philippe du Plessis-Mornay and Hubert Languet as the most likely writers. The former was also a member of the well-educated nobility and served in prominent diplomatic and military positions on behalf of French Protestants. The latter was his younger friend. This treatise was published in 1579, though written perhaps several years earlier.[15]

---

13. For recent biographical material on Beza, see Scott M. Manetsch, *Theodore Beza and the Quest for Peace in France, 1572-1598* (Leiden: Brill, 2000). For a recent study on important aspects of Beza's legal and political thought, see John Witte, Jr., *The Reformation of Rights: Law, Religion, and Human Rights in Early Modern Calvinism* (Cambridge: Cambridge University Press, 2007), ch. 2; this chapter also deals, more briefly, with all of the other authors and their resistance theories considered in the present chapter.

14. For Hotman's biography, see Donald R. Kelley, *François Hotman: A Revolutionary's Ordeal* (Princeton: Princeton University Press, 1973). For helpful material on the composition of this treatise, also see Ralph E. Giesey and J. H. M. Salmon, "Introduction," in François Hotman, *Francogallia*, ed. Ralph E. Giesey and J. H. M. Salmon, trans. J. H. M. Salmon (Cambridge: Cambridge University Press, 1972), 38-39.

15. See, e.g., *Constitutionalism and Resistance in the Sixteenth Century: Three Treatises by Hotman, Beza, & Mornay*, ed. and trans. Julian H. Franklin (New York: Pegasus, 1969), 39, 138-40. For a detailed discussion of the issue of authorship, see George Garnett, "Editor's introduction," in Stephanus Junius Brutus, the Celt, *Vindiciae, contra tyrannos: or, concerning the legitimate power of a prince over the people, and of the people over a prince*, ed. and trans. George Garnett (Cambridge: Cambridge University Press, 1994), lv-lxxvi.

These treatises also bear their distinctive marks. *Francogallia*[16] is a study of French constitutional history in which Hotman attempts to show the elective nature of the French monarchy and the wisdom of traditional limitations on regal authority. Readers were left to themselves to discern implications for contemporary controversies. Beza's *Concerning the Rights of Rulers*[17] picks up on Hotman's historical work in a number of places, but also offers a more theoretical study of the obligation of obedience towards magistrates, the duties of magistrates towards their laws, and the proper response toward tyranny. Finally, *Vindiciae contra Tyrannos*,[18] the last and perhaps most comprehensive of these treatises, takes up similar subjects. The author addresses the obligation of subjects towards decrees contradicting God's law, the permissibility of resisting rulers who oppress the church or commonwealth, and whether neighboring princes may or ought to aid those suffering under tyranny.

Before I turn to the main concern of this chapter, a description and analysis of the use of natural law by these resistance theorists, a brief survey of scholarly opinion on certain pertinent matters may put some of this chapter's contentions in context. First, certain scholars accuse some of the writers under consideration here — particularly the British exiles — of biblicism, that is, an over-emphasis or even exclusive emphasis upon the Bible over against other sources of knowledge and authority. One writer, for example, in discussing Knox, speaks of "the intense biblicism which is the true hallmark of his thought" and "the closed world of biblical precept and precedent inhabited by John Knox."[19] Another scholar claims that, "in the main, Knox sought to make Scripture the sole basis for his authority. . . ."[20] Others make reference to the "pronounced literalness" or "literalism"[21] in his use of

16. For a modern critical edition in Latin and English translation, see *Francogallia,* ed. Giesey and Salmon. Subsequent citations to this work are to the English text of this edition.

17. For English translation (based upon the 1595 Latin edition rather than the original French), see Theodore Beza, *Concerning the Rights of Rulers over Their Subjects and the Duty of Subjects Towards their Rulers,* trans. Henri-Louis Gonin, ed. A. H. Murray (Cape Town: H.A.U.M., 1956). Subsequent citations to this work are to this edition.

18. For a modern critical edition, see *Vindiciae,* ed. Garnett. Subsequent citations to this work are to this edition. Abridged versions of all three Huguenot treatises in English translation are included in *Constitutionalism and Resistance,* trans. and ed. Franklin.

19. Mason, "Introduction," in *On Rebellion,* xxiv.

20. Richard L. Greaves, *Theology and Revolution in the Scottish Reformation: Studies in the Thought of John Knox* (Grand Rapids: Christian University Press, 1980), 4.

21. See Richard Kyle, "John Knox and the Purification of Religion: The Intellectual Aspects of His Crusade against Idolatry," *Archiv für Reformationsgeschichte* 77 (1986): 275; and Roger A.

Scripture and his pressing "the doctrine of *sola scriptura* to extremes."[22] A number of scholars liken the views of Knox to those of Goodman, though they often portray Goodman in an even more extreme light.[23] One writer goes so far as to say that Goodman's *Superior Powers* "relied exclusively on biblical precepts, turning its back on arguments from secular history, the writers of antiquity, Church Fathers or constitutional law. Since scripture was the revealed word of God, it made no sense to Goodman to look farther."[24] Though the Huguenot writers generally receive fewer accusations of biblicism, even they do not escape completely.[25] It must also be said, however, that many scholars, even some of those cited just above, also acknowledge a role for natural law (as well as an appreciation for humanism and other extra-biblical learning) in these resistance theorists.[26]

Mason, *Kingship and the Commonweal: Political Thought in Renaissance and Reformation Scotland* (East Lothian: Tuckwell, 1998), 143.

22. Mason, *Kingship and Commonweal*, 142-43. Somewhat similar, with acknowledgement of Knox's use of non-biblical sources too, is Arthur H. Williamson, "British Israel and Roman Britain: The Jews and Scottish Models of Polity from George Buchanan to Samuel Rutherford," in *Jewish Christians and Christian Jews: From the Renaissance to the Enlightenment,* ed. Richard H. Popkin and Gordon M. Weiner (Dordrecht: Kluwer, 1994), 106.

23. E.g., see Dan G. Danner, "Christopher Goodman and the English Protestant Tradition of Civil Disobedience," *Sixteenth Century Journal* 8, no. 3 (1977): 70; and Jane E. A. Dawson, "Trumpeting Resistance: Christopher Goodman and John Knox," in *John Knox and the British Reformations,* ed. Roger A. Mason (Aldershot: Ashgate, 1998), 135-36. See also Danner's relevant comments on Goodman in "Resistance and the Ungodly Magistrate," 475.

24. Gerry Bowler, "Marian Protestants and the Idea of Violent Resistance to Tyranny," in *Protestantism and the National Church in Sixteenth Century England,* ed. Peter Lake and Maria Dowling (New York: Croom Helm, 1987), 138.

25. E.g., after Roger A. Mason and Martin S. Smith refer to the "biblical literalism of Knox and Goodman," they also mention "the rather less shrill Biblicism of Beza and the authors of the *Vindiciae.*" See "Introduction," in *A Dialogue on the Law of Kingship among the Scots: A Critical Edition and Translation of George Buchanan's De Iure Regni apud Scotos Dialogus,* ed. Roger A. Mason and Martin S. Smith (Burlington, VT: Ashgate, 2004), xlvi.

26. For discussion of the place of natural law in the writings of the Marian exiles, from various points of view, see, e.g., Michael Walzer, *The Revolution of the Saints: A Study in the Origins of Radical Politics* (Cambridge: Harvard University Press, 1965; London: Weidenfeld and Nicolson, 1966), 36; J. H. Burns, *The True Law of Kingship: Concepts of Monarchy in Early-Modern Scotland* (Oxford: Clarendon, 1996), 146; Jane E. A. Dawson, "The Two John Knoxes: England, Scotland and the 1558 Tracts," *Journal of Ecclesiastical History* 42 (Oct 1991): 563; Greaves, *Theology and Revolution,* 12, 152; Bowler, "Marian Protestants," 135, 139; Mason, "Knox, Resistance and the Royal Supremacy," in *John Knox and the British Reformations,* ed. Mason, 166; Hudson, *John Ponet,* 134-41; Danner, "Christopher Goodman," 473-75; and Danner, "Resistance and the Ungodly Magistrate," 70. On the importance of humanism and extra-biblical learning in these writers, see, e.g., Roger A.

Another relevant matter discussed in the scholarly literature is the relationship among the various treatises under consideration. One common school of thought highlights the differences between the three Marian exiles and the three French Huguenots. These alleged differences occur along various lines, including the more aristocratic origins of the French writers[27] and the more radical character of the British exiles.[28] Many writers have also explored the mutual dependence among these resistance theorists, not only among fellow countrymen but also between the British and French.[29]

Another point of interest in the scholarly conversation concerns the place of these theorists in the larger tradition of Christian thinking on law, politics, and rebellion. A number of scholars stress the decisive character of these resistance works. Whether in the form of recognizing their originality[30]

Mason, "Covenant and Commonweal: The Language of Politics in Reformation Scotland," in *Church, Politics and Society: Scotland 1408-1929,* ed. Norman MacDougall (Edinburgh: John Donald, 1983), 99-100; Reid, *Trumpeter of God,* 18; Barrett L. Beer, "John Ponet's *Shorte Treatise of Politike Power* Reassessed," *Sixteenth Century Journal* 21, no. 3 (1990): 374; Hudson, *John Ponet,* 5-7, 105, 131-32; David H. Wollman, "The Biblical Justification for Resistance to Authority in Ponet's and Goodman's Polemics," *Sixteenth Century Journal* 13, no. 4 (1982): 31; Esther Hildebrandt, "The Magdeburg Bekenntnis as Possible Link Between German and English Resistance Theories in the Sixteenth Century," *Archiv für Reformationsgeschichte* 71 (1980): 241-42; Manetsch, *Theodore Beza,* 10-11, 69; Giesey and Salmon, "Introduction," in Hotman, *Francogallia,* 3-5, 105-6; Keith L. Griffin, *Revolution and Religion: American Revolutionary War and the Reformed Clergy* (New York: Paragon House, 1994), 10-13; and Kelley, *François Hotman,* vii-xi, 18, 186-87, 190, 203-4, 246. Quentin Skinner, in fact, speaks persuasively about the broadness of appeal that the Huguenots hoped to achieve through eschewing exclusive "sectarian ideology," reaching not only fellow Calvinists but also moderate Roman Catholics; see Quentin Skinner, *The Foundations of Modern Political Thought,* vol. 2, *The Age of Reformation* (Cambridge: Cambridge University Press, 1978), 254-55, 310-14. For interesting commentary on the results of some of this intentionally broad appeal, see Giesey and Salmon, "Introduction," in Hotman, *Francogallia,* 91-92.

27. E.g., see Walzer, *Revolution of the Saints,* 68-69, 96.

28. E.g., see Walzer, *Revolution of the Saints,* 68; Dawson, "Trumpeting Resistance," 137; and Richard C. Gamble, "The Christian and the Tyrant: Beza and Knox on Political Resistance Theory," *Westminster Theological Journal* 46 (Spring 1984): 130.

29. E.g., see Gamble, "The Christian and the Tyrant," 129-30; Hildebrandt, "The Magdeburg Bekenntnis," 246; W. Stanford Reid, "John Knox's Theology of Political Government," *Sixteenth Century Journal* 19, no. 4 (1988): 540; Hudson, *John Ponet,* 196-200; Danner, "Christopher Goodman," 72-73; A. A. van Schelven, "Introduction," in Beza, *Concerning the Rights of Rulers,* 9; Manetsch, *Theodore Beza,* 66-67; and Kelley, *François Hotman,* 93.

30. See, e.g., Charles H. McIlwain, "Bibliographical Note," in Goodman, *How superior Powers,* unpaginated; W. Stanford Reid, "John Knox: The First of the Monarchomachs?" (Philadelphia: Center for the Study of Federalism, 1981), 2-3; Hudson, *John Ponet,* 180; Danner, "Christopher Goodman," 73; and Gamble, "The Christian and the Tyrant," 134.

or stressing the revolutionary character of Calvinism,[31] many scholars afford these treatises a very important place in the history of Western social thought. On the other hand, some writers, Quentin Skinner perhaps most prominently, have questioned this popular interpretation. They have emphasized instead how much these Reformed writers borrowed from earlier Lutheran or medieval sources and, therefore, how Reformed resistance theory does not rest on a distinctively Reformed theology.[32]

Although these various issues debated in the scholarly literature are not of equal concern to the present study, the question of natural law in the resistance treatises has relevance for them all. In particular, the way these writers used natural law suggests that accusations of biblicism must be severely qualified, that there was a significant degree of harmony among these six authors, and that there were important strands of continuity between them and their Reformation and even medieval predecessors. To this I return in the chapter's conclusion.

The Coordination of Natural Law and Scripture

The first point at which to observe the natural law views of the six resistance theorists is the way that they coordinate natural law and biblical morality. These authors were committed to the authority of Scripture, yet this commitment did not prevent them from making appeals to natural law and other non-biblical sources. In these treatises, natural law supplements and illustrates the arguments from Scripture and at times even shapes the biblical exegesis itself. Looking briefly at examples from each of the six writers provides extensive evidence for this claim.

A first example is John Knox's coordination of natural law and Scripture in his political tracts. Early in the *First Blast,* Knox introduces his principal theme, that women ought not wield civil authority. He concedes that he will not give every argument that supports his view, but he does identify three

---

31. Most importantly, see Walzer, *Revolution of the Saints,* generally, and especially ch. 2. Certain strains of this line of thought are evident in the classic work of Ernst Troeltsch, *The Social Teachings of the Christian Churches,* vol. 2, trans. Olive Wyon (New York: Macmillan, 1931), ch. 3.

32. See Skinner, *The Foundations of Modern Political Thought,* 206-9, 321; Burns, *The True Law,* 123; Hildebrandt, "The Magdeburg Bekenntnis," generally; Myriam Yardeni, "French Calvinist Political Thought, 1534-1715," in *International Calvinism, 1541-1715,* ed. Menna Prestwich (Oxford: Clarendon, 1985), 321; Greaves, *Theology and Revolution,* 176; and Giesey and Salmon, "Introduction," in Hotman, *Francogallia,* 18-19.

sources for his forthcoming discussion: nature, Scripture, and the Church Fathers. He writes that he will "stand content with a simple proof of every member, bringing in for my witness God's ordinance in nature, His plain will revealed in His Word, and the minds of such as be most ancient amongst godly writers."[33] In what follows in this tract, Knox evidently sees no contradiction among these various sources, but expression of the same moral standard. Though the *First Blast* represents Knox's most extensive foray into non-biblical sources of authority, as often recognized, statements in other treatises display a similar view of the harmony between biblical and natural law sources. For example, in his *Letter to the Regent* Knox commends various virtues for monarchs "which not only God's Scriptures, but also writers illuminated only with the light of nature require in godly rulers."[34] Thus, Knox happily found convergence between the sacred and profane writers on matters of moral virtue.

John Ponet's *Short Treatise* demonstrates the same point. In the second chapter of this work, Ponet asks whether rulers possess absolute authority over their subjects. He describes rulers claiming such power as those who "freely and without correction or offence do contrary to the laws of nature, and other Gods Lawes, and the positive lawes and customes of their Countries. . . ."[35] Ponet, therefore, views regular violation of natural law alongside of violation of God's law (presumably, Scripture) as a characteristic of tyranny. Also, the fact that he refers to "other Gods Lawes" implies that he views natural law as given by God as well. Ponet similarly coordinates Scripture and natural law in the next chapter, where his chief concern is with rulers' subjection to the law, both God's and their country's. He says by way of summary at the close of the chapter that kings, unless given explicit exemption by the legislator, should obey what "is taught by God's law, the law of nature, man's law, and good reason."[36] Ponet thus effortlessly brings natural law (and "good reason," common natural law terminology) into his discussion of divine and civil law. Finally, near the end of his treatise, he commends the coordination of biblical and natural morality. He warns his readers that kings cannot always be trusted and that they should be suspicious and wise in evaluating the grand promises that rulers make to them. The wisdom of which Ponet speaks is not narrowly biblical, but a wisdom that both natural

33. Knox, *First Blast*, 8.
34. Knox, "The Letter to the Regent," in *On Rebellion*, 61.
35. Ponet, *Short Treatise*, 11.
36. Ponet, *Short Treatise*, 22.

law and Scripture commend: "To sue such honest wisdom and fore-sight, is permitted both by Gods Word and nature. Yea, God Word and nature command honest men to use it."[37]

This harmony between the moral order of Scripture and natural law that Knox and Ponet observe is also evident in the third Marian exile, Christopher Goodman. Goodman, though sometimes accused of radical biblicism, frequently supplements appeals to Scripture with references to natural law. In the first chapter of *Superior Powers*, Goodman recounts the story in Acts 4 in which the Jewish leaders threaten the apostles. Goodman, without appeal to the biblical text itself, remarks that these threats were against both reason and God's word.[38] A similar coordination appears in chapter 3, where Goodman claims that God sends tyrants over people to punish them for their wickedness, specifically their sins "contrarie to nature and the many feste worde of God."[39]

A third example from Goodman's treatise closely resembles the first. Here he identifies two aspects of the instructions about royal appointments in Deuteronomy 17 as consistent with the teaching of nature. Deuteronomy 17 commanded Israel to choose a king "from among his brothers." In part, says Goodman, this was because foreigners would not have a "natural zeal" for the people and, especially, because Israel was to avoid "that monster in nature," namely, the rule of women.[40] At this point, therefore, natural law considerations actually shape the exegetical conclusions. Goodman's subsequent tirade also goes beyond taking natural law as supplemental. He writes that if God's word and the authority of the realm cannot convince someone, then "let nature teach you the absurditie therof."[41] Goodman, therefore, like his British cohorts, understood nature and Scripture in close harmony. What God's law forbids, nature abhors.[42]

Turning to the Huguenot resistance theorists reveals a similar approach to the coordination of natural law and Scripture. Theodore Beza's treatise offers a number of examples. In Question 5 of *Concerning the Rights of Rulers*, Beza offers a vigorous argument that rulers are ordained for the good of the people, and does so by weaving together appeals from the Old Testa-

---

37. Ponet, *Short Treatise*, 66-67.

38. Goodman, *Superior Powers*, 15-20.

39. He adds just later that these wicked rulers devour God's people "agaynst nature" (Goodman, *Superior Powers*, 34-35).

40. Goodman, *Superior Powers*, 51-52.

41. Goodman, *Superior Powers*, 53. See also 80 (actually 79, but mispaginated).

42. See Goodman, *Superior Powers*, 96.

ment, New Testament, nature, and various pagan writers. Of particular interest is the way in which he speaks of the Apostle Paul *confirming* what the natural philosophers long taught: "And this is what not only Plato, Aristotle and the other natural philosophers — furnished with the light of human reason alone — have taught and proved, but God Himself by the utterance of St. Paul writing to the Romans, the rulers of almost the entire world, confirmed with clear words."[43] Throughout the treatise Beza continues this alternation between biblical and the non-biblical sources. When speaking about the authority of inferior magistrates, he recalls a saying of Marcus Aurelius and the actions of Trajan, and then turns immediately to biblical examples.[44] Shortly thereafter, Beza argues that the authority of all magistrates rests on the public authority of those who raised them to power. He first ponders examples from Rome and Greece and then turns to Scripture's teaching on the Israelite monarchy, before appealing back to natural reason later in the discussion.[45] A final example from Beza comes in his treatment of remedies for tyranny in Question 7. At one point he offers several lines of historical evidence for a point he makes, drawing freely from biblical, Roman, and French history.[46] Beza, it is clear, frequently integrated his biblical, natural law, and other non-biblical sources.

A second Huguenot treatise, François Hotman's *Francogallia,* offers few specific examples of the coordination of natural law and biblical morality. The fact that Hotman's work is designed as a study of French political history, from which constructive application can usually only be implied, means that the very scope of his project eliminates appeals to Scripture. Nevertheless, at the end of *Francogallia* Hotman offers a perspective not unlike that of his fellow Huguenot writers. After providing copious argument from the actions of their French ancestors — whose wisdom he frequently praises — he closes his treatise by calling for the authority of the Bible to prevail in France and for the French youth to devote themselves to studying it.[47] Given the force of the entire treatise, Hotman obviously viewed such a forceful appeal to the importance of Scripture as completely compatible with studying and learning from the history and customs of his own people.

The final treatise, *Vindiciae contra Tyrannos,* combines appeals to Scrip-

---

43. Beza, *Rights of Rulers,* 30-31.
44. Beza, *Rights of Rulers,* 41-42.
45. Beza, *Rights of Rulers,* 48-49.
46. Beza, *Rights of Rulers,* 73.
47. Hotman, *Francogallia,* 523, 525.

ture and nature in many places, often in ways quite similar to Beza's. The pseudonymous author states early in the treatise that the Bible primarily will give resolution to questions concerning the obligations of subjects when their prince's orders contradict God's law.[48] Though the authority of Scripture is placed front and center, this author also does not hesitate to combine appeals to Scripture with appeals to natural law or other non-biblical sources. One of the most evident ways is the author's use of biblical history alongside of ancient and more recent history to illustrate his points. For example, to support his claim that kings ought to be appointed by representative assemblies, the author appeals first to the history of Israel and then to that of Egypt, Rome, Germany, Poland, France, Spain, England, and Scotland.[49] Similarly, he tries to show the original purpose of kings by combining arguments first from divine and profane history, and then from the Old Testament followed by Aristotle, Cicero, the Medes, and other classical sources.[50] Various other matters, such as the supremacy of law or the responsibilities of kings in regard to public finance, are resolved in similar ways.[51]

In addition to supplementing biblical arguments with natural law appeals, the author of *Vindiciae* uses non-biblical considerations to illustrate and even to mold his biblical exegesis. For example, he illustrates his own interpretation of certain words of the prophet Samuel by reference to Herodotus.[52] In addition, natural law type of thinking clearly shapes his understanding of the crucial passage Romans 13:1-7. When interpreting these verses, he analogizes to the general relationship of masters and servants to show that God must be obeyed above kings. At a later point, he elaborates his assertion of right "implanted by nature" by noting that Romans 13 speaks of kings as ministers of God for the good, in order to defend the idea that a king who uses taxes to enrich himself is unworthy of his title.[53] This author then, together with the other five, clearly refused to limit his argumentation to Scripture, but frequently resorted to a wide variety of natural law and other non-biblical sources to buttress, illustrate, and shape biblical claims.

---

48. *Vindiciae*, 16.
49. *Vindiciae*, 78-89.
50. *Vindiciae*, 94-96.
51. E.g., see *Vindiciae*, 99-103, 115-18, 126-27, 160-63.
52. *Vindiciae*, 129.
53. *Vindiciae*, 32-33, 114-15.

The Character and Content of Natural Law

Another important issue to be explored is the view of these writers on the character and content of natural law. Though none of the treatises under consideration contains systematic presentations of natural law, their passing comments on and use of natural law display a perhaps surprisingly generous and broad view of it. Beginning with some basic descriptions of natural law already common to early Reformed theology, these resistance theorists provide an extensive account of natural law's moral content. In addition to seeing natural law as teaching general principles of morality and justice, they believe that it constrains rulers' authority and provides various remedies against tyrants.

First, the authors shared similar convictions on the basic character of natural law. Like Calvin and other theological predecessors, most of them explicitly associated natural law with the testimony of conscience and the law of God written on the heart, appealing to Romans 2:14-15. Knox, for example, speaks on several occasions of what nature has "printed" on human beings, or even in one case upon "all beasts."[54] Ponet writes of the natural law as "planted and grafted" on the human mind at creation and, similarly, as "not written in Bookes, but grafted in the hearts of men . . . which we have not learned, received, or read: but have taken, sucked and drawne it out of nature; whereunto we are not taught, but made; not instructed, but seasoned. . . . This Law testifieth to every mans conscience. . . ."[55] Adopting almost identical language, Goodman writes of God's "holie Lawes and preceptes" which people have "ingrafted naturally in their hartes."[56] Among the Huguenot writers, Beza comes closest to the Marian exiles' language. He declares null and void obligations contracted because of violence or deceit, and he labels this a "general rule of law and justice." Beza calls such a rule one of "the common principles of nature, which still linger in man after the fall however corrupt. . . ."[57]

Two important points of clarification of this view of natural law as printed or ingrafted in the human heart must be made, however. The first point is that this natural law was not some sort of autonomous or natural*istic* phenomenon. Though natural in the sense of being inherent in the hu-

---

54. Knox, *First Blast*, 25, 31.
55. Ponet, *Short Treatise*, 3, 50.
56. Goodman, *Superior Powers*, 11-12.
57. Beza, *Rights of Rulers*, 64-65.

man person, the natural law is divinely ordained and implanted. Ponet, for example, states clearly that the natural law is "not made by man, but ordained by God. . . ."[58] A second point of clarification is that these writers, obviously reflecting their Reformed theological perspective, viewed human reason itself as badly corrupted. Though nature confronts all people with the divine law, reason as a human faculty is not inherently trustworthy. Ponet, in fact, at the beginning of his treatise, claims that the corruption of humanity means that people cannot rule themselves by reason and, therefore, that those who argue that commonwealths are the product of reason are incorrect.[59] What reason *ought* to comprehend by nature and what it actually does are therefore different things for these writers.

In regard to the actual content of this natural law written on the human heart, the resistance theorists make remarkable affirmations. The natural law, for these writers, is no bare or minimalist moral standard, but declares an extensive and detailed morality. Certainly, no two writers identify exactly the same things as taught in natural law, but there are many points of overlap and rarely does one author affirm something that another contradicts. Both general affirmations and specific applications of natural law may be discerned in these resistance treatises.

The broad, general affirmations about the content of natural law tend to reflect emphases again common in Calvin and other earlier theologians. Ponet writes early in his treatise that the natural law, originally planted and grafted "onely" in the human mind, was subsequently "set forth in writing in the ten Commandments."[60] Ponet goes on immediately to draw the logical conclusion that Christ's summaries of the Mosaic law also provide insight into the content of natural law. Hence, the Decalogue, the written summary of the natural law, was itself summarized in the command to love God and neighbor and in the so-called Golden Rule, to do unto others what you would have them do to you.[61] Other general summaries of the content of natural law reflect broader, catholic ideas[62] that were not emphasized by a figure such as Calvin. For example, *Vindiciae* at several places speaks of natural law as teaching a principle of self-preservation: "nature instructs us to

58. Ponet, *Short Treatise*, 50.
59. Ponet, *Short Treatise*, 3.
60. Ponet, *Short Treatise*, 3.
61. Ponet, *Short Treatise*, 3.
62. For example, Thomas Aquinas speaks of the inclination to self-preservation as part of natural law, in accord with the nature that humans share in common with all substances; see *Summae Theologiae*, 1a2ae 94.2.

defend our lives and our liberty, without which life is hardly life at all."[63] This adoption of an old strain of natural law thinking is also reflected in the author's previous affirmation of a natural human instinct to be a ruler rather than to be ruled: "men are free by nature, impatient of servitude, and are born more to command than to obey."[64]

A final way in which these resistance writers speak in general terms of the content of natural law is by recognizing the basic principles of justice revealed in it. Here again, by grounding civil law in natural law, they display significant continuity with Calvin and the older theological traditions. Several of the writers address this point directly. For example, Beza admits a distinction between the natural law common to all nations and the public law of particular places. While these two need not be identical, Beza finds in natural law "general equity and fairness" such that any polity forsaking them ought to be "utterly condemned and cast off."[65] Alternatively, *Vindiciae* asserts that human nature teaches two main principles of justice, namely, that none should be harmed and that the interests of all people should be advanced as far as possible.[66] Perhaps most enthusiastically, Ponet declares that natural law, as summarized in Scripture, comprehends "all justice," is the "onely stay to maintain every Commonwealth," and that by it "all mens laws [must] be discerned."[67] In saying this, however, Ponet retains a degree of subtlety also found in the earlier traditions. He gives examples of how natural law serves as the standard for civil law by stressing its different application in different circumstances — a particular law might be a just application of natural law in one place and unjust in another, and thus much is "left to the discresion of the people."[68]

These Reformed resistance theorists also believed that natural law addresses more specific moral issues, particularly in regard to their principal topic, the nature of political rule and the right to resist tyranny. One matter that several writers addressed was how natural law prescribed the duties of kings. Beza, for example, arguing that monarchs themselves are bound to the law, appeals to "so many weighty maxims of the jurists of old, derived from

---

63. *Vindiciae*, 149; see also 104-5.

64. *Vindiciae*, 92.

65. Beza, *Rights of Rulers*, 68. At another point in his treatise, Beza states that in certain circumstances rulers have the obligation to examine and defend "what elements of reason and justice" are found in particular civil laws; see *Rights of Rulers*, 27.

66. *Vindiciae*, 181.

67. Ponet, *Short Treatise*, 4.

68. Ponet, *Short Treatise*, 4-5.

the law of nature." Among the maxims in mind are that legislators are bound to the laws, that all people must observe what they have decreed against others, that kings' submission to the law is beneficial to imperial power, and that rulers profess themselves to be subject to the laws.[69] The author of *Vindiciae* adds his own maxims derived from natural law, asserting at one point that reason infuses a hatred of tyranny into good kings.[70] Along similar lines, he appeals to the "law of nature" to demonstrate that kings were ordained to govern rather than ruin commonwealths.[71] More specifically, he even subsumes public finance under natural law, reasoning that "just as this element of right is implanted by nature, so it is approved by the practice of almost all nations that it is unlawful for a king to diminish the commonwealth at his own whim. . . ."[72]

Given that kings often do not follow their natural law responsibilities — as the very existence of these treatises illustrates — these writers also turn to natural law for remedies against tyranny. They discover in natural law both ordinary checks on the power of rulers and extraordinary remedies in extreme circumstances. In regard to the former, *Vindiciae* makes the programmatic claim that the people exist prior to kings and that kings are originally established by the people. The author arrives at this conclusion by reasoning that no one is born a king or is a king by nature "in himself" and that a king cannot rule without a people.[73] Following a similar train of thought, Beza argues that rulers are instituted for the good of the people and not vice versa, "as indeed Nature herself seems to proclaim with a loud voice."[74] Given this limited authority of monarchs, Beza later draws the conclusion that monarchical rule ruins and destroys a people unless "curbed by certain reins. . . ." This fact was recognized by "the philosophers enlightened by natural reason alone. . . ."[75] Beza provides examples of such reins. He claims that mutual compacts and covenants between parties are not necessarily absolute. Arguing from natural law and equity, he says that such compacts can be annulled by parties agreeing to do so, by the clear violation of them, or by later recognition that their obligations are against natural law.[76] The author of

69. Beza, *Rights of Rulers*, 68.

70. *Vindiciae*, 67.

71. *Vindiciae*, 127.

72. *Vindiciae*, 114.

73. *Vindiciae*, 71.

74. Beza, *Rights of Rulers*, 31.

75. Beza, *Rights of Rulers*, 49.

76. Beza, *Rights of Rulers*, 64-65.

the *Vindiciae* picks up on the same point. He finds it "in conflict with nature" that the people should be considered bound by promises extracted by violence, especially if such promises were "contrary to good practices . . . and the law of nature." All of this, again, is grounded on the conviction that nothing can be more "in keeping with nature" than that kings were ordained by the people on condition of governing well.[77]

What does natural law indicate if such ordinary checks on rulers do not successfully curb the tyranny? These resistance writers find a number of extraordinary remedies commended in natural law. According to Goodman, that God is to be obeyed rather than human beings when their commands contradict is something "that there can be nonen so malitious or ignorante, whom verie nature will not compel to confesse it, if he had no further knowledge."[78] At a later point he extends this reasoning to conclude that the people ought to stand up to tyrants rather than passively endure them, based on the fact that they are "reasonable creatures" rather than "brute beasts."[79] This means that civil disobedience is necessary at times, as others of the resistance theorists agree. Beza finds civil disobedience in a case concerning obligatory attendance at Mass commendable "both by the law of God and by the law of nature. . . ."[80] Yet Beza also applies such reasoning to matters beyond specifically religious concern. He writes that civil polities that act against the general fairness and equity of natural law must "be utterly condemned and cast off."[81] Ponet states the most stark conclusion: it is lawful "to kill a tyrant," as known even by heathen "indued [only] with the knowledge of the Law of nature."[82]

This section, taken in its entirety, provides extensive evidence that these Reformed resistance theorists held a quite expansive view of the content of natural law. This is not to say that all of their interpretations of the content of natural law are palatable to most contemporary readers. Knox's condemnation of the rule of women as a "monster in" and "repugnant to" nature is a case in point.[83] Nevertheless, these writers were clearly committed to a broad

---

77. *Vindiciae*, 138-40.

78. Goodman, *Superior Powers*, 41-42; see also 85.

79. Goodman, *Superior Powers*, 146-49.

80. Beza, *Rights of Rulers*, 28.

81. Beza, *Rights of Rulers*, 68.

82. Ponet, *Short Treatise*, 50.

83. Knox, *First Blast*, 4, 8, and many similar statements elsewhere. Goodman, *How Superior Powers*, 52, 96, repeats much of Knox's language. Many scholars have noted that his sentiments on female rule were shared by most writers contemporary to him, of whatever religious affilia-

understanding of natural law that reflected considerable agreement with their Reformation and even medieval predecessors.

The Method of Natural Law Argument

Another issue to be considered is the method by which the early Reformed resistance theorists made their appeals to and arguments from natural law. One thing that is evident perhaps above everything else is that these writers were not narrow in their utilization of non-biblical sources. In augmenting, illustrating, and forming their biblical arguments, the resistance theorists drew on a wide variety of analogies, non-Christian authors, and historical evidence, and also appealed to experience and expediency. The following paragraphs take up their use of these various sources and demonstrate once again their broad view of natural law.

First, these resistance theorists appealed to natural law by evoking a variety of analogies to support their claims. For instance, they analogized mundane aspects of human behavior to human behavior in the legal or political realm. In doing so, these writers seem to assume that an understanding of relatively obvious characteristics of human behavior aids understanding of other, more complex areas such as civil life. Knox uses such reasoning in several of his political treatises. For example, he analogizes women's rule to the blind leading those with sight, the sick caring for the strong, and the foolish counseling the sober-minded.[84] On the more specific point of response to tyranny, Knox justifies political rebellion by analogizing it to children rising up against a father who had become insane and was about to kill them.[85] In both cases, Knox encourages his readers to see the likeness of the particular point of controversy with other aspects of human relationship whose evaluation is more obvious. The author of *Vindiciae* analogizes different realms of human action by multiple comparisons of political life to life

---

tion. See, e.g., Burns, *The True Law*, 146; Greaves, *Theology and Revolution*, 157-58; and Mason, *Kingship and the Commonweal*, 151. A number of contemporary scholars also have spoken positively about Knox's concrete relationships with women he knew. See, e.g., Susan M. Felch, "The Rhetoric of Biblical Authority: John Knox and the Question of Women," *Sixteenth Century Journal* 26, no. 4 (1995): 805-22; Greaves, *Theology and Revolution*, 160; Stewart Lamont, *The Swordbearer: John Knox and the European Reformation* (London: Hodder & Stoughton, 1991), 88-92; and Reid, *Trumpeter of God*, 80-81.

84. Knox, *First Blast*, 8-9.

85. Knox, "Knox and Mary Queen of Scots," in *On Rebellion*, 178-79.

on a ship. In arguing that the people as a whole are greater than their kings, he likens a monarch to a pilot that is appointed by the owner of a ship as one servant among many servant sailors.[86] At another point, the author returns to the maritime analogy, arguing that officers in a kingdom may depose a tyrannical ruler just as officers on a ship may assume command from a drunken pilot.[87] Hotman also makes use of such reasoning. He cites favorably Plutarch's analogy that as hunters prefer a fine dog or horse to one that is well bred, so those constituting a commonwealth ought to seek a ruler of quality over one of royal birth. Elsewhere, Hotman utilizes analogy in his argument that the king exists for the sake of the kingdom, not vice versa. The relationship of king and kingdom, he says, is like that of tutor and student, guardian and ward, pilot and passengers, pastor and flock, and commander and army. In all of these examples, the obvious from everyday life provides the political conclusion.

A second kind of analogy that these writers used is comparison of society to the human body. Ponet, for example, in his defense of tyrannicide, asserts that society can kill a tyrant just as a person can cut away an incurable part of the body that otherwise would destroy the whole.[88] Hotman speaks similarly, reasoning that just as bodies that are dislocated by a blow do not become healthy until each member is restored to its natural place, so the French commonwealth would not become healthy again until its ancient and natural state was restored.[89] Knox likewise, in his attempt to connect the rule of males with good order, says that men are to society as the head is to the body.[90]

A third and quite common analogy employed by these resistance theorists is that of human political life to various features of the animal kingdom. Knox sees shame in the fact that men allow themselves to be ruled by women when "no man ever saw the lion make obedience and stoop before the lioness, neither yet can it be proved that the hind taketh the conducting of the herd amongst the harts."[91] Another such analogy, invoked in passing

---

86. *Vindiciae,* 74-75.
87. *Vindiciae,* 164-65.
88. Ponet, *Short Treatise,* 50.
89. Hotman, *Francogallia,* 143.
90. Knox, *First Blast,* 22-23.
91. Knox, *First Blast,* 25. Knox, perhaps the most aggressive of the analogizers among the resistance theorists, also makes a comparison of sorts between human behavior and non-sentient and even inanimate forces of nature. In his diatribe against women's rule he analogizes the impossibility of a female monarch not becoming proud with the impossibility of the weak reed or turning weathercock not being moved by the wind. See *First Blast,* 16.

in *Vindiciae*, is that nature imprints on good kings as much hatred of tyrants as it imprints hatred of wolves in dogs.[92] Of particular importance, however, is the way these writers use animal analogies to defend resistance against tyrants. Goodman states that nature teaches all creatures to flee from dangers and desire things that do them good: "And when God hath made this comon to all beastes, and inferior creatures, paynefully to seeke their preservation: hathe he denied the same to man, whome above all others he will have preserved?"[93] The author of *Vindiciae* speaks of a related human trait that can be discerned through analogy to animals, the desire to defend oneself. He writes, "Nature implants this in dogs against wolves, in bulls against lions, in doves against hawks, and in chicks against kites: all the more so in man against man himself, if he has become a wolf to himself. So he who disputes whether it is lawful to fight back seems to be fighting nature itself." He applies this, predictably, to the lawfulness of resisting tyrants.[94] Conversely, these writers make their points at times by appealing to the *dissimilarity* between human beings and animals evident in nature. On this score, Hotman provides an example in asserting that no tyrannical government has existed in which "the citizens are treated like cattle rather than human beings."[95]

Another method by which these resistance theorists make non-biblical arguments is by regular appeal to heathen writers. Though such appeals may not appear at first to be natural law arguments, these authors often note explicitly that their sources were enlightened by natural law alone. Even when they do not make such comments, their very willingness to appeal to such writers displays their understanding of the worth of (even indirect) appeals to rational, non-biblical argumentation, though they also continue to note its limitations.[96] Beza gives his own judgment on why such appeals are helpful. He explains that he uses heathen examples not as a rule for conscience, but because they are "famous and very well known to most people" and because "they are not so far removed from the standard of justice that it may not justifiably be said that justice was on one side and injustice on the other."[97]

Sometimes these appeals assume only a general shape. Ponet, for example, cites what was known to the "Ethnics" who had only knowledge of the

92. *Vindiciae*, 67.

93. Goodman, *Superior Powers*, 158-59.

94. *Vindiciae*, 149.

95. Hotman, *Francogallia*, 415.

96. On the limitations of such appeals, see, e.g., Beza, *Rights of Rulers*, 83.

97. Beza, *Rights of Rulers*, 33.

law of nature, and Goodman references the teaching of the "verie Gentils with out God [who] were taught so muche of nature" and "the Gentils, wich lyue besides the Lawe. . . ."[98] The French writers also speak at times in general terms. Beza refers to "the excellent maxim expressed by a heathen" and the author of *Vindiciae* asserts that "we may learn, even from the heathens, what human society and the common nature of all require of us in this matter."[99] When these writers turn to more specific references, they prefer Aristotle to all other non-Christian sources. Knox, Goodman, Beza, Hotman, and the author of *Vindiciae* all appeal to him, in some cases multiple times.[100] Another source of appeal is the Roman law or various Roman jurists. The popularity of this source is much more evident among the Huguenot authors, due probably to their more extensive legal training and to the greater importance of Roman law for the French legal system than for the British. Among the Roman lawyers that they cite are Bartolus, Ulpian, and Papinian (the latter, comments Beza, "though he was no Christian").[101] The author of *Vindiciae* appeals more generally to a rule "well known amongst the jurisconsults."[102] In addition to these frequent sources, the resistance writers intersperse their works with an impressive array of citations from other classical Greek and Roman authors. Among the Greeks, they appeal at various points to Homer, Aesop, Herodotus, Solon, Socrates, Plato, Xenophon, Polybius, and Plutarch.[103] Romans Augustus, Trajan, Marcus Aurelius, Severus, Seneca, and Cicero also make appearances.[104] The combined effect is an undeniable interest in and respect for the wisdom of pagan antiquity.

Furthermore, the Calvinist resistance theorists make non-biblical arguments by combining their appeals to heathen writings and actions with references to evidence from secular history, both ancient and contemporary. The Marian exiles took this approach on occasion, but the Huguenot au-

---

98. Ponet, *Short Treatise,* 50; and Goodman, *Superior Powers,* 91, 93-94.

99. Beza, *Rights of Rulers,* 80; and *Vindiciae,* 181.

100. See Knox, *First Blast,* 9; Goodman, *Superior Powers,* 155-56; Beza, *Rights of Rulers,* 31, 54; Hotman, *Francogallia,* 155, 287; and *Vindiciae,* 94, 98.

101. See *Vindiciae,* 156; Hotman, *Francogallia,* 399; and Beza, *Rights of Rulers,* 27-28. Knox, a Scot, does refer to Roman law and, specifically, to the *Corpus Juris Civilis,* the Emperor Justinian's monumental compilation of Roman law. The latter was the product of Christians, not pagans. See Knox, *First Blast,* 9-11.

102. *Vindiciae,* 111.

103. See Beza, *Rights of Rulers,* 31; *Vindiciae,* 92, 102-3, 129; and Hotman, *Francogallia,* 155, 201, 399, 401, 403, 405.

104. See Ponet, *Superior Powers,* 21; Beza, *Rights of Rulers,* 41-42; *Vindiciae,* 92-93, 94, 96, 102, 105, 181; and Hotman, *Francogallia,* 155, 403, 405.

thors especially favored it. Beza makes historical appeals less than the other two, but he at times calls upon Greek and Roman history for support of his claims.[105] Hotman's *Francogallia* is literally permeated with historical examples — it is, after all, a study in French constitutional history. This fact might seem to question the identification of his historical citations with a kind of natural law thinking. However, Hotman reveals on a number of occasions his view of the history he discusses. In his preface, he not only speaks of the wisdom of their ancestors in constituting the commonwealth as they did, but he also expresses his own confidence that "the most certain remedy for our great afflictions should be sought in the constitution."[106] Throughout this work, then, despite its posture as an objective historical study, Hotman repeats his praise of their ancestors' wisdom.[107] *Vindiciae* is also enamored with historical example. Probably with great reliance on Hotman's scholarship, this treatise appeals at times to French history.[108] But it also cites ancient history and the history of other European countries. In defending the idea that representative assemblies ought to appoint kings, he refers to the practices of Egypt, Rome, Germany, Poland, Spain, England, and Scotland, as well as France.[109] In another place he even cites the history of the Medes.[110] These writers took historical events as weighty precedents and helpful models.

A final point to mention briefly in this section is that these resistance theorists also occasionally make appeals to experience and expediency. Knox, for instance, calls upon experience to vindicate his claim that women make poor rulers, and Goodman cites it as proof that the common fool makes a better ruler than an idolatrous tyrant.[111] Both Beza and the author of *Vindiciae* appeal to expediency in order to temper undue haste toward rebellion. The former demands that no remedy against tyranny be sought until what is both permissible and expedient has been examined. The latter, similarly, warns that it is not always expedient for the people to do all that is lawful against a tyrant, lest the medicine prove worse than the disease.[112]

The various strains of argument and appeal surveyed in this section to-

---

105. E.g., see Beza, *Rights of Rulers*, 45-48.

106. Hotman, *Francogallia*, 143.

107. See Hotman, *Francogallia*, 201, 221, 237, 261, 289, 297, 323, 333, 399.

108. E.g., see *Vindiciae*, 57-58.

109. *Vindiciae*, 80-89.

110. *Vindiciae*, 94.

111. Knox, *First Blast*, 9; and Goodman, *Superior Powers*, 144.

112. Beza, *Rights of Rulers*, 73-74, 86; and *Vindiciae*, 155.

gether provide extensive evidence of the variety and flexibility of the resistance theorists' recourse to natural law and non-biblical reasoning more generally. All told, this evidence further demonstrates that these writers, despite their commitment to biblical authority, eschewed any narrow biblicism. In making diverse analogies, appealing to non-Christian authors, citing historical examples, and noting concerns of experience and expediency, they appealed to natural law freely, widely, and comfortably.

Pre-Conclusion Postscript:
Natural Law in Other Reformed Resistance Treatises

Though the resistance treatises of the three Marian exiles and the three Huguenots are the most famous Reformed treatments of the subject, they were certainly not the only ones. As observed above, a number of the earliest and most influential Reformed theologians, such as Calvin and Vermigli, addressed ideas of civil obedience and rebellion. Other Reformed writers produced important treatises both contemporaneous to the authors discussed above and in the following century. A significant example of the former is George Buchanan's *A Dialogue on the Law of Kingship among the Scots* (originally written in 1567 and published in 1579) and of the latter is Samuel Rutherford's *Lex, Rex* (1644). Once again, the purpose of this section is not to consider these treatises as such, holistically, nor to examine their place in the development of Western political thought more generally. What this section does seek to provide is a brief account of the role of natural law in them both, as a way to illustrate further the theology and practical use of natural law in the early years of Reformed Christianity, along the lines of topics considered in previous sections.

Buchanan (1506-82), a Scot, enjoyed friendship and correspondence with most of the six resistance theorists examined above. His treatise (also referred to by the beginning of its Latin title, *De Iure*) is sometimes contrasted with other Reformed resistance treatises in being less biblical and theological and more secular and humanist in its argumentation, as well as in being more populist and hence more radical.[113] Nevertheless, Buchanan did work

---

113. E.g., see Mason and Smith, "Introduction," in *Dialogue*, xlvi-lxiii. For a somewhat different view of Buchanan, particularly in regard to his understanding of and reliance upon Scottish history, see also H. R. Trevor-Roper, *George Buchanan and the Ancient Scottish Constitution* (London: Longmans, 1966). In regard to the question of the secular or biblical character of his work, however, Trevor-Roper concludes similarly: "He drew his ideas not from the books of Judges and

knowledgably within the Reformed orbit and, whatever differences in themes and emphases with the other treatises, the fact that he was committed to biblical authority and that the other authors used non-biblical sources makes differences between them probably more a matter of degree than of substance. One way or another, Buchanan's *Dialogue* provides yet another example of the great importance of natural law and other non-biblical sources for Reformed social thinkers in the post-Reformation era.

Though Buchanan's resistance treatise is less overtly biblical than many of the others, he affirms the priority of Scripture over philosophical and legal sources, provided that it is properly interpreted.[114] But he notes that civil laws do not require explicit prescription in Scripture in order to be acceptable and beneficial,[115] and in fact he roughly equates biblical morality with natural law (and useful human moral teaching).[116] Concerning natural law, Buchanan speaks of a "force of nature" that is "deeply imprinted in many by nature" that makes human beings social animals and is summarized in the commands to love God and neighbor. Yet he is also clear that the natural law is given by God, at one point even declaring that "the voice of God and of nature is the same."[117] Buchanan not only echoes the other resistance theorists in many of these points, but also does so in pointing to nature as teaching the impropriety of tyranny and even as providing remedies for tyranny when it arises.[118] Finally, Buchanan resembles the other resistance theorists

---

Kings but from the classics of pagan antiquity. In the dialogue *de Jure Regni* barely so much as lip-service is paid to religion. The authority of St. Paul is mentioned only to be brushed aside in favour of the older and (it seems) better authority of Aristotle. The quotations are almost exclusively from classical authors." See *George Buchanan*, 9. Arthur H. Williamson describes the common verdict (which he generally affirms but nuances), comparing Knox and Buchanan specifically, in "British Israel and Roman Britain," 97: "Both were revolutionaries and leading apologists for the upheavals of the 1560s. But their views of these events and of the place of religion in society differed drastically." He adds that according to conventional wisdom Buchanan "approached society in his enormously influential political writings from a position which might well be described as anti-scriptural."

114. Buchanan, *Dialogue*, 110-111. This seems to be evidence contrary to the claim of many that Buchanan placed biblical and classical sources on a par, or even the latter above the former; see "Introduction," in *Dialogue*, lvii. Also note John Coffey's "sharp contrast" of Buchanan and Rutherford in terms of the latter's appeal to biblical examples and the former's relativizing of them through humanist exegesis; see *Politics, Religion and the British Revolutions: The Mind of Samuel Rutherford* (Cambridge: Cambridge University Press, 1997), 80.

115. Buchanan, *Dialogue*, 124-125.

116. Buchanan, *Dialogue*, 18-21.

117. Buchanan, *Dialogue*, 16-21, 50-51.

118. E.g., see Buchanan, *Dialogue*, 26-27, 84-85, 96-99.

in pointing to a wide range of non-biblical sources to make his arguments. He cites numerous Greek and Roman writers[119] and makes many noteworthy claims along the way, including the statement that the Greeks were the "most distinguished in all the liberal arts" and even that Aristotle made Paul's point in Romans 2:14-15 before Paul.[120]

Samuel Rutherford (1600-1661), another Scot, composed his famous work, *Lex, Rex,* in the midst of the English Civil War, as novel matters of civil rebellion and even regicide faced Reformed thinkers. Rutherford was a Reformed scholastic theologian of high repute. Since he will be one of the several writers on whom attention will focus in the next chapter, I do not elaborate here at great length on his use of natural law. Nevertheless, a brief account of Rutherford's use of natural law in *Lex, Rex* — and it quite literally pervades this lengthy work — contributes to this chapter considerable evidence that natural law continued to be a central source for Reformed resistance thinking even into the mid-seventeenth century.

Rutherford seems to have been influenced by some of the resistance thinkers studied above.[121] Whatever the actual degree of influence, his utilization of natural law places him in line with them on many points. Rutherford often closely coordinates his appeals to Scripture and natural law[122] and identifies the latter's content with the commands to love God and neighbor.[123] With the greatest clarity he treats natural law as God's law (though he made certain distinctions between fallen and unfallen nature[124]), even stating at the opening of his book: "What is warranted by the direction of nature's light is warranted by the law of nature, and consequently by a divine law; for who can deny the law of nature to be a divine law?"[125] Like so many of his predecessors, he also grounds civil law in the law

---

119. Among those cited at various places in the *Dialogue* are Aristotle, Cicero, Horace, Seneca, Theodosius, Valentinian, and Xenophon. See also Roger Mason, "Rex Stoicus: George Buchanan, James VI and the Scottish Polity," in *New Perspectives on the Politics and Culture of Early Modern Scotland,* ed. John Dwyer et al. (Edinburgh: John Donald, 1982), 9-33.

120. Buchanan, *Dialogue,* 40-41, 50-51.

121. The influence of the *Vindiciae* on Rutherford, e.g., is discussed in J. F. Maclear, "Samuel Rutherford: The Law and the King," in *Calvinism and the Political Order,* ed. George L. Hunt (Philadelphia: Westminster, 1965), 75-76.

122. E.g., see Samuel Rutherford, *Lex, Rex* (1644; reprinted, Harrisonburg, VA: Sprinkle, 1982), 59-60, 138, 203.

123. Rutherford, *Lex, Rex,* 162.

124. E.g., see Rutherford, *Lex, Rex,* 227-28. He also notes, however, that civility and grace do not destroy nature, but perfect it; see *Lex, Rex,* 68.

125. Rutherford, *Lex, Rex,* 1; see also, e.g., 53, 97, 233.

of nature,[126] and he writes in various ways of how natural law underlies the very formation of civil authority, even among the heathen.[127] For Rutherford, natural law inclines people to society[128] and commands the safety of the whole.[129] Innumerable times, he speaks of natural law as inclining people to self-preservation and self-defense, and he uses this idea to explain his anti-tyrannical opinion that people can choose their own rulers[130] and that they cannot give absolute authority to their kings.[131] He further bolsters his polemic against tyranny by arguing that, by nature, all people are born free from civil (if not parental) authority[132] and that the universality of reason constrains royal authority.[133] Furthermore, when tyranny does arise, natural law permits the tyrant to be overthrown even as it permits the people to set up their ruler in the first place.[134] As a final point at which similarities exist between Rutherford and many of the earlier Reformed resistance theorists, he makes natural law and other non-biblical arguments by analogy,[135] by appealing to animal life,[136] and by citing a wide range of sources, including classical and medieval and even contemporary Arminian and Roman Catholic.[137]

Conclusion

Some conclusions may be drawn as we arrive at the end of this chapter. Most significantly for purposes of the present study, this chapter's investigations of the resistance theorists display numerous points of continuity with both

126. E.g., see Rutherford, *Lex, Rex*, 35, 68.

127. E.g., see Rutherford, *Lex, Rex*, 22-23, 30, 38, 129, 204-7.

128. E.g., see Rutherford, *Lex, Rex*, 34, 52, 104.

129. E.g., see Rutherford, *Lex, Rex*, 124, 137.

130. E.g., see Rutherford, *Lex, Rex*, 43-44.

131. E.g., see Rutherford, *Lex, Rex*, 46, 104, 123. Rutherford also mentions this point numerous times apart from the context of self-defense; e.g., see *Lex, Rex*, 66, 81-82, 118.

132. E.g., see Rutherford, *Lex, Rex*, 50-54, 62, 71, 126, 230.

133. E.g., see Rutherford, *Lex, Rex*, 65. Rutherford also denies that natural law teaches monarchy to be the best form of government; see *Lex, Rex*, q. 38.

134. E.g., see Rutherford, *Lex, Rex*, 129, 132.

135. E.g, see Rutherford, *Lex, Rex*, 141-42, 162-63, 210.

136. E.g., see Rutherford, *Lex, Rex*, 45-46, 51-52, 160.

137. Among the sources that Rutherford cites in *Lex, Rex* are Aristotle (e.g., 50, 62), the Twelve Tables (119), Thomas Aquinas (50-51), Hugo Grotius (66, 72), and Roman Catholics such as Luis Molina, Francisco Suarez, Fernando Vasquez, and Francisco Vitoria (e.g., 1-5, 52-54, 207).

the early Reformed theology of natural law and that of the medieval traditions. Though these resistance writers addressed specific circumstances of their own day and developed distinctive arguments in order to deal with them, they appealed to many standard natural law ideas in the articulation of their theories. Among ideas common to both Reformation and medieval traditions that these resistance theorists affirmed and utilized are the divine origin of natural law, Romans 2:14-15 as biblical proof-text, the grounding of civil law in natural law, and the use of natural law to understand the Mosaic law and its contemporary relevance. In regard to ideas more typically (though not necessarily exclusively) characteristic of the Reformation traditions, the Reformed resistance writers associated natural law with the conscience, identified the content of natural law especially with the Decalogue and the commands to love God and neighbor, and recognized the corruption of reason and its understanding of nature. Therefore, the works discussed in this chapter seem to indicate that natural law played a central role in the development of early post-Reformation Reformed social thought and did so in a way displaying significant continuity with earlier Reformation and medieval theological traditions.

Another conclusion that can be drawn is that the early Reformed tradition represented not a miserly use of natural law but a broad and creative use of it. These resistance theorists made natural law arguments in a variety of ways and plumbed the wisdom of classical antiquity in order to explore the question of civil disobedience and resistance and to construct persuasive arguments. For all of the confidence in and utilization of Scripture on the part of these authors, biblical authority did not prevent them from doing what Calvin exhorted, namely, to appreciate truth wherever it might be found.

In light of these primary conclusions, I close this chapter with a few observations that interact with several points of scholarly debate about the Reformed resistance theorists. First, while many scholars acknowledge the obvious truth that these resistance writers spoke about natural law, several also label at least some of them biblicists. All of these writers professed the authority of Scripture and most of them incorporated extensive biblical argumentation into their treatises, yet any claim that they were biblicists must be severely qualified in the light of this chapter's explorations. Second, some of the scholarly literature on these resistance theorists has discussed the relationship of these writers and their treatises to each other, often finding significant differences among them, particularly between the Marian exiles on the one hand and the Huguenots on the other. While there are undeniable differences among these treatises and their authors, and even general distinctions between the British and French authors, this chapter's conclusions suggest that in their use of natural law (not an obscure aspect of their treatises) these treatises display a great deal of similarity with each other and continuity with earlier theological traditions. Hence, natural law provides perhaps overlooked evidence for why dissimilarity among these treatises should not be overemphasized. Finally, an earlier section of the chapter noted the scholarly debates among those who see these Reformed resistance treatises as innovative and immensely influential in the creation of modern Western political thought and those who emphasize the elements of continuity with earlier Reformed, Lutheran, and medieval thinking about obedience and rebellion. While it is beyond the scope of the chapter to probe this issue in depth, it is perhaps worth suggesting that the conclusions I have drawn in the preceding paragraphs add important evidence for those arguing a continuity thesis. Whatever the precise degree of innovation of the particular arguments that these resistance writers made, their use of natural law in Reformation and medieval hues points to conservative and non-innovative aspects of their work.

In regard to natural law, therefore, the Reformed resistance theorists had much in common with each other, with their Reformation forebears, and with the medieval traditions. Having seen these important elements of continuity among medieval, Reformation, and early post-Reformation Reformed natural law theologies, we now turn to explore this line of thought in the development of Reformed orthodox theology in the decades ahead.

CHAPTER 5

The Age of Orthodoxy:
Natural Law and the Two Kingdoms in Reformed Doctrine and Practice

In this chapter attention turns to the age of Protestant orthodoxy and the fate of the natural law and two kingdoms doctrines in the Reformed thought of this era. One prominent scholar of Reformed orthodoxy has identified the years 1565-1640 as roughly the period of "early" orthodoxy and the years 1640-1725 as that of "high" orthodoxy,[1] and thus this chapter approaches a potentially long duration of time and therefore a great many theologians. For obvious reasons, then, I must be selective in order to make this chapter a feasible endeavor, and selectivity also requires a more tentative conclusion than a more comprehensive study might provide. That being said, I hope to provide significant evidence here that the Reformation natural law and two kingdoms doctrines remained alive and at work in the subsequent orthodox era and, therefore, that there was significant continuity, alongside development, in the handling of these issues over the first two centuries of Reformed Christianity.

The study of Reformed orthodoxy has undergone a rather major re-examination in recent years, as mentioned briefly in Chapter 3. Not long ago, prevailing wisdom tended to see a gaping gulf between John Calvin and the "Calvinist" theologians of subsequent generations.[2] Advocates of such a view often portray Calvin in a positive light, as a biblical and humanist theo-

---

1. See Richard A. Muller, *Post-Reformation Reformed Dogmatics: The Rise and Development of Reformed Orthodoxy, ca. 1520 to ca. 1725,* vol. 1, *Prolegomena to Theology,* 2d ed. (Grand Rapids: Baker, 2003), 30-32.

2. Among influential works generally advocating a Calvin vs. the Calvinists approach are Brian G. Armstrong, *Calvinism and the Amyraut Heresy: Protestant Scholasticism and Humanism in Seventeenth-Century France* (Madison: University of Wisconsin Press, 1969); and R. T. Kendall, *Calvin and English Calvinism to 1649* (Oxford: Oxford University Press, 1979).

logian, while describing the later Calvinists negatively as speculative and rationalist in their theology, giving pride of place to reason and having less interest in Scripture. Significantly, a number of writers have identified natural law as one of the areas in which the differences between Calvin and the Calvinists were pronounced, as will be discussed below. In the past couple of decades, however, many competent scholars have put the Calvin versus the Calvinists thesis to the test and found it seriously wanting.[3] While not denying development and therefore differences between Calvin and later Reformed theologians, these scholars have identified fundamental continuities between Reformation and post-Reformation theologies and thus have argued for a variegated yet single Reformed theological tradition. The present chapter permits giving little more than a cursory account of this new perspective on Reformed orthodoxy. Among its important features are a much greater recognition of the orthodox theologians' immersion in biblical studies,[4] of their scholasticism as more a development of method than a change in theological substance,[5] of the international character of Reformed orthodoxy,[6] and of the complex and variegated character of Reformed theology

---

3. Generally, see Richard A. Muller, *After Calvin: Studies in the Development of a Theological Tradition* (Oxford: Oxford University Press, 2003); Richard A. Muller, *Post-Reformation Reformed Dogmatics: The Rise and Development of Reformed Orthodoxy, ca. 1520 to ca. 1725,* 4 vols. (Grand Rapids: Baker, 2003); *Reformation and Scholasticism: An Ecumenical Enterprise,* ed. Willem J. van Asselt and Eef Dekker (Grand Rapids: Baker, 2001); *Protestant Scholasticism: Essays in Reassessment,* ed. Carl Trueman and R. Scott Clark (Carlisle: Paternoster, 1999); and Paul Helm, *Calvin and the Calvinists* (Edinburgh: Banner of Truth, 1982).

4. E.g., in *After Calvin,* 10, Muller writes: "One of the erroneous contrasts often made between the theology of the Reformers and that of their orthodox and scholastic successors presents the theology of the Reformation as a biblical and exegetical theology and that of the Reformed orthodox as a highly dogmatic and rational theology, largely negligent of exegetical issues. It is important to remove this fiction explicitly and entirely." For an example of a recent critical examination of the accusations of rationalism against one particular prominent Reformed scholastic theologian (and a focus of the present chapter), see Sebastian Rehnman, "Alleged Rationalism: Francis Turretin on Reason," *Calvin Theological Journal* 37 (2002): 255-69.

5. See, e.g., Willem J. van Asselt and Eef Dekker, "Introduction," in *Reformation and Scholasticism,* 13; Willem van't Spijker, "Reformation and Scholasticism," in *Reformation and Scholasticism,* 79-98; Antoine Vos, "Scholasticism and Reformation," in *Reformation and Scholasticism,* 99-119; Muller, *After Calvin,* ch. 2; and Muller, *Post-Reformation,* 1.30, 34-37. Readers should note that though the term "Reformed scholasticism" is sometimes used interchangeably with "Reformed orthodoxy," the terms are certainly not synonyms; Reformation-era theologians such as Jerome Zanchi were scholastic in their method and many orthodox-era theologians wrote in non-scholastic ways.

6. E.g., see Muller, *Post-Reformation,* 1.28, 66-67.

within a single tradition,[7] which includes the conviction that Calvin, despite his importance, should never be taken as the sole standard for assessing later Reformed thought.[8]

Though the present chapter does not seek to contribute directly to this scholarly debate, its conclusions certainly add supporting evidence to the case for continuity between Reformation and post-Reformation Reformed theology and for early Reformed theology as a variegated yet single tradition. I argue that the treatment of natural law and the two kingdoms doctrines, and related issues, among the several orthodox-era Reformed thinkers and confessional documents examined here displays significant continuity with the treatment of these issues by the earlier Reformed writers examined in the previous two chapters. A point of particular significance for the present study is that these Reformed orthodox writers, through their natural law and two kingdoms doctrines, affirmed and developed the idea that social and political life is grounded in God's work of creation and providence rather than in his work of redemption.

Readers should keep in mind that though I sometimes refer to "Reformed orthodoxy" generally in this chapter, I am not claiming to set forth *the* views of Reformed orthodoxy, for which a much more comprehensive study would be necessary. I consider other theologians and documents here and there, but I focus upon the writings of three individuals (Johannes Althusius, Samuel Rutherford, and Francis Turretin) and upon the *Westminster Confession of Faith and Catechisms* (1646-47). Thus I am setting forth the views of *representative* figures and documents. Yet the representative figures and documents were not chosen arbitrarily and certainly provide a very helpful window into a larger world. The three individuals all dealt with the matters at issue here at some length in their major writings.[9] Furthermore,

---

7. E.g., see van Asselt and Dekker, "Introduction," 13; Muller, *After Calvin,* 7-8; and Muller, *Post-Reformation,* 1.28.

8. E.g., see Muller, *Post-Reformation,* 1.38, 45; and van Asselt and Dekker, "Introduction," 33.

9. I will focus here upon Francis Turretin's *magnum opus,* originally published in 1679-85 as *Institutio theologiae elencticae,* which appears in English translation as *Institutes of Elenctic Theology,* 3 vols., trans. George Musgrave Giger, ed. James T. Dennison, Jr. (Phillipsburg, NJ: P&R, 1992-1997); upon Johannes Althusius's influential work, originally published in 1603 as *Politica methodice digesta,* which appears in abridged English translation as *Politica (Politics Methodically Set Forth and Illustrated with Sacred and Profane Examples),* trans. and ed. Frederick S. Carney (Boston: Beacon, 1964; Indianapolis: Liberty Fund, 1995), with some scattered references as well to his monumental *Dicaeologicae* of 1617, of which small selections appear in English translation by Jeffrey J. Veenstra in "Selections from the *Dicaeologicae,*" *Journal of Markets and Morality* 9, no. 2 (2006): 429-84; and upon not only Samuel Rutherford's major political work considered briefly in

Rutherford (1600-61) and Turretin (1623-87) are appropriate subjects for study due to their position as leading scholastic theologians, the former in Britain and the latter on the continent (in Geneva), in the midst of the vibrant and mature Reformed orthodoxy of the mid-seventeenth century.[10] Althusius (1557-1638) not only provides a view of our topics at a somewhat earlier point chronologically and from a different geographical location (Emden, near the German-Dutch border), but also offers his Reformed treatment from the perspective of a trained legal (rather than theological) scholar. Althusius was a major figure throughout Western Europe in his own time, and his best-known work, the *Politica*, "was one of the most widely read and, by some, the most despised book of its day."[11] He also serves as an interesting link between other figures considered in this book. In regard to the matters at issue here, he himself was influenced significantly by Jerome Zanchi, considered in Chapter 3, and he in turn appears to have influenced Rutherford.[12] In addition to these three, whose work will be considered throughout the whole of this chapter, I also give some attention to the eminent Puritan theologian John Owen (1616-83) in regard to natural law and to

the previous chapter, *Lex, Rex* (1644; reprinted, Harrisonburg, VA: Sprinkle, 1982), but also upon his massive ecclesiological work, *The Divine Right of Church-Government and Excommunication* (London, 1646). References to Turretin and Althusius will be to the English translations.

10. The prominence of Turretin as Reformed scholastic theologian is perhaps better appreciated than that of Rutherford. Of the latter, however, note the comment by John Coffey in *Politics, Religion and the British Revolutions: The Mind of Samuel Rutherford* (Cambridge: Cambridge University Press, 1997), 114: Rutherford "was the most distinguished theologian among the Scottish Covenanters, with an international reputation as a champion of Reformed orthodoxy." Another recent writer has identified Rutherford's thinking on (at least) natural law as representative of that of the British Puritans of his day; see Peter Judson Richards, "'The Law Written in Their Hearts'?: Rutherford and Locke on Nature, Government and Resistance," *Journal of Law and Religion* 18, no. 1 (2002): 184.

11. Stephen J. Grabill, *Rediscovering the Natural Law in Reformed Theological Ethics* (Grand Rapids: Eerdmans, 2006), 123. In this context Grabill also provides a succinct bibliographical survey of recent scholarship on Althusius; see *Rediscovering the Natural Law,* 122-29. For a subsequent study of Althusius, which treats him as a major Reformed figure in respect to many of the issues considered in the present chapter, particularly natural law, see John Witte, Jr., *The Reformation of Rights: Law, Religion, and Human Rights in Early Modern Calvinism* (Cambridge: Cambridge University Press, 2007), ch. 3.

12. Zanchi's influence on Althusius is evident throughout the latter's work; see, e.g., *Politica,* 144; see also the discussion in Grabill, *Rediscovering the Natural Law,* 132-42. On Althusius's influence on Rutherford, see, e.g., the comments in Coffey, *Politics, Religion and the British Revolutions,* 180; and John D. Ford, "*Lex, rex iusto posita:* Samuel Rutherford on the Origins of Government," in *Scots and Britons: Scottish Political Thought and the Union of 1603,* ed. Roger A. Mason (Cambridge: Cambridge University Press, 1994), 282.

Rutherford's Scottish colleague George Gillespie (1613-48) in regard to the two kingdoms, both of whom made contributions to Reformed thinking on these respective issues.

The *Westminster Confession and Catechisms* (drafted by the Westminster Assembly during the English civil war of the 1640s) seem appropriate and important for study in the present context for several reasons. First, as confessional documents, they represent not the opinions of individual theologians but the consensus of many theologians and indeed of the church as a whole (in this case, of the British Reformed theologians and churches). Hence, insofar as the conclusions of the individual writers considered here are reflected in such confessional standards, we have a greater degree of certainty that these conclusions were widely shared among the Reformed. Second, the *Westminster Confession and Catechisms* address the topic of natural law explicitly and frequently and the two kingdoms doctrine indirectly though significantly. Third, they are more usefully examined in this chapter than other significant Reformed confessional documents such as the *Heidelberg Catechism, Belgic Confession,* and *Canons of Dort* (which are commonly referred to as the "Three Forms of Unity" and function as the doctrinal standards for many continental Reformed churches), both because they deal at greater length with natural law and the two kingdoms and because they represent a more detailed exposition of Reformed doctrine at a later and more mature point in the development of Protestant theology.

With this background in view, we may now turn to consider our topics specifically. Though in Chapters 2 and 3 I considered two kingdoms issues first and then matters related to natural law, here I reverse the order in the interests of clarity.

Natural Law in Reformed Orthodoxy

As mentioned in the introduction to this chapter, the issue of natural law is one point at which many writers favoring some sort of Calvin versus the Calvinists approach have posited a great difference between the Reformation and subsequent Reformed orthodoxy.[13] They assert that the genius of

13. As cited in Chapter 3, among various examples are Karl Barth, "No!," in *Natural Theology,* trans. Peter Fraenkel (London: Geoffrey Bles: Centenary, 1946), 67-128; Karl Barth, *The Knowledge of God and the Service of God According to the Teaching of the Reformation,* trans. J. L. M. Haire and Ian Henderson (London: Hodder and Stoughton, 1938); T. H. L. Parker, *The Doctrine of the Knowledge of God: A Study in the Theology of John Calvin* (Edinburgh: Oliver and Boyd, 1952), ch. 2;

Calvin's theology was essentially hostile to natural law but that later Reformed scholastic theologians tried to reintroduce it into Reformed theology. I have addressed and refuted the alleged hostility of Calvin toward natural law in a previous chapter. The present chapter of course does not dispute the idea that Reformed orthodoxy ascribed a positive view to natural law as it incorporated this notion into its theology and ethics. What it does is add further evidence against the Calvin versus the Calvinist thesis by displaying numerous points of continuity concerning natural law between eminent representatives of Reformed orthodoxy on the one hand and, on the other hand, Calvin and other Reformation figures (and the medieval traditions before them), even as certain points were developed and elaborated.[14] In particular, on issues such as the divine origin of natural law, the implanting of the natural law on the human heart in connection with the conscience, the close connection of natural law with the moral law and Decalogue, natural law as the basis and standard for civil law, and natural law as test for the continuing applicability of the Mosaic law, substantial continuity with the earlier Reformed tradition is evident. What is more, I

T. H. L. Parker, *Calvin: An Introduction to His Thought* (Louisville: Westminster John Knox, 1995), Part 1; Edward A. Dowey, *The Knowledge of God in Calvin's Theology* (New York: Columbia University Press, 1952); James Torrance, "Interpreting the Word by the Light of Christ or the Light of Nature? Calvin, Calvinism, and Barth," in *Calviniana: Ideas and Influence of Jean Calvin*, ed. Robert V. Schnucker (Kirksville, MO: Sixteenth Century Journal Publishers, 1988), 255-67; August Lang, "The Reformation and Natural Law," trans. J. Gresham Machen, in *Calvin and the Reformation: Four Studies* (New York: Fleming H. Revell, 1909), 56-98; Michael Walzer, *The Revolution of the Saints: A Study in the Origins of Radical Politics* (Cambridge: Harvard University Press, 1965; London: Weidenfeld and Nicolson, 1966), 30-31; I. John Hesselink, *Calvin's Concept of the Law* (Allison Park, PA: Pickwick Publications, 1992), 67-70; and Josef Fuchs, S.J, *Natural Law: A Theological Investigation,* trans. Helmut Reckter, S.J. and John A. Dowling (New York: Sheed and Ward, 1965), 10-11, 46-47, 62-63.

14. Though there is certainly more work to be done in testing and developing this claim, some scholars have already made significant contributions in this regard. See Chapter 3 for bibliographic material on Calvin and natural law. For material on natural law and the natural knowledge of God more generally in the age of Reformed orthodoxy, see Grabill, *Rediscovering the Natural Law,* chs. 5-6; Muller, *Post-Reformation,* vol. 1, ch. 6; and John Platt, *Reformed Thought and Scholasticism: The Arguments for the Existence of God in Dutch Theology, 1575-1650* (Leiden: Brill, 1982). Among recent specialized studies of the natural law thought of particular Reformed figures examined here, see John L. Marshall, "Natural Law and the Covenant: The Place of the Covenantal Framework of Samuel Rutherford's *Lex, Rex*" (Ph.D. dissertation, Westminster Theological Seminary, 1995); Stephen J. Grabill, "Natural Law and the Noetic Effects of Sin: The Faculty of Reason in Francis Turretin's Theological Anthropology," *Westminster Theological Journal* 67 (Fall 2005): 261-79; and (regarding John Owen) Paul Helm, "Calvin and Natural Law," *Scottish Bulletin of Evangelical Theology* 2 (1984): 13-16.

suggest and offer evidence for the claim that Reformed orthodoxy incorporated natural law into its system of doctrine as a whole, such that natural law, in touching so many points of doctrine, was integral to Reformed orthodox theology and could not be excised from it without wreaking havoc upon its intellectual and practical integrity.

The Nature and Divine Origin of Natural Law

This opening subsection considers the basic understanding of natural law among our Reformed orthodox thinkers and its origin in God himself. In the midst of a nuanced and detailed discussion, Turretin offers a precise definition of natural law, writing that orthodox Reformed theologians

> affirm that there is a natural law, not arising from a voluntary contract of law of society, but from a divine obligation being impressed by God upon the conscience of man in his very creation, on which the difference between right and wrong is founded and which contains the practical principles of immovable truth (such as: 'God should be worshipped,' 'parents honored,' 'we should live virtuously,' 'injure no one,' 'do to others what we would wish them to do to us' and the like). Also that so many remains and evidences of this law are still left in our nature (although it has been in different ways corrupted and obscured by sin) that there is no mortal who cannot feel its force either more or less.[15]

Owen also expressed care in defining natural law. He rejects what he says is a common definition of natural law, namely, "the dictates of right reason. Which all men, or men generally, consent in and agree about. . . ." He is unhappy with this definition for a number of reasons, primarily because even the wisest people disagree about what the dictates of right reason are, whereas the natural law must be uniform and the same in all people.[16] Owen suggests this alternative definition:

> By the law of nature, then, I intend, not a law which *our nature gives unto all our actions,* but a law *given unto our nature,* as a rule and measure unto

---

15. Turretin, *Institutes*, 2.3.

16. John Owen, "Exercitations concerning the name, original, nature, use, and continuance, of a day of sacred rest," in *The Works of John Owen,* vol. 11, *An Exposition of the Epistle to the Hebrews,* ed. William H. Goold (London/Edinburgh, 1850; Philadelphia: Leighton, 1869), 338-42.

our moral actions. It is 'lex naturae naturantis,' and not 'naturae naturatae.'. . . . And this respect alone can give it the nature of a law, — that is, an obliging force and power. . . . This law, therefore, is that rule which God hath given unto human nature, in all the individual partakers of it, for all its moral actions, in the state and condition wherein it was by him created and placed, with respect unto his own government of it and judgment concerning it; which rule is made known in them and to them by their inward constitution and outward condition wherein they were placed of God.[17]

Though I will address these matters at more length below, already one can observe some important characteristics of these writers' understanding of natural law that echo concerns of earlier Reformed thought: the natural law is known by nature apart from special revelation, it teaches the basic content of the moral law, it is written on the heart of every human being and roughly associated with the conscience, and assures everyone's accountability before God.

One of the points made by both Turretin and Owen that is worth emphasis and elaboration is that God himself establishes the natural law and thus natural law is God's law. Turretin, arguing against Thomas Hobbes' contractual understanding of natural law among other things, proceeds to explain that Reformed theologians do not call the natural law natural because "it has its origin from bare nature" because in fact "it depends upon God the supreme lawgiver."[18] The opening section of Rutherford's *Lex, Rex* makes this same point explicitly and pointedly: "What is warranted by the direction of nature's light is warranted by the law of nature, and consequently by a divine law; for who can deny the law of nature to be a divine law?"[19]

A more difficult matter touching upon natural law's divine origin is the relation of natural law to God's own moral character. As mentioned in Chapter 2, the degree to which natural law reflects God's moral nature and/ or his will, and the related questions of whether God could have made the natural law other than it is or can make exceptions to it, were points of debate and disagreement among medieval theologians, particularly in their identifications with the realist or voluntarist schools of thought. Calvin, as

17. Owen, "Exercitations," 342. For some similar definitions of natural law, see Althusius, "*Dicaeologicae*," 439-40.

18. Turretin, *Institutes*, 2.2-3.

19. Rutherford, *Lex, Rex*, 1. See also *Lex, Rex*, 53, 97, 233.

observed in Chapter 3, emphasized the supremacy of God's will in setting the moral standard for his creation, but he did so also insisting that God is not *ex lex* and calling the principles of God's law a reflection of his own holiness. This displays similarity between Calvin and the realist medieval tradition and distinguishes him from at least more extreme forms of the voluntarist tradition. Reformed orthodox theologians were not of one mind on this question. Turretin presents a nuanced analysis of it in his discussion of the natural and positive right of God, the former of which he defines as that which God cannot command otherwise without prejudice to his nature, perfection, and holiness. He identifies three positions. One extreme position, which he associates with William Ockham and the Socinians (what we might consider a radical voluntarist view), is that the precepts of the moral law are founded on positive right alone and thus that God may change them at his pleasure. A second, middle position, associated with Duns Scotus and Gabriel Biel, is that "three precepts of the first table are indispensable; that the fourth, however, is partly dispensable; and that all the others of the second table are dispensable." Finally, the third position, associated with Thomas Aquinas and several others, is that "the moral law as to all its precepts is simply indispensable because it contains the intrinsic reason of justice and duty; not as proceeding from the law, but as founded on the nature of God." Turretin states that though some Reformed theologians adopt the second view, the third view is "the more common opinion of the orthodox." He does make a qualification: some of the precepts flow absolutely from the nature of God while others "depend upon the constitution of the nature of things (the free will of God coming in between) so that they should not be thought to hold an equal degree of necessity and immutability." The latter, while not strictly dispensable, may be given different interpretations as circumstances change.[20]

Turretin, who had previously claimed that natural law is founded in God's very own holiness, wisdom, and justice,[21] goes on to defend the third view, which he associates with most of the Reformed orthodox. Among other arguments, he claims that, at least with regard to some of the commands of the Decalogue, for God to command otherwise would result in him "denying himself and doing violence to his own nature," and he claims that "the moral law (which is the pattern of God's image in man) ought to correspond with the eternal and archetypal law in God, since it is its copy

20. Turretin, *Institutes*, 2.9-10.
21. Turretin, *Institutes*, 2.2.

and shadow . . . , in which he has manifested his justice and holiness."[22] It is interesting to note his language of "eternal law," a concept present in Thomas Aquinas and going back to Augustine, yet absent in later nominalist theologians as well as in Reformers Luther and Calvin. Turretin uses not only Thomas's language but also, in some respects, his concept.

Among the other Reformed orthodox theologians under consideration here, Owen, at least in his later writings, expresses convictions sounding similar to Turretin's. He says, for example, that the moral laws (in distinction from divine positive laws) are those that "are good from their respect to the nature of God himself, and from that nature and order of all things which he hath placed in the creation. So that this sort of laws is but declarative of the absolute goodness of what they do require."[23] Elsewhere he claims that Christ's atoning sacrifice was necessary if human sins were to be forgiven, on account of God's inherently just character. He argues that all human beings have an innate sense of justice by which they know God's moral standard and perceive the fact that their sin must either be punished or atoned for, and by which they understand that this punitive or vindicatory justice is natural to God.[24] The Westminster Standards also affirm that the natural moral law reflects the divine character. All three of the documents speak clearly of holiness as a defining attribute of God's character (Westminster Confession of Faith [WCF] 2.1; Westminster Larger Catechism [WLC] 7; Westminster Shorter Catechism [WSC] 4). As considered below, the Westminster Standards identify natural law with the moral law, and WLC 95 states that the moral law "is of use to all men, to inform them of the *holy nature* and will of God . . ." (95). The "duties of holiness and righteousness which he oweth to God and man" (WLC 93) are reflective of that holiness which marks God's own nature.

Althusius and Rutherford, however, seem to offer evidence for what Turretin concedes, namely, that the Reformed tradition was not unanimous on this issue. Althusius, arguing a position similar to that of Scotus (the sec-

---

22. Turretin, *Institutes,* 2.11-12.

23. Owen, "Exercitations," 329. See also relevant material in "Exercitations," 336-37.

24. John Owen, "A Dissertation on Divine Justice," in *The Works of John Owen,* vol. 10, ed. William H. Goold (reprinted, Edinburgh: Banner of Truth, 1967), 483-624. Owen attempts to demonstrate this claim by extensive appeals to non-Christian opinion and practice, including even the reprehensible but common practice of human sacrifice; see especially "Dissertation," 512-41. For a helpful recent study of this work and of Owen's conception of justice and the divine nature, see Carl R. Trueman, "John Owen's *Dissertation on Divine Justice:* An Exercise in Christocentric Scholasticism," *Calvin Theological Journal* 33 (1998): 87-103.

ond opinion identified by Turretin), asserts that the "precepts of the first table can never be set aside or relaxed, and not even God himself is able to reject them" and then shortly thereafter adds that "God sometimes relaxes the
fifth, sixth, and eighth precepts, and out of his great wisdom sets aside the
things that ought to be done according to them."[25] Rutherford takes a position perhaps further from Turretin than Althusius. One scholar has called
Rutherford an "intense" and "extreme" voluntarist, and there is evidence
that he at least tended in this direction.[26] It is noteworthy that Owen, generally a theological ally of Rutherford, singles him out for special critique for
his deficient view of justice and the divine nature.[27] All in all it seems fair to
say that Reformed orthodoxy contained within itself differences on this issue
that mirrored differences present many centuries earlier in medieval theology, although, assuming Turretin appraised the situation accurately, the
view closely associating natural law with the divine nature had the upper
hand in the mid-seventeenth century.

Natural Law and Conscience

The natural law theology of Reformed orthodoxy quite distinctly reflects
prior Christian thought in its understanding of natural law as impressed
upon the human heart and known through conscience. As a confessional affirmation, the Westminster Standards speak of human beings as "having the
law of God written in their hearts" (WCF 4.2; WLC 17). Many individual
theologians adopt and elaborate this sentiment. Turretin writes: "We find in
man a natural law written upon each one's conscience excusing and accusing
them in good and bad actions, which therefore necessarily implies the
knowledge of God, the legislator, by whose authority it binds men to obedience and proposes rewards or punishments."[28] Later he writes somewhat
more concisely of natural law as "impressed by God upon the conscience of

---

25. Althusius, *Politica*, 141-43.

26. Coffey makes this claim about Rutherford in *Politics, Religion and the British Revolutions*,
129. He also makes such assertions about Calvin, a claim that I have disputed. An example of
Rutherford's voluntarist language is found in *Lex, Rex*, 110: "God may command against the law of
nature, and God's commandment maketh subjection lawful."

27. See especially Owen, "Dissertation," 607-18. At other places he acknowledges Rutherford
as a "learned man" yet claims that he "blunders miserably" and calls him a "mere novice" regarding issues of justice and the nature of God; see "Dissertation," 523, 539.

28. Turretin, *Institutes*, 1.7.

man."[29] Althusius speaks similarly when he asserts that "common law [natural law] . . . has been naturally implanted by God in all men" and that "by this knowledge imprinted within us by God, which is called conscience, man knows and understands law . . . and the means to be employed or avoided for maintaining obedience to law. By this innate inclination, or secret impulse of nature, man is urged to perform what he understands to be just, and to avoid what he knows to be wicked."[30] Likewise, Owen says of the law of our creation that there were and are "general notions of good and evil indelibly planted on the faculties of our souls."[31]

Such statements indicate that these prominent Reformed orthodox figures shared the Reformation and medieval conviction that natural law was inscribed or impressed by God himself upon the human heart. Furthermore, these statements show that they shared the more distinctively Reformed association of natural law with the conscience. Finally, these theologians continued to follow the Reformation and medieval understanding of Romans 2:14-15 as key biblical proof for the idea of a divine natural law implanted on the heart.[32]

Natural Law as Moral Standard

Implied in the matters already considered is the role of natural law as moral standard for the human race. Various issues related to this point are worth exploring in some more detail. First, following Reformation and even much medieval precedent, Reformed orthodoxy associated natural law very closely with the moral law and the Decalogue. The Westminster Standards, which speak of the Decalogue as a summary of the moral law (WSC 41; WLC 98), clearly identify the written moral law and unwritten natural law as to their substance. This is evident in comparing WCF 4.2 with WLC 92, which concern God's dealings with Adam and Eve before the fall into sin. WCF 4.2 states: "Besides *this law written in their hearts,* they received a command, not to eat of the tree of the knowledge of good and evil. . . ." WLC 92, on the other hand, reads: "The rule of obedience revealed to Adam in the estate of

29. Turretin, *Institutes,* 2.3.
30. Althusius, *Politica,* 139-40.
31. Owen, "Exercitations," 388. For discussion of Rutherford's view of natural law and conscience, see Marshall, "Natural Law and the Covenant," ch. 3.
32. E.g., see Turretin, *Institutes,* 1.577; 2.4; and Althusius, *Politica,* 140. Romans 2:14-15 was also an original proof text for the statement about the law of God written in the heart in WCF 4.2 and WLC 17.

innocence, and to all mankind in him, besides a special command not to eat of the fruit of the tree of the knowledge of good and evil, was *the moral law.*" Evidently, the moral law and natural law both describe the general obligation of the first human beings. This substantive identity of the moral and natural laws is confirmed by comparison of the language of WCF 21.1 on the light of nature with WSC 41-42 on the summary of the moral law. This perspective of the Westminster Standards simply reflected the common teaching of Reformed orthodox theology, which equated the content of the natural law with the moral law (as summarized in the Decalogue). More technical discussions distinguished the natural and moral laws insofar as the former was unwritten and known through general revelation and the latter was written and known through special revelation. In Turretin's words, they differ not in substance or principles, but in "mode of delivery."[33]

In addition to this substantive identification of natural law and moral law, a common conviction in both Reformation and medieval theology, the Reformed orthodoxy thinkers also adopted the more distinctively Reformation move of associating natural law also with the commands to love God and neighbor (rather than seeing the latter as higher or supernatural precepts). Confessionally, Reformed orthodoxy viewed the love commands as a summary of the summary (the Decalogue) of the moral law (WSC 42; WLC 102, 122). Among individual writers, Althusius, for example, specifically relates natural law and love: "In this common law [natural law] . . . is set forth for all men nothing other than the general theory and practice of love, both for God and for one's neighbor."[34]

This function of natural law as the fundamental, basic moral standard was true already in creation and continues to bind all people after the fall into sin, even apart from Christ's work of redemption, according to the common teaching of Reformed orthodoxy. This is a crucial teaching for the claims of this book. Discussion of this point is therefore necessary and in fact gives some indication of the extent to which the idea of natural law had become intimately incorporated into the broader Reformed system of doctrine.

First, Reformed orthodoxy taught that the natural law was implanted on

33. See Turretin, *Institutes,* 2.6-7. See also Althusius, *Politica,* 139-40, 144; Rutherford, *Divine Right,* 75, 79; and Owen, "Exercitations," 366-69, 395.

34. Althusius, *Politica,* 140. Rutherford too associates natural law and love. Related to his strong conviction that natural law teaches a principle of self-preservation, however, he emphasizes that natural law commands love for ourselves above love for our neighbor. He writes, for example: "Nature's law teacheth every man to love God best of all, and next ourselves more than our neighbour" (*Lex, Rex,* 162).

the human heart at creation, as an aspect of the image of God. WCF 4.2 and WLC 17 describe God creating man male and female, with reasonable and immortal souls, and after his own image. Following these affirmations, they speak of human beings as "having the law of God written in their hearts, and power to fulfil it." Various theologians agree in pointing to creation as the origin of the natural law.[35] What is of even more profound theological interest is that many Reformed theologians viewed natural law as an essential aspect of the covenant of works. The doctrine of the covenant of works, which became a standard feature of Reformed orthodox theology, teaches that God, at creation, promised Adam a reward of everlasting, eschatological life on condition of his perfect obedience during a probationary period (and threatened everlasting punishment upon disobedience). Far from being considered an obscure point of doctrine, the covenant of works idea served to anchor the broader covenant theology that was a major organizing principle within Reformed theology and that became a significant distinctive feature of Reformed thought in comparison to other Christian traditions.[36] The key role of natural law in the covenant of works is evident in Turretin, for example. In speaking of different characteristics of the covenant of

---

35. For example, see Turretin, *Institutes,* 2.3; and Owen, "Exercitations," 388.

36. The Westminster Standards offer a mature Reformed confessional expression of this doctrine in WCF 7.2; WLC 20; WSC 12. The whole of WCF 7 is helpful for seeing the place of the covenant of works doctrine in the light of a broader Reformed covenant theology. The words of the eminent Wilhelmus à Brakel (1635-1711) illustrate how important many Reformed orthodox theologians considered the doctrine of the covenant of works: "Acquaintance with this covenant is of the greatest importance, for whoever errs here or denies the existence of the covenant of works, will not understand the covenant of grace, and will readily err concerning the mediatorship of the Lord Jesus." See *The Christian's Reasonable Service,* 4 vols., trans. Bartel Elshout (Ligonier, PA: Soli Deo Gloria, 1992-95), 1.355. Among Reformed orthodox theologians, one of the most thorough and competent expositions of the covenant of works doctrine, in its broader place in covenant theology and Reformed theology more generally, is a work originally published in Latin in 1677: Herman Witsius, *The Economy of the Covenants between God and Man: Comprehending a Complete Body of Divinity,* 2 vols., trans. William Crookshank (1822; reprinted Phillipsburg, NJ: P&R, 1990). For a study of the covenant of works in early Reformed theology, see David Alexander Weir, "*Foedus Naturale:* The Origins of Federal Theology in Sixteenth Century Reformation Thought" (Ph.D. thesis, University of Saint Andrews, 1984). For recent explanations and defenses of the Reformed doctrine of the covenant of works, see Bryan D. Estelle, "The Covenant of Works in Moses and Paul," in *Covenant, Justification, and Pastoral Ministry: Essays by the Faculty of Westminster Seminary California,* ed. R. Scott Clark (Phillipsburg, NJ: P&R, 2007), 89-135; and John Bolt, "Why the Covenant of Works Is a Necessary Doctrine: Revisiting the Objections to a Venerable Reformed Doctrine," in *By Faith Alone: Answering the Challenges to the Doctrine of Justification,* ed. Gary L. Johnson and Guy P. Waters (Wheaton: Crossway, 2006), 171-89.

works, he says: "It is also called 'legal' because the condition on man's part was the observation of the law of nature engraved within him."[37] Shortly thereafter he says of the covenant of works: "The whole duty was partly general, partly special (according to the twofold law given to him: the moral or natural and the symbolic). . . . The former was founded on the law of nature not written in a book, but engraven and stamped upon the heart."[38] Statements by many other early Reformed theologians similarly associate natural law with the covenant of works.[39]

The idea that the creation of human beings with the natural law written on their hearts was itself a covenantal act of God represents a significant development of earlier Christian natural law thought. Human perception of the natural law never occurred except in the context of a determined, established relationship with God, according to this line of thought. At the same time, this idea was apparently not developed with rigorous consistency in the era of Reformed orthodoxy, and even the Westminster Standards reflect some ambiguity on the subject.[40] Later Reformed writers would explore this idea at greater length, as later chapters will discuss.

To the extent that Reformed orthodox figures did indeed associate natural law with the covenant of works, they possessed a powerful theological

---

37. Turretin, *Institutes*, 1.575.

38. Turretin, *Institutes*, 1.577. For a study of Turretin's doctrine of the covenant of works, including points discussed here, see Stephen R. Spencer, "Francis Turretin's Concept of the Covenant of Nature," in *Later Calvinism: International Perspectives,* ed. W. Fred Graham (Kirksville, MO: Sixteenth Century Journal Publishers, 1994), 71-91. For discussion of such ideas in other Reformed theologians, see, e.g., Marshall, "Natural Law and the Covenant," 23, in regard to Rutherford; in regard to important theologians of the next generation, Herman Witsius and Wilhelmus à Brakel, see Muller, *After Calvin,* 183.

39. E.g., see Question & Answer 36 of the Larger Catechism of Zacharias Ursinus (1534-83) in Lyle D. Bierma, with Charles D. Gunnoe Jr., Karin Y. Maag, and Paul W. Fields, *An Introduction to the Heidelberg Catechism: Sources, History, and Theology* (Grand Rapids: Baker Academic, 2005), 168-69; Owen, "Exercitations," 388; and Witsius, *The Economy of the Covenants,* 1.72. See discussion of this issue in David VanDrunen, "Natural Law and the Works Principle under Adam and Moses," in *The Law Is Not of Faith: Essays on Works and Grace in the Mosaic Covenant,* ed. Bryan D. Estelle, J. V. Fesko, and David VanDrunen (Phillipsburg, NJ: P&R, 2009), 286-91.

40. WCF 19.1-3 may suggest that human beings were created in covenant and with the natural law implanted within them. WCF 19.1 speaks of God giving to Adam "a law" at his creation, which is finally identified in 19.3 as the moral law. According to 19.1, God gave this law to Adam "as a covenant of works, by which he bound him and all his posterity to personal, entire, exact, and perpetual obedience. . . ." On the other hand, WCF 7.1 contemplates at least the theoretical possibility that the relationship between human beings endowed with reason and God the creator could be conceived apart from a covenantal arrangement.

tool for affirming a point explored in Chapter 3 with regard to Calvin. The covenant of works was understood as an act of *creation* distinct from and independent of God's work of *redemption* in the "covenant of grace" after the fall into sin. Insofar as natural law originated in the covenant of works, therefore, Reformed orthodox theologians grounded it in God's *creating* work rather than in his *redeeming* work.

Even after the fall into sin, natural law continued to be grounded in the work of creation (and the providential sustaining of creation) rather than in redemption, according to Reformed orthodox theologians. Though they taught that Adam broke the covenant of works and that its terms now held out no possibility of attaining everlasting life, since sin made perfect obedience impossible, they also affirmed that natural law continues to be written on all human hearts and to make known a perfect moral standard even to those without faith in Christ. In other words, natural law serves to sustain moral life in the world without itself offering a means for attaining to a life beyond this world. As considered in previous chapters, medieval theology recognized the effects of sin upon human knowledge of the natural law, and Reformation theology made this point with greater emphasis. Reformed orthodoxy also acknowledged these dire consequences of sin, speaking, for example, both of the hampered ability of sinners to draw specific conclusions from natural law principles and of the difference in nature itself before and after Adam's fall.[41] But despite the various ways in which sin hinders people from obeying the natural law, Reformed theologians and confessions in the age of orthodoxy granted natural law a significant role in the postlapsarian world. For one thing, they speak of natural law as an enduring and universal moral standard binding all people. Turretin again provides a helpful example of Reformed thinking on this point. Viewing knowledge of the natural law as innate (and also acquired), he explains that, despite sin, there are so many evidences and remains of natural law that no person can fail to feel its force.[42] In defending these claims, Turretin appeals to standard proof-texts such as Rom 1:19 and 2:14-15.[43] Elsewhere he defends at some length the immutable character of the moral standard set forth in the natural law.[44] The

41. On these two points respectively, see, e.g., Turretin, *Institutes*, 2.4; and Rutherford, *Lex, Rex*, 227-28. For discussion of how Rutherford's robust view of sin affected his understanding of natural law, in contrast to later thinkers such as John Locke often thought to be influenced by him, see Richards, "'The Law Written in Their Hearts'?"

42. Turretin, *Institutes*, 1.5; 2.3.

43. Turretin, *Institutes*, 1.577; 2.4.

44. See Turretin, *Institutes*, 2.12-18.

practical consequences of such things for Turretin are evident in his exposition of the Decalogue, in which he makes recourse to natural law in his explanation of each one of the commandments of the second table.[45]

Clear evidence demonstrates that the Westminster Standards saw the *substantive content* of the natural law as continuing to bind all people as the rule for moral living. For example, the Standards describe the moral law (substantively identical to the natural law) as the permanent standard for human conduct (WCF 19.2; WLC 93), summarily comprehended in the precepts of the Decalogue (WLC 98; WSC 41). Yet the Standards elsewhere make clear that more than simply the content of natural law continues to oblige, but also the natural law as such. This is perhaps most evident in the opening sentence of WCF 21.1: "The light of nature showeth that there is a God, who hath lordship and sovereignty over all, is good, and doth good unto all, and is therefore to be feared, loved, praised, called upon, trusted in, and served, with all the heart, and with all the soul, and with all the might." Though the burden of WCF 21 is to focus upon worship and Sabbath, these opening words of the chapter are striking for their comprehensive description of the moral duty owed by human beings to God as known by natural revelation.

As this continuing and universal moral standard, the natural law also serves to secure the universal liability of all people to the divine judgment, according to Reformed orthodoxy. According to the Westminster Standards, God is righteous and just (WCF 2.1; WLC 7; WSC 4), but also condemns all unbelievers to hell (WCF 33.2; WLC 89), whether or not they have had access to biblical revelation. Questions about God's justice that such teaching raises are answered in the opening words of the WCF: "Although the light of nature, and the works of creation and providence do so far manifest the goodness, wisdom, and power of God, as to leave men unexcusable. . . ." (1.1) According to Reformed orthodox theology, therefore, the light of nature, which includes the natural law, explains how God can be just in condemning even those never exposed to the Christian gospel.

Natural Law and Civil Law

We come now to two matters that have been of particular concern in previous chapters, namely, the relation of natural law to civil law and the law of Moses. Those chapters offered abundant evidence that the various medieval

---

45. Turretin, *Institutes,* 2.104-37.

schools as well as the Lutheran and Reformed wings of the Reformation pointed to natural law as the standard for civil law, such that civil laws inconsistent with or not somehow based upon the natural law were deemed unjust. This conviction continued unabated in the era of Reformed orthodoxy. Althusius, expressing his reliance on Zanchi, defines proper law as "nothing other than the practice of this proper common natural law . . . as adapted to a particular polity" and shortly thereafter writes: "Common [natural] law commands in general. Proper law makes these commands specific. . . ."[46] Rutherford writes similarly, asserting that the community's law is the natural law, rather than arbitrary lust. Hence, absolute power is against nature and is thus unlawful.[47] Whatever interpretation of civil law "swerveth either from fundamental laws of policy, or from the law of nature, and the law of nations, and especially from the safety of the public, is to be rejected as a perverting of the law."[48] Elsewhere, Rutherford speaks of the law of nations as founded upon the law of nature.[49] Turretin's understanding is no different. Describing the view of the "orthodox" over against the "libertines," he affirms that "there is such a natural law of God obtaining among all (as the rule of justice and injustice) antecedently to the positive laws of men" and hence denies that "justice and virtue depend upon man's will alone and spring from the consent of human society and are to be measured by each one's own utility."[50] Yet, like Calvin and many others, Turretin affirms that human legislators have flexibility and discretion in putting natural law into concrete legal form in particular circumstances. For instance, he deems the "manner and degree of punishment" of crimes to be "mutable."[51]

Natural Law and the Mosaic Law

In regard to the relationship of natural law and Mosaic law, the previous chapters have also described a broad consensus among medieval and Reformation traditions. This consensus classifies the Mosaic laws into moral, ceremonial, and civil, identifying the moral law with the natural law (and hence deeming it of perpetual obligation) and making natural law the test for the

46. Althusius, *Politica*, 144, 146.
47. Rutherford, *Rex, Lex*, 35, 104.
48. Rutherford, *Rex, Lex*, 137.
49. Rutherford, *Rex, Lex*, 68.
50. Turretin, *Institutes*, 2.2.
51. Turretin, *Institutes*, 2.167.

continuing applicability of the civil law. As with the related question of natural law and civil law, the Reformed orthodox confessions and theologians examined here upheld and developed this consensus position.

First, Reformed orthodoxy continued to affirm the threefold division of the Mosaic law into moral, ceremonial, and civil (or judicial) as a standard theological axiom. Turretin, for example, writes: "The law given by Moses is usually distinguished into three species: moral (treating of morals or of perpetual duties towards God and our neighbor); ceremonial (of the ceremonies or rites about the sacred things to be observed under the Old Testament); and civil, constituting the civil government of the Israelite people."[52] While the moral law was substantively identified with the natural law and thus considered of perpetual obligation, as considered above, and the ceremonial law was viewed as abrogated through Christ's redemptive work, the civil law's continuing applicability required a more nuanced analysis. The basic approach of Reformed orthodoxy, like that of the Reformation and medieval traditions, was to proclaim the civil law generally abrogated following the coming of Christ, but also to acknowledge a relevance of the Mosaic civil law for contemporary civil law insofar as the former reflected the law of nature. This perspective, of course, corresponds closely to the idea that natural law is the standard for contemporary civil law.

Althusius provides a helpful first example of this approach among Reformed orthodox thinkers. He says that in similar circumstances civil law should not depart from the polity of the Jews.[53] But his qualification regarding circumstances is crucial. Later he writes: "The forensic [civil] law was the means by which the Jews were informed and instructed to observe and obey both tables, or the common [natural] law, for the cultivation of human society among them in their polity, according to the circumstances of things, persons, place, and time. . . . What is moral in such a law is perpetual; what is judicial can be changed by the change of circumstances." Then, after associating moral equity with the natural law, Althusius explains that the magistrate "is required to conform to everything therein [the Old Testament judicial law] that is in harmony with common [natural] law. But he is by no means required to conform in those things in which the proper law of Moses, in order to be accommodated to the polity of the Jews, differs from the common [natural] law." From a somewhat different, and more forceful, angle, he concludes: "The magistrate who makes the proper law of Moses com-

52. Turretin, *Institutes,* 2.145; see also WCF 19.2-4.
53. Althusius, *Politica,* 13.

pulsory in his commonwealth sins grievously. For those particular circumstances and considerations because of which the Jewish proper law was promulgated should bear no weight in his commonwealth."[54]

These thoughts had taken on very precise form by the middle of the seventeenth century. Turretin's discussion is striking for its conceptual clarity. Turretin claims the middle ground for Reformed orthodoxy between those who think that the Old Testament judicial law was abrogated in every sense and those who believe it is still in force.[55] With an artist's precision, he distinguishes between those elements of the civil law that were founded upon the particular circumstances of the Jews and those that were founded upon the natural law, and he argued that the former, but not the latter, were abrogated. He writes: "The forensic [civil] law may be viewed either formally, as it was enacted for the Jews (and so is abrogated); or materially, inasmuch as it agrees with the natural law and is founded on it (and thus it still remains)." Therefore, contemporary magistrates have discretion in shaping civil law, so long as it is derived from natural law:

> The forensic law is better than other laws, not affirmatively, but negatively because it was determined to certain circumstances which do not now exist. Then again it is better than human laws (simply as human), but not inasmuch as they are founded upon the natural law, whose source is God. Therefore, when the Roman laws are preferred to the Mosaic, they are not preferred simply as enacted by men, but as derived from natural and common right they can be more suitable to places, times and persons.[56]

Rutherford echoes these sentiments: "But we conceive, the whole bulk of the judicial law, as judicial, as it concerned the republic of the Jews only, is abolished, though the moral equity of all those be not abolished."[57] In determining which punishments set forth in the judicial law are binding today, Rutherford's criterion is therefore whether they are "moral and perpetual."[58] It is worth noting, at the same time, that his views on this topic (and those of his Reformed contemporaries) are "complex," for they demanded "discerning the moral and permanent element in particular judicial laws." For Rutherford, perhaps surprisingly to contemporary readers, "the Old Testa-

---

54. Althusius, *Politica*, 146, 148.
55. Turretin, *Institutes*, 2.166.
56. Turretin, *Institutes*, 2.167.
57. Rutherford, *Divine Right*, 493.
58. Rutherford, *Divine Right*, 493-94.

ment laws concerning national covenanting and the magistrate's duty to defend true religion were still binding on Christians."[59] Many of his Reformed contemporaries held similar convictions.[60] I will deal with this issue further in the discussion of the two kingdoms doctrine below.

The Reformed orthodox approach to the relation of natural law and Mosaic civil law found confessional expression in WCF 19.4. This section states that to Old Testament Israel, "as a body politic, he [God] gave sundry judicial laws, which expired together with the state of that people; not obliging any other now, further than the general equity thereof may require." Though the language here is not explicit, almost certainly the terminology of "general equity" is, for all intents and purposes, a reference to natural law. This makes natural law the standard for the Mosaic civil law's continuing applicability in the WCF. I suggest two lines of argument in defense of this claim. Both revolve around the fact that the Westminster Standards were consensus documents and therefore that the theologians who constructed them (of whom Rutherford himself was a prominent member) sought to enshrine, as far as possible, common and broadly-held views of Reformed churches and theologians of the day. The first line of argument then, is the simple reminder that, as the previous paragraphs explored with regard to Althusius, Turretin, and Rutherford, Reformed orthodox theology widely affirmed that indeed natural law was the criterion for whether and how Mosaic civil laws ought to be applied in the present. The framers of the Westminster Standards surely were not attempting to strike out on a new course.

The second line of argument is that Reformed orthodox writers regularly associated the ideas of natural law and equity very closely. A couple of articles in recent years on WCF 19.4 have provided generally helpful treatment of the meaning of "general equity."[61] Both contain good discussion of

---

59. Coffey, *Politics, Religion and the British Revolutions*, 156-57.

60. Pertinent here may be the comments of Thomas O. Hueglin in "Covenant and Federalism in the Politics of Althusius," in *The Covenant Connection: From Federal Theology to Modern Federalism,* ed. Daniel J. Elazar and John Kincaid (Lanham: Lexington, 2000), 41: "Althusius did not wish to set forth a political theory of theocracy, nor anything like a religious state. The exclusive sovereignty of God is the normative category which constitutes mutuality and self-regulation among humans. If such self-regulated human existence also appears as the rational consequence of a social philosophy based on natural law, then Althusius sought to demonstrate that Christian religion and natural law are identical points of reference for a rationally constructed theory of politics."

61. Sinclair B. Ferguson, "An Assembly of Theonomists? The Teaching of the Westminster Divines on the Law of God," in *Theonomy: A Reformed Critique,* ed. William S. Barker and W. Robert Godfrey (Grand Rapids: Zondervan, 1990), 315-49; A. Craig Troxel and Peter J. Wallace,

the philosophical and juridical background of the idea of equity as denoting the fairness or justice lying behind the letter of the law. One of these articles also presents helpful material on the interpretation of general equity against the background of English legal history. It rightly points out that the English legal system was divided between courts of common law and courts of equity, the latter providing recourse to justice in cases where the common law courts, with their more narrow range of remedies, could not provide a fair outcome. "General equity," then, is "a *terminus technicus* consistent with the concept in English and American jurisprudence."[62] One matter that these two articles do not address in great detail, however, is the relation of natural law and general equity in the interpretation of WCF 19.4.[63] Following the line of thought indicated by Calvin,[64] the Reformed orthodox often treated equity and natural law as virtual synonyms. Althusius, for example, writes: "There is no civil law, nor can there be any, in which something of natural and divine immutable equity has not been mixed. If it departs entirely from the judgment of natural and divine law . . . , it is not to be called law. . . . It is entirely unworthy of this name, and can obligate no one against natural and divine equity."[65] His subsequent words are even more to the point: "The magistrate is obligated in the administration of the commonwealth to the proper law of Moses so far as moral equity or common [natural] law are expressed therein."[66] Some years later, writing shortly after the Westminster Assembly, Turretin continues to associate these ideas tightly. After commenting that equity is the mind of the law as well as the aim, rule, and end of all law, he notes that "the law of nature (the fountain of all other laws, because it is the most equitable) is also the most majestic."[67]

In light of this evidence, I suggest that the most plausible reading of WCF 19.4 concurs with the general sentiments of the Reformed orthodox

---

"Men in Combat over the Civil Law: 'General Equity' in WCF 19.4," *Westminster Theological Journal* 64 (Fall 2002): 307-18.

62. Troxel and Wallace, "Men in Combat," 312; see also Ferguson, "An Assembly," 330.

63. See, however, the brief discussion in Troxel and Wallace, "Men in Combat," 311.

64. See Calvin, *Institutes*, 4.20.16. After explaining that equity ought to be proposed in all civil laws, and that civil laws in different places may rightly be diverse, "provided they all alike aim at equity as their end," Calvin points to natural law as where this equity is defined: "Now, as it is evident that the law of God which we call moral, is nothing else than the testimony of natural law, and of that conscience which God has engraven on the minds of men, the whole of this equity of which we now speak is prescribed in it."

65. Althusius, *Politica*, 72.

66. Althusius, *Politica*, 148.

67. Turretin, *Institutes*, 2.137-38.

writers being studied in this chapter. The civil or judicial law of Moses has been abrogated with the coming of Christ, yet has continuing applicability insofar as it reflects the natural law. For Reformed orthodoxy, as for the Reformation and medieval traditions of the past, civil magistrates ought not impose the Mosaic civil law *as such* upon contemporary societies. Yet at times they will implement Mosaic civil laws, not because they are Mosaic laws but because they are particular applications of the natural law still appropriate under present circumstances.

Other Aspects of the Reformed Orthodox Doctrine of Natural Law

Before bringing this section on natural law to a conclusion, I note here a few additional points of similarity to earlier Reformed natural law thought. The things highlighted in this subsection all concern characteristics of the natural law theology of the Reformed resistance theorists considered in the previous chapter. At the end of the previous chapter I called attention to how Rutherford's *Lex, Rex,* a resistance treatise in its own right, picked up on these themes. Here I note how these themes also appear in other Reformed thinkers considered in this chapter.

First, Reformed orthodox writers affirmed that human beings are social animals by nature.[68] Second, they posited that all creatures by nature seek self-preservation, and hence that a certain right of self-defense is taught by natural law.[69] Third, they believed that natural law establishes a certain equality among all people. This, in turn, makes the people as a whole prior to and superior to their civil rulers, with significant repercussions for political life.[70] Fourth, they used analogies from nature to make natural law claims, including the notion of the superiority of the people over their princes.[71] The examples could undoubtedly be enumerated, but as a final

---

68. E.g., see Althusius, *Politica,* 24-25. Though I note here similarities regarding natural law between Althusius and the resistance theorists of the previous chapter, scholars have also noted various differences between them on political and legal issues more generally. For example, Hueglin writes in "Covenant and Federalism," 45: "A principal difference between Althusius and earlier pamphleteers lies in the constitutional stabilization of what had formerly been only a strategic argument of resistance, and what now appeared as a means for a popularly controlled exercise of mandatory government."

69. E.g., see Turretin, *Institutes,* 2.116-17; and Althusius, *"Dicaeologicae,"* 441-42.

70. E.g., see Althusius, *Politica,* 93-102.

71. E.g., see Althusius, *Politica,* 96-97.

matter I note that these Reformed orthodox thinkers, like the resistance theorists, had a high enough view of natural law to weave together arguments drawn from a wide range of sources. As is amply demonstrated by a simple perusal of their works that are considered in this chapter, and as much recent scholarship has discussed, they utilize not only biblical and Reformed sources, but also patristic, medieval, and contemporary Roman Catholic sources, as well as (and most significantly for present concerns) all sorts of classical, pagan writings as they attempt to defend their claims, though they do not do so uncritically.[72] They continue the Reformed tradition of receiving truth gratefully wherever it may be found.[73]

Conclusion

In this section, I have set forth evidence on a variety of points indicating the importance that Reformed orthodoxy ascribed to natural law for a number of theological and moral issues as well as the significant degree of similarity of Reformed orthodoxy's teaching on natural law not only with earlier Reformation teaching but also with that of the medieval traditions before. On the basis of the evidence accrued from the theologians and confessional documents studied here, I conclude that there is marked continuity with Reformation doctrine and in many cases the medieval traditions in Reformed orthodoxy's teaching on natural law in relation to its character and divine origin, on the witness to natural law in Romans 2:14-15, on the association of natural law and conscience, on the identification of natural law with the moral law and love commands, on natural law as the standard for civil law, on natural law as test for the continuing applicability of the Mosaic law, and on a variety of other issues. Furthermore, the incorporation of the idea of natural law into a number of other doctrinal issues by Reformed orthodox theologians suggests that they developed the idea into something crucial and integral to the Reformed system of doctrine. In addition to the integration of natural law into the key doctrine of the covenant of works, as described

72. Among writings that discuss the wide variety of sources utilized by the Reformed thinkers considered here, see, e.g., Richards, "'The Law Written in Their Hearts'?"; Marshall, "Natural Law and the Covenant," 113, 147; Coffey, *Politics, Religion and the British Revolutions*, 27, 69-77; Sebastian Rehnman, "John Owen: A Reformed Scholastic at Oxford," in *Reformation and Scholasticism*, 181-203; Frederick S. Carney, "Translator's Introduction," in *Politica*, xxiv-xxvii.

73. E.g., Turretin appeals to classical literature, but only to "the wiser among the heathen" (among whom he includes Pythagoras, Plato, Aristotle, Seneca, and Cicero); see *Institutes*, 2.117.

above, one might also mention the importance of natural law for Reformed orthodox thought on doctrines precious to the Reformed such as the Sabbath,[74] Christian liberty,[75] and the ordering of worship and church government.[76] Clearly, natural law was not an aspect of Reformed orthodox theology and ethics that could be eliminated without serious ramifications for the system of Reformed thought as a whole.

The Two Kingdoms Doctrine in Reformed Orthodoxy

As explored in Chapter 3, John Calvin taught a doctrine of the two kingdoms. In so doing, he continued and developed a line of thought first articulated explicitly by Martin Luther though related to much previous Christian thought. The question that confronts us now is what happened to the two kingdoms idea in subsequent Reformed thought. Through a continuing investigation of Althusius, Rutherford, and Turretin, as well as the Westminster Standards and other theologians and ecclesiastical documents, I conclude that Reformed theology in the age of orthodoxy continued to articulate and apply the two kingdoms idea (though not always explicitly using "two kingdoms" terminology), not only to pressing matters of civil and ecclesiastical authority but also to a variety of other moral, theological, and ecclesiological issues. It did so, in fact, in many ways similar to Calvin,

74. What is commonly referred to as the "Puritan" doctrine of the Sabbath holds that the general obligation to keep one day in seven as a day of rest and worship remains binding on all people despite the change from the seventh to first day of the week and the ceremonial/typological aspects of the fourth commandment. Reformed theologians who defended this doctrine developed a nuanced account of the fourth commandment distinguishing its natural, moral, and positive aspects, in order to specify which parts of the commandment are still binding and which have expired with Christ's coming. This classification of natural, moral, and positive aspects of the fourth commandment are clearly evident in WCF 21.7 and are evident throughout Owen's discussion in "Exercitations." On the prevalence of such thinking among many Puritan theologians of this era, see generally James T. Dennison, Jr., *Market Day of the Soul: The Puritan Doctrine of the Sabbath in England, 1532-1700* (Lanham: University Press of America, 1983). For evidence that this way of thinking was not confined to British Puritan theologians, but was manifest in continental Reformed theologians as well, compare the discussion of the fourth commandment in Turretin, *Institutes*, 2.84-89.

75. E.g., see WCF 20.4. This point will be discussed in more detail below, in light of the importance of both natural law and the two kingdoms doctrine for the Reformed articulation of Christian liberty.

76. E.g., see WCF 1.6. Again, as this point touches upon the relationship of natural law and the two kingdoms doctrine, it will be discussed at more length below.

though it also developed and extrapolated his basic ideas on certain issues. At the same time, the sorts of tensions that I observed between Calvin's two kingdoms doctrine and his understanding of concrete relations between church and state continue to emerge in later Reformed thought. To put the main point simply: Calvin did not hold a contemporary Reformed one-kingdom view in which the redemptive kingdom of Christ embraces all areas of life, and neither did these eminent thinkers and confessional documents of Reformed orthodoxy.

Perhaps the context within the later sixteenth- and seventeenth-century Reformed world that is best known for defending a two kingdoms doctrine is the Scottish church of the late 1500s. Many historians of this period have commented on the advocacy of a two kingdoms idea among certain Scottish church leaders, though they have offered quite different interpretations of the idea's significance.[77] Andrew Melville is often most associated with the doctrine, though he is wrongly credited with being the first Scot to articulate it.[78] Melville and others adopted the terminology of "two kingdoms" particularly in confronting the royal crown with the limits of its power and the rights and authority of the church.[79] The ideas at work here, if not the "two

77. Some scholars have argued that the Scottish two kingdoms doctrine was essentially a theocratic, one kingdom doctrine that made the church functionally supreme over the state, while other scholars understand it to teach a genuine dual authority. For examples of the former interpretation, see Gordon Donaldson, *Scottish Church History* (Edinburgh: Scottish Academic Press, 1985), 234-36; and Francis Lyall, *Of Presbyters and Kings: Church and State in the Law of Scotland* (Aberdeen: Aberdeen University Press, 1980), 17; for examples of the latter, see James Kirk, *Patterns of Reform: Continuity and Change in the Reformation Kirk* (Edinburgh: T&T Clark, 1989), 237-38; and Coffey, *Politics, Religion and the British Revolutions,* 208. Among studies of the practical outworking of the Scottish two kingdoms doctrine and debates surrounding it, see Alan R. MacDonald, "Ecclesiastical Representation in Parliament in Post-Reformation Scotland: The Two Kingdoms Theory in Practice," *Journal of Ecclesiastical History* 50 (January 1999): 38-61; K. M. Brown, "In Search of the Godly Magistrate in Reformation Scotland," *Journal of Ecclesiastical History* 40 (Oct 1989): 553-81; and Michael Graham, "The Civil Sword and the Scottish Kirk, 1560-1600," in *Later Calvinism,* 237-48. For an extensive analysis generally of the effects of the Reformation on Scottish ecclesiastical and social life, see Margo Todd, *The Culture of Protestantism in Early Modern Scotland* (New Haven: Yale University Press, 2002).

78. Kirk makes this point in discussing a statement sent by the Lords of the Congregation to Mary of Guise, the queen regent, in 1559, decades before Melville's famous articulation of the doctrine in 1596, in which a two kingdoms distinction is clearly made; see *Patterns of Reform,* 235-36.

79. The 1559 statement to Mary of Guise, for example, distinguishes between "ane kingdome temporall" and "Christis kingdome" (the latter identified with the church) and between the governments of "the spirituall and hevinlie kingdome"; as quoted in Kirk, *Patterns of Reform,* 235. Andrew Melville's 1596 statement claimed that "thair is twa Kings and twa Kingdomes in Scot-

kingdoms" terminology itself, found ecclesiastical expression in the Scottish General Assembly's 1578 *Second Book of Discipline,* which defined with some precision the respective spheres of civil and ecclesiastical authority and which will receive some attention in the subsections below.

The two kingdoms doctrine continued to be of great importance to the seventeenth-century Scottish Presbyterians, particularly in defense of the authority of the church over against state encroachment. Samuel Rutherford and his colleague George Gillespie provide prominent examples.[80] Rutherford writes: "How does this confound the two kingdoms? The kingdom that is of this world, and fights with the sword; and the kingdom that is not of this world, and fights not with the sword?"[81] In many other places he makes a similar distinction, between, for example, "the magistrate's kingdom" and "the church and kingdom of Christ" or between "the kingdom of this world" and "Christ's other kingdom, that is not of this world."[82] Gillespie writes of "the twofold kingdom of Jesus Christ" over against the Socinians (and others), who "stiffly hold that Christ hath but one kingdom."[83] Significant Reformed orthodox theologians from the continent such as Turretin also utilized the language and concepts of the "two kingdoms" and thereby stood in continuity with the Scottish churchmen and Calvin before them. For instance, early in his discussion of the kingdom of Christ, Turretin states that "before all things we must distinguish the twofold kingdom, belonging to Christ; one natural or essential; the other mediatorial and economical."[84] Later in the same discussion, from a some-

---

land"; see James Melville, *The Autobiography and Diary of Mr. James Melvill,* ed. Robert Pitcairn (Edinburgh: Wodrow Society, 1842), 370.

80. Rutherford's *Divine Right,* which will be cited frequently below, was a massive ecclesiological work designed in large part to defend the church's authority, and often did so with appeal to the two kingdoms doctrine. Precisely the same description applies to one of Gillespie's major works, *Aaron's Rod Blossoming; or, the Divine Ordinance of Church Government Vindicated* (London, 1646; reprinted Harrisonburg, VA: Sprinkle, 1985). For recent discussions of Rutherford and especially Gillespie on these matters, see David McKay, "From Popery to Principle: Covenanters and the Kingship of Christ," in *The Faith Once Delivered: Essays in Honor of Dr. Wayne Spear,* ed. Anthony T. Selvaggio (Phillipsburg, NJ: P&R, 2007), 136-42; and W. D. J. McKay, *An Ecclesiastical Republic: Church Government in the Writings of George Gillespie* (Carlisle: Paternoster, 1997), ch. 2. Other scholars have remarked on the continuity between the Reformers and the later sixteenth-century Scots (e.g., see Kirk, *Patterns of Reform,* 236-37) and between the sixteenth-century Scots and Rutherford (e.g., see Coffey, *Politics, Religion and the British Revolutions,* 208).

81. Rutherford, *Divine Right,* 555.

82. E.g., see Rutherford, *Divine Right,* 532, 564.

83. Gillespie, *Aaron's Rod Blossoming,* 90 (2.V).

84. Turretin, *Institutes,* 2.486.

what different angle, he contrasts the "kingdom of Christ" with the "kingdoms of the world" or "temporal kingdoms."[85] Both Rutherford and Turretin, we will see, apply this two kingdoms distinction to delicate matters of church and state.

The Nature and Attributes of the Two Kingdoms

As we now begin a more detailed consideration of the two kingdoms doctrine in Reformed orthodox thought, it seems helpful first to discuss how Reformed writers of this era articulated the nature and attributes of the two kingdoms, particularly in terms of one kingdom's distinction from the other. Turretin, in characteristic fashion, offers a nuanced and relevant discussion of Christ's kingship similar to that of other Reformed orthodox theologians,[86] and thus his treatment serves as a useful focus for this subsection.

Turretin begins his exposition of Christ's kingship with a crucial distinction that shapes his subsequent articulation of matters pertaining to the two kingdoms doctrine: "Before all things we must distinguish the twofold kingdom, belonging to Christ: one natural or essential; the other mediatorial and economical." As clearly indicated in the discussion that follows this statement, Turretin is in effect identifying what Calvin referred to as the civil kingdom and the spiritual kingdom. Turretin proceeds to make a series of distinctions in order to differentiate one kingdom from the other. The "natural or essential" kingdom is "over all creatures" while the "mediatorial and economical" kingdom is "terminated specially on the church." Christ possesses the former as the eternal Son (along with the Father and Holy Spirit) and administers the latter "in a peculiar manner as God-man." The former "is founded on the decree of providence" and the latter "on the decree of election." Christ exercises kingship over the former "inasmuch as he is God . . . and the Logos" and over the latter "inasmuch as he is God-man." In a summary statement, Turretin explains: "Hence it is called his 'mediatorial and economical kingdom' because it is a dominion peculiar to the Mediator and as it were his own according to the dispensation of grace. The other belongs to him by nature and is on that account called 'natural.'"[87]

---

85. Turretin, *Institutes,* 2.489.

86. See and compare the summaries and quotations of Reformed orthodox teaching on Christ's kingship and kingdom in Heinrich Heppe, *Reformed Dogmatics,* rev. and ed. Ernst Bizer, trans. G. T. Thomson (1950; reprinted London: Wakeman, n.d.), 481-83.

87. Turretin, *Institutes,* 2.486. On the prominence of this Christological distinction in

This material alone provides substantial evidence not simply for remnants of a Reformation two kingdoms doctrine in Reformed orthodoxy, but for a well thought out and developed theology of the two kingdoms incorporated into larger questions of Christology. It is worth lingering for a moment and highlighting Turretin's claims here. Christ rules the one kingdom as *eternal God,* as *the agent of creation and providence,* and *over all creatures.* Christ rules the other kingdom as *the incarnate God-man,* as *the agent of redemption,* and *over the church.* The latter kingdom is redemptive, the former is non-redemptive. The latter is exclusive, the former is inclusive. To my knowledge, Calvin never put things in quite this organized, detailed, and nuanced a way. But Turretin's exposition seems very much to express the ideas that Calvin articulated, as discussed in Chapter 3, but in a more developed and theologically integrated fashion.

One of the matters that Turretin is intent on emphasizing in his subsequent discussion is the spiritual and heavenly nature of Christ's mediatorial, redemptive kingdom in distinction from the earthly and mundane nature of the natural, essential kingdom, thereby echoing an important theme for Calvin.[88] The specific question that he poses "concerns the manner of that [mediatorial] kingdom — whether it should be mundane and earthly, or spiritual and heavenly." His answer is that "the orthodox infer that his kingdom is not mundane and earthly, but spiritual and celestial." He identifies the contrary opinion with the Jews, echoing Calvin's sentiment that finding Christ's kingdom in earthly things is a "Jewish vanity."[89] Turretin proceeds to offer six biblical and theological reasons in support of this claim, pointing especially to Old Testament prophecies and types and to New Testament teaching about the Messiah and his kingdom. In this discussion he asserts that "all that pertains to this kingdom is spiritual, not mundane and earthly," mentioning its king, throne, scepter, subjects, mode of administration, laws, and blessings.[90]

A few years earlier, Rutherford and Gillespie also embraced many of these key points. Like Turretin, Rutherford distinguished between one kingdom ruled by God *as creator* (and hence temporal and mundane) and the other kingdom ruled by God *as redeemer* (and hence spiritual and heavenly). For example, in speaking about the institutional expression of these two

---

seventeenth-century Reformed thought, see McKay, *An Ecclesiastic Republic,* 42-60; and McKay, "From Popery to Principle," 136-42.

88. Compare Calvin, *Institutes,* 2.15.3, 5; 4.20.1.

89. Turretin, *Institutes,* 2.487. Compare Calvin, *Institutes,* 4.20.1.

90. Turretin, *Institutes,* 2.487-89.

kingdoms in state and church, Rutherford says: "these two powers are so different, as spiritual and temporal, carnal of this world, spiritual not of this world, the one subject as supreme immediately to God creator, the other supreme immediately subject to God the redeemer." Shortly thereafter he contrasts "Christ's kingdom" and "the magistrate's kingdom" and, precisely because of the spirituality of the former, concludes that the magistrate's kingdom "is not a part of his [Christ's] kingdom."[91] The only evident difference between Rutherford's and Turretin's language here is that while Turretin speaks of the temporal kingdom as ruled by Christ as God, with the Father and Spirit, Rutherford simply speaks of this kingdom as ruled by God (the creator). But the theological idea expressed by these theologians is substantively identical. Gillespie affirms the same doctrine, writing, in language more similar to Turretin's, of "a twofold kingdom of Jesus Christ: one, as he is the eternal Son of God, reigning together with the Father and the Holy Ghost over all things . . . ; another, as Mediator and Head of the church."[92]

In discussing the spiritual, redemptive kingdom of Christ, Turretin argues that its administration and exercise consist principally in four things: the calling and gathering of the church, the conservation and government of the church, the protection and defense of the church, and the full glorification of the church.[93] One matter that is particularly striking for the present study is the close association of the church and Christ's spiritual kingdom. Turretin mentions only the church as the place where the kingdom is administered and exercised, which suggests that he viewed the church as *the only* present institutional expression of the essentially heavenly kingdom of Christ. The way Turretin speaks elsewhere bolsters such a conclusion. He writes, for example, that "the church is the kingdom of heaven" and that Christ's redemptive, mediatorial kingship is "terminated specially on the church." In fact, he adds that the mediatorial kingship belongs to Christ "because he [God] constituted him King over the church (Ps. 2:6)."[94] Gillespie's language is concise and unambiguous: "Christ, as Mediator, is King of the church only."[95] Such an exclusive identity of the redemptive, spiritual kingdom with the church was no novelty in Reformed theology. As observed in Chapter 3, Calvin taught this same doctrine, contrary to commonly received

---

91. Rutherford, *Divine Right,* 510-11.

92. Gillespie, *Aaron's Rod Blossoming,* 90 (2.V).

93. Turretin, *Institutes,* 2.487.

94. See Turretin, *Institutes,* 3.280; 2.486.

95. Gillespie, *Aaron's Rod Blossoming,* 90 (2.V). With these words Gillespie contrasts his own position with that of one of his opponents.

opinion about him. Likewise, the Scottish ecclesiastics of 1559, after referring to the "spirituall and hevinlie kingdome," clarified by adding: "the kirk of God we mein."[96] It is no surprise, then, that Heinrich Heppe writes, in summarizing the opinion of Reformed orthodoxy generally, that "it is not right, when it is said that according to Reformed doctrine the kingship of Christ also extends over the extra-Church sphere (of nature). Of course Christ has power over this also, but only for the purpose of exercising his mediating Kingship over the Church."[97] This aspect of the two kingdoms doctrine found confessional expression in the Westminster Standards. WLC 45 speaks primarily of Christ's kingship in terms of the church: "Christ executeth the office of a king, in calling out of the world a people to himself, and giving them officers, laws, and censures, by which he visibly governs them; in bestowing saving grace upon his elect, rewarding their obedience, and correcting them for their sins, preserving and supporting them under all their temptations and sufferings. . . ." At this point it goes on to speak of his kingship over those outside of the church, not in redemptive terms but only, as Heppe says, for the sake of his people or for wreaking vengeance: "restraining and overcoming all their enemies, and powerfully ordering all things for his own glory, and their good; and also in taking vengeance on the rest, who know not God, and obey not the gospel." Succinctly, but along the same lines, WCF 25.2 states that the visible church "is the kingdom of the Lord Jesus Christ."

It is worth noting that these Reformed orthodox views of the church as the redemptive kingdom of Christ and of this kingdom as spiritual did not mean that the church itself should have no external government. In this matter the Reformed tradition differed from typical Lutheran two kingdoms theology, which, in seeing the church's spiritual character as precluding an external government, was content to hand external administrative matters of the church over to the state. Closer to home for the Reformed, Swiss physician and University of Heidelberg professor Thomas Erastus (1524-83) is often associated with similar views. Erastus denied the right of the church to excommunicate and the term "Erastian" came to connote the idea that the state should control the church.[98] Not only did Calvin affirm the necessity of a spiritual yet externally organized ecclesiastical government and discipline,

---

96. As quoted in Kirk, *Patterns of Reform*, 235.

97. Heppe, *Reformed Dogmatics*, 482.

98. For a study of Erastus, see Charles Dewey Gunnoe, Jr., "Thomas Erastus in Heidelberg: A Renaissance Physician during the Second Reformation, 1558-1580" (Ph.D. dissertation, University of Virginia, 1998).

as discussed in Chapter 3, but later Reformed theology and practice also typically called for such. This was in fact a major concern of Turretin, Rutherford, and Gillespie.[99] If the Reformed two kingdoms doctrine meant anything it meant that the external government and discipline of the church was not left to the civil magistrate.

One final matter remains for the present subsection. The clear distinction between the two kingdoms that Turretin and other Reformed orthodox luminaries articulated raises the important yet difficult question of just how, or even whether, Christ rules the civil kingdom (or, more concretely, particular earthly kingdoms). Turretin makes clear that he does, yet makes several qualifications in explaining how. One hesitates to call them "qualifications," but they seem important enough to warrant the term. First, as seen above, Turretin makes quite clear that Christ rules over the temporal kingdom not as the incarnate mediator but as the Logos, the eternal Son of God, and hence as creator and sustainer but not as redeemer.[100] Later in his discussion he elaborates on the question before us by specifying the different ways in which Christ reigns in these distinct capacities. Though Christ reigns always in a "spiritual" and not an "earthly" way, Turretin explains: "Indeed he reigns differently in the pious and the wicked: in the former by the sweet and healthful influence of the Spirit, as head; in the latter, by his own powerful virtue as Lord."[101] Turretin's exposition here might be suspected of harboring some confusion, insofar as the distinction between the two kingdoms that he previously set forth is not a strict distinction between the "pious" and the "wicked." The pious live in the civil as well as the spiritual kingdom (and some wicked people hold external membership in the church). Despite what thus may be a brief confusion of categories, Turretin's sentiments here seem a logical extension of his earlier comments: as creator and sustainer, Christ rules the temporal kingdom as the sovereign lord of all; as incarnate

99. E.g., see Rutherford, *Divine Right*, 13, 104-5, 220-37, 421, 510-11; Turretin, *Institutes*, 3.274, 293-303 (Turretin calls Erastus "the insane man"); and Gillespie, *Aaron's Rod Blossoming*, Book 3. The "Erastian" faction was a leading foe of Scottish Presbyterians such as Rutherford and Gillespie at the Westminster Assembly. For a description of this Erastian party, see, e.g., Robert S. Paul, *The Assembly of the Lord: Politics and Religion in the Westminster Assembly and the 'Grand Debate'* (Edinburgh: T&T Clark, 1985), 127-32; see also various discussions in J. R. de Witt, *Jus Divinum: The Westminster Assembly and the Divine Right of Church Government* (Kampen: Kok, 1969). For a study of a leading Erastian at the Assembly, see Reid Barbour, *John Selden: Measures of the Holy Commonwealth in Seventeenth-Century England* (Toronto: University of Toronto Press, 2003).

100. Turretin, *Institutes*, 2.486.

101. Turretin, *Institutes*, 2.489-90.

redeemer, Christ rules the spiritual kingdom as a tender savior. Hence would seem to follow Turretin's conclusion elsewhere: "The political magistrate as such does not serve properly and formally in promoting the kingdom of Christ."[102] Gillespie frequently speaks in the same way as Turretin.[103]

Rutherford's language is similar though not identical to Turretin's, and their substantive theological claims are the same. As noted above, Rutherford put the temporal kingdom under "God the creator" and spiritual kingdom under "Christ the Redeemer and Head of the Church."[104] In speaking further about the former, he writes that it is "not a part" of Christ's spiritual kingdom and thus states bluntly that the civil magistrate "is not subordinate to Christ as mediator and head of the church."[105] Along similar lines, he says later that "magistrates as magistrates" are not "the ambassadors of Christ" but "the deputy of God as the God of order, and as the creator."[106] Still later he adds that "the magistrate as a magistrate is not the vicar nor deputy of Jesus Christ as mediator" and that "the magistrate as such is not a vicar of Christ's mediatory kingdom."[107] There are nuances and qualifications to these claims, some of which will be discussed below.[108]

In light of this evidence, I suggest that Turretin and Rutherford teach the same doctrine in these passages, though from somewhat different angles. Turretin answers Yes to the question whether Christ rules the temporal kingdom, but with qualifications (i.e., that he does so only as eternal God, with the Father and Holy Spirit, as creator/sustainer); Rutherford answer No to the same question, but with qualifications (i.e., that God the creator does rule this kingdom). When the qualifications of each are compared to the other's, the effect is the same. To put it as precisely as possible, they both teach that the Son of God rules the temporal kingdom as an eternal member of the Divine Trinity but does not rule it in his capacity as the incarnate mediator/redeemer.

---

102. Turretin, *Institutes*, 3.278.

103. E.g., see Gillespie, *Aaron's Rod Blossoming*, 97 (2.VI), where, in stating the point of controversy between him and his opponent, he denies that it concerns the question whether the magistrate is Christ's deputy in every sense. Thus, the question is not "Whether the magistrate be Christ's deputy, as Christ is God, and as he exerciseth an universal dominion over all things, as the Father and the Holy Ghost doth? Here likewise I hold the affirmative."

104. Rutherford, *Divine Right*, 510.

105. Rutherford, *Divine Right*, 511.

106. Rutherford, *Divine Right*, 550-51.

107. Rutherford, *Divine Right*, 601, 604.

108. E.g., see his comments on the similarities and differences between magistrates who are Christians and those who are not in *Divine Right*, 547-48, 601-8.

This theological distinction is crucial for the story being narrated in this book. Chapter 3 noted that Calvin's so-called *extra Calvinisticum* Christology gave him theological categories for distinguishing Christ's divine work of creation and providence from his work of redemption as God-man and mediator, even after the incarnation. Reformed orthodox theologians also recognized Christ's continuing distinct identities as creator/sustainer and as redeemer and developed this idea in the ways observed above, tying it specifically to the two kingdoms doctrine. As they grounded natural law in the covenant of works, and hence in creation rather than in redemption, so they also grounded the civil kingdom in creation rather than in redemption. Subsequent chapters will explore how later Reformed theologians continued to distinguish between Christ's creating/sustaining work and his redeeming work and retained a two kingdoms doctrine by doing so, but later chapters will also identify rejection of this distinction as a major factor in the recent Reformed abandonment of the two kingdoms doctrine.

The Distinctions between Civil and Ecclesiastical Authority

At this point attention appropriately turns to the concrete relationship of church and state, considered especially under the rubric of civil and ecclesiastical authority. As considered in the previous subsection, many prominent Reformed orthodox writers believed that the two kingdoms find present institutional expression in church and state. Calvin wrote similarly, though he also saw a broad range of social and cultural activities as falling within the purview of the civil kingdom. The Reformed orthodox did not deny that the civil kingdom has a broader scope, but their emphasis certainly fell upon the state. In this subsection, I discuss how Reformed orthodoxy articulated distinctions between the institutions of church and state as an application of the theological distinction between the two kingdoms.

In regard to the distinction between church and state generally, Turretin expresses common Reformed orthodox sentiment in warning that "the duties of the ecclesiastical and political order be not confounded, but the due parts be left to each."[109] Foundational for understanding this concern is the association of church and state with the two kingdoms and therefore with the starkly different natures — spiritual and carnal — that these institutions respectively exhibit. Speaking of the magistrate and church, Rutherford

---

109. Turretin, *Institutes*, 3.316.

writes: "The former is carnal, and of the kingdom of this world; the latter spiritual and of Christ's other kingdom, that is not of this world."[110] Hence Rutherford's characteristic concern: "That presbyteries meddle with civil business, is a slander. They meddle with public scandals that offendeth in Christ's kingdom."[111]

Turretin unpacks these general concerns more specifically by identifying seven ways in which ecclesiastical and civil authorities differ. The other writers under consideration here offer similar sentiments on most of these points, and I will compare them along the way as we consider Turretin's organized treatment.

First, Turretin asserts that ecclesiastical and civil authorities differ as to *origin*. In short, civil authority originates in *God the Creator* and ecclesiastical authority in *Christ the Mediator*. His language here is reminiscent of that observed above and serves further to demonstrate the intimate association of church and state with the spiritual and civil kingdoms: "Political power was instituted by God, the Creator, and supreme ruler of the world; but ecclesiastical power was instituted by Jesus Christ, the supreme head of the church and its Lord and governor. The political magistrate as such does not serve properly and formally in promoting the kingdom of Christ, nor does he discharge his office in his name, as appears in the heathen magistrate; but ministers are sent by Christ for the establishing of his kingdom and act in his name."[112] Rutherford speaks similarly: "Two powers so different as spiritual and temporal: 2. As power carnal of this world, and spiritual not of this world: And 3. Both immediately subject, the one to God the creator, the other to Christ the Redeemer and Head of the Church."[113] Gillespie writes, concerning Christ's "twofold kingdom," that "as he is the eternal Son of God" so "the magistrate is his vicegerent, and holds his office of and under him," but that he is also "Mediator and Head of the church," in which capacity "the magistrate doth not hold his office of and under Christ as his vicegerent."[114] The *Second Book of Discipline* expressed this same position in defining the church's "policy" and its difference from "civil policy." It affirms that "this power ecclesiastical is an authority granted by God the Father, through the Mediator Jesus Christ" (1.2) and later adds that "this ecclesiastical power flows immediately from God, and the Mediator Jesus Christ" (1.5).

110. Rutherford, *Divine Right*, 564.
111. Rutherford, *Lex, Rex,* 216.
112. Turretin, *Institutes*, 3.278.
113. Rutherford, *Divine Right*, 510.
114. Gillespie, *Aaron's Rod Blossoming*, 90 (2.V).

Second, Turretin explains that civil and ecclesiastical powers differ in regard to their *subject*. In other words, different criteria exist for what sort of people can exercise authority in these respective realms. The first thing he mentions seems a logical consequence of his identification of church and state with the two kingdoms: "Political power can be in the hands of heathen and strangers to the covenant, but not ecclesiastical."[115] Interestingly, he acknowledges that the spiritual state of the church may sometimes be better when the magistrate is not a Christian.[116] Other Reformed orthodox sources agree that Christian faith is not a requirement for holding political authority,[117] a position emphasized by William of Ockham against papal pretensions many years before. The second thing that Turretin mentions is not as obvious logically: "The former can be exercised by women; the latter not."[118] He offers no explanation or defense of this (and no apology to John Knox), but it probably rests not in the two kingdoms distinction itself but in biblical prohibitions of women holding ecclesiastical office, prohibitions lacking in regard to political office.

The third difference that Turretin identifies between civil and ecclesiastical power regards their *form:* "Political power is controlling . . . and absolute . . . , which implies dominion and sway. But ecclesiastical is ministerial . . . and economical . . . and serving . . . , which consists in service alone without any sway and dominion properly so called." Crucial here, as Turretin goes on to explain, is the magistrate's "lawmaking power," by which he can make, improve, and change laws as necessary. But ministers in the church have no such power: "They can and ought to promulgate the laws of Christ and to apply them to certain cases. They can make canons for the preservation of good order . . . ; but they can make no laws properly so called. Christ alone is the legislator, whose laws can neither be changed nor remodeled by ministers." This was a theological claim of considerable practical significance in the early Reformed tradition, a claim already evident in Calvin, as seen in Chapter 3. It would also prove to be a crucial idea for certain American Presbyterian debates to be considered in the next chapter. Civil magis-

---

115. Turretin, *Institutes,* 3.278.

116. Turretin, *Institutes,* 3.280.

117. E.g., see Rutherford's comments in *Divine Right,* 606, where he discusses whether the responsibilities of Christian and non-Christian magistrates differ. In this context he writes: "Those magistrates among the Americans and other heathen, who never by any rumor heard of Jesus Christ, are essentially and formally magistrates." Gillespie also emphasized this point; see *Aaron's Rod Blossoming,* 107-108 (2.VII). See also WCF 23.4.

118. Turretin, *Institutes,* 3.278.

trates have a legislative discretion that officers of the church simply do not have. The latter may only enunciate and apply laws that are already given, by *Christ* in *Scripture.* Beyond this they may not go.[119] Later Turretin makes this same point by contrasting the power of state and church in terms of "dominion" and "ministry."[120] Rutherford, speaking as a Scottish Presbyterian for whom such issues were of great importance, expresses the same sentiment: "But we desire to know, what mediate acts of law-giving which is essential to kings and parliaments in civil things, does agree to kings, parliaments, and synods; Christ has not made pastors under-kings to create any laws morally obliging the conscience to obedience in the court of God, which God has not made to their hand."[121] The *Second Book of Discipline* sought to express this idea in concrete polity by asserting that "It is proper to kings, princes, and magistrates to be called lords and dominators over their subjects, whom they govern civilly, but it is proper to Christ only to be called Lord and Master in the spiritual government of the kirk; and all others that bear office therein ought not to usurp dominion therein, nor be called lords, but only ministers, disciples, and servants" (1.8). WCF 20.2 also speaks directly to this point, as will be discussed below.

Fourth, Turretin says that civil and ecclesiastical authorities differ as to their *end.* Again, his comments here follow unsurprisingly from his theology of the two kingdoms and his association of these kingdoms with the civil and ecclesiastical realms. The supreme end of the civil magistrate "as such," that is, in his capacity as civil magistrate, is "the glory of God, the Creator, conservator of the human race, and the ruler of the world." The magistrate's subordinate end is "the public peace and tranquility, the external and temporal good of the state." "As a magistrate," he ought not "advance the kingdom of Christ" (though he should "as a Christian"). On the other hand, the supreme end of the church's ministry is "not only the glory of the Creator, but also the glory of Christ, the Mediator, and the King and head of the church." Its subordinate end is "the peace and safety of the church, the preservation and propagation of the mediatorial kingdom of Christ."[122] Again, Turretin's Reformed cohorts conveyed similar ideas. Althusius speaks of the "ecclesiastical communion of the realm" (in distinction from the "secular") as "the process by which those means that pertain to the public organizing

---

119. Turretin, *Institutes*, 3.278; see also *Institutes*, 3.285-93.

120. Turretin, *Institutes*, 3.280-81.

121. Rutherford, *Divine Right*, 25; see also Rutherford, *Lex, Rex*, 210.

122. Turretin, *Institutes*, 3.278-79.

and conserving of the kingdom of Christ . . . are established, undertaken, and communicated according to his will."[123] Later he explains that ecclesiastical, in distinction from secular, functions are "the means whereby the kingdom of God . . . is introduced, promoted, cared for, and conserved in the commonwealth."[124] God "administers his kingdom, which is not of this world, through his ministers of the Word," not through magistrates.[125] Rutherford, in speaking about civil magistrates "as magistrates," makes them not "ambassadors of Christ" but "deput[ies] of God as the God of order, and as the creator."[126]

Fifth, Turretin differentiated between civil and ecclesiastical authority in regard to *object*. Here he again echoes opinions of Calvin concerning their distinctive jurisdictions on external matters and internal matters of the soul. Turretin writes: "Civil power has for its object things, actions and persons which and inasmuch as they pertain to the animal life and public companionship or the external man; but ecclesiastical power has for its object sacred things, persons and actions as such, under this formal reduplication, inasmuch as they are both ordained and can be ordained to union with God in Christ and to eternal salvation."[127] In Althusius's detailed taxonomy of authority and responsibilities in church and state, he reflects such views in a variety of contexts. For example, after asserting that "the care and administration of ecclesiastical things and functions belong not to the secular magistrate, but to the collegium of these presbyters," he writes that this ecclesiastical administration concerns "things necessary for the welfare of the soul." "The secular order," in distinction, concerns "the body, food, clothing, and other things that pertain to this life."[128] Later he makes a similar distinction, entrusting "religion and piety, which pertain to the welfare and eternal life of the soul," to the ecclesiastical communion and "justice, which concerns the use of the body and of this life," to the secular communion.[129] Hence his

---

123. Althusius, *Politica*, 75.

124. Althusius, *Politica*, 160.

125. Althusius, *Politica*, 172.

126. Rutherford, *Divine Right*, 550-51.

127. Turretin, *Institutes*, 3.279. Elsewhere Turretin enumerates the three parts to ecclesiastical power: the dogmatic (consisting in doctrines, preaching, and sacraments), the ordinating (consisting of ecclesiastical laws and constitutions), and the judicial and disciplinary (consisting of censures, excommunication, and restoration); see *Institutes*, 3.275.

128. Althusius, *Politica*, 59-60.

129. Althusius, *Politica*, 74-75. Shortly thereafter he also speaks of the "secular and political communion" as pertaining to "a common life of justice" and to "those things that relate to use of this life," training people "how to live justly in the present world"; see *Politica*, 79. Elsewhere

claim is understandable that while the ecclesiastical order produces pious, learned, wise, and good people, the political or secular order produces strong, militant, and brave people.[130] Similarly, Rutherford assigns to state and church, respectively, responsibility for "all civil things" and "soul-matters."[131] This same sort of distinction was captured in the *Second Book of Discipline,* where the Scottish church affirmed: "The magistrate commands external things for external peace and quietness amongst the subjects; the minister handles external things only for conscience cause. . . . The magistrate handles external things only, and actions done before men; but the spiritual ruler judges both inward affections and external actions, in respect of conscience, by the word of God" (1.11-12). I note briefly that Turretin, in his discussion of this matter, goes on to mention that civil power has a certain concern for "sacred and ecclesiastical things," a judgment shared by Althusius and Rutherford. Later in this chapter I discuss what they meant by this, the qualifications they made, and how it fit into their broader discussions.

Turretin treats briefly his sixth distinction between civil and ecclesiastical authority, that concerning *effects.* The magistrate, he says, in dealing with things politically and for political ends, has "homogeneous effects," among which he includes "political and civil laws, civil punishments and fines and by these means civil peace and tranquility." On the other hand, he goes on, "the ecclesiastical power as it is occupied with a spiritual object in a spiritual manner and for a spiritual end, also has spiritual effects," though he does not specify what these spiritual effects are.[132] The reference to "civil peace and tranquility" is noteworthy in light of the material discussed in Chapter 3 regarding Calvin's strong statements on "common peace and safety" being the magistrate's "only study."[133] Althusius also resembled Calvin in such concerns. When discussing the "secular administration" by which civil magistrates attend to civil functions, Althusius puts special emphasis upon matters such as "good order," "conserving justice, peace, tranquility, and discipline," and the preservation of "concord," while treating "civil disturbances" as a "sickness."[134]

Althusius lists the church's responsibilities as examination of doctrine, public reverence and divine worship, schools, ecclesiastical goods, and the poor; see *Politica,* 55-56.

130. Althusius, *Politica,* 61.
131. Rutherford, *Divine Right,* 560.
132. Turretin, *Institutes,* 3.279.
133. See Calvin, *Institutes,* 4.20.9.
134. Althusius, *Politica,* 175-76, 181.

Turretin's seventh and final distinction between civil and ecclesiastical authority is that of *mode*. After reiterating the difference between these two authorities in terms of external and internal matters, he explains that these two therefore have distinctive standards governing them and distinctive weapons for accomplishing their purposes. He writes: "The latter [ecclesiastical power] is not regulated by natural reason, civil laws and human statutes, by which states are governed; but by the word of God alone and the canon of the Scriptures dictated by the Holy Spirit. It is not exercised in a political and worldly, but in a spiritual and mystical manner by the keys of the kingdom of heaven and by the sword of the Spirit and other similar weapons; not carnal. . . . It administers the sacraments, which are seals, not of any earthly and civil privilege, but of mystical union with Christ and of his spiritual benefits. Nor does it regard any other end than the edification of the body of Christ, the establishment of his kingdom and the salvation of sinners."[135] A number of important matters are raised here, some of which we will consider again below. The state looks to natural reason and civil laws, the church looks to Scripture alone. The state takes up carnal weapons, such as the sword, while the church has spiritual and mystical weapons, the keys of the kingdom. These are certainly differences with far-reaching implications if put into practice.

Once again, similar ideas emanated from other Reformed orthodox circles. The *Second Book of Discipline,* for example, teaches that the ecclesiastical power is grounded (only) in Scripture (1.2, 7). Furthermore, it states: "The civil power is called the power of the sword, and the other the power of the keys" (1.9); and "The civil magistrate craves and gets obedience by the sword and other external means, but the ministry by the spiritual sword and spiritual means" (1.13). From a different angle, "The magistrate neither ought to preach, minister the sacraments, nor execute the censures of the kirk, nor yet prescribe any rule how it should be done. . . . The ministers exercise not the civil jurisdiction" (1.14). Gillespie associates the rule of natural law with the state but not the church: "Government and authority which hath a foundation in the law of nature and nations . . . cannot be held of, and under, and managed for Christ, as he is Mediator. But magistracy or civil government hath a foundation in the law of nature and nations."[136] Rutherford too points to Scripture as the church's standard, saying, for example, that in Scripture the church has a "perfect platform" for church gov-

---

135. Turretin, *Institutes,* 3.279.
136. Gillespie, *Aaron's Rod Blossoming,* 113 (2.VII).

ernment.[137] In regard to civil authority, he denies to the magistrate "power in matters of Christ's kingdom or the government thereof" and explains that "magistrates as magistrates do punish sins with the sword . . . but not forgive sin, nor bind and loose in earth or heaven, nor exercise any spiritual power, nor deal with the consciences of men."[138] The very essence of the magistrate's kingdom is bearing the sword, and hence his office is not a part of the kingdom of Christ nor can he be head of the church.[139]

As this subsection has laid out in considerable detail, Reformed orthodox writers made numerous, interrelated distinctions between the character, functions, and goals of civil authority on the one hand and ecclesiastical authority on the other. In expositing such distinctions, these writers demonstrated the practical significance of their two kingdoms distinction and of their identification of these two kingdoms particularly with church and state. Comparison of this material with the related discussion in Chapter 3 should manifest the great concurrence between Calvin and his theological heirs in articulating the differences between these two institutions. Immediately following the enumeration of his seven distinctions, Turretin offers a conclusion that seems a fitting finale to this subsection: "Therefore, since this ecclesiastical power is spiritual and differs in so many ways from the political, it follows that it is not formally and specifically civil and secular, but distinct from it in species."[140]

The Two Kingdoms and the Broader Reformed System of Theology and Practice

Before moving on to the difficult issue of the civil state and enforcement of true religion, I note in this subsection a few additional issues that seem pertinent in a discussion of the two kingdoms doctrine in the age of Reformed orthodoxy. Though matters of church and state probably deserve the most attention when implications of the two kingdoms doctrine are considered, it is not as if these are its only implications. Though a more detailed study than provided here would be necessary to assert the claim with full confidence, I suggest that the two kingdoms doctrine, like the doctrine of natural law, was

---

137. Rutherford, *Divine Right,* §1.
138. Rutherford, *Divine Right,* 528-29.
139. Rutherford, *Divine Right,* 511-12.
140. Turretin, *Institutes,* 3.279.

embedded into Reformed orthodox theology and practice — in theological, moral, and ecclesiastical life — in such a way as to make it, though often implicitly rather than explicitly, an intimate part of the system of doctrine that could not be excised from it without serious consequences for the whole. The evidence that I present to make this suggestion at least plausible is drawn from the WCF and focuses upon the related matters of conscience, Christian liberty, and worship.

In Chapter 3, I noted the importance of the doctrine of Christian liberty for understanding Calvin's two kingdoms doctrine. In *Institutes* 3.19, Calvin identifies Christian liberty as an essential aspect of a believer's salvation in Christ. Among the many benefits of Christian liberty is freedom from the obligation to do or not to do things that are in and of themselves morally indifferent. But in order to dissuade readers from the conclusion that this truth entails rejection of all earthly authority, he appeals to the two kingdoms doctrine. Here in *Institutes* 3.19, alongside 4.11 and 4.20, Calvin lays down the principle that while ecclesiastical authorities cannot bind the conscience of believers in anything *beyond* what Scripture teaches, civil authorities do in fact bind consciences when they command anything that is not *contrary* to biblical teaching (however unwise many of these commands may be). In other words, Christians are bound to obey ecclesiastical authorities only insofar as they command what Scripture commands, while Christians are bound to obey civil authorities in everything except when their commands contradict a responsibility that Scripture places upon them.

WCF 20 teaches this doctrine, in a way more explicit and taut than Calvin did, as far as I am aware. WCF 20.1 begins by laying out at some length what Christian liberty is generally, namely, the Calvin-like conviction that Christian liberty is of the essence of the believer's salvation in Christ. Then WCF 20.2 offers a succinct statement crucial for present concerns, the first part of which reads: "God alone is Lord of the conscience, and hath left it free from the doctrines and commandments of men, which are, in anything, contrary to his Word; or beside it, if matters of faith, or worship." The WCF, therefore, makes a sharp distinction between the liberty enjoyed by Christians in two different areas, "matters of faith and worship" on the one hand and everything else on the other. The former are the province of the church, not the state, and the latter are the concern of the state, not the church, as other statements in the WCF indicate.[141] Thus, the application of Christian

---

141. WCF 23.3 prohibits the civil magistrate from assuming "the administration of the word and sacraments, or the power of the keys of the kingdom of heaven." WCF 31.3 gives church synods

liberty to the believer is determined by means of the two kingdoms doctrine. In the spiritual kingdom of the church, ecclesiastical authorities, dealing only with spiritual things, have no power to bind consciences beyond the declaration of what Scripture itself teaches (a "ministerial" authority) and believers have no conscientious obligation to believe or do anything that the church says otherwise. Believers are free from anything "beside" the word of God. In the civil kingdom and with respect to civil matters, however, believers are free only from commands "contrary" to Scripture, meaning that they are conscientiously bound to do all things that the magistrate commands (however disagreeable) so long as they do not contradict some biblical teaching. Thus, in both Calvin and Reformed orthodoxy one sees the significance of the two kingdoms doctrine for so central a theological matter as the Christian liberty bestowed in salvation.

One area in which these matters of Christian liberty and conscience had significant implications for Reformed churches was that of worship. The Reformed development of the "regulative principle of worship" (RPW) was certainly a distinguishing feature of the Reformed from other Christian traditions. There are a number of important nuances that would need to be elaborated for a complete explanation of the RPW, but its basic idea can be articulated briefly. The RPW states that the public worship of the church may consist only of those elements that the New Testament itself teaches are proper elements of worship.[142] Reformed theologians distinguished this doctrine from an approach to worship (which it associated with Lutheranism) in which the church has freedom to worship as it deems right so long as it does not do things prohibited by Scripture. At the heart of this distinctive Reformed doctrine was its two kingdoms–driven conception of Christian liberty and conscience. Because the church has no power to impose any-

---

and councils authority over "controversies of faith" and "the better ordering of the public worship of God" while WCF 31.5 forbids synods and councils "to intermeddle with civil affairs, which concern the commonwealth." Also significant here is the emphasis in WCF 31.3 that ecclesiastical authority is exercised only "ministerially," that is, merely declaring what Scripture says. It should be noted here that most American Presbyterian churches have modified the WCF on matters of the magistrate and religion, and hence the sections cited here as WCF 31.3 and 31.5 may be found in American versions as 31.2 and 31.4.

142. WCF 21.1 articulates the RPW in this way: "The acceptable way of worshiping the true God is instituted by himself, and so limited by his own revealed will, that he may not be worshiped according to the imaginations and devices of men, or the suggestions of Satan, under any visible representation, or any other way not prescribed in the Holy Scripture." For discussion of the RPW in the seventeenth-century context in connection with questions of church power and the two kingdoms, see McKay, *An Ecclesiastical Republic*, 88-96.

thing beyond the teaching of Scripture upon the consciences of believers, it has no power to demand that believers worship God in any way other than what Scripture ordains. The church must demand that believers gather for corporate worship (because Scripture commands such), but when Christians are so gathered (being a captive audience of sorts) the church may not then impose non-biblical elements of worship, no matter how pious or edifying they may seem, lest believers' consciences be burdened beyond proper limits. Reformed worship, therefore, characterized by a unique simplicity in comparison with other Christian traditions, was therefore in significant respect a logical application of the Reformed understanding of the two kingdoms doctrine.

Though I have offered just this limited set of examples, it offers at least plausibility, I believe, to the claim that the two kingdoms doctrine, like the doctrine of natural law, was an intimate part of the larger system of Reformed doctrine and practice. At the heart of Reformed theology (the doctrine of salvation) and at the heart of Reformed practice (worship) the two kingdoms doctrine played a crucial role. The two kingdoms doctrine could not be expunged from Reformed orthodox Christianity without beginning to unravel its holistic understanding of Christian faith and life.

The Relationship of Church and State and the Question of State Involvement in Religious Affairs

Previous material in this section has put forward a case for the continuity and elaboration of the two kingdoms doctrine and its implications for an understanding of church and state from Calvin through the age of Reformed orthodoxy. A couple of matters in Calvin upon which I reflected at some length in Chapter 3 have not yet been dealt with in this chapter, however. Specifically, Chapter 3 considered Calvin's views on the collaborative relationship of church and state as well as his often troubling attributions of religious concern to civil magistrates. It is time now to consider these subjects in Reformed orthodox thought. As should be of little surprise by this point, Reformed orthodoxy generally shared Calvin's view of church-state collaboration and his attribution of certain qualified religious responsibilities to the state.

In light of this, some scholars of the period have concluded, from various angles, that advocates of the two kingdoms and natural law doctrines were inconsistent with themselves when arguing for state involvement in religious affairs.[143] As with Calvin, I suggest that quick and facile dismissal of such views as starkly inconsistent with a two kingdoms doctrine is unfair. Nevertheless, in my judgment, even a sympathetic reading of these Reformed orthodox sources cannot completely eliminate the sense that they have not applied their two kingdoms distinction (and natural law doctrine) with entire consistency at every point.

As it was when considering Calvin, this is a very difficult issue to tackle. The Reformed orthodox writers lived in vastly different social circumstances from that of the contemporary Western world. The medieval Christendom assumptions about a unified Christian society lived on into the seventeenth century. All kings of that day considered themselves Christians and were interested in the affairs of the church. Despite the Reformation, in most jurisdictions there was only one church recognized as legitimate by most people. The Reformed orthodox writers gave instructions about the relationship of church and state geared toward their own concrete setting and considered contexts like our own of religious liberty and ecclesiastical disestablishment (if they did so at all) only in passing and theoretically. In addition, those people in their own day who did advocate religious liberty tended to be theologically and socially suspect, which made the cause of religious liberty all the less attractive.[144] These things must be kept in mind in the following discussion, and I attempt to consider their theology and categories on their own terms as far as possible.

An initial matter to consider touching the relationship of the civil magistrate to religion is that the clear and sharp distinctions between the civil and ecclesiastical realms discussed in the previous subsection were never meant to suggest that church and state were to operate in complete independence from one another, without acknowledgement of each other's existence. Rather, Reformed orthodox views on church and state, like Calvin's,

---

143. An example of this in regard to Rutherford may be found in Coffey, *Religion, Politics and the British Revolutions,* chapters 6-8 generally and pages 183-87, 227, 248, 251-52, 255 perhaps most particularly. He concludes that there were tension and ambiguity between Rutherford's natural law constitutionalism and his advocacy of national covenanting and its consequences (about which more below), and that the latter aspect of his thought ultimately triumphed. Discussion of various related points may also be found throughout Marshall, "Natural Law and the Covenant."

144. Turretin, e.g., mentions their great theological adversaries, the Socinians, as opponents of Geneva's execution of Servetus; see *Institutes,* 3.336. Paul notes that "a few Republicans, Levellers and other radicals" were the ones promoting religious freedom in Britain at the time of the Westminster Assembly, though they were also joined (perhaps often for pragmatic reasons) later by many Independents, ecclesiological rivals of the Presbyterians; see *The Assembly of the Lord,* 15, 121-24.

contained a strong desire to see these institutions execute their responsibilities in a harmonious, collaborative, and mutually beneficial relationship.

The *Second Book of Discipline* had particular concern for this issue (though the crown was never impressed enough to embrace its conclusions) and thus it may serve as a helpful focus for treatment of this issue. Though it made the common Reformed affirmation[145] that the same person should not ordinarily hold the offices of both magistrate and minister (1.9), a seemingly prudent application of two kingdoms theology, it envisioned a friendly relationship between the offices. One of its important claims is that the church's ministers and the civil magistrates stand in a posture of mutual submission in matters of their respective competencies. "The ministers and others of the ecclesiastical estate are subject to the civil magistrate" and "the person of the magistrate" is "subject to the kirk spiritually, and in ecclesiastical government" (1.9). Later it adds in more detail: "As ministers are subject to the judgment and punishment of the magistrate in external things, if they offend; so ought the magistrates to submit themselves to the discipline of the kirk, if they transgress in matters of conscience and religion" (1.15). Regarding the magistrate's submission, Althusius speaks somewhat more specifically about how ministers may exercise their authority by stating that, toward the ecclesiastical administration, "even the magistrate is subject with respect to warnings, censures, and other things necessary for the welfare of the soul."[146] In addition to such mutual submission, the *Second Book of Discipline* commends each authority to "assist" the other in its work: "The magistrate ought to assist, maintain, and fortify the jurisdiction of the kirk. The ministers should assist their princes in all things agreeable to the word, provided they neglect not their own charge by involving themselves in civil affairs" (1.15). Finally, each authority is to command the other to do *its own* work properly: "The civil power should command the spiritual to exercise and do their office according to the word of God. The spiritual rulers should require the Christian magistrate to minister justice and punish vice, and to maintain the liberty and quietness of the kirk within their bounds" (1.10). This statement reads as though little more than mutual exhortation were in mind, leaving each authority to make its own determinations about how it is to do its job. Later, however, the *Second Book of Discipline* seems to take a significant and striking step beyond this, adding that though "ministers exercise not the civil jurisdiction," they ought to "teach the magistrate how it

---

145. E.g., see Turretin, *Institutes*, 3.321; and, as discussed in Chapter 3, Calvin, *Institutes*, 4.11.8.
146. Althusius, *Politica*, 59.

should be exercised according to the word" (1.14). The church, then, is actually to teach magistrates *how* to do their own work, not simply to remind them *that* they ought to do it. Significantly, this pedagogical responsibility only runs in one direction, from the church toward the state. This fact has been a leading cause for suspicion that the sixteenth-century Scottish two kingdoms doctrine was theocracy in disguise.[147] One other matter pertinent to the collaboration of church and state worth mentioning briefly is Rutherford's contention that a person may *complain* to magistrates about an unjust judgment of the church. Yet he does not permit such a person to *make an appeal* to the magistrate, as that would imply going from one judge to a higher judge.[148] Here seems to be an attempt to affirm mutual relation while enunciating the incommensurability of these authorities, as the two kingdoms doctrine might suggest.

The practices described in the previous paragraph do raise a couple of legitimate questions about the consistency with which Reformed orthodoxy held the two kingdoms doctrine. The requirement that the civil magistrate submit to and assist the church is practically possible provided that there is no dispute in a given jurisdiction about which institution is the true church. Where there are competing claims, one might wonder, on two kingdoms premises, how the civil magistrate attains the expertise and authority to determine true church from false, especially if competing claims on finer points of theology are at stake. Furthermore, the idea that the spiritual authority should tell the civil authority how to do its job also seems difficult to reconcile with the Reformed two kingdoms doctrine. If politics is a kind of art that requires particular skill and prudence, as a thinker such as Althusius so clearly believes, and if there are even different primary standards of authority in the civil and ecclesiastical realms (natural law and Scripture, respectively), then there seems to be reason to doubt that ministers, whose training lies in spiritual things, have the competence to offer useful and even authoritative instruction on political matters.

Nevertheless, the two kingdoms doctrine would seem reasonably able, as a general matter, to undergird a system in which church and state, minister and magistrate, coexist in relative harmony. More difficult to systematize is the Reformed orthodox theology of the two kingdoms and corresponding church-state distinctions with its support of state intervention on religious matters. Before we return to the question of whether and how these ideas

---

147. E.g., see Donaldson, *Scottish Church History*, 235; and Lyall, *Of Presbyters and Kings*, 17.
148. Rutherford, *Divine Right*, 580.

might be harmonized, some description of what representative Reformed orthodox writers wrote on the subject of magistrates and religion is necessary.

Althusius, first, deals with this question at some length in his chapter on "Ecclesiastical Administration." After explaining that the administration of the public functions of the realm is either ecclesiastical or secular, he asserts that "both are of concern to the magistrate." The supreme magistrate's interest in the ecclesiastical administration "consists in his inspection, defense, care, and direction of ecclesiastical matters," duties "imposed upon the magistrate by the mandate of God" and also supported "by arguments from reason."[149] In the execution of these duties, the magistrate ought to introduce "orthodox religious doctrine and practice in the realm" and ensure its preservation and transmission to the next generation.[150] This requires of the magistrate "the establishment of a sacred ministry and of schools." Related duties include establishing penalties for those who do not properly acknowledge and worship God, validating orthodox doctrine by law, and calling ecclesiastical synods.[151] He writes: "From these things it is apparent that the supreme magistrate has a responsibility to judge concerning the knowledge, discernment, direction, definition, and promulgation of the doctrine of faith."[152] The magistrate must "announce and hold ecclesiastical assemblies and visitations in every province of the realm" and execute a host of other religious duties.[153] Although Althusius counseled a certain restraint in the persecution of those deviating from the true religion, he exhorted magistrates to establish and permit only the true religion in the realm and to expel atheist, impious, and obstinate people.[154]

Rutherford's views were similar. He grants to magistrates "a care of matters of religion," which includes "a power to examine heretics and false doc-

149. Althusius, *Politica*, 159-60.

150. Althusius, *Politica*, 162.

151. Althusius, *Politica*, 165-66.

152. Althusius, *Politica*, 167.

153. Althusius, *Politica*, 168-70.

154. See Althusius, *Politica*, 170-74. Some examples of his restraint include allowing Jews and Roman Catholics to live in the realm, though without the liberty to engage in their religious worship (a certainly ungenerous toleration by our contemporary standards, though not by his own), and the distinguishing among different sorts of heretics, some of whom should be executed or exiled and others not. A certain pragmatism, about which I comment further below, is evident when he writes: "He should not, however, permit the practice of a wicked religion lest what occurred to Solomon may happen to him. But if he cannot prohibit it without hazard to the commonwealth, he is to suffer it to exist in order that he not bring ruin to the commonwealth" (173).

trine" and administer appropriate "bodily punishment with the sword," though their judgment should be subsequent to the church's judgment. The magistrate also "may command the pastor to preach, and the synod and presbytery to use the keys of Christ's kingdom according to the rules of the word."[155] Similarly, Rutherford elsewhere urges magistrates to be sure that there are preachers and other ecclesiastical office-bearers to preach, administer sacraments, and discipline. Furthermore, they should command people to serve Christ and profess the gospel and should punish blasphemy.[156] Turretin's views are again similar. In rejecting the two extremes of giving magistrates all ecclesiastical power and removing all care of ecclesiastical things from them, Turretin claims that "a multiple right concerning sacred things belongs to the magistrate."[157] In a helpful summary statement, he includes in the magistrate's religious duties the establishing and maintaining sacred doctrine and pure worship according to Scripture, protecting the church, restraining heretics, providing for and cherishing the ministry of the word, opening schools, ensuring that ministers do their duties, causing forms of church confession and government to be established and protected, and constituting ecclesiastical conventions for matters of doctrine, discipline, and order.[158] Although Turretin refutes the view that magistrates can compel faith of their subjects and counsels neither "an excessive severity or too great mildness" in dealing with heretics, he also teaches that magistrates can "restrain and check" and "coerce" heretics, and even kill arch-heretics.[159]

Among this era's most noteworthy instances of Reformed advocacy of the magistrate's involvement in religious affairs was the subscription of the National Covenant in 1638 by the Scottish church and nobility and of the Solemn League and Covenant in 1643 by the Scottish church, civil authorities in England and Scotland, and the Westminster Assembly.[160] In the National Covenant, "the kirk of Scotland, the King's Majesty, and the three estates of this realm" swore their allegiance to Reformed Christianity and the

155. Rutherford, *Divine Right,* 503-4.

156. E.g., see Rutherford, *Divine Right,* 543, 547, 552.

157. Turretin, *Institutes,* 3.316.

158. Turretin, *Institutes,* 3.320.

159. Turretin, *Institutes,* 3.323-33.

160. For description of these, see, e.g., *Dictionary of Scottish Church History and Theology,* ed. Nigel M. de S. Cameron (Downers Grove: InterVarsity Press, 1993), 620, 786-87; and Paul, *The Assembly of the Lord,* 87-100. For a hagiographic account of them, see Edwin Nisbet Moore, *Our Covenant Heritage: The Covenanters' Struggle for Unity in Truth as Revealed in the Memoir of James Nisbet and Sermons of John Nevay* (Ross-shire: Christian Focus, 2000), 31-38.

abhorring and detesting of "all contrary religion and doctrine, but chiefly all kind of Papistry."[161] They recall various acts of Parliament "conceived for maintenance of God's true and Christian religion, and the purity thereof." One example notes that "Seeing the cause of God's true religion and his Highness's authority are so joined, as the hurt of the one is common to both; that none shall be reputed as loyal and faithful subjects to our sovereign Lord, or his authority, but be punishable as rebellers and gainstanders of the same, who shall not give their confession, and make their profession of the said true religion."[162] The National Covenant lists two reasons for entering into such a covenant, "for defending the true religion" and "for maintaining the King's Majesty, his person and estate; the true worship of God and the King's authority being so straitly joined, as that they had the same friends and common enemies, and did stand and fall together."[163] The signers thus solemnly declared "that with our whole heart we agree, and resolve all the days of our life constantly to adhere unto and to defend the foresaid true religion" and swore "to continue in the profession and obedience of the foresaid religion; and that we shall defend the same, and resist all these contrary errors and corruptions, according to our vocation, and to the uttermost of that power that God hath put in our hands, all the days of our life."[164] The Solemn League and Covenant, more concisely, swore to seek "the preservation of the reformed religion in the Church of Scotland," to "endeavour the extirpation of Popery, Prelacy, . . . superstition, heresy, schism, profaneness, and whatsoever shall be found to be contrary to sound doctrine," to "endeavour the discovery of all such as have been or shall be incendiaries, malignants, or evil instruments, by hindering the reformation of religion," and to "assist and defend all those that enter into this League and Covenant."[165] It is worth noting that this idea of a covenant between the people and their rulers was nothing original to Reformed thought in this era. The idea was developed by Huguenot resistance theorists such as Theodore Beza and the author of the *Vindiciae contra Tyrannos*, examined in the preceding chapter, and by thinkers such as Althusius and Rutherford.[166] Among the important ideas espoused by a Scottish covenanter like Rutherford was

---

161. See "The National Covenant; or, the Confession of Faith," in *Westminster Confession of Faith* (Glasgow: Free Presbyterian Publications, 1990), 347.

162. "National Covenant," 350-51.

163. "National Covenant," 352.

164. "National Covenant," 352-53.

165. "The Solemn League and Covenant," in *Westminster Confession*, 358-59.

166. E.g., see Althusius, *Politica*, 162-63; and Rutherford's argument generally in *Lex, Rex*.

that the making of such a covenant could put religious obligations upon civil magistrates that they did not have before.[167]

How do these beliefs square with the convictions of Reformed orthodoxy examined earlier in the chapter, such as the idea that natural law is the standard for civil law and that, according to the two kingdoms doctrine, civil magistrates in their official capacity are not servants of the mediator Jesus Christ and do not advance Christ's kingdom? The easy answer is that Reformed orthodox theology was simply inconsistent at this point. Though ultimately I believe that there was inconsistency, there are in fact clear indications that Reformed advocates of the civil magistrate's involvement in religious affairs recognized the danger of self-contradiction and in fact took pains to articulate the magistrate's religious duties in light of their natural law and two kingdoms convictions.

First, a fairly large amount of evidence suggests that Reformed orthodox thinkers such as Althusius, Rutherford, and Turretin tried consciously to articulate their views on the magistrate's religious duties in light of the theological boundaries provided by the two kingdoms doctrine. They did so by making numerous twofold distinctions in the way that a magistrate's religious responsibilities might be executed. Among these distinctions are between caring for religious affairs *civilly* or spiritually, *externally* or internally, with respect to the *body* or the soul. Repeatedly, Reformed orthodox writers permitted the magistrate care of religion only in a civil, external, bodily way, never in a spiritual, internal, or soulish way.

In the midst of an extended discussion advocating a long list of religious matters on which the magistrate should promulgate law, Althusius makes a move illustrative of a common Reformed orthodox approach, writing: "But the political magistrate should be very careful in this activity not to apply his own hands to these matters, but commit and entrust them to the clergy. He should concern himself only that the external actions of men conform to laws."[168] Shortly thereafter he makes a similar point by reminding magistrates that they should "not claim imperium over faith and religion of men, which exist only in the soul and conscience" but should "reserve to himself what God has given him, namely, imperium over bodies."[169] Rutherford used similar language to Althusius in regard to the exter-

---

167. For further discussion, see, e.g., Coffey, *Religion, Politics and the British Revolutions,* ch. 6.

168. Althusius, *Politica,* 170.

169. Althusius, *Politica,* 172-73.

nal character of the magistrate's care for religion. In a discussion of whether and how magistrates' duties change when they become Christians, Rutherford insists that they are not obliged to promote the mediatorial kingdom of Christ nor punish blasphemers of Christ as such, but can punish blasphemies "only as such obedience and such blasphemies, may promote the external safety, prosperity, and peace of the civil society, whereof he is head, or may dissolve the sinews and nerves of that society." Shortly thereafter he adds: "At no time, and in no state, has the magistrate's sword any influence in the mediatory kingdom at all, but is so far as the sword may procure external peace to the society of that kingdom as they are a civil body."[170] Another relevant distinction that Rutherford makes is between the "material" and "formal," only the former of which pertains to the magistrate in his religious duties. He writes, for example: "The magistrate may serve Christ as Christ, and promote and advance the kingdom of Jesus Christ as mediator, when he contributes his power to those things that materially conduce to a supernatural end, though he does not contribute any thing that formally conducts to such an end." Later he says similarly: "Though the material object of the magistrate's sword be the spiritual kingdom of Christ, yet the formal object is the natural and civil peace of this kingdom, as a civil society."[171]

This material/formal distinction is one that Turretin utilized as well.[172] Numerous other distinctions served the same purpose for him: civil magistrates have the "care," but not the "administration," of religious things; they look after such things "extrinsically" (or "externally"), "materially," "indirectly," and "objectively," not "intrinsically" (or "internally"), "formally," and "directly," all of which latter things characterize the work of the church.[173] He is concerned, immediately upon raising the issue of the magistrate's care of religion, to note that "this right should be circumscribed within certain limits that the duties of the ecclesiastical and political order be not confounded, but the due parts be left to each."[174] This means that magistrates, in light of the external and indirect nature of their tasks, cannot make new articles of faith, enjoin new worship, preach the word, administer sacraments, or exercise church discipline.[175] Even the covenanting documents give hints of

170. Rutherford, *Divine Right*, 607-8.
171. Rutherford, *Divine Right*, 600, 608.
172. See Turretin, *Institutes*, 3.280-81.
173. See Turretin, *Institutes*, 3.275, 279, 280-81, 318-19.
174. Turretin, *Institutes*, 3.316.
175. Turretin, *Institutes*, 3.319-20.

attention to the distinctions required by the two kingdoms doctrine when, for instance, the subscribers pledge to defend doctrine and the church "according to our vocation and power" and "places and callings."[176]

The evidence offered above provides strong evidence that Reformed orthodox reflection on magistrates' religious responsibilities took specific account of the two kingdoms doctrine. The very same language used to distinguish the two kingdoms, in terms of civil and spiritual, external and internal, were used to distinguish the magistrate's from the minister's duties toward religious things. But it was not simply sensitivity to the two kingdoms doctrine that constrained their language. There is also evidence that points to the fact that their doctrine of natural law provided guidance for their articulation of these matters and that these Reformed thinkers saw their understanding of magistrates' religious responsibilities as consistent with the view of natural law as the standard for civil law.

One piece of evidence that supports this point is the fact that these Reformed orthodox writers believed, as noted earlier in the chapter, that the Decalogue as a whole provides a concise summary of the demands of the natural law. Therefore, since natural law teaches the first as well as the second table of the Decalogue, and since natural law is the standard for civil law, a logical conclusion was that magistrates were to have concerns of the first table within their purview. The writers under consideration in this chapter clearly adopted this view.[177] In light of this, they could claim to have a natural law basis for entrusting the magistrate with the establishment and enforcement of laws concerning atheism, idolatry, blasphemy, and worship, which relate to the demands of the first four commandments.

In addition to this basic point, these Reformed orthodox thinkers also made the effort to offer what Althusius refers to as "arguments from reason" for magistrates' religious responsibilities. Althusius calls such arguments "weighty and significant." In his sight, reason commends the magistrate's concern for religion because such concern promotes the general well-being of society. He writes: "For a sound worship and fear of God in the commonwealth is the cause, origin, and fountain of private and public happiness. On the other hand, the contempt of God, and the neglect of divine worship, are the cause of all evil and misfortune. . . . [Sound religion] nourishes peace and concord, disapproves all scandals, and makes men pious and just." In fact, he says, "the profession and practice of orthodox religion are the cause

---

176. "National Covenant," 348; "Solemn League and Covenant," 358-59.
177. E.g., see Rutherford, *Divine Right,* 503.

of all public and private happiness."[178] Turretin presents a similar argument from reason, a kind of natural law appeal. As one line of proof for his thesis that magistrates should have a concern for religious things, he notes that magistrates are entrusted with the safety of society and of all things that pertain to it. Religion, he continues, is in fact one of the things pertaining to it, and he cites non-Christian, classical sources (Aristotle, Plato, and Cicero) for support.[179] Even pagan writers, the argument seems to be, working only from reason and natural law, recognized the need for magistrates to concern themselves with religion because of religion's effect on the public well-being. Also interesting is that Althusius counsels magistrates to refrain from religious persecution when it would in fact harm the public peace.[180] This suggests that magistrates' duty to enforce the external practice of the true religion is subordinate to and contingent upon the higher, general natural law requirement that they promote the public welfare. This is a similar dynamic to that observed in Calvin's thought in Chapter 3.

A final piece of evidence indicating that Reformed orthodoxy tried to see magistrates' religious duties as a requirement of natural law is found in the way in which they appealed to Scripture to support their position. This may be initially counter-intuitive, since their appeals to biblical examples seem in fact to lie in tension with their assertions that natural law is the standard for civil law. While these Reformed orthodox writers cannot in fact escape this criticism entirely, once again they were sensitive to this as potentially problematic and took steps to address the concern. That these writers looked to biblical examples — especially Old Testament examples, given the paucity of New Testament material supporting their position — to bolster their case for the magistrate's involvement in religious affairs is very clear.[181] But such appeals could be theologically consistent with their assertions that the Old Testament law is not binding upon New Testament Christians nor

178. Althusius, *Politica*, 161.

179. Turretin, *Institutes*, 3.317.

180. Althusius, *Politica*, 173.

181. E.g., see Althusius's appeals to the examples of Moses, Gideon, David, Hezekiah, and Josiah in *Politica*, 160-61; and Turretin's numerous biblical (almost exclusively Old Testament) appeals in his discussion of the subject in *Institutes*, 3.316-18. Charles James Butler, *Covenant Theology and the Development of Religious Liberty* (Philadelphia: Center for the Study of Federalism, 1980), 16-17, has interesting discussion of how Reformed writers of this era who understood the Mosaic covenant as a covenant of works, and in that sense discontinuous with the new covenant proclaimed by Christ, tended to favor religious toleration and to decline using Old Testament Israel as a contemporary model.

the contemporary civil state, provided that they took these Old Testament rules and precedents as not specific to the Israelite theocracy but as applications of the natural law with a more general relevance.

There is evidence that Reformed orthodox writers took this theological axiom into consideration when defending magistrates' religious responsibilities from the Old Testament. For example, in the midst of Althusius's appeals to Old Testament texts in order to advocate religious covenants among the people and their rulers, he addresses an objection. Over against the objector who claimed that such religious covenants were made only during certain unordinary times of Israelite history and were therefore not generally applicable, Althusius not only counters by saying that these covenants occurred during other, ordinary times of Israelite history but also by claiming that the texts he cites "demonstrate that the nature and purpose of this compact is such that it is useful and necessary in any type of commonwealth."[182] Granted, there is no specific appeal here to natural law or a related concept such as general equity, but the reasoning seems to presuppose it. Another example, perhaps better though it also requires some inference, comes from Turretin. In his defense of the magistrate's responsibility to punish heretics, he cites Old Testament material exclusively.[183] Sympathetic to the objection that Old Testament precedent is not itself sufficient proof for his position, he comments: "Now although we do not deny that these had something peculiar by reason of the more rigid Mosaic polity (which does not belong to us living under a milder economy), still it is certain that they have also their use in general among us and two things can rightly be gathered thence. First, since defection from religion, which was established by the word of God, and persuasion to defection are punished by the civil magistrate, the same crimes ought not to remain unpunished, but ought to be punished now also. Again, since no reason can be given why the majesty of God and the safety of the church and state should be of less weight with us than it was formerly among the Jews . . . , Christians can have less excuse if they despise the true religion or defend it with less zeal than the Jews."[184]

One might plausibly disagree with the conclusion that these Old Testament examples represent general moral and social obligations rather than specific obligations restricted to the unique Mosaic theocracy. What seems clear, however, is that these Reformed writers did not violate their general

---

182. Althusius, *Politica*, 164.
183. See Turretin, *Institutes*, 3.327-36.
184. Turretin, *Institutes*, 3.333.

principles about natural and civil law in such discussions. They did not, at least in their more reflective moments, take Mosaic law *per se*, as Mosaic law, to be binding; the mere fact that the Old Testament commended magistrates' concern for religious affairs did not itself establish the same practice in the present. Instead, they recognized their theological need to connect these Old Testament laws and examples with more general moral duties, and therefore with the natural law.

The considerations raised in this subsection offer strong reason, I believe, not to speak too quickly of the dissonance between Reformed orthodoxy's view of natural law and the two kingdoms and its view of magistrates' religious duties. The latter position was affirmed with the former in mind. In my judgment, nevertheless, certain tensions or even inconsistencies remain, which even the most sympathetic readings cannot entirely overcome. I offer here two brief examples.

First, though Reformed orthodox writers often used the external/internal distinction to confine magistrates' religious duties within two kingdoms bounds, there is reason to wonder whether they always did so coherently. Althusius's *Politica* provides an example. Althusius makes clear that the ecclesiastical communion and ecclesiastical functions concern the kingdom of Christ and matters of religion, piety, the soul, and the first table of the law. He also says that the ecclesiastical administration (the process by which ecclesiastical functions are administered)[185] concerns things necessary for the welfare of the soul, in distinction from the secular order that has to do with things of the body, this life, justice, and the second table of the law.[186] Ecclesiastical things, he claims, do not belong to the secular magistrate but to the church's presbyters.[187] Yet later in this work he divides the ecclesiastical administration itself into two parts, one of which concerns external things and is entrusted to the magistrate.[188] Althusius, then, having already distinguished the secular and ecclesiastical realms precisely in terms of external/ internal, body/soul distinctions, proceeds to distinguish the ecclesiastical itself in precisely the same terms. This sort of move seems to underlie other contentions that are difficult to reconcile, such as the claim that God only administers his kingdom through ministers of the word[189] compared with the claim that the magistrate can raise up and preserve the kingdom of

---

185. See Althusius, *Politica*, 160.
186. Althusius, *Politica*, 60, 74-75.
187. Althusius, *Politica*, 59.
188. Althusius, *Politica*, 159-74.
189. See Althusius, *Politica*, 172.

God.[190] To put the question briefly, is it coherent to differentiate secular and ecclesiastical (and thereby identify where the kingdom of Christ is and is not) by means of a distinction that in turn differentiates aspects of the ecclesiastical realm itself and opens a fairly wide door for magistrates' involvement?

Related to this consideration is a question about these writers' very use of the distinctions between external and internal and between body and soul as a way to differentiate the kingdoms. Are such distinctions helpful and do they in fact capture what Reformed orthodox theology was seeking to capture by its two kingdoms doctrine? Clearly these writers did not wish to say that the spiritual kingdom of Christ had nothing to do with external, bodily things, for they talked at length about the church's government, its ministry of the word, and its administration of the sacraments. As with Calvin, it is perhaps not surprising that they were unable to carry through their external/internal and body/soul distinctions in a consistent manner.

One other example of a lingering tension not easily resolved is the burden of judgment placed upon magistrates by their responsibilities in religious affairs. Turretin's list of magistrates' religious duties recounted above surely must make a reader wonder at the very least how magistrates attain the competence to make the necessary judgments these duties require.[191] Maintaining sound doctrine, pure worship, a properly functioning ministry, and other such things certainly demand considerable theological acumen in order to ascertain precisely what makes such religious affairs sound, pure, and properly functioning. As long as some ideal situation persists in which the Christian church in a particular jurisdiction is perfectly united among its ministers and elders, presumably magistrates could make such judgments by simply following the counsel of the church, thus presuming no special theological competence on their part. Of course, such an ideal situation, if ever actually attained for a moment, is certainly ephemeral. What is more, the very fact that the magistrate is called upon to enforce externally right doctrine, worship, and ministerial function seems to presume the ever-present threat of dissenting belief and practice. When theologically trained ministers are themselves divided on an issue, even to the point of division in the church, how is a magistrate without special theological training to be expected to adjudicate the dispute? Why should one expect a magistrate, whose knowledge and skills are devoted to political leadership, to determine

---

190. See Althusius, *Politica*, 162.
191. This list appears in Turretin, *Institutes*, 3.320.

when ministers are doing their job properly better than ministers themselves? The National Covenant calls upon the king to root out all heretics who shall be convicted by the true church.[192] Again, this satisfactorily addresses the question for a moment, but determining true church from false has frequently been an issue in ecclesiastical history and, at least by Reformed lights, requires theological judgment to decide. Why should one expect the civil magistrate to have the special theological skill to referee such a dispute and make what would inevitably be a decisive judgment on the matter? One can imagine a magistrate's proper concern, on a natural law basis, for atheism, idolatry, and blasphemy on a very general level. But how does enforcement of a specifically Christian and even narrowly Reformed understanding of church and doctrine comport with the responsibilities of a magistrate who operates with a natural law standard and holds authority as an officer of a non-redemptive, creation-order civil kingdom?

Conclusion

In the concluding subsection of this chapter's discussion of natural law in Reformed orthodoxy, I maintained that the evidence indicates that the view of natural law in Reformed orthodoxy stands in considerable continuity with that of Calvin and other early Reformed theologians, and therefore also, on many points, with that of the Lutheran and medieval traditions. In this concluding subsection concerning the two kingdoms doctrine in Reformed orthodoxy, I maintain that the evidence points again to a significant degree of continuity with the thought of Calvin, and therefore also with Luther on many points. Like Calvin, the representative Reformed orthodox writers examined here articulated the two kingdoms doctrine through a variety of distinctions (such as between the internal and external, earthly and heavenly, body and soul) and applied this distinction to their concrete expositions of the duties and relationship of church and state. For them, the kingdom of Christ found expression in but one present institution, the church. Furthermore, they, like Calvin, used the two kingdoms doctrine to explain the crucial nuances of the central soteriological issue of Christian liberty, and even developed this in more explicit ways than Calvin as they applied it to matters such as the different authority of magistrate and minister with respect to conscience and the unique Reformed understanding of worship. Like Calvin also,

192. See "National Covenant," 351-52.

they kept attentive to the two kingdoms and natural law doctrines in their advocacy of state involvement in religious affairs, though internal tension or even contradiction persists in their thought at this point. To anticipate discussion in later chapters, it may be stated clearly that these representative Reformed orthodox figures and their ecclesiastical confessions did not hold that the kingdom of Christ extends to all institutions and spheres of life at present, as commonly taught by many contemporary Reformed writers.

This close relation to Calvin's theology also leads to the conclusion that the Reformed orthodox doctrine of the two kingdoms in certain ways combined aspects of Luther's two kingdoms idea with a Gelasian two swords idea. The Reformed orthodox writers studied in this chapter, like Gelasius, understood the world as governed by two powers, each with respective jurisdictions and each offering mutual submission to the other in matters of the other's competency. As I suggested in Chapter 3 with respect to Calvin, this combination of two kingdoms and two swords conceptions is able to function coherently on many points, but does leave matters somewhat clouded on an issue of central importance to this book. Did the Reformed orthodox thinkers understand the civil kingdom in terms of *commonality* or *Christianity*? Is the civil kingdom a realm common to Christians and non-Christians or a realm meant to be one part of a unified Christian society? These writers certainly laid theoretical ground for seeing the civil kingdom as a realm marked by commonality. They spoke of the civil kingdom as governed by natural law and as established by God as creator rather than redeemer, they appealed to non-Christian sources and examples in discussing it, and they did not think that a Christian profession adds any degree of legitimacy to a magistrate in his civil office. But practically they did not make the move from their doctrine of the civil kingdom to a conception of a society common to believers and unbelievers, and instead they retained the Christendom assumption of a unified Christian society. They clearly believed that having Christian magistrates is ideal (and thus they laid down extensive instructions for them) and encouraged Christian magistrates to enforce external adherence to Christian doctrine and worship in society by force of the sword. They desired magistrates not simply to defend religion in general, but the *true* religion. Thus Reformed orthodoxy, like Calvin, seems to waver between two ways of speaking. It speaks in Diognetian, Augustinian terms of a civil realm whose characteristics imply a common area between Christians and non-Christians, and it speaks in Gelasian terms of the civil realm as part of a unified Christian society which, alongside the spiritual realm, is governed by two complementary authorities.

The Relation of Natural Law and the
Two Kingdoms in Reformed Orthodoxy

Before concluding this chapter it seems appropriate to reflect briefly on the relationship of the natural law and two kingdoms doctrines in the age of Reformed orthodoxy. I have argued that Reformed orthodox writers not only affirmed these doctrines but also saw many implications of them and incorporated them as critical aspects of their larger system of doctrine and practice. But was affirmation of one of these doctrines necessarily related to affirmation of the other? In Chapter 3, I maintained that the two doctrines were in fact vitally related for Calvin. Here I also argue that the two doctrines were important in large part in relation to each other.

A first respect in which the natural law and two kingdoms doctrines were related in Reformed orthodoxy is that both natural law and the civil kingdom were grounded in God's work of creation and providence rather than in his work of redemption. As considered above, the Reformed orthodox writers perceived natural law to be given originally in the creational covenant of works and sustained among sinful human beings even apart from the redemptive covenant of grace. Similarly, they understood the civil kingdom to be established and governed by the triune God as creator but not by Christ in his specific role as mediator of redemption.

This fundamental relationship between the Reformed orthodox natural law and two kingdoms doctrines is important background for the next point: natural law was considered the primary standard for the civil kingdom but not for the spiritual kingdom, where Scripture was primary. Earlier in this chapter I pointed to statements in Althusius, Rutherford, Turretin, and WCF 19.4 which asserted that civil law should be grounded in natural law, even to the point that the present applicability of Mosaic civil laws is determined by their relation to the law of nature. In this, Reformed orthodoxy made a claim common to the Reformation and medieval traditions before it. That this grounding of civil law in natural law was closely related to and even incorporated into the two kingdoms doctrine is evident in Turretin's sevenfold distinction between civil and ecclesiastical power, in which he contrasts civil power as that which is regulated by "natural reason, civil laws and human statutes" and ecclesiastical power as that which is regulated by "the word of God alone."[193]

By such statements, Turretin and other Reformed orthodox writers did

---

193. Turretin, *Institutes*, 3.279.

not mean to say that Scripture is irrelevant for the civil kingdom nor natural law for the spiritual kingdom. As discussed above, they drew instruction on civil concerns from the Mosaic law and Old Testament history. Nevertheless, they applied these things to the contemporary situation, at least in their more theoretically reflective moments, when they believed that they were rooted in natural law and therefore generally applicable rather than uniquely suited to the Mosaic theocracy. On the other side, they also believed that natural law has relevance for the spiritual kingdom, as illustrated in WCF 1.6. The first part of 1.6 affirms the Protestant doctrine of the sufficiency or perspicuity of Scripture: "The whole counsel of God concerning all things necessary for his own glory, man's salvation, faith and life, is either expressly set down in Scripture, or by good and necessary consequence may be deduced from Scripture: unto which nothing at any time is to be added, whether by new revelations of the Spirit, or traditions of men." This general affirmation of *sola Scriptura,* or Scripture alone, is immediately qualified: "Nevertheless, we acknowledge the inward illumination of the Spirit of God to be necessary for the saving understanding of such things as are revealed in the Word: and that there are some circumstances concerning the worship of God, and government of the church, common to human actions and societies, which are to be ordered by the light of nature, and Christian prudence, according to the general rules of the Word, which are always to be observed." The second part of this qualification demonstrates the (albeit subordinate) role that natural law plays in the spiritual kingdom. Though Scripture alone is to determine the elements of worship (see the discussion of the RPW above) and church government, there are circumstances, or incidentals, related to such things that Scripture does not and need not regulate. For example, Scripture commands corporate worship but does not say at what time of day it should occur; Scripture commands Presbyterian church government but does not provide rules of order for moderating a presbytery meeting. Scripture does not need to do so because such concerns are "*common* to human actions and societies." They are, in other words, the sorts of matters that also concern civil kingdom affairs and non-Christians. In such things, "the light of nature," as understood through "prudence," is the guide. But natural law in the spiritual kingdom is always subordinate, being tested by "the general rules of the Word."[194]

---

194. Among the writers receiving particular attention in this chapter, Rutherford deals with such issues perhaps most thoroughly; e.g., see his *Divine Right,* 4-5, 127 and elsewhere throughout this work.

One other matter pertaining to the relationship of natural law and the two kingdoms in Reformed orthodoxy is the ability that natural law, when seen through two kingdoms lenses, provides for making relative judgments about the good achieved by non-Christians. In Chapter 3 I argued that Calvin viewed non-Christians as able to accomplish remarkable things by the light of nature when evaluated from the perspective of the civil kingdom, but as unable to attain the slightest commendation from God by the light of nature when evaluated from the perspective of the spiritual kingdom. The Reformed orthodox theologians of course shared Calvin's conviction that non-Christians can do nothing that gains them everlasting reward in Christ's heavenly kingdom. But they also shared Calvin's conviction that, when viewed from the perspective of the civil kingdom, unbelievers armed only with nature's light could achieve marvelous things and even receive praise as morally upright. Their frequent citation of classical authors to support their claims about civil magistrates and their duties offer one line of proof for this claim. But Reformed orthodox writers also reflected explicitly on this point. Althusius, for instance, after discussing how natural law determines present applicability of the Mosaic civil law and is summarized in the Decalogue, says that the deeds of the Decalogue, when done out of faith, are pleasing to God. But if, he continues, "they are performed by an infidel or heathen, to whom the Apostle Paul indeed ascribes a natural knowledge of and inclination towards the Decalogue, these works are not able to please God. But in political life even an infidel may be called just, innocent, and upright because of them."[195] Like Calvin, then, Reformed orthodox writers relied upon the two kingdoms doctrine to explicate the doctrine of natural law and its uses among unbelievers. In doing so, they indeed provide a distinctive Reformed articulation of the Diognetian and Augustinian affirmation of both *antithesis* (in terms of eternal things and the spiritual kingdom) and *commonality* (in terms of temporal things and the civil kingdom) between Christians and non-Christians, even if often ambiguously on the latter prong.

Conclusion

This chapter, building upon Chapters 3-4, has presented a case for a continuous, developing Reformed tradition on the natural law and two kingdoms

---

195. Althusius, *Politica*, 147.

doctrines in the sixteenth and seventeenth centuries. Not only did Reformed orthodox thinkers affirm these doctrines in ways very similar to Calvin and other early Reformed theologians, but they also appreciated the intimate relation and mutual dependence of these two doctrines even as Calvin did. There remained some lingering tension or even contradiction in their thought as they advocated religious responsibilities for civil magistrates alongside of and even in light of their natural law and two kingdoms doctrines. They were therefore also ambiguous on whether the civil kingdom is to be viewed as a common realm or a Christian realm. Despite this, they presented a generally lucid and powerful account of natural law and the two kingdoms in the light of larger theological concerns and, in doing so, a generally lucid and powerful perspective on the nature and purposes of social and political life. It now remains for us to examine what Reformed thinkers in other places and of subsequent centuries saw fit to do with such an inheritance.

CHAPTER 6

Theocratic New England, Disestablished Virginia, and the Spirituality of the Church

In the mid-nineteenth century, the prominent Kentucky Presbyterian pastor and theologian Stuart Robinson (1814-1881) made a provocative claim. Two traditions on church-state relations exist in America, he explained, the New England model and the Virginia model. The former, which flourished in colonial days and in the early years of the Republic, comprised a theocratic, Erastian vision in which religious matters and the state's affairs are intertwined and the church is viewed as an arm of the state. The latter, which came to expression in the years immediately following the Declaration of Independence and became the inspiration for the First Amendment of the United States Constitution, freed the church from state control and granted religious liberty to all citizens.[1] This sharp distinction between the early Puritan vision for New England and the enlightened vision of revolutionary Virginia is not in itself uncommon nor particularly noteworthy.[2] But Robinson gave this distinction an arresting twist that raises all sorts of important questions for the present study: while the New England model reflects an

---

1. E.g., see Stuart Robinson, "Relation of the Temporal and Spiritual Powers Historically Considered: The Scoto-American Theory" (originally published in 1867), in Preston D. Graham, Jr., *A Kingdom Not of This World: Stuart Robinson's Struggle to Distinguish the Sacred from the Secular during the Civil War* (Macon: Mercer University Press, 2002), 200-218, especially 202, 212-17; and Stuart Robinson, "Two Theories: The True American, as Contrasted with the New England Doctrine Touching the Relation of the Civil to the Spiritual" (originally published in 1862), in Graham, *A Kingdom Not of This World*, 223-30. In the latter he writes that "Massachusetts and Virginia stand as two great antagonist types of ideas in 'irrepressible conflict'" (228).

2. See similar distinction in Thomas J. Curry, "Church and State in Seventeenth and Eighteenth Century America," *Journal of Law and Religion* 7, no. 2 (1989): 266-68; and Fred J. Hood, *Reformed America: The Middle and Southern States, 1783-1837* (University, AL: University of Alabama Press, 1980), 2-3, 28-30.

originally pagan view of religion and the state that has corrupted Christianity since at least the days of Constantine, the Virginia model reflects the original vision of the Scottish Reformation as expressed in the *Second Book of Discipline* (considered in the previous chapter), but which the Scottish reformers and other Reformed people had never been able to put into practice consistently as they continued to fuse the roles of church and state.[3] What makes Robinson's claim here so intriguing in the present context is how remarkably similar his analysis is to the suggestions made in Chapters 1 and 5 above, where I argued that the early Reformed tradition's granting the magistrate authority over religious affairs could not be fully reconciled to its clear distinction between the two kingdoms. Robinson, in fact, distinguished civil and ecclesiastical authority by explicit appeal to many of the standard Reformed natural law and two kingdoms categories explored in previous chapters and held out the American experiment as a unique opportunity for Reformed churches to express the genius of their doctrine of the church, as a distinct institution from the state.

Evaluating Robinson's claims in the context of the broader story of the development of the natural law and two kingdoms doctrines in the Reformed tradition is a major focus of this chapter. How did the English Puritans' attempt to build a city on a hill in colonial New England comport with their own Reformed heritage on the matters of natural law and the two kingdoms? What role did the Presbyterians play in the achievement of religious freedom in Virginia and why did they align themselves with this historically momentous event? And how do certain later American Presbyterians, like Stuart Robinson, represent a further development in Reformed thinking on these issues as they articulated doctrines such as the spirituality of the church?

This chapter consists of three major sections. First, I consider the early days of the New England experiment through a study of its most accomplished apologist, John Cotton (1584-1652), and his place within the Reformed natural law and two kingdoms tradition. Then I turn to Revolutionary-era Virginia and examine the attitude and actions of the state's Presbyterians in the movement toward disestablishment and religious liberty, primarily through a consideration of the series of memorials that the

---

3. See, e.g., Stuart Robinson, *The Church of God as an Essential Element of the Gospel, and the Idea, Structure, and Functions Thereof* (Philadelphia: Joseph M. Wilson, 1858; reprinted Greenville: Greenville Presbyterian Theological Seminary Press, 1995), 9-10, 28, 64-65, 127-129; and Robinson, "Two Theories," 223, 228-29.

Hanover Presbytery sent to the state legislature. Finally, I discuss the mid-nineteenth-century Presbyterian debates over the doctrine of the spirituality of the church and the related notion of *jure divino* Presbyterianism, especially through the writings of Robinson and his eminent contemporaries Charles Hodge and James Henley Thornwell. In this last section I not only reflect upon the relation of the spirituality doctrine to the earlier Reformed two kingdoms theology but also discuss briefly the popular Reformed utilization of common sense realist philosophy during this era and its relation to earlier Reformed ideas about natural law.

This makes for a lengthy chapter covering a long period of time — from John Cotton, an older contemporary of major figures considered in the previous chapter, Samuel Rutherford and Francis Turretin, to American Presbyterians writing more than two centuries later. Yet the desire to evaluate Robinson's claims about seventeenth-century New England, eighteenth-century Virginia, and his own nineteenth-century context provides the reason for comprehending these three in a single chapter. This chapter argues that Robinson was generally correct in his understanding of the New England and Virginia models with respect to the earlier Reformed tradition and that his own doctrine of the spirituality of the church is indeed deeply rooted in the historic Reformed natural law and two kingdoms doctrines, without many of its classic incoherencies. Nevertheless, this chapter also argues that Robinson's sharp dichotomy between New England and Virginia requires a number of nuances to make it more helpful and accurate and that the spirituality doctrine that he and some contemporaries enunciated left some questions of its own unanswered.

John Cotton, New England Theocracy, and the Reformed Natural Law and Two Kingdoms Doctrines

The early New England colonies, and Massachusetts in particular, are often seen as the pinnacle expression of Reformed theocratic tendencies. From John Winthrop's vision of the City on a Hill to the expulsion of Roger Williams to the Salem witch trials, Massachusetts represents to many an extreme attempt to achieve a religiously uniform society ruled and inhabited by the saints. There is of course much truth in this. Though not all of them were "Puritan" in the technical sense of that term, the early Massachusetts colonists were by and large deeply committed to Reformed doctrine and practice and troubled in various ways by the only partially reformed Anglican establishment in England. The societies that they sought to create and in some measure did create were marked by high degrees of religious uniformity, enforced by the erection of serious social disabilities, or worse, for non-members of the approved churches. The fact that these were attempts to establish new societies rather than adjustments to already-existing societies opened up possibilities for realizing ideals that other early Reformed people did not have and probably contributed to the radical edge that their vision conveyed.

Such a context would seemingly offer barren soil for natural law and two kingdoms doctrines and would perhaps provide the best evidence for an interpretation of the Reformed tradition different from that defended in this book. Indeed, a scholar such as Mark Noll, in describing the early American Puritans as an English Protestant extension of Christendom committed to the necessity of coercive civil and religious integration, goes in this direction. He emphasizes how crucial it was that they came under the influence of Reformed ideas about the organic unity of the world under God and the normativity of Scripture for all of life *over against* Lutheran ideas about the two kingdoms.[4] In a similar vein, Greg Bahnsen, a twentieth-century Reformed advocate of making the Mosaic judicial law the standard for contemporary civil law, saw in John Cotton not only a supporter of the idea that Christ's kingdom should come to expression in all areas of society but also of the idea that the Mosaic laws are universal, for all nations and not just Old Testament Israel.[5]

Though Cotton did not come to Massachusetts with the very first wave of settlers, when he did arrive he quickly established himself as its leading intellectual figure and chief defender. Given his wide influence and copious writings, there seems to be no better choice than Cotton as representative figure of early New England.[6] Certainly contributing to his influential status

---

4. See Mark Noll, *America's God: From Jonathan Edwards to Abraham Lincoln* (New York: Oxford University Press, 2002), 33-36. On this point it is interesting to note the discussion of Philip Hamburger, who acknowledges that John Calvin as well as Martin Luther taught a two kingdoms doctrine and includes these two along with the early New England figures as examples of how those who recognized a distinction between church and state could still support a religious establishment; see *Separation of Church and State* (Cambridge: Harvard University Press, 2002), 22-23.

5. Greg L. Bahnsen, *Theonomy in Christian Ethics* (Nutley, NJ: Craig, 1979), 549-50, 552-53, 556.

6. On the significance and influence of Cotton in early Massachusetts, see, e.g., Larzer Ziff, *The Career of John Cotton: Puritanism and the American Experience* (Princeton: Princeton University Press, 1962), ch. 6; Everett H. Emerson, *John Cotton* (New Haven: College & University Press, 1965), 7, 17; Darren Staloff, *The Making of an American Thinking Class: Intellectuals and Intelligent-*

when he took his position in Massachusetts was the fact that Cotton was a very well-educated man for his day. He studied for many years at Cambridge University, receiving extensive training in the classics, Ramist logic, Aristotelian ethics, and Reformed theology. During his university years he also came under the influence of several significant Puritan leaders, including William Perkins and Richard Sibbes, the latter to whom he credited his conversion. After serving for over twenty years as a vicar in an Anglican church in England, during which time he established himself as a leading non-conformist and came under the scrutiny of Bishop Laud, he sailed for America in 1633 and took up his position in Boston. During the nearly twenty remaining years of his life, Cotton would become a major player in the banishment of Roger Williams (and especially its aftermath) and the excommunication of Anne Hutchinson in the so-called Antinomian affair, serve on several committees erected to draft civil laws for the colony, turn down an invitation to attend the Westminster Assembly, and become the colony's leading spokesman not only for the New England arrangement of church and state but also for Congregational, or Independent, church government.[7]

This section of the chapter will explore Cotton's thought, particularly as it pertains to the Reformed two kingdoms and natural law traditions. My conclusion is that Cotton's views on most issues were quite similar to those of his Reformed orthodox colleagues discussed in the previous chapter. While this may be surprising to some readers, Cotton was, despite his move across the Atlantic, thoroughly immersed in the world of early to mid-seventeenth-century Reformed theology and hence his congruence with that world ought not be shocking. We will see, in fact, that he resembled his Reformed contemporaries in regard to both the doctrinal categories that he employed and the theological and practical inconsistencies created by his ascribing significant religious responsibilities to the civil magistrate.

Cotton and the Two Kingdoms

John Cotton, despite his understandable reputation as a New England theocrat, espoused many views reflecting the commonplace Reformed two king-

---

sia in Puritan Massachusetts (New York: Oxford University Press, 1998), 27; Lisa M. Gordis, Opening Scripture: Bible Reading and Interpretive Authority in Puritan New England (Chicago: University of Chicago Press, 2003), 37; and Hamburger, Separation of Church and State, 39.

7. For detailed studies of Cotton's life, see Emerson, John Cotton; and Ziff, The Career of John Cotton.

doms theology of his day. In this subsection, I discuss various places in his writings where he adopts this point of view. When this is accomplished I will turn to his infamous views on the magistrate and religion and reflect upon how they cohere with his two kingdoms categories.

One way in which Cotton reflected the two kingdoms teaching of the early Reformed tradition was by identifying the church as the earthly manifestation of the kingdom of Christ. For example, when discussing the keys of the kingdom of heaven, he writes: "By the kingdom of heaven is here meant both the kingdom of grace, which is the church; and the kingdom of glory, which is in the highest heavens."[8] This church, according to Cotton, is a "spiritual" body, and as such it stands in distinction from the state, whose competence concerns "civil" things. He explains that the "only wise God hath fitted and appointed two sorts of Administrations, *Ecclesiastical and Civil*," corresponding to the inward and outward conditions of the human person, with each having power suitable to its character. Each administration must do its business "without confounding those two different states."[9] Cotton goes on to differentiate them by calling the church "a Divine Order appointed to believers for holy communion of holy things" and the state a "Humane Order appointed by God to man for Civil Fellowship of humane things."[10] As Timothy Hall notes, it may seem baffling to modern readers to see New England Puritans such as Cotton distinguishing civil and ecclesiastical authority so clearly, but they do seem to have "learned from John Calvin that 'Christ's spiritual kingdom and the civil jurisdiction are things completely distinct.'"[11]

Cotton proceeds to identify four specific differences between the civil and ecclesiastical authorities that closely resemble the distinctions that Turretin would make a couple of decades later in Geneva, as observed in the previous chapter. First, Cotton asserts that while the church has an "economical" power only, with Christ alone possessing legislative power within it, the state has "lordly" power over its subjects.[12] Elsewhere Cotton unpacks

---

8. John Cotton, "The Keys of the Kingdom of Heaven" (originally published in 1644), in *John Cotton on the Churches of New England*, ed. Larzer Ziff (Cambridge: Belknap/Harvard University Press, 1968), 87-88; see also 95.

9. John Cotton, *A Discourse about Civil Government in a New Plantation Whose Design Is Religion* (Cambridge: Samuel Green and Marmaduke Johnson, 1663), 5.

10. Cotton, *Discourse about Civil Government*, 5-6.

11. Timothy L. Hall, *Separating Church and State: Roger Williams and Religious Liberty* (Urbana: University of Illinois Press, 1998), 63.

12. Cotton, *Discourse about Civil Government*, 6.

this distinction at greater length, defining the economical power of the church also as "ministerial" and "stewardly," meaning that church courts, in contrast to the wide discretion possessed by the state, have no authority to command things that are indifferent but are confined to enjoining those things for which Christ (in Scripture) has given "injunctions" and "commission."[13] This limitation of church authority to ministering the things found in Scripture was grounded in classic Reformed notions of the Christian liberty of believers in regard to spiritual things, which was itself grounded in the two kingdoms doctrine, as also considered in previous chapters.[14] Cotton's second difference between civil and ecclesiastical authority concerns the distinct ways in which the same people are subjects under these two authorities. The subject of the state is "Man by Nature being a Reasonable and Sociable Creature, capable of Civil Order." The subject of the church, on the other hand, is "Man by Grace called out of the world to fellowship with Jesus Christ." This means, for Cotton, that all people are subjects of the state but only Christians are subjects of the church. Believers are subject to the church in their "inward man" while in their "outward man" they are "subject to the Civil Power in common with other men."[15]

While this second difference concerns the people who are subject to the two authorities, the third difference concerns God who is "the efficient and author of them both," yet in distinct ways. God is author of the civil administration "as the Creator and Governor of the world" but is author of the ecclesiastical administration "as in Covenant with his People in Christ." Cotton further explains this distinction with words reminiscent of figures such as Rutherford and Turretin concerning Christ's twofold kingship over creation and redemption, as discussed in the previous chapter. He speaks of Christ being "the Efficient and Fountain of Civil Order & Administrations" insofar as he is "the Essential Word and Wisdom of God creating and governing the World" and speaks of him establishing the ecclesiastical order insofar as he is "Mediator of the New Covenant, & Head of the Church."[16] Thus, for Cotton as for other Reformed orthodox theologians, the Son rules the state as God and creator and rules the church as God-Man and redeemer. The fourth difference between the civil and ecclesiastical administrations that Cotton identifies concerns their respective ends. Though the ultimate end of both is the

13. See Cotton, "Keys of the Kingdom," 88, 121-23, 125-26.

14. For more on Cotton's views on church authority and Christian liberty, see Emerson, *John Cotton*, 23, 69.

15. Cotton, *Discourse about Civil Government*, 6.

16. Cotton, *Discourse about Civil Government*, 6.

glory of God, their penultimate ends differ. The end of civil administration is the "Preservations of Humane Societies in outward Honor, Justice and Peace" while the end of ecclesiastical administration is the "Conservation, Edification, and Salvation of Souls, Pardon of Sins, Power against Sin, Peace with God, &c." Hence, the objects of these two administrations also differ, the civil power having concern for "bodies" and "the things of this life" and the ecclesiastical power for "the Souls and Consciences of men, the Doctrine and Worship of God, the Communion of the Saints."[17]

In addition to these basic distinctions, Cotton elsewhere notes another key distinction that also reflects common Reformed notions, that of the different weapons belonging to church and state. Cotton associates the "sword" with the civil authority, insofar as it deals with "bodily life and death." He prohibits the church from wielding the sword, however, and instead recognizes the "keys of the kingdom of heaven" as the "ordinances which Christ hath instituted, to be administered in his church," namely preaching, sacraments, and ecclesiastical censures.[18]

Having made such distinctions, Cotton appeals for a "joint harmony" to be kept between the two orders and administrations. He warns against two extremes. The first is "confounding" them, such as by giving "Spiritual Power" to the civil magistrate (an error which he identifies as Erastian) or by giving "Civil Power" to the officers of the church, "who are called to attend only to Spiritual matters" and ought not "be distracted from them by Secular entanglements." Here he also distinguishes between church officers and church members, the latter of whom may be employed in the things of this life "to carry on all worldly and civil business" but the former of whom ought not to have civil power. The second extreme is that of setting the civil and ecclesiastical orders "in opposition as contraries." Instead, he calls for them to provide mutual help for each other and to be subject to each other in their respective competencies. Thus, civil magistrates must be submissive to church authority in spiritual things even while the church ought not to interfere with their exercise of civil authority. Cotton quotes his Reformed forebear Franciscus Junius to show that "as a Christian" the magistrate is a "holy sheep of Christ's holy flock" but that "as a Magistrate" he is a "preserver of public order."[19] In all of these matters, Cotton sets forth common sixteenth- and seventeenth-century Reformed two kingdoms sentiments.

---

17. Cotton, *Discourse about Civil Government*, 7.
18. Cotton, "Keys of the Kingdom," 88.
19. Cotton, *Discourse about Civil Government*, 7-9.

Yet it is not as if Cotton is always perfectly clear even in his use of these categories. For instance, in a difficult passage to interpret found in his exchanges with Roger Williams, Cotton affirms that "Church and Commonwealth are still distinct Kingdoms, the one of this world, the other of Heaven," and denies that "a Civil and temporal Israel" is to be established today. Nevertheless, he also asserts that "Christ hath enjoyed (even as Mediator) an everlasting Kingdom, not only in the Church, but in the Government of all the Kingdoms of the earth." He defends this assertion, which seems to contradict the third of his four basic distinctions between civil and ecclesiastical authority discussed above, by stating that "the Kingdoms of the earth are then said to be the Kingdoms of our Lord, when they submit their laws to the laws of his word."[20] Though Cotton does not cite a Scripture text here, it is likely that he is referring to Revelation 11:15, which speaks of the kingdoms of the world becoming the kingdom of the Lord and of his Christ.[21] This declaration in Revelation 11:15, however, occurs in the context of the seventh trumpet, seemingly pointing to God's own action at the end of history with the return of Christ. Cotton, therefore, while elsewhere claiming that the spiritual kingdom is ruled by Christ as mediator of redemption and that the civil kingdom is ruled by him as creator, has apparently moved into history — even into his own day — the transfer of civil kingdoms into a single, overarching kingdom ruled by Christ as mediator, accomplished not by the divine act of Christ's return but by the human act of civil states submitting their laws to Scripture.[22] In order to trace the contours of Cotton's thought more broadly in this area, I now turn to consider his view of civil magistrates and their religious responsibilities, a view that relativizes, though does not completely nullify, the distinctions between civil and ecclesiastical authorities described above.

20. John Cotton, *The Bloody Tenet Washed and Made White in the Blood of the Lamb*, 92-93, in *The Complete Writings of Roger Williams*, vol. 3, ed. Samuel L. Caldwell (New York: Russell & Russell, 1963).

21. Not only is Cotton's language similar to the text of Revelation 11:15, but he cites this text in other places in this treatise to defend similar points; e.g., see *The Bloody Tenet Washed*, 105, 159.

22. On the practice of Cotton and Puritans more generally of reading the visions of Revelation as references to historical events of their own day, see Harry S. Stout, *The New England Soul: Preaching and Religious Culture in Colonial New England* (New York: Oxford University Press, 1986), 48-49.

Religion and the Civil Magistrate

That the early New England state was heavily invested in the religious affairs of its citizenry is a well-known fact of history. Although the involvement of New England churches in civil affairs, in matters such as the preaching of election day sermons[23] and Cotton's own service on committees to draft civil legal codes, could raise a similar set of questions, it is the state's entanglement in religious affairs that will engage us in this subsection. Here, as in Chapters 3 and 5, the magistrate's religious responsibilities raise serious questions about the application of the two kingdoms doctrine in early Reformed theology and the coherence of its social thought.

Immediately after setting forth the fourfold distinction between civil and ecclesiastical administration in his *Discourse about Civil Government*, Cotton makes a key move that is determinative for much else that he writes about magistrates and religion. He reads Romans 13:1-7, which requires Christians to submit to heathen magistrates, as Paul's counsel to an already-established civil order. But he distinguishes this from a situation in which a new civil order is being established — the situation, of course, of the Massachusetts colonies. Were Paul addressing the latter context, Cotton explains, he would have spoken differently and advised them to choose as magistrates only those who are members of the church. Cotton, anticipating what must indeed be the immediate reaction of so many of his readers, seeks to deflect the charge that his reading of Paul is "a flight and uncertain conjecture" by quoting several other Pauline passages that he believes show that Christians should prefer being judged by other Christians than by unbelievers.[24] Cotton clarifies that where a new civil order is established and most residents are not Christians, then appointing heathen magistrates is "good enough," but in their own New England context, where most profess Christ, they must heed the advice that Paul would have given: the pool of potential civil magistrates consists of members of the church.[25]

---

23. On election day sermons, see, e.g., Stout, *The New England Soul,* 29-30.

24. Cotton, *Discourse about Civil Government,* 9-10.

25. Cotton, *Discourse about Civil Government,* 12-13. On various issues pertaining to the establishment of new civil communities in New England and the importance of religious covenants for their identity, see the comprehensive study of David A. Weir, *Early New England: A Covenanted Society* (Grand Rapids: Eerdmans, 2005). More recently, see also John Witte, Jr., *God's Joust, God's Justice: Law and Religion in the Western Tradition* (Grand Rapids: Eerdmans, 2006), 143-68; and John Witte, Jr., *The Reformation of Rights: Law, Religion, and Human Rights in Early Modern Calvinism* (Cambridge: Cambridge University Press, 2007), ch. 5.

Having thus dismissed the potentially troublesome Romans 13 passage, Cotton turns to expounding how things ought to work in a newly established Christian commonwealth such as his own in Massachusetts. One point that Cotton emphasizes, as already seen, is that only members of the church should serve as civil magistrates. In his *Discourse about Civil Government* he lists six arguments in support of this position.[26] While it may be tedious to spell out all of these, it is interesting to note where he finds biblical support in making these arguments. One key line of biblical evidence for Cotton is the fact that Old Testament Israel was a "theocracy" and thus is the best form of government. He finds other Old Testament support in places such as Psalm 2:10-12, which calls upon the kings of the earth to "kiss the Son," and Isaiah 49:23, which speaks of kings being foster fathers and queens being nursing mothers for God's people.[27] Regarding the New Testament, Cotton claims that drawing civil magistrates from the rolls of the church best gives Christ his "due preeminence," as prescribed in Ephesians 1:21-22 and Colossians 1:15-19, and best respects Paul's injunction in 1 Corinthians 6:1-18 that believers ought to seek judgment from believers rather than unbelievers whenever possible. Cotton goes on to add, as a sort of icing on the cake of his six arguments, that he could "easily . . . add the Consent of all Nations" as evidence for his case. He gives examples from Protestant and Roman Catholic countries as well as examples from non-Christian nations that also have religious tests for their magistrates, referring his readers to "Turkey itself" and "these very Indians that Worship the Devil."[28]

Another matter that Cotton emphasizes is that, in a Christian commonwealth such as his own, the civil magistrate ought to have a care for religion. In one place he calls on the state to exercise its power of the sword to establish and reform true religion in terms of doctrine, worship, and government, even asserting that the church's ministerial power of the keys ought to submit to the civil sword in such matters insofar as they concern civil peace.[29] Elsewhere he assures civil magistrates that they need not fear that they have exceeded the bounds of their office if they "meddle with the spiritual affairs of the Church in God's way."[30] And just as he appealed to non-Christian lands for examples of the principle that only Christians should hold civil of-

26. Cotton, *Discourses about Civil Government*, 16-23.

27. Cotton appeals to these two passages in a number of other places as well; see, e.g., *The Bloody Tenet Washed*, 60-61.

28. Cotton, *Discourse about Civil Government*, 23-24.

29. Cotton, "Keys of the Kingdom," 153-54.

30. Cotton, *The Bloody Tenet Washed*, 162.

fice, so Cotton also appealed to the "light of nature" and to "profane Authors" to show that magistrates should have a care for religion and to shame Christians who might exhibit less zeal for the true God than pagans for their idols.[31]

Finally, and building off the previous point, Cotton took great pains to defend the right and duty of the civil magistrate, in certain circumstances, to punish with the sword those who practice false religion. This brings us most directly into the midst of his famous dialogue with Roger Williams (1603-1684). Williams had clashed with the Massachusetts authorities on a number of issues, culminating in his opposition to requiring (religious) oaths as a condition for (civil) citizenship, and he was banished from the colony in the winter of 1636-37. Though Cotton's name has become indelibly linked to Williams', Cotton himself disavowed involvement in the decision to banish Williams, and several modern scholars have indeed argued that Cotton had some sympathy for him and tried to arbitrate between him and the civil court that effected his exile.[32] Nevertheless, it was Cotton at whom Williams aimed his polemical arrow, and Cotton was not timid about firing back. Their exchanges are an illuminating debate on liberty of conscience and established religion.

The matter of liberty of conscience was a crucial aspect of this debate, and without understanding Cotton's view of this issue one will not understand the rest. Cotton did not dispute in general that liberty of conscience must be respected, but he made several distinctions that landed him in a much different position from Williams'. In response to Williams' strong appeal to liberty of conscience, Cotton first distinguished between matters of doctrine and practice that are fundamental and those that are circumstantial or less principal. In regard to the latter he made a further distinction, between people holding such views meekly and those holding them in a way that disturbs civil peace. Another important distinction that Cotton makes is between persecution of a conscience that is rightly informed and persecu-

---

31. Cotton, *The Bloody Tenet Washed,* 108-9. For discussion of a sermon, attributed to Cotton though perhaps more likely delivered by John Davenport, that appeals to the consent of the nations and cites a variety of Christian and non-Christian sources to show that religion ought to be established, see Frank Lambert, *The Founding Fathers and the Place of Religion in America* (Princeton: Princeton University Press, 2003), 85.

32. E.g., see James Calvin Davis, *The Moral Theology of Roger Williams: Christian Conviction and Public Ethics* (Louisville: Westminster John Knox, 2004), 10-11; and Irwin H. Polishook, *Roger Williams, John Cotton and Religious Freedom: A Controversy in New and Old England* (Englewood Cliffs: Prentice-Hall, 1967), 15.

tion of a conscience that is erroneous or blind.[33] He denies, unsurprisingly, that he favors persecution of one whose conscience is rightly informed and who holds and practices correct views. People who have erroneous or blind consciences and who err on fundamental, weighty matters must not be punished immediately, but must first be admonished. Then, if they persist in their error and are punished by the magistrate, they are not in fact persecuted for conscience's sake but for their sin *against conscience* (since it has now been properly informed).[34] Thus, if Williams was not suffering for a righteous cause, as Cotton insisted he was not, then he was not being "persecuted."[35] Finally, Cotton asserted that those erring in lesser, non-principal matters ought to be tolerated as long as they do so meekly and not in an arrogant way that disturbs the civil peace.[36]

Against this background we may observe a number of related reasons that Cotton used against Williams to justify the civil magistrate's punishment of those adhering to false religious beliefs and practices. One key consideration for Cotton was the danger that such people would seduce others. Cotton admits that people cannot be constrained to believe, but they may be restrained from seducing the populace. Thus, he permits toleration of those who hold to false religions (including submissive Indians), but not if they seduce Christians to apostatize or embrace their religions.[37] Cotton finds it absurd and merciless that one would pity those who are "incurably contagious" and not the "many scores or hundreds of the souls of such, as will be infected and destroyed by the toleration of the other."[38]

A second line of argument employed by Cotton is an appeal to the need for civil order. This argument took a variety of forms for Cotton, but on the whole his reasoning here resembles that of Calvin in justifying, at least in part, the civil suppression of religious heterodoxy for the sake of social

33. John Cotton, "The Answer of Mr. John Cotton of Boston in New-England, to the aforesaid Arguments against Persecution for Cause of Conscience," 41-42, in *The Complete Writings of Roger Williams,* vol. 3.

34. Cotton, "Answer," 42. See also Cotton, *The Bloody Tenet Washed,* 21-22, 27, 83, 172. For discussion of these claims of Cotton, see, e.g., Emerson, *John Cotton,* 138; and Stout, *The New England Soul,* 21.

35. See John Cotton, *A Reply to Mr. Williams his Examination; and Answer of the Letters sent to him,* 13-14, in *The Complete Writings of Roger Williams,* vol. 2.

36. Cotton, "Answer," 42-43. See also Hall, *Separating Church and State,* 61.

37. Among many examples, see Cotton, "Answer," 47; and Cotton, *The Bloody Tenet Washed,* 18, 27, 33, 81-82, 88, 94-95, 155.

38. Cotton, *The Bloody Tenet Washed,* 35; see also 83. On this point see also Hall, *Separating Church and State,* 59.

peace. One form of this argument is *a fortiori:* since civil government is about keeping peace and order, if it is concerned about the peace of societies of merchants and the like, how much more about that of the church![39] He admits that the peace of the commonwealth is "Civil and humane," yet this sort of peace is destroyed when spiritual purity and peace are disturbed.[40] He explains later that it is impossible for one who is religiously a "wolf" to keep civil peace or for spiritual whoredom and witchcraft to coexist with it.[41] Elsewhere, again to justify the magistrate's duty to punish religious seducers, he states that religion is the best good of the city and that people prosper in their outward estate when pursuing God's kingdom and righteousness.[42] This requires, he recognizes, that magistrates make judgments about what is genuine godliness, as far as such tends to uphold the public peace.[43] One can sense Cotton's urgency. Those who destroy religion are "disturbers" of the civil state;[44] civil states that despise or neglect God's grace "cannot long expect bodily health";[45] and not having civil laws protecting true religion "may bring the wrath of God," while punishing seducers brings divine blessing.[46]

In addition to all of these other arguments, Cotton is not above making personal appeals to win consent to his position. "Surely," he writes, "if everyone be bound to put forth himself to his utmost power in God's Business, then civil Magistrates are bound to put forth their civil power, in defending the Faith of Jesus."[47]

As with the discussions in previous chapters regarding Calvin and the Reformed orthodox, Cotton's earnest defense of civil punishment of religious deviance raises serious questions about the coherence of his two kingdoms theology with his concrete social vision. In Chapters 3 and 5 I offered some initial caveats about too quickly dismissing these thinkers' thought as blatantly inconsistent, and the same seems appropriate here too. At least three considerations indicate that Cotton did not lose total sight of his two kingdoms doctrine even while polemicizing against Williams. First, Cotton,

---

39. Cotton, *The Bloody Tenet Washed*, 10-11; see also 104.

40. Cotton, *The Bloody Tenet Washed*, 13.

41. Cotton, *The Bloody Tenet Washed*, 88-89.

42. Cotton, *The Bloody Tenet Washed*, 151, 163.

43. Cotton, *The Bloody Tenet Washed*, 62; see also 94.

44. Cotton, *The Bloody Tenet Washed*, 91-92.

45. Cotton, *The Bloody Tenet Washed*, 164.

46. Cotton, *The Bloody Tenet Washed*, 150-51, 138.

47. Cotton, *The Bloody Tenet Washed*, 59.

like many of his Reformed contemporaries and predecessors, stated that the punishments that magistrates inflict upon religious offenders are "merely Civil."[48] In other words, they do not touch the soul or conscience but merely the outward estate. Second, Cotton distinguished the actions of Christians as they constitute the church from the actions of Christians in their civil capacities.[49] Hence Christians' duty to promote the cause of Christ in both church and state was to retain a distinction between their action in one and action in the other. The third consideration is again familiar from preceding chapters. Cotton appeals not only to Scripture in support of magistrates' religious responsibilities but also to natural law. As seen above, he defended his position by pointing to the "light of nature" and he also argued, as will be considered in more detail below, that the Mosaic legislation prescribing execution of blasphemers and those seducing people to idolatry is part of the permanently binding moral equity of the Old Testament law.[50]

Despite these indications of a continuing sensitivity to the two kingdoms doctrine, Cotton, like his fellow early Reformed theologians, cannot escape suspicion of lingering tension and even inconsistency in his thought. Though others might be added, I suggest four points which remain unresolved in Cotton's theology and social practice. The first involves a matter noted briefly above. After differentiating the civil from the ecclesiastical administration in that the former is ruled by the Son as God and creator and the latter by the Son as God-Man and mediator of redemption, he proceeds to claim that a state that adopts biblical law becomes the kingdom of Christ "even as Mediator."[51] In this context and elsewhere it is clear that Cotton does not wish to extinguish the distinction between the civil and ecclesiastical administrations, yet this claim, based (dubiously) on Revelation 11:15, is clearly important for Cotton's justification of the magistrate's enforcement of religious purity. Cotton, however, does not explain if or how exactly a state's embrace of Christianity changes its essential nature. Whether the state continues to be ruled by God specifically as creator or a unilateral action of the state changes that remains an ambiguity in Cotton's theology.

Second, Cotton exhibits a surprising lack of confidence in the power of the church's appointed means of exercising its authority, particularly the preaching of the word. For example, he makes the following statement:

48. Cotton, *The Bloody Tenet Washed*, 69.
49. Cotton, *Discourse about Civil Government*, 12.
50. Cotton, *The Bloody Tenet Washed*, 108-9, 55.
51. Cotton, *The Bloody Tenet Washed*, 92-93.

"Though the Spiritual weapons be absolutely sufficient to the end for which God hath appointed them . . . : yet if an Heretic still continue obstinate, and persist in seducing, creep into Houses, lead captive silly souls, and destroy the faith of some, . . . such *Gangrenes* would be cut off by another Sword, which in the hand of the Magistrate is not borne in vain."[52] What in fact are the ends for which God has appointed the spiritual weapons? The *Westminster Shorter Catechism,* a document that Cotton could have helped to compose had he been able to accept the invitation to attend the Westminster Assembly, expresses the consensus Reformed view of the era in stating that "The Spirit of God maketh the reading, but especially the preaching of the Word, an effectual means of convincing and converting sinners, and of building them up in holiness and comfort, through faith, unto salvation" (Answer 89). If the spiritual word of God was indeed "absolutely sufficient" for such a task, then Cotton's conviction, expressed here and so many other places, that the civil sword was also necessary for the protection of "silly souls" seems to be an inconsistent element in his thought.

The third point is that he speaks inconsistently in regard to whether the state's authority extends only to external, temporal things or also to internal matters of the soul. In previous chapters I have suggested that the common Reformed practice of distinguishing the two kingdoms in terms of body/soul and external/internal was not entirely felicitous for capturing the point of the distinction and that this may have contributed to failure to put the two kingdoms doctrine into consistent practice. Similar observations apply to Cotton. In his typically Reformed fourfold distinction between civil and ecclesiastical authority, Cotton puts the "outward man" and his "outward Honour, Justice and Peace" under the jurisdiction of the civil administration, while he reserves the "Inward man" and the "Conservation, Edification, and Salvation of Souls" to the jurisdiction of the ecclesiastical administration.[53] Yet in his debate with Williams he also claims that "It is a carnal and worldly, and indeed, an ungodly imagination, to confine the Magistrate's charge, to the bodies, and goods of the Subject, and to exclude them from the care of their souls."[54] These two claims stand in rather forthright contra-

---

52. Cotton, *The Bloody Tenet Washed,* 155.

53. Cotton, *Discourse about Civil Government,* 6-7.

54. Cotton, *The Bloody Tenet Washed,* 67-68. Later in this treatise Cotton takes a somewhat mediating position between these two contradictory affirmations, stating "that though the Government of the civil Magistrate do extend no further than over the bodies and goods of his Subjects, yet he may and ought to improve that power over their bodies and goods, to the good of

diction, yet both seem crucial for various other affirmations that Cotton makes throughout his writings. Here again, therefore, one finds inconsistent claims in Cotton's thought.

Finally, Cotton's thought runs into internal tension in placing a great burden of spiritual discernment upon civil magistrates. When one considers the various aspects of Cotton's social vision presented above, it is evident that magistrates, in order to determine whether or not people should be punished for religious belief or practice, must determine whether a person does in fact hold an erroneous view and whether an error is fundamental or peripheral. Much of what Cotton wrote against Williams, in fact, concerned the purity of the church and what sort of obligation Christians had to separate from the Church of England. And this was necessary for their debate, since Williams built so much of his own case on his quest for religious purity.[55] Yet the very people best trained to deal with such theological disputes, the ministers, were the very ones that Cotton excluded from holding civil office. Cotton entrusted those not having advanced training in theology and possessing competence in other areas with tasks such as reforming the church in its doctrine, worship, and government and even in judging disputes between trained theologians such as Cotton and Williams.

Like so many of his Reformed contemporaries, therefore, John Cotton lived with a number of theological and practical inconsistencies stemming from his dual assertion of the two kingdoms doctrine and the task of the civil magistrate to guard religious purity. Though he never abandoned the institutional distinction between church and state and advocated some differentiation of their functions, in the end it is difficult to avoid the conclusion that these ideas tended to fade into the background in the face of his zeal to defend civil religion against the threat that Williams posed. To exacerbate these tendencies, Cotton embraced a strong postmillennial eschatology, readily looked to Old Testament Israel as a model for his social vision (in striking contrast to an Augustine who looked to Israel in Babylonian exile as the model for understanding present Christian existence), and did not develop an understanding of the Christian life as a pilgrimage away from one's true home (an idea that tempered even Calvin's this-worldly energy). In short, Cotton's writings evidence both the continuing presence of the two

---

their souls"; see *The Bloody Tenet Washed,* 161. Here the state seems charged not with direct care for the soul but with the support of the church in its care for the soul.

55. On Williams' radical views on religious purity, which eventually led him to reject all visible gatherings of the church, see, e.g., Davis, *The Moral Theology of Roger Williams,* 35-41; Ziff, *The Career of John Cotton,* 222; and Hamburger, *Separation of Church and State,* 51-52.

kingdoms doctrine in seventeenth-century Reformed thought and the frequent failure of this theological tradition to apply it consistently in social matters.

John Cotton and the Reformed Natural Law Tradition

There is less extant material from John Cotton pertaining to the issue of natural law, and thus treatment of the issue here may be briefer. Despite some apparent evidence to the contrary, a number of things in Cotton's writings suggest that he held many traditional Reformed and broader Christian views on natural law, including its relation to the Mosaic judicial law. Though surely less sanguine about the role of natural law than many of his Reformed contemporaries, Cotton on the whole remained within his own tradition on this issue.

The New England Puritans are often viewed as biblicists whose interest in any non-Scriptural sources for moral and political guidance was minimal. While the importance of Scripture for them is obvious, a number of scholars writing in recent years have recognized that natural law, along with other non-biblical sources such as the English common law, played a role in early New England ethics and jurisprudence.[56] Some of these scholars call upon Cotton for evidence, and indeed he drew upon the idea of natural law in a number of contexts. Most significantly for the present study, Cotton appealed to natural law as a normative standard for civil law. Some examples of this appeared in the previous subsection under discussion of the magistrate's religious responsibilities. Cotton cited the "light of nature" directly and also indirectly through appeals to "profane Authors" and "the Consent of all Nations" in defending his position.[57] On a very different aspect of civil law, the law of inheritance, he also pointed explicitly to the "law of nature" as indicating that inheritances should "naturally" descend to the next of kin

---

56. For example, see the study of John D. Eusden, "Natural Law and Covenant Theology in New England, 1620-1670," *Natural Law Forum* 6 (1960): 1-30, who identifies frequent use of natural law among the New England Puritans, though he finds it often imprecise and locates these Puritans within the natural law tradition only with "severe qualifications." Other writers finding significant use of natural law among them include Keith L. Griffin, *Revolution and Religion: American Revolutionary War and the Reformed Clergy* (New York: Paragon House, 1994), 26; and George Lee Haskins, *Law and Authority in Early Massachusetts: A Study in Tradition and Design* (New York: Macmillan, 1960), 118-19.

57. Cotton, *Discourse about Civil Government*, 23-24; Cotton, *The Bloody Tenet Washed*, 108-9.

and that a double portion should be assigned to the eldest son.[58] In regard to a third issue, Jesper Rosenmeier argues that Cotton made use of a wide variety of sources to argue against usury, including reason and notions of common justice and equity, in addition to classical authors and contemporary legal practice.[59] Such examples indicate that Cotton, with the broader Christian tradition, felt comfortable citing natural law and that he viewed it as at least one normative standard for civil law.

Some very difficult questions arise, however, regarding Cotton's view of the Mosaic judicial law and its relation to natural law. At least one recent writer has appealed to Cotton as precedent for his own conviction that the Mosaic judicial law as such (and not natural law) ought to be the standard for contemporary civil law.[60] Such a view of the Mosaic law is clearly not the historic Reformed — or broader Christian — position, as argued at length in previous chapters, but one can make a plausible case for this being Cotton's position, and Rosenmeier, for one, claims that Cotton diverged from Calvin on this issue.[61] But as will be seen below, Rosenmeier does not account for all of the evidence, and George Haskins' conclusions seem accurate. He places the early New England Puritans well within the Reformed consensus, though he sees different emphases among the various figures, finding an important figure such as John Winthrop more in the center of this consensus and Cotton on one fringe of it, due to the great extent of the Mosaic judicial law that he viewed as universally binding.[62]

Perhaps the best evidence that Cotton falls within the mainstream of early Reformed thought on the relation of Mosaic judicial law and natural law is his utilization of the standard Reformed test for the continuing applicability of the former. In short, like his Reformed contemporaries, he argued for the universal character of those aspects of Mosaic judicial law that reflect "moral equity," terminology used by Calvin and the Reformed orthodox as a virtual equivalent of natural law. He wrote, for example, that "Natural Judicials bind all; of moral equity."[63] In his debate with Williams, further-

58. John Cotton, "An Abstract of the Laws of New-England, as They Are Now Established" (originally published, 1641), in Bahnsen, *Theonomy in Christian Ethics*, 563.

59. Jesper Rosenmeier, "John Cotton on Usury," *William and Mary Quarterly* 47 (October 1990): 548-65.

60. As cited above, see Bahnsen, *Theonomy in Christian Ethics*, 549-50, 552-53, 556.

61. Rosenmeir, "John Cotton on Usury," 556.

62. See Haskins, *Law and Authority*, 151-61.

63. John Cotton, "How Far Moses Judicialls Bind Mass[achusetts]," reprinted in *Proceedings of the Massachusetts Historical Society*, Second Series 16 (October 1902): 282.

more, he denied that a Christian commonwealth was bound to "all the judicial Laws of Moses" rather than "only [to] those of Moral, and perpetual equity." Christ never abolished "the Judicial Laws of Moses, which were of Moral equity."[64] On the other hand, those Old Testament judicial laws that were "peculiar to that state" and concerned Israel "as they were a peculiar church & none besides them in the world & sequestered from all people under heaven" were not to be enforced in contemporary civil law.[65]

All of this reflects common Reformed conviction. Judged by the standard of traditional Reformed categories, however, Cotton's views do appear somewhat deficient in at least two respects. First, though Cotton obviously works with the category of judicial law (along with moral and ceremonial law), it seems that he viewed particular judicial laws as being either moral or ceremonial, without remainder. In other words, he argued for the continuing applicability of judicial laws that are moral and the expiration of judicial laws that are ceremonial (i.e., that pointed to and found their fulfillment in Christ and his work), as if there were no other category in which to place them.[66] Though figures such as Calvin before Cotton and Turretin shortly after him perhaps did not articulate this with conscious clarity, they seemed to recognize that certain Mosaic judicial laws were neither strictly moral nor strictly ceremonial, but were simply not appropriate for the particular circumstances of their contemporary European societies. Second, one does not find Cotton making the general affirmation that the Mosaic judicial law has expired, as do so many of his Reformed cohorts. While others spoke generally of the abrogation of the judicial law and secondarily of its contemporary applicability when moral equity so indicates, Cotton seemed intent on finding the judicial law primarily of universal application and its expired aspects the exception. Part of the dynamics here undoubtedly must be understood in the context of his need to refute Williams. Cotton saw the social arrangement of Old Testament Israel as key justification for the New England way, particularly in the role that Israel's kings played in protecting true religion. In this context, Cotton set a very high bar for seeing typology in the Old Testament law, that is, for seeing aspects of the Mosaic law as inapplicable to Christians because they pointed to and were fulfilled by Christ. In all of this, Cotton assumed continuity between Old

---

64. Cotton, *The Bloody Tenet Washed*, 92-93, 126.

65. Cotton, "How Far Moses," 282.

66. In my judgment, Cotton's discussions in "How Far Moses," 282-84, support this interpretation. Compare Emerson's similar conclusion in *John Cotton*, 144.

and New Testaments and accepted that Mosaic judicial laws had expired only in limited circumstances.[67]

Two examples from Cotton's work that offer perhaps the best evidence that he stands outside of the Reformed consensus on these issues may serve to test the general conclusions drawn in the preceding paragraphs. The first example is the model for Massachusetts law that he drew up which, though never itself enacted, became influential in the colony. This relatively brief document contains copious citation of texts from the Mosaic law to support the laws that it proposes and many sections virtually copy rules right out of Scripture. In the midst of this, there are striking examples of violation of his own principle that ceremonial or typological laws are no longer applicable[68] and examples of ecclesiastical censures applied to the civil context.[69] All of this points to a quite straightforward thrusting of Mosaic law onto New England without even some of the nuanced qualifications that Cotton expresses elsewhere. But even here there is countervailing evidence. Some lengthy sections of the document do not cite Mosaic law at all and in fact pertain to things of particular concern to New England and irrelevant to Old Testament Israel. For example, Cotton proposes laws protecting the fishing trade and requiring every person to live within a mile from the church meeting-place.[70] Cotton also appeals to natural law to help to justify a couple of provisions.[71] Other laws deal with matters peculiar to the English common law tradition, such as the regulation of jury selection.[72] And some laws, like the prohibition of selling to the Indians goods that might be used against the colonists, simply seem to reflect common sense.[73] It is difficult to

---

67. Perhaps no single statement sums up Cotton's attitude better than this: "It is a part of the happiness of Christian nations that they are subject to the Laws of that commonwealth of Israel"; see Cotton, "How Far Moses," 284. His writings offer numerous examples of attempts to constrain appeals to typology, over against Williams; see, e.g., Cotton, *A Reply to Mr. Williams,* 42-43; and Cotton, *The Bloody Tenet Washed,* 67, 72, 113, 177. For helpful discussions of the importance of typology in Williams' case for differentiating the contemporary social order from that of Old Testament Israel, in contrast to Cotton's views, see, e.g., Davis, *The Moral Theology of Roger Williams,* 29-33; Emerson, *John Cotton,* 139; and Polishook, *Roger Williams,* 32-33.

68. E.g., the requirement in section IV.8 that no land in a town be sold to people outside of that town; see Cotton, "Abstract," 563.

69. E.g., the requirement in section VII.8, based on appeal to 1 Corinthians 5:5, that revilers of religion and the church be banished; see Cotton, "Abstract," 566.

70. See sections III.2 and IV.4 in Cotton, "Abstract," 561, 562-63.

71. See sections IV.5-6 in Cotton, "Abstract," 565.

72. See section IX.3 in Cotton, "Abstract," 568.

73. See section V.2 in Cotton, "Abstract," 564.

make dogmatic conclusions about this document, but I suggest, based upon all of the evidence taken together, that this is an eclectic collection of laws derived from various sources, Mosaic law of course being particularly prominent.[74] The provisions deal with a variety of issues from those universal to human society to those quite particular to the needs of colonial New England. With a few exceptions, nothing in them is fundamentally inconsistent with Cotton's theoretical position regarding judicial and natural law outlined above.

The second test case for the claim that Cotton was within the Reformed natural law tradition comes from some comments that he makes to Williams: "Seeing he [God] hath expressly authorized civil Magistracy in the New-Testament, and hath given no express Laws or Rules of Righteousness for them to walk by in Administration of civil Justice, therefore either he leaveth them to act and rule without a Rule (which derogateth from the perfection of Scripture:) or else they must fetch their rules of Righteousness from the Law of Moses and from the Prophets, who have expounded him in the Old-Testament."[75] To put it colloquially, Cotton seems to say that since the New Testament is silent on civil law, it is Moses or nothing. By suggesting that refusal to make Moses the standard for civil law leaves no biblical standard and hence compromises the perfection of Scripture (i.e., its sufficiency), he implies that the doctrine of *sola scriptura* applies to the matter of civil law. Clearly this was not the sixteenth- and seventeenth-century Reformed view. If Cotton's words here are taken at face-value, then he expresses a position out of Reformed bounds. But fairness suggests that this statement be read in the context of all else that he writes, and this suggestion is bolstered by the fact that when he repeats a short while later that it is Moses or nothing he then adds the usual qualifier about moral equity.[76]

In conclusion, Cotton's relation to the Reformed natural law tradition is similar to his relation to the Reformed two kingdoms tradition. He is clearly influenced by the common Reformed categories of his day and utilizes them in many places in his corpus. Yet his zeal to defend the New England way

---

74. See relevant comments by Ziff, *The Career of John Cotton*, 104; Haskins, *Law and Authority*, 111; and Emerson, *John Cotton*, 144. For discussion more generally about the fallacy of an overly-biblicistic interpretation of early New England law and the other relevant legal sources, such as the common law, see, e.g., Haskins, *Law and Authority*, 4-7, and ch. 9; Eusden, "Natural Law and Covenant Theology," 3, 12-15; Emerson, *John Cotton*, 146; and Hall, *Separating Church and State*, 54-55.

75. Cotton, *The Bloody Tenet Washed*, 177-78.

76. Cotton, *The Bloody Tenet Washed*, 193.

with its civil enforcement of religious purity produced a less than fully consistent presentation of the issues and resulted in lingering tensions in his discussions of the social controversies of his day.

Virginia Presbyterians and Religious Disestablishment

At the beginning of this chapter, I posed Stuart Robinson's claim that there were two traditions on church-state relations in America, the New England and Virginia models, and that the latter, not the former, was the true heir to the original sixteenth-century Scottish Presbyterian vision. In the preceding study of John Cotton, we observed the continuing presence of the Reformed natural law and two kingdoms traditions in New England, albeit in sometimes ambiguous and inconsistent form, mixed as they were with the vigorous defense of civil enforcement of religious purity. Now we turn to the Virginia model in order to test further the Robinson proposal.

This section, then, will primarily examine the remarkable actions of the Hanover Presbytery in Virginia as it presented numerous memorials to the state legislature in the decade after the Declaration of Independence and played a crucial role in the eventual disestablishment of the Anglican church in Virginia and in passage of the Statute for Religious Freedom, which was championed especially by Thomas Jefferson and James Madison and served as a model for the First Amendment of the United States Constitution. I argue here that while the Virginia Presbyterians certainly came to support a greatly different social vision from that of the New England Puritans, they seem often to have been driven less by theological principle than by pragmatic concerns driven by various political winds. In the end, Presbyterians in Virginia and throughout America came somewhat hesitantly to embrace the idea that civil government should stay out of the church's affairs (even while continuing to promote general Protestant Christianity informally), but they did not come to any strong convictions that the church should refrain from offering its own wisdom to the state concerning its handling of civil affairs.

The Early American and Virginian Presbyterian Experience

Before specific consideration of the post-Revolutionary Virginia Presbyterians, a few comments about the origins of American Presbyterianism, particularly in Virginia, may be helpful for understanding later events. The story of American Presbyterianism often begins with the work of Francis Mackemie (1658-1708), an immigrant from Ulster who did pioneering work in Virginia and elsewhere in the American colonies.[77] For present purposes, perhaps the most significant thing to note about Mackemie's labors is the shadow of repression under which they were done. When Mackemie ministered in Virginia all dissenters from the Church of England found themselves in an unfavorable legal situation and those wishing to preach required special permission from the colonial government, which Mackemie secured in 1699. Under even more trying circumstances, Mackemie was actually prosecuted in New York on the charge of preaching without a license and using rites in a worship service not found in the Anglican Book of Common Prayer. Though acquitted of the charge, he was required to pay fees to the court and prosecutors.[78] The American Presbyterian experience began as a legally burdened dissenting group.

That these original American Presbyterians' experience as dissenters may have begun eroding some common Reformed views on church and state at an early date finds support in certain events surrounding the Adopting Act of 1729. This Act by the Synod of Philadelphia made subscription to the Westminster Standards a requirement for its ministers and sought to define the meaning of such subscription. Though members of this gathering did not entirely agree amongst themselves as to what confessional subscription ought to mean, there was broad consensus that scruples about the Confession of Faith's statements about the civil magistrate were permissible for ministers in good standing.[79]

The origins of what was to become the first presbytery in Virginia can be traced to a small group in Hanover County in the late 1730s. Having fallen under the influence of revival-friendly New Light Presbyterian preachers and of transcripts of some sermons by the great evangelist George Whitefield, this group adopted generally Reformed convictions, dissented from the Anglican church, and was summoned by Governor Gooch to ac-

---

77. See Leonard J. Trinterud, *The Forming of an American Tradition: A Re-examination of Colonial Presbyterianism* (Philadelphia: Westminster, 1949), 29-34; Ernst Trice Thompson, *Presbyterians in the South*, vol. 1: *1607-1861* (Richmond: John Knox, 1963), 20-25; and William Henry Foote, *Sketches of Virginia: Historical and Biographical* (1850; reprinted Richmond: John Knox, 1966), 40-41.

78. See Foote, *Sketches of Virginia*, 48-49, ch. 3; and Trinterud, *The Forming of an American Tradition*, 33.

79. See Trinterud, *The Forming of an American Tradition*, 48-50; and D. G. Hart, "American Presbyterianism: Exceptional," *Journal of Presbyterian History* 84, no. 1 (Spring/Summer 2006), 13.

count for their actions. Gooch recognized them as Presbyterians (though they were not yet actually such) and granted them official toleration. New Light Presbyterian churches from the middle colonies soon sent some itinerant preachers to organize and support this fledgling group. The work of these preachers and perhaps especially the itinerant character of their ministry apparently aroused considerable opposition among the religious and civil authorities, and by April of 1747 the governor had promulgated a decree forbidding them to hold religious services or other meetings.[80]

Crucial for the maturing of this group, which was eventually organized as the Hanover Presbytery in 1755, was the arrival of the recently ordained Samuel Davies (1723-61) in 1748. By all accounts an intelligent, refined, and winsome man, Davies labored in Virginia for eleven years until he accepted the presidency of the Log College in Princeton shortly before his untimely death at age 37. During those eleven years, Davies not only ministered to the spiritual needs of the Virginia Presbyterians but also became their chief advocate in an ongoing and tedious battle for religious toleration. Among the key matters of dispute was whether the English Toleration Act of 1689, which granted dissenters certain rights within the broader framework of an Anglican establishment, applied in Virginia and, if so, how its requirements that dissenting preachers be licensed and their houses of worship be registered should be implemented. Though their legal struggles with the established church in Virginia would continue for several more decades, Davies is widely credited with advancing the Presbyterians' cause in significant ways and plowing the soil for their later efforts to secure much broader religious liberty.[81] Some scholars, in fact, have seen Davies' influence not only in his

---

80. For discussion of the early days of the Hanover Presbytery, see, e.g., Trinterud, *The Forming of an American Tradition*, 129-30; George William Pilcher, *Samuel Davies: Apostle of Dissent in Colonial Virginia* (Knoxville: University of Tennessee Press, 1971), ch. 2; Rhys Isaac, *The Transformation of Virginia: 1740-1790* (New York: W. W. Norton & Company, 1982), 148-50; Philip N. Mulder, "Converting the New Light: Presbyterian Evangelicalism in Hanover, Virginia," *Journal of Presbyterian History* 75, no. 3 (Fall 1997): 141-47; and Foote, *Sketches of Virginia*, chs. 7-8. On the particularly provocative effect of their itinerant preaching, see also Lambert, *The Founding Fathers*, 125, and ch. 5.

81. On the life and work of Davies generally, see Pilcher, *Samuel Davies*. For additional discussion of his perennial legal struggles over toleration for Presbyterians, see also Mulder, "Converting the New Light," 147-49; Trinterud, *The Forming of an American Tradition*, 130, 231-32; Foote, *Sketches of Virginia*, ch. 10; Isaac, *The Transformation of Virginia*, 151-54; and Dan M. Hockman, "Hellish and Malicious Incendiaries: Commissary William Dawson and Dissent in Colonial Virginia, 1743-1752," *Anglican and Episcopal History* 59, no. 2 (1990): 150-80. For other studies indicating the breadth of Davies' interests and accomplishments, see, e.g., Richard M. Gummere,

often successful legal argumentation before civil officials but also in his rousing of patriotic sentiments. Allegedly he spurred military recruiting among Presbyterians during the French and Indian War, whose effects were felt especially hard in some areas of Virginia where Presbyterianism was strong. Such efforts, it is argued, softened many Anglican hearts toward these dissenters who contributed valiantly to this civil cause.[82]

Against this background it is not surprising that some have seen the early Virginia Presbyterians as champions of the separation of church and state as this idea came to be popularly understood later in American history. A considerable amount of countervailing evidence clouds this idealistic picture, however. As a number of scholars have explored, many Presbyterian ministers in Virginia and elsewhere used their pulpits to promote political causes and spurred on their congregations with visions of an earthly millennial kingdom that the church would help to usher in.[83] As the Revolution approached, an increasing number of American Presbyterians also came to embrace Whig and republican political sentiments, and though these sentiments strongly favored the cause of religious liberty, they also intertwined religious and civil liberty in ways that tended to make the causes of (the Protestant) church and (the nascent American) state a unified cause.[84]

"Samuel Davies: Classical Champion of Religious Freedom," *Journal of Presbyterian History* 40, no. 2 (June 1962): 67-74; and Jeffrey H. Richards, "Samuel Davies and the Transatlantic Campaign for Slave Literacy in Virginia," *The Virginia Magazine of History and Biography* 111, no. 4 (2003): 333-78.

82. On Davies' recruiting role in the French and Indian War, see Pilcher, *Samuel Davies*, 76, 85, 164-67; H. J. Eckenrode, *Separation of Church and State in Virginia: A Study in the Development of the Revolution* (1910; reprinted New York: Da Capo, 1971), 34; and Foote, *Sketches of Virginia*, 307-9; but for a less sanguine view of the importance of this activity for the cause of Presbyterian religious liberty, see Isaac, *The Transformation of Virginia*, 153-54.

83. On Davies' linkage of Christianity and patriotism, even from the pulpit, see, e.g., Pilcher, *Samuel Davies*, 76, 85, 164-67; Foote, *Sketches of Virginia*, 282-84; Alan Heimert, *Religion and the American Mind: From the Great Awakening to the Revolution* (Cambridge: Harvard University Press, 1966), 96, 327-30; and an excerpt from a Davies sermon in 1760 that includes a gushing eulogy for King George II upon his recent demise, in "Presbyterians and the American Revolution: A Documentary Account," *Journal of Presbyterian History* 52, no. 4 (Winter 1974): 325-27. On the preaching of politics from the pulpit by John Witherspoon, the widely influential Scot who served as president of Princeton, see, e.g., Trinterud, *The Forming of an American Tradition*, 249-50.

84. On the growing attachment of Presbyterians to Whig and republican politics, including Witherspoon's important role in this development, see, e.g., Lambert, ch. 7 and 207, 243-44; Hood, *Reformed America*, 12, 53-54, 126; Noll, *America's God*, ch. 5; Trinterud, *The Forming of an American Tradition*, 252, 256-57; Darryl Hart, *A Secular Faith: Why Christianity Favors the Separation of Church and State* (Chicago: Ivan R. Dee, 2006), 46-52; James H. Smylie, "We, the Presbyterian Peo-

Given Davies' embodiment of many of these various factors and his significance for the development of Virginia Presbyterianism, especially regarding its identity as a dissenting group constantly struggling to protect and expand its rights, a brief discussion of his theological perspective on church and state may provide helpful background for later developments among the churches he served. A recently republished sermon that Davies preached in 1756, at the outset of the French and Indian War, is particularly revealing for purposes of the present study. In it one can see expressed, here in the unique cultural circumstances of mid-eighteenth-century colonial Virginia, much of the classical Reformed perspective, including even that of Cotton's New England, on matters of religion and social life.

One striking aspect of this sermon, based generally on Jesus' declaration of his own kingship before Pilate in John 18:37, is its vibrant articulation of the traditional Reformed two kingdoms doctrine. Early in the sermon he announces that his purpose is to inquire into the nature of the "kingdom of Christ" considered "in contrast with the kingdoms of the earth."[85] After echoing the sentiments of Calvin some two centuries earlier that Jewish expectations of a "secular prince" were "carnal" and "unhappy prejudices,"[86] Davies makes the by now familiar distinction between the "mediatorial kingdom of Christ" and the kingdom that he exercises "as God . . . over all the works of his hands." It is the former kingdom, he says, that is "an empire of grace," that secures "salvation of fallen sinners of our race by the gospel," and that is "the kingdom of heaven."[87] While the kingdoms of the world have laws that extend "only to outward actions," the kingdom of Christ has laws that "reach the heart, and the principle of action within."[88] Kings of the earth have their own ministers of state but Christ has angels and "ministers, of an humbler form," to whom he entrusts "the ministry of reconciliation" and appoints "to preach his word, to administer his ordinances, and to manage the affairs of his kingdom."[89] Again reflecting the theological inheritance

ple: On Celebrating the Constitution of the U.S.A.," *American Presbyterians* 65, no. 4 (Winter 1987): 245-46; and Thomas E. Buckley, S.J., *Church and State in Revolutionary Virginia, 1776-1787* (Charlottesville: University Press of Virginia, 1977), 15.

85. Samuel Davies, "The Mediatorial Kingdom and Glories of Jesus Christ," in *Political Sermons of the American Founding Era, 1730-1805*, ed. Ellis Sandoz (Indianapolis: LibertyPress, 1991), 186.

86. Davies, "The Mediatorial Kingdom," 188.

87. Davies, "The Mediatorial Kingdom," 190.

88. Davies, "The Mediatorial Kingdom," 193-94.

89. Davies, "The Mediatorial Kingdom," 194.

of Reformed orthodoxy, Davies asserts that Christ's mediatorial authority extends over all people, but in different ways depending on their character. On the one hand, the wicked rebel against Christ's authority and yet Christ constrains them in order to make all things subservient to his redemptive purposes. Over the righteous, on the other hand, Christ exercises a government of special grace in order to make them happy subjects of the coming kingdom of glory.[90] Davies also makes the classic Reformed distinction between the two kingdoms in terms of their different weapons, and he does so with moving eloquence: "Other kingdoms are often founded in blood, and many lives are lost on both sides in acquiring them. The kingdom of Christ, too, was founded in blood; but it was the blood of his own heart: life was lost in the conflict; but it was his own; his own life lost, to purchase life for his people. Others have waded to empire through the blood of mankind, and even of their own subjects, but Christ shed only his own blood to spare that of his soldiers. . . . How amiable does his character appear, in contrast with that of the kings of the earth!"[91] And shortly thereafter he adds: "Other kings have their arms, their swords, their cannons, and other instruments of destruction; and with these they acquire and defend their dominions. Jesus, our king, has his arms too, but O! of how different a kind! The force of evidence and conviction in his doctrine, attested with miracles, the energy of his dying love, the gentle, and yet efficacious influence of his holy spirit; these are the weapons with which he conquered the world. His gospel is the great magazine from whence his apostles, the first founders of his kingdom, drew their arms; and with these they subdued the nations to the obedience of faith."[92]

Davies had apparently learned his Reformed two kingdoms theology well. But this sermon reveals that he had also absorbed other aspects of the Reformed tradition, especially those readily embraced by the New England Puritans. Though Davies expresses in this sermon a strong measure of Calvin's conception of the Christian life as a pilgrimage of suffering in the midst of a violent world,[93] he ends his message on a triumphalistic, postmillennial note. He envisions Virginia submitting itself to Christ and therefore being released from the French threat. Then he extends his vision and looks forward to the kingdoms of the earth becoming the kingdoms of Christ, the

90. Davies, "The Mediatorial Kingdom," 192-93.
91. Davies, "The Mediatorial Kingdom," 197.
92. Davies, "The Mediatorial Kingdom," 201.
93. E.g., see Davies, "The Mediatorial Kingdom," 183, 197-99.

conversion of the Jews, and the gospel's "triumph over heathenism, Mahometism, Judaism, popery, and all those dangerous errors that have infected the Christian church."[94] Thus, alongside his two kingdoms doctrine, Davies anticipates a perhaps imminent day in human history when the distinction between them seems to fade and widespread embrace of Protestant Christianity results in worldly prosperity for the saints.

An interesting confluence of influences, therefore, shaped the early decades of Virginia Presbyterianism. It was weaned on the vicissitudes of life as a dissenting body with a growing list of grievances against the Anglican establishment and heard from its most esteemed spiritual father both the historic Reformed two kingdoms (as well as natural law)[95] doctrine and an exuberant expectation of the triumph of Christianity among the nations of the world. Presbyterians in Virginia and elsewhere in America were growing suspicious of state involvement in the church, increasingly embraced Whig and republican political views for the sake of both religious and civil liberty, and continued to use their pulpits to promote political ends. Surely all of these factors played a role in shaping the Presbyterians' remarkable role in post-Revolutionary Virginia.

The Post-Revolution Memorials of the Hanover Presbytery

By 1785, the Hanover Presbytery unanimously supported Thomas Jefferson's Statute for Religious Freedom. Given the critical importance of the Presbyterians for the enactment of this statute[96] and the importance of these events in Virginia for the articulation of the First Amendment of the United States Constitution,[97] the Virginia Presbyterians may plausibly lay claim to

94. Davies, "The Mediatorial Kingdoms," 203-6.

95. On the role of natural law in the generally pro-Revolutionary thought of the American Reformed clergy, including some discussion of Davies, see especially Griffin, *Revolution and Religion*, 32, 37-38, 52, 60-61, 70.

96. On the crucial role of the Presbyterians generally in these events in Virginia, including their intriguing alliance with men such as Jefferson and James Madison, see, e.g., Lambert, *The Founding Fathers*, ch. 6 and 209; Buckley, *Church and State*, 164, 175-76; Isaac, *The Transformation of Virginia*, 291-93; Thompson, *Presbyterians in the South*, vol. 1, 97; and Trinterud, *The Forming of an American Tradition*, 269-70. On the role of another important dissenting group in Virginia, the Baptists, see generally Charles F. James, *Documentary History of the Struggle for Religious Liberty in Virginia* (1900; reprinted New York: Da Capo, 1971).

97. Buckley, *Church and State*, ix, states: "Ultimately the Old Dominion separated church and state in a way substantially identifiable with later America law and practice, for in its articula-

being leaders in shaping the emerging American consensus on religious freedom and the separation of church and state. Such a claim of course concurs with Stuart Robinson's thesis about the two American traditions, and some others have argued along these lines.[98] Many other scholars, however, have complicated this portrayal of things by noting the ambiguities, internal divisions, and waffling displayed by the Hanover Presbytery in response to the very concrete events that they faced over nearly a decade.[99] This evidence suggests that the Virginia Presbyterians were not nearly as principled as might be suspected (or perhaps hoped) but operated, along with some significant theological doctrines, with a considerable degree of self-interest and sought something less than modern notions of the separation of church and state. An examination of the series of memorials that the Presbytery sent to the state legislature between 1776 and 1785 seems to confirm the latter interpretation.

I turn now to this examination. A first thing to notice about the five memorials under consideration is that they were not all addressing the same specific questions nor always taking the same position when they were. The first, from October, 1776, primarily argued against having any religious establishment in the newly independent American state. In April, 1777, the Presbytery's second memorial urged the legislature not to impose any general assessment, that is, a tax to support religious activity. Seven years later, however, the third memorial was not really concerned about getting the state out of religion but instead berated the legislature for failure to remove all civil preferences given to the Episcopalian church. This subtle change in focus became more explicit in the fourth memorial, of October, 1784. Whereas the second memorial had rejected entirely the idea of a general assessment,

---

tion of the issues and their ultimate resolution, Virginia provided the rationale and the preliminary draft for the First Amendment and its later interpretation."

98. E.g., Foote, *Sketches of Virginia*, 341. Foote was a mentor of Robinson in his youth, as described by Graham, *A Kingdom Not of This World*, 14-15. Foote's interpretation is reflected in Robinson's take on these events in, e.g., "Relation of the Temporal and Spiritual Powers," 214-16; and "Two Theories," 224-27. Also see Thompson, *Presbyterians in the South*, vol. 1, 104-5; and Eckenrode, *Separation of Church and State*, 88-91, for attempts to minimize the significance of apparent change of opinion by the Hanover Presbytery on key issues.

99. For relevant discussion and argument of this interpretation, see, e.g., Hamburger, *Separation of Church and State*, 9-10, ch. 4; Fred J. Hood, "Revolution and Religious Liberty: The Conservation of the Theocratic Concept in Virginia," *Church History* 40, no. 2 (June 1971): 170-81; James, *A Documentary History*, 47; Thomas E. Buckley, S.J., "Church-State Settlement in Virginia: The Presbyterian Contribution," *Journal of Presbyterian History* 54, no. 1 (Spring 1976): 105-19; Buckley, *Church and State*, 175-82; and Curry, "Church and State," 261-73.

the fourth rejected a call for the incorporation of clergy from all denominations but gave its approval to a general assessment that promised to benefit them along with the Episcopalians on an equitable basis. Yet less than a year later, in August of 1785, the Presbytery changed its advice and again rejected the general assessment and called for adoption of the Statute for Religious Freedom.[100] To put this decade-long drama in brief, the Virginia Presbyterians initially called for no established church and no state support for any church, then turned their attention to complain about state preference for the Episcopalians and to support a general assessment so long as they were included, and then reverted back to their original sentiments.

This suggests that though they were certainly never shy about seeking their own interests, the Virginia Presbyterians lacked a clear and consistent view of what church-state relations ought to look like. This raises the question as to what rationales the Presbytery presented to the legislature in making its various appeals. The answer is that it offered a great number of them, from theological and ecclesiological arguments grounded in the Reformed tradition to political and pragmatic concerns geared to win sympathy to their cause at the moment. Though their ways of reasoning might well be classified in different ways, I identify at least six distinct sorts of arguments that could be categorized as political or pragmatic and at least five as theological or ecclesiological.

The three sorts of arguments that I identify as political are notable for owing more to the rhetoric of the European Enlightenment than to anything emanating from traditional Reformed circles. In fact, one sort, utilized on several occasions, reminded the legislature that they live in an "enlightened age" and should exercise "philosophic and liberal discernment" in considering the contemporary issues.[101] Second, the Presbytery twice called upon the lawmakers to recognize the "unalienable" right of all people to practice religion according to the dictates of their conscience.[102] And third, these Presbyterians repeatedly asserted the popular Whig contention concerning the necessary connection between civil and religious liberty: protecting the latter supports the former, and the revolutionary spirit of Virginia entails the promotion of both.[103]

The three sorts of pragmatic arguments support, as one might expect,

---

100. The texts of these memorials may be found in several sources, including Foote, *Sketches of Virginia*, 323-44.

101. See Memorials 1, 3, and 4; in Foote, *Sketches of Virginia*, 323, 334, 337.

102. See Memorials 1, 2, and 5 ; in Foote, *Sketches of Virginia*, 324, 327, 342.

103. See Memorials 1, 2, and 3; in Foote, *Sketches of Virginia*, 323, 326, 333-34.

different positions depending on the need of the hour. On the one hand, when seeking to persuade the state to get its hands off the church and its affairs in the first and last memorials, the Presbytery instructed the legislature that religious establishments tend to harm the common good.[104] On the other hand, when positioning itself to get a share of the revenue from a general assessment, the Presbytery asserted that the state should "seek its [the churches'] alliance and solicit its aid in a civil view," on the grounds that churches have a positive effect upon public morality and encourage oaths to be taken more seriously.[105] In a different vein, it utilized what might be considered a kind of *reductio ad absurdum* argument, essentially warning the legislature that once they embraced rationales to support and favor one religious group those same rationales could serve to justify all sorts of results that they would never desire. Moving in different directions, it argued both that any argument that could support the establishment of Christianity could also support the establishment of Islam and that making the state competent to judge between Christianity and other religions would also make it competent to judge between different forms of Christianity.[106]

Many of the theological and ecclesiological rationales utilized by the Presbytery reflect the Reformed two kingdoms tradition of which they were heirs. First, they appealed to the spiritual nature of Christ's kingdom.[107] Conversely, and secondly, they also reminded the legislature that its own authority was only "civil" and "temporal."[108] A third sort of argument gets to an issue which I have noted as a point of incoherence among several earlier Reformed theologians. Whereas Cotton and many of his contemporaries required (non–theologically trained) magistrates to make rather precise theological judgments in order to carry out their duty to protect religious purity, the Hanover Presbytery on at least one occasion dismissed the civil magistrate as incompetent to judge which of the different Christian churches de-

104. See Memorials 1 and 5; in Foote, *Sketches of Virginia,* 324, 343.

105. See Memorial 4; in Foote, *Sketches of Virginia,* 337.

106. See Memorials 1 and 5, in Foote, *Sketches of Virginia,* 323-24, 343.

107. See Memorials 1 and 4, in Foote, *Sketches of Virginia,* 324, 337. In the former, the Presbytery states: "We rather conceive that when our blessed Saviour declares his *kingdom is not of this world,* he renounces all dependence upon state power, and as his *weapons are spiritual,* and were only designed to have influence on the judgment, and heart of man."

108. See Memorials 1, 2, 4, and 5; in Foote, *Sketches of Virginia,* 324, 326-27, 337, 342. The first is typical: "We would humbly represent, that the only proper objects of civil government, are the happiness and protection of men in the present state of existence; the security of the life, liberty, and property of the citizens; and to restrain the vicious and encourage the virtuous by wholesome laws, equally extending to every individual."

served preference, without, that is, "erecting a chair of infallibility, which would lead us back to the church of Rome."[109] A fourth sort of theological argument is also noteworthy in that it too corrects a matter that I have identified as a point of seeming incoherence in the earlier Reformed tradition. Whereas their Reformed forebears had turned to the civil magistrate's sword to protect the flock from religious seduction, the Virginia Presbyterians in almost all of their memorials asserted that the church and its gospel, resting on the providence and promises of God, did not need the magistrate's assistance in order to accomplish its divinely appointed tasks.[110] Finally, the Presbytery argued vigorously against a proposal to incorporate, or give special legal recognition to, ministers of the gospel, even if ministers of all Protestant denominations were included. Asserting that ministers derive their authority from a higher source than the civil government and are entrusted with the care of souls and other spiritual things, it denied to the state the power to make a distinction among citizens (laical and clerical) "on account of something entirely foreign from civil merit."[111]

In summary, the arguments employed by the Hanover Presbytery seem nothing if not eclectic. They take considerations drawn from the Reformed two kingdoms tradition, even seeing their application with greater clarity than many of their predecessors, and combine them with appeals drawn from philosophical notions of the European Enlightenment and from pragmatic hunches about the ill effects of potential courses of action. Sometimes the different lines of argument are combined in ways that seem amusing in hindsight. For example, the Presbytery at one point spoke about the spiritual nature of the ministerial office and duties — an undeniably theological claim — and then appealed to the legislature's "philosophical and liberal discernment" as reason why they should understand this.[112] Though an argument can certainly be made that these Virginia Presbyterians began to see implications of the two kingdoms framework that their earlier tradition had not perceived, one must also account for the fact that they were at least sorely tempted throughout the process to bless direct civil promotion of religion on the condition that no other denomination was given preference over them.

---

109. See Memorial 1; in Foote, *Sketches of Virginia*, 323-24.
110. See Memorials 1, 2, 4, and 5; in Foote, *Sketches of Virginia*, 324, 327, 337, 342.
111. See Memorial 4; in Foote, *Sketches of Virginia*, 336.
112. See Memorial 4; in Foote, *Sketches of Virginia*, 337.

American Revision of the Westminster Confession

However groping the approach of the Virginia Presbyterians may seem to a twenty-first-century reader, by the mid 1780s they had publicly and unmistakably identified themselves with the burgeoning liberal American approach to church-state relations. Yet what exactly was this emerging approach to which the Hanover Presbytery gave their assent? It seems safe to say that this approach broke with the past in excluding the state from any direct control or support of the churches. And this was indeed a significant break from so much earlier Reformed doctrine and practice. But clearly the Virginia Presbyterians did not move in the opposite direction, for they continued to serve the state with a regular dose of counsel. Indeed, the very fact that they helped to secure religious freedom in their state by repeatedly sending memorials to the state legislature telling it what it ought to do offers ample proof of this observation.

The extant evidence suggests that Presbyterians throughout the new American states had come to share the convictions of their Virginia colleagues, both in their desire to keep the civil government out of ecclesiastical affairs and in their expectation that the church would remain an active participant in civil affairs. The former conviction enmeshed serious Presbyterians in an ecclesiastical difficulty, however, for their Confession of Faith, to which Presbyterian ministers and elders had subscribed under oath for nearly a century and a half, explicitly entrusted the magistrate with responsibilities to protect true religion. Though scruples to these confessional provisions had been permitted in America for many decades, something more drastic seemed necessary since this could no longer be considered the view of the church. Not surprisingly, then, the highest judicatory of the American Presbyterian Church, the Synod of New York and Philadelphia, in 1788 officially revised the *Westminster Confession of Faith* (WCF) on several points pertaining to the civil magistrate. Though the change was so significant, the revision seems to have generated little controversy — and proportionately little scholarly study from that day to the present.[113]

The revisions themselves seem perfectly in line with the perspective of the Hanover Presbytery as interpreted above. In modifying chapters 20, 23, and 31 of the WCF, the church consistently stripped magistrates of authority

---

113. One recent article explores and analyzes the confessional revision at some length; see Hart, "American Presbyterianism." Trinterud, *The Forming of an American Tradition*, 305, amazingly dedicates just one sentence to this event.

over the church's affairs and bound them to protect the good name of all people no matter what their religious affiliations.[114] What the revisions did not do was address issues pertaining to the church's involvement in civil affairs. The WCF, explicitly and implicitly, already said things about this subject, but it would remain to mid-nineteenth-century Presbyterians to joust over how this teaching was to apply,[115] a topic to which we will turn our attention momentarily. For the time being, American Presbyterians seemed content to keep their churches on the forefront of social life in order to contribute to the civil good and to hasten the onset of the millennial kingdom permeated by Christian ideals. In addition, many Presbyterians of the early nineteenth century eagerly participated in the work of inter-denominational voluntary societies designed to achieve similar goals through promotion of a variety of religious and civil activities. Their vision was clearly far from that of a secularized nation or naked public square.[116]

At the end of this section it is interesting to reflect upon all of this in the light of contemporary debates about broader American church-state relations. While scholars such as Frank Lambert, Isaac Kramnick, and R. Laurence Moore present a case for a secular reading of the First Amendment that gives no special place to Christianity, Philip Hamburger argues that the First Amendment was intended to protect a religious liberty very different from the Jeffersonian and common contemporary notion of a wall of separation between church and state.[117] Though the complex historical

114. For discussion of these points, see Hart, "American Presbyterianism," 14.

115. A possible objection to this blanket statement is the fact that in 1788 the Synod also approved its Plan of Government, which made a strong affirmation that the church's power is only ministerial and declarative and that the church may legislate no rules binding on the conscience, remarking that it is more dangerous for the church to grasp legislative power than for it to misinterpret biblical laws; see Trinterud, *The Forming of an American Tradition*, 297-98. Though such statements have great bearing on the question of ecclesiastical involvement in civil affairs, the possible extent of the implications of such statements did not seem to trouble American Presbyterians seriously for many more decades.

116. Of particular importance here is the study of Hood, *Reformed America*, who treats these developments in the late-eighteenth- and early-nineteenth-century middle and southern states in considerable detail. See also Buckley, *Church and State*, 179-82 on the Virginia Presbyterians. On John Witherspoon's influential views concerning civil religion, see Jeffry H. Morrison, *John Witherspoon and the Founding of the American Republic* (Notre Dame: University of Notre Dame Press, 2005), ch. 2. On American Presbyterians more broadly, see Hart, "American Presbyterianism," 15; and Griffin, *Revolution and Religion*, ch. 6.

117. See Lambert, *The Founding Fathers;* Isaac Kramnick and R. Laurence Moore, *The Godless Constitution: A Moral Defense of the Secular State* (New York: W. W. Norton, 2005); and Hamburger, *Separation of Church and State.*

and normative issues at stake in this debate are beyond the pale of the present book, the preceding discussion at least confirms Hamburger's claim that most dissenters at the American Founding (in this case, the Presbyterians) were concerned to eliminate religious establishments rather than to erect a secular Jeffersonian wall of separation. The events in Virginia and the subsequent adoption of the First Amendment gave to Presbyterians their wish of a church generally free of state control. But their church continued to project its voice in the affairs of the state and other social organizations, though this activity would soon come to be challenged from within.

Nineteenth-Century Presbyterianism and the Spirituality of the Church

A key idea that served to challenge this activity was the doctrine of the spirituality of the church, an issue that came to prominence in some Presbyterian debates during the Civil War era. The spirituality doctrine was closely related to the idea of *jure divino* Presbyterianism, a matter that had reared its head at about the same time. The connection between these doctrines was that both placed significant constraints upon the power of the church to speak and act. *Jure divino,* or divine right, Presbyterianism asserted that, in Scripture, God had ordained Presbyterian church government, commissioned the church and its officers to perform certain functions, and prescribed the modes by which it could carry out these functions. The church was not only obliged to organize itself and exercise its responsibilities according to this biblical teaching but was also prohibited from adding anything to it. The doctrine of the spirituality of the church, on the other hand, indicated that the church's only concern was with spiritual (as opposed to temporal or civil) things, and thus that the church was generally prohibited from expressing views about civil affairs. A concise summary might be to say that these two doctrines ascribed to the church authority to exist and act according to Scripture only and to address itself to spiritual matters only.

This section will discuss these issues through an examination of three significant mid-nineteenth-century American Presbyterian theologians. First, I look at the writings of Kentucky professor and pastor Stuart Robinson, a leading voice among border-state Presbyterians and later a respected figure in the Southern Presbyterian church.[118] Then I examine the ex-

118. Robinson's stature is indicated by the fact that the 1869 Southern Presbyterian General

changes on both *jure divino* Presbyterianism and the spirituality of the church between probably the two greatest American Presbyterian theologians of the era, Charles Hodge of Princeton Seminary and James Henley Thornwell of South Carolina. Of particular interest here for purposes of the present book is how advocates of these doctrines, though in some cases cutting against the grain of much historic Reformed practice, grounded the doctrines in the Reformed theological tradition and especially in Reformed two kingdoms categories, both explicitly and implicitly. The provenance of these doctrines, especially spirituality, exercised not only mid-nineteenth-century Presbyterians but also many subsequent scholars looking back upon the debates of this era. While some have tended to view the spirituality doctrine as a creation of the Southern and/or border states for the purpose of keeping the church from condemning slavery, others have tended to see its advocates as more principled and as genuinely trying to apply historic Reformed ideas.[119]

Assembly, which received a great number of the border-state churches (including Robinson's) into their number, elected him to be its moderator; see Graham, *A Kingdom Not of This World,* 166.

119. For studies of the spirituality doctrine in nineteenth-century Presbyterianism that tend to see the strong positions of a Robinson or Thornwell as an innovation in relation to the Reformed tradition and the Southern embrace of the doctrine as largely motivated by the slavery issue, see, e.g., Ernst Trice Thompson, *The Spirituality of the Church: A Distinctive Doctrine of the Presbyterian Church in the United States* (Richmond: John Knox, 1961); Ernst Trice Thompson, *Presbyterians in the South,* vol. 2: *1861-1890* (Richmond: John Knox, 1973), ch. 15; Jack P. Maddex, "From Theocracy to Spirituality: The Southern Presbyterian Reversal on Church and State," *Journal of Presbyterian History* 54 (Winter 1976): 438-57; Robert Ellis Thompson, *The American Church History Series,* vol. 6, *A History of the Presbyterian Church in the United States* (New York: Charles Scribner's Sons, 1900), 153-55, 168-71; Alan D. Strange, "2001 Preface to Charles Hodge's *The Church and Its Polity,*" *Mid-America Journal of Theology* 13 (2002): 32-33; and E. Brooks Holifield, *The Gentlemen Theologians: American Theology in Southern Culture, 1795-1860* (Durham: Duke University Press, 1978), 154. For studies of the spirituality doctrine that tend to see it as rooted in the Reformed tradition and as part of Southern Presbyterian convictions not simply because of slavery, see Graham, *A Kingdom Not of This World;* and D. G. Hart, *Recovering Mother Kirk: The Case for Liturgy in the Reformed Tradition* (Grand Rapids: Baker Academic, 2003), ch. 3. Taking somewhat neutral positions on the origins of spirituality doctrine in the Southern Presbyterian church are James Oscar Farmer, Jr., *The Metaphysical Confederacy: John Henley Thornwell and the Synthesis of Southern Values* (Macon: Mercer University Press, 1986), 256-60 (though see 160, 259-60 for his conviction that this doctrine was a departure from the older Reformed tradition); and Joe L. Coker, "The Sinnott Case of 1910: The Changing Views of Southern Presbyterians on Temperance, Prohibition, and the Spirituality of the Church," *Journal of Presbyterian History* 77, no. 4 (Winter 1999): 248-49. For studies from different perspectives of the *jure divino* Presbyterianism issue as it came to a head in debates about church boards, to be discussed below, see A. Craig

The consistency of and motivation for Southern Presbyterian advocacy of the spirituality of the church are interesting and difficult questions, but this section will delve into them only lightly. I will argue, however, that the advocates of *jure divino* Presbyterianism and the spirituality of the church had a strong claim to seeing these doctrines as applications of historic Reformed categories and that in teaching them they avoided several of the common inconsistencies that befell their Reformed predecessors in their handling of the two kingdoms doctrine. The advocates of these doctrines, therefore, attempted to complete the re-thinking of the application of the Reformed two kingdoms doctrine begun by their eighteenth-century American Presbyterian predecessors, not only by removing the state more thoroughly from the affairs of the church but also by removing the church from the affairs of the state and other civil organizations.

Stuart Robinson on the Nature and the Authority of the Church

Stuart Robinson was born in 1814 in northern Ireland and immigrated to the United States at an early age. He received some of his primary education under William Henry Foote, chronicler of the Virginia Presbyterians' role in forging the distinctively American view of church and state, and later went to Princeton Seminary for theological training. Identified with the Old School Presbyterians (like Hodge and Thornwell), he served pastorates in Virginia, Kentucky, and Baltimore, was a professor for a brief time at the Presbyterian seminary in Danville, Kentucky, and served for many years as pastor of Second Presbyterian Church in Louisville. Robinson became well-known as a champion of the doctrine of the spirituality of the church during a time, the Civil War, when politics and patriotism were fixtures of American church life, and he promoted the doctrine for a number of years through two periodicals, the *Presbyterial Critic* and the *True Presbyterian*. His advocacy of this doctrine and, from the distinctive border-state context, his refusal to use his pulpit to promote either the Northern or Southern political cause brought him under serious social pressure that compelled him to flee to Canada in 1862 until the end of the war. In the late 1860s, the spirituality doctrine was also the moving cause in the realigning of most of the Ken-

---

Troxel, "Charles Hodge on Church Boards: A Case Study in Ecclesiology," *Westminster Theological Journal* 58 (1996): 183-207; Thompson, *Presbyterians in the South,* vol. 1, ch. 33; Farmer, *The Metaphysical Confederacy,* 185-86; and Strange, "2001 Preface," 26-27.

tucky Old School Presbyterian churches (including Robinson's) with the Southern Presbyterian church, which had embraced this doctrine over against the Old School Presbyterians of the North (the Old School churches in the Southern states had broken with those of the Northern states in 1861 to form a separate denomination).[120]

Of primary concern for Robinson in much of his writings was developing a sound ecclesiology. The very title of his most significant work indicates this: *The Church of God as an Essential Element of the Gospel, and the Idea, Structure, and Functions Thereof.* He refers in this work to "the truth that a divinely-constituted Church on earth is a fundamental fact of the revealed counsels of God"[121] and devotes Part I to showing how certain sorts of ecclesiology have corresponded historically to certain sorts of theologies. In an appendix to another one of his books from several years later, Robinson claimed that where historically the church has been purest in doctrine and practice, it has developed consciousness of the distinction between the two powers, that of church and state.[122] Through the rest of *The Church of God* Robinson does much to explore this distinction from his Reformed theological perspective, a perspective that involves much debt to the two kingdoms doctrine.

In Part II, Robinson's two kingdoms convictions begin to come to the fore as he examines the successive covenants revealed through biblical history. He claims that underlying all of these covenants is the idea that God separates a portion of the human race from the rest of it, so that when Jesus Christ, the King, comes, he does not lay claim to direct headship over the world at large, but over a kingdom not of this world.[123] God has made every revelation, ordinance, promise, and covenant not to "men as men, or as constituting nations, but to and with the Church, as such," and these revelations come "not from God as Creator to men as creatures, but from Messiah as Prophet and King over his Church to his own peculiar people.[124] All of the covenants, furthermore, have "primarily a spiritual" significance.[125] Thus

120. For extensive biographical material on Robinson, see especially Graham, *A Kingdom Not of This World.* For additional material on his context in Kentucky in the Civil War era, see also Louis B. Weeks, *Kentucky Presbyterians* (Atlanta: John Knox, 1983), chs. 5-6.

121. Robinson, *The Church of God,* 26. On the importance of ecclesiology generally for him, also see Stuart Robinson, "Our Idea" (originally published in 1855), in Graham, *A Kingdom Not of This World,* 195.

122. Robinson, "Relation of the Temporal and Spiritual Powers," 209.

123. Robinson, *The Church of God,* 49-50.

124. Robinson, *The Church of God,* 67.

125. Robinson, *The Church of God,* 55.

Robinson already expresses here the historic Reformed distinction between God's rule over all people as Creator and his spiritual rule over his church for redemptive, spiritual purposes.

In Part III, this debt to the Reformed two kingdoms tradition becomes even more evident. He affirms that the source of all power in the church is "Jesus Christ, the Mediator," who delegates this power to the church as such, to be administered by "office-bearing members" who are to rule "ministerially" in his name.[126] Reflecting both the *jure divino* and spirituality concerns described above, Robinson explains that in light of Christ being the source of all church power and his kingdom being "not of this world," the power of the church is "limited in the mode of its exercise" and "limited as to its end." The mode of its exercise is "wholly ministerial" and its end is "wholly spiritual," the latter of which means that it is "for the edification of his people, and for the Lord's business; for the peace and harmony of the Church, for the extension of the Church, and for Jehovah's glory."[127] Toward the end of this work he adds important considerations that unpack some of the implications. There he explains that "as the affairs of the spiritual kingdom of Christ are of such a nature as to preclude any human devices in the way of means and instrumentalities for administration, so also the divinely appointed agencies for the administration of these affairs preclude the idea of the use of these agencies and the power accompanying them for any other purposes than the one great purpose of the kingdom itself." That purpose is the evangelization of the world and the gathering of the elect. Thus he rejects "the too common conception of the Church as power to be used directly for the promotion of mere humanly devised reforms" or the use of preaching "as an instrumentality to rectify wrong public opinion, wrong moral views of social and civil affairs; or the conception of the courts of the Church as agencies through which to reach directly and reform civil evils and to arraign the State on national wrong-doing." All of this is "inconsistent with the fundamental nature of the Church itself." This kingdom "contemplates men only in relation to Jesus the Mediator" and "ignores all strifes and parties of the kingdom of Caesar."[128] Here the principles of *jure divino* Presbyterianism in general and the spirituality of the church in particular are spelled out by distinguishing the church as the kingdom of Christ from the kingdom of Caesar and by assigning to the former characteristics famil-

---

126. Robinson, *The Church of God*, 79-81.
127. Robinson, *The Church of God*, 84.
128. Robinson, *The Church of God*, 123-24.

iar from earlier two kingdoms theology, such as the ministerial nature of its authority and its spiritual ends.

The most striking aspect of Part III of *The Church of God* for present purposes, however, is his utilization of classic Reformed two kingdoms categories in laying out five ways in which the civil and ecclesiastical powers "differ fundamentally." First, the one "derives its authority from God as the Author of nature" and the other only "from Jesus as Mediator." Second, the rule of guidance for the one is "the light of nature and reason" as revealed by "the Author of nature" and for the other is "that light which, as Prophet of the Church, Jesus Christ has revealed in his word." Third, Robinson turns to their "scope and aim." Those of the civil power are "things seen and temporal," things "political," while those of the ecclesiastical power are "things unseen and spiritual," or "religious." Except indirectly and incidentally, "the things pertaining to the kingdom of Christ are things concerning which Caesar can have rightfully no cognizance" and "the things pertaining to the kingdom of Caesar are matters of which the Church of Christ as an organic government can have no cognizance." Fourth, they differ in that "the significant symbol of the civil power is the sword" and "its government is a government of force" while "the significant symbol of Church power is the keys, its government only ministerial." Finally, the two powers differ "in that civil power may be exercised as a *several* power by one judge, magistrate, or governor; but all ecclesiastical power pertaining to government is a joint power only," since Christ has not conferred "spiritual power of jurisdiction in any form upon a single man."[129] Though Robinson specifically identifies these five distinctions, there seems also to be a sixth that he adds shortly thereafter. There he explains that the one power is "ordained of God . . . in the mercy and forebearance of the Author of nature toward the apostate race at large, to hold in check the outworking of that devilish nature consequent upon the apostasy" and to furnish a platform upon which the scheme of redemption could be accomplished. The other power "is designed to constitute of the families of earth that call upon his name, and into the hearts of which his grace has *put* enmity toward Satan and his seed, a nation of priests, a peculiar nation, not reckoned among the nations, of whom Jehovah is the God and they are his people."[130]

Robinson made similar distinctions in many other places in his writings. For example, in a letter sent to Abraham Lincoln from his Canadian ex-

129. Robinson, *The Church of God*, 84-86.
130. Robinson, *The Church of God*, 87.

ile he quotes the sixteenth-century Scot Andrew Melville, mentioned in the previous chapter, in order to remind the president of "God's two kingdoms," one of "divine authority" to coerce obedience by the power of the sword and the other "ordained of Christ the Mediator" which possesses the "power of the keys." The one "is derived from God the Author of Nature and has cognizance only of the interests that pertain to the present life of men" and the other, the "spiritual government of the Church," "is derived from Christ the mediator as its source, and can take cognizance only of men's eternal interests." The one, to which Lincoln's government belongs, "has for its rule of guidance the light of nature and reason common to all nations," which is true "whether among Christian or Heathen people" and "whether enlightened by revelation or not." The other, the "spiritual government," instead "has for its *only rule* of guidance the positive statute law in the revealed statute book of its great founder and Ruler."[131] This last distinction, the same as the second distinction in *The Church of God,* is of course of special interest for the present study, and Robinson emphasizes it in still other places. For example, he condemns as an "*unscriptural* proposition" that the "revealed will of Christ, rather than the law of nature, is the supreme law of the land — a political rule of faith and practice."[132]

It is worth noting that for Robinson these distinctions between the two kingdoms are not theological luxuries but vital to the health of Christianity. The five distinctions in *The Church of God,* he writes, "are neither accidental nor arbitrary, but spring out of those fundamental truths concerning the nature of the Church itself, and of its relations to the gospel."[133] If connecting the two kingdoms doctrine to the gospel seems exaggerated, one may recall from previous chapters that Calvin and the Reformed orthodox made the same connection, particularly through their close association of the two kingdoms doctrine with the idea of Christian liberty, which Calvin called an "appendix" to the doctrine of justification.

Alongside this connection of the two kingdoms doctrine with the gospel, Robinson also asserted that his distinctions between the "secular and spiritual" orders were essential and distinctive to "Presbyterianism as a Church

---

131. Stuart Robinson, "Rev. Stuart Robinson to President Lincoln," in Graham, *A Kingdom Not of This World,* 263-64.

132. Stuart Robinson, "The Movement for an Orthodox Constitution of the U.S. Officially Endorsed Another Stride in the Erastian Apostasy," in Graham, *A Kingdom Not of This World,* 253. For comments on Robinson's confinement of the state to general revelation only, see Graham, *A Kingdom Not of This World,* 122.

133. Robinson, *The Church of God,* 87.

Government."[134] They captured the sentiment of the Presbyterian members of the Westminster Assembly[135] and, before them, the Presbyterian convictions of the Scottish fathers and martyrs, whose ideas he was striving to carry through to their full application.[136] Yet in claiming the heritage of his Presbyterian ancestors, Robinson forthrightly and adamantly rejected their confusing of the concerns of church and state as a poisonous corruption of their true principles. Since this topic has been of significant concern over the past several chapters, Robinson's views on the matter are worth some consideration.

For Robinson, the church was to stay out of all things "political" and the state out of all things "spiritual." As seen above, the spiritual nature of the church meant that it could have "no cognizance" of the "things pertaining to the kingdom of Caesar" and should "ignore all strifes and parties of the kingdom of Caesar."[137] He had in mind, perhaps, statements like the one quoted in the previous chapter from the Scot Samuel Rutherford: "That presbyteries meddle with civil business, is a slander."[138] From the other direction, Robinson advocated remarkable positions, even by American standards. For example, he questioned the authority of the civil government to call upon churches to observe fast-days and stated that the church which he pastored had never acknowledged them. More significantly, he strongly opposed calls to amend the United States Constitution by including acknowledgement of God as the source of all power and Jesus Christ as governor of the nations. This was not only because of what he called "the political absurdity, injustice and inexpediency" of making a constitution that would require most of the population to perjure themselves when swearing to it and the "theological absurdity and danger of accepting a half creed." More importantly, it involved "heretical doctrines." He denies that it is "a function of the State in its political constitution, as of the Church in her creed, to testify the Gospel truth, that Jesus Christ the mediator, is King of nations, and has revealed his will to men." He also denies that Scripture is "a political rule of faith and practice" and rejects the notion that it is the state's duty to establish a "Christian government."[139]

---

134. See Stuart Robinson, "Prefatory to the *True Presbyterian*," in Graham, *A Kingdom Not of This World*, 222.

135. See Robinson, "Two Theories," 223.

136. E.g., see Robinson, *The Church of God*, 9-10, 64-65, 128-29; Robinson, "Two Theories," 228-29; and Robinson, "The Movement for an Orthodox Constitution," 254-55. For further comments, see Graham, *A Kingdom Not of This World*, 29.

137. Robinson, *The Church of God*, 86, 123-24.

138. Samuel Rutherford, *Lex, Rex* (1644; reprinted, Harrisonburg, VA: Sprinkle, 1982), 216.

139. Robinson, "The Movement for an Orthodox Constitution," 252-53.

In his letter to President Lincoln he spoke in similar ways, but perhaps more precisely, by saying that, though it was proper for civil government to "recognize a God — a truth of natural religion," it ought not go beyond this to acknowledge also "the revealed doctrine of the supreme divinity of Jesus Christ, the inspiration of the scriptures, and their authority as the foundation of civil government."[140] In other words, to acknowledge the existence of God as revealed in nature was acceptable but acknowledging the authority of Christ and the Scriptures was beyond the competence of the civil magistrate. Elsewhere Robinson made an interesting departure from many of his Reformed predecessors in regard to the historical fact that many pagan nations used religion for state purposes. Whereas many of the figures examined earlier in this book saw this evidence as testimony to some sort of natural law principle, Robinson saw it as evidence that the state's garbing itself in religion was of pagan rather than Christian origin (and had crept into the church in the days of Constantine).[141]

What happened then, that Reformed people, despite the clear distinction between the two kingdoms inherent in their Presbyterian polity, had so largely embraced these pagan ideas? Why had the Reformation's "views of the doctrine and order of the church," which should "have led to a restoration of the spiritual independence of Christ's kingdom," not been "permitted to work out their logical results?"[142] He blamed Calvin's inconsistency on his training as a lawyer, which had imbued him "with the ideas of the Justinian code."[143] In regard to the Scots, he notes that they lived in "a time of peril, and it seemed to human vision impossible that the Church could exist without the aid of, much less in direct conflict with, the civil power." They "did not penetrate fully" the meaning of Jesus' declaration that his kingdom was not of this world and bought "their peace with the State till the Lord might open the way before them."[144] Elsewhere he spoke of the "seductions and arts of the civil power" that cheated the Scottish church out of what was hers and he identified four reasons why "there was a general failure to actualize the theory": the Reformation was a political as well as spiritual revolution, the church was not permitted to develop their ideas since it was compelled to take shelter under the civil power, the jealousy of the civil powers squelched any attempt that was made to develop them, and the widespread

140. Robinson, "The Rev. Stuart Robinson to President Lincoln," 269.
141. Robinson, "Relation of the Temporal and Spiritual Powers," 203-5.
142. Robinson, "Relation of the Temporal and Spiritual Powers," 206.
143. Robinson, "Relation of the Temporal and Spiritual Powers," 207.
144. Robinson, *The Church of God*, 127-28.

legal notion (of the Theodosian and Justinian codes) that the state had the right to employ religion.[145] Whatever the reasons, Robinson could not have been more clear about how serious this degeneration of theory and practice was. He believed that "any form, or any degree of this error . . . must inevitably work out the slavery of the church and the corruption of the faith."[146] Elsewhere he added that "any degree of confusion in respect of this distinction is proportionably dangerous and corrupting" and that it "must ultimately work out only confusion and corruption."[147]

It is worth noting that Robinson's insistence that the church stay out of civil affairs did not mean that individual Christians, in their private, civil capacities should be socially uninvolved. Robinson himself was an entrepreneur and advised political candidates, though not in his capacity as a minister of the gospel.[148] Like his Reformed predecessors, he too had a high view of secular occupations and callings.

Stuart Robinson, then, attempted to set forth in both systematic and occasional writings a traditional Reformed two kingdoms doctrine, brought to its proper practical conclusions and purged of the inconsistent practices that his Reformed predecessors had allowed to corrupt it. I will offer some evaluation of his attempt after exploring how two of his Old School Presbyterian contemporaries, Hodge and Thornwell, addressed these sorts of issues in concrete ecclesiastical controversies, at times in debate with each other.

Hodge and Thornwell on the Limits of Ecclesiastical Authority

Charles Hodge (1787-1878) and James Henley Thornwell (1812-1862) were almost certainly the two greatest Old School Presbyterian theologians of the mid-nineteenth century, Hodge the greatest of the Northern states and Thornwell the greatest of the Southern.[149] Though allies on most of the great

---

145. Robinson, "Relation of the Temporal and Spiritual Powers," 209. See also Stuart Robinson, "The Battle of Scottish Presbyterianism during Three Centuries for a Free Christian Commonwealth," in Graham, *A Kingdom Not of This World*, 237, where his explanation was "the wily kings craft of James, his violation of pledges, his apostasy from the faith of his early life, his corrupt purchase of false ministers and his hoodwinking of moderate men," but even more "the error which the Scotch reformers retained in connection with their great truths concerning the crown rights of Jesus Christ."

146. Robinson, "The Battle of Scottish Presbyterianism," 237.

147. Robinson, *The Church of God*, 87-88, 123-24.

148. See Graham, *A Kingdom Not of This World*, 31-32.

149. For studies on Thornwell's thought, see, e.g., Farmer, *The Metaphysical Confederacy;*

theological issues of the day, they clashed on two major ecclesiastical matters in the 1850s and 1860s. One dealt with church boards and the other with the right of the church to speak about social and political issues, but both directly involved questions about the extent of the church's authority and at least indirectly the Reformed two kingdoms legacy. Thornwell advocated a position basically identical to Robinson's while Hodge, though closer to the Robinson-Thornwell position than many other American Presbyterians of his day, countered Thornwell on both matters, dismissing his Robinsonesque claim to be applying consistently the great principles of Presbyterianism. In this subsection I discuss the contribution of Hodge and Thornwell to these debates and offer some evaluation of their different interpretations of the Reformed tradition.

The church boards controversy did not immediately concern the relation of church and state, but did get to crucial questions about ecclesiastical authority that had important ramifications for the nature of the church's relations with social institutions. This controversy had its roots in the early nineteenth-century formation of a variety of voluntary societies in which many American Presbyterians participated along with Christians from other denominations. Many of these voluntary societies promoted social reform causes, but some also dealt with issues that Presbyterians had traditionally seen as the work of the church itself, such as foreign missions. While New School Presbyterians tended to be great defenders of the voluntary societies, Old School Presbyterians were concerned to defend the church's right to send out missionaries and to take up the tasks that were rightly hers. Some of these debates became moot after the New School–Old School split of 1837, but the Old School, to which Hodge and Thornwell both belonged, continued to in-fight on related issues. In the Old School Presbyterian church, church boards had taken up responsibility for missions and the like from the voluntary societies, but now some leaders in the church, Thornwell a leading light among them, began to question whether these boards, which existed semi-autonomously from the General Assembly, were the proper instru-

---

John H. Leith, "James Henley Thornwell and the Shaping of the Reformed Tradition in the South," in *Probing the Reformed Tradition: Historical Studies in Honor of Edward A. Dowey, Jr.,* ed. Elsie Anne McKee and Brian G. Armstrong (Louisville: Westminster John Knox, 1989), 424-47; and Morton H. Smith, *Studies in Southern Presbyterian Theology* (1962; reprinted Phillipsburg, NJ: P&R, 1987), 121-82. For a variety of studies on the thought of Hodge, see, e.g., *Charles Hodge Revisited: A Critical Appraisal of His Life and Work,* ed. John W. Stewart and James H. Moorhead (Grand Rapids: Eerdmans, 2002); for material in this collection particularly relevant in the present context, see Richard J. Carwardine, "The Politics of Charles Hodge," 247-97.

ments for carrying out the church's work. These issues came to a head at the 1860 General Assembly with a proposed reorganization of the Board of Domestic Missions. While Thornwell argued that the church itself had to do the work of missions and had no discretion to delegate it to other agencies, Hodge argued that such was indeed within the scope of the church's authority.[150] The Assembly sided with Hodge, but the two major figures traded journal articles publicizing their respective positions in the aftermath of this decision.

Much of Hodge's article attempted to state the basic principles of Presbyterianism over against Thornwell's view. Hodge defined the main issue in regard to church boards as whether the boards were against Christ's divine rule of the church or were both useful and entirely within the discretion that Christ had granted to the church. Specifically, according to Hodge, the debate was whether the church is wholly tied to the organizations or organs prescribed in the New Testament, such that everything relating to the government and action of the church is laid down in detail in Scripture.[151] Hodge condemned Thornwell's position, which affirmed this doctrine, as both "a peculiar theory of Presbyterianism" without historical precedent and as impossible to be put into practice even by its advocates.[152] A central aspect of Hodge's argument was the doctrine of Christian liberty. He claimed that Thornwell's idea "ties down" the government and action of the church to what is prescribed in the New Testament and, toward the end of his article, he writes: "There is as much difference between this extreme doctrine of divine right, this idea that everything is forbidden which is not commanded, as there is between this free, exultant Church of ours, and the mummified forms of mediaeval Christianity."[153]

Before turning to Thornwell's response, I note something immediately odd about Hodge's claims in the light of preceding chapters. The Reformed doctrine of Christian liberty was never about the church being freed to do things (such as create boards to which it could delegate the work of missions) about which Scripture was silent. Instead, with direct reference to the

---

150. For various studies of the rise of the voluntary societies and the church boards controversy, see Troxel, "Charles Hodge on Church Boards"; Hood, *Reformed America*, chs. 6-8; Thompson, *Presbyterians in the South*, vol. 1, ch. 33; Farmer, *Metaphysical Confederacy*, 185-86; Strange, "2001 Preface," 26-27.

151. Charles Hodge, "Presbyterianism" (originally published in 1860), in *Discussions in Church Polity* (New York: Charles Scribner's Sons, 1878), 118-19.

152. Hodge, "Presbyterianism," 118, 131-32.

153. Hodge, "Presbyterianism," 118-19, 133.

two kingdoms doctrine, Reformed theologians and confessions spoke of Christian liberty in regard to the justified individual, who was freed in the civil kingdom from any obligation to do things *contrary* to the teaching of Scripture and in the spiritual kingdom from any obligation to do things *beside* the teaching of Scripture.[154] In other words, the state has a wide discretionary authority, such that Christians must obey its commands except when they contradict Scripture, while the church has a more circumscribed authority, such that Christians must obey its commands only when its commands are the commands of Scripture. Where Scripture is silent, neither commanding nor prohibiting, the church cannot burden the conscience of Christians. This was the doctrine lying behind the distinction between the state's "legislative" power and the church's "ministerial" authority. Thus, when Hodge taught, as the Presbyterian doctrine of Christian liberty, that the church is permitted to do what is not forbidden in Scripture, he was in fact transferring the traditional Reformed standard for the civil kingdom to the spiritual kingdom and thus giving the church precisely the power (speaking and acting beyond the teaching of Scripture) that the Reformed tradition had tried to take from it.

Thornwell recognized exactly this flaw in Hodge's reasoning and relentlessly exposed it in an incisive, biting, and at times humorous response. He paid respect to Hodge's general greatness as a theologian, but lamented on the one hand the lack of candor and honor in his article and, on the other hand, his ineptness in regard to ecclesiology.[155] Key to his case was the argument that Hodge had things backwards. Hodge's principle that the church is permitted to do all that Scripture does not forbid it to do was not the Reformed principle of Christian liberty over against Rome but the principle of Rome which the Reformed doctrine of Christian liberty sought to overthrow.[156] He rejected Hodge's claim that his own position took away all discretion from the church, explaining that it was not a question of whether the church had discretion but of what sort. For Hodge, the church had discretion in regard to actions themselves, having freedom to do or not to do actions about which Scripture is silent. In contrast, Thornwell asserted that the church had no discretion in terms of its actions, for it must do only those things that Scripture commands it to do (since it has only ministerial author-

---

154. E.g., see Calvin, *Institutes*, 3.19.15-16, 4.11; and WCF, 20.2.

155. James Henley Thornwell, "Church-Boards and Presbyterianism" (originally published in 1861), in *The Collected Writings of James Henley Thornwell*, vol. 4, ed. B. M. Palmer (1875; reprinted Edinburgh: Banner of Truth, 1986), 242-44.

156. Thornwell, "Church-Boards and Presbyterianism," 253-58.

ity), but certainly did have discretion regarding *circumstances* concerning *how* it carried out its actions. Thus, the church has no discretion to create boards and to delegate its proper work to them, but so long as the church itself is doing its own work it does have discretion to erect committees *by which* the church as a whole may accomplish its divinely-mandated tasks.[157] This distinction between semi-autonomous boards to which the Church delegates its responsibilities and committees of the church whereby the church itself carries out its own responsibilities may seem to be overly subtle — Hodge certainly thought so. But whatever one thinks of the particular application, Hodge and Thornwell were reasoning from significantly different theological premises, and Thornwell seems to have had the much surer grip on the historic principles of Presbyterianism and the Reformed two kingdoms doctrine. He not only appealed perceptively to the WCF 1.6 regarding the difference between actions and circumstances and 20.2 regarding Christian liberty, but also to Calvin, the Puritans, and his Scottish Presbyterian contemporary William Cunningham to show his view's Reformed lineage. "If we have erred," he wrote, "we have no reason to be ashamed of our company."[158]

In this church boards controversy, therefore, Thornwell sought to limit the government and action of the church to the prescriptions of the Bible *only*, and did so with reference to historic Reformed convictions about the church's ministerial authority and about Christian liberty, both of which were dependent on its two kingdoms doctrine. The other area in which Hodge and Thornwell sparred during this time was the spirituality of the church. Here again the question was about the extent of the church's authority. In this case, Hodge and Thornwell wrestled with whether the church's authority was limited to addressing *spiritual* matters or whether it also extended to addressing *civil* matters. Thornwell is open to the charge of some theoretical inconsistency, was certainly guilty of practical hypocrisy,[159] and

---

157. Thornwell, "Church-Boards and Presbyterianism," 244-53.

158. Thornwell, "Church-Boards and Presbyterianism," 245-50.

159. Thornwell's practical hypocrisy is perhaps best seen in his sermon of November, 1860 encouraging secession and resistance to Northern aggression. For accounts of this sermon (and sermons of other Southern proponents of the spirituality doctrine), see Farmer, *The Metaphysical Confederacy*, 261-64; Thompson, *The Spirituality of the Church*, 28; and Thompson, *Presbyterians in the South*, vol. 2, 13. See also discussions of Thornwell's desire for the Southern Presbyterian General Assembly to send a memorial to the Confederate Congress in support of a constitutional article recognizing Christianity and the Southern Assembly's profession of loyalty to the Confederacy in Farmer, *The Metaphysical Confederacy*, 276, 280; and Thompson, *Presbyterians in the South*, vol. 2, ch. 1.

undoubtedly was in part motivated to espouse his doctrine because it prohibited the church from taking a political stance against slavery. He did, however, set forth a serious *theological* argument for confining the church's authority solely to spiritual affairs, an argument that in itself is distinguishable from his personal hypocrisy and defense of a now universally-condemned institution. He made this argument, significantly, by appealing to many aspects of the traditional Reformed two kingdoms doctrine. Hodge, who taught a doctrine of the spirituality of the church only in a looser and thinner sense, condemned Thornwell's position (perhaps not entirely fairly), though in practice their views may have been somewhat closer than often realized.

Thornwell's views on the spirituality of the church are perhaps most helpfully seen in his contributions to General Assembly debates about whether the church should support certain non-ecclesiastical social organizations, namely, the American Temperance Union and the African Colonization Society. Thornwell rejected the church's endorsement of these organizations, and "all other secular institutions for moral ends," not because he was opposed to their work but because of the nature of the church and its divinely-given authority. He explicitly hearkened back to the Reformed two kingdoms doctrine in identifying the church as "the kingdom of God" and as "a kingdom not of this world."[160] The church's only "legitimate business," therefore, were the things that "belong to His kingdom," for it had "no mission to care for the things, and to become entangled with the kingdoms and the policy, of this world."[161] In defending these assertions, Thornwell appealed to numerous considerations that were standard features of traditional Reformed two kingdoms doctrine. He appealed, for example, to the spiritual as opposed to the civil character of the church. It is a "spiritual body," a "spiritual organization, and possesses none but spiritual power." Hence it "has nothing to do with the voluntary associations of men for various civil and social purposes."[162] He also appealed to the different ends which God ordained for ecclesiastical and civil institutions. The church's ends are "spiritual," consisting of "holiness and life, to the manifestation of

---

160. James Henley Thornwell, "Societies for Moral Reform" (originally a committee report submitted to the 1848 General Assembly), in *Collected Writings*, vol. 4, 469; and James Henley Thornwell, "Speech on African Colonization" (originally a speech delivered at the 1858 General Assembly), in *Collected Writings*, vol. 4, 477.

161. Thornwell, "Speech on African Colonization," 472-73.

162. Thornwell, "Societies for Moral Reform," 469; and "Speech on African Colonization," 473.

the riches and glory of Divine grace," and not the civil ends of "morality, decency and good order, which may to some extent be secured without faith in the Redeemer."[163] Furthermore, Thornwell stated that "the only rule of faith and manners" in the church (in distinction from civil institutions, he implies) is Scripture.[164] Connected to this last point and the *jure divino* issue considered above, he again affirmed that the church's authority is "only ministerial and declarative."[165]

Finally, Thornwell drew upon the Reformed two kingdoms tradition by appealing to its notion of Christian liberty. Whether or not Christians participate in organizations for social reform is "a matter of Christian liberty" such that "Christian people may choose to adopt this particular mode of attempting to achieve the good at which all Moral Societies profess to aim." The church must "leave the whole matter where the Scriptures leave it, to the prudence, philanthropy, and good sense of God's children; each man having a right to do as to him shall seem good."[166] Here Thornwell appeals to the Reformed idea of Christian liberty as he did in his fight against church boards (contrary to Hodge's appeal), namely, as protection of the freedom of Christians from the tyranny of the church speaking where Scripture is silent. Here, then, as elsewhere, Thornwell resembles Robinson in maintaining a positive view of individual Christians' involvement in cultural matters. His conviction that the church should stay out of civil matters did not prevent him from having interest in and opinions on all of the major social and intellectual controversies of his day[167] and expecting individual Christians, trained by the church's teaching, to contribute powerfully to the health of all civil institutions.[168] Though a "court of the Lord Jesus Christ" could not of-

163. Thornwell, "Societies for Moral Reform," 469; and "Speech on African Colonization," 477.

164. Thornwell, "Societies for Moral Reform," 469-70; and "Speech on African Colonization," 472.

165. Thornwell, "Speech on African Colonization," 477.

166. Thornwell, "Societies for Moral Reform," 470; and "Speech on African Colonization," 476.

167. E.g., see Elizabeth Fox-Genovese and Eugene D. Genovese, "The Divine Sanction of Social Order: Religious Foundations of the Southern Slaveholders' World View," *Journal of the American Academy of Religion* 55, no. 2 (Summer 1987): 217-18; Leith, "James Henley Thornwell," 442-43; Farmer, *The Metaphysical Confederacy*, especially ch. 3 and 154; and Holifield, *The Gentlemen Theologians*, 3-4, 154.

168. Thornwell, "Speech on African Colonization," 475. Here he even refers to the "Christianization" of all social institutions, an idea whose consistency with the spirituality doctrine is open to question. The idea sounds similar to the vision promoted by Abraham Kuyper, which will be the focus of the next chapter.

fer its judgments on social affairs, a "body of Christian gentlemen" certainly could.[169]

Thornwell, therefore, seems to have done little else than apply the Reformed two kingdoms doctrine as he developed his spirituality doctrine — and without some of the practical inconsistencies of his Reformed predecessors. Hodge, however, had harsh words about Thornwell's doctrine of the spirituality of the church. He called it "new," "ambiguous," "extreme," and "palpably unsound and untenable."[170] Though he disagreed with Thornwell's position on a number of practical issues, Hodge at times seemed to be a fellow proponent of the spirituality doctrine. Hodge's defining moment as an advocate of the spirituality of the church came during the 1861 General Assembly, which met after the Southern states had seceded but before the Presbyterian churches in these states had withdrawn to found their own denomination (though relatively few Southerners attended this Assembly). Hodge filed a protest against the Assembly's adoption of the Gardiner Spring Resolutions, which expressed loyalty to the Constitution and the Federal government. This protest was admirable as a principled action, for Hodge was in fact a strong supporter of the Union and was subject to vilification in some quarters for being a Southern sympathizer. But Hodge explained that his protest was not an indication of his political views but of his conviction that the General Assembly was not to decide such a "political question." Though the church, on the basis of Scripture, should teach its members to submit to the civil magistrate, Northerners and Southerners did not disagree on that point but on *which* civil magistrate was due allegiance, that is, whether allegiance was due primarily to the state or to the federal government. In the Spring Resolutions the church "pronounces or assumes a particular interpretation of the Constitution. This is a matter clearly beyond the jurisdiction of the Assembly."[171]

Thus far Hodge seems to echo the concerns of Thornwell. But it is important to note here that Hodge viewed this question as "purely a political question, for the decision of which the word of God gives no direction." Though he does not lay it out quite this explicitly, it seems that Hodge's driving principle is that the church's silence on political issues applies only to "pure" political issues, by which he means issues about which Scripture says

169. See Thornwell, "Speech on African Colonization," 472.

170. Charles Hodge, "The General Assembly," *Biblical Repertory and Princeton Review* 33 (July 1861): 556-57; and Charles Hodge, "The Princeton Review on the State of the Country and of the Church," *Biblical Repertory and Princeton Review* 37 (October 1865): 645.

171. See Hodge, "The General Assembly," 548-50; and "The Princeton Review," 642-44.

absolutely nothing. He included among pure political issues not only the question whether Americans owed primary obligation to their state or to the federal government but also what form of civil government is best and how the state should regulate its commercial affairs. According to Hodge, Scripture says nothing about such things and thus neither should the church. But there were a range of issues that were of overlapping concern to both church and state. On such issues, such as marriage and divorce, the Bible does speak and the political question depends upon the "moral" question that Scripture addresses. Hodge insisted that the church has a right to speak on such matters. In fact, the church, "as witness of God, is bound to bear her testimony against all sin and error, and in favour of all truth and righteousness, agreeably to the Scriptures. . . . If the laws of the community under which we live, with regard to slavery, the slave-trade, to marriage and divorce, and the like, are contrary to the word of God, then the church is bound so to teach and so to preach." "Everything to which that teaching applies is within her legitimate cognizance."[172] In staking what he saw as a middle position, Hodge rebuked the proponents of the Spring Resolutions for making the church speak beyond what Scripture says but also rebuked those who would not allow the church to speak to political and other civil issues about which Scripture did speak. Hodge's animating principle was that the church should say only, but also all, that the Scriptures say.

Hodge explicitly denounced Thornwell for unduly limiting what the church could say. He interpreted him as claiming that the church, as spiritual, cannot "express any judgment for or against any act of the civil government" and that it can speak only "the method of salvation" and not "the law of God."[173] The first part of this charge, that the church ought not express any judgment concerning civil government, does seem to be a fair reading of Thornwell's principles, and this interpretation of Thornwell is repeated today.[174] In fact, however, Thornwell said certain things that point in a different direction — and made him sound much like Hodge himself. In his statements to the General Assembly regarding both the temperance and African colonization societies, he opened the door surprisingly wide in Hodge's direction. In the course of his arguments Thornwell appealed to WCF 31.4, which limits the church to "ecclesiastical" business and forbids it from intermeddling "with civil affairs which concern the commonwealth." But

---

172. See Hodge, "The Princeton Review," 642-45; and also "The General Assembly," 557, 560.
173. Hodge, "The General Assembly," 556; and "The Princeton Review," 645.
174. E.g., see Strange, "2001 Preface," 32-34.

31.4 also states the following qualification: "unless by way of humble petition in cases extraordinary; or, by way of advice, for satisfaction of conscience, if they be thereunto required by the civil magistrate." Thornwell made an explicit reference to the legitimacy of the church offering such a petition to the state, but arguably gave it the duty to do even more than this. He writes that when societies for moral reform "proclaim principles that are scriptural and sound, it is not denied that the Church has a right, and under certain circumstances may be bound, to bear testimony in their favour; and when, on the other hand, they inculcate doctrines which are infidel, heretical and dangerous, the Church has a right to condemn them." Thus, with reference to the American Temperance Union, the church could approve "of abstinence from intoxicating drinks as a matter of Christian expediency."[175]

Hodge apparently did not account for these words of Thornwell. But even so, he did expose an ambiguity and even inconsistency in Thornwell's thought. In general, Thornwell's doctrine suggests that one can make a real distinction between affairs that are spiritual and affairs that are civil, and hence that distinct jurisdictions can be assigned to the church on the one hand and to the state and other social organizations on the other hand. But in his statements discussed in the preceding paragraph, Thornwell suggests a position quite similar to Hodge's, namely, that though there may be a relatively small class of "purely political" issues, there are a wide range of issues for which the church and state have overlapping jurisdiction, namely, civil issues about which the Bible has something to say.

Perhaps one cannot blame Thornwell too much for tripping on this matter, for the matter of assigning respective jurisdictions to church and state had tripped his Reformation and Reformed orthodox predecessors as well. As discussed in previous chapters, their incoherence involved enunciating the two kingdoms doctrine and then trying to find a *civil* aspect to *religious* concerns and thus entrusting magistrates with protecting religious purity as a civil responsibility. The issue here with Hodge and Thornwell entailed the reverse scenario. American Presbyterians had in significant ways (though not entirely) rejected the idea that the state was to enforce religious purity as a civil task. But Hodge, despite his stance against the Spring Resolutions, held on to common American Presbyterian notions that the church

---

175. Thornwell, "Societies for Moral Reform," 470-71; see also "Speech on African Colonization," 475. Thompson discusses some relevant points regarding a speech of Thornwell's at the first General Assembly of the Southern Presbyterian church following its split from the Northern churches, in *Presbyterians in the South*, vol. 2, 30.

should project its voice directly into political and other cultural affairs. Insofar as Thornwell echoed similar concerns after enunciating his spirituality doctrine, he lapsed into incoherence by finding a *religious* aspect to *civil* concerns and thus entrusting the church with promotion of civil good as a spiritual responsibility. Thus, Thornwell's thought illustrates the continuing difficulty with which Reformed theologians sought to apply their two kingdoms doctrine in a theoretically and practically consistent way.

Concluding Reflections on the Doctrine of Spirituality in American Presbyterianism

Eminent nineteenth-century American theologians such as Stuart Robinson and James Thornwell articulated a doctrine of the spirituality of the church that self-consciously relied upon the classic distinctions of Reformed two kingdoms theology. In doing so, Robinson attempted to move the American Presbyterian church further down the road which their eighteenth-century predecessors had taken in regard to getting the state out of the affairs of the church. Embracing the disestablishment mentality of the Virginia Presbyterians, Robinson, through traditional Reformed two kingdoms distinctions, also condemned the lingering enticement of unofficial state establishment of general Christianity, as expressed, for example, in proposals to acknowledge Christ in the U.S. Constitution. Hence Robinson, like Calvin and the Reformed orthodox writers before him, grounded social and political life in the work of God as creator, not in the work of Christ as redeemer. But Robinson also distinguished himself from his Reformed predecessors — but hearkened back to a Diognetian and Augustinian theme — by having a stronger sense of the civil kingdom as universal and hence *common* to believers and unbelievers, in distinction from the exclusive character of the spiritual kingdom. Both he and Thornwell, furthermore, challenged the Presbyterian church in the other direction, regarding the church's interference in the state's affairs, a matter that eighteenth-century events had largely overlooked. By asserting the principle of divine right Presbyterianism and the spirituality of the church, and both of these in connection to Reformed two kingdoms distinctions, Robinson and Thornwell urged the Presbyterian church to abstain from involvement in political and other civil affairs. As previous chapters have considered, in claiming that the church as the kingdom of Christ is *spiritual* these theologians echoed a doctrine that Calvin himself had articulated. And in claiming that the state but *not* the church should involve itself in civil and temporal matters, they reflected the theological (if not always practical) precedent established not only by numerous early Reformed theologians but also by patristic and medieval figures such as Gelasius and Ockham.

Though the purpose of this book is not to evaluate the Reformed two kingdoms doctrine itself, it has been concerned to evaluate the consistency with which Reformed thinkers propounded this doctrine. As discussed above, Thornwell's own treatment of these matters betrayed an inconsistency and ambiguity of its own. Yet the achievement of figures such as Robinson and Thornwell in eliminating many perennial tensions in Reformed two kingdoms theology and practice deserves recognition. Not only did they apply the two kingdoms doctrine more consistently than their predecessors by wrenching the church away from civil politics and the state away from spiritual affairs, but they also did so without any suggestion that Christians should withdraw from life in the cultural realm. In light of Robinson's and Thornwell's positive perspective on the involvement of individual Christians in cultural activities, as observed above, the accusation that advocates of the spirituality doctrine were "pietistic" is thoroughly misleading.[176] In fact, they preserved the Reformed tradition's high view of cultural activity and secular vocations. However frustrating it may be to see proponents of the spirituality doctrine such as Thornwell violate their own principles by preaching politics from the pulpit or use the doctrine for the cause of preserving chattel slavery, the doctrine itself, though not completely shorn of ambiguities, seems a creative and largely coherent development of the Reformed theological tradition.

Natural Law in Early American Presbyterianism

The previous two sections of this chapter, concerning eighteenth- and nineteenth-century American Presbyterianism, largely focused on issues pertaining to the two kingdoms doctrine and very little on natural law. This section addresses the topic of natural law in early American Presbyterianism, though only in a cursory way. The pieces of evidence upon which I draw suggest that the Reformed natural law tradition certainly remained alive during this era.

176. Among those making this charge are Maddex, "From Theocracy to Spirituality," 446; Thompson, *The Spirituality of the Church*, 40; and Thompson, *A History of the Presbyterian Church*, 154-55.

One place in which the issue of natural law did arise in the previous section of this chapter was the discussion of Stuart Robinson's thought. In several places, Robinson made the classic Reformed two kingdoms distinction between the civil and ecclesiastical administrations in terms of their respective standards: while the state is governed by Scripture only, the church is governed by the law of nature. Robinson, therefore, closely connected the doctrines of natural law and the two kingdoms and thereby reflected common sentiments of the earlier Reformed tradition. If such sentiments remained alive in early American Presbyterianism, it raises the question about how Reformed people utilized natural law in concrete moral and social endeavors in the civil kingdom. One important part of the answer to this question involves the popularity of Scottish common sense realist philosophy. This is an enormous subject, but evidence clearly exists that a number of important Presbyterian theologians of this era carried on significant aspects of the Reformed natural law tradition precisely through their utilization of common sense realism. John Witherspoon (1722-1794) and James Thornwell offer two good examples.

Before looking specifically at how this was true for Witherspoon and Thornwell, I offer a few brief words about the origins of common sense realism in the Scottish Enlightenment. The immediate background against which common sense realism was developed was the skepticism — especially epistemological — present in contemporary British philosophy. For prominent figures such as David Hume and George Berkeley, the only immediate objects of knowledge were one's own ideas and perceptions of sensory data. Hence the accusations of epistemological skepticism: if Hume and Berkeley were correct, then people have no certain, direct, objective knowledge of a real world outside of their own consciousness. In response to such skepticism, the Scottish common sense realists defended human beings' trustworthy and objective knowledge of the real world outside of themselves. Human intellectual judgment was fundamentally reliable, a reliability that extended beyond general epistemology to include moral judgment. The principles of common sense that these Scottish realists promoted were things that all people take for granted and cannot deny without lapsing into absurdity. The principal figure with whom the common sense realist philosophy is associated is Thomas Reid (1710-1796),[177] though some other Scot-

___

177. For recent studies of various aspects of Reid's thought relevant to the present study, see, e.g., Nicholas Wolterstorff, *Thomas Reid and the Story of Epistemology* (Cambridge: Cambridge University Press, 2001) (particularly regarding his epistemology); Knud Haakonssen, *Natural Law*

tish thinkers such as Francis Hutcheson (1694-1746)[178] and Dugald Stewart (1753-1828)[179] played an influential role in its American reception.

The widespread American embrace of Scottish common sense realism in the late eighteenth and nineteenth centuries has been extensively chronicled.[180] One place in which it came to have particular influence was in the courses on moral philosophy offered at many American colleges and universities in this period, courses which were often taught by the president of the institution to students at the culmination of their studies.[181] John Witherspoon, a Scot who immigrated to America to assume the presidency of the College of New Jersey (Princeton), taught such a course, and his students included an impressive array of future American religious and political leaders. Thornwell, in his position at the influential South Carolina College, also offered such a course. Since Witherspoon was such a key figure for both the American reception of the Scottish philosophy and the development of American Presbyterianism,[182] and since Thornwell has already

and Moral Philosophy: From Grotius to the Scottish Enlightenment (Cambridge: Cambridge University Press, 1996), ch. 6 (particularly regarding his moral and political philosophy); and William C. Davis, *Thomas Reid's Ethics: Moral Epistemology on Legal Foundations* (New York: Continuum, 2006) (particularly regarding his ethics).

178. Noll, *America's God*, 105-10, discusses the greater influence of Hutcheson than Reid on Witherspoon and thereby on the subsequent development of common sense realism in America. For a study of the development of Hutcheson's thought in relation to Reformed orthodox theology, see James Moore, "The Two Systems of Francis Hutcheson: On the Origins of the Scottish Enlightenment," in *Studies in the Philosophy of the Scottish Enlightenment*, ed. M. A. Stewart (Oxford: Clarendon, 1990), 37-59.

179. See Holifield, *The Gentlemen Theologians*, 117, on the influence of Stewart on the American clergy. For a broader study on Stewart's thought, see Haakonssen, *Natural Law and Moral Philosophy*, ch. 7.

180. Among many studies, see, e.g., Daniel Walker Howe, *Making the American Self: Jonathan Edwards to Abraham Lincoln* (Cambridge: Harvard University Press, 1997), ch. 2; Haakonssen, *Natural Law and Moral Philosophy*, ch. 10; Holifield, *The Gentlemen Theologians*, ch. 5; and the briefer comments of George M. Marsden, *Fundamentalism and American Culture: The Shaping of Twentieth-Century Evangelicalism: 1870-1925* (New York: Oxford University Press, 1980), 14-16.

181. On the required lectures on moral philosophy, especially in the South, and the endeavor of moral philosophy more generally, see Holifield, *The Gentlemen Theologians*, 119, 127-28. For a more reserved portrayal of the dominance of the Scottish philosophy in nineteenth-century collegiate philosophy, see Bruce Kuklick, *Churchmen and Philosophers: From Jonathan Edwards to John Dewey* (New Haven: Yale University Press, 1985), ch. 9.

182. See Morrison, *John Witherspoon*, ch. 3, on Witherspoon as conduit of common sense realism in America and his lectures on moral philosophy at Princeton. For other discussion of Witherspoon and common sense realism, see, e.g., Douglas Sloan, *The Scottish Enlightenment and the American College Ideal* (New York: Teachers College Press, 1971), ch. 4; Hood, *Reformed Amer-*

played an important role in this chapter in regard to the two kingdoms doctrine, it may be helpful to consider the topic of common sense realism and the Reformed natural law tradition by taking a brief look at their lectures on moral philosophy.

Witherspoon's lectures were published posthumously and without his consent. Though they are not particularly lengthy, they do cover an impressive range of topics. The only point of concern at present, however, is the lectures' connection to the Reformed natural law tradition, and there is a fair bit of evidence that Witherspoon was carrying on significant aspects of this tradition in these lectures. A first matter to note is his definition and defense of what he was doing: moral *philosophy*. He did not say enough about this to enable a thorough analysis, but his words seem basically consistent with traditional Reformed views. His task was philosophy because he was inquiring into moral obligation on the basis of reason, not revelation. His Reformed predecessors certainly made a similar distinction (though they might also have distinguished philosophy as based on *general revelation* from theology as based on *special revelation*). Likewise, his assertions that the discoveries of reason and Scripture cannot contradict each other but that the former may illustrate and confirm the latter would have been unexceptional observations to his forebears, provided that he meant the *correct* discoveries of reason and acknowledged that reason can err.[183] And this he certainly did. When he went on to assert that moral philosophy is nothing else but the knowledge of human nature, he immediately claimed that discerning human nature is difficult, due especially to depravity. The original dictates of (unfallen) human nature, not present sinful propensities, are the source of moral philosophy.[184] Thus, like the Reformed natural law tradition generally, Witherspoon desired to account for the sinful condition of humanity.

A number of other things that Witherspoon said in these lectures also reflect the Reformed natural law tradition. Drawing on common sense realism, he spoke of an internal sense of morality and perception of moral excellence as one of the internal senses that human beings have. But he identified

---

ica, 13-15; and Noll, *America's God*, 105-6. On the significance of common sense realism for his lectures on moral philosophy, see also Haakonssen, *Natural Law and Moral Philosophy*, 333-36. On Witherspoon's commitment to historic Reformed theology, see discussions in Kuklick, *Churchmen and Philosophers*, 68-70; and Noll, *America's God*, 125-27.

183. John Witherspoon, "Lectures on Moral Philosophy," in *The Works of the Rev. John Witherspoon*, vol. 3, 2nd ed. (Philadelphia: William W. Woodward, 1802; reprinted Bristol: Toemmes, 2003), 367.

184. Witherspoon, "Lectures on Moral Philosophy," 367-70.

this with "conscience" and, alluding to the standard Reformed proof-text, Romans 2:14-15, with "the law which our Maker has written upon our hearts, and [which] both intimates and enforces duty, previous to all reasoning." It is those who oppose "the law of nature" who deny this moral sense.[185] Furthermore, Witherspoon affirmed a traditional Reformed view of the applicability of the Mosaic judicial law: "The political law of the Jews contains many noble principles of equity, and excellent examples to future lawgivers; yet it was so local and peculiar, that certainly it was never intended to be immutable and universal." Scripture, he says, "was never intended to teach us every thing."[186] Along similar lines, he recognized with his Reformed predecessors that lawmakers have discretion in creating civil law, based upon considerations of "public utility." The kind and degree of punishment of crimes must vary from nation to nation.[187] Another point at which Witherspoon reflected traditional Reformed natural law notions (at least in many theologians) was his teaching that the natural law, perceived through conscience, is grounded in God's own character, it being "as deeply founded as the nature of God himself, being a transcript of his moral excellence."[188] The final point that I mention here is an intriguing one. While Witherspoon could perhaps be faulted for falling short of the Reformed tradition in failing to connect explicitly his ideas about natural law with Reformed covenant theology (though since he was doing moral philosophy and not theology this may not be a fair critique), he did make an important implicit connection between them. As earlier Reformed orthodox theologians affirmed that the natural law was part of the original obligation of the covenant of works at creation, so Witherspoon expressed in several places his belief that conscience conveys not a sense of bare obligation but "an apprehension or belief that reward and punishment will follow, according as we shall act in the one way, or in the other." He also wrote that there is a "universal" human belief in "a future state of rewards and punishments," that is, that the law has a "sanction."[189] Though he did not say it explicitly, then, Witherspoon's understanding of conscience was very similar to the older Reformed view that the natural law proclaims the strict connection between one's deeds and their deserts, according to the creational covenant of works.

Thornwell's published lectures, originally chapel addresses at South

---

185. Witherspoon, "Lectures on Moral Philosophy," 379.

186. Witherspoon, "Lectures on Moral Philosophy," 369.

187. Witherspoon, "Lectures on Moral Philosophy," 454.

188. Witherspoon, "Lectures on Moral Philosophy," 388.

189. Witherspoon, "Lectures on Moral Philosophy," 382, 390.

Carolina College, addressed fewer of these issues of Reformed natural law theology than Witherspoon's, but several things indicate that Thornwell too was working within this tradition even as he utilized common sense realist philosophy.[190] Early in these lectures, after warning that both the necessity of reason and the sufficiency of reason can be exaggerated, he defends the idea that morality "is a subject which falls within the province of natural light." He then quotes the common Reformed proof-text, Romans 2:14, and states: "The elemental principles of right . . . which are involved in the very conception of a moral nature, must be conceded to man as man. They are the birthrights of his being, and not the legacy of a subsequent revelation."[191] But Thornwell, like Witherspoon and his Reformed predecessors, also pointed to the great effect of sin on the ability to discern this natural light: "In our present fallen condition, it is impossible to excogitate a standard of duty which shall be warped by none of our prejudices, distorted by none of our passions, and corrupted by none of our habits. . . . The elements of reason have no power to secure their just application."[192] For Thornwell, the Scriptures "guard against these defects" in that they "prescribe the law in its fullness and integrity" and "indicate the prejudices which are likely to pervert us." In their infallible teaching of morality the Scriptures "are of inestimable value to the moral philosopher himself."[193] Thornwell goes on to explain, again in typical Reformed fashion, that the Bible both clarifies what nature teaches and teaches things that could never be known by the "principles of natural light," especially the "scheme of redemption."[194]

The above considerations, however brief, suggest that early American Presbyterian proponents of common sense realism incorporated the Scottish philosophy into their thought in ways that concurred with their own tradition's teaching on natural law. Much more work could be done on this subject, to be sure, but this conclusion points in a somewhat different direction from the claims of those who conclude that common sense realism and Reformed theology were at odds, particularly in their respectively optimistic

190. On Thornwell and common sense realism, see, e.g., Leith, "James Henley Thornwell," 435-36; Farmer, *The Metaphysical Confederacy*, 92-98, ch. 4; and Holifield, *The Gentlemen Theologians*, 120-22. For brief discussion of Thornwell's lectures on moral philosophy, see Farmer, *The Metaphysical Confederacy*, 162; and Holifield, *The Gentlemen Theologians*, 127.

191. James H. Thornwell, *Discourses on Truth* (New York: Robert Carter & Brothers, 1855), 15-16.

192. Thornwell, *Discourses on Truth*, 17.

193. Thornwell, *Discourses on Truth*, 19.

194. Thornwell, *Discourses on Truth*, 26-53.

and pessimistic views about human nature and the possibility of free will.[195] Common sense realism and Reformed theology in general certainly did have different views on such issues, but, as discussed above, figures such as Witherspoon and Thornwell did not accept the Scottish philosophy's anthropology uncritically, but warned that incorrect moral conclusions would result from ignoring the dire effects of human depravity. There is at least a plausible argument to be made that these Reformed theologians made use of the Scottish philosophy as their predecessors had made use of other philosophical systems, never uncritically but insofar as they provided ways of explaining and defending things important to them. In the case of common sense realism, the American Presbyterians certainly found attractive its affirmations of a moral sense present in all people everywhere and of the objectivity of knowledge over against contemporary skepticism.[196] Just how well

195. For presentation of this view, see, e.g., Marsden, *Fundamentalism and American Culture*, 16; Noll, *America's God*, ch. 6. John C. Vander Stelt, *Philosophy and Scripture: A Study in Old Princeton and Westminster Theology* (Marlton, NJ: Mack, 1978), 67, 74-75, is similar, speaking of Witherspoon "uncritically accepting certain fundamental notions of common sense philosophy." Vander Stelt's sustained polemic about the corrupting influence of common sense realism on American Presbyterian theology shoots wide of the mark at several other places too. E.g., in faulting Presbyterians for utilizing common sense realism though it was an "inherently dualistic philosophy" in terms of anthropology and the natural-supernatural distinction, he does not sufficiently account for the body-soul and natural-supernatural distinctions that Reformed theology and the Westminster Standards themselves made; see *Philosophy and Scripture*, 271-72. Marsden and Noll also point critically to the mutual lack of historical consciousness in common sense realism and much Old School Presbyterian theology; see Marsden, *Fundamentalism and American Culture*, 110-14; and Mark A. Noll, "Introduction," in *The Princeton Theology 1812-1921: Scripture, Science, and Theological Method from Archibald Alexander to Benjamin Breckinridge Warfield*, ed. Mark A. Noll (Grand Rapids: Baker, 2001), 31; on this point, also see James Turner, "Charles Hodge in the Intellectual Weather of the Nineteenth Century" in *Charles Hodge Revisited*, 58-61; and related discussion in Haakonssen, *Natural Law and Moral Philosophy*, 61-62. For a critique of the view that common sense realism corrupted American Presbyterian theology along the lines suggested by Vander Stelt, see, e.g., Paul Kjoss Helseth, "Moral Character and Moral Certainty: The Subjective State of the Soul and J. G. Machen's Critique of Theological Liberalism" (Ph.D. dissertation, Marquette University, 1997).

196. On these points and other suggestions as to why some Reformed theologians found common sense realism attractive, see Paul Helm, "Thomas Reid, Common Sense and Calvinism," in *Rationality in the Calvinian Tradition*, ed. Hendrik Hart, Johan Van der Hoeven, and Nicholas Wolterstorff (Lanham: University Press of America, 1983), 71-89. Helm concludes that the connection between the two is "at best tenuous and adventitious" and that while Calvinism rules out certain epistemologies, it does not require one in particular. Interestingly, Helm views Reid's epistemology as foundationalist while Wolterstorff views it as non-foundationalist; see Wolsterstorff, *Thomas Reid*, x, ch. 8. For an example of a contemporary philosopher finding attraction in Reid's

and faithfully these theologians implemented their tradition in these matters is open to debate. But at least it may be said that on issues such as human sinfulness in which tension existed between Reformed theology and common sense philosophy, they attempted to resolve the tension in favor of their theology.

Some scholars have also contrasted the American Presbyterian advocates of common sense realism with the emerging Dutch renewal of Reformed theology in the late nineteenth century spearheaded by great figures such as Abraham Kuyper and Herman Bavinck. These scholars have pointed to the Dutch thinkers' greater consciousness of human sinfulness, the antithesis that they posited between Christian and non-Christian thought, and their rejection of evidentialist apologetics as key factors distinguishing them from the American realists.[197] There is certainly truth to such claims. The Dutch figures addressed many issues in notably distinct ways and did, in particular, reject the apologetic method typical of nineteenth-century American Presbyterians by which they argued for the existence of God, the reliability of Scripture, and other such matters. But, as will be considered in detail in the next chapter, these Dutch theologians continued to affirm both the existence of natural law as an aspect of Reformed theology and also its great importance for cultural and political issues. On this matter, at least, both the American Presbyterians and the Dutch Reformed were part of a common Reformed tradition.

Conclusion

At the beginning of this chapter, I raised the claim of Stuart Robinson that there were two great American traditions of church-state relations, that of New England and that of Virginia. Robinson associated the New England theocratic model with the pagan, Constantinian, Erastian view that religion is an arm of the state and associated the dissestablishment Virginia model with the original Reformation and Scottish Presbyterian view that church and state are separate institutions with different origins, standards, and pur-

---

thought at least in part because of a shared Reformed theology, see Davis, *Thomas Reid's Ethics*, 15. For consideration of the developing Protestant natural law tradition as background for the development of Scottish common sense realism, see especially Haakonssen, *Natural Law and Moral Philosophy*, ch. 1.

197. E.g., see Noll, "Introduction," 32, 41; Marsden, *Fundamentalism and American Culture*, 115.

poses. As we come at last to the conclusion of this chapter, how should we evaluate Robinson's claims in the light of our study of the Reformed natural law and two kingdoms traditions?

In broad lines, I believe that Robinson was largely correct, but the claims of this chapter suggest that his scheme requires a number of nuances to qualify its black-and-white assertions. As I have argued, Robinson's own position (which he identified with the Virginia model) did exhibit great continuity with the natural law and two kingdoms tradition that shaped the teaching of the Reformation and early Scottish Presbyterianism. Among other relevant issues for the present study, Robinson grounded social and political life in the work of God as creator rather than in the work of Christ as redeemer. Moreover, his own doctrine of church and state maintained this tradition without several of the persistent inconsistencies that had troubled his Reformed predecessors. His conviction that the state should not profess Christianity or Christ as savior, for instance, dealt with the civil kingdom as a realm of genuine *commonality* among all people rather than as one aspect of a holistic *Christian* society. A full account of New England Puritanism, however, as exemplified by its chief early defender, John Cotton, must recognize that it too taught standard Reformed natural law and two kingdoms categories, though it fell into inconsistencies similar to those of Calvin and leading Reformed orthodox theologians. A balanced account of the Virginia Presbyterians, furthermore, must recognize that they came to hold only part of the position later advocated in their name by Robinson, and that with some hesitation and ambiguity. And, finally, though Robinson and other proponents of the spirituality of the church went farther still than the Virginians in distinguishing church from state and the spiritual from the civil, and thereby brought the Reformed natural law and two kingdoms tradition to its most coherent expression yet achieved, even here some unresolved tensions remained. In particular, the Hodge-Thornwell disputes revealed some lingering ambiguity about how the distinction between spiritual and civil affairs was to be understood and how church and state respectively ought to take jurisdiction over them.

Thus, the Reformed natural law and two kingdoms traditions continued on into the early American experiment and even attained greater degrees of clarity among some theologians amidst the greatly changing social and intellectual contexts. We now move a few more decades ahead chronologically and back across the Atlantic to examine the fate of those traditions amidst another very different set of circumstances.

CHAPTER 7

An Ambiguous Transition:
Abraham Kuyper on Natural Law
and the Two Kingdoms

The present chapter brings us to what is undeniably a crucial subject for any examination of the development of Reformed social thought: the cultural and political vision of Dutch polymath Abraham Kuyper (1837-1920). Kuyper was an extraordinary figure who began his career in the pastoral ministry and later served as a university founder, theology professor, newspaper editor, political party leader, member of Parliament, and Prime Minister of the Netherlands.[1] His energetic intellectual and practical endeavors included a voluminous corpus of writing on a broad range of theological, political, and broader cultural issues. Kuyper's profound and relentless pursuit of a theologically sound, Christ-honoring cultural and political agenda perhaps inevitably made him a larger-than-life figure in the development of Reformed thought. Historically, his labors did not provide the final word for Reformed thought, however. I conclude in this chapter (and those that follow) that Kuyper was a transitional figure. He was rather traditional in many aspects of his cultural and political vision. Yet in Kuyper's wake, and in significant degree under his inspiration, a great deal of subsequent Reformed theology moved in a direction decisively different from that of the earlier Reformed tradition as interpreted in previous chapters.

In line with the concerns of the present work, I expound and interpret Kuyper's work here in light of the traditional Reformed doctrines of natural law and the two kingdoms. Kuyper did not use explicit language of "natural

---

1. Many secondary works on Kuyper include biographical information. Among extended biographical studies are Louis Praamsma, *Let Christ Be King: Reflections on the Life and Times of Abraham Kuyper* (Jordan Station: Paideia, 1985); Frank Vanden Berg, *Abraham Kuyper* (Grand Rapids: Eerdmans, 1950); and P. Kasteel, *Abraham Kuyper* (Kok: Kampen, 1938).

law" and the "two kingdoms" as organizing principles of his cultural and political thought. There are plenty of contextual considerations that may suggest why he would have been wary of such terms, relevant as they surely were for his interests.[2] Kuyper was probably the first significant Reformed theologian to confront directly what is now called a post-Christian culture. No longer were Reformed Christians threatened primarily by the hegemony of other Christian traditions, such as Roman Catholicism. His writings make abundantly clear that he regarded Christian faith of any sort as marginalized in his beloved Dutch society and that he viewed Christianity, both practically and intellectually, as under sustained assault by variations of an explicitly *anti*-Christian worldview, which he often rooted especially in the French Revolution and saw embodied in a host of modern philosophies such as modernism, evolutionism, and pantheism.[3] As Kuyper sought to embolden Dutch Reformed Christians for cultural and political activism and a counter-assault on the worldview of the French Revolution, perhaps it is understandable why terminology of "natural law" and "two kingdoms" did not conduce to his purposes. Kuyper judged that his day was one in which God's rule and God's claims needed to be asserted in a social context that did not simply argue about what these meant but actually challenged their validity altogether. Therefore paradigms such as "divine ordinances" and the distinction between "common grace" and "special grace" at least arguably served better Kuyper's desire to express explicitly the activity of God in all of life and the consequent responsibility of human beings to serve him everywhere.

I argue in this chapter, however, that Kuyper's very use of such catego-

2. Among helpful recent studies of Kuyper's context and the relation of his thought to the intellectual trends of his day, see Peter S. Heslam, *Creating a Christian Worldview: Abraham Kuyper on Calvinism* (Grand Rapids: Eerdmans, 1998); John Bolt, *A Free Church, a Holy Nation: Abraham Kuyper's American Public Theology* (Grand Rapids: Eerdmans, 2001), especially ch. 1; and James D. Bratt, "Abraham Kuyper: Puritan, Victorian, Modern," in *Religion, Pluralism, and Public Life: Abraham Kuyper's Legacy for the Twenty-First Century*, ed. Luis E. Lugo (Grand Rapids: Eerdmans, 2000), 3-21. For an interesting example of differing interpretations of Kuyper's relation to one particular trend, Romanticism, see Edward E. Ericson, "Abraham Kuyper: Cultural Critic," *Calvin Theological Journal* 22 (Nov 1987): 210-27; and Jan de Bruijn, "Calvinism and Romanticism: Abraham Kuyper as a Calvinist Politician," in *Religion, Pluralism, and Public Life*, 45-58.

3. In regard to these sentiments, a key precursor of Kuyper was Guillaume Groen van Prinsterer (1801-76), a leading figure in the Dutch anti-revolutionary movement that spawned the Anti-revolutionary political party that Kuyper led for many years. For a study of Groen and his thought, see Harry Van Dyke, *Groen Van Prinsterer's Lectures on Unbelief and Revolution* (Jordan Station, Ontario: Wedge, 1989), 1-269.

ries as the divine ordinances and common and special grace bore very significant resemblances to earlier Reformed use of the natural law and two kingdoms categories. Like his Reformed predecessors, Kuyper's theological foundation in large part grounded cultural and political life in the creation order as sustained in a sinful world rather than in Christ's work of redemption. He also developed such doctrines in constructive ways, such as by opposing the idea of a national church and generally supporting religious liberty (in this way resembling some of the American Presbyterians considered in Chapter 6) and by giving a more nuanced account of the civil kingdom than did older Reformed figures. Nevertheless, I also argue that at times Kuyper spoke and acted in ways that suggest tension with these basic convictions, though the tensions in his thought emerged elsewhere than where they appeared in his forebears. Kuyper, therefore, stood somewhat ambiguously in the Reformed natural law and two kingdoms tradition. As I begin to argue in this chapter and will continue to argue in subsequent chapters, later Reformed thinkers resolved the ambiguity in Kuyper's thought in a direction that in fact rejected the Reformed natural law and two kingdoms tradition, and with it the traditional creation-order foundation of cultural and political life, in favor of a redemptive-christological and/or eschatological foundation.

Kuyper and Natural Law

In this chapter I first examine Kuyper's relation to the Reformed natural law tradition. Kuyper, to be sure, is not ordinarily associated with a doctrine of natural law, and with plausible reason. His program is usually remembered as a vibrant attempt to bring a distinctively biblical worldview to bear upon social life and, as we will observe below, Kuyper at times speaks in grand terms of how Scripture provides instruction for all areas of existence. Furthermore, Kuyper also reflected critically on what he perceived as an increasing emphasis on natural theology through the early centuries of the Reformed tradition. To his mind, this development had damaged Reformed theology and distanced it from Calvin.[4] Nevertheless, strong countervailing evidence exists

4. E.g., see Abraham Kuyper, *Principles of Sacred Theology,* trans. J. Hendrik De Vries (Grand Rapids: Eerdmans, 1954), 372-74. Among helpful studies cited in Chapter 5 of the early development of Reformed understanding of the natural knowledge of God, see Richard A. Muller, *Post-Reformation Reformed Dogmatics: The Rise and Development of Reformed Orthodoxy, ca. 1520 to ca. 1725,* vol. 1, *Prolegomena to Theology,* 2d ed. (Grand Rapids: Baker, 2003), ch. 6; J. V. Fesko and

that Kuyper in fact stood in substantial continuity with his Reformed prede cessors, both Calvin and the Reformed orthodox figures examined in Chapter 5, on matters pertaining to natural law. He not only held a high view of general revelation broadly speaking, but also affirmed that God himself wrote his law on the heart of every person and that knowledge of this law was to play a crucial role in the development of a sound social and political life. Though Kuyper did not describe his own approach in terms of a natural law theory, I argue in this section that what he said on this subject, though different in certain respects, was surprisingly harmonious with the early Reformed and broader Christian traditions as examined in previous chapters. This argument is the first line of evidence that Kuyper, though not with entire consistency, embraced an approach to social and political life based in the creation order, rather than the redemptive and eschatological order.

Kuyper on General and Special Revelation

Before examining in particular Kuyper's views on the moral knowledge accessible to human beings in nature, it may be helpful first to survey his theology of general and special revelation more broadly. Kuyper made a traditional Reformed distinction between the general revelation that comes in nature and the special revelation coming in Scripture. Yet within this traditional framework his theology of revelation bears distinctive marks.

Kuyper believed, with his Reformed theological predecessors, that God revealed himself to human beings in nature already before the fall into sin. But he makes the unexpected assertion that God communicated *only* through general revelation in the pre-lapsarian state. God spoke, as it were, by an inner word, and Adam received it in an immediate fashion through direct insight. Kuyper calls this the "natural principium" and describes it as the "normal" way in which God communicates with human beings.[5] After the

---

Guy M. Richard, "Natural Theology and the Westminster Confession of Faith," *The Westminster Confession into the 21st Century: Essays in Remembrance of the 350th Anniversary of the Westminster Assembly*, vol. 3, ed. J. Ligon Duncan (Fearn: Mentor, 2009), 233-66; and John Platt, *Reformed Thought and Scholasticism: The Arguments for the Existence of God in Dutch Theology, 1575-1650* (Leiden: Brill, 1982). For a study of later development of this theme at the end of the age of Reformed orthodoxy, see Martin I. Klauber, *Between Reformed Scholasticism and Pan-Protestantism: Jean-Alphonse Turretin (1671-1737) and Enlightened Orthodoxy at the Academy of Geneva* (Selinsgrove, PA: Susquehanna University Press, 1994).

5. Abraham Kuyper, *Lectures on Calvinism* (Grand Rapids: Ecrdmans, 1931), 56; Kuyper, *Prin-*

fall, however, sin damaged this inner instinct, and though God continues to give general revelation, it is no longer able to provide people with any new, pure, or sufficient knowledge about God.[6] Sin affects not only the will, but also the intellect.[7] In response to the ravages of sin, God introduced special revelation, what Kuyper called the "special principium" and the "abnormal" means of God's communication. For Kuyper, special revelation is absolutely necessary after the fall, both as remedial and auxiliary. But it works toward the same goal that general revelation had before the advent of sin, that of eternal blessedness and the glorified state, in which God will again communicate to his people by the natural, normal way of direct communication. Special revelation, therefore, is only for the time in which sin is present in the world, between the fall and Christ's second coming.[8] Corresponding to this, religion's soteriological, or salvific, character is "abnormal," pertaining only to the era after the fall and before the consummation. Salvation was not necessary before the fall and will not be necessary after Christ returns.[9] Salvation is important, but the broader glory of God much greater.[10]

In the post-lapsarian world, life is not divided into compartments known by general revelation and those known by special revelation. Rather, Kuyper asserts that there is one knowledge, drawn from general and special revelation, sources "whose waters have mingled themselves." From this idea flow several consequences. Special revelation is not limited to matters of salvation, but extends to those matters made known in general revelation.[11] Further, natural knowledge becomes of service only with the help of special revelation.[12] In the other direction, however, "special theology" is never sufficient to itself, but must always be considered in connection with "natural theology," its "twin sister."[13] Hence Kuyper seeks to free theology from any "dualism" breaching the two principia.[14]

---

ciples, 369-70; Abraham Kuyper, "Common Grace in Science," in *Abraham Kuyper: A Centennial Reader*, ed. James D. Bratt (Grand Rapids: Eerdmans, 1998), 451.

6. Kuyper, *Principles*, 361, 373.

7. Kuyper, *Principles*, 107.

8. Kuyper, *Principles*, 361-62, 369-70; Kuyper, *Lectures*, 55-56.

9. Kuyper, *Lectures*, 54-56.

10. Kuyper, *Lectures*, 119.

11. Kuyper, *Principles*, 377-78; Kuyper, "Common Grace in Science," 459-60; Kuyper, "Sphere Sovereignty," in *Centennial Reader*, 487. See also Kuyper, *Lectures*, 120-21.

12. Kuyper, *Principles*, 378.

13. Kuyper, *Principles*, 372-73, 381.

14. Kuyper, *Principles*, 380-81; see also Kuyper, *Lectures*, 53-54.

Kuyper on the Divine Ordinances

Kuyper expressed these sentiments in various forums through his life, both in his theological writing and in his broader interaction with cultural issues. But how did they work out in practice, and especially in regard to his approach to politics and other social questions? Or, to put it differently, how did his views of general and special revelation relate to the question of natural law and its moral authority in social life? One of Kuyper's most illuminating discussions of this subject is a series of newspaper articles that he penned early in his political career, seeking to explain the position of his Anti-revolutionary party and to address some common objections and mischaracterizations of its position.[15] Some scholars have questioned whether Kuyper's views on this subject remained steady throughout his career.[16] Though it would be impetuous to rule out all development in his handling of questions pertaining to natural law, the harmony of the convictions expressed in these newspaper articles with his theological account of revelation in his *Principles of Sacred Theology,* as well as with his Stone Lectures at Princeton, indicates that, though certain emphases may have shifted over time, his basic views on the subject did not undergo any great change.

In these articles, Kuyper frequently uses the term "divine ordinances," which he admits has been frequently misunderstood by friend and foe alike.[17] As he unpacks what his use of this term really means, it seems clear that he describes a concept of natural law. In his Stone Lectures twenty-five years later, in fact, Kuyper continues to use this terminology, explicitly identifying the "divine ordinances" with the "laws of Nature," which he associates with the conscience and believes to be written on the heart of every person and renewed by God through Moses on Mount Sinai.[18] Kuyper's earlier exposition of the divine ordinances stresses that they are of divine origin. They do not simply emerge "from the constitution of our human nature" but

---

15. These articles appeared in 1873 in *De Standaard.* Excerpts of these articles appear in English translation under the title "The Ordinances of God" in *Political Order and the Plural Structure of Society,* ed. James W. Skillen and Rockne M. McCarthy (Atlanta: Scholars, 1991), 242-57. Subsequent citations of these articles will be to this translation. For a recent discussion of these articles, see Vincent E. Bacote, *The Spirit in Public Theology: Appropriating the Legacy of Abraham Kuyper* (Grand Rapids: Baker Academic, 2005), 57-61.

16. E.g., see the discussion in Heslam, *Creating a Christian Worldview,* 164.

17. See Kuyper, "The Ordinances of God," 242.

18. Kuyper, *Lectures,* 70-72.

"from the will of a personal, living God."[19] Kuyper reiterated this point also in his Stone Lectures, where he insists that the divine ordinances, or "laws of nature," are imposed upon nature by God and are not merely derived from nature.[20]

Kuyper's conviction expressed in the Stone Lectures that "many divine potencies . . . were hidden away in the bosom of mankind from our very creation"[21] seems to have been at the root of his earlier explanation of the apprehension and use of these divine ordinances in human society. He writes of the divine ordinances that "all the givens that govern the political life of the nations were present in human nature at its creation" and that these "laws governing life reveal themselves spontaneously in life." That is, by engaging in the various activities of human culture, people by reflection may come to understand the divine ordinances and may attain "scientific discovery of the laws that rule the lives of nations." "Life comes first; afterward reflection on that life." Remarkably, Kuyper mentions art, scholarship, commerce, industry, and politics and remarks that "it enters no one's mind to consult the Bible or ecclesiastical authorities" when seeking to know what their purposes are. In fact, Kuyper comments, in sentiments that clearly reflect his broader theology of revelation as surveyed above, that, were it not for sin, human discovery of these divine ordinances "would be completely adequate to establish an unsurpassable constitutional law."[22]

Of course, Kuyper the Reformed theologian believed that sin most certainly had to be accounted for. Indeed, he judged that recognition of the effects of sin on human perception of the ordinances was the chief dividing line between the Christian approach of his Anti-revolutionary party and their opponents, the advocates of "the Revolution."[23] For Kuyper, observation of and reflection upon the experience of life in order to apprehend the divine ordinances are no longer sufficient for a perfect understanding of political existence: "Sin makes futile every effort to found political theory solely on the observation of life and causes it to fail."[24]

Precisely at this point, however, Kuyper strongly rejects what today might be called a biblicist approach to social life. Though many in Dutch society took the Anti-revolutionary party's view of sin and its effects as an en-

---

19. Kuyper, "The Ordinances of God," 244.
20. Kuyper, *Lectures,* 70-71.
21. Kuyper, *Lectures,* 9.
22. Kuyper, "The Ordinances of God," 245-46.
23. Kuyper, "The Ordinances of God," 246-47.
24. Kuyper, "The Ordinances of God," 247-48.

dorsement of the exclusive use of Scripture for development of public policy, Kuyper forcefully rejects such a position. He writes: "Does it follow, therefore, that the sooner we stop our observation of life the better, so that we can seek the rules of state polity outside life in Holy Scripture? This is how some mistakenly think that we reason. . . . However, the opposite is true. Calvinism has never supported this untenable position but has always opposed it with might and main. A state polity that dismisses and scorns the observation of life and simply wishes to duplicate the situation of Israel, taking Holy Scripture as a complete code of Christian law for the state, would, according to the spiritual fathers of Calvinism, be the epitome of absurdity. Accordingly, in their opposition to Anabaptism as well as the Quakers, they expressed unreservedly their repugnance for this extremely dangerous and impractical theory."[25] Kuyper goes on to probe the sorts of ill consequences that would follow were one to adopt the biblicist approach that he rejects. He states, for example: "If we considered the political life of the nations as something unholy, unclean and wrong in itself, it would lie outside of human nature. Then the state would have to be seen as a purely external means of compulsion, and every attempt to discover even a trace of God's ordinances in our own nature would be absurd. Only special revelation would then be capable of imparting to us the standards for that external means of discipline. Wherever, thus, this special revelation is absent, as in the heathen world, nothing but sin and distortion would prevail, which would therefore not even be worth the trouble of our observation. . . . However, if we open the works of Calvin, Bullinger, Beza and Marnix van St. Aldegonde, it becomes obvious that Calvinism consciously chooses sides against this viewpoint. The experience of the states of antiquity, the practical wisdom of their laws, and the deep insight of their statesmen and philosophers is held in esteem by these men, and these are cited in support of their own affirmations and consciously related to the ordinances of God. The earnest intent of the political life of many nations can be explained in terms of the principles of justice and morality that spoke in their consciences. They cannot be explained simply as blindness brought on by the Evil One; on the contrary, in the excellence of their political efforts we encounter a divine ray of light."[26]

Kuyper goes on repeatedly to emphasize the continuing necessity of recourse to the divine ordinances, or natural law. He reiterates his repudiation of the view "that one should turn to the political order of Israel as a model

---

25. Kuyper, "The Ordinances of God," 248.
26. Kuyper, "The Ordinances of God," 249.

by which the nations ought to be guided in all times and latitudes" and appeals to Calvin's *Institutes* 4.20 for support.[27] He asserts that "with proper rights we contradict the argument that Holy Scripture should be seen as the source from which a knowledge of the best civil laws flows. The supporters of this position talk as though after the Fall nature, human life, and history have ceased being a revelation of God and as though, with the closing of this book, another book, called Holy Scriptures, was opened for us. Calvinism has never defended this untenable position and will never acknowledge it as its own."[28] Finally, he comes to the conclusion: "We have refuted the notion that we entertain the foolish effort to patch together civil laws from Bible texts, and we have declared unconditionally that psychology, ethnology, history and statistics are also for us givens which, by the light of God's Word, must determine the standards for state polity."[29]

Kuyper, therefore, rejects any view that excludes utilization of natural law in social life as well as any view that thinks recourse to natural law alone is able to produce a *perfect* constitutional polity. This early view of Kuyper, therefore, sits coherently beside his theological exposition in *Principles,* in which he argues that neither general nor special revelation is completely independent of the other. But then how practically did Kuyper envision his Anti-revolutionary party using both Scripture and natural law in public life? He admits that the answer is "far from simple."[30] Scripture, he posits, clarifies the things revealed in nature and allows people again to perceive "the ground rules, the primary relationships, the principles that govern man's life together and his relationship to the most holy God."[31] Among these basic principles that Scripture clarifies, he includes "knowing what man is, knowing what a nation is and the purpose of the nations, knowing the source of justice and authority, knowing too where the claim to freedom and progress derives its impulse."[32] From this point, Kuyper lets reflection upon the divine ordinances, natural law, take over. He even uses exclusive language to describe the role of natural law in developing a concrete public policy from the general principles: "What the application of these principles to contemporary issues should be, however, how they ought to be adapted to the nature of various times and peoples, what kind of expression they should find

27. Kuyper, "The Ordinances of God," 249-50.
28. Kuyper, "The Ordinances of God," 250.
29. Kuyper, "The Ordinances of God," 251.
30. Kuyper, "The Ordinances of God," 254.
31. Kuyper, "The Ordinances of God," 250.
32. Kuyper, "The Ordinances of God," 256.

in the laws and decisions of government, must be regulated so exclusively by the phenomena of life that Holy Scripture does not even opt for any single form of government, and allows Christian constitutional law to consider a monarchy as well as a commonwealth, an aristocratic republic as well as a democratic federation."[33] Later he comments in the same vein: "One of the implications of this method, however, is that it is impossible to supply a handbook for Christian political theory that is valid for all nations and all times. The Christian statesman cannot placidly accept such neglect of the differences among nations and the changing times. Each nation, he finds, has its own character, and in the course of time he finds a perpetual fluctuation of circumstance. These facts demand attention. He wishes not to be speculative or doctrinaire, but historical, because reality constrains him to be so. Only the principles for which he stands up are eternal, valid for all nations and in force for all times."[34]

Kuyper expresses similar sentiments in another section of this same work (though not included in the translation utilized above). He distinguishes the natural from the revealed knowledge of God, the former of which can be found in creation, the human person, and the organism of the nation. Claiming continuity with the older Reformed tradition, he points to this natural rather than revealed knowledge of God as that which should set the direction for public policy.[35]

Kuyper's subsequent writings, even when emphasizing the importance of biblical truths for social life, do not indicate that he abandoned this position in later years. An address that he gave in 1891 expresses what might be read initially as the kind of biblicist approach that Kuyper attacked two decades earlier. There he writes, for example, that "On almost every point in regard to the social question, God's Word gives us the most positive direction" and that the "principles by which we are obliged to test the existing situation and existing juridical relationships lie clearly expressed in the Word of God."[36] Yet Kuyper's focus on "principles" here, and not upon concrete details of public policy, suggests that he saw a similar role for Scripture at this time as he did earlier (whatever difference in emphasis there

---

33. Kuyper, "The Ordinances of God," 250.

34. Kuyper, "The Ordinances of God," 255.

35. Abraham Kuyper, *Ons Program* (Amsterdam: J. A. Wormser, 1892), 79.

36. Abraham Kuyper, *The Problem of Poverty,* ed. James W. Skillen (Grand Rapids: Baker, 1991), 68, 72. A helpful treatment of the socio-political context of this address appears in Harry Van Dyke, "How Abraham Kuyper became a Christian Democrat," *Calvin Theological Journal* 33 (Nov 1998): 420-35.

may be).[37] Furthermore, attentive readers must be struck by Kuyper's repeated appeals to things natural and organic in his 1898 Stone Lectures, particularly in the lecture on politics. For instance, he writes in this third lecture that "the impulse to form states arises from man's social nature" and speaks of "the very innate thirst for liberty" and of the "God-consciousness innate in every man."[38] In addition, he had already asserted in the second lecture that the natural laws are moral ordinances of the most particular detail rather than general rules.[39] This is perhaps a puzzling statement when isolated from the rest of Kuyper's thought. But it seems to cohere with his earlier affirmation that the divine ordinances (not Scripture) are meant to provide the concrete application of general principles in particular circumstances. Therefore, that Kuyper did not abandon the principal ideas of his earlier position, even when particularly concerned to articulate biblical principles and a biblical worldview, seems to be a fair conclusion.

Kuyper, Natural Law, and the Reformed Tradition

I turn now to address the question of how Kuyper's approach to such issues relates to the doctrine of natural law taught by his Reformed predecessors, particularly Calvin and the Reformed orthodox thinkers of whom Kuyper saw himself as heir. I argue here that though Kuyper formulated his ideas on this subject in distinctive ways, he in fact expressed standard Reformed views on most of the key features of early Reformed natural law theology examined in previous chapters. Kuyper's unique development of the Reformed natural law tradition must be acknowledged, but it is erroneous to exclude him from the tradition. Whether he caused himself undue difficulties by not embracing or interacting with a natural law tradition that he in some re-

37. J. Budziszewski refers to this very quotation to suggest that readers would expect Kuyper to develop his social theory (particularly, his doctrine of sphere sovereignty) through special revelation. He then goes on to note how much Kuyper's exposition of sphere sovereignty in fact depends upon general revelation. See *Evangelicals in the Public Square: Four Formative Voices on Political Thought and Action* (Grand Rapids: Baker Academic, 2006), 63-64. My analysis here suggests that in the context of Kuyper's thought there is certainly difference in rhetoric here but not necessarily the substantive incongruity suggested by Budziszewski. In other words, what Budziszewski sees as an unwitting sort of natural law view on Kuyper's part may not have been quite as unwitting as he suggests.

38. Kuyper, *Lectures*, 79, 80, 103.

39. Kuyper, *Lectures*, 70-71.

spects belonged to, but instead building a theory from scratch, as one recent writer has suggested, is nevertheless a good question.[40]

A few words about Kuyper's unique use of the Reformed natural law inheritance are perhaps appropriate at the outset. One distinctive feature of Kuyper's position is terminological. He clearly preferred the language of "divine ordinances" to that of "natural law," though, as observed above, he does in fact use the latter terminology at times. The former term was perhaps more amenable to Kuyper in light of his understanding of his contemporary context. As suggested in the introduction to the present chapter, in an age in which his bitter opponents, the apologists for the French Revolution and the worldviews that it reflected and spawned, could speak glowingly about things natural, the language of "divine ordinances" was perhaps better suited to express a key truth that his opponents denied, namely, that the natural law was not simply natural but was imposed upon nature by God. In addition to the distinctiveness of Kuyper's language, he also expressed certain substantive views that seem to be out of accord with earlier Reformed teaching. An example is his insistence that general revelation is "normal" and special revelation "abnormal," deriving from his conviction that there was no special revelation, but only general revelation, before the fall into sin and that the same will be true in the consummate state following Christ's return. To my knowledge, this position does not find any significant precedent in the Reformed tradition. Its practical consequences for the use of natural law in the present world, however, are probably minimal.

On questions of special concern to this book, Kuyper's views as discussed in the previous subsections display significant continuity with the Reformed natural law tradition and, therefore, with the broader Christian natural law tradition. In fact, Kuyper believed that his views reflected earlier Reformed teaching.[41] Like his predecessors, Kuyper not only affirmed the existence of natural law but also emphasized its divine origin and hence divine authority. The law of nature is the law of God. Kuyper also spoke of the law of nature as written upon the human heart, associated it with the conscience, and identified it with the Decalogue. Furthermore, he followed Reformed precedent in expressing qualified yet apparently genuine appreciation for the cultural accomplishments of non-Christian, heathen people without access to special revelation, even while strongly emphasizing the dire effects of sin upon human perception of the natural law.

---

40. See Budziszewski, *Evangelicals in the Public Square,* 64.

41. As cited above, see Kuyper, *Ons Program,* 79.

On the relation of natural law and civil law, a matter receiving considerable attention in previous chapters, Kuyper again expressed views that seem consonant with the earlier Reformed tradition. He affirmed that as an objective matter natural law reveals everything necessary for forming a perfect political order. Though Scripture, very significantly, clarifies general principles of the natural law obscured by sin, the concrete application of even these principles requires recourse to natural law and not Scripture. For Kuyper, then, natural law serves as the standard for civil law, though the clarifying lens of Scripture greatly aids the understanding of this standard. Of course, as noted above, Kuyper at times spoke of Scripture's role in political life in ways that seem overstated in comparison with the position he articulated elsewhere. But even here the previous chapters would suggest that he had Reformed precedent. Kuyper also followed in the train of his Reformed predecessors in emphasizing the flexibility with which natural law is to be applied in the formation of civil law, due to changing circumstances in different times and places. On the related question of the applicability of Mosaic laws to present social life, he articulated a view again in line with the Reformed and broader Christian traditions. He rejected any simplistic appeal to Old Testament civil laws as the standard for contemporary law and pointed to the appropriate application of natural law (as clarified through general principles revealed in Scripture) as the alternative.

In addition to all of these standard points of Reformed doctrine, Kuyper also expressed views similar to many of his Reformed predecessors in explicating certain convictions regarding human nature with important political implications. Though not limited to the Reformed resistance theorists discussed in Chapter 4, these sorts of sentiments were highlighted by them in particularly strong ways. Among examples considered above are Kuyper's belief that human beings have a social nature and his judgment that each person has an innate desire for liberty.

A final consideration may add to the plausibility of my argument that Kuyper's position on issues related to natural law placed him in basic continuity with the earlier Reformed tradition. One of Kuyper's most eminent colleagues and fellow travelers was the systematic theologian Herman Bavinck, professor first at the theological seminary in Kampen and then later at Kuyper's own Free University of Amsterdam. Bavinck articulated a doctrine of general revelation at considerable length in his *magnum opus,* the *Gereformeerde Dogmatiek.*[42]

---

42. See generally chapters 10 and 12 in Herman Bavinck, *Reformed Dogmatics,* vol. 1, *Prolegomena,* ed. John Bolt, trans. John Vriend (Grand Rapids: Baker, 2003).

Bavinck's position is nuanced, yet certainly must be taken as a standard, historic Reformed presentation of this subject. Among his affirmations typical of confessional Reformed theology is the reality of God's revelation "in the heart and conscience of every individual," a claim he supports by reference to Romans 2:14-15 along with other biblical verses.[43] He also echoes the view of many Reformed orthodox theologians that the natural law was part of the original obligation of the human race in the creational covenant of works.[44] At times his presentation reflects concerns similar to Kuyper's about the early development of the Reformed tradition. For example, he speaks of how Reformed theologians increasingly granted independence to general revelation and reason.[45] But even when Bavinck disagreed with Kuyper, such as on the latter's claim that there was no special revelation before the fall,[46] it was in defense of traditional Reformed views. Though Bavinck's views are of course not proof of what Kuyper's were, the fact that the preeminent theological voice among Kuyper's most respected colleagues was traditionally Reformed on general revelation may add additional weight to the claim that Kuyper stood in considerable continuity with the broader Reformed on such matters and did not intend to strike out on a radically different path.

Kuyper and the Two Kingdoms

Kuyper's place in the Reformed natural law tradition provides one line of evidence that he, like his Reformed predecessors, adopted an approach to political and social life fundamentally grounded in the creation order as sustained in a sinful world rather than in the redemptive, eschatological order. In this next section I argue that his place in the Reformed two kingdoms tradition provides another line of evidence. Addressing this new issue in Kuyper is, I believe, more difficult than the previous, and the argument I

---

43. Bavinck, *Reformed Dogmatics*, 1.310.

44. Herman Bavinck, *Reformed Dogmatics*, vol. 2, *God and Creation*, trans. John Vriend, ed. John Bolt (Grand Rapids: Baker, 2004), 567. He writes: "It was called 'covenant of nature,' not because it was deemed to flow automatically and naturally from the nature of God or the nature of man, but because the foundation on which the covenant rested, that is, the moral law, was known to man by nature, and because it was made with man in his original state and could be kept by man with the powers bestowed on him in the creation, without the assistance of supernatural grace."

45. Bavinck, *Reformed Dogmatics*, 1.305-6.

46. See Bavinck, *Reformed Dogmatics*, 1.358.

make also more difficult. One thing that makes Kuyper difficult to place in terms of the Reformed two kingdoms tradition is that while he certainly addressed all of the major issues touching upon the two kingdoms doctrine, he did so with a very different set of terms and concepts. Another thing making this analysis difficult is the tension or even inconsistency in Kuyper's thought on these issues that many writers — even some of his devoted disciples — have perceived.[47] Despite these difficulties, I argue here that Kuyper's theological description of cultural and political life and the Christian's place within it does in fact place him broadly within the Reformed two kingdoms tradition, despite certain ambiguous aspects of his thought that have, indeed, been taken in a quite different direction by many of his followers. This argument, then, supports the general contention of this chapter that Kuyper, like his Reformed predecessors, looked primarily to the creation order, rather than the redemptive, eschatological order, to understand the nature of cultural and political life.

Because Kuyper worked with a set of terms and concepts which were in large part unknown or at least unutilized in the early Reformed tradition, it seems appropriate first to let Kuyper's vision speak for itself before asking how it compares to the terms and concepts of the traditional Reformed two kingdoms doctrine. In the following subsections, therefore, I attempt to describe in some detail Kuyper's thought on cultural and political issues. After doing so, I then reflect upon its place in the broader Reformed tradition.

Regeneration, Worldview, and Antithesis

The discussion of Kuyper and natural law above noted that sin necessitated the introduction of special revelation. Kuyper also argued, however, that the fall into sin necessitated the divine act of regeneration upon human persons if they are to know God and understand the world truly.[48] In this first subsection, I discuss Kuyper's view of regeneration and the implications that he

---

47. E.g., see an essay that will be discussed below, S. U. Zuidema, "Common Grace and Christian Action in Abraham Kuyper," in *Communication and Confrontation* (Toronto: Wedge, 1972), 52-105. Bolt's argument that Kuyper should be considered as a rhetorician and poet, rather than simply as an intellectual, brings a helpful perspective to the question of how to read Kuyper and what to expect of him in terms of intellectual consistency; see Bolt, *A Free Church*, ch. 1.

48. Kuyper, *Principles*, 151-52; Abraham Kuyper, "The Blurring of the Boundaries," in *Centennial Reader*, 398-400.

drew from this doctrine in order to develop his crucial concepts of worldview and antithesis.

For Kuyper, regeneration, a sovereign divine action of renewing the human heart, is necessary because all knowledge flows out of a basic starting-point. For true knowledge, this basic starting-point must be that God in Christ is sovereign over all.[49] Kuyper did not believe that formal thought processes have been attacked by sin, nor that the beginnings of scientific investigation, such as primary observation through weights, measures, or numbers, are affected by regeneration.[50] Given the primacy of empirical observation in the hard sciences, the effects of sin are less prominent here than with the disciplines of "the spirit," in which the wrong starting-point tends to make wrong conclusions much more immediately obvious.[51] But as knowledge develops into science, he asserts that all thought that does not begin from the conviction that God is sovereign must consistently diverge from the truth.[52] Only through regeneration, then, can one affirm God's sovereignty and hence pursue true knowledge.

Kuyper teaches, therefore, that there are two kinds of science. On the one hand is a Christian science;[53] or, better, a Calvinist science that begins, through regeneration, from the conviction that Christ is sovereign. On the other hand is a non-Christian science that begins, apart from regeneration, from the conviction that humanity and the cosmos as presently constituted are in a normal condition.[54] One of Kuyper's many poetic images helps to capture why he thought that each branch of learning must proceed on a distinctively Christian basis: "As truly as every plant has a root, so truly does a principle hide under every manifestation of life."[55] Different worldviews emerge from these different principial starting-points.[56] Hence arises the crucial Kuyperian concept of the *antithesis,* the radical contrast between truth and falsehood, between Christian and non-Christian principles, that,

49. See Kuyper, *Lectures,* 79, 155; Abraham Kuyper, "Calvinism: Source and Stronghold of Our Constitutional Liberties," in *Centennial Reader,* 307; Kuyper, "Sphere Sovereignty," 480.

50. See Kuyper, *Principles,* 159.

51. Kuyper, *Principles,* 116-17, 157-58, 161-62, 166-68; Kuyper, "Common Grace in Science," 450, 454.

52. Kuyper, *Principles,* 155.

53. Kuyper, *Principles,* 181.

54. Kuyper, *Principles,* 154-55; Kuyper, *Lectures,* 130-34; Kuyper, "Common Grace in Science," 458.

55. Kuyper, *Lectures,* 189.

56. Kuyper develops the idea of worldview (also called "life-system" and other similar terms) in many places. Perhaps most importantly, see *Lectures,* ch. 1.

when played out, means that "school will form itself against school, system against system, world-view against world-view."[57] Among the consequences following from this two-fold science and the antithesis between Christian and non-Christian thought are the rejection of apologetics[58] and the conviction that Calvinists (and people of other worldviews) should establish their own circles in science and all spheres of life in order to work out theory and practice from their distinctive starting-points.[59]

Kuyper's approach to these issues was intimately related to his view of Western history. He was convinced that history proceeded in large part through the working out of key ideas or starting-point principles. Kuyper seemed to think that, given the prominence of a key idea, historical events are set in motion in an inevitable and perhaps even predictable way.[60] This sort of analysis of history played an important role in Kuyper's broader polemics against the intellectual and social problems of his day and in favor of a Calvinist renewal. A brief account of his perspective on history may give a sense of this dynamic. First, Kuyper analyzed the medieval era primarily in terms of the Roman Catholic worldview, characterized by the nature-grace dichotomy as its principal idea. This entailed the separation of the lower and higher realms of life, the devaluing of the temporal realm for the sake of the spiritual, and the requirement that every temporal endeavor seek blessing from the church.[61] For Kuyper, this represented a lower stage in the development of human history.[62] Though he

57. Kuyper, *Principles*, 117.

58. Kuyper, *Principles*, 394-96. Kuyper, interacting with what now might be termed a "classical" or "evidentialist" view of apologetics, explains that "no argument will avail where Reason is both a party to the dispute and its judge." For discussion of the differences between Kuyper and B. B. Warfield on apologetics, see Heslam, *Creating a Christian Worldview*, 123-32.

59. Kuyper, *Lectures*, 138-41; Kuyper, "The Blurring of the Boundaries," 400; Kuyper, "Sphere Sovereignty," 484-86.

60. The third chapter of his *The Problem of Poverty* may serve to illustrate this tendency in Kuyper's thought. He describes how the French Revolution changed "people's consciousness and view of life" (43) and goes on to explain the various consequences spawned by the social system it produced. At one point he asserts that this system gave birth to the social-democratic movement "with equally rigorous necessity" (47). James D. Bratt provides helpful, critical comments on Kuyper's principial thinking and how he viewed history as explicable through the development of ruling ideas, bordering at times on legerdemain; see *Dutch Calvinism in Modern America: A History of a Conservative Subculture* (Grand Rapids: Eerdmans, 1984), 17-18, 21.

61. Kuyper, *Lectures*, 122-23, 127-28. See also his comparison of the nature-grace view with his own view of common grace in Abraham Kuyper, "Common Grace," in *Centennial Reader*, 174.

62. Kuyper, *Lectures*, 186. Kuyper did, however, make political alliance with Roman Catholic parties at various times in his career; for an account of this see, for example, Heslam, *Creating a Christian Worldview*, 52-53.

perceived noble things in earlier ages of history, Kuyper saw the Calvinist Reformation as the great turning-point. It is only slight exaggeration to say that Kuyper believed Calvinism to be the fount or at least the stimulant of nearly every beneficial aspect of modern culture. He identified Calvinism as the source of constitutional liberties[63] and the spur of revivals in science, art, and commerce, among other things.[64] As may be evident, Kuyper admitted that the term "Calvinism" could carry several definitions, but he used the term to denote a world-and-life view, hence encompassing all areas of existence and not merely doctrinal or ecclesiastical matters.[65] In fact, it was precisely this worldview element of Calvinism, with its starting-point in the sovereignty of God, that constituted its superiority over Lutheranism, with its narrower focus on obtaining salvation.[66]

Kuyper saw subsequent European history as defined, in large part, by a series of destructive "isms" that, despite their internal differences, shared common anti-Christian presuppositions. The turn away from God and toward man that these "isms" represented was already expressed by the Deists and the Philosophes. The great enemy, however, was the French Revolution, which embraced and worked out the anti-Christian, atheistic position with often terrifying consistency and completely changed people's perception of life.[67] The French Revolution often consumed Kuyper's attention and passions; one scholar makes the very believable claim that Kuyper referred to the French Revolution more than to any other historical event.[68] Among other movements following in the wake of the French Revolution were pantheism, evolutionary thought, and modernism, all of which derived from non-Christian starting-points. Kuyper identified pantheism with the perni-

63. Kuyper, "Calvinism: Source and Stronghold," 279-317; Kuyper, *Lectures,* 40, 49, 94.

64. Kuyper, *Lectures,* 40, 110. Bratt, *Dutch Calvinism,* 16, summarizes Kuyper's view of Calvinism's effect on Western culture: "By destroying the medieval church's tyranny . . . , it could take credit for the development of modern European civilization and its finest fruits: progressive science and emancipated art; constitutional, republican government and civil liberties; thriving agriculture, commerce, and industry; and a purified family life." Bratt also asserts, however, that Kuyper, in claiming this, facilely identified Christianity with one or another piece of European civilization and thus fell prey to the very kinds of criticisms he leveled against his opponents; see *Dutch Calvinism,* 20.

65. See especially Kuyper, *Lectures,* ch. 1.

66. For helpful discussion, see Heslam, *Creating a Christian Worldview,* 114.

67. Among many discussions, see Kuyper, *Lectures,* 10-11, 85-88, 151, 175-77; Kuyper, "Calvinism: Source and Stronghold," 312-13 and generally; Abraham Kuyper, "Uniformity: The Curse of Modern Life," in *Centennial Reader,* 24; Kuyper, "Sphere Sovereignty," 470; Kuyper, *Problem of Poverty,* 43.

68. Heslam, *Creating a Christian Worldview,* 97.

cious idea of state sovereignty.[69] Evolutionary theory derived from pantheism, according to Kuyper, though was in fact even worse, since the theory of evolution and the Christian religion are "two mutually exclusive systems . . . antipodes that can be neither reconciled nor compared."[70] At other points in his career Kuyper treated modernism as the chief adversary,[71] rooted in the French Revolution.[72] In the theological world, modernism was the great enemy of doctrinal orthodoxy.[73] More generally, modernism erred fundamentally by dealing with humanity as unfallen.[74] For Kuyper, Calvinism was the only manifestation of the Christian principle that could stand up effectively to oppose the modernist worldview.[75]

It is not immediately obvious whether Kuyper's doctrine of the antithesis drove his reading of Western history or whether the crisis of Western history that he felt in his own social context compelled him to develop his doctrine of the antithesis. Certainly these two aspects of Kuyper's thought, his doctrine of the antithesis and his sense of the contemporary degeneration of Western thought, cannot be separated and were in fact mutually reinforcing.

Common Grace

As important as these matters of antithesis and worldview are for understanding Kuyper's thought, no less important are his views on common grace. Kuyper makes a crucial distinction between saving grace and common grace, which he defines in the following way:

69. Kuyper, *Lectures*, 34, 85-89; more generally, see Kuyper, "Blurring of the Boundaries."

70. See generally Abraham Kuyper, "Evolution," in *Centennial Reader*, especially 412-13, 439-40. See also Kuyper, *Lectures*, 178; and Kuyper, "Blurring of the Boundaries," 375. For a sympathetic critique of Kuyper's "Evolution" by a contemporary scientist, see Clarence Menninga, "Critical Reflections on Abraham Kuyper's *Evolutie* Address," *Calvin Theological Journal* 33 (1998): 435-53.

71. In one of his influential early addresses, Kuyper described modernism as the most forceful and coherent system of the polemic against Christianity; see Abraham Kuyper, "Modernism: A Fata Morgana in the Christian Domain," in *Centennial Reader*, 88-89.

72. Kuyper, "Modernism," 89; Kuyper, *Lectures*, 23.

73. See generally "Modernism." Though in this address Kuyper deals with modernism primarily as a theological phenomenon, in later work he treated it as a more general movement. This approach is particularly evident in his Stone Lectures. Heslam notes that in the Stone Lectures he used the terminology of modernism to describe a comprehensive worldview; see *Creating a Christian Worldview*, 96.

74. Kuyper, *Lectures*, 11; Kuyper, "Modernism," 103-4.

75. Kuyper, *Lectures*, 12.

We must distinguish two dimensions in this manifestation of grace: 1. a *saving* grace, which in the end abolishes sin and completely undoes its consequences; and 2. a *temporal restraining* grace, which holds back and blocks the effect of sin. The former . . . is in the nature of the case *special* and restricted to God's elect. The second . . . is extended to the whole of our human life.[76]

While special grace brings in something new for God's people, a re-creation, there is never anything new in common grace, which preserves and develops the original creation.[77] Common grace plays a critical role in the historical development of culture. It prevents unbelievers from playing out their anti-Christian starting-point (and their total depravity) to its full consequences.[78] Common grace, therefore, allows a measure of cooperation among believers and unbelievers in cultural life, despite the ever-present reality of the antithesis and without eliminating the need for distinctive Christian endeavors in individual fields of activity.[79] Alongside of this, it may be noted parenthetically, Kuyper identifies a variety of factors that explain the presence of commonness in the sciences: regeneration does not immediately work itself out among believers, regeneration does not immediately impel toward scientific investigation, and unbelievers have made use of special revelation through much of history.[80]

One important aspect of Kuyper's theology of common grace is his insistence that common grace does not exist solely for the benefit of special grace, simply to provide a necessary backdrop for the history of redemption. Instead, common grace also has its own independent purposes — chief among them is giving glory to God in its own right.[81] This happens as common grace ensures the continuing development of the potentialities with which human beings were originally created, despite the evil effects of sin. Through common grace, the human race constructs an edifice of human culture to greet Christ at his return.[82]

---

76. Kuyper, "Common Grace," 168.

77. Kuyper, "Common Grace," 174.

78. Kuyper, *Lectures,* 124-25; Kuyper, "Common Grace in Science," 448.

79. Kuyper, *Principles,* 159-60. Kuyper makes some puzzling statements on this score in regard to art; see *Lectures,* 160-61. For further reflection on Kuyper on art, see Bacote, *The Spirit in Public Theology,* 83; and especially Heslam, *Creating a Christian Worldview,* ch. 8.

80. Kuyper, *Principles,* 162-66.

81. Kuyper, "Common Grace," 169.

82. Kuyper, "Common Grace," 174-79.

Kuyper, therefore, presents a grand picture of the fulfillment of the creation mandate through the blessing of common grace, which he clearly distinguishes from special, saving grace. By doing so, Kuyper does not mean to keep matters of salvation and Christianity out of the broader cultural arena, which would seem at considerable odds with his understanding of revelation and epistemology explicated above. On the contrary, Kuyper also demands that special grace leaven common grace for its better functioning. The Christian spirit, he says, must modify, transform, and Christianize the various organic connections of human life upheld by common grace.[83] Key to this idea is his conception of the church *as organism*, which makes the Christian religion shine beyond the walls of the visible, institutional church, even — remarkably — where all personal faith is lacking.[84] In order to unpack Kuyper's distinctive ecclesiology, however, it is necessary to take a detour through his theory of "sphere sovereignty" before returning to the subject of common grace.

Sphere Sovereignty and Ecclesiology

Kuyper viewed cultural life as constituted by multiple spheres of human activity, including art, science, politics, education, commerce, and many others.[85] He believed that the basic Calvinist principle of divine sovereignty entailed the idea of "sphere sovereignty." To put it simply, Christ is the

83. Kuyper, "Common Grace," 188-89.

84. Kuyper, "Common Grace," 194-97, 199.

85. For example, see Kuyper, "Sphere Sovereignty," 467. Though this seems to be the primary meaning of "sphere" in Kuyper's mind, at times he also used the term to denote the different levels of *political* authority ranging from the local to the national, a point at which even Kuyperians have criticized him. See, for example, L. Kalsbeek, *Contours of a Christian Philosophy: An Introduction to Herman Dooyeweerd's Thought*, ed. Bernard and Josina Zylstra (Toronto: Wedge, 1975), 93. Heslam also identifies another variation in Kuyper's terminology, in which he spoke of sphere sovereignty as the freedom of confessional and ideological groups to form their own independent associations; see *Creating a Christian Worldview*, 159-60. Budziszewski probes a number of inconsistencies in Kuyper's doctrine of sphere sovereignty; see *Evangelicals in the Public Square*, 62-69. John Bolt expresses general agreement with Budziszewski's analysis, though he also argues that Kuyper's doctrine should be read more as a vision or orientation than as a detailed political theory; see "Abraham Kuyper and the Search for an Evangelical Public Theology," in *Evangelicals in the Public Square*, 144-45. Among thoughtful historical and constructive analyses of Kuyper's doctrine of sphere sovereignty generally, also see Richard J. Mouw, "Some Reflections on Sphere Sovereignty," in *Religion, Pluralism, and Public Life*, 87-109; and Gordon J. Spykman, "Sphere-Sovereignty in Calvin and the Calvinist Tradition," in *Exploring the Heritage of John Calvin*, ed. David E. Holwerda (Grand Rapids: Baker, 1976), 163-208.

sovereign Lord of each sphere, and no sphere may usurp the authority of another sphere and thus act as its lord. For Kuyper, this was a great bulwark against the tyrannical power of the state, which he considered a great danger, but sphere sovereignty was meant to halt any sphere threatening to encroach upon the territory of another.[86]

Though the state is the sphere most prone and most able to usurp the functions of other spheres, it has a critical task in the realization of sphere sovereignty. The state's distinctive role is to keep the other spheres within their God-given boundaries of authority.[87] Hence, the existence of the state presupposes sin and is thus only a post-lapsarian institution. Yet its authority comes from God's sovereignty alone, not by any social contract or other device of human invention.[88] For Kuyper, then, the state is distinctively "mechanical," in contrast to the "organic" life of the other spheres in society. In other words, it grows not spontaneously from the potentialities built into the human race at creation, but is imposed from without, by God, as a remedy for the effects of sin.[89] The state, however, supervises these other, organic, spheres and seeks to promote their flourishing within prescribed bounds. The organic development in each sphere is to reflect the richness and diversity of human life. Human society is complex, not uniform.[90] Human beings achieve cultural goods through their instinctive and spontaneous capacities, not simply their reflective or intellectual ones.[91] Hence, a truly natural or organic process of development will respect and value a broad spectrum of human potential. In light of this, it is perhaps not surprising that Kuyper believed the Calvinist worldview to be generally supportive of a wholesome democratic conception of social life.[92]

Intimately connected with this vision of sphere sovereignty in Kuyper's program is his distinction between the church as organism and church as institution, a distinction mentioned above in the (interrupted) discussion of common grace. Kuyper defined the church as institution as the organized, visible church community with its ordained officers, discipline, services of worship, and the ministry of word and sacraments. The church as organism, on

---

86. See generally Kuyper, "Sphere Sovereignty"; also see Kuyper, *Lectures,* 90, 94-96, 157.

87. Kuyper, *Lectures,* 97; Kuyper, "Sphere Sovereignty," 467-68.

88. Kuyper, *Lectures,* 80-82, 91-93, 98.

89. Kuyper, *Lectures,* 91-93.

90. Kuyper, *Lectures,* 80, 84, 126-29; Kuyper, "Common Grace in Science," 445-47; Kuyper, "Sphere Sovereignty," 467; and generally, see Kuyper, "Uniformity," 19-44.

91. See generally Abraham Kuyper, "Our Instinctive Life," in *Centennial Reader,* 255-77.

92. Kuyper, *Lectures,* 27-28.

the other hand, invisibly and mysteriously permeates all of life as Christian principles and Christian people have their effect on the various spheres.[93] As an institution, the church is a heavenly and "spiritual organism" that deals with matters related to eternal salvation.[94] It is to be a city on a hill, free in its own sphere and hence rising organically from the bottom up.[95] This organic development of the institutional church makes the multiformity of the church an inevitable and good thing. Christian ideas, even Calvinist ideas, take different forms in different places, and one manifestation of them can correct deficiencies or one-sidedness in another.[96] This institutional church ought not be a national church, according to Kuyper. Supporters of the national church rightly desired the church to work for the whole of society, but they failed to make the institute/organism distinction and hence to promote the church's influence in the proper way.[97] For Kuyper, the church is fundamentally organism, not institution, and should pervade every aspect of society precisely as organism, working its influence on the realm of common grace.[98]

Common Grace (Revisited) and the Church as Organism

Here we return to the subject of common grace, temporarily set aside several paragraphs ago. A seeming incongruity was observed: Kuyper associates the ongoing cultural task with the blessings of common grace, which he has clearly distinguished from special, saving grace, yet he goes on to speak of the influence of special grace on common grace and even the Christianization of the cultural spheres. The resolution of this incongruity, in Kuyper's mind, lay centrally in the church's identity as organism. The organic church, but not the institutional church as such, penetrates the common grace arena. With rhetorical flourish, Kuyper writes:

> This institute does not cover everything that is Christian. Though the lamp of the Christian religion only burns within that institute's walls, its

---

93. For a basic statement by Kuyper, see, for example, "Common Grace," 187-88.

94. Kuyper, *Lectures*, 59-60.

95. Kuyper, *Lectures*, 62-63, 190.

96. Kuyper, *Lectures*, 63-64.

97. Kuyper, "Common Grace," 189-90.

98. Kuyper, "Common Grace," 194-96. On the more fundamental character of the church as organism, he writes: "That church, after all, exists before the institute; it lies behind the institute; it alone gives substance and value to that institute" (195).

light shines out through its windows to areas far beyond, illumining all the sectors and associations that appear across the wide range of human life and activity. Justice, law, the home and family, business, vocation, public opinion and literature, art and science, and so much more are all illuminated by that light, and that illumination will be stronger and more penetrating as the lamp of the gospel is allowed to shine more brightly and clearly in the church institute.[99]

Shortly thereafter he adds that "a sanctifying and purifying influence must proceed from the church of the Lord to impact the whole society amid which it operates" and then that "it must purify and ennoble the ideas in general circulation, elevate public opinion, introduce more solid principles, and so raise the view of life prevailing in state, society, and the family."[100] Peter Heslam provides a useful summary of this dynamic:

> His purpose in adopting and emphasizing the concept of the church as organism, in contrast to the church as institute, is clear. It allowed him to restrict the activity of the church as institute to its ecclesiastical offices such as the ministry of the Word and sacraments, alms-giving, and church discipline . . . , and thereby to lay stress on the far broader task of the church as organism, which was the transformation of human society by bringing it into harmony with the insights provided by the Christian faith. The formation of a Christian mind or disposition, for instance, as well as Christian social organizations, Christian science, and Christian art, came into the realm of activity belonging to the church as organism. . . . In adopting and advocating the concept of the church as organism and institute, Kuyper aimed, therefore, to encourage both the Christianization of society and society's complete separation from the institutional church. The Christianization of society would involve bringing all aspects of human life into conformity with Christian principles, and the separation of society from the institutional church would help to purify the church from its corrupting involvement in the world.[101]

From the parameters of this perspective, Kuyper can define more clearly what he means by the Christianization of culture and the social spheres. Use of terms such as a "Christian country" or "Christian society" does not sup-

99. Kuyper, "Common Grace," 194.
100. Kuyper, "Common Grace," 195.
101. Heslam, *Creating a Christian Worldview*, 134-35.

pose that a nation is mostly populated by regenerate people, Kuyper explains. Instead, "it means that in such a country special grace in the church and among believers exerted so strong a formative influence on common grace that common grace thereby attained its highest development." In fact, Kuyper contemplates the possibility of a society in which the spiritual state of its people is very low, perhaps even where personal faith is absent altogether, yet which could still be labeled "Christian," witnessing "to the fact that public opinion, the general mind-set, the ruling ideas, the moral norms, the laws and customs there clearly betoken the influence of the Christian faith."[102] Kuyper discusses the Christian character of society at various places. He defends ideas of "Christian" medicine and art.[103] He calls for a specifically Christian response to the problem of poverty.[104] And he asserts that the state, though not theocratic except in ancient Israel,[105] has religious responsibilities and must be governed in a "Christian way," in accord with the principles of statecraft that flow from Christ.[106]

What is described in the preceding paragraph pertains to what Kuyper calls "the terrain of common grace that is illumined by the light emitted by the lamp of special grace." This is to be distinguished, however, from another terrain, that of "special grace that has utilized the data of common grace."[107] Kuyper explains that this latter terrain appears where the church as organism manifests itself. By this he refers to believers forming their own circles, that is, their own institutions and associations, and allowing the principles of special revelation to control the life of common grace. In this terrain, he speaks of Christian art, Christian schools, or a Christian press, but wants to communicate something quite different from his use of "Christian" in the former terrain, that of the "Christian society" or "Christian nation," controlled by common grace illumined by special grace.[108] To summarize, "Christian" nations or societies exist on the plane of common grace, influenced by special grace but not presupposing faith on the part of the mem-

---

102. Kuyper, "Common Grace," 199. On the last point, see also "Common Grace," 195: "The church as organism may even manifest itself where all personal faith is missing but where nevertheless some of the golden glow of eternal life is reflected on the ordinary facades of the great edifice of human life."

103. E.g., see Kuyper, "Sphere Sovereignty," 487.

104. E.g., see Kuyper, *Problem of Poverty*, 24-28, 64-67, 75, 78.

105. Kuyper, *Lectures*, 85.

106. See Kuyper, *Lectures*, 103-4.

107. Kuyper, "Common Grace," 199.

108. Kuyper, "Common Grace," 200.

bers of the nation or society; a "Christian" school or press, in distinction, exists on the plane of special grace, as believers form their own associations in the various societal spheres and seek to let special revelation control common grace activities.

These are obviously quite different understandings of what makes something "Christian." Yet Kuyper has reasons for wanting to use the same word in both instances. He believes that Christ stands behind both common grace and special grace, and thus holds them together in a higher unity, despite the necessary distinctions between them. The key is that Christ is both redeemer and creator. It was Christ, not as Son of man or as the incarnate Word, but as the Eternal Word, who created all things, and thus the eternal Son of God stands behind both common and special grace. This should prevent Christians from falling into the Anabaptist trap and making "the word 'Christian' . . . appropriate to you only when it concerns certain matters of faith or things directly connected with the faith." According to Kuyper, this dangerous approach results in "living in two distinct circles of thought" and consigning scholarship, art, and commerce to unholy territory. Rejecting this mindset, Kuyper states:

> common grace must have a formative impact on special grace and vice versa. All separation of the two must be vigorously opposed. Temporal and eternal life, our life in the world and our life in the church, religion and civil life, church and state, and so much more must go hand in hand. They may not be separated.

For Kuyper, the connection must be maintained by sharply distinguishing between them, yet never forgetting that their intimate connection derives from the same Christ.[109]

Under the inspiration of such ideas, Kuyper makes some of the statements for which he is most well known. "Oh, no single piece of our mental world is to be hermetically sealed off from the rest, and there is not a square inch in the whole domain of our human existence over which Christ, who is Sovereign over *all*, does not cry: 'Mine!'"[110] All of life belongs to Christ. Calvinism must reject any "dualism" that threatens the standard of "religious monism" and seek instead to "impress the stamp of *one-ness* upon *all* human life."[111]

109. See Kuyper, "Common Grace," 171-73, 183-87.
110. Kuyper, "Sphere Sovereignty," 488.
111. Kuyper, *Lectures*, 53-54.

Kuyper, the Two Kingdoms, and the Reformed Tradition

I come now to the arduous task of locating Kuyper with respect to the Reformed two kingdoms tradition. Perhaps what makes it most arduous is the fact that Kuyper, as a self-consciously Reformed thinker, developed a new set of terms and concepts (and poured new content into certain older terms) in order to articulate his approach to cultural and political life. In other words, he sought to promote a distinctively Reformed cultural and political program with recourse primarily to an innovative collection of foundational terms and concepts. The claim that Kuyper was merely a "copyist" of Calvin and never deviated from his theology seems widely overstated.[112] On the other hand, neither is it immediately obvious that Kuyper's work represents a "radical reinterpretation and reapplication" of the central tenets of traditional Reformed theology.[113] The conclusion that I proffer in this subsection is that much of the foundation of Kuyper's cultural and political thought is similar to and a development of the Reformed two kingdoms tradition and, as such, an approach based in the creation order rather than in the redemptive or eschatological order. Nevertheless, I argue, there were other aspects of Kuyper's thought that pointed in a rather different direction, one that many of his followers would exploit. Hence, Kuyper stood ambiguously in the Reformed two kingdoms tradition, belonging there in many important respects but inspiring a legacy that wished to read him and use him in a quite different way.

112. E.g., see William Masselink, *General Revelation and Common Grace: A Defense of the Historic Reformed Faith Over Against the Theology and Philosophy of the So-called "Reconstructionist" Movement* (Grand Rapids: Eerdmans, 1953), 187. A helpful discussion generally of debates over Kuyper's relation to the earlier Reformed tradition appears in Bolt, *A Free Church*, 443-64.

113. Heslam states, in *Creating a Christian Worldview*, 259-60: "Kuyper's treatment of traditional Reformed doctrine amounted to a radical reinterpretation and reapplication of its central tenets. His aim was to emphasize its significance for the whole of human existence, and thereby to challenge Reformed theologians . . . to regard it not as a collection of independent dogmas of chief importance to the church and to private morality, but as a system of dynamic and creative principles, able to provide consistent answers to the most fundamental questions of human existence, and to transform human life and culture." And shortly thereafter he asserts that the result of Kuyper's "modernization may justifiably be called 'neo-Calvinism' and cannot be taken as an accurate and reliable guide to the theology of John Calvin." Taking a rather different approach (through a focus on covenant theology) but also asserting stark differences between Kuyper (with the neo-Calvinist tradition) and historic Reformed theology is William Young, "Historic Calvinism and Neo-Calvinism," *Westminster Theological Journal* 36 (Fall 1973): 48-63 and continued in *Westminster Theological Journal* 36 (Winter 1974): 156-73.

I begin the present argument by noting briefly Kuyper's account of the antithesis. One doctrine observed already in the thought of early forerunners of a two kingdoms approach, such as the author of the *Epistle to Diognetus* and Augustine, was the existence of a fundamental antithesis between Christians and non-Christians as to their morality, identity, and destiny in regard to spiritual, eternal realities. In previous chapters on the early Reformed tradition, I noted that this doctrine continued in Calvin and his Reformed orthodox successors. Among places where it found especially fertile soil there was the doctrine of sin, which taught that apart from salvation in Christ no human being can do any truly good work in God's sight. In Kuyper this doctrine that I have previously described in terms of the "antithesis" comes to be called exactly that. As seen above, Kuyper explicitly posited an antithesis between believer and unbeliever that was at its root epistemological, deriving from the different starting-points of their thought, a radical contrast inevitably finding expression, to various extents, in all areas of human endeavor. From this conviction, Kuyper developed his idea of competing Christian and non-Christian worldviews, so crucial for his cultural and political program as a whole.

In articulating these ideas, it seems fair to say that Kuyper developed and extrapolated upon an accepted theme in Reformed theology. The Reformed tradition had commonly taught that unbelievers live in fundamental hostility toward God (despite sometimes outwardly admirable behavior), unable ultimately to please him in thought, word, or deed, in contrast with believers in Christ who have been reconciled to God and are recipients of the Holy Spirit's sanctifying work. It is true that earlier Reformed theologians had not articulated the idea of an epistemological antithesis in the explicit way that Kuyper did, nor did they use any inchoate antithesis doctrine as a key organizing principle for their social thought or see their religion in terms of an intellectual worldview competing against others. The idea of a Christian worldview will be revisited below when certain tensions and ambiguities in Kuyper's thought are examined. For now I suggest that his basic assertion of a fundamental antithesis between Christians and non-Christians bears significant similarity to earlier Reformed teaching on the devastating effects of sin on every aspect of the human person and on the crucial moral reorientation of those brought to faith in Christ.

While Kuyper's theology clearly reflects the antithesis idea that underlies a traditional Reformed two kingdoms doctrine, the two kingdoms distinction itself may certainly seem more elusive in his cultural and political thought. But his doctrine of common grace bears striking resemblance at many points to important themes in the Reformed two kingdoms tradition, and, given the prominence of common grace in Kuyper's cultural and political writings, this is not a connection that can be ignored. Common grace is another doctrine articulated by Kuyper that finds no exact precedent in the Reformed tradition. Though of course earlier Reformed theologians spoke of God's sustaining the world in general and his preservation and blessing of civil society in particular, they did not use common grace as a distinct and organizing category.[114] Some aspects of Kuyper's common grace doctrine discussed above, however, manifest similarity to traditional two kingdoms thought. To put it concisely, Kuyper's distinction between God's work of common grace and his work of special grace bears close resemblance to earlier Reformed theology's distinction between God's work in the civil kingdom and his work in the spiritual kingdom.

A first relevant aspect of Kuyper's common grace doctrine pertains to its distinction between the (institutional) church and the other institutions and activities of human life. Kuyper identified special grace as saving and re-creating grace, and he identified the institutional church as "spiritual," the place where the message of salvation and re-creation is proclaimed and the ministry of the gospel exercised. He viewed all of the other spheres of human life as the arena of common grace, and though special grace was to have its leavening impact upon these other spheres, this was the arena not of re-creation but of the development of the potencies instilled in the original creation. Both the two kingdoms doctrine and the doctrine of common grace posit a clear distinction between the church and the rest of life, and for both doctrines the chief distinction lies in that the former is the place where salvation is ministered and the latter a place where it is not. For the present study it is interesting to note the similarities of Kuyper's concerns with the ecclesiological concerns especially of the American Presbyterians considered in Chapter 6 and their Scottish predecessors such as Rutherford and Gillespie considered in Chapter 5. All of these parties emphasized the spiritual and salvific nature of the church in distinction from other social institu-

---

114. Various writers have attempted to find the doctrine of common grace, in some form or another, in earlier Reformed thought; see especially Herman Kuiper, *Calvin on Common Grace* (Grand Rapids: Smitter, 1928). But whatever seeds of Kuyper's doctrine may have been present in previous centuries, at least this much must be said: "The first real impetus to a thorough study and systematization of this doctrine was given therefore by Abraham Kuyper. . . . To Kuyper belongs the credit of gathering the historic material, especially from the works of John Calvin, arranging this material in a system, and showing its practical bearing upon every day life." See Masselink, *General Revelation*, 187.

tions and the freedom of the church from state control. Furthermore, when Kuyper described non-ecclesiastical institutions he did not hesitate to distinguish them from the kingdom of God, precisely as earlier two kingdoms doctrine taught. "De 'Staat' is niet het 'Koninkrijk Gods'" — the state is not the kingdom of God.[115]

These broad points of similarity between a traditional two kingdoms doctrine and Kuyper's common grace doctrine are closely related to another important point of similarity: their shared distinction between the Son of God's twofold role as creator and redeemer. As noted above, Kuyper grounded the gift of common grace in Christ's identity as the Eternal Word, the creator of the world, while he grounded the gift of special grace in his identity as the Incarnate Word, the redeemer of his people. This is a key reason why Kuyper believed that there is nothing new in common grace while special grace is about a new creation. The traditional Reformed two kingdoms doctrine, as discussed especially in Chapters 5 and 6, likewise distinguished the Son's work as creator from his work as redeemer, and it grounded the civil kingdom in the former and the spiritual kingdom in the latter. In both doctrines, the common, non-redemptive character of the areas of life outside the church is rooted in the Son's work of creation, while the special, redemptive character of the church's life and ministry is rooted in the Son's work of salvation.

A final point of similarity that I mention between Kuyper's common grace doctrine and the traditional Reformed two kingdoms doctrine is somewhat less certain, but nevertheless important: the idea of an independent purpose for the life of common grace, or the civil kingdom. As highlighted above, Kuyper taught that common grace did not simply exist for the benefit of special grace. Society and the world in general were not preserved and allowed to flourish only for the purpose of helping to achieve God's saving work in Christ. Rather, the life of common grace permitted God's original designs for the world in the creation mandate to be accomplished to some extent and thus served in its own right to bring him glory. Even apart from matters of redemption in Christ, therefore, the life of common grace had a positive and God-intended purpose. Earlier Reformed theologians never articulated things in quite this way. Nevertheless, they arguably viewed the civil kingdom as not merely a means for facilitating the establishment of the spiritual kingdom but as having positive purposes of its own. According to them, it is a realm for maintaining a measure of justice, peace, and pros-

---

115. Kuyper, *Ons Program*, 80.

perity in the world — good things in their own right. Furthermore, theologians such as Calvin were clear that the accomplishments of pagans were manifestations of the lingering image of God and of the gifts of the Holy Spirit — things which would seem, therefore, to bring glory to God even apart from his saving work. At the very least, they did not, to my knowledge, reduce the relatively good accomplishments of the civil kingdom to the *sole* purpose of serving God's redemptive plans. Along these lines, then, Kuyper's insistence on an independent purpose of the life of common grace bears similarities to the way that the earlier Reformed tradition described the life of the civil kingdom.

In addition to bearing these basic similarities to the earlier two kingdoms tradition, Kuyper's doctrine of common and special grace developed this tradition in a number of constructive ways. One way in which he did so mirrored the work of many of the American Presbyterians considered in Chapter 6. He affirmed religious liberty for all people in society to a degree far beyond that of the earlier Reformed tradition and broke quite decisively from a Christendom mindset by rejecting the idea of a national church and supporting the ecclesiastical modification of Article 36 of the *Belgic Confession*, one of his church's doctrinal standards.[116] He also rejected the idea that the church was competent to instruct the state in determining public policy,[117] a conviction resembling the nineteenth-century American Presbyterian doctrine of the spirituality of the church. Here, it would seem, is a perspective taking seriously not only the idea that the church is sovereign in its

---

116. For recent discussions of Kuyper's views on religious liberty, see John Witte, Jr., *The Reformation of Rights: Law, Religion, and Human Rights in Early Modern Calvinism* (Cambridge: Cambridge University Press, 2007), ch. 6; and Budziszewski, *Evangelicals in the Public Square*, 59-62, 67-69. James W. Skillen has developed the idea of "principled pluralism" to describe a Kuyperian view of social life. He uses the term to indicate a commitment to religious freedom grounded not in anti-religious motives but in biblical and theological motives. E.g., see Skillen's "From Covenant of Grace to Equitable Public Pluralism: The Dutch Calvinist Contribution," *Calvin Theological Journal* 31 (1996): 67-96. The original Article 36 of the *Belgic Confession* included references to the civil magistrate's responsibility to remove all obstacles to the preaching of the gospel and exercise of divine worship, with a view toward advancing the kingdom of Christ and resisting every anti-Christian power. For discussion of Kuyper's role in the modification of this article, see Bolt, *A Free Church*, 321-32. Kuyper did, however, continue to advocate the state's responsibility to restrain blasphemy, confess God's name in the constitution, maintain the Sabbath, and proclaim days of prayer and thanksgiving. It is interesting to note in view of the discussion of natural law above, though, that Kuyper grounds the state's right to restrain blasphemy in the innate God-consciousness in every person. See Kuyper, *Lectures*, 103.

117. For discussion of this point, see Bolt, *A Free Church*, 308-9.

own affairs over against the state but also the idea that the state is a non-redemptive, common grace institution. These, of course, were issues that raised extended discussion in earlier chapters about the internal consistency of Reformation and Reformed orthodox two kingdoms teaching. It is true that Kuyper's affirmation of religious liberty and rejection of the national church idea were intimately related to his doctrine of sphere sovereignty and his distinctive ecclesiology. Neither of these were taught in the earlier tradition and in fact raise their own set of questions about Kuyper's relation to his Reformed heritage.[118] But here it is worth noting not only that Kuyper affirmed something very much like a classic two kingdoms doctrine but also that he avoided perennial tensions in the earlier tradition by removing enforcement of true religion from the hands of the magistrate as well as by rejecting the church's role as pedagogue of the state.

Kuyper's theology of common grace also revived and wrestled with, as its very name suggests, the idea of commonality, that is, the mutual social life of believers and unbelievers. As discussed in Chapter 2, earlier Christian literature such as the *Epistle to Diognetus* and Augustine's *City of God* reflected upon the things that Christians may and must hold in common with non-Christians in the broader world. In the early centuries of the Reformed tradition, the doctrine of the two kingdoms provided theological foundation for developing the idea of commonality but, as previous chapters have also suggested, the lingering reality of Christendom made the idea of a mixed, religiously plural society rather remote. Stuart Robinson, embracing the American experiment in religious liberty as consonant with the Reformed two kingdoms doctrine, worked with the idea of commonality in a much more explicit way. And now Kuyper, living in an increasingly post-Christendom world, confronted the necessity of wrestling with what Christians and non-Christians could and should hold in common in social life. Here his doctrine of common grace did what the related doctrine of the civil kingdom also could have done, and in fact began to do in Robinson's thought, namely, define the nature and extent of that commonality.

118. Some comments on the relation of Kuyper's doctrine of sphere sovereignty to the earlier Reformed tradition appear above. On the question of his ecclesiology, Reformed theologians indeed made important distinctions between the visible and invisible church, but however much their idea of the visible church may correspond with Kuyper's idea of the institutional church, their concept of the invisible church (that body of all the elect known now only to God) was not developed in terms of a mysterious, organic penetration and transformation of all the realms of social life. Additional reflections on the relationship that Kuyper posits between the institutional and organic churches, in comparison to the teaching of the earlier Reformed tradition, appear below.

Another area in which Kuyper developed the historic Reformed two kingdoms doctrine in a constructive manner was through his idea of the multiple social spheres. While previous Reformed two kingdoms thought tended to focus upon the institutions of church and state, Kuyper emphasized that the realm of common grace (the civil kingdom) consists of many institutions and fields of endeavor and warned against the state usurping authority over the others. Furthermore, Kuyper's insistence that each sphere is sovereign over its own affairs seems to be a step forward in the ongoing Reformed struggle to define coherently the respective jurisdictions of the ecclesiastical and civil realms, a struggle that continued to plague even the American Presbyterian theologians considered in Chapter 6 who affirmed religious liberty and the spirituality of the church.

This reading of Kuyper as a two kingdoms theologian differs from many conventional accounts of his work. Bolstering the argument that this is indeed a fair reading is the fact that a number of scholars have also interpreted Kuyper in the same way, including scholars who deem themselves his followers and *do not particularly like* these aspects of his thought. In other words, even some of those who have no interest or agenda in seeing Kuyper in this light have admitted that he takes such views. One very clear and poignant example of a critic of Kuyper who reads him, and laments him, as a two kingdoms theologian is Jeremy Begbie. On several points, Begbie critiques Kuyper for the "damaging gulf" that "opens up between the orders of creation and redemption" in his theology. Especially problematic is the doctrine of common grace, according to Begbie: "The notion of common grace only deepens the split, for it is usually rendered in impersonal and abstract terms as an expression and enactment of God's will in the world at large, in contrast to special grace which reveals God's unmerited love in saving his chosen people."[119] Another difficulty in Kuyper's thought, in Begbie's judgment, is the distinction "between Christ as Mediator of creation as the second Person of the Trinity, and Christ as Mediator of our salvation as Son of God and *man*."[120] Drawing upon such evidence, Begbie concludes, to his own dismay, that Kuyper is a proponent of a two kingdoms approach: "It is hard to avoid the conclusion that the Christian functions in two realms: the

---

119. Jeremy Begbie, "Creation, Christ, and Culture in Dutch Neo-Calvinism," in *Christ in Our Place: The Humanity of God in Christ for the Reconciliation of the World,* ed. Trevor Hart and Daniel Thimell (Allison Park, PA: Pickwick, 1989), 126. In this essay, Begbie critiques Kuyper along with Bavinck and Herman Dooyeweerd (the latter to be considered in Chapter 9), as part of a general Dutch neo-Calvinist school of thought.

120. Begbie, "Creation, Christ, and Culture," 127.

one which includes his earthly cultural pursuits and the other which concerns his salvation."[121] Throughout his article, Begbie's solution to this perceived problem in Kuyper is to commend the theology of Karl Barth, whose christocentric understanding of creation allegedly eliminates this regrettable two kingdoms dualism. Begbie's interpretation, therefore, effectively places Kuyper in the earlier two kingdoms tradition and makes Barth's theology the decisive break with this tradition. Though interaction with Barth must wait until the next chapter, this claim is exceedingly relevant for the present book. Begbie sees Kuyper, as a two kingdoms theologian, grounding cultural activity in the creation order and Barth grounding cultural activity in a redemptively christological order.

Dutch philosopher S. U. Zuidema provides another example of someone interpreting Kuyper as a two kingdoms theologian. Like Begbie, Zuidema sees these themes in Kuyper and does not find them attractive, but his solution is different, namely, identifying inconsistency within Kuyper's own thought and proposing that Kuyper himself overcame his two kingdoms–like tendencies. What I have called Zuidema's "two kingdoms" reading of Kuyper (he himself never uses exactly that term) is grounded in the same themes that I highlighted above in my own interpretation of Kuyper. For example, Zuidema states that Kuyper "repeatedly taught that God's common grace has an independent purpose," that he spoke of a "contrast" between common and special grace, and that for Kuyper "common grace rests in Christ the Son of God as the Mediator of Creation; particular grace is rooted in Christ as the Incarnate Word, the Mediator of Redemption."[122] Based upon such ideas, says Zuidema, Kuyper does not see the terrain of common grace as the kingdom of heaven or as "Christian," but rather as "a secular affair."[123] Almost using two kingdoms language, Zuidema states, "When giving a more exact description of the relation between the two domains of common grace and particular grace, Kuyper talks in terms of an opposition."[124] But Zuidema also sees in Kuyper a strong desire to overcome this distinction or even opposition. Kuyper envisioned special, particular grace as having a strong influence on the realm of common grace and desired the Christianization of the different societal spheres. Hence Zuidema perceives that Kuyper wrestled with a "haunting dilemma" and

---

121. Begbie, "Creation, Christ, and Culture," 128.
122. Zuidema, "Common Grace," 53, 68.
123. Zuidema, "Common Grace," 69, 72.
124. Zuidema, "Common Grace," 68.

"vacillated between these two positions."[125] "Obviously Kuyper can thus be fought with Kuyper. The Kuyper of the antithesis is then fought off with the Kuyper of common grace."[126] Nevertheless, this latter strain in Kuyper triumphed in the end, though without ever completely eliminating the former strain. Kuyper was "forced to correct himself" and in fact "the happy hour arrived that he set forth that Christ as the Mediator of Redemption not only may lay claim to the central, spiritual core of man, but also is in principle the new Root of all created reality and the Head, the new Head, of the 'human race.' With that, Kuyper had broken with his own polarly dualistic contrast between particular grace and common grace."[127] Transcending this dualism and emphasizing particular grace corresponded to Kuyper's "deepest beliefs," was "closest to Kuyper's heart," "finally weighs the most with Kuyper," and "has priority in Kuyper."[128] What is the import of all of this for purposes of the present book? A careful, deeply sympathetic reader and follower of Kuyper, who wished himself to avoid a two kingdoms–like "dualism" between the domains of common grace and special grace and wished to rescue Kuyper from such a position, could not do otherwise than affirm clearly that Kuyper in fact expressed such a position, however much he may have struggled against it and partially transcended it. Other writers working in the Kuyperian tradition have made very similar claims.[129]

If Kuyper's theology indeed bore this strong resemblance to a traditional Reformed two kingdoms approach, what should be said about the question that Zuidema raises so clearly, namely, that of Kuyper's own consistency in advocating such a position? In the paragraphs that follow I discuss four considerations suggesting that there are indeed tensions in Kuyper's thought that, in the end, do make him an ambiguous proponent of the two kingdoms tradition. Like his Reformed predecessors, Kuyper does not seem

---

125. Zuidema, "Common Grace," 100, 95-96.

126. Zuidema, "Common Grace," 94.

127. Zuidema, "Common Grace," 95-96.

128. Zuidema, "Common Grace," 53, 56, 57, 94.

129. E.g., see C. van der Kooi, "A Theology of Culture. A Critical Appraisal of Kuyper's Doctrine of Common Grace," in *Kuyper Reconsidered: Aspects of His Life and Work*, ed. Cornelis van der Kooi and Jan de Bruijn (Amsterdam: VU Uitgeverij, 1999), 98-100; and Jacob Klapwijk, "Antithesis and Common Grace," in *Bringing into Captivity Every Thought: Capita Selecta in the History of Christian Evaluations of Non-Christian Philosophy*, ed. Jacob Klapwijk, Sander Griffioen, and Gerben Groenewoud (Lanham: University Press of America, 1991), 170-79. In this latter article, Klapwijk explicitly associates Kuyper with the two kingdoms tradition, noting that "Kuyper elaborates the doctrine of common and particular grace in terms of a theory of two realms"; see "Antithesis and Common Grace," 177.

to carry through his two kingdoms theology with full consistency, though his lack of consistency does not lie precisely where theirs was.

A first issue that suggests tension in Kuyper's thought is the jarring language he uses in some of his political rhetoric in order to elicit support from Christians for his own political platform. As explored above in the section on natural law, Kuyper, in a manner seemingly consistent with his view of politics as a common grace sphere of human activity, looked to Scripture in the political realm only for general principles and insisted that his Anti-revolutionary party looked exclusively to the divine ordinances (natural law), interpreted through life experience, in putting concrete policies into place. These concrete policies, he explained, would vary considerably in different times and places. This public insistence upon a flexible, prudential approach, however, did not stop Kuyper from rallying the members of his party by invoking the threat of divine judgment upon Christians who chose to vote for parties other than his own. In one address shortly before an election he proclaimed: "Whether it's you or your children who experience it, when Christ returns on the clouds *yours* will be the guilt before God that the wrath of the returning One will erupt also against our country, a country richly blessed by God and steeped in an abundance of grace. Therefore I beg you to abandon all petty calculations. Remove from your midst all that might contribute to dividing God's people at the ballot box."[130] If concrete public policy is merely a prudential application of general biblical principles through reflective experience on general revelation, as Kuyper had said, then the question seems fairly posed as to the source of Kuyper's overflowing confidence in his ability to define a political platform that can bind the consciences of Christian voters before the throne of God's final judgment.

One might appeal to the passion of the political moment to explain such apparent excesses of rhetoric. Undoubtedly there would be truth in such an appeal.[131] But such an appeal begs a further question, a second consideration suggesting tension in Kuyper's thought on the issues before us. This question concerns the degree of emphasis, even the priority, that Kuyper affords to a cultural-political agenda. I have in mind here not primarily the fact that Kuyper resigned from his pastoral duties and demitted his ministerial ordination in order to devote himself to cultural and political activity, though surely this is not an irrelevant matter. Rather, I note his theological decision not only

---

130. Kuyper, "Maranatha," in *Centennial Reader*, 226.

131. For discussion of the political and rhetorical aspect of this address and its ambiguously theocratic tenor, see Bolt, *A Free Church*, 319-21.

to make a distinction between the institutional and organic church, but also to posit priority for the latter. As discussed above, Kuyper saw the organic church, whose task was to pervade all of life's spheres with Christian influence, as existing before, lying behind, and alone giving substance and value to the institutional church. Since, according to Kuyper's own claims, the means of grace — the preaching of the word and administration of the sacraments — are received only in the institutional church, one might wonder how, apart from the institutional church, the organic church would attain any resources to support its own existence. Beyond this difficulty that Kuyper's ecclesiology creates, it must be asked how the priority of the Christian's labors in the non-ecclesiastical cultural spheres comports with Kuyper's theology of common and special grace. If only special grace bestows salvation and ushers in the eschatological new creation, and if it is in the institutional church that this grace is received and the eschaton anticipated, then making the institutional church secondary to the organic church, which strives to improve the working of common grace for this life only, is rather puzzling. Is the proclamation of eternal salvation of secondary importance to the purifying of temporal life? How, one might ask further, does this comport not only with other emphases of Kuyper but also with the insistence of earlier Reformed two kingdoms theology that the present life is but a pilgrimage, the Christian's true hope and encouragement deriving from the life that is to come? Finally, what is the significance of Kuyper's emphasis upon religion not as primarily a message of salvation or in terms of ecclesiastical life and doctrine, but as a worldview, something that can be described as "Calvin*ism*," in the light of a traditionally Reformed two kingdoms perspective?[132]

The final two issues, I believe, may bring us closer to the heart of the matter theologically. The third consideration, then, that betrays tension in Kuyper's thought is his advocacy of the "Christianization" of culture. As discussed above, he used the adjective "Christian" in different ways in different contexts. One way in which he used it, in reference to "Christian" societies or nations, for example, was meant to describe the terrain of common grace as it had been leavened and purified by special grace.[133] Kuyper believed that

132. A related issue worth further reflection concerns how consistent Kuyper's (and later neo-Calvinism's) advocacy of a Christian worldview is with traditional Reformed ideas about Christian liberty, as explored in previous chapters. If all fields of human endeavor are to be pursued in distinctively Christian ways, yet the church has no authority to bind its members' consciences in matters on which Scripture is silent, then how "Christian" can the many cultural activities really be for which the church can advocate no position?

133. This was his tempered use of such terminology, at least. In a political address cited

societies and nations could be "Christian" even if few true Christians were in them, so long as Christianity had had a formative influence on the character of their culture. The point of tension is that the cultural life of such a society or nation is then both "common" and "Christian" simultaneously. Since it exists on the terrain of common grace there is never anything new in it, as it simply develops the potencies inscribed in the original creation. Special grace, that is, the "Christian" influence, serves merely to help the common realm develop these potencies better than it otherwise would. This is therefore a non-redemptive "Christian" influence, a "Christianization" that does not save or pertain to *re*-creation. Though Kuyper here is careful not to confuse the salvation or re-creation that is administered in the institutional church with the common preservation of the original creation in the other spheres of human endeavor, his use of "Christian" terminology for both seems at best confusing.

This leads to the fourth issue displaying tension in Kuyper's thought. As noted above, Kuyper defended the awkward notion of a non-redemptive yet "Christianized" common grace realm by an appeal to the doctrine that Christ is mediator of both creation and redemption, of both common grace and special grace. Though common and special grace must be clearly distinguished, he says, they derive from the same Christ. Has Kuyper rescued himself from confusion and even inconsistency regarding "Christianization" with this move? The answer, I would argue, is negative. Some interpreters of Kuyper, like Begbie, disprove of his traditional Reformed distinction between these two mediatorships of the Son of God. But once Kuyper makes this distinction and seeks to use it to construct his cultural and political program, theological coherence and clarity require considerably more precision in language than Kuyper exhibits. To distinguish between the Son as creator and the Son as redeemer entails that the title of "Christ" belongs only to the latter. Biblically, the Son is accorded the language of "Christ," or "Messiah" — the Anointed One — in his special mission of becoming incarnate for the particular work of saving his people. The Son redeemed the world, but did not create the world, as the Messiah, the Christ. Therefore, for Kuyper to make the traditional distinction between two mediatorships and then to de-

---

above, Kuyper can speak of the Netherlands as a "baptized nation" and claim that Christ "compels the nations to choose also as nations for or against him." See "Maranatha," 211-12. This certainly seems to be something more than the idea of special grace leavening the realm of common grace even apart from the lively faith or Christian profession of a society's inhabitants, and also something other than Kuyper's promotion of "Christian" associations, formed by Christians of their own free volition to engage in various cultural tasks from a Christian perspective.

fend the idea of the "Christianization" of the common grace realm because it is the work of "Christ," is to confuse categories and language precisely where categories and language are at issue. If the Son of God creates in a different capacity from his capacity as redeemer, then he does not create as "Christ," and the terrain of common grace, grounded in the creation order, is not "Christian," no matter how noble it becomes. In fairness to Kuyper, it is worth mentioning that his eminent Reformed predecessors such as Turretin also used the language of "Christ" imprecisely, as noted in Chapter 5. But since Kuyper, unlike the Reformed orthodox, used this imprecise terminology to defend a notion of "Christianizing" society, the matter seems to become more significant with Kuyper's work.

Here, in my judgment, is a knife's edge upon which much subsequent Reformed social thought would be determined. Theological coherence demands that one cannot have both traditional two kingdoms–related concepts like the distinct, dual mediatorship of the Son as well as the notion of a "Christianized" culture. In different ways, the two dominant paradigms in the twentieth century among those wishing to develop a self-consciously Reformed theological approach to cultural and political issues, the Barthian and the neo-Calvinist, both rejected the two kingdoms perspective (explicitly or not) and pursued a more consistent vision of a Christianized culture. Kuyper articulated an approach to cultural and political issues grounded largely in the creation order, like his Reformed predecessors, yet opened the door for an approach grounded in a soteriological christology and/or eschatology. As Chapters 8 and 9 will explore, Barth and the neo-Calvinists walked through this door boldly.

Conclusion

Abraham Kuyper's theological vision of cultural and political life is arguably the most thorough and complex ever constructed in the history of Reformed Christianity. In this chapter I have attempted to explicate important aspects of this vision as they pertain to the development of the Reformed traditions of natural law and the two kingdoms. My conclusion, as perhaps befits the subject matter, is itself somewhat complex. I have argued that Kuyper, contrary to what is often taken to be characteristically "Kuyperian," in fact laid a great deal of theological foundation that placed him squarely and comfortably in the Reformed natural law and two kingdoms traditions, particularly through his doctrines of the divine ordinances and common grace. He not only affirmed many traditional Reformed categories but also developed these in constructive ways, often paralleling the developments of the American Presbyterians considered in Chapter 6. But I have also claimed that Kuyper, in both his practical political rhetoric and his theological handling of matters such as the Christianization of culture and Christ's two mediatorships, acted and reasoned in ways that are in tension with his traditional Reformed foundations.

My claim that theological coherence militates against the co-existence of both of these aspects of Kuyper's thought and therefore demands the choosing of one rather than the other seems to be borne out by subsequent Reformed reflection on cultural and political matters. Both Karl Barth and the ongoing development of neo-Calvinism have rejected a traditional Reformed two kingdoms theological foundation and pursued various visions of a Christian culture. Kuyper may have grounded cultural endeavors in the creation order, but he did so ambiguously. Much subsequent thought in Reformed circles has resolved the ambiguity in ways unfriendly to this traditional creation order approach. Thus it now lies for the next two chapters to unravel the decisive turn in Reformed social thought accomplished by Barth and the neo-Calvinists.

CHAPTER 8

The Christological Critique:
The Thought of Karl Barth

This chapter brings us to consideration of probably the most significant Christian theologian of the twentieth century, Karl Barth (1886-1968).[1] After finishing his theological studies at the University of Marburg in 1909, Barth pastored churches in Geneva and Safenwil in his native Switzerland. He came to the attention of the broader theological world with the publication of his commentary on *Romans* in 1918, followed a few years later by a substantially revised second edition. In this work, Barth made a sharp break from the regnant classical liberal theology of his teachers such as Wilhelm Hermann and expressed a "dialectical" theology which, according to many recent scholars, he developed over the rest of his life but never substantively abandoned.[2] He

---

1. A standard biographical account of Barth is Eberhard Busch, *Karl Barth: His Life From Letters and Autobiographical Texts* (Grand Rapids: Eerdmans, 1994).

2. An older, received paradigm portrayed Barth as moving away from his dialectical theology toward an analogical theology during the 1920s, a move sealed in his 1931 work on Anselm, *Fides Quaerens Intellectum: Anselm's Proof for the Existence of God in the Context of His Theological Scheme* (London: SCM, 1960). The classic expression of this paradigm is found in Hans Urs von Balthasar, *The Theology of Karl Barth: Exposition and Interpretation,* trans. Edward T. Oakes, S.J. (San Francisco: Ignatius, 1992). Bruce L. McCormack, building on the work of German scholars Eberhard Jüngel, Ingrid Spieckermann, and Michael Beintker, has argued that there was in fact no turn to analogy from dialectic in Barth's thought, but that he became a "critically realistic dialectical theologian" at his initial break from liberalism and remained such throughout his life (though this volume examines only his thought until 1936); see *Karl Barth's Critically Realistic Dialectical Theology: Its Genesis and Development 1909-1936* (Oxford: Clarendon, 1995). Other recent studies of the development of Barth's thought that support and build upon McCormack's thesis are John Webster, *Barth* (New York: Continuum, 2000) (see especially 22-24); John W. Hart, *Karl Barth vs. Emil Brunner: The Formation and Dissolution of a Theological Alliance, 1916-1936* (New York: Peter Lang, 2001); and, in regard to Barth's ethics in particular, David Clough, *Ethics in Crisis: Interpreting Barth's Ethics* (Burlington: Ashgate, 2005).

began his professorial career in 1921 at Göttingen and subsequently took positions in Münster in 1925 and Bonn in 1930. In 1935, upon refusing to swear an oath of loyalty prescribed by the Nazi government, he left Germany and took a professorship in Basel, where he would remain for the rest of his teaching career.

In this study of the development of the natural law and two kingdoms doctrines in the *Reformed* theological tradition, the inclusion of a chapter on Barth deserves at least a brief comment. Barth clearly was not a Reformed theologian in the classic, confessional sense that the thinkers studied in the previous five chapters were. One recent writer has argued that Barth was not a "neo-Reformationist" (an updater of the Reformers) like his contemporary Emil Brunner, because he took what he liked from them and developed it radically.[3] Bruce McCormack has labeled Barth's theology a *critically* realistic dialectical theology precisely because it was modern and not a return to the naïve, metaphysically grounded realism of classical theology. According to McCormack, he always presupposed the validity of Immanuel Kant's epistemology and critique of metaphysics.[4] And more conservative, confessional Reformed theologians offered sharp critiques of Barth's theology which distinguished it clearly from the earlier Reformed tradition.[5] Nevertheless, Barth identified himself as a Reformed theologian and was and is regularly regarded as such. His first academic post was in fact a newly-established professorship in Reformed Theology at Göttingen. When he looked for a source to help him develop his lectures on Reformed theology in Göttingen he turned to Heinrich Heppe's compilation of Reformed thought in the sixteenth and seventeenth centuries, *Reformed Dogmatics*.[6] In his Gifford Lectures of 1937-38, Barth took up his task in his "calling as a theologian of the Reformed Church, a calling which I cannot well exchange for any other" and called upon a Reformed confessional document, the *Scottish Confession* of 1560, to aid his mostly indirect polemic against natural theology.[7] And Barth posted two pictures

---

3. Hart, *Karl Barth,* 215-16.

4. McCormack, *Karl Barth's Critically Realistic Dialectical Theology,* 130.

5. E.g., see Cornelius Van Til, *Christianity and Barthianism* (Philadelphia: Presbyterian and Reformed, 1962). For a more gentle Reformed critique, see G. C. Berkouwer, *The Triumph of Grace in the Theology of Karl Barth* (Grand Rapids: Eerdmans, 1956).

6. This work was originally published in German in 1861 and exists in translation as Heinrich Heppe, *Reformed Dogmatics,* rev. and ed. Ernst Bizer, trans. G. T. Thomson (London: Wakeman, n.d.).

7. Karl Barth, *The Knowledge of God and the Service of God According to the Teaching of the*

side-by-side in his office, not only of his beloved Wolfgang Amadeus Mozart but also of John Calvin.[8]

The purpose of the present study of Barth is not to offer a comprehensive placement of Barth within or outside the Reformed tradition. Instead, I will assume the common identification of Barth as a Reformed theologian and explore his relation to the Reformed tradition at two particular (and closely related) points, the natural law and two kingdoms doctrines. One thing that should be kept in mind throughout this chapter, however, though it will not itself be explored in much depth, is that Barth's interaction with and critique of the earlier tradition were forged most immediately by his own rejection of the nineteenth-century Protestant liberal theology or culture Protestantism in which he was trained. He saw the earlier tradition's acceptance of natural law and two kingdoms doctrines as serious flaws that had opened the door to many fundamental errors of recent Protestant theology.

I argue that Barth was in fact sharply critical of these two doctrines and therefore made a significant break with the Reformed tradition here, despite some ambiguity in his own writings on exactly where he stood in regard to this tradition on such matters. Yet this rejection of natural law (and of the natural knowledge of God more generally) and the two kingdoms doctrine did not mean that Barth repudiated the value of non-Christian thought or life outside of the church. On the contrary, he was remarkably "appreciative and indulgent of this world," as one unlikely commentator, the novelist John Updike, has put it.[9] Both Barth's aversion to the natural law and two kingdoms doctrines and his receptivity to the non-Christian world, in fact, were grounded in his attempt to make theology thoroughly christocentric, a christocentrism that penetrated to his doctrines of divine revelation and creation as well as to reconciliation. It is important to note up front that the earlier Reformed tradition as studied in previous chapters was certainly christocentric, as exemplified in the doctrine of the Son's dual mediatorship over creation and redemption. But Barth's christocentrism was of a different sort and, I argue, differentiated him from earlier Reformed theology. Readers should keep this in mind as I use inevitably ambiguous terms such as "christocentric" and even "Christological" in the following pages.[10] This

---

Reformation, trans. J. L. M. Haire and Ian Henderson (London: Hodder and Stoughton, 1938) (especially 5).

8. See Theodore A. Gill, "Barth and Mozart," *Theology Today* 43 (October 1986): 405.

9. John Updike, "Foreword," in Karl Barth, *Wolfgang Amadeus Mozart,* trans. Clarence K. Pott (Grand Rapids: Eerdmans, 1986), 7.

10. Richard A. Muller's brief but convincing article should be mentioned in this regard: "A

chapter will explore, then, how Barth's christocentric reworking of Reformed doctrine produced an approach to cultural and social life distinct from the creation-order approach of the earlier tradition.

In order to accomplish this, I first survey several aspects of Barth's theology that provide an overview of key elements of his thought relevant to the questions at issue in this book. Then I turn to examine specifically where these aspects of Barth's theology place him in relation to the earlier Reformed natural law and two kingdoms tradition. In this chapter I draw upon a number of different writings of Barth over several decades of his career. Specifically, I use Barth's *Ethics,* his exchange with Brunner on natural theology, his Gifford Lectures, his three essays collected in the volume *Community, State, and Church,* his several essays on the music of Mozart, and of course various sections from his *magnum opus,* the unfinished *Church Dogmatics* [hereafter *CD*].[11] Though there is certainly other relevant material throughout the voluminous corpus of Barth's writings, I have attempted to choose a representative sampling of important discussions that give a fair presentation of his thought both in its general outlines and in its relevant nuances.

Note on 'Christocentrism' and the Imprudent Use of Such Terminology," *Westminster Theological Journal* 68 (Fall 2006): 253-60. Muller wryly observes that every *Christian* theologian worthy of the name, of whatever theological tradition, has striven to be christocentric. In light especially of recent neo-orthodox attempts to evaluate early Reformed theology in terms of a Barth-like christocentrism, Muller finds the term "christocentric" itself basically meaningless in discussions of sixteenth- and seventeenth-century Reformed thought.

11. See Karl Barth, *Ethics,* ed. Dietrich Braun, trans. Geoffrey W. Bromiley (New York: Seabury, 1981); Karl Barth, "No!" in *Natural Theology: Comprising 'Nature and Grace' by Professor Dr. Emil Brunner and the Reply 'No!' by Dr. Karl Barth,* trans. Peter Fraenkel (London: Geoffrey Bles: Centenary, 1946); Barth, *The Knowledge of God;* Karl Barth, *Community, State, and Church: Three Essays* (Gloucester, MA: Peter Smith, 1968) [this volume consists of three separate essays, "Gospel and Law" (1935), "Church and State" (1938), and "The Christian Community and the Civil Community" (1946)]; Barth, *Wolfgang Amadeus Mozart;* and from the *Church Dogmatics* [hereafter *CD*] especially (but not exclusively) Karl Barth, *Church Dogmatics,* II/1, *The Doctrine of God,* ed. G. W. Bromiley and T. F. Torrance, trans. T. H. L. Parker, W. B. Johnston, Harold Knight, J. L. M. Haire (Edinburgh: T&T Clark, 1957); Karl Barth, *Church Dogmatics,* II/2, *The Doctrine of God,* trans. G. W. Bromiley, J. C. Campbell, Iain Wilson, J. Strathearn McNab, Harold Knight, R. A. Stewart, ed. G. W. Bromiley and T. F. Torrence (New York: T&T Clark, 1957); and Karl Barth, *Church Dogmatics,* IV/3/1, *The Doctrine of Reconciliation,* trans. G. W. Bromiley, ed. G. W. Bromiley and T. F. Torrance (New York: T&T Clark, 1961).

Aspects of Barth's Theology of Culture and Social Life

In this opening section, before placing Barth's thought in relation to the Reformed natural law and two kingdoms traditions, I try to let his theology speak for itself, on its own terms, particularly as it relates to his approach to cultural and social life. Though there are numerous aspects of his theology that might be examined here, I highlight three specifically: his theology of revelation, his idea of "secular parables of truth," and his understanding of the civil state. In all three areas Barth's Christological reworking of theology is evident.

Barth's Theology of Revelation

The first of the major issues that I identify as foundational for his social thought (and certainly for his thought as a whole) is his theology of revelation.[12] In the CD, Barth affirms that there is true human knowledge of God, but that such knowledge comes only through the Word of God, that is, through the revelation of Jesus Christ. It is, therefore, mediated knowledge.[13] Elsewhere Barth states that God makes himself known in Jesus Christ and not in any other way.[14] We can know "absolutely nothing" about God, the world, or human beings except through revelation in Jesus Christ. Everything else leads astray.[15] "The fact that man stands before the God who gives Himself to be known in His Word, and therefore to be known mediately, definitely means that we have to understand man's knowledge of God as the knowledge of faith."[16] For Barth this also means that we can never approach God on our own initiative or from our own resources, but that we know him only as he gives himself to be known.[17]

---

12. For recent discussion of Barth's theology of revelation, see generally Webster, *Barth*, ch. 3; Eberhard Busch, *The Great Passion: An Introduction to Karl Barth's Theology,* trans. Geoffrey W. Bromiley (Grand Rapids: Eerdmans, 2004), ch. 1; and Trevor Hart, "Revelation," in *The Cambridge Companion to Karl Barth,* ed. John Webster (Cambridge: Cambridge University Press, 2000), 37-56.

13. Barth, *CD,* II/1, 7-10.

14. Barth, *The Knowledge of God,* 21.

15. Barth, *The Knowledge of God,* 43-44. This affirmation that God reveals himself only in Jesus Christ is a key aspect of the "objectivism" that George Hunsinger identifies as one of the central motifs of Barth's theology; e.g., see *How to Read Karl Barth: The Shape of His Theology* (Oxford: Oxford University Press, 1991), 36-37, 76, 100.

16. Barth, *CD,* II/1, 12.

17. Barth, *CD,* II/1, 41.

It is important to note that Barth's claim that God is known truly only in the revelation of himself in the Word of God refers to Jesus Christ alone and not to Scripture. Scripture is a crucial aspect of Barth's theology of revelation, but Scripture itself is not the Word of God, nor is it itself revelation. Scripture witnesses or bears testimony to Jesus Christ, the one Word of God. Barth explains: "By the Word of God the Scottish Confession and the whole Reformed church means the *Holy Scriptures* of the Old and New Testaments, in so far as these Scriptures are the concrete form of Jesus Christ." By this the church does not mean "the book, as a book," but rather means "by the Word of God Him to Whom this book and this book alone bears testimony."[18] More than twenty years later Barth had expanded this point, rather significantly for present purposes, claiming that in fact the Bible does not *alone* bear testimony to Jesus Christ. Instead, "the message, activity and life of the Christian Church" also witnesses of Christ, as does the "history of the gifts and operations of Jesus Christ" and even "the luminous sphere in which His attestation takes place and His impulses are in some way visible."[19] This witness to Christ outside of Scripture and the church will be considered further below. For now, it is sufficient to note that God's revelation of himself in Jesus Christ takes place mediately or indirectly,[20] *especially* in Scripture for people today, but that the words of Scripture themselves are not revelation. Christians do not possess the Word of God in a book that they carry with them.

Rather than this revelation of God in Jesus Christ being something we possess, in Scripture or elsewhere, Barth explains that it takes the form of an encounter, an action of grace, of free bestowal. As such, it always contains something new and surprising and the object of knowledge does not become something at our disposal.[21] Our knowledge of God is never conclusive, but is something of which we can speak, again and again, infinitely often, as God in Jesus Christ graciously encounters us in revelation.[22] Thus, as George Hunsinger explains, "in Barth's theology truth is always conceived as an event. Truth is not a static datum, nor is it a fixed and deposited state of affairs."[23] Barth places this emphasis on revelation as an encounter and hence on knowing truth as an event not only for doctrine or theology, but

---

18. Barth, *The Knowledge of God*, 177-78.
19. Barth, *CD*, IV/3/1, 96.
20. Barth, *CD*, II/1, 199.
21. Barth, *CD*, II/1, 21-23.
22. Barth, *CD*, II/1, 250.
23. Hunsinger, *How To Read Karl Barth*, 67 (see also Part II of this work generally).

for ethics as well. He viewed ethics not as a separate discipline from theology but as an intimate part of the theological task across the spectrum of doctrines.[24] Hence it is little surprise that when he begins his lengthy treatment of ethics in chapter 8 of his discussion of the Doctrine of God he reminds readers of his common theme: "God is not known and is not knowable except in Jesus Christ."[25] And this particular section concludes with the exhortation that the "first thing that theological ethics has to show, and to develop as a basic and all-comprehensive truth, is the fact and extent that this command of God is an event." Ethics concerns "not a reality which is, but a reality which occurs," and thus no refuge can be sought in the "safe shelter of a general theory."[26] Therefore, Barth often emphasizes that proper human action cannot be derived or applied from a knowledge of being or of human nature, but that good is determined wholly by the command of God: the "reality of the command of God" is "the sum of the good."[27] Good is done as obedience is rendered to the command of God as it comes again and again, never to be comprehended in a tight and sufficient moral system. This view of ethics has prompted some to critique Barth as an occasionalist, unable to account for the continuity in a person's moral life or to provide a place for moral reasoning, though others have defended Barth on this charge.[28]

Another important aspect of Barth's understanding of revelation is important to note for present purposes. As seen above, people know God in revelation by a share in the truth. Yet this is not a partial knowledge, as if one might wait for another or higher revelation, for in revelation God is known in his entirety, as Father, Son, and Holy Spirit, as creator, reconciler, and redeemer. God is either known in his entirety or he is not known at all.[29] Barth

---

24. For recent treatment of Barth's ethics, see e.g. Clough, *Ethics in Crisis;* Nigel Biggar, "Barth's Trinitarian Ethics," in *The Cambridge Companion to Karl Barth*, 212-27; Nigel Biggar, *The Hastening That Waits: Karl Barth's Ethics* (Oxford: Clarendon, 1993); John Webster, *Barth's Moral Theology: Human Action in Barth's Thought* (Grand Rapids: Eerdmans, 1998); John Webster, *Barth's Ethics of Reconciliation* (Cambridge: Cambridge University Press, 1995); Webster, *Barth*, ch. 7; Busch, *The Great Passion*, ch. 5; Paul D. Matheny, *Dogmatics and Ethics: The Theological Realism and Ethics of Karl Barth's* Church Dogmatics (New York: Peter Lang, 1990); and Robin W. Lovin, *Christian Faith and Public Choices: The Social Ethics of Barth, Brunner, and Bonhoeffer* (Philadelphia: Fortress, 1984), ch. 2.

25. Barth, *CD*, II/2, 509.

26. Barth, *CD*, II/2, 548.

27. Barth, *CD*, II/2, 536.

28. For discussion of these themes in Barth, see e.g. Biggar, *The Hastening That Waits*, ch. 1; Clough, *Ethics in Crisis*, ch. 3 and 5; and Webster, *Barth's Moral Theology*, 51.

29. Barth, *CD*, II/1, 51.

does not want to collapse the categories of creation and reconciliation, but neither will he grant them any independent existence. Simply put, the orders of creation and reconciliation are united in Jesus Christ.[30] To know God as creator is also to know him as redeemer. For Barth, then, creation itself is a Christological category.[31] Barth's refusal to consider the doctrine of creation independently of Christology was certainly a key aspect of his dispute with Brunner, which will be addressed further below.[32] But perhaps most notably, Barth viewed his insistence on a Christological doctrine of creation as separating him decisively from the Roman Catholic theological tradition. It is along these lines that Barth offers some of his harshest critiques of Rome, accusing it of partitioning the one God into creator and redeemer, which he calls an intolerable abstraction. He condemns this as "the introduction of a foreign god into the sphere of the Church," an attempt to unite Yahweh with Baal, the triune God of Holy Scripture with the concept of being of Aristotelian and Stoic philosophy."[33]

Barth's views on a number of other matters are related to these convictions. Since not only reconciliation comes in Christ but creation as well, Barth repudiated common tendencies in Christian theology to ascribe to some matters a certain independence from Christology through grounding them in the creation order. As already considered, all revelation comes in Jesus Christ and is therefore grace and salvation.[34] No revelation comes in creation that is not also gracious and soteriological. Likewise, human persons cannot be viewed solely from their status as created beings nor be afforded a role independent of Christ — there is only the Christological. Everything that can be said about a human being can be said only from the point of view of his being in Jesus Christ.[35] Any supposed human independence is an illusion.[36] Similar things were true for Barth in regard to ethics and law, which cannot be grounded in the creation order independent of Jesus

30. Barth, *CD*, IV/3/1, 41.

31. On the Christological nature of creation (and providence) in Barth's thought, see e.g. Kathryn Tanner, "Creation and Providence," in *The Cambridge Companion to Karl Barth*, 111-26; Webster, *Barth*, ch. 5; and Busch, *The Great Passion*, ch. 5. Also see McCormack, *Karl Barth's Critically Realistic Dialectical Theology*, 454.

32. On this point, see Hart, *Karl Barth*, 119.

33. Barth, *CD*, II/1, 84 (see generally 79-84). Elsewhere, however, Barth acknowledged that Roman Catholic thought sees things such as natural rights (an idea closely related to that of an independent creation order) as having divine origin; e.g., see Barth, *The Knowledge of God*, 126-27.

34. E.g., see Barth, *CD*, II/1, 197-98.

35. E.g., see Barth, *CD*, II/1, 162.

36. Barth, *CD*, II/1, 165.

Christ. Ethics, as observed above, consists in obedience to the command of God that comes in Christ. It can only be a response to God's grace.[37] In regard to law, Barth insisted that the common order of law and gospel be reversed. Law has no existence, in creation or otherwise, independent of the gospel. We must speak of the gospel and its content (Jesus Christ and his grace) before we speak of the law, else the law is not the law of *God*.[38] The publication of God's grace in Jesus Christ in fact establishes the law.[39] For Barth, the gospel is that Christ fulfilled the law for us, and by faith in Jesus Christ we can fulfill the law.[40]

Secular Parables of Truth

Barth, therefore, believed that all true knowledge comes through revelation, that is, revelation of God the creator, reconciler, and redeemer in Jesus Christ. As Barth put it, Jesus Christ is *the,* one and only, light of life.[41] This affirmation brings us to the second of the major themes that I identify in this section as foundational for his social thought. Though Barth believed that all truth is Christological, he did not thereby mean, contrary to what one might expect from such an affirmation, to grant a special, exclusive privilege to Christians, the church, or Christianity.[42] Rather, he believed that much truth was to be found and heard among non-Christians and outside the church. In order to account for this in a way consistent with his Christological understanding of knowledge and truth, Barth introduced the idea of "secular parables of truth," true words spoken *extra muros ecclesiae*.[43] True words may be spoken in the world and not merely in the Bible or in the church. Jesus Christ, however, is the only Word of God and hence he delimits all other words, whether in the Bible, church, or world.[44] The truth of Jesus

37. E.g., see Barth, *CD*, II/2, 539.
38. Barth, "Gospel and Law," 71-73.
39. Barth, "Gospel and Law," 78.
40. Barth, "Gospel and Law," 81, 84.
41. Barth, *CD*, IV/3/1, 86.
42. Barth, *CD*, IV/3/1, 91.

43. For discussion of this topic in Barth's theology, see especially Hunsinger, *How To Read Karl Barth*, Epilogue; and Biggar, *The Hastening That Waits*, ch. 5. For a briefer discussion, see e.g. Joseph Mangina, *Karl Barth: Theologian of Christian Witness* (Louisville: Westminster John Knox, 2004), 133.

44. Barth, *CD*, IV/3/1, 97.

Christ can never be combined with some other truth into a higher system, but it can enter into conjunction and union with other words.[45] If they are indeed to be true, such words must say the same thing as the Word of God and be true for that reason, and this happens when the Word of God allows itself to be reflected and reproduced in them.[46] Though they must be tested by the Word of God, Barth urges that they really be heard, for they can illumine, accentuate, or explain the biblical witness in a particular time or situation.[47] Among the criteria for testing these secular words, Barth includes their correspondence to Scripture (which remains the primary witness to revelation), the fruits they have produced, and the way that they address the church (calling the church to repentance yet always in a way that affirms and strengthens it).[48] Yet, in a way consistent with his general theology of revelation, Barth emphasizes that these words, these secular parables of truth, are never valid for all times and all places, and should thus never be collected into a kind of second Bible.[49]

Important to emphasize for present purposes is that the existence of such true secular words is explained, and guaranteed, christologically. Barth points specifically to the resurrection of Christ, to all things being put under his feet, to the idea that the sphere of his dominion is greater than that of all the Christian community. This is what permits us, he explains, to "eavesdrop" in the world at large.[50] Barth also affirms that the created order itself has a true speech of its own, a witness to its creator. But this too he says is never independent of the epiphany of Jesus Christ.[51] The things of creation still bear witness concerning creation, but do so concretely rather than abstractly, always in harmony with what God himself says about his actions toward human beings.[52] It may be appropriate to mention here, then, that just as there is no continuing voice of creation that is independent of God's work in Christ, so there is no common, preserving grace in the creation that is independent of it. In response to Brunner, Barth acknowledged the existence of a preserving grace but, as with the voice of creation, he denied that it is "abstract." Instead, this preserving grace must be understood as the work of

---

45. Barth, *CD*, IV/3/1, 101.
46. Barth, *CD*, IV/3/1, 111.
47. Barth, *CD*, IV/3/1, 115.
48. Barth, *CD*, IV/3/1, 126-30.
49. Barth, *CD*, IV/3/1, 130-33.
50. Barth, *CD*, IV/3/1, 116-17.
51. Barth, *CD*, IV/3/1, 139.
52. Barth, *CD*, IV/3/1, 164.

the one true God only insofar as through it "man is preserved through Christ for Christ, for repentance, for faith, for obedience, for the preservation of the Church."[53] Hence, Barth permits attributing the goodness and truth of non-Christians to a preserving grace, but such a preserving grace is itself Christological and is ultimately not distinct from saving grace.[54]

Perhaps the most fascinating example of Barth finding truth (and goodness and beauty!) outside of the expected biblical and ecclesiastical channels is his fascination with Wolfgang Amadeus Mozart. Barth confessed: "I have for years and years begun each day with Mozart, and only then (aside from the daily newspaper) turned to my *Dogmatics*."[55] This is perhaps not the perfect example, since Mozart, whatever his spiritual state, did live within the confines of Christianity. Nevertheless, Barth viewed Mozart as making music in an entirely non-theological, non-dogmatic way, yet in his music he presented the world as it really is. In fact, Barth asked himself how he could have the sort of positive view of Mozart that he did, in light of his own theological convictions: "How can I as an evangelical Christian and theologian proclaim Mozart? After all he was so Catholic, even a Freemason, and for the rest no more than a musician, albeit a complete one." His answer was to appeal precisely to the parable idea (though he does not use the terminology of "secular" parable): "He who has ears has certainly heard. May I ask all those others who may be shaking their heads in astonishment and anxiety to be content for the moment with the general reminder that the New Testament speaks not only of the kingdom of heaven but also of *parables* of the kingdom of heaven?"[56] How, then, did Barth view the non-theological, simply musical Mozart?

One thing to be said is that Barth found Mozart's music to be personally

---

53. Barth, "No!" 83-85. In light of this, a response might be offered to Theodore A. Gill, who reflects on how useful the category of common grace would have been for Barth to explain his admiration of Mozart. Gill states that this category would have allowed Barth to sidestep both natural revelation and redemption, but that Barth seems never to have considered it; see "Barth and Mozart," 405. However, the evidence just cited suggests that Barth did consider the possibility of such a common grace, but adamantly rejected it.

54. Here Biggar comments, regarding Barth's idea of "virtual Christianity" among those not making an explicit Christian confession, that "Barth is able to affirm both the dependence of the goodness of human action upon a rightly ordered relationship with God, and the possibility of genuine virtue among (apparent) pagans; and to do so without recourse to the Thomist distinction between nature and grace or the Calvinist distinction between common and saving grace." See *The Hastening That Waits*, 91.

55. Barth, *Wolfgang Amadeus Mozart*, 16.

56. Barth, *Wolfgang Amadeus Mozart*, 57.

edifying and uplifting. As he put it once: "Whenever I listen to you, I am transported to the threshold of a world which in sunlight and storm, by day and by night, is a good and ordered world. Then, as a human being of the twentieth century, I always find myself blessed with courage (not arrogance), with tempo (not an exaggerated tempo), with purity (not a wearisome purity), with peace (not a slothful peace). With an ear open to your musical dialectic, one can be young and become old, can work and rest, be content and sad: in short, one can live."[57] But this was more than just a utilitarian appreciation of music that was of subjective benefit. Much more remarkably, Barth wrote of Mozart's music as something that, in an ultimately inexplicable way, presented reality in its universal wholeness, the world as it really is. He identified the profundity of his music in that "it evidently comes from on high, where (since everything is known there) the right and the left of existence and therefore its joy and sorrow, good and evil, life and death, are experienced in their reality but also in their limitation."[58] According to Barth, "what he translated into music was real life in all its discord." And yet "neither does he let himself go; he is never guilty of excess. Imposing limits, he tells us how everything is. Therein lies the beauty of his beneficient and moving music."[59] Barth goes on to call Mozart "universal" and to say that "everything comes to expression in him." What Mozart concerns himself with he does "not only partially but fully," for he "has apprehended the cosmos and now, functioning only as a medium, brings it into song!"[60] Yet equally important for Barth was the fact that Mozart did this remarkable thing without preaching a doctrine, promoting an ideology, communicating a message: "Mozart does not wish to *say* anything: he just sings and sounds. He does not force anything on the listener, does not demand that he make any decisions or take any positions; he simply leaves him free."[61] Mozart always had "something to say," yet his music should never be burdened with "doctrines and ideologies," for in Mozart there is no "moral to the story."[62]

How did Mozart do this, especially given the fact that he seemed to know so relatively little about general culture and the real world? Barth's attempted answers were little less than appeals to the miraculous or supernatural: "He must have had organs which, as if to belie that extraordinary seclu-

57. Barth, *Wolfgang Amadeus Mozart*, 22.
58. Barth, *Wolfgang Amadeus Mozart*, 32-33.
59. Barth, *Wolfgang Amadeus Mozart*, 33-34.
60. Barth, *Wolfgang Amadeus Mozart*, 34-35.
61. Barth, *Wolfgang Amadeus Mozart*, 37.
62. Barth, *Wolfgang Amadeus Mozart*, 51.

sion from the external world, made it in fact possible for him to apprehend universally what he was able to state universally." But his basic response even here was ignorance: "I do not know the answer."[63] Elsewhere he mused that "Mozart's rich work, together with his brief, busy life, can never be satisfactorily accounted for; one could say it is a mystery," such that "whoever has discovered Mozart even to a small degree and then tries to speak about him falls quickly into what seems rapturous stammering."[64] To one who demands further explanation, Barth simply points to the reality of "parables of the kingdom."

Barth's passion for Mozart then does appear to reveal important things about his perspective on truth, goodness, and beauty in matters other than Scripture, church, and things specifically "Christian." Barth, it seems, could genuinely appreciate the secular, the Word revealed in unusual sources. He did not demand an explicit profession of Christ from these sources and could receive them in a way that withheld critical judgment. As is clear in the case of Mozart, he did not even demand of himself a coherent explanation of how Christ, the Word of God, was speaking in such sources (though Barth was convinced that he was). Barth encouraged the testing of all secular parables of truth by the Scriptures, yet this was not meant to stifle the secular voices that the Word chose to use or to dampen the appreciation of Christians who heard.

Barth's Conception of the State

The third and final topic that I discuss in this section is Barth's view of the civil state. Barth's relation to the state in both practice and theory is not a simple matter. From his involvement with socialist movements during his pastoral ministry in Switzerland to his refusal to capitulate to Nazi demands upon German civil servants and later to his alleged (though disputed) tendencies toward pacifism, Barth's life and thought bore the marks of his wrestling with the character of the state.[65] Many related issues cannot be dealt

---

63. Barth, *Wolfgang Amadeus Mozart*, 37.

64. Barth, *Wolfgang Amadeus Mozart*, 26-27.

65. Much discussion of the impact of Barth's socialist activism on his thought was triggered by Friedrich Wilhelm Marquardt, *Theologie und Sozialismus: Das Beispiel Karl Barths* (Munich: Kaiser, 1972). Similar stimulus was provided in regard to Barth's relation to pacifism by John Howard Yoder, *Karl Barth and the Problem of War* (Nashville: Abingdon, 1970). For recent general studies of Barth's political thought and activity, see David Haddorff, "Karl Barth's Theological

with here. In this subsection I focus upon matters that bear especially upon his christocentric theology and the relation of the state to the church and to Christianity generally. I attempt to set forth his claims in a general and broad way, while acknowledging that Barth often finely nuanced and qualified his claims.

Barth affirmed a generally positive view of the state and, consistently with the rest of his theology, demanded that it be considered christologically. Contrary to much traditional Christian thought, the God of Romans 13 cannot be understood as simply creator and ruler, apart from the person and work of Jesus Christ. Instead, the New Testament speaks of the State in the Christological sphere.[66] The state as such belongs originally and ultimately to Jesus Christ.[67] Related to such affirmations is Barth's rather complex and nuanced articulation of the relationship of the state to the kingdom of God (and the church).[68] The state is not the kingdom of God (and neither is the church), but the state has something to do with the kingdom. Barth speaks in a variety of ways at this point which are not easy to summarize in brief fashion. One way in which Barth puts it is that the church is the inner circle of the kingdom and the State the outer circle.[69] Though Barth rejected the idea that the state is an anticipation of the kingdom, he did speak of it as an allegory, or correspondence, or analogue to the kingdom.[70] The kingdom is the original and final pattern of the civil order.[71] Yet the state is an outward, not an inward and spiritual, order of justice and, as such, constitutes the

---

Politics," in a new edition of Karl Barth, *Community, State, and Church: Three Essays* (Eugene: Wipf and Stock, 2004), 1-69; and William Werpehowski, "Karl Barth and Politics," in *The Cambridge Companion to Karl Barth*, 228-42.

66. Barth, "Church and State," 120.

67. Barth, "Church and State," 118. See also the discussion in Werpehowski, "Karl Barth and Politics," 232. For consideration of Barth's understanding of gospel and law (rather than law and gospel) and its relation to his christological understanding of the state, see Jesse Couenhoven, "Law and Gospel, or the Law of the Gospel? Karl Barth's Political Theology Compared with Luther and Calvin," *Journal of Religious Ethics* 30, no. 2 (Summer 2002): 181-205.

68. Among discussions of these matters, see e.g. George Hunsinger, *Disruptive Grace: Studies in the Theology of Karl Barth* (Grand Rapids: Eerdmans, 2000), ch. 5; and Werpehowski, "Karl Barth and Politics," 232-33.

69. Barth, "The Christian Community," 157-59. For discussion of how neither church nor state is the kingdom, yet how the kingdom is hidden in both, see Busch, *The Great Passion*, 171. Hunsinger suggests that, for Barth, the church is no more sanctified than the world, but that both share a solidarity in sin and grace that is more significant than any difference that arises from their different responses to Jesus Christ; see *Disruptive Grace*, 123.

70. Barth, "The Christian Community," 168-69.

71. Barth, "The Christian Community," 154.

promise of the eternal kingdom without being that kingdom.[72] Even when the state takes demonic form, which Barth believed does happen at times, it is constrained to do good, becomes an instrument of justification, and serves the kingdom of Christ.[73]

Barth's Christological interpretation of the state bears certain similar features to his treatment of secular parables of truth. For example, Barth did not intend to grant a special privilege to Christians or the church with respect to the state and its functioning. Nor did he expect or ask the State to make an explicit affirmation of Jesus Christ. Thus, for Barth, though the church is to claim the political order for obedience to God, it should do so in a way appropriate to a sphere that is not yet under the obedience of faith.[74] Similarly, Christians are to work in both the inner and outer spheres of the kingdom — church and state — yet their works of faith, hope, and love must assume different forms in each one.[75] It is interesting to note that Barth, even while offering his Christological interpretation of the state, opposed the formation of Christian political parties. Among other rationales for this, he noted that in the political sphere Christians should bring in their Christianity only indirectly and anonymously.[76]

As for the state itself, its service to God is not to be measured by whether its rulers profess Jesus Christ. Rather, its service is simply to do the business entrusted to it, that is, obeying God's commands and abiding within the bounds of justice.[77] The state, as State, knows nothing of the Holy Spirit, of love, of forgiveness. Instead, it bears the sword, enforcing and guaranteeing human law by force, which is necessary because of sin.[78] Furthermore, the state, unlike the church, embraces everyone within its bounds and thus shares no common awareness of a relationship to God and can make no appeal to the Word or Spirit in carrying out its affairs. Its tasks are external, relative, and provisional, and tolerance is its ultimate wisdom.[79] Barth believed

---

72. Barth, *The Knowledge of God*, 221.

73. Barth, "Church and State," 110-12, 115-18.

74. Barth, *The Knowledge of God*, 221-22.

75. Barth, "The Christian Community," 158-59.

76. Barth, "The Christian Community," 182-84, 187-88. See also Barth, *The Knowledge of God*, 94-95.

77. Barth, *The Knowledge of God*, 223-24.

78. See Barth, "Church and State," 132, 142; and Barth, "The Christian Community," 154. This point involves issues about Barth's alleged movement toward pacifism in his later years, a debate provoked especially by Yoder's *Karl Barth and the Problem of War*. For recent comments on Yoder's claims and subsequent debates, see, e.g., Clough, *Ethics in Crisis*, ch. 7; Biggar, *The Hastening That Waits*, 180-81; and Werpehowski, "Karl Barth and Politics," 237-40.

79. Barth, "The Christian Community," 151.

that there is no such thing as the Christian State, despite the state's existence within the kingdom. There is also no exclusively Christian political form or system nor any political achievement that should be mistaken for the kingdom. Such things are only brought about by human insight.[80] For Barth, dreams of a State-Church should be abandoned.[81] Intended for the "world not yet redeemed," the state, *as such*, is "neutral, pagan, ignorant" and "knows nothing of the kingdom of God." It remains "ignorant of the mystery of the kingdom of God."[82]

In light of this dynamic, Barth advocated several responsibilities of the church toward the state. The first service of the church to the state is prayer, which encompasses all the rest of its service.[83] Elsewhere he says that the church's best service to the state is simply to be the church.[84] It provides a "wholesomely disturbing presence" to the state, which in itself is ignorant of the kingdom, and thereby reminds the state of things of which the state cannot remind itself.[85] On the other hand, it must endure the injustice of the state and, when necessary, resist it. This too is part of the church's service to the state.[86] Yet in doing these things it must not try to turn the state into the church, making the former subservient to the latter.[87]

Barth's Critique of the Natural Law and Two Kingdoms Doctrines

I come now to the second main section of this chapter, a consideration of Barth's relation to the Reformed natural law and two kingdoms traditions. I focus especially on Barth's explicit comments on the issues of natural law and the two kingdoms, but do so by attempting to relate them to his foundational theological convictions explored in the previous section. Also of interest in this section is Barth's own perception of where his critique of natural law and the two kingdoms doctrines situated him in relation to the Reformed tradition. I argue that while Barth clearly differentiated himself from tendencies of post-Reformation theology, he generally attempted to portray

80. Barth, "The Christian Community," 160-61.
81. Barth, "The Christian Community," 166.
82. Barth, "The Christian Community," 167-70.
83. Barth, "Church and State," 136.
84. Barth, "Church and State," 141; and Barth, "The Christian Community," 158.
85. Barth, "The Christian Community," 169-70.
86. Barth, "Church and State," 138-39; and Barth, *The Knowledge of God*, 227-35.
87. Barth, "The Christian Community," 166.

himself as sharing the basic convictions of the Reformers. Nevertheless, he also at times critiques the Reformers themselves, including Calvin, for undue sympathy to natural law and two kingdoms ideas. As a whole, this section argues that Barth set out to reject the natural law and two kingdoms doctrines quite explicitly, even being willing to separate himself from the Reformers on this issue when necessary, and that he did so as a direct consequence of his Christological understanding of revelation, secular truth, and the state.

Before I examine matters pertaining to natural law and the two kingdoms in particular, it may be helpful to note one metaphor that Barth applies on several occasions to express his difficulty with both of these two doctrines, in historical perspective: the metaphor of a "dual system of book-keeping" or simply "double book-keeping." In one use of this metaphor Barth specifically identified natural law and the two kingdoms ideas as his target. In advocating an independent consideration of sanctifying grace (alongside of justifying grace), he laments the temptation that "we begin to look for the indispensable norm of the Christian way of life elsewhere than in the Gospel (in which we think we have only the consoling word of justifying grace), and are forced to seek and grasp a law formed either by considerations drawn from the Bible or natural law, or by historical convenience. But this means that we are involved in double book-keeping, and either tacitly or openly we are subjected to other lords in a kingdom on the left as well as to the Lord Jesus Christ whose competence extends only, as we think, to the forgiveness of sins."[88] Where does such a mistake land a person historically? In another use of this metaphor, Barth describes the "dual system of book-keeping" as essentially Roman Catholic, and warns that approval of this system makes escape from the Roman Catholic tradition impossible. "The Reformers themselves" adopted this system "to some extent" and "the Lutheran and Reformed fathers" did so more categorically. The Enlightenment, then, exploited this fundamental weakness in Protestant theology, ruthlessly exposing "what must always come to light sooner or later when this double system is used." And what is this consequence? "When the two books are juxtaposed as sources of our knowledge of the Creator and creation, it is quite useless to recommend the book of grace. . . . The co-existence of an earthly pleasure with the heavenly necessarily makes the latter superfluous. To set that which is human, worldly and rational alongside that which is Christian

---

88. Karl Barth, *Church Dogmatics*, IV/2, *The Doctrine of Reconciliation*, trans. G. W. Bromiley, ed. G. W. Bromiley and T. F. Torrance (New York: T&T Clark, 1958), 504.

is inevitably to expel the latter. No man can serve two masters."[89] This, in summary, captures Barth's basic objection to the natural law and two kingdoms doctrines in light of his broader concerns and the historical dynamic in which he believed that he voiced this objection. Now I turn to reflect on things he said about each of these doctrines particularly.

Barth and Natural Law

In considering Barth's opposition to natural law, it may first be helpful to comment on his related rejection of natural theology. As noted in the opening chapter of this book, natural theology is of course not the same thing as natural law. Both are species of the natural knowledge of God, the former about God and his character and the latter about the law of God that obligates humanity. Barth's critique of natural law was simply one aspect of his more general critique of the idea of the natural knowledge of God, and thus his discussions of natural theology are pertinent in the present context. As considered above, Barth claimed that all true knowledge comes through the revelation of God in Jesus Christ, and as such is gracious. This truth, he asserted in his famous dispute with Brunner, demands a rejection of all natural theology.[90] Barth dismissed natural theology because it is a system differing from, and speculation concerning something other than, the revelation of God in Jesus Christ.[91] His affirmation that humans can never possess the knowledge of God, but are constantly dependent on receiving it anew as a gift of grace, was closely associated with this rejection of natural theology.[92] Sensitive to claims that Scripture itself speaks favorably of natural theology in a number of places, Barth surveys relevant passages at great length and concludes that biblical witness to "man in the cosmos" is intimately related to revelation and for the sake of revelation.[93] At times he steps back from

---

89. Karl Barth, *Church Dogmatics,* III/1, *The Doctrine of Creation,* trans. J. W. Edwards, O. Bussey, and H. Knight, ed. G. W. Bromiley and T. F. Torrance (New York: T&T Clark, 1958), 414.

90. Barth, "No!" 71. For an argument that Barth's opposition to natural theology arose from theological, not political, reasons, see generally Hart, *Karl Barth.*

91. Barth, "No!" 74-75.

92. See the helpful comments here in Mangina, *Karl Barth,* 62. Hunsinger comments that Barth rejected natural theology because it is not mediated through Jesus Christ, because it is natural rather than miraculous, and because it is generally accessible rather than unique in kind; see *How to Read Karl Barth,* 96.

93. Barth, *CD,* II/1, 99-124.

critiquing the idea of natural theology and just dismisses it as something to which the church is simply indifferent, something it regards as superfluous. For Barth, the church can do so since it is so taken with its task of proclaiming the true existence of human beings in Jesus Christ.[94] These basic considerations have practical implications for how the church deals with the world. For example, the church refuses to try to lead unbelievers to the truth by means of natural theology, which is in fact deceptive and hardens them toward the truth.[95] Furthermore, as considered above, given that the church recognizes secular parables of truth in the broader world and thus can eavesdrop in the world at large because the Word of God allows itself to be reflected in such words, the church does not need recourse to a "pitiful" natural theology in order to explain the existence of truth outside of its walls.[96] In other words, the Christological basis for truth in the secular world rules out the need for natural theology precisely in the place where one might be most tempted to find it.

In addition to the idea of natural theology, the concept of ordinances or orders of creation is also closely related to natural law. In fact, the claim that there are ordinances built into and comprehensible in the creation order is practically indistinguishable from many definitions of natural law itself. This seems to be the case in Brunner's defense of natural theology to which Barth offered his famous response. Brunner argued that there were such ordinances (e.g., marriage being an ordinance of creation and the state an ordinance of preservation, the former existing independent of sin), which he insisted were "divine ordinances of *nature*," and he posited that they are a basic part of all ethical problems.[97] Barth's response to Brunner at this point was a decisive rejection of his idea of creation ordinances. He argues that different people's reason and instinct provide different answers as to what the creation ordinances are and that there is nothing that could raise the constants of human history to the level of commandment. Brunner's claim that these ordinances allow people to make at least a few positive steps toward God compromises the doctrines of *sola gratia* and the utter sinfulness of the human race.[98] Though Barth's rejection of the creation ordinance idea seems rather absolute here, the matter is somewhat more complicated when

94. Barth, *CD*, II/1, 168.

95. Barth, *CD*, II/1, 93-95.

96. Barth, *CD*, IV/3/1, 117.

97. Emil Brunner, "Nature and Grace," in *Natural Theology*, 29-31. Brunner also said, however, that these creation ordinances can only be understood rightly by faith.

98. Barth, "No!" 85-87.

Barth's theological development as a whole is considered, especially in the light of his historical context. As a number of commentators have noted, the idea of ordinances or orders of creation was employed by some of the "German Christians" in defense of aspects of the National Socialist, Nazi ideology, such as the "blood and soil" doctrine. Barth did in fact use the notion of orders of creation earlier in his career and would admit later that such language could be helpfully employed were it not for the danger of misunderstanding. As discussed above, Barth did not deny that God witnesses to himself and to his will in creation, but he identifies even this witness with the one gracious witness in Jesus Christ. As Nigel Biggar concludes: "had it not been for a certain bias in the hearing of his audience, Barth would have considered it appropriate to designate the relationship between Creator and creature as an 'order of creation.'"[99]

Another topic intimately related to the topic of natural law is that of conscience. Barth defended the concept of conscience, though here again his treatment of this idea reflected his broader Christological theology of revelation and ethics. He dealt with conscience at some length in his *Ethics,* completed shortly before embarking on the *Church Dogmatics,* and revisited the issue in this latter work. Barth's stated thesis regarding conscience in the *Ethics* is: "God's command strikes me as my own strictly moment-by-moment co-knowledge of the necessity of what I should do or not do in its relation to his coming eternal kingdom. In this concrete fellowship of mine with God the Redeemer it claims me and I have to listen to it."[100] For Barth, conscience is the command of God to which the response must be obedience. It is not something that human beings possess by nature, part of "man's constitution by creation," a thing that they have in their possession.[101] "What conscience tells us relates, strictly speaking, only to the present in the strict sense, only

---

99. Biggar, *The Hastening That Waits,* 57. For discussion of these issues, see generally Biggar, *The Hastening That Waits,* 49-62, 164-65; Biggar, "Barth's Trinitarian Ethics," 218-18; Hart, *Karl Barth,* 117; and Busch, *The Great Passion,* 26, 50.

100. Barth, *Ethics,* 475. The larger section on conscience in this work is found on pages 475-97.

101. Barth, *Ethics,* 475. Note the similar concerns in Karl Barth, *Church Dogmatics,* III/4, *The Doctrine of Creation,* trans. A. T. MacKay, T. H. L. Parker, H. Knight, H. A. Kennedy, J. Marks, ed. G. W. Bromiley and T. F. Torrance (New York: T&T Clark, 1961), 9-10: "There is no such thing as a casuistical ethics: no fixation of the divine command in a great or small text of ethical law; no method or technique of applying this text to the plenitude of conditions and possibilities of the activity of all men; no means of deducing good or evil in the particular instance of human conduct from the truth of this text presupposed as a universal rule and equated with the command of God" (9-10).

to the given moment. Like God's command in general — and on the basis of conscience one may say this of God's command in general — it is a Word that God speaks personally. It is thus an event and not a thing. It does not exist; it takes place."[102] Were it otherwise, it would be only a person speaking to himself, a "mutual self-accusing and self-excusing," which, Barth says interestingly, is what Paul describes in Romans 2:15. This can be no more than a witness to or prototype of the true conscience, which is "captive to the Word of God."[103] As such, this true conscience concerns knowledge of God the Redeemer and has to do with the relation of acts to the coming kingdom of God.[104] Hence, Barth rejected the idea of conscience as a universal, constant, creation-order bestowal upon human nature by God that witnesses to the moral law, in favor of a notion of conscience as a human co-knowledge of that one, gracious, Christological Word of God spoken to human beings.

In addition to these considerations regarding natural theology, ordinances of creation, and conscience, Barth also dealt explicitly with the concept of natural law. A number of different examples could be given, such as his comments relating to "double book-keeping" noted above. But some of his most interesting comments on natural law occur in his discussion of the state. Since his view of the state has been an issue before us, and since previous chapters have had particular interest in the relation of natural law to civil law, it may be useful to focus attention here. In general, Barth rejected the idea that natural law is the proper standard for State action. At times, however, he did grant it a certain place in the governing of civil society, though always with reminders about its virtual worthlessness for this task.

Barth provides the following definition of natural law: "By 'natural law' we mean the embodiment of what man is alleged to regard as universally right and wrong, as necessary, permissible, and forbidden 'by nature,' that is, on any conceivable premise. It has been connected with a natural revelation of God, that is, with a revelation known to man by natural means."[105] Barth's basic po-

---

102. Barth, *Ethics*, 495. Barth affirms a similar understanding of conscience in *CD*, III/4, 9: "If it is meaningful to understand by 'conscience' this encounter of God's command and human action, then it is true that in each moment and act of his conduct every man finds himself in a *casus conscientiae*. And the decision in each of these 'cases of conscience' is taken in such a way that God's general command for all men in every situation is as such also the highly particular, concrete and special command for this or that man in the 'case of conscience' of his particular situation, and therefore the measure by which the goodness or evil of his action is to be assessed."

103. Barth, *Ethics*, 477.

104. Barth, *Ethics*, 485-91.

105. Barth, "The Christian Community," 163-64.

sition was that such a natural law should not be regarded as the standard for the state and its law, as it has so often in Christian theology. For example, he argues that the commands given in Romans 13:1-7 cannot be taken as dealing with natural law, falling as they do within the context of instructions that presuppose Christian existence.[106] For Christians to base their decisions in the political sphere on natural law is to adopt the methods of the pagan state when what the state lacks is precisely a better motivation for decisions than natural law can provide.[107] The concrete law of freedom that the church claims for its Word, then, not natural law, is the measure for the law that the State is to establish.[108] Apart from the church, in fact, there is no fundamental knowledge of what makes the state legitimate and necessary.[109] When the state conducts itself properly, it is not evidence of having discovered the true natural law, but of the fact that the state is in the kingdom of God and that all politics is founded on God's gracious ordinance.[110] Here, then, the implications of Barth's Christological understanding of the state come to bear.

These sorts of affirmations from Barth do need to be balanced against other claims that seem to leave a certain inevitable place for natural law in the life of the state. For example, though he said that Christians should not base their political decisions upon natural law, Barth also states that the civil community "as such" has no other choice but to think, speak, and act on the basis of natural law, or at least upon what is passed off as natural law. In this, however, the State is reduced to guessing and groping.[111] The state — again, as Barth says, "as such" — is neutral, ignorant, and pagan and thus knows nothing of the kingdom of God, cannot grow into it, and, at best, knows of various ideals based on natural law.[112] "As a purely civil community," the state, ignorant of the mystery of the kingdom, can draw only from "the porous wells of the so-called natural law."[113] Important to note here, however, is that by the state "as such" Barth referred to "the civil community which is not yet or is no longer illuminated from its centre."[114] What seems to be driving these sentiments, therefore, is the idea that the state, left to its own

106. Barth, "Church and State," 134.
107. Barth, "The Christian Community," 163.
108. Barth, "Church and State," 147.
109. Barth, "Church and State," 140.
110. Barth, "The Christian Community," 164; see also 181.
111. Barth, "The Christian Community," 163-64.
112. Barth, "The Christian Community," 167.
113. Barth, "The Christian Community," 169-70.
114. Barth, "The Christian Community," 163-64.

resources, can rely upon nothing but natural law, as vacuous as it is; however, Christians and the church ought to offer a Christological witness to the state that reveals to it its true character and the true standard for its judgment, a witness that eschews natural law in favor of the truth that is found in the Word of God, Jesus Christ. Where this witness is given, even if it is anonymous and indirect, as Barth suggests elsewhere, natural law seems to fade into irrelevance in much the same way that natural theology, according to Barth, becomes irrelevant for the Christian who receives the gracious revelation of the Word of God.

In taking these positions, how did Barth himself view his relation to the earlier Reformed tradition? As evident above in the discussion of Barth on "double book-keeping," his basic perception seemed to be that his rejection of the natural knowledge of God put him in line with the spirit of the Reformation but starkly out of accord with later Reformed thought. Nevertheless, in some of the very discussions in which he aligned himself with the Reformation over against subsequent Reformed theology, he also expressed reservations about the Reformers themselves. While the "Lutheran and Reformed fathers" worked with the system of double book-keeping, the "Reformers themselves" adopted it "to some extent."[115]

A similar perspective is evident in some earlier writings of Barth. At the opening of his Gifford Lectures, Barth invokes his identity as a Reformed theologian as the very thing that obligates him to oppose natural theology, claiming that the Reformation and natural theology are in "antithesis."[116] Furthermore, he claims that Brunner's appeal to Calvin was the one unforgivable aspect of his defense of natural theology.[117] Barth condemns Brunner as a representative not of the Reformation but of the "rational orthodoxy" of the late seventeenth and early eighteenth centuries, which he sees exemplified, among others, by Jean Alphonse Turretin, son of Francis, who, along with many contemporaries, "tried to achieve a pious and sensible alliance between revelation and reason" and thus inhabited an "interesting intermediary period" between the Reformation and the Enlightenment.[118] Nevertheless, Barth admits here as well that elements of natural theology encroached upon Calvin's own thought. This he attributes primarily to the historical circumstances in which Calvin wrote rather than to the motives of his

---

115. Barth, *CD*, III/1, 414.
116. Barth, *The Knowledge of God*, 5-6, 8-9.
117. Barth, "No!" 105.
118. Barth, "No!" 110.

theology. Calvin and the Reformers fought against Pelagianizing tendencies of later nominalism, but were unaware of the "superior" theology of Thomas Aquinas, which requires a much sharper and more thorough critique. There was a "practical non-existence of St. Thomas in the sixteenth century." But in light of the rediscovery of Thomas in recent years, Barth writes, the opening chapters of Calvin's *Institutes* need to be rewritten so that no one such as Erich Przywara (his one-time Roman Catholic colleague) could any longer find material in it for his own ends.[119] Among later Reformed theologians, it is interesting to note that Barth on occasion mentions Abraham Kuyper. Barth identified Kuyper's interpretation of Calvin with Brunner's and therefore associated Kuyper with a defense of natural theology. He regarded him as naïve, if well-meaning, in defending the importance of Scripture only alongside of reason.[120]

Barth and the Two Kingdoms

Barth advocated a number of ideas that appear consistent with or even suggestive of a two kingdoms doctrine. To mention a few examples discussed above, he taught that the state should embrace Christians and non-Christians in common, that its tasks are external and provisional, and that desire for both a state-church and a Christian state should be abandoned. Nevertheless, Barth clearly critiqued the two kingdoms idea, though he sometimes seems to caricature the doctrine — at least if we take Reformation-era definitions of the doctrine as the baseline. His historical understanding aside, the direction of his theology is decidedly contrary to the two kingdoms idea at important points, particularly in regard to his christocentrism.[121]

---

119. See Barth's larger discussion of this in "No!" 94-109. His claim about "the practical non-existence of St. Thomas in the sixteenth century" is obviously crucial to his argument here.

120. See Barth, "No!" 103; and Barth, *CD*, II/1, 173.

121. One relevant issue regarding Barth and the two kingdoms doctrine that I do not explore here is the place of the two kingdoms doctrine in the Barmen Declaration of 1934. For a discussion of this issue, see Wolfgang Huber, "The Barmen Theological Declaration and the Two Kingdom Doctrine. Historico-Systematic Reflections," in *Lutheran Churches — Salt or Mirror of Society? Case Studies on the Theory and Practice of the Two Kingdoms Doctrine*, ed. Ulrich Duchrow (Geneva: Lutheran World Federation, 1977), 28-48. For discussion of Barth and the Barmen Declaration relevant to the discussion above concerning Barth's understanding of natural law, see also Jordan J. Ballor, "The Aryan clause, the Confessing Church, and the ecumenical movement: Barth and Bonhoeffer on natural theology, 1933-1935," *Scottish Journal of Theology* 59, no. 3 (2006): 263-80.

Some initial examples appear in his Gifford Lectures, where Barth implicitly separates himself from the two kingdoms doctrine. Fairly early in these lectures, on the topic of the ascension, Barth distinguishes between the kingdom of God and the kingdom of the world. He defines the latter as "the realm of all strange and false gods, the realms of nature and spirit, fate and arbitrary power." It is not absolutely clear that Barth is addressing a classic two kingdoms view here, though there are good reasons to think that this is at least one of the things within his purview. This distinction, and his definition of the kingdom of the world, clearly rest upon his christocentrism. He says that the kingdom of God is the kingdom of Jesus Christ, apart from which there is no other kingdom and no other power about which Christians need concern themselves.[122] A classic two kingdoms view, in asserting a civil (or left-hand) kingdom that is a kingdom of God without being the kingdom of Jesus Christ as mediator of redemption, seems clearly rejected by such claims. Barth also seems to make an indirect critique of the two kingdoms idea later in the Gifford Lectures when speaking of the Christian life.[123]

More direct interaction with the two kingdoms doctrine, I believe, appears in some comments he makes toward the end of the Lectures, when dealing with the Scottish Confession on "The State's Service of God." Barth distinguishes the Reformed view expressed in the Scottish Confession with two others, one that of an unnamed sixteenth-century movement (surely he had in mind certain Anabaptists) that urged Christians to have no interest in and to withdraw from the world and the other that of the Lutherans, which acknowledged "a certain independence of the Kingdom of the world over against the Kingdom of Jesus Christ." According to Barth, Reformed theology rejected both withdrawing from the world and recognizing its independence. He comments: "these two realms are indeed to be distinguished, but

---

122. Barth, *The Knowledge of God,* 93.

123. See Barth, *The Knowledge of God,* 142-43. He asks: "Once our relation to God has been set in order by faith in Jesus Christ, does there not perhaps exist apart from faith a sphere of life, or even many such spheres in which our action is subject to chance, or indeed to the moral law or to other laws as well (perhaps to those of biology, aesthetics, economics or politics)? These would be spheres of life in which we, while recognizing and acknowledging the imperfection of this world, could yet remain satisfied with our honest endeavour after perfection of many kinds." His answer is clearly negative: "Our life as such, our human life in its total extent, our ways of thought and of action, our outward and inward achievements, could not have a more intensive and complete claim made upon them than is made by our believing in Jesus Christ and by His being thus our life."

are nonetheless one, in so far as Jesus Christ is Lord not only of the church but also of the world."[124]

Barth explicitly interacted with the two kingdoms doctrine in his *Church Dogmatics.* As noted above, in his discussion of double book-keeping he rejected the idea that Christians might be subject to lords "in a kingdom on the left," clearly an allusion to Luther's two kingdoms theology.[125] Another example comes in his discussion of secular parables of truth. Though Barth does commend making a "sharp and clear distinction" between the spheres of creation and reconciliation, he warns against being content with merely asserting their difference, which "might well lead to the unfortunate doctrine of two kingdoms."[126] Barth's further discussion of this point makes clear that his conclusion rests upon the conviction, discussed above, that the order of creation, just as much as that of reconciliation, is christologically grounded. He emphasizes that the spheres of creation and reconciliation "derive their force from the same God." Shortly thereafter, in another obvious allusion to Luther's language, he speaks of the two kingdoms doctrine as presenting God "on the right hand" and the world "on the left," which he terms "Gnosticism."[127]

As with his critique of natural law, the question may be posed as to how Barth viewed himself in regard to the Reformed tradition in his rejection of the two kingdoms doctrine. In the case of the two kingdoms, Barth clearly distanced himself from Luther, though there are reasons at times to question how accurately he portrays the Lutheran position. His view of Calvin with regard to the two kingdoms doctrine is somewhat ambiguous. Sometimes he portrays the Reformed tradition in contrast to the Lutheran but at other times finds fault with Calvin too on this issue.

In the material on secular parables of truth discussed two paragraphs above, Barth's rejection of Luther on the two kingdoms is evident in his dismissal of the two kingdoms doctrine as Gnosticism in light of its distinction between the "right hand" and the "left," Luther's famous terminology.[128] Yet Barth speaks of these two hands as though one presents God and the other presents the world. This description does not accurately capture Luther's position, in which *both* hands belonged to God, who is both creator and reconciler. Nevertheless, this rather misleading characterization of Luther's teach-

124. Barth, *The Knowledge of God,* 220-21.
125. Barth, *CD,* IV/2, 504.
126. Barth, *CD,* IV/3/1, 151.
127. Barth, *CD,* IV/3/1, 151-52.
128. Barth, *CD,* IV/3/1, 151-52.

ing does not make Barth's dispute with the two kingdoms idea any less real. For Barth, affirming that God, but not God in Jesus Christ the redeemer, is the creator is tantamount to ascribing creation to a false God. In this light, Barth's misrepresentation of classic two kingdoms doctrine is explainable: speaking of God's right and left hands in a classic two kingdoms way is, fundamentally, an elimination of the true God from the affairs of the left.

Barth also objected to the Lutheran two kingdoms doctrine in another passage examined a few paragraphs above, where he contrasted its assertion of the independence of the kingdom of the world and the kingdom of Jesus Christ with the Reformed view as expressed in the Scottish Confession.[129] In doing so, he explicitly set the early Reformed tradition over against the Lutheran, apparently because he believed that the early Reformed tradition had christocentric concerns similar to his own. It is interesting to note, however, that Article 24 of the Scottish Confession, which Barth is allegedly expounding at this point, clearly speaks of the state as an ordinance of God, but never of Jesus Christ specifically. It never mentions Christ and certainly does not give the state a Christological basis in any explicit way. In this case, therefore, one may suspect that Barth is reading certain theological assumptions into this early Reformed confessional document that were not necessarily there. For Barth, a genuine affirmation that the state is an ordinance of God entails that it is therefore an ordinance of Jesus Christ the redeemer. But the same entailment cannot be read into the Scottish Confession's affirmation that the state is an ordinance of God, at least if my interpretation of early Reformed theology offered in earlier chapters is accurate.

Another place in which Barth engaged in some interpretation of the early Reformed tradition on two kingdoms–related issues was his essay "Church and State." Though published in the very same year as his Gifford Lectures, here Barth seems more careful to avoid reading his own theological presuppositions into the early Reformed tradition, particularly in regard to his christocentrism, and therefore is not only more accurate in his historical understanding but also more critical of the early Reformed tradition than he is elsewhere. Barth generally praised the Reformers' view of the relation of church and state, but at the same time explicitly faulted them on certain matters. The Reformers, including Calvin, did not articulate properly the connection between the two institutions and did not explain what Christ has to do with the state. They did not, he says, build upon a gospel or Christological foundation. Barth says that Calvin, in *Institutes* 4.20, fails at

---

129. Barth, *The Knowledge of God*, 220-21.

precisely this point, though he attributes it not to a fundamental flaw in his theology but to a failure to carry out the agenda that he followed elsewhere.[130]

Conclusion: Barth and the Reformed Natural Law and Two Kingdoms Tradition

This chapter has explored several themes in Karl Barth's theology relevant to the doctrines of natural law and the two kingdoms, particularly his version of a Christological understanding of revelation and its implications for his understanding of truth in the secular world and of the nature and role of civil government. Furthermore, this chapter has discussed Barth's more direct treatment of natural law and the two kingdoms and argued that he offered a sharp critique of these doctrines, a critique very much grounded in his broader Christological understanding of revelation, the secular world, and the state. In this concluding section I attempt to place Barth's critique of the natural law and two kingdoms doctrines in its relation to the earlier Reformed tradition. My conclusion is that while Barth in many ways shared a classic Reformed appreciation for the truth and goodness to be found outside of Christianity and the church, and in some ways even heightened it, he did so from a fundamentally different theological foundation.

Perhaps this conclusion can best be described and defended by a brief review of some of the major themes in the earlier Reformed tradition observed in previous chapters. For the earlier tradition, the two kingdoms doctrine consisted in a distinction between two reigns of God, one a redemptive reign over his church and the other a providential, non-redemptive reign over civil society and the broader cultural realm. This distinction often involved the corresponding distinction between the Son as eternal God (and, as such, as the creator and sustainer of all things) and the Son as the incarnate mediator, the Lord Jesus Christ (and, as such, the redeemer of his people). As the eternal Son of God he reigns over the civil kingdom and as the incarnate mediator of redemption he reigns over the spiritual kingdom. Connected to this basic theological framework was the conviction that creation was an act of God, and therefore an act of the Son, but not a redemptive act of the mediator Christ. The older Reformed perspective viewed creation as well as redemption "christologically" or "christocentrically" in this

---

130. Barth, "Church and State," 102-4.

sense. At creation God established a covenant of works with Adam and, through him, with all of creation. In this covenant, God gave to Adam the law (i.e., commanding him what to do) and held out the hope of eschatological life upon his obedience to the law. This law that God gave to Adam at creation included the natural law. Natural law was therefore not an abstract concept but was grounded in God's covenantal creation of the world as a whole and especially of human beings as his image-bearers. In this creation covenant, however, God did not give the gospel (i.e., the gracious promise that God himself had accomplished what he demanded of his creatures, a promise to be received by faith). The Son of God became incarnate as the Lord Jesus Christ and the gospel message was proclaimed only as a result of the fall into sin. After the fall, God not only initiated the covenant of grace for the purpose of establishing the spiritual kingdom but also preserved the creation order through the establishment of the civil kingdom. In this upholding of the creation order in the civil kingdom God also preserved the witness of natural law, which continues to serve as the primary standard for this civil kingdom. In Abraham Kuyper's somewhat revised version of this theological framework, the distinction between the Son as creator and the Son as redemptive mediator served to undergird the distinction between the realms of common grace and special grace, this latter distinction being similar in important respects to the older Reformed distinction between the two kingdoms.

Barth's theology, as discussed in this chapter, constitutes a rejection of the traditional Reformed natural law and two kingdoms doctrines precisely because it rejects the theological foundation traditionally undergirding these doctrines. Barth distinguished God's work of creation from his work of redemption, but he did so only while insisting that they are both Christological in a way such that they can never be separated. The orders of creation and redemption are united in Christ and to know God as creator is also to know him as redeemer. To deny this, according to Barth, is to speak of two gods, to combine Yahweh and Baal. In following this line of thought, Barth separated himself from the traditional Reformed distinction between the two mediatorships of the Son of God, one of creation and providence and the other of redemption, and its corresponding doctrine that the original creation did in fact exist independently of redemption. And he thereby also separated himself from the traditional understanding of creation being "Christological" and theology being "christocentric." He likewise rejected the doctrine of a creational covenant of works in which the law was given without the gospel. For Barth, as creation is Christological in a way that it can never be accorded an existence independent of redemption, so the law can never come apart from the gospel, the latter of which must take precedence. There never was a historical covenant of works at creation proclaiming the law (without the gospel), nor was there a historical fall into sin which alone provoked the necessity of the gospel and of the Son of God becoming the Christ. Along the same lines, as Barth rejected any independent existence of the creation order, so he rejected any witness to God in the creation order independent of the redemptive revelation of his grace. Natural law cannot exist, as it did for the earlier Reformed tradition, as a creation-based but not redemptively-Christological witness to God's moral truth. Barth himself understood that the older Reformed ideas about a pre-incarnate Son (the so-called *logos insarkos*), the distinction between a protological covenant of works and a subsequent covenant of grace, and the natural law were intertwined and to be rejected together.[131]

Likewise, as Barth rejected the traditional Reformed idea of an original non-redemptively-Christological creation order in which law but not gospel was proclaimed, so he rejected the traditional Reformed idea of a post-fall distinction between a non-redemptive, providentially sustained civil kingdom and a redemptive, Christ-secured spiritual kingdom. The church and the secular world, or the church and the state, could be distinguished, but they possessed a higher unity in that both were part of the kingdom of God (though neither itself constituted it) and that both were christologically grounded. Barth agreed with the earlier Reformed tradition that both Christians in the church and non-Christians in the secular world could speak truth. But Barth rejected the idea that the former did so under the saving influence of the Holy Spirit speaking in Scripture while the latter did so through the non-redemptive preservation of their humanity and the non-redemptive testimony of general revelation. Instead, for Barth, both spoke truth insofar as God witnessed to himself in the Word of God, Jesus Christ. For the earlier Reformed tradition, then, God has dealt and continues in some situations to deal with people as creator but *not* as redeemer, while for Barth God deals with all people all the time as both creator and redeemer. In this matter there is great insight in Hunsinger's observation regarding the recognition of truth in non-Christian writers: what Calvin (and, I would

---

131. An illuminating place where Barth brings these various themes together in a critique of classic Reformed covenant theology is Karl Barth, *Church Dogmatics*, IV/1, *The Doctrine of Reconciliation*, trans. G. W. Bromiley, ed. G. W. Bromiley and T. F. Torrance (New York: T&T Clark, 1956), 54-66.

add, the subsequent Reformed tradition) defined anthropologically, Barth defined Christologically.[132] Further, while the earlier Reformed tradition also placed a significant epistemological gulf between the Christian and the non-Christian amidst the lingering commonness, thanks to the regenerating, sanctifying influence of the Holy Spirit, Barth often relativized this gulf between them in the light of their mutual Christological existence, denying any advantage that the Christian may have in the political realm, for example. In brief, while the earlier Reformed tradition traced the presence of truth and goodness in non-Christians to the non-redemptive preservation of the creation order (including natural law), and thereby identified the commonness between Christians and non-Christians in their mutual existence as creatures of God, Barth traced the presence of truth and goodness in non-Christians to the gracious, electing, redemptive Word of God witnessing to and through them, and thereby identified the commonness between Christians and non-Christians in their mutual existence under the reign of Christ.[133] In so doing, Barth also lessened the traditional Reformed distinction more generally between the Christian's knowledge and existence and that of the non-Christian.

In light of this, the conclusions at the end of the previous chapter can be put into better perspective. I argued there that Kuyper in significant ways stood within the earlier Reformed tradition through his doctrines of the divine ordinances and common and special grace, grounded in his traditional distinction between the two mediatorships of the Son of God. Though Kuyper advocated the "Christianization" of culture and could even speak of common grace being grounded in "Christ," I suggested that he spoke here in a way that stood in some tension with these other fundamental theological affirmations. Kuyper advocated a "Christian" culture, but attempted to do so (though arguably without entire coherence) within a fairly traditional Reformed natural law and two kingdoms theological framework. I also suggested in the previous chapter that much subsequent Reformed thought has advocated the idea of a Christian culture, though in a more consistent way, one that involved the rejection of at least some of the traditional Reformed theological framework that Kuyper himself affirmed.

---

132. See Hunsinger, *How to Read Karl Barth*, 234-35.

133. The reference to election here raises an important and relevant issue that I have not addressed due to constraints of space. For helpful discussion of Barth's doctrine of election in relation to many of the matters that this chapter has discussed, see, e.g., Michael S. Horton, "Covenant and Christology in the Theology of Karl Barth," in *Contemporary Investigations in Karl Barth's Theology and Significance*, ed. Bruce McCormack (Grand Rapids: Eerdmans, forthcoming).

This chapter has presented one example of how subsequent thinkers in the Reformed tradition have gone in this direction. Barth presented a view of what might well be called a "Christian" culture. He did not mean this in Kuyper's sense, which rested both upon a common-special grace distinction and an understanding of a sharp epistemological antithesis between Christians and non-Christians (both, in innovative ways, developed from traditional Reformed ideas). Instead, Barth understood the cultural realm to be good and true insofar as it was indeed "Christian," that is, a part of the kingdom of God and grounded in Christological grace (even apart from any explicitly Christian profession). He affirmed this while rejecting the idea of a non-redemptive preserving grace and any privileging of the Christian in cultural affairs, the very things Kuyper embraced. Barth, I believe insightfully, identified Kuyper with the older Reformed tradition in his view of the natural knowledge of God and, it would seem, of what Barth condemned as double book-keeping. Barth aligned Kuyper with the way of thought that he rejected. He himself eliminated the idea of a dual mediatorship of the Son of God, and with it the two kingdoms doctrine and an independent natural law, in favor of his own distinctive Christological understanding of all reality, and thereby affirmed the "Christian" character of culture insofar as any goodness or truth was found within it, for all of its goodness and truth must be due to the creating and redeeming work of Christ.

Barth, therefore, represents a rather radical break from the earlier Reformed tradition, not only with the natural law and two kingdoms doctrines themselves, but from their traditional theological underpinnings. In the next chapter we will examine the legacy of Kuyper himself and see, particularly in the contemporary neo-Calvinists, another version of a break with the earlier Reformed tradition, one which Kuyper himself hinted at but never made.

CHAPTER 9

The Kuyperian Legacy (I):
Herman Dooyeweerd and
North American Neo-Calvinism

In Chapter 7, I argued that Abraham Kuyper's approach to Christians' cultural engagement, particularly through his notions of the divine ordinances and common grace, in many ways resembled the earlier Reformed natural law and two kingdoms traditions. Like his Reformed predecessors, Kuyper grounded the Christian's cultural task and the standard for pursuing that task in the creation order, not the redemptive order. Yet I also suggested in that chapter that Kuyper did so only with a certain inconsistency. His rhetoric of the "Christianization" of the various cultural spheres and activities, for example, sat in tension with his notion that these spheres and activities belong to the realm of common grace, and hence are rooted in the Eternal Son's mediatorship of creation and not in his incarnate mediatorship of redemption.

In much post-Kuyper, Reformed reflection on Christian cultural engagement, such tensions have been avoided through (implicit or explicit) rejection of the doctrine of the two mediatorships of Christ and other ideas that linked Kuyper to the earlier Reformed natural law and two kingdoms doctrines. As observed in Chapter 8, Karl Barth rejected the idea that the world ever has any dealings with God except as he is the God who reveals himself graciously in Jesus Christ. For Barth, there is no knowledge of God as creator except as he is also redeemer. Hence, Barth quite consistently repudiated doctrines such as natural law and the two kingdoms and argued that all revelation of God's law and all human cultural endeavors, including the political, must be grounded in the gracious, reconciling work of Christ.

But what about Reformed figures who, unlike Barth, were self-consciously indebted to Kuyper's thought and sought to develop his work constructively? Certainly one of the most important and profound Kuyperian thinkers, especially on matters of culture and social life, was the Dutch philosopher and legal theorist Herman Dooyeweerd (1894-1977), to whom this chapter turns attention. Dooyeweerd offered a sharp critique of Barth for allowing redemption to swallow up creation in his theology, and he affirmed the integrity of creation in relation to redemption, thereby hearkening back to Kuyper and the earlier Reformed tradition. Yet I argue in this chapter that he rejected traditional Reformed ideas that grounded the cultural task in God's creating work but not in his redeeming work and — like Barth, ironically — set forth a view of culture and social life rooted in both creation and redemption in Christ. In so doing, he placed himself at odds, at least implicitly, with central aspects of the Reformed natural law and two kingdoms traditions.

In addition to an examination of Dooyeweerd's thought, this chapter also explores the work of several contemporary North American Reformed figures who have done significant thinking about matters of culture and social life in terms of some of Dooyeweerd's basic concepts. For reasons explained below, I will refer to them by the common moniker "neo-Calvinist." I argue that they make a similar attempt to ground culture in creation *as it is being redeemed* and perceive only *one* kingdom of God, thereby setting forth a program for Christian participation in culture with fundamental theological differences from the earlier Reformed natural law and two kingdoms traditions.

Furthermore, I also argue here that Dooyeweerd and representative North American neo-Calvinists, in their grounding of culture in creation as it is being redeemed, have placed an eschatological burden upon the cultural task that was not present in earlier Reformed thought and that further distinguishes their thought from earlier ideas of natural law and the two kingdoms. The Reformed tradition, through its doctrine of the covenant of works, indeed connected the attainment of the eschatological age to come with Adam's obedience before the fall into sin. But after the fall, the earlier tradition affirmed that this covenant was broken and that, in the subsequently established covenant of grace, only the obedient work of Jesus Christ has attained and established the eschatological kingdom. It maintained that Christians now belong to that kingdom by faith and have fellowship with it through the ministry of the church, but that their cultural labors, pursued according to the basic standard of the natural law in the civil kingdom (the original creation order as preserved from the full effects of sin), are good and legitimate but for a temporal, not an eschatological, end. For Dooyeweerd and contemporary neo-Calvinism, on the other hand, redemption tends to be identified with the restoration of the original creation order and the re-enabling of human beings to develop the potentialities in creation toward an eschatological goal. The Christian's task is Adam's task reestablished. Cultural activity and the investigation of the laws of creation are therefore specifically Christian tasks, to be accomplished according to a Christian world-and-life view, with the goal of building even now the material for the age to come.

In order to explain and defend these conclusions, I divide this chapter into two main sections. First I consider the thought of Herman Dooyeweerd and then that of five representative neo-Calvinists, four of whom have had particular influence in recent years through their publication of introductory books designed for use among students at (especially historically Reformed) Christian colleges.

Natural Law and the Two Kingdoms
in the Thought of Herman Dooyeweerd

Herman Dooyeweerd was raised in circles sympathetic to Kuyper and his activities and was educated at Kuyper's Free University of Amsterdam, where he received a doctoral degree in law. He was involved in the Anti-revolutionary Party through much of his life and served from 1926 until his retirement as professor of law at the Free University. Though he taught and wrote on various legal subjects, he is best known for his attempt to develop a comprehensive Calvinist philosophy, which he undertook in interaction with a vast range of thinkers through Western history, including leading European legal and philosophical theorists of his own day.[1] In light of his wide-

1. His *magnum opus* is Herman Dooyeweerd, *A New Critique of Theoretical Thought*, 4 vols., 2d ed., trans. David H. Freeman and William S. Young (Philadelphia: Presbyterian and Reformed, 1969). On the various influences under which Dooyeweerd worked, one writer, arguably too simplistically, says that Dooyeweerd's "labyrinthian system is in essence no more than an extension of Kuyper's theory of a universal law pervading the created order." See Jeremy Begbie, "Creation, Christ, and Culture in Dutch Neo-Calvinism," in *Christ in Our Place: The Humanity of God in Christ for the Reconciliation of the World,* ed. Trevor Hart and Daniel Thimell (Allison Park, PA: Pickwick, 1989), 120-21. A more thorough, yet still concise, examination of the influence of Kuyper and Dutch neo-Calvinism more generally, as well as of German neo-Kantianism and phenomenology, on Dooyeweerd appears in Albert M. Wolters, "The Intellectual Milieu of Herman Dooyeweerd," in *The Legacy of Herman Dooyeweerd: Reflections on Critical Philosophy in the Christian Tradition,* ed. C. T. McIntire (Lanham: University Press of America, 1985), 2-15. For other helpful contextual discussion, see Jonathan Chaplin, *Herman Dooyeweerd: Christian Philosopher of State and Civil Society* (forthcoming), ch. 2.

ranging interest in the Christian's engagement and development of culture, as well as his considerable impact not only in the Netherlands but also in North America, Dooyeweerd seems an important figure to consider in the present volume.

I begin this section with an overview of Dooyeweerd's broader thought, only within which his relation to the Reformed natural law and two kingdoms traditions can be understood. Following this overview, I attempt specifically to place his thought in relation to these earlier traditions. I conclude that Dooyeweerd diverged from Kuyper at some of the very points that, as explored in Chapter 7, linked Kuyper most specifically to the earlier Reformed two kingdoms doctrine. Dooyeweerd, therefore, presented a theory that is distinct in significant respects from a two kingdoms view. I also conclude that though Dooyeweerd accorded a very important place in his thought to the ordinances of creation, and therefore might in some sense be characterized as a natural law thinker, his use of the idea of creational laws is significantly different from that of the earlier Reformed natural law tradition. I suggest therefore that Dooyeweerd attempted to construct a Calvinist philosophy that struck out in different paths from that of much of the earlier Reformed tradition on matters related to natural law and the two kingdoms.

An Overview of Dooyeweerd's Thought

Though it is difficult to know where to initiate a brief exposition of Dooyeweerd's thought, perhaps the present section would begin most helpfully with consideration of his idea of a transcendental critique of theoretical thought. Dooyeweerd's philosophy took special aim at what he viewed as the tyranny and autonomy of theoretical thought over pre-theoretical, "naïve," thought.[2] In order to expose such errors, he launched a radical criticism of the dogma of autonomy. He did this by subjecting theoretical, philosophical thought to what he called a "transcendental" critique. This was different from a "transcendent" critique. For Dooyeweerd, a transcendent

2. Concerning the potentially misleading terminology of "naïve," Dooyeweerd writes: "Naïve experience is not at all a theory which may be refuted by scientific and epistemological arguments. It does not identify empirical reality with its abstract sensory aspect and it lacks the metaphysical notion of an objective world of things in themselves beyond the world of experience. Naïve experience is much rather a pre-theoretical datum, corresponding with the integral structure of our experimental horizon in its temporal order." See Herman Dooyeweerd, *In the Twilight of Western Thought* (Philadelphia: Presbyterian and Reformed, 1960), 18.

critique criticizes a philosophy from a perspective lying beyond that philosophy's point of view. That is, it critiques a philosophical theory from a different philosophical standpoint or from a theological standpoint. A transcendental critique, on the contrary, concerns itself with the inner structure of philosophical thought itself. It inquires into the universally valid conditions that alone make theoretical thought possible and that are required by the inner nature of thought. This critical inquiry, penetrating to the root of theoretical thought, reveals presuppositions that surpass its boundaries. Hence, contrary to the traditional "dogmatic" view of theoretical thought, the starting-point of philosophy must be found beyond philosophy itself.[3] Interestingly, Dooyeweerd believed that this transcendental critique, by examining the inner nature of a philosophy rather than critiquing it from the outside, is able to become an effective common basis for a philosophical discussion among those of different starting-points, in a way that using transcendent critique cannot.[4] A number of commentators, with different overall assessments of Dooyeweerd, have agreed with this contention, though others, such as Cornelius Van Til, were sharply critical of it.[5]

3. See Dooyeweerd, *Twilight*, 1-5. For Dooyeweerd's further explanation of his approach, in dialogue with Cornelius Van Til, see Herman Dooyeweerd, "Cornelius Van Til and the Transcendental Critique of Theoretical Thought," in *Jerusalem and Athens: Critical Discussions on the Philosophy and Apologetics of Cornelius Van Til,* ed. E. R. Geehan (Nutley, NJ: Presbyterian and Reformed, 1971), 74-89. A helpful general description of Dooyeweerd's transcendental critique can be found in Chaplin, *Herman Dooyeweerd*, ch. 3; and L. Kalsbeek, *Contours of a Christian Philosophy* (Toronto: Wedge, 1975), ch. 22. Some recent commentators have found anticipations of postmodernist concerns in this aspect of Dooyeweerd's (and his followers') thought. For example, see James K. A. Smith, *Introducing Radical Orthodoxy: Mapping a Post-secular Theology* (Grand Rapids: Baker Academic, 2004), 40-41; Jim Olthuis, "Of Webs and Whirlwinds; Me, Myself and I," in *Contemporary Reflections on the Philosophy of Herman Dooyeweerd*, ed. D. F. M. Strauss and Michelle Botting (Lewiston, NY: Edwin Mellen, 2000), 31-48; Hendrik Hart, "Notes on Dooyeweerd, Reason, and Order," in *Contemporary Reflections*, 125-46; and Guenther Haas, "Kuyper's Legacy for Christian Ethics," *Calvin Theological Journal* 33 (Nov 1998): 320-49;

4. Dooyeweerd explains his reasoning in, for example, *Twilight*, 54-56. At one point he states: "Those who participate in such a discussion should penetrate to each other's supra-theoretical presuppositions, in order to be able to exercise a truly immanent criticism of each other's philosophical views. Then they will also be prepared to learn from one another by testing their divergent philosophical conceptions of the empirical world by the real states of affairs within the structural order of human experience, which order is a common condition of every philosophy." This will "introduce a new critical mind of mutual understanding into the philosophical debate."

5. Among those agreeing with Dooyeweerd, see Kalsbeek, *Contour*, 48-49; and G. E. Langemeijer, "An Assessment of Herman Dooyeweerd," in *Contours*, 12. On the other hand, Van Til believed that Dooyeweerd's transcendental approach was inconsistent, due to his refusal to tell non-Christians at the very outset of their conversation that their thought is futile if not based

For Dooyeweerd, then, the starting-point of philosophy lies outside of theoretical thought itself, hence belying the tyrannical claims of autonomy so often exerted by theoretical thought over pre-theoretical, naïve thought. Dooyeweerd identifies this starting-point as the religious ground motive. This religious ground motive operates in the ego as the center of our temporal horizon of experience, yet cannot itself become the object of theoretical inquiry, lying as it does beyond the pale of philosophy.[6] By analyzing the different religious ground motives at work through the history of thought, therefore, Dooyeweerd is able to identify the antithesis between Christian and non-Christian thought, an antithesis that at its deepest root is not theoretical or scientific, but religious.[7]

According to Dooyeweerd, the ground motives that underlie every religion and system of thought are a spiritual force that govern all of life's temporal expressions and determine one's whole worldview.[8] Dooyeweerd identified four principal religious ground motives that have, at different times, dominated the development of western culture. All three of the non-Christian ground motives are internally dualistic, pushing life in opposite poles without the ability to synthesize them and bearing the seeds of a religious dialectic. Religious dialectics arise when one part of created reality is deified or absolutized, or when the Christian ground motive is synthesized with another ground motive. Thus what is at stake, for Dooyeweerd, is the relation between religion and temporal life, with the danger that the religious dialectic will cause an absolute division or opposition between Christian and non-Christian areas of life.[9]

Dooyeweerd described the Christian ground motive as creation-fall-redemption. Creation means that human life in every aspect ought to be directed to its ultimate origin in self-surrender.[10] Fall means that sin and apostasy is radical, touching the religious center of human beings.[11] Yet though

---

upon Christian presuppositions; see Cornelius Van Til, "Response by C. Van Til," in *Jerusalem and Athens,* 89-127. For an extended analysis of the exchange between Van Til and Dooyeweerd on this issue, see Scott Oliphint, "Jerusalem and Athens Revisited," *Westminster Theological Journal* 49 (1987): 65-90.

6. Dooyeweerd, *Twilight,* 32-34.

7. See Herman Dooyeweerd, *Roots of Western Culture* (Toronto: Wedge, 1979), 5-6. For a recent discussion of Dooyeweerd on the ground motives, see Chaplin, *Herman Dooyeweerd,* ch. 3.

8. Dooyeweerd, *Roots,* 8-9.

9. Dooyeweerd, *Roots,* 11-15; Dooyeweerd, *Twilight,* 35-36.

10. Dooyeweerd, *Roots,* 30.

11. Dooyeweerd, *Roots,* 36.

the fall redirected the human heart, it did not change the creation ordinances, for God preserves these ordinances through common grace. Redemption too reaches all aspects of life and hence, for Dooyeweerd, creation, fall, and redemption are inseparable.[12] Since all three touch all areas of life, the Christian ground motive avoids the dualisms and religious dialectics of the non-Christian ground motives. Thus the Christian ground motive is a leaven that ought to permeate all things, radically changing a person's view of the state and other societal spheres as it comes to acknowledge their true principles. This ground motive permits no dualistic ambiguity, for Dooyeweerd; it either works radically in people's lives or they serve other gods.[13]

As noted above, each of the three principal religious ground motives besides the Christian bears an internal dualism, opposing poles that the ground motive itself cannot reconcile. First, the Greco-Roman ground motive hovers between the poles of form and matter, its idea of the state tending toward totalitarianism.[14] Second, the medieval scholastic or Thomistic ground motive was that of nature and grace. It attempted a synthesis between the Christian and Greco-Roman worldviews. According to Dooyeweerd, it held to the autonomy of human thought, also tended toward totalitarianism, despite its doctrine of subsidiarity, and looked for the unity of society in the institutional church.[15] Though Dooyeweerd thought that Ockham and Luther broke drastically with the medieval synthesis, he also believed that the nature-grace ground motive continued to permeate their thought. He thought that Calvin offered a true alternative to it, but the nature-grace ground motive reasserted itself in Philipp Melanchthon's attempt at a new synthesis of Christianity and Greek culture, which led to the corruptions of Protestant scholasticism. Dooyeweerd also believed that both Karl Barth and Emil Brunner, his contemporaries, were significantly influenced by the nature-grace ground motive, despite their own differences on creation and its ordinances.[16] Finally, Dooyeweerd identified the humanist ground motive as that of nature and freedom.[17]

As noted above, Dooyeweerd identified the antithesis between Christian

12. Dooyeweerd, *Roots,* 59-60.

13. Dooyeweerd, *Roots,* 47, 109.

14. Dooyeweerd, *Roots,* 16-28; *Twilight,* 38-41.

15. Dooyeweerd, *Roots,* ch. 5; *Twilight,* 43-45; and see also Herman Dooyeweerd, *The Christian Idea of the State* (Nutley, NJ: Craig, 1968), 7-8. This was originally a lecture delivered in 1936.

16. See Dooyeweerd, *Roots,* 137-47; *Christian Idea,* 14-21.

17. Dooyeweerd, *Roots,* ch. 6; Dooyeweerd, *Twilight,* 45-51.

and non-Christian thought through analysis of these ground motives. His use of the concept of antithesis did not mirror common use of the term in philosophical literature. He meant it not in a dialectical way, indicating a relative antithesis to be resolved into a higher synthesis. Instead, he referred to an absolute antithesis that touches the religious root of all temporal life. In fact, he was convinced that identifying the antithesis between Christian and non-Christian thought and understanding its implications was not only the responsibility of theoretical thinkers such as himself but also the responsibility of every human being. In both theoretical and practical life, motives were to be brought out into the open.[18] Dooyeweerd made such assertions against the Dutch National Movement in the years shortly following the Second World War. This movement claimed that the well-being of the Netherlands required the synthesis of Christian and humanist views of life rather than assertion of the antithesis between them through the formation of different political parties. In this context, Dooyeweerd issued a resounding call for the continuing need to proclaim the antithesis and felt compelled to argue that Christianity "does indeed draw a permanent dividing line of essential significance not only for one's personal faith but for one's whole view of society."[19] Appealing to the ideas that God is creator and that Christ is the ruler of the kings of the earth, Dooyeweerd in fact calls for Christians "to strive for the consolidation of power in organizations that aim at applying christian principles to society."[20] This was not a new theme for Dooyeweerd. Before the war also he decried "the weakening synthesis, the spirit of compromise with the world" and called for an uncompromising affirmation of the antithesis in delineating a Christian view of the state.[21] For Dooyeweerd, discerning and acting upon the antithesis was a task for every Christian.

As noted above, in discussion of the dualisms and religious dialectics present in the non-Christian ground motives, Dooyeweerd believed that working with an apostate ground motive pushes one to absolutize one aspect or mode of created reality, which in turn produces a false view of reality as a whole.[22] In contrast, the Christian ground motive is characterized by the crucial ideas of the modal aspects of reality and sphere sovereignty. Dooyeweerd thought that the temporal order consists of a wide variety of distinct modes or aspects of being, which are displayed in "created reality":

18. Dooyeweerd, *Roots*, 5-6, 14-15.
19. Dooyeweerd, *Roots*, 2; and see also 3-4.
20. Dooyeweerd, *Roots*, 66-67.
21. Dooyeweerd, *Christian Idea*.
22. On this point, see also Dooyeweerd, *Roots*, 41-42.

They are basically the fields investigated by the various modern special sciences: mathematics, the natural sciences (physics and chemistry), biology (the science of organic life), psychology, logic, history, linguistics, sociology, economics, aesthetics, legal theory, ethics or moral science, and theology which studies divine revelation in christian and nonchristian faith. Each special science considers reality in only one of its aspects.[23]

A central element of this vision is that no modal aspect can be reduced to any other, an idea captured in the doctrine of sphere sovereignty. Dooyeweerd's use of the "sphere sovereignty" terminology can be confusing. Though he clearly drew inspiration from Kuyper's doctrine, he often did not mean the same thing by the term as did Kuyper. Kuyper used the term to convey the different responsibilities and independence of the various social institutions, and through this idea enriched the earlier Reformed analysis that had tended to focus on the relationship of church and state. Sometimes Dooyeweerd referred to this term in the same way and credited Kuyper with grounding this notion of sphere sovereignty in the creation order. He urged Dutch society to recover such an idea in his own day.[24] But Dooyeweerd also used the term "sphere sovereignty" to assert that no modal aspect of reality can be reduced to another, which is precisely what non-Christian thought attempts to do. The modal aspects are mutually irreducible, innerconnected, and inseparably coherent.[25] Thus, on the one hand he affirmed the integrity of each mode against encroachment from another, insofar as the original authority of each sphere derives directly from God himself, not from any other sphere. Each sphere has "an intrinsic nature and law of life."[26] On the other hand he asserted "sphere universality," the idea that each modal aspect expresses "the universal coherence of all the aspects in its own particular structure."[27] Dooyeweerd believed that the idea of sphere sovereignty was intimately connected with the ideas of the kingdom of God and the Christian view of the state, about which more will be said below.[28]

23. Dooyeweerd, *Roots,* 40-41. For extended discussion of Dooyeweerd's understanding of the modal aspects, see Chaplin, *Herman Dooyeweerd,* ch. 4.

24. E.g., see Dooyeweerd, *Roots,* 49-55. Kalsbeek describes Dooyeweerd's views on sphere sovereignty at some length in *Contours,* chapters 9-11.

25. Dooyeweerd, *Roots,* 43.

26. Dooyeweerd, *Roots,* 48. Dooyeweerd, accordingly, concluded that to seek a starting-point for thought in any particular aspect of temporal reality constitutes a denial of sphere sovereignty; see *Christian Idea,* 27.

27. Dooyeweerd, *Roots,* 45-46; Dooyeweerd, *Christian Idea,* 33.

28. Dooyeweerd, *Christian Idea,* 11, 27.

In this theory of sphere sovereignty, the discipline of philosophy plays a crucial role, and a more central role than theology. Philosophy alone is able to give insight into the inner nature, structure, relation, and coherence of the various modal aspects.[29] Thus Christian philosophy must be sharply distinguished from, and not draw its fundamentals from, theology (understood "in a scientific sense"), which pertains to but one modal aspect (that of faith) and is as unable to give a theoretically holistic view of things as biology.[30] In fact, theology must have a philosophical foundation, and the only question is whether that philosophy will be Christian or not.[31]

As discussed above, however, Dooyeweerd defended the importance of "naïve" thought and experience over against the tyranny of theoretical thought. Thus, true knowledge of God and ourselves surpasses all theoretical thought and is acquired by the operation of Scripture and the Holy Spirit on the heart, at the religious root of one's existence. As such, this knowledge is the object of neither philosophy nor theology, but serves as the presupposition of both.[32] For Dooyeweerd, then, there is no intellectual discipline, including theology, that deals with the very root or foundation of knowledge, be it of God or ourselves. As he explains, real self-knowledge comes not through theology but through the Word-revelation operating by the Spirit in the heart, the religious center of our existence.[33] This Word-revelation explains all natural revelation and is the foundation for the whole Christian life, practical and scientific.[34] It constitutes a direct communication, of the most fundamental knowledge, from Scripture to the human heart, apart from the mediation of theology or any other discipline. Dooyeweerd in fact warned against elevating the disciplines of dogmatics or biblical exegesis too highly and thereby making them a necessary mediator between Scripture and the believer.[35] By asserting these ideas, Dooyeweerd sought to preserve the independence of each modal

---

29. Dooyeweerd, *Twilight*, 152. For discussion of the relationship of philosophy and theology for Dooyeweerd, see also Chaplin, *Herman Dooyeweerd*, ch. 2.

30. Dooyeweerd, *Twilight*, 113, 130, 133.

31. Dooyeweerd, *Twilight*, 152, 157.

32. Dooyeweerd, *Twilight*, 120; see also Dooyeweerd, "Cornelius Van Til," 77, 84-85.

33. Dooyeweerd, *Twilight*, 184-85.

34. See Dooyeweerd, *Roots*, 99; and Dooyeweerd, *Twilight*, 132.

35. See Dooyeweerd, *Twilight*, 133-36. For discussion of these issues, see also Kalsbeek, *Contours*, 66. John M. Frame says that, for Dooyeweerd, this direct communication of the Word is non-conceptual, and he wonders how the central message of Scripture can really govern all of human life when it has no conceptual content; see *Cornelius Van Til: An Analysis of His Thought* (Phillipsburg, NJ: P&R, 1995), 375-76. I am not convinced, however, that Dooyeweerd in fact believed that this direct communication is non-conceptual.

aspect. No science pertaining to any modal aspect has primacy over another, even in receiving the message of Scripture. Each scientific discipline and each modal aspect receives its direction from Scripture directly. All disciplines therefore have equal competence to interpret Scripture, each for its own sphere. The central religious command to love God and neighbor comes to each aspect of temporal existence. Therefore, says Dooyeweerd, there is "no room for any neutral sphere in life, which could be withdrawn from the central commandment in the kingdom of God."[36]

These affirmations lead to another subject particularly important for the present study, namely, the relationship of the social spheres and the kingdom of God. Dooyeweerd equated the kingdom of God and the invisible church, which are grounded in the created world order and are the "religious root-community" of the human race. He speaks of this reality as the supra-temporal root of all societal structures. All social relationships, therefore, are but temporal manifestations or expressions of the invisible church/kingdom of God.[37] He writes, "The various structures of temporal society and their sphere-sovereignty can be viewed only from society's deeper root-community which is the kingdom of God in Christ Jesus' invisible church."[38] The deeper unity of these social structures is thus found only in Christ.[39] The difference between the visible, institutional church and the other spheres, then, lies not in their relationship to the kingdom, but in the fact that the church has a confession of faith, whereas the state should make only the more general affirmation of God's sovereignty.[40] As L. Kalsbeek says of Dooyeweerd's view, the state is indeed to be of Christian character, but this concerns not its relationship to the church so much as its own internal structure and particular expression of the lordship of Christ. Scripture is normative for political life, but the state does not seek biblical guidance through the church and its confessions.[41]

A final topic to consider in this summary of Dooyeweerd's thought is that of common grace. Dooyeweerd articulated his belief in the reality of common grace alongside his strenuous defense of the antithesis and of the kingdom of God as the root of all societal spheres. One important role that he saw for common grace was its upholding the creation ordinances. Critiquing

36. Dooyeweerd, *Twilight*, 188-90.
37. Dooyeweerd, *Christian Idea*, 9-10.
38. Dooyeweerd, *Christian Idea*, 29.
39. Dooyeweerd, *Christian Idea*, 32.
40. Dooyeweerd, *Christian Idea*, 46.
41. See Kalsbeek, *Contours*, 232-34.

Barth, he insisted that creational structures are not changed by the fall into sin.[42] Furthermore, Dooyeweerd asserted that common grace curbs the effects of sin and allows traces of God's goodness, truth, and the like to radiate even in cultures bent toward apostasy. It bestows upon particular people individual talents and gifts that benefit the human race (though common grace should be seen not as grace merely for the apostate individual, but as grace for the whole of humanity). Dooyeweerd explained that even the most antigodly rulers must submit themselves to God's decrees in order to see good results from their labors, though any obedience to them that is not rendered in the light of their religious root will always be incidental and piecemeal.[43]

One additional point on common grace is particularly important for present purposes. Dooyeweerd warned against making any sharp, dualistic separation between the realms of common grace and special grace.[44] Common grace should not be attributed simply to God as creator, which forces a wedge into the Christian ground motive between creation and redemption. Instead, Dooyeweerd claimed that Jesus Christ is the religious root of common grace and thus is the king over the entire domain that it influences.[45]

Dooyeweerd and the Natural Law and Two Kingdoms Traditions

Dooyeweerd's place in the Reformed natural law and two kingdoms traditions may now be considered. In regard to the two kingdoms, I conclude that Dooyeweerd's conceptions of the societal spheres, the kingdom of God, and common grace represent an approach to issues of Christian cultural engagement that distinguishes him clearly from many aspects of the earlier two kingdoms doctrine. His relation to the natural law tradition is more complex. Dooyeweerd developed an extensive and complex theory of the creational laws that might be termed a kind of sophisticated natural law approach. Nevertheless, I argue that the philosophical and theological context in which he developed his treatment of the laws of creation (a context that includes, importantly, an implicit repudiation of the two kingdoms doctrine) makes his theory significantly different from the idea and role of natural law in the earlier Reformed tradition. In order to unpack and defend

42. Dooyeweerd, *Roots*, 59-60.

43. Dooyeweerd, *Roots*, 37-38.

44. Dooyeweerd, *Christian Idea*, 32.

45. Dooyeweerd, *Roots*, 38. For discussion of Dooyeweerd's grounding of common grace in Christ's kingship, see also Chaplin, *Herman Dooyeweerd*, ch. 3.

these basic claims, I first discuss his thought in relation to the two kingdoms and then to natural law.

First, then, fundamental differences between Dooyeweerd's thought and the Reformed two kingdoms tradition can be observed from several angles. Most obviously, as discussed above, Dooyeweerd viewed all social relationships and spheres as temporal manifestations of the one kingdom of God in Christ, which is the "invisible church" and the "religious root-community" of the human race. This stands in clear distinction from much of the earlier Reformed tradition, which posited two distinct kingdoms and two distinct ways in which God governs them. For the earlier tradition, the whole human race exists in common only in the civil kingdom, and the invisible church, as the body of all the elect, is identified only with the spiritual kingdom. Whereas the earlier tradition distinguished state and church in terms of God's kingship over creation and his kingship over redemption, Dooyeweerd asserted their deeper unity "in Christ" and distinguished them in terms of the church alone having a confession of faith.

Closely related to these issues is Dooyeweerd's understanding of common grace. Much of what he said about this subject sounds similar to the views of Kuyper. But Dooyeweerd also spoke of common grace in ways that differentiated him from Kuyper on some of the very issues that tied him to the earlier two kingdoms tradition. Kuyper grounded common grace in the Son of God's mediatorship over creation and special grace in his mediatorship over redemption. Dooyeweerd, in contrast, though semantically similar to Kuyper in finding a higher unity of common and special grace "in Christ," argued that common grace should in fact not be attributed to God only as creator. As noted above, he believed that this illegitimately forced a wedge between creation and redemption in the Christian ground motive. As an observer of these Dutch thinkers has stated, in defending Dooyeweerd over Kuyper, "Kuyper did not adequately stress that God does all this [upholding the world and the creation ordinances through common grace] for the sake of Christ. Kuyper stated that the earth (common grace) bears the Cross (particular grace); he often did not see that in a deeper sense the reverse is true: the Cross bears the earth. Now, Dooyeweerd's contribution has been to re-formulate Kuyper's view of common grace on such a christocentric basis. The doctrine of common grace can be kept unsoiled by the stubborn tradition of the two-realms theory on condition that it be anchored christocentrically alone."[46] As Jacob Klapwijk implicitly notes here,

46. Jacob Klapwijk, "Antithesis and Common Grace," in *Bringing into Captivity Every*

and as I argued in Chapter 7, Kuyper's ideas of the two mediatorships of the Son of God and an independent purpose of the life of common grace links him strongly to the two kingdoms tradition. Dooyeweerd's attempted "re-formulation" of Kuyper on these issues constituted a break with earlier two kingdoms theology.

Dooyeweerd's views on these matters are interesting — and perhaps ironic — to consider in light of his critique of Barth. Dooyeweerd believed that Barth allowed the creation motive to disappear from sight for the sake of asserting the motives of fall and redemption in Christ, and thus he had no use for the idea of creation ordinances as guidelines for life in the world. Yet Dooyeweerd rejected one of the ways in which classic Reformed theology made distinction between creation and redemption, that of the two mediatorships of the Son of God. A related matter that is also somewhat ironic is Dooyeweerd's evaluation of Brunner in relation to his debates with Barth. According to Dooyeweerd, Brunner did acknowledge the validity of the creation ordinances as upheld by common grace, but erred in placing them in dialectical polarity with the commandment of divine love. Brunner thereby fell into the "lutheran contrast between law and gospel." The seeming irony here is that the law-gospel contrast historically was just as much a Reformed doctrine as a Lutheran,[47] and that one of the distinctive Reformed ways of utilizing this doctrine was in order to distinguish God's work of creation (in which, in the covenant of works with Adam, God gave the law but no gospel) from his work of redemption (in which, in the covenant of grace, God gave the gospel and commanded obedience to the law in response to the gospel). Furthermore, the earlier Reformed tradition, while acknowledging the continuing importance of the laws of nature for the civil kingdom, did in fact teach that the love command given to Christians flowing out of the gospel is, *in certain respects,* distinct from the ethic of these laws of nature, as evidenced in its assertion that the civil kingdom enforces its laws through the physical sword while the spiritual kingdom does not. What Dooyeweerd's interaction with Barth and Brunner reveals, then, is his rejection of Barth's non-Reformed collapsing of creation and redemption alongside of his own rejection of historic Reformed categories that served to clarify the distinction between creation and redemption (and between the two kingdoms)

Thought: Capita Selecta in the History of Christian Evaluations of Non-Christian Philosophy, ed. Jacob Klapwijk, Sander Griffioen, and Gerben Groenewoud (Lanham: University Press of America, 1991), 183.

47. As cited in a previous chapter, see, e.g., Michael S. Horton, "Calvin and the Law-Gospel Hermeneutic," *Pro Ecclesia* 6 (Winter 1997): 27-42.

that Barth's theology endangered. In following this route, Dooyeweerd ended up evaluating culture in at least one way strikingly similar to Barth and dissimilar to the earlier Reformed tradition: through the lens of redemption in Christ.[48]

I make some additional observations about Dooyeweerd and the two kingdoms tradition below, but I now turn more specifically to his relation to the natural law traditions. As views about natural law and the two kingdoms were related in the thought of earlier Reformed theologians, so I believe that they were related in Dooyeweerd's thought. Though not considered in depth or detail in the previous subsection, his philosophy of the modal aspects of reality and related issues represents a massive and elaborate attempt to investigate general revelation and the laws inherent in the creation order. In light of this, Dooyeweerd clearly stands in some relation to the earlier Reformed and broader Christian natural law traditions. Nevertheless, his account of the creational laws ends up in a different place from that of earlier Reformed thinking on natural law. As John Witte relates, early in his career Dooyeweerd in fact articulated a fairly traditional Reformed natural law basis for civil law and civil rights. But his thinking developed in a different direction as he became convinced that this traditional approach was too vague to provide a satisfactory grounding for a concrete account of what civil law ought to look like.[49] The material in many previous chapters does indicate that while Reformed theologians often defended particular positions with appeals to natural law and offered theological and biblical defenses for the existence and character of natural law, they were often short on specifics as to how one could determine precisely what natural law teaches and how natural law ought to translate into civil law. Dooyeweerd's mature thought must therefore be seen at least as a momumentally more ambitious project than his Reformed predecessors attempted.

But how more specifically to place Dooyeweerd in relation to earlier natural law thinking? In his mature thought, he expressed some positive appreciation for older theories of natural law. His analysis of the Greco-Roman ground motive, for example, addressed the development of the concept of a universal civil law in the Roman legal tradition. Needing to find a basis for the empire's law on something more fundamental than the family or Roman community, the Romans called upon the idea of natural law from Greek phi-

---

48. For his interaction with Barth and Brunner, see, e.g., Dooyeweerd, *Roots*, 143-47.

49. See John Witte Jr., "The Development of Herman Dooyeweerd's Concept of Rights," *The South African Law Journal* 110 (Nov 1993): 544-49.

losophy. Despite the essentially apostate ground motive underlying their ef forts, Dooyeweerd praised this development: "The Roman jurists based the *ius gentium* on this *ius naturale*. In doing so, they made an outstanding dis covery. . . . The Roman *ius gentium* was a gift of God's common grace to western culture. The Roman jurists masterfully developed its form with a great sensitivity to practical needs."[50] Furthermore, Dooyeweerd at times also made significant distinctions among older natural law thinkers, all of whom he sharply criticized at other times. For example, in differentiating Hugo Grotius's understanding of natural law from that of Thomas Aquinas, Dooyeweerd writes: "Grotius's standpoint was completely different from the position of Thomas Aquinas. . . . Thomas and the other scholastics would never think of searching for an autonomously valid ground of natural law in 'natural human reason' alone, a ground independent of even the existence of God."[51]

Despite these sentiments of (relative) appreciation for older natural law thought, and discrimination among various expressions of it, Dooyeweerd's interpretation of the development of Western thought leaves his readers with a decidedly negative impression of the natural law tradition. He does not always single out the idea of "natural law" specifically, but Dooyeweerd focused with particular zeal on the deficient views of nature exhibited by many of the Christian thinkers most associated with natural law thinking. He critiqued many Christian writers for synthesizing Christianity (the creation-fall-redemption ground motive) with the Greco-Roman form- matter ground motive, a tendency he often termed "scholasticism" and which he accused of adhering to human autonomy in its understanding of nature. He perceived the presence of this nature-grace ground motive among many already in the patristic era, thought that it flourished in the high Middle Ages, and claimed that it revived in the era of Protestant Ortho- doxy under the inspiration of men such as Philipp Melanchthon and Theo- dore Beza.[52] Thomas Aquinas and the subsequent "Thomism" of the Roman Catholic tradition are the object of particular critique, a critique that ex- tends to their appeals to Romans 1:19-20 and 2:14-15 in support of their un- derstanding of nature.[53] But Dooyeweerd also spoke sharply against

---

50. See Dooyeweerd, *Roots,* 26-27, 37.

51. Dooyeweerd, *Roots,* 158.

52. See generally, e.g., Dooyeweerd, *Roots,* ch. 5.

53. In *Roots,* 119-21, Dooyeweerd claims that Paul, in Romans 1-2, speaks of God's general rev- elation to sinners, not of the natural light of reason, as understood by Thomas and Roman Ca- tholicism. Insofar as he emphasizes that the things known in and by nature are revelatory, he

Protestant scholasticism, labeling it the (unintended) beginning of "the process of decay of Reformation theology."[54] Through these long centuries, Dooyeweerd set apart Calvin as practically the one exemplary figure, poised between the deviations of medieval and Protestant scholasticism, particularly on his understanding of "nature."[55]

In this analysis, Dooyeweerd certainly identified some important points of divergence between, broadly speaking, medieval and Reformation thought. If the analysis in Chapters 2-5 above (and of much other contemporary scholarship) is correct, however, then Dooyeweerd also failed to account for the many lines of similarity that also exist between medieval and Reformation accounts of nature and especially between Reformation and post-Reformation accounts. In particular, as several previous chapters have explored (and whatever the accuracy of Dooyeweerd's evaluation of medieval thought), not only the Reformation but also the mainstream of post-Reformation Reformed thought repudiated any idea that nature is autonomous. Post-Reformation Reformed orthodoxy, in fact, developed the doctrine of the covenant of works to describe the dependence of creation on God from the beginning of history and to explain the context in which the law written upon the heart was bestowed on human beings. Reformed orthodox theologians always affirmed that the natural law is the law of God. Whatever impression to the contrary Dooyeweerd's analysis suggests, rejecting the idea that nature is autonomous gives no reason to reject the historic Reformed doctrine of natural law.

Beyond Dooyeweerd's historical analysis and its negative implications for evaluating the earlier natural law traditions, his constructive understanding of the creational laws distinguishes him in important ways from the natural law of his Reformed predecessors. His interaction with Barth and

---

seems to reflect a common Reformed teaching. Earlier Reformed thinkers, however, as evident in many previous chapters, did not see general revelation and the light of reason as contrasting alternatives, as Dooyeweerd seems to do. One potentially confusing aspect of Dooyeweerd's analysis here is his insistence that revelation must be received by *faith* (which underlies his critique of Thomas and Rome for emphasizing the importance of *reason* in this context). His understanding of faith here, as with his understanding of faith as one of the modal aspects of reality, is not what Paul meant by "faith" throughout Romans nor how classic Reformed theology usually understood "faith." Paul and the Reformed tradition ordinarily used "faith" to designate a trust in Christ for salvation, and hence a response not to revelation generally, but to the gospel made known in special revelation particularly. E.g., see *Heidelberg Catechism*, Q&A 21; *Westminster Larger Catechism*, Q&A 72; and *Westminster Confession of Faith*, 14.2.

54. See Dooyeweerd, *Twilight*, 158.

55. E.g., see Dooyeweerd, *Christian Idea*, 19-20, in the context of his larger argument.

Brunner, discussed above, demonstrates that his critique of the understanding of nature in so many previous Christian thinkers did not entail a rejection of the idea of general revelation nor of the idea that there are binding, normative laws instilled by God in the creation order and preserved despite the fall into sin. Yet this interaction with these Swiss theologians also demonstrates that he did reject the idea that the laws of creation are to be distinguished from the law that comes to believers in Scripture and the Christian religion: Christ's law of love and the normative creational laws do not stand in contrast to each other. Certainly most earlier Reformed theologians would have agreed in regard to the general moral content of natural and biblical law, but they also recognized that these laws were promulgated in different contexts. The former (though clarified by the latter) is the primary governor of the creation-based civil kingdom and the latter is governor of the redemption-based spiritual kingdom. Because of these different contexts, the similar moral substance of these two laws came to quite distinct forms of expression, according to the earlier tradition. This is evident in common Reformed handling of the difference between the Mosaic law and the natural law, and of the difference between the non-sword-bearing character of ecclesiastical government and the sword-bearing character of civil government.

In these matters, I believe a subtle, yet significant, difference can be identified between Dooyeweerd and the earlier tradition. Dooyeweerd did not see biblical law as a law distinct from (even if having the same basic moral substance as) the natural law in light of its purpose of governing a different kingdom, but saw the natural, creational laws as the universally governing laws that, thanks to redemption in Christ, Christians are now once again enabled to pursue rightly. Redemption restores human beings in accomplishing the task that they were meant to accomplish from the beginning, prior to the fall into sin: to obey the creational laws and thereby to develop the potentialities of creation in the unfolding of human culture. Pursuing the ordinances of creation *is* the Christian task, for Dooyeweerd. In his conception of things, therefore, interpretation and application of the natural law is central to a specifically Christian worldview. The Bible does not provide concrete instruction for going about cultural work. Instead, it provides a general direction and imparts a certain attitude so that the Christian may undertake properly the arduous task of investigating the creational laws and thereby discovering concrete paths for cultural development.[56] In-

56. See Dooyeweerd, *Roots*, 58-59. He writes: "Those who think they can derive truly scriptural *principles* for political policy strictly from explicit bible texts have a very mistaken notion of

terpreting and applying the laws of nature are, then, about developing a comprehensive Christian program. It is not that Dooyeweerd looked upon non-Christian investigation of the creational laws as worthless, but apart from investigating them through the grid of the creation-fall-redemption ground motive learned in Scripture, the conclusions will be too vague, indeterminate, and laced with error to guide such a program.

Dooyeweerd's Reformed predecessors certainly appealed to natural law in connection with their understanding of Scripture and would never have advocated their dissociation. Kuyper said things very similar to Dooyeweerd in asserting that Scripture provides general principles for public policy while investigating the divine ordinances in nature provides the details, as well as in his developing a public policy program for his Christian political party. But the earlier tradition, at least, looked at natural law as providing something definitely short of a comprehensive, redemptive Christian program. The great value of natural law was found in the civil kingdom of God the creator, not in the spiritual kingdom of Christ the redeemer. In the spiritual kingdom it was Scripture *alone* that set the parameters for Christian government and worship. The earlier theologians appealed freely to pagan laws and practices to ground their appeals to natural law and their claims about public policy. They viewed the natural laws as universal, not in Dooyeweerd's sense that they make manifest to all people the invisible church and kingdom of God that is being restored through redemption in Christ, but in the sense that all people have been created and temporarily preserved by God, with his law written on their hearts. Surely they would not have denied that Christians should be able to interpret the natural law better than non-Christians, in theory at least, and, in their Christendom context, they did not reflect at great length on the nature of life in a religiously-pluralistic society. But their doctrine of the civil kingdom suggested that the interpretation and utilization of natural law is largely a *common* task of humanity, pursued by believers and unbelievers alike, due to a common divine creation and preservation. For Dooyeweerd, on the other hand, interpreting and utilizing the creational laws is a specifically *Christian* task, something restored in redemption, directed by Scripture, and generating a comprehensive Christian program and worldview.

---

scripture. They see only the letter, forgetting that the Word of God is spirit and power which must penetrate our whole attitude of life and thought. God's Word-revelation puts men to work. . . . One needs insight into the specific ordinances that God established for historical development. There is no easy path to such insight. It requires investigation. Our search will be protected against derailment if the creation motive of God's Word claims our life and thought integrally."

This subtle, yet theologically significant, difference between Dooyeweerd and the earlier Reformed tradition may be viewed from a slightly different angle. Due to his divergent conception of the kingdom of God and common grace, Dooyeweerd freighted the creational laws and their interpretation with an eschatological burden. For Dooyeweerd, human beings from the beginning were to develop the creational laws toward the full flowering of the cultural potentialities that God had placed within them. This same eschatologically oriented task is restored in redemption and thus constitutes the Christian program of the present day. For the earlier tradition, there was no equivalent eschatological burdening of natural law and its interpretation.[57] It certainly held that the original creation was given an eschatological destiny, a conviction expressed through the doctrine of the covenant of works. It also ascribed a role to natural law in this covenant, for this law written on the heart constituted part of the original obedience that Adam was to render to God. Upon the breaking of this covenant, human beings became unable to achieve their eschatological destiny, but Christ has achieved it for them. That eschatological destiny — the spiritual kingdom of Christ — is reserved in heaven for believers, and present participation in this kingdom occurs only *in the (visible) church.* Heeding the laws of nature is still required of every person and is decisive for the health of the civil kingdom, but it does not manifest the spiritual kingdom of Christ and therefore it has no eschatological goal. Natural law's beneficent effects in the civil kingdom (or realm of common grace) serve to preserve a world in which God acts redemptively and, in Kuyper's language, serve purposes independent of redemption, but conformity to natural law does not contribute to attainment of the eschaton.

This is not to say that eschatologically-charged language never appeared in the earlier tradition's Christendom-influenced discussions of civil society. But the theological foundation of natural law in the context of a two king-

---

57. There is certainly some similarity of Kuyper to Dooyeweerd on this issue. Kuyper too believed that the godly products of our cultural work may be carried over into the eschaton, a point at which he was critiqued by some later Dutch Reformed theologians; e.g., see Henry R. Van Til, *The Calvinistic Concept of Culture* (1959; Grand Rapids: Baker, 2001), 148-49; and K. Schilder, *Heaven: What Is It?* trans. Marian M. Schoolland (Grand Rapids: Eerdmans, 1950), 109-11. Interestingly, however, Kuyper saw these cultural products as produced in the realm of common grace, rooted in the work of the Son as creator, not redeemer. He himself at one point stated, concerning our cultural products: "Whether or not this will subsequently be consumed in the coming cosmic conflagration does not matter"; see Abraham Kuyper, "Common Grace," in *Abraham Kuyper: A Centennial Reader,* ed. James D. Bratt (Grand Rapids: Eerdmans, 1998), 179. It seems at least that Dooyeweerd has gone beyond Kuyper and further beyond the earlier tradition.

doms doctrine, as developed by many Reformed theologians examined in previous chapters, strips the eschatological context from the task of interpreting and utilizing natural law, and here Dooyeweerd appears in a different light. Dooyeweerd, striving to see the one, eschatologically oriented kingdom of God made manifest in the pursuing of the creational laws, developed a comprehensive account of them as part of a biblically-driven Christian worldview. In distinction, earlier Reformed theologians, seeing the eschatological, spiritual kingdom as purchased by Christ, stored up in heaven, and enjoyed now in the church, made (often imprecise) appeals to the natural law, interspersed with pagan references, in order to promote a measure of justice in the civil kingdom of the present world. One suspects that they could be content with somewhat imprecise appeals to natural law given the relative modesty of their goal in making such appeals.

Natural Law and the Two Kingdoms in North American Neo-Calvinism

This second section of the chapter brings into focus living, contemporary authors for the first time in this book. I use the terminology of "neo-Calvinism" to describe these authors, not meaning thereby to categorize their thought prematurely or to be pejorative. But as this term is often applied to refer to those who are self-consciously indebted to the thought of Kuyper, often mediated through the philosophy of Dooyeweerd, and who attempt to apply their perspective to contemporary issues, particularly those concerning the relationship of Christianity and culture, it seems a convenient and appropriate term to utilize here.[58] In this section I focus upon the work of five scholars: Henry Stob, Cornelius Plantinga, Albert Wolters, Craig Bartholomew, and Michael Goheen. I interact first with Stob, who was much older than the others and is now deceased, as an important figure in communicating Dooyeweerd's thought to the North American Reformed community from his professorial post at Calvin College and Seminary in Michigan beginning in the middle of the last century. Then I deal with Plantinga, a later (and current) voice at Calvin College and Seminary. Finally, I interact with Wolters and then Bartholomew and Goheen, professors at Redeemer University College in Ontario

---

58. For a discussion of some of the early use of and debates about the term "neo-Calvinism," see John Bolt, *A Free Church, A Holy Nation: Abraham Kuyper's American Public Theology* (Grand Rapids: Eerdmans, 2001), 443-64.

(Goheen has recently moved to a different position). There are any number of figures who would be legitimate subjects of investigation here. I have chosen to investigate Stob because of his important role in mediating Dooyeweerd to a North American audience which has included these later four authors. I have chosen the latter four out of many possible candidates because they have all produced significant works since the turn of the twenty-first century intended to be introductions to Reformed worldview thinking aimed at college students, particularly those at historically Reformed institutions.[59] Though it is difficult to prove such a broad claim, I believe that the perspectives promulgated in these volumes are representative of many widely-shared beliefs among self-consciously Reformed North Americans of the present day, along various points of the left-to-right theological spectrum. Certainly the promotion of these books to thousands of students at Reformed colleges each year indicates their importance for both the present and future of Reformed Christianity. Though they are not (and were not intended to be) the most academically rigorous examples of North American neo-Calvinism, they do give a helpful sense of how it is being popularized. It should be noted that I do not offer here any comprehensive analysis of these authors or their books, but simply look at some of their key ideas in light of the Reformed natural law and two kingdoms doctrines under investigation in this study.

I argue in this section that these neo-Calvinist writers, sometimes explicitly and very often implicitly, show the considerable influence of Dooyeweerd upon their thought. Though they also at times express their appreciation for Kuyper, they, like Dooyeweerd, do not pick up on themes that linked Kuyper to the earlier Reformed natural law and two kingdoms traditions. Instead, they follow Dooyeweerd in taking Kuyperian thought in a distinctively different direction, one standing at some distance from earlier Reformed theology on these issues. They show little awareness of the two kingdoms doctrine in classic Reformed thought and propound a vision of a Reformed worldview that rests decisively on the presence of but one kingdom of God. Likewise, they display small interest in the Reformed natural law tradition but promote investigation of creational laws as part of an over-

---

59. These books are: Albert M. Wolters, *Creation Regained: Biblical Basics for a Reformational Worldview* (Grand Rapids: Eerdmans, 1985), and the second edition, Albert M. Wolters, *Creation Regained: Biblical Basics for a Reformational Worldview,* 2d ed. (Grand Rapids: Eerdmans, 2005) (citations to this work, unless otherwise noted, are to the first edition, due to its long use and familiarity); Craig G. Bartholomew and Michael W. Goheen, *The Drama of Scripture: Finding Our Place in the Biblical Story* (Grand Rapids: Baker, 2004); and Cornelius Plantinga Jr., *Engaging God's World: A Christian Vision of Faith, Learning, and Living* (Grand Rapids: Eerdmans, 2002).

arching, one-kingdom Christian worldview. As I observed with regard to Dooyeweerd in the previous section, these neo-Calvinists agree with their Reformed predecessors on the goodness and legitimacy of work outside of the church in all sorts of cultural endeavors, but, unlike their predecessors, load cultural work and investigation of the laws of creation with an eschatological burden.[60] For them, there are no independent purposes of a civil kingdom or realm of common grace. In the end, what is advertised as a Reformed or reformational view of culture and the world rests on central convictions markedly different from much traditional Reformed and (more generally) Reformation thought.

Henry Stob

Henry Stob (1908-1996) was educated at Calvin College and Seminary and, after finishing doctoral work at the University of Göttingen in Germany, spent a year of post-graduate study with Dooyeweerd and his colleague D. H. Th. Vollenhoven in Amsterdam. He undertook this work reluctantly and only upon being urged to do so by some influential figures at Calvin.[61] When he returned to the United States, Stob immediately began a long career of teaching at Calvin, and he put his exposure to these Dutch figures to use. As he explained later in life, he was instrumental in the formation of a faculty philosophy club dedicated to exploring their thought and was glad to introduce their ideas and to respond to questions about them.[62] Stob clearly had a pivotal role in the penetration of Dooyeweerdian thought into the intellectual milieu of Calvin College and Seminary, institutions that would later train Plantinga and Wolters (the latter of whom had significant influence upon Bartholomew and Goheen).

Stob's writings display the impact of Dooyeweerd at many points. Not only did he enthusiastically review and commend the Dutchman's first English-language book,[63] but common Dooyeweerdian themes discussed in

---

60. For another study that explores this theme in neo-Calvinism, see William D. Dennison, "Dutch Neo-Calvinism and the Roots for Transformation: An Introductory Essay," *Journal of the Evangelical Theological Society* 42, no. 2 (June 1999): 271-91.

61. See Henry Stob, *Summoning Up Remembrance* (Grand Rapids: Eerdmans, 1995), 167.

62. See Stob, *Summoning Up Remembrance*, 213-14.

63. See Henry Stob, review of Herman Dooyeweerd, *Transcendental Problems of Philosophic Thought: An Inquiry into the Transcendental Conditions of Philosophy,* in *Calvin Forum* 14 (October 1948): 53-54.

the previous section appear throughout his works. For example, he empha-sized the creation-fall-redemption motif. He saw this as central to Calvinist thought over against Roman Catholicism (and Lutheranism to a lesser ex-tent) and he used it, for instance, to structure his analysis of the relationship of the church and the kingdom.[64] Dooyeweerd's influence is also evident in his claim that all philosophical thought has a pre-theoretical, religious root and in his repudiation of the autonomy of philosophy from religion.[65]

In light of the general importance of Dooyeweerd for Stob, it is perhaps not surprising to find that Stob displayed little interest in the Reformed nat-ural law and two kingdoms traditions, though he wrote on many issues re-lated to these doctrines. First, Stob's writings indicate a general ignorance of the presence of the two kingdoms doctrine in his Reformed heritage. At times he uses the very terminology of the "two kingdoms," but, in a manner that seems to have become characteristic of contemporary neo-Calvinism, he employs this category as a synonym for Augustine's "two cities." As dis-cussed in Chapter 2, Augustine's "two cities" referred to the antithetical cities of God and Satan, of which Christians belong only to the former. Thus, Au-gustine's idea is distinct from (though not incompatible with) the Reformed idea of the "two kingdoms," according to which God rules both kingdoms and Christians are citizens of both. Stob, however, seems unaware of the "two kingdoms" as a distinct Reformed category and collapses the idea into Augustine's two cities.[66] Another interesting and perhaps revealing item in Stob's writings is his interaction with H. Richard Niebuhr's famous classifi-cation of historic Christian approaches to the relation of Christianity and culture. Not only does Stob agree with Niebuhr's interpretation of Calvin as a transformer of culture, but he also, when mentioning Niebuhr's categories, mentions only four of them, leaving out entirely the "paradox" category for which Martin Luther's two kingdoms theology was the prime example.[67] Be-yond this indirect evidence that the historic Reformed two kingdoms doc-trine was outside of his frame of reference, there is also positive evidence

---

64. E.g., see Henry Stob, *Theological Reflections: Essays on Related Themes* (Grand Rapids: Eerdmans, 1981), 129-30; and Henry Stob, *Ethical Reflections: Essays on Moral Themes* (Grand Rapids: Eerdmans, 1978), ch. 5.

65. E.g., see Stob, *Theological Reflections*, 176-79.

66. E.g., see Stob, *Ethical Reflections*, 63-64, 68-69; and Henry Stob, "Observations on the Concept of the Antithesis," in *Perspectives on the Christian Reformed Church: Studies in Its History, Theology, and Ecumenicity*, ed. Peter De Klerk and Richard R. De Ridder (Grand Rapids: Baker, 1983), 242.

67. Stob, *Theological Reflections*, 129-30.

that Stob's understanding of the kingdom was different from that of many of his Reformed predecessors. Like Dooyeweerd, he affirmed but one kingdom of God that is "universal or worldwide." One of the things that he meant by this is that it embraces "the whole of human society." Though Stob speaks of the centrality of the church for the kingdom in a way that hearkens back to the earlier Reformed tradition, he also claims that the church is narrower than the kingdom. Christians are called "to work upon socio-political structures and institutions" and, in doing so, set up "signs and tokens" of the presence of the kingdom and serve its ends. The kingdom is operative "wherever the Spirit blows, wherever the Word is taught or preached, and wherever Christ's healing ministry is undertaken — in the latter case whether it is done in his name or not."[68]

Stob's thought also displays a seeming ignorance of, or at least indifference toward, the Reformed natural law tradition. This is curious as well, in light of the fact that Stob on at least one occasion took up explicitly an evaluation of "natural law ethics." In this article, he affirms a number of things about moral revelation in nature that would seem to place him squarely within the earlier Reformed tradition. He acknowledges that all people reside under the moral law, that this moral law is summarized in the Decalogue, that all people are aware of this law by nature, and that Romans 1 and 2 offer biblical support for this universal awareness of the law.[69] Shortly thereafter he writes: "Formally speaking, enough is known to leave all men and women without excuse of ignorance when judgment comes. Materially speaking, enough is known to enable us to distinguish between right and wrong, to organize our personal lives in the pattern of external decency, and to establish with others a tolerably just social and political order."[70] In light of many previous chapters in this book, one might argue that this is precisely what the earlier Reformed tradition taught in regard to natural law. But Stob immediately proceeds to say that the real question is whether more than this can be known apart from Christ. While some people, especially Roman

68. See Stob, *Ethical Reflections*, 68-69. This last quotation, dealing with the promotion of Christ's kingdom apart from the intention of the one promoting it, resembles certain themes in Barth's theology, as examined in Chapter 8. Though I cannot take up any extended consideration of the impact of Barth's thought on Stob, I note briefly that Stob expressed cautious appreciation for Barth and expressed clear disappointment in Cornelius Van Til's sharp critique of him. E.g., see Stob, *Summoning Up Remembrance*, 139, 295; and Stob, *Ethical Reflections*, ch. 8.

69. Henry Stob, "Natural Law Ethics: An Appraisal," *Calvin Theological Journal* 20, no. 1 (1985): 58-59.

70. Stob, "Natural Law Ethics," 60.

Catholics, think that the answer is yes, Stob argues that the answer is no: the "natural man," by "the light of reason operating independently of the revealed Word," cannot "construct an ethic thoroughly adequate for mundane affairs and quite fit to be incorporated whole and without amendment into the Christian scheme."[71] Put this way, Stob's answer again seems quite in line with classical Reformed thinking about natural law.[72] From the standpoint of the present book, however, what is rather perplexing and misleading about Stob's analysis is that "natural law ethics" is identified with the "Roman Catholic" and "Thomistic" position that he rejects, giving no indication that centuries of Reformed thought embraced "natural law" terminology and certainly developed a certain sort of natural law ethic. Stob relegates the very language of "natural law" to a description of a Roman Catholic approach that elevates reason at the expense of Scripture.

One final observation about Stob's evaluation of natural law seems relevant in the present context. Similar to Dooyeweerd, Stob emphasizes the oneness of the moral law known in nature and the law known in Scripture.[73] As I noted toward the end of the previous section, there is Reformed precedent for such a claim in regard to the basic moral content of natural and biblical law. But whereas the earlier tradition also emphasized important differences between the applications of the moral law in the different kingdoms, this additional emphasis is lacking in Stob, as it was also in Dooyeweerd.

Cornelius Plantinga

I turn now to a subsequent figure that has held several positions at Calvin College and Seminary, Cornelius Plantinga. His recent work, *Engaging God's World: A Christian Vision of Faith, Learning, and Living,* is aimed particularly at college students and attempts to reflect with them on the nature and task of education at Christian colleges. In this work, Plantinga aims at a broader audience, yet expresses special appreciation for the Reformed tradition and its interest in developing a worldview and establishing institutions of higher education.[74] Plantinga, however, displays no awareness of, or at least no in-

---

71. Stob, "Natural Law Ethics," 60.

72. See, however, Stephen Grabill's interaction with Stob's three specific criticisms of natural law ethics in this article in Stephen J. Grabill, *Rediscovering the Natural Law in Reformed Theological Ethics* (Grand Rapids: Eerdmans, 2006), 43-47.

73. See Stob, "Natural Law Ethics," 59.

74. E.g., see Plantinga, *Engaging God's World*, ix-xix.

terest in, the Reformed natural law and two kingdoms doctrines, even as he deals with issues very much related to them. In fact, he presents a constructive position that stands at some variance with these Reformed doctrines, often along the lines suggested by Dooyeweerd.

Among the key Dooyeweerdian themes that are explicitly central to Plantinga's view of Christian cultural engagement are the creation-fall-redemption motif (which helps to distinguish Reformed higher education from Lutheran and Anabaptist) and the importance and necessity of a worldview.[75] He develops these ideas in ways indifferent to, and different from, the Reformed two kingdoms doctrine. First, his (limited) use of two "kingdoms" terminology mirrors Stob's. In appealing to Kuyper's idea of the antithesis and to Augustine's "two cities" idea, Plantinga writes that "the kingdom of God and the kingdom of this world are sworn foes." Of course, there is biblical precedent for such language, but though Plantinga also appeals to Calvin along with Augustine and Kuyper as teaching this antithetical "clashing of the kingdoms," he does not acknowledge the fact that Calvin's "two kingdoms" doctrine had a different sense.[76] It is also interesting to note that while Plantinga speaks of "Jesus Christ" as the mediator of both creation and redemption and hints at the older Reformed distinction between the former as his work as the eternal Son of God and the latter as his work as the incarnate God-man, he does not use these ideas to ground a two kingdoms doctrine nor even a common grace–special grace distinction.[77] Instead, he develops an approach to cultural engagement that embraces the idea of but one kingdom of God and effectively rejects the kingdom theology underlying much of earlier Reformed thought.

This is evident very prominently in the way that he grounds all of the Christian's cultural work in the resurrection of Christ and his consequent call for Christians to reform and redeem all areas of life.[78] Cultural activity is rooted in creation, to be sure, but precisely creation as it is being redeemed. And the redemption that God's people long for is a righteousness throughout the land, the coming of the kingdom of God.[79] This kingdom is the sphere of his sovereignty, which means that it has been in existence forever

75. On the creation-fall-redemption motif, see Plantinga, *Engaging God's World*, xiv-xv, as well as his structuring the central chapters 2-4 of this book around these three themes. On the importance of worldview, see, e.g., *Engaging God's World*, xvi, 67-68, 127.

76. See Plantinga, *Engaging God's World*, 111.

77. See Plantinga, *Engaging God's World*, 19-22.

78. E.g., see Plantinga, *Engaging God's World*, 80, 94-100, 117.

79. Plantinga, *Engaging God's World*, 103.

and is constituted by the whole universe.[80] Plantinga is therefore under-standably emphatic that it is not just the church that builds the kingdom, but social institutions of all sorts, and not only those that are Christian. Among these other institutions are the state (here he appeals to Calvin, though Calvin himself clearly asserted that civil government was not part of the kingdom of Christ), hospitals, schools, recreational clubs, and Habitat for Humanity.[81] And though Plantinga warns against triumphalism, he calls "prime citizens of the kingdom" those who are reform-minded in looking to address the deformities of life and culture.[82] He repudiates the distinction between "a sacred realm and a secular realm" in which redemption pertains only to the former. He appeals again here to Calvin, as well as to the Puritans, "who got really fired up about the need for redemption in every place and structure," and he claims that Christian college programs are designed pre-cisely to avoid such a sacred-secular distinction.[83] This rejection of a sacred-secular realm distinction in which only the former is redeemed is certainly consistent with Plantinga's kingdom theology, though this distinction is ar-guably exactly what the earlier Reformed two kingdoms doctrine was meant to uphold.

As with Dooyeweerd, Plantinga's distaste for two kingdoms kinds of ideas is obvious while his view of natural law is somewhat ambiguous. Plantinga's book does not address the idea of natural law explicitly, though he makes a number of affirmations related to natural law that reflect historic Reformed convictions. He recognizes that truth is found not only in Scrip-ture but also in many places, appealing (correctly) to Calvin. He also states that general and special revelation are always consistent and compatible, even if we do not always understand how. Furthermore, he writes that though the Bible provides principles for our task of redeeming creation, we must go beyond explicit biblical teaching in order to work out this task cre-atively.[84] Plantinga, like Dooyeweerd, clearly has a robust view of the testi-mony of creation to God and his laws. Nevertheless, though in general this places him in line with the earlier Reformed tradition, I believe that some of the same observations made above regarding the distinctiveness of Dooyeweerd's view of natural law-related issues in comparison to the earlier tradition can be made about Plantinga's view.

80. Plantinga, *Engaging God's World*, 104-5.
81. See Plantinga, *Engaging God's World*, 109-13.
82. Plantinga, *Engaging God's World*, 117, 119.
83. See Plantinga, *Engaging God's World*, 96, 123.
84. See Plantinga, *Engaging God's World*, x, 66, 99.

The most basic observation is that Plantinga places an eschatological burden upon natural law (and cultural work more generally) that the earlier Reformed tradition did not. Plantinga, resembling Dooyeweerd, speaks of cultural work as the task of developing the potentialities imparted to human beings in creation. Cultural work now, after the fall, is a project of restoration, in that redemption re-enables people to do the cultural tasks to which they were called before the entrance into sin. This cultural work, furthermore, not only builds the kingdom of God here and now but also builds the new earth. In fact, "we may think of the holy city as the garden of Eden plus the fullness of the centuries."[85] Whereas the earlier Reformed tradition taught, in its doctrine of the covenant of works at creation, that human obedience in its cultural mandate would have resulted in eschatological consummation, but that after the fall into sin only the obedience of Jesus Christ could bring such a result, Plantinga speaks as though the original eschatologically-driven cultural task is reestablished in redemption for all believers. Whereas much of the earlier Reformed tradition placed post-fall cultural work within the civil kingdom, a temporal and provisional realm originating in creation, preserved by God but not redeemed by Christ, Plantinga places it within the one, redemptive kingdom of God such that Christians are called to produce things that will carry over into the age to come. Whereas the earlier Reformed tradition placed investigation of creation and the laws of nature within the civil kingdom, for purposes of promoting a measure of truth, justice, and order among all people in the present age, Plantinga places such investigation within the outworking of a Christian worldview that builds the stuff of the new Jerusalem.[86] In comparison with the earlier tradition, then, Plantinga affirms a similar general revelation but views its purposes within a much different context.

To conclude this subsection on Plantinga, perhaps it is helpful here to return to an issue discussed above in regard to Dooyeweerd and Stob. These two figures asserted the identity of the creation laws and the biblical laws and therefore of the moral obligation of all people. I argued above that this is a historically Reformed assertion in so far as it speaks to the basic moral con-

---

85. See Plantinga, *Engaging God's World*, xii, 31-33, 137-38. Plantinga appeals here to two other works influential in neo-Calvinist circles: Anthony A. Hoekema, *The Bible and the Future* (Grand Rapids: Eerdmans, 1979); and Richard J. Mouw, *When the Kings Come Marching In: Isaiah and the New Jerusalem* (Grand Rapids: Eerdmans, 1983).

86. This point may also put into better perspective Plantinga's decisively negative assessment of education at "secular" colleges and universities, in comparison to that at Christian institutions; see *Engaging God's World*, 121-23.

tent of natural and biblical law, but that it seems to differ from earlier Re
formed thinking in not paying sufficient attention to differences between
the outworking of this basic moral content in the distinct contexts of different kingdoms. Plantinga, I suggest, displays an outlook similar to these two
predecessors. Evidence of this appears in many places in *Engaging God's
World* in which Plantinga appeals to the most general virtues and practices
(those certainly known *by the natural laws of creation*) to describe how
Christians can bring in the *kingdom* to all areas of life. Pursuing "top-notch"
work, telling the truth, doing ordinary jobs "conscientiously," learning a second language, and cultivating diligence are all means for ushering in the
kingdom in our cultural work.[87] From the theological perspective of the two
kingdoms, all of these things are indeed good, but they are known to be good
by natural law (not just by Scripture) and in this sense are common moral
obligations of the human race as a whole. There is therefore nothing *distinctively Christian* about these things: Christians demand that their non-
Christian neighbors be honest and conscientious too. Being honest and conscientious at work is excellent but it does not bring in the redemptive kingdom of Christ. For Plantinga, following Dooyeweerdian trajectories, these
are "Christian" tasks because the Christian task is really nothing more than
the common human task, purified and redeemed. The law of Scripture does
not teach, first and foremost, an ethic of a new creation and coming kingdom distinct from the kingdom by which God rules the world now, but
teaches precisely how to understand and follow the laws of this creation as
they were meant to be kept all along.

Albert Wolters

I come now to the third neo-Calvinist writer to be examined in this section, Albert Wolters. Though Wolters too was trained at Calvin College, he represents
an expression of a neo-Calvinist approach to culture promulgated out of another historically Reformed institution, Redeemer University College in Ontario. Wolters' short but influential presentation of neo-Calvinist cultural engagement, *Creation Regained: Biblical Basics for a Reformational Worldview,* has
challenged students at many Christian colleges for more than 20 years, and its
recent re-issuance in a second edition testifies to its significance. In my judgment, Wolters' work requires a very similar evaluation to that offered of

---

87. See Plantinga, *Engaging God's World,* 120-21, 129-32.

Plantinga's work immediately above. In this subsection, therefore, I mention some salient features of Wolters' presentation and discuss briefly their disjunction from earlier Reformed natural law and two kingdoms doctrines.

Wolters' thought, like that of Stob and Plantinga, bears evidence of the influence of Dooyeweerd. Wolters too emphasizes, and indeed structures his whole argument around, the creation-fall-redemption motif and stresses the idea of a worldview.[88] He also appeals to the generally Kuyperian theme of sphere sovereignty and the more specifically Dooyeweerdian distinction between theoretical or scientific knowledge on the one hand and pre-theoretical or pre-scientific knowledge on the other.[89] At the beginning of his work, Wolters explicitly acknowledges that he is carrying on the work of Dooyeweerd (as well as Vollenhoven, Kuyper, and Herman Bavinck), and he states in the second edition that his book was meant to introduce the philosophy of Dooyeweerd and Vollenhoven (Kuyper and Bavinck being here unmentioned).[90]

As with the others drawing inspiration from Dooyeweerd, Wolters does not display awareness of the historic Reformed two kingdoms doctrine and presents a constructive view that repudiates a two-kingdoms-like perspective and propounds a single, universal kingdom of God. In regard to his lack of interaction with earlier Reformed views, it may be noted first that when he does use the language of "two kingdoms," he uses it, like Stob and Plantinga, to refer to the Augustinian "two cities" or the Kuyperian antithesis between God and the Satan, with no acknowledgement of a different historic meaning in Reformed theology.[91] Moreover, Wolters writes as if there is no third option besides the choices of shunning the world and seeing the world as being redeemed by Christ, when it is precisely a third option that the two kingdoms doctrine provided in his own Reformed tradition.[92] Furthermore, though he teaches that "Christ" is the mediator of creation and preservation as well as of redemption, he makes no traditional Reformed distinction between his work as the eternal Son and his work as the incarnate God-man nor acknowledges the use of this distinction in grounding doctrines of the two kingdoms and common and special grace.[93]

---

88. On creation-fall-redemption, see Wolters, *Creation Regained*, 10-11, as well as the titles and organization of chapters 2-4. On worldview, see *Creation Regained*, ch. 1.

89. On these two themes respectively, see Wolters, *Creation Regained*, 80-84 and 8-9.

90. See Wolters, *Creation Regained*, 1; and Wolters, *Creation Regained*, 2nd ed., 119.

91. See Wolters, *Creation Regained*, 67-70.

92. See Wolters, *Creation Regained*, 58.

93. See Wolters, *Creation Regained*, 20-21.

Beyond generally overlooking the Reformed two kingdoms tradition, Wolters explicitly adopts a one kingdom view that stands in clear contrast to this tradition. He suggests that people's view of the kingdom is crucial for their worldview,[94] and indeed he makes a kingdom theology central to his. For Wolters, redemption is the restoration of creation, and the restoration of creation is the same thing as the coming of the kingdom. This kingdom of God is universal, for nothing is excluded from its scope.[95] He is adamant that a "two realms" theory (which he calls at various times "dualistic" and a "deep-rooted Gnostic tendency") is *not* consistent with a "Reformational" worldview and asserts, in fact, that Anabaptists, Roman Catholics, and liberal Protestants all succumb to the temptation to fall into a two realms theory.[96] What exactly is such a pernicious "two realms" theory? He describes it as a view that separates "the kingdom of God and the church from 'the world,'" such that the church belongs to one realm and things such as family, politics, and business to the other. In other words, it looks very much like a Reformation two kingdoms view, though Wolters has characterized it as precisely the opposite of a "Reformational" view. He also claims that the "Reformational" worldview opposes all attempts to divide the world into realms of the sacred and the profane/secular.[97] In so doing, Wolters treats the concepts of "profane" and "secular" as though they denoted something unqualifiedly wicked, again despite the Reformation's teaching, via its two kingdoms doctrine, that the civil realm could be God-ordained and legitimate without being sacred and in the process of being redeemed. The examples of Wolters' condemning as anti-Reformational what the Reformation in fact taught could be multiplied. One last remarkable example is this: "Other traditions curtail the scope of Christ's kingship by identifying the kingdom with the institutional church. Though this identification is traditionally thought of as being Roman Catholic, its Protestant adherents are numerous. This view holds that only clergymen and missionaries engage in 'full-time kingdom work' and that the laity are involved in kingdom activity only to the degree that they are engaged in church work."[98] As argued in previous chapters, much early Reformed thought saw Christ's redemptive kingdom as expressed institutionally in the present age only in the church, precisely what

---

94. Wolters, *Creation Regained*, 64-65.

95. See Wolters, *Creation Regained*, 60-61, 63.

96. E.g., see Wolters, *Creation Regained*, 10-11, 54, 65.

97. E.g., see Wolters, *Creation Regained*, 53-54, 56, 58, 74. He writes, for example, that "sin profanes all things, making them 'worldly,' 'secular,' 'earthly.'"

98. Wolters, *Creation Regained*, 65.

Wolters condemns as Roman Catholic. Early Reformed theology would indeed not have considered all occupations as equally kingdom work, but would never have thereby suggested anything second-class or illegitimate about work outside of the church, as Wolters seems to assume. Whether Wolters' theology of the kingdom is theologically correct or not, to insist that it is "Reformational" is historically dubious.

In regard to issues relevant to natural law, Wolters has a better case for being an heir of the Reformation. Speaking more from a scientific than from an ethical perspective, he defines "laws of nature" in terms of the physical laws discoverable through the natural sciences.[99] Nevertheless, Wolters also believes that God's will is made known in laws manifest in general revelation, and his view of general revelation is quite robust.[100] His discussion of conscience and of the law written on the heart reflects common Reformed teaching.[101] Furthermore, his interpretation of the relation between "creational law" and the law of Moses also mirrors the view of historic Reformed theology.[102] And though he emphasizes the authority of Scripture over all areas of life in a way that lacks some of the significant nuances of earlier Reformed thought,[103] he suggests important nuances of his own later, such as the need to exercise wisdom when Scripture is silent.[104]

Without meaning to belabor a point already discussed at some length above, I note that Wolters, like Plantinga and Dooyeweerd, freights the interpretation and use of the creational laws with an eschatological burden that the earlier Reformed doctrine did not.[105] Picking up on the Dooyeweerdian theme also emphasized by Plantinga, Wolters speaks of redemption and salvation as constituted by the restoration of creation. From the beginning, human beings were to develop the original creation toward maturity.[106] They "botched" their original mandate but are now given a "second chance," "reinstated" as God's managers. The only thing new in redemption therefore is rem-

---

99. See Wolters, *Creation Regained*, 13-15.

100. E.g., see Wolters, *Creation Regained*, 24, 28, 31-35.

101. E.g., see Wolters, *Creation Regained*, 25.

102. See Wolters, *Creation Regained*, 34-35.

103. E.g., see Wolters, *Creation Regained*, 6-8.

104. See Wolters, *Creation Regained*, 29-30.

105. This is a key reason why my interpretation of Wolters and natural law ultimately differs from that of Thomas K. Johnson, *Natural Law Ethics: An Evangelical Proposal* (Bonn: Verlag für Kultur und Wissenschaft, 2005), 116-24, who points to Wolters' thought as pointing the way to a contemporary recovery of Reformed natural law ideas.

106. See Wolters, *Creation Regained*, 37-41.

edy for sin. Redemption is universal and Christians are to "promote renewal" everywhere.[107] This does not mean going back to Eden, but developing the creation as originally intended.[108] As creation was meant to progress from its original state toward a state of glory through this human development, so also redemption now enables this same progress, such that our cultural achievements will survive into the new, glorified earth.[109] Wolters claims that the kingdom advances in this cultural development toward the new creation precisely as the natural law is obeyed: "wherever family life, for example, grows in obedience and conformity to God's creational law, there the kingdom advances and the world is pushed back."[110] The original connection between general human cultural achievement and eschatological attainment is therefore established again by grace, not, as in the older Reformed doctrine of the covenant of works, lost once and for all in the fall such that believers must look to Christ alone as the one whose obedience brings in the eschatological state.

For Wolters, then, as for many of his neo-Calvinist contemporaries, interpretation and utilization of the natural law is not for the primary purpose of discovering and achieving a relative, temporal justice, peace, and order in this present life, as in much of the earlier Reformed tradition. Neither is it part of a common cultural task among believers and unbelievers, as suggested by the doctrine of the civil kingdom (if often not articulated in that way). Instead, it is a task for redeemed believers, striving to implement a fully biblical world-and-life view, looking to produce ultimate, everlasting cultural achievements that will carry over into the age to come.

Craig Bartholomew and Michael Goheen

The work of Craig Bartholomew and Michael Goheen, *The Drama of Scripture: Finding Our Place in the Biblical Story,* is closely related to that of Wolters considered immediately above. Not only do these authors dedicate their book to Wolters, claiming his "formative influence" upon them, but also the new preface to the second edition of Wolters' book (which Wolters co-authored with Goheen) states that the revised *Creation Regained* would serve as an "excellent companion volume" to *The Drama of Scripture*.[111] The

---

107. E.g., see Wolters, *Creation Regained*, 11, 57-60.
108. Wolters, *Creation Regained*, 63-64.
109. See Wolters, *Creation Regained*, 40-41.
110. Wolters, *Creation Regained*, 67.
111. Wolters, *Creation Regained*, 2nd ed., x.

latter volume is distinctive from any of the other literature considered in this chapter, however, in its biblical-theological focus. In other words, it develops its argument through a survey of the progress of biblical history and of the revelation given by God in the different eras of his dealings with his people. With Wolters and other neo-Calvinist literature, Bartholomew and Goheen affirm common Dooyeweerdian themes such as the centrality of worldview and of the creation-fall-redemption motif.[112] And their relation to the Reformed natural law and two kingdoms doctrines seems similar to those of the other neo-Calvinist authors.

As with the others, an understanding of the kingdom of God is crucial for their perspective. Along with the concept of covenant, they use the kingdom idea to structure the book.[113] Rejecting any view that would restrict Christ's kingdom to certain areas of life over against other areas (though they make no mention of a traditional Reformed two kingdoms theology), they strongly assert the universality of this kingdom in the world: "God's kingdom has no boundaries of any kind. Jesus does not merely sit on the throne of our hearts and reign there: that is much too narrow a concept of his authority. Jesus reigns over *all* of human life, all history, and all nations."[114] While acknowledging that the church's evangelism is "important," they emphasize that "witness to God's kingdom is as wide as creation. Witness will mean embodying God's renewing power in politics and citizenship, economics and business, education and scholarship, family and neighborhood, media and art, leisure and play."[115] In this context, they seem to capture a historic Reformed concern that working in various areas of life is not made legitimate simply by evangelizing in them. Their alternative, however, is a conception of but one, universal kingdom of God, not two.

In their kingdom theology, Bartholomew and Goheen follow writers such as Plantinga and Wolters in perceiving a commission to the human race from the beginning to rule and "to develop the riches of creation" over time.[116] Despite the fall into sin, this cultural development continued in compromised form in the post-lapsarian world.[117] Again, like Dooyeweerd and other neo-Calvinists, Bartholomew and Goheen describe God's redemptive work as comprehensive and fundamentally *restorative:* in Christ

---

112. See Bartholomew and Goheen, *The Drama of Scripture,* 11-12, and throughout.
113. Bartholomew and Goheen, *The Drama of Scripture,* 24.
114. Bartholomew and Goheen, *The Drama of Scripture,* 172.
115. Bartholomew and Goheen, *The Drama of Scripture,* 201.
116. See Bartholomew and Goheen, *The Drama of Scripture,* 37, 40.
117. See Bartholomew and Goheen, *The Drama of Scripture,* 48.

human beings work to restore the creation that was marred and work again toward the positive cultural development of this world. After the fall, God set out on a "salvage mission."[118] They write: "We stress the comprehensive scope of God's redemptive work in creation. The biblical story does not move toward the destruction of the world and our own 'rescue' to heaven. Instead, it culminates in the restoration of the entire creation to its original goodness."[119] Through their book, they write of the various major events through biblical history — the covenant with Noah, the covenant with Abraham, Israel's entering the land, the establishing of the tabernacle, Jesus' proclamation of the kingdom, Jesus' death and resurrection, and the church's proclamation of that resurrection — as steps along the way to the restoration of creation. Bartholomew and Goheen, with other neo-Calvinists, emphasize the continuity of this world and its cultural achievements with the world to come, though they also acknowledge that there will be "some elements" of discontinuity as well. Human cultural development of creation will continue, in fact, after consummation in the new earth.[120]

These themes, I would argue, are again important for considering these authors' relation to the natural law traditions. As with other neo-Calvinist writers examined above, Bartholomew and Goheen do not interact explicitly with earlier Christian reflection on natural law. They do offer limited reflection upon laws in the creation order and upon other matters related to natural law, and in doing so often express views quite consonant with traditional Reformed teaching.[121] Clearly these authors have a high view of God's revelation in creation and the importance of investigating it in the task of cultural development. But they impose upon this task the neo-Calvinist eschatological burden. In an illustrative section toward the end of their book, Bartholomew and Goheen consider several practical examples of Christians who have taken up their cultural work as kingdom service by excelling in their fields and doing good to people and to the broader creation. They believe that this sort of vision helps to save people from thinking that only their specifically religious exercises constitute kingdom or Christian service. In an earlier Reformed natural law and two kingdoms perspective, following the laws of nature and pursuing cultural endeavors with excellence were indeed legitimate and God-glorifying activities. Yet these were activities of the

---

118. Bartholomew and Goheen, *The Drama of Scripture*, 129.

119. Bartholomew and Goheen, *The Drama of Scripture*, 12.

120. See Bartholomew and Goheen, *The Drama of Scripture*, 211-13.

121. E.g., see their discussion of the Mosaic law and the wisdom literature in Bartholomew and Goheen, *The Drama of Scripture*, 69, 96.

civil kingdom, grounded in creation but not redemption, serving relative, temporal purposes. For Bartholomew and Goheen, there is no traditional Reformed distinction between these cultural activities and the spiritual, redemptive activities of the church, because evangelism and pursuing the creational laws in business or environmental work are all part of one grand, redemptive program of creation restoration and kingdom building. Discovering and following the laws of the created order aim at nothing less than moving all of creation toward its fulfillment in the age to come.

Conclusion

This chapter has considered perhaps the most profound Kuyperian thinker of the twentieth century, Herman Dooyeweerd, and several prominent contemporary North American Reformed writers significantly influenced by his thought. In these writers one can see a great many historically Reformed and particularly Kuyperian convictions articulated. They continue the long-standing Reformed concern for matters of culture and social life, for the goodness of all sorts of occupations, and for investigation of the various aspects of creation, and they do so seeking to address both sophisticated intellectual conversations and ordinary Christians involved in mundane tasks.

Yet despite these many links to historic Reformed Christianity, I have argued in this chapter that Dooyeweerd and these representative neo-Calvinists have, in other ways, taken a Reformed, and particularly Kuyperian, approach to cultural engagement in directions different from that provided by much of the earlier tradition through the doctrines of natural law and the two kingdoms. They reject, modify, or simply pass over traditional Reformed articulation of ideas such as the two mediatorships of the Son of God and the covenant of works and, in so doing, come to ground the cultural task in both the creating and redeeming work of God. They follow Kuyper's lead in seeking to make the spheres and activities of culture "Christian," yet without his nuances and qualifications that defined such Christianization in light of the reality of a common grace rooted in creation but not in redemption. Furthermore, in Dooyeweerd and especially in his North American disciples, one sees an eschatological burdening of cultural work in which such work becomes a specifically Christian task, pursued through a comprehensive Christian world-and-life view and with the goal of bringing the kingdom of God to eschatological fulfillment. The earlier Reformed view of cultural activity as a temporal task of the civil kingdom, theoretically a common endeavor among believers and unbelievers, governed primarily though a natural law to which all people had access and insight, has thus been significantly redirected. For the neo-Calvinists considered here, there are no independent purposes of common grace or a civil kingdom, but all is subsumed under the purposes of redemption and eschatological consummation.

CHAPTER 10

The Kuyperian Legacy (II):
Cornelius Van Til and the Van Tillians

In this final chapter, I investigate another stream of the Kuyperian tradition, that forged by Cornelius Van Til (1895-1987) and some of his disciples. As already evident in the previous chapter, the legacy of Abraham Kuyper for Reformed Christianity has been a fertile one. Though there was mutual interaction between Herman Dooyeweerd and Van Til and many points of similarity between the ways in which they developed Kuyper's (and earlier Reformed) thought, there are enough significant points of difference to suggest a separate chapter. The relation of Van Til's thought to the Reformed natural law and two kingdoms traditions is, however, in many ways more difficult to identify than the relation of Dooyeweerd and the North American neo-Calvinists to these traditions.

Van Til, like Dooyeweerd, was born in the Netherlands but immigrated at a young age to Indiana. Raised in the Christian Reformed Church, a historically Dutch-American denomination, he attended its denominational schools, Calvin College and Seminary, before pursing further degrees in theology and philosophy at Princeton Seminary and University. After brief stints as an instructor at Princeton Seminary and as a pastor in Michigan, Van Til joined several of his Princeton colleagues in establishing Westminster Theological Seminary in 1929, in Philadelphia, in response to a reorganization of the Princeton board that, in their judgment, gave undue influence to theological modernists. Seeking with his Westminster colleagues to teach and defend historic, confessional Reformed theology, Van Til labored his entire career at Westminster as professor of apologetics (the intellectual defense of the Christian faith), where his primary interest was applying Reformed doctrine consistently to apologetic method.[1]

---

1. For detailed discussion of Van Til's life, context, influence, and academic and ecclesiastical work, see the new biography, John R. Muether, *Cornelius Van Til: Reformed Apologist* (Phillips-

Van Til was in some ways an obscure figure, whose influence was primarily confined to small, conservative, confessional Reformed and Presbyterian denominations in North America. Furthermore, his writings were almost entirely devoted to apologetics or matters directly related to this theological discipline; he did not write any sustained treatment of social life or political or legal affairs. There are, nevertheless, several reasons for including a chapter in the present study on Van Til and his followers. First, in many corners of the conservative, confessional end of the contemporary Reformed spectrum, Van Til has evoked a devoted following, in which consideration of social issues regularly occurs through the theological grid that he provided. He did, in fact, offer one of the most ambitious attempts to apply classic Reformed and Kuyperian theology in the twentieth century, and he addressed many topics of direct importance for the Reformed natural law and two kingdoms traditions. Second, beyond his own confessional Reformed circles, Van Til was recognized in the mid-twentieth century in the broader conservative Protestant world as one of the earliest and most relentless critics of the theology of Karl Barth, and his critique focused on matters of central relevance for the present study.[2] And still today some scholars from very different theological perspectives acknowledge Van Til's contribution to twentieth-century theological discussions.[3] Finally, one of Van Til's devoted disciples, Meredith G. Kline (1922-2007), offered one of the twentieth century's few Reformed accounts of social and cultural life that arguably

---

burg, NJ: P&R, 2008). Among large-scale attempts to wrestle generally with Van Til's thought, see John M. Frame, *Cornelius Van Til: An Analysis of His Thought* (Phillipsburg, NJ: P&R, 1995); and Greg L. Bahnsen, *Van Til's Apologetic: Readings and Analysis* (Phillipsburg, NJ: P&R, 1998). A shorter study of Van Til's views on apologetic methodology through his career can be found in Scott Oliphint, "The Consistency of Van Til's Methodology," *Westminster Theological Journal* 52 (1990): 27-49. For a recent proposal concerning Van Til's contribution to the discipline of Christian apologetics, also see K. Scott Oliphint, "Cornelius Van Til and the Reformation of Christian Apologetics," in *Revelation and Reason: New Essays in Reformed Apologetics*, ed. K. Scott Oliphint and Lane G. Tipton (Phillipsburg, NJ: P&R, 2007), 279-303.

2. The culmination of his sustained critique of Barth was arguably his *magnum opus*: Cornelius Van Til, *Christianity and Barthianism* (Philadelphia: Presbyterian and Reformed, 1962). For helpful discussion of Van Til's interest in Barth, and the enthusiastic support and sharp disagreement that his critique of Barth evoked among his contemporaries, see Muether, *Cornelius Van Til*, ch. 5.

3. E.g., see the Roman Catholic William M. Shea's recent work, in which he identifies Van Til as one of the century's most interesting and penetrating Evangelical critics of Roman Catholic theology: *The Lion and the Lamb: Evangelicals and Catholics in America* (New York: Oxford University Press, 2004), 151-55.

recovers and constructively develops many notions of the older natural law and two kingdoms traditions. Kline's work is worth a brief exploration in its own right, but it is difficult to appreciate without some background in Van Til's thought. For such reasons, an investigation of Van Til's writings and his relation to the Reformed natural law and two kingdoms traditions is offered in the present chapter.

Placing Van Til in relation to these traditions is not an easy task and my conclusions are — necessarily, I believe — somewhat ambiguous. Though he addressed a host of issues pertaining to the present study of Reformed natural law and two kingdoms doctrine, he was not a social theorist and his forays into cultural matters were occasional and scattered. Furthermore, he had limited historical interests beyond discussing some of the major theological and philosophical writers of the Western world, whom he tended to portray in broad, general terms for the purpose of setting the stage for his own constructive work. Therefore, while dealing with many matters relevant to natural law and the two kingdoms in a self-consciously Reformed way, Van Til usually did not reflect at length upon them in the light of the Reformed historical context under investigation in this book. An argument can be made that the tenor of Van Til's thought inclines against the natural law and two kingdoms traditions. Though indebted to Kuyper in many ways, some of the few points at which he explicitly diverged from Kuyper were on matters identified in Chapter 7 as linking Kuyper strongly to earlier Reformed natural law and two kingdoms doctrines. These disagreements with Kuyper, alongside of his occasional specific comments on social and cultural affairs, might suggest that Van Til, like so many other representatives of twentieth-century Reformed thought, viewed such affairs as grounded in Christ's work of redemption rather than in God's work of creation and preservation in distinction from redemption. Some of Van Til's admirers, such as the so-called theonomists, who will be described briefly below, have pursued a social and cultural agenda to a much greater degree than he and have landed in a very different place from the Reformed natural law and two kingdoms tradition.

But if one recognizes that Reformed social ethics was an undeveloped aspect of Van Til's thought and that the historic Reformed natural law and two kingdoms doctrine was outside of his immediate purview, a less clear-cut conclusion seems appropriate. One could very well adopt Van Til's method of apologetics as an attempt at a consistent application of Kuyper's notion of the antithesis between Christian and non-Christian thought (a concept present in earlier Reformed theology and dating back to Augustine's two cities model) and at the same time acknowledge that in a range of cultural affairs believers must live in common with unbelievers and pursue shared projects for provisional, temporal ends — much as Augustine himself did. In other words, adopting Van Til's apologetics in order to show the conflict between Christian and non-Christian thought in regard to ultimate, spiritual concerns does not seem to prohibit recognizing a civil kingdom, under God's authority through the natural law and hence neither autonomous nor morally neutral, in which people of all faiths must live in peace in regard to penultimate, mundane concerns. This, in broad outline, resembles the approach of Kline.

In this chapter, therefore, I first give an overview of Van Til's thought and then place it in relation to the historic Reformed natural law and two kingdoms doctrines. Next I consider briefly the way in which Greg L. Bahnsen (1948-1999), as a representative of the theonomic school, took his Van Tillian moorings in developing a Reformed account of social ethics. Finally, I explore in somewhat more detail the way in which Kline took his Van Tillian moorings to develop a strikingly different Reformed account of the Christian's role in cultural life. I conclude that Van Til's thought, apparently unfriendly to the historic Reformed natural law and two kingdoms doctrines in certain respects, left room for varied expressions of the Christian's place in society, such that a devotee of Van Tillian apologetics such as Kline could develop an original, yet two-kingdoms-like, theology of Christianity and culture.

An Overview of Van Til's Thought

Van Til's theology of revelation may be a helpful place to begin this discussion. Van Til stood broadly in the Reformed tradition in affirming the existence of both general and special revelation. He identified special revelation with Scripture, though he also believed that God gave special revelation to Adam before the fall into sin. Though he did not write with entire consistency on this matter, he explained that *all* of created reality, including the activity of subjective, sinful human moral consciousness, is God's general revelation.[4] This pertains immediately to a crucial aspect of Van Til's thought

---

4. E.g., see Cornelius Van Til, *An Introduction to Systematic Theology* (Phillipsburg, NJ: P&R, 1974), 63-64. Van Til discusses matters of human moral consciousness (conscience) as revelation in many other places, including Cornelius Van Til, "Nature and Scripture," in *The Infallible Word,*

and a central point of his critique of Roman Catholic theology. He emphasized that there exists no autonomous or neutral area of reality and no space for an autonomous human response to that reality, because everything that exists proclaims God and God's own interpretation of things. For Van Til, this teaching stood in contrast to Rome's, which left space, following Aristotle, for affirmation of "being in general" and "knowledge in general" and hence also for the autonomy of the human will before needing to face the existence and claims of God.[5]

Like Kuyper, Van Til stressed the interrelation and interdependence of general and special revelation through history, though he extended this emphasis beyond Kuyper in claiming that special revelation accompanied general revelation even before the fall into sin.[6] For Van Til, "revelation in nature and revelation in Scripture are mutually meaningless without one another and mutually fruitful when taken together."[7] Before the fall, natural, rational theology was not meant to function apart from theology proper, for natural revelation was always insufficient without special revelation. Hence, Van Til claims that natural revelation never existed by itself, and to separate natural from supernatural revelation is to deal with abstractions rather than the concrete situation.[8] Van Til writes that Adam, in the pre-lapsarian state, had a perfect moral consciousness and, moreover, that his very nature was revelational. Nevertheless, Adam had to listen to what God told him by special revelation concerning the facts of nature and the scope of God's moral

---

ed. N. B. Stonehouse and Paul Woolley (Grand Rapids: Eerdmans, 1946), 265-67; Cornelius Van Til, *Common Grace and the Gospel* (Nutley, NJ: P&R, 1977), 175-76; Cornelius Van Til, *Christian Apologetics* (Phillipsburg, NJ: P&R, 1976), 33; and Cornelius Van Til, *In Defense of the Faith*, vol. 3, *Christian Theistic Ethics* (Phillipsburg, NJ: P&R, 1980), 139-40. Van Til's teaching on conscience and its authority is not lucid. At times he speaks of every response of human moral consciousness, even sinful responses, as revelational and hence authoritative "in their very abnormality." At other times, however, and in the same context as these other statements, Van Til identifies moral consciousness as revelational and authoritative "to the extent that its voice is still the voice of God" despite the sinner's efforts to suppress it.

5. Among many examples, see Van Til, *Christian Apologetics*, 8-14.

6. Van Til's most extended and focused treatments of general revelation, particularly in its relation to special revelation, are found in *Introduction*, chapters 7-10; and "Nature and Scripture," 255-93. For discussions of Van Til on general revelation, see, e.g., Frame, *Cornelius Van Til*, ch. 9; and William D. Dennison, "Natural and Special Revelation: A Reassessment," *Kerux* 21 (Sept 2006): 15-19.

7. Van Til, "Nature and Scripture," 261.

8. See Van Til, *Introduction*, 74; Van Til, *Christian Apologetics*, 33, 55; Van Til, *Common Grace*, 69; and Cornelius Van Til, *The Defense of the Faith* (Philadelphia: Presbyterian and Reformed, 1955), 203.

purpose, and thus supernatural revelation had to supplement the revelation in nature.[9] Van Til insisted on this point strongly in enough places to leave little doubt that he meant it, though he did not always express this view consistently. For example, he writes in other places — even within the same works cited immediately above — that human sinfulness necessitated special revelation, and Scripture in particular.[10] When Van Til writes about the post-lapsarian state he also expresses the relationship between general and special revelation as one of mutual dependence. He states in one place, for instance, that the two forms of revelation supplement and presuppose one another, each needing the other to be meaningful.[11] Not only does Van Til believe that post-lapsarian general revelation continues to reveal God's glory, but he also suggests that fallen nature reveals more than before the fall, since it also reveals God's wrath. Things are thus more complex and obscure in the present age.[12] Yet people must always be attentive to general revelation, and he warns against a "biblicism" that "underestimates the value of God's general revelation."[13]

In one of his discussions of natural revelation, Van Til speaks of its necessity in terms of "regularity," in distinction from the "exceptional." Both before and after the fall, nature reveals a regularity that appears in distinction from and serves as a presupposition for the exceptional, that is, special revelation. Hence, before the fall the regularity revealed in nature functioned to highlight the arbitrary character of the special command regarding the tree of the knowledge of good and evil, an arbitrariness necessary for this command to fulfill its particular purpose. Likewise, after the fall, nature reveals a regularity that includes the curse of God upon sin, so that post-lapsarian special revelation might appear exceptional in its redemptive character. In connection with his broader theology of common grace, to be explored further below, Van Til describes this ongoing historical dynamic of

9. Van Til, *Christian Theistic Ethics*, 21-22, 129-30.

10. See Van Til, *Introduction*, 110; and Van Til, *Christian Theistic Ethics*, 23. At least an aspect of Van Til's concern here is to pinpoint sinfulness *rather than ontological necessity* as the reason for special revelation (though certainly he viewed the ontological difference between God and human beings as the reason why, in general, revelation is necessary for humans to know anything). This raises important theological issues, and matters significant to Van Til's thought more generally, but there does seem to be a lack of precision in his writing on this topic.

11. Van Til, *Christian Apologetics*, 29-30.

12. Van Til, *Introduction*, 79.

13. Van Til, *Defense of the Faith*, 203. Note, however, that Van Til makes this statement in the midst of a consideration of some of his critics' position. He goes on immediately to defend the necessity of special revelation for understanding general revelation.

the giving of natural and special revelation in terms of the response of human beings through the passage of time and the consequent differentiation of those who respond positively from those who do not.[14] "To the believer the natural or regular with all its complexity always appears as the playground for the process of differentiation which leads ever onward to the fullness of the glory of God."[15] Shortly thereafter, he adds that the revelation of regularity in nature is a "limiting notion," sufficient historically for the purpose that God intended it to serve, which is precisely that it be this playground for the process of differentiation.[16]

In light of the above, Van Til's position is clearly that special revelation can never be understood apart from general revelation. "Scripture does not claim to speak to man, even as fallen, in any other way than in conjunction with nature."[17] The emphasis in his thought, however, lies upon Scripture as starting-point and upon the necessity of recourse to Scripture for understanding anything and everything.[18] Consequently, Van Til also stresses that Scripture speaks to all matters pertaining to ethics.[19] At times, Van Til even slips into claims that, at least on the surface, contradict his other assertions about the necessity of general revelation. He says, for example, that after the fall "it is Scripture, and Scripture only, in the light of which all moral questions must be answered."[20]

These convictions of Van Til regarding objective divine revelation are closely connected to his understanding of subjective human knowing. He says, as noted above in regard to moral consciousness, that even human knowing is itself revelation. More fundamentally, he asserts that revelation must be the foundation upon which all knowledge rests. Of primary importance is that God is the one who knows all things comprehensively. Human beings cannot know things comprehensively, but they can nonetheless know things truly. To do so, however, they must respect the principle of revelation and be "*derivative* interpreters or re-interpreters."[21] God has interpreted all things first and all things perfectly, and human beings must strive to reflect his interpretation in a finite manner. Knowing any fact truly, and even ratio-

---

14. Van Til, "Nature and Scripture," 261-64.

15. Van Til, "Nature and Scripture," 264; see also 259-60.

16. Van Til, "Nature and Scripture," 268.

17. Van Til, "Nature and Scripture," 255.

18. E.g., see Van Til, *Christian Apologetics*, 2, 27; and Van Til, *Defense of the Faith*, 203-4.

19. E.g., see Van Til, *Christian Theistic Ethics*, 5, 16, 139-40, 143; and Van Til, *Introduction*, 197.

20. Van Til, *Christian Theistic Ethics*, 22-23.

21. Van Til, *Introduction*, 24.

nality itself, requires one to presuppose God's existence and his plan for the universe.[22] Both facts and universals are what they are only because of their common dependence upon the ontological Trinity.[23] One interpreter of Van Til summarizes his epistemology in this way: "to understand, know, and interpret the facts correctly one must begin with the one who creates the facts."[24]

For Van Til, therefore, God knows and interprets all things comprehensively. Human beings cannot know and interpret anything unless God reveals it to them. As God reveals, they know and interpret truly, though not comprehensively, provided that they know and interpret as derivative knowers and interpreters; that is, they must think God's thoughts after him and interpret all aspects of reality according to God's own interpretation of it. These key convictions are related to Van Til's interest in the common Kuyperian theme of worldview. The Christian world and life view, according to Van Til, presents an absolutely comprehensive interpretation of human experience.[25] The *summum bonum* taught in Scripture is absolute, giving a comprehensive program and all-embracing plan of God.[26] Without Christian presuppositions, there is no meaning or coherence in anything.[27]

These ideas have many implications. There is no Christian theology without a Christian philosophy, and Christian theology in turn provides the necessary prerequisites for science. Philosophers and scientists, as well as theologians, must look to Scripture for fundamental information about their disciplines.[28] In regard to science specifically, Van Til decries the notion that contemporary science is neutral and non-metaphysical. On the contrary, it is anti-Christian.[29] Though he thought that Kuyper was correct to speak about two kinds of science, one Christian and the other non-Christian, Van Til laments that Kuyper did not follow through consistently enough on this basic insight.[30] The believing scientist has a responsibility to

22. Van Til, *Introduction*, 22; Van Til, *Common Grace*, 9-10.

23. Van Til, *Common Grace*, 64.

24. William D. Dennison, "Analytic Philosophy and Van Til's Epistemology," *Westminster Theological Journal* 57 (1995): 40-41.

25. Van Til, *Christian Apologetics*, 38.

26. Van Til, *Christian Theistic Ethics*, 77.

27. Van Til, *Christian Apologetics*, 99.

28. Van Til, *Christian Apologetics*, 23-25.

29. Van Til, *Common Grace*, 3.

30. Van Til, *Common Grace*, 35-44. Van Til believed that Kuyper ended up ceding areas of neutrality and commonness to unbelievers in lower aspects of the natural sciences (such as measuring and counting), which Kuyper did not think affected by sin or regeneration. Van Til even ac-

witness in the lab before unbelieving colleagues that science is possible and meaningful only if Christianity is true.[31] Van Til, in fact, spoke of a comprehensive task of believers to eliminate sin from the universe, though he warned that this would never be fully accomplished in this life.[32] The moral task given to Christians pertains not merely to them or to a defined segment of life. Instead, the redemptive standard is always the absolute standard, addressing "man as such" and reestablishing the creation ordinances.[33] The believer may never compromise the Christian ethical program, since the non-Christian ethical program is a straightforward denial of it.[34] In order to pursue this all-embracing worldview, encompassing such scientific and ethical questions, Van Til, like Kuyper, believed it necessary for Christians to establish their own schools and to be able to defend their reason for existence.[35] No genuine education takes place "outside of a Christian-theistic atmosphere," and thus Christian education is "the only education that is fit for a covenant child."[36] When he surveyed the Christian tradition as a whole, he concluded that only Reformed churches had carried out the idea of Christ's kingship over every sphere of life (rather than focus primarily on saving souls).[37]

This raises serious questions, important for the present study, concerning the state of unbelievers' knowledge and what, if anything, they can know or accomplish in this world. Van Til sometimes speaks as though unbelievers know absolutely nothing, while elsewhere he offers a perhaps surprisingly positive evaluation of their knowing and doing. He presented these two poles in terms of the Kuyperian categories of antithesis and common grace. Van Til's sympathizers have wondered whether he juxtaposed these themes

---

cused Kuyper of Kantian proclivities at this point. Further description of Van Til's critique of Kuyper on the two kinds of sciences can be found in Jan van Vliet, "From Condition to State: Critical Reflections on Cornelius Van Til's Doctrine of Common Grace," *Westminster Theological Journal* 61 (1999): 76-77.

31. Van Til, *Common Grace*, 143-45.

32. Van Til, *Christian Theistic Ethics*, 86-88.

33. See Van Til, *Christian Theistic Ethics*, 65, 120, 138.

34. Van Til, *Christian Theistic Ethics*, 115.

35. See especially the four essays of Van Til included in *Foundations of Christian Education: Addresses to Christian Teachers*, ed. Dennis E. Johnson (Phillipsburg, NJ: P&R, 1990). Among other examples, see Van Til, *Common Grace*, 195.

36. Cornelius Van Til, "Antithesis in Education," in *Foundations of Christian Education*, 17; and Cornelius Van Til, "*Faith*: Faith and Our Program," in *Foundations of Christian Education*, 100.

37. Van Til, *Christian Theistic Ethics*, 115.

in a fully consistent manner,[38] and he himself acknowledged that it was impossible to give a wholly adequate account of the knowledge of the unbeliever, calling this "a very complex situation."[39] Nevertheless, Van Til was conscious of the need to affirm both antithesis and common grace in order to give a satisfactory account of the state of the unbeliever.

When describing unbelievers' knowledge in terms of the antithesis, he portrays them very literally as getting everything wrong. In contrast to Christians, non-Christians think of this world as self-existent and self-meaningful, of the human mind as ethically normal rather than depraved, and of human reason as functioning univocally rather than analogically.[40] They affirm being in general and knowledge in general, they view themselves as their own law-givers, and they look at the current human ethical situation as normal, not as fallen from an originally perfect creation.[41] Van Til can say that from the *"ultimate point of view"* the non-Christian is in absolute ethical antithesis to God. Because all knowledge is inter-related, requiring a person to know all things truly in order to know one thing truly, non-Christians know nothing as they should, nothing truly.[42] Hence, in an essay on education, he states that a basic fact such as two times two equals four means something different to believers and unbelievers. Shortly thereafter he explains: "The ground for the necessity of Christian schools lies in this very thing, that no fact can be known unless it be known in its relationship to God. And once this point is clearly seen, the doubt as to the value of teaching arithmetic in Christian schools falls out of the picture. Of course arithmetic must be taught in a Christian school. It cannot be taught anywhere else."[43]

Yet Van Til, relying upon his doctrine of common grace, also acknowledges a point of view other than the "ultimate." From a "relative point of view," the non-Christian actually "knows all things *after a fashion.*" This is the case because God objectively impresses his truth upon non-Christians' consciousness, and though they always try to suppress it, they can never fully succeed. Hence, they remain inconsistent with their unbelieving, monistic

---

38. E.g., see Frame, *Cornelius Van Til,* 189-92. Frame calls Van Til an "apostle of antithesis" who, in the spirit of heroes such as Kuyper and J. Gresham Machen, felt responsible for maintaining an antithesis mentality, despite a fairly flexible use of the antithesis idea in practice; see *Cornelius Van Til,* 187-88, 210-11.

39. Van Til, *Introduction,* 26-27, 94-95.

40. See Van Til, *Introduction,* 23-25, 101.

41. See Van Til, *Christian Apologetics,* 8-12; and Van Til, *Christian Theistic Ethics,* 59-61.

42. Van Til, *Introduction,* 26, 82.

43. Van Til, "Antithesis in Education," 7, 18.

starting-point, and therefore the real-life situation of the non-Christian is a perpetual mixture of truth and error.[44] God's will is heard in human moral consciousness despite sin, and sinful people, at bottom, recognize truth, which penetrates their minds in spite of themselves.[45] Because of this enduring revelation from God, "deep down" they know that theism is true — indeed, that the one and only God exists — and that their own views are false.[46]

Van Til contemplates this situation at some length, particularly in regard to the physical sciences and other mundane areas of life, given his conviction that, from the "relative" point of view, unbelievers know about earthly things better than they know about God.[47] An important aspect of Van Til's evaluation of the situation is his notion of "borrowed" or "stolen" capital. Unbelievers have indeed been very successful in scientific pursuits and have discovered many true states of affairs, but this is only "adventitious." They have not applied their own presuppositions consistently, but have instead borrowed or stolen the truth that rightly belongs only to Christians working with the correct presuppositions.[48] Van Til calls it "absurd" to say that non-Christians do not discover truth by their methods — though Van Til actually says such things himself. The reality is simply that they cannot employ their own methods consistently. They unwittingly presuppose Christian truth for the sake of their own accomplishments.[49] Common grace, a subject to be explored more explicitly below, keeps people from working out their own principles consistently.[50] Because of this inconsistency with his own principles, the "natural man" does many "good" things.[51]

In evaluating unbelievers through the twin ideas of antithesis and common grace, Van Til strives for balance. Though Christians know that all non-Christians will be lost forever, they cannot be indifferent to whether non-Christians are murderers or upstanding citizens, to whether they are more

---

44. Van Til, *Introduction*, 26-27, 82-83.

45. Van Til, *Introduction*, 95; Van Til, *Christian Theistic Ethics*, 23.

46. Van Til, *Introduction*, 41; Van Til, *Common Grace*, 130-31.

47. See Van Til, *Introduction*, 83. He draws these conclusions, in part, from his interaction with Calvin in 2.2.13 of the *Institutes*.

48. Van Til, *Introduction*, 84; and Cornelius Van Til, "Response by C. Van Til," in *Jerusalem and Athens: Critical Discussions on the Philosophy and Apologetics of Cornelius Van Til*, ed. E. R. Geehan (Nutley, NJ: Presbyterian and Reformed, 1971), 91.

49. Van Til, *Christian Apologetics*, 64.

50. Van Til, *Common Grace*, 117-18.

51. Van Til, *Common Grace*, 196-97.

or less consistent in their unbelieving interpretation of life.[52] The unbeliever has no truly good purpose or motive, yet often continues to do what appears externally to be obedience to God's law.[53] Were Christians and non-Christians both to be epistemologically self-conscious, they would have absolutely nothing in common. This applies, contra Kuyper, even to weighing and measuring, activities which are part of the single whole that constitutes interpretation of reality.[54] And yet God restrains the unbeliever's epistemological self-consciousness.

Van Til's doctrine of common grace, however, for which he received significant criticism in his own day,[55] was not concerned merely with the epistemological restraint of unbelievers, but was rooted in a broader philosophy of history. Though he was certainly indebted to Kuyper in making common grace a major organizing category of his thought, Van Til's doctrine was in many ways quite different from Kuyper's. Very significantly, Van Til states that common grace is not an end in itself, but *only* a means for preparing a field for the operation of special grace.[56] Here he consciously diverges from Kuyper. Following the critique of Jochem Douma, Van Til rejects Kuyper's account of an organic development of creation through an independent stream of common grace. He adds, along similar lines, that Kuyper was wrong to distinguish between Christ as mediator of creation and as mediator of redemption.[57]

---

52. Van Til, *Introduction,* 93.

53. Van Til, *Introduction,* 105.

54. Van Til, *Common Grace,* 5, 44.

55. For example, within the span of two calendar years two significant figures in the Christian Reformed Church, in which Van Til had been raised and with which he maintained close ties throughout his life, leveled strong attacks on his doctrine of common grace. See William Masselink, *General Revelation and Common Grace: A Defense of the Historic Reformed Faith over against the Theology and Philosophy of the So-Called "Reconstructionist" Movement* (Grand Rapids: Eerdmans, 1953); and James Daane, *A Theology of Grace: An Inquiry into and Evaluation of Dr. C. Van Til's Doctrine of Common Grace* (Grand Rapids: Eerdmans, 1954). It may also be noted that Van Til offered his own pointed criticism of the common grace views of many figures, particularly those from his native Dutch Reformed circles, including Kuyper, Dooyeweerd, Herman Bavinck, Valentin Hepp, Klaas Schilder, and Herman Hoeksema, as well as replies to criticisms of those such as Masselink and Daane.

56. Van Til, *Introduction,* 80. Perhaps an important appendix to this claim is Van Til's statement that God speaks only redemptively after the fall; see *Christian Theistic Ethics,* 144. This statement, however, seems contradictory to his assertion elsewhere that God's wrath is also revealed after the fall; e.g., see "Nature and Scripture," 260.

57. Van Til, *Common Grace,* 228-29. Muether notes that Van Til, when asked about issues of cultural analysis, often referred inquirers to a book written by his nephew, Henry Van Til; see

Thinking in terms of a philosophy of history, Van Til views common grace as common in the sense of being *earlier*. At the earliest stage of history, all grace is common. After the fall, non-saving common grace is distinguished from saving, special grace. Common grace pertains, however, to all dimensions of life, not just to those termed lower, and pertains to them in the same way at all stages of history. Van Til understands common grace to be God's gift by which good things, whether rain and sunshine or the preaching of the gospel, come to people in common, whether believer or unbeliever. As history moves along, a process of differentiation occurs. Both Christians and non-Christians, as they respond differently to common grace, become increasingly self-conscious epistemologically, and hence the commonness between them gradually diminishes. Van Til admits here that the process of differentiation has proceeded further in the higher than in the lower dimensions of life, hence meaning that there remains more commonness in mathematics than in theology, for example. In either case, common grace diminishes over time, as history reaches toward its consummation and people make more choices and commit more actions in response to the common grace. When the process of differentiation through epistemological self-consciousness reaches its maximum, the "crack of doom has come." Thus Van Til explains:

> All common grace is earlier grace. Its commonness lies in its earliness. It pertains not merely to the lower dimensions of life. It pertains to all dimensions, and to these dimensions in the same way at all stages of history. It pertains to all the dimensions of life, but to all these dimensions ever decreasingly as the time of history goes on. . . . With every conditional act the remaining significance of the conditional is reduced. God allows men to follow the path of their self-chosen rejection of Him more rapidly than ever toward the final consummation. God increases His attitude of wrath upon the reprobate as time goes on, until at the end of time, at the great consummation of history, their condition has caught up with their state.[58]

Muether, *Cornelius Van Til*, 154-55. In this book, Henry Van Til makes the same criticisms of Kuyper on this issue that his uncle did; see *The Calvinistic Concept of Culture* (1959; Grand Rapids: Baker, 2001), 236-37.

58. Van Til, *Common Grace*, 82-83. This theology of common grace as I have summarized it in this paragraph is perhaps most fully set out in chapter 3 of *Common Grace*, particularly on pages 72-95. Some detailed critique of this doctrine of common grace embedded in a philosophy of history appears in van Vliet, "From Condition to State."

How does this vision shape Van Til's understanding of believers' responsibilities in the present age, in regard both to their interaction with unbelievers and to their cultural endeavors? Regarding the former, Van Til states quite clearly that Christians are to seek to hasten the process of differentiation. Part of the task of apologetics is to make people more self-consciously covenant breakers or covenant keepers. Elsewhere he writes that they are to "make men epistemologically self-conscious all along the line."[59] Van Til places believers in a somewhat awkward situation: they are grateful for the "day of undeveloped differentiation," which enables Christian influence on society and the state, yet at the same time they must exert every effort to hasten the differentiation.[60]

How then does he view the Christian's cultural task? He acknowledges a place for Christians to engage in "legitimate cooperation," "'as if' cooperation," with non-Christians.[61] But for Van Til, pursuing the cultural mandate, originally established at creation, is not a mutual task shared in common by believers and unbelievers. It is a task for Christians, who in turn utilize non-Christians for their own purposes. Van Til explains that common grace puts non-Christians at the service of Christians, who are taking up the cultural mandate anew. Christians — covenant keepers — have "one great plan of accomplishing the cultural tasks that God has given to man." They "are in control of the situation." "Yet that it may be the earth and the *fulness* thereof that is developed, the covenant keepers will make use of the works of the covenant breakers which these have been able and compelled to perform in spite of themselves."[62] Van Til allows believers to be generous and cooperative with unbelievers, but only when believers are being epistemologically self-conscious and pressing the Christian claim at every point. In regard to the cultural edifice, Van Til says that "we own the title."[63] And so even when conversion of unbelievers seems to be out of the question, Christians, in fulfillment of their comprehensive goal of eliminating sin, must perform their task of destroying evil in the field of common grace.[64]

---

59. Van Til, *Common Grace*, 85; see also Van Til, *Christian Apologetics*, 27.
60. Van Til, *Common Grace*, 85.
61. Van Til, *Common Grace*, 44.
62. Van Til, *Common Grace*, 117-19.
63. Van Til, *Common Grace*, 95.
64. Van Til, *Christian Theistic Ethics*, 87.

Van Til and the Natural Law and Two Kingdoms Tradition

I now turn to place Van Til's thought in relation to the Reformed natural law and two kingdoms traditions. As noted in the introduction to this chapter, Van Til never explicitly interacted with these doctrines as expressed in his own theological heritage, nor did he devote much sustained attention to ordinary matters of culture and social life. Though he wrote about many issues relevant to natural law and the two kingdoms, and to the relation of Christianity and culture generally, these were undeveloped areas of his thought. Nevertheless, even if his apologetics method is not determinative for an approach to culture and social life, some conclusions can be drawn about his relation to the earlier tradition, first in regard to the two kingdoms and then natural law.

To begin, then, a number of aspects of Van Til's theology suggest a fundamental sympathy with the concerns of the Reformed two kingdoms tradition. His critique of Barth provides an excellent case in point, for he homed in precisely upon issues identified in Chapter 8 as foundational for Barth's rejection of both the two kingdoms and natural law ideas. Following the suggestion of G. C. Berkouwer, Van Til claimed that Barth's theology has no place for a "transition from wrath to grace in history." According to Van Til, Barth says that God is only known in his revelation in Christ, a revelation of grace and reconciliation. Van Til writes of Barth: "The original relation of every man is therefore that of his election in Christ. Christ as the only real man is before Adam. Therefore man's acceptance with God is an accomplished fact before his creation. His redemption has taken place in God before he exists."[65] In distinction from this position, Van Til affirmed what he took as the historic Reformed and biblical view that there was a historical man Adam who lived originally in an unfallen world and later fell into sin, and that in these historical events God revealed himself to Adam apart from the message of grace and reconciliation in the incarnate Christ. The revelation of redemption in Christ comes only as a response to the historical fall of the human race into sin, and the wrath of God continues to be revealed in nature in a way distinct from the supernatural revelation of God's mercy in Christ. In light of these fundamental disagreements with Barth, Van Til clearly rejected the Christological reworking of Reformed theology on which Barth's critique of the Reformed tradition on natural law and the two kingdoms rested.

65. Van Til, *Christianity and Barthianism*, 62-63.

Several other aspects of Van Til's thought explored above also suggest fundamental sympathy for the Reformed two kingdoms tradition. Van Til embraced the doctrine of common grace, which, as argued in Chapter 7, Kuyper before him had developed as a means for expressing historic Reformed two kingdoms concerns. Furthermore, Van Til also acknowledged that non-Christians know many true things and that Christians should engage in common tasks with them, through his ideas about a "relative" (in distinction from an "ultimate") perspective and "as if" cooperation. Finally, he refused to be indifferent about whether non-Christians were respectable or base citizens. All of this suggests that Van Til had the same sorts of concerns as did the earlier Reformed tradition in positing a civil kingdom distinct from the spiritual kingdom and pertaining to temporal, mundane matters of universal human existence.

Yet other aspects of Van Til's thought stand in some tension with historic two kingdoms doctrine. Though he never explicitly critiqued the Reformed two kingdoms categories, his unnuanced statements about Christ's kingship over every sphere of life indicate that Van Til was operating without his theological ancestors' distinctions between God's two kingdoms and the different ways in which Christ reigns over them. The fact that he regularly recommended a book on Christian cultural engagement that specifically repudiated a "two realms" approach would seem to confirm this conclusion.[66] Van Til also at times spoke of Christians taking up again the original cultural task given to the human race at creation, a common theme among the neo-Calvinists considered in the previous chapter. Beyond these sorts of observations, intriguing for present purposes is how Van Til, for all of his admiration for Kuyper, expressly disagreed with him on three points pertaining to the doctrine of common grace, all of which, as argued in Chapter 7, connected Kuyper to the earlier Reformed two kingdoms tradition: the distinction between the two mediatorships of Christ, the identification of a realm of common grace, and the independent purposes of common grace beyond its service to the purposes of special grace. These three

---

66. As noted in a footnote above, Van Til recommended his nephew's book to inquirers about cultural issues. In this work, Henry Van Til uses "two kingdoms" language only as equivalent to Augustine's "two cities" doctrine, which he finds a helpful idea (see *Calvinistic Concept,* ch. 6). He does not interact with Calvin's two kingdoms doctrine but does contrast Calvin to Luther in ways suggesting a greater difference between these Reformers than that suggested in Chapters 2 and 3 above; see *Calvinistic Concept,* 20, 226-27. Henry Van Til rejects a "two realms" approach, which he associates with a medieval nature-grace view and Luther's position, but not Calvin's; see *Calvinistic Concept,* 237-39.

ideas were intimately connected for Kuyper. It was precisely because different areas of life are grounded in two distinct works of the Son (creation and redemption) that the (common grace) areas of life grounded in creation could have purposes independent of the purposes of the (special grace) areas of life grounded in redemption. The purposes of common grace could not be reduced to the purposes of special grace because the purposes of the Son's creative work could not be reduced to the purposes of his redemptive work. Van Til's rejection of these three aspects of Kuyper's common grace theology also bore an inner consistency. In rejecting the distinction between the Son's two mediatorships he also refused to see a distinction between primarily common grace spheres of life and primarily special grace spheres and thus to acknowledge that the former has purposes independent from the latter.

These three points of critique of Kuyper on common grace may be viewed briefly in turn. First, Van Til rejected the distinction between the two mediatorships of the Son over creation and redemption as he found it in Kuyper (but which, perhaps unbeknownst to Van Til, was also taught by such other Reformed theologians discussed above as Stuart Robinson, Francis Turretin, John Cotton, George Gillespie, and Samuel Rutherford). Instead, Van Til sided with Dutch theologian Klaas Schilder in rejecting "Kuyper's distinction between Christ as the mediator of creation and as the mediator of redemption. We must unite the idea of creation in Christ with that of His redemption of all things."[67] Van Til, therefore, rejected what, historically, was perhaps the most basic theological foundation for the Reformed two kingdoms doctrine. That Van Til would make this move is, in my judgment, not at all obvious. It was Barth's uniting of Christ's creating and redeeming work that drove his rejection of the two mediatorships idea and hence also the two kingdoms doctrine, as explored in Chapter 8. Yet for all of his theological criticism of Barth for his unwillingness to distinguish creation and redemption sufficiently and make room for historical transitions in God's dealings with the human race, Van Til expressed this semantic similarity with Barth and rejected an aspect of Reformed doctrine that was intended historically to protect the integrity of God's creating and sustaining work in distinction from his work of redemption.[68]

67. Van Til, *Common Grace,* 228-29. In the book Van Til recommended on cultural engagement, Henry Van Til agreed in choosing Schilder over Kuyper on this issue; see *Calvinistic Concept,* 134-35, 236-37.

68. For a recent attempt to defend and develop Van Til's apologetic method through biblical exegesis, exploring the Christological dimension of both creation and redemption (though without

Second, Van Til also differed with Kuyper in the way that Kuyper identified a realm or terrain of common grace, namely, that of the nation or broader society with its shared cultural pursuits. This difference, I suggest, was implicit rather than explicit on Van Til's part. Kuyper viewed the institutional church (and the organic church insofar as it formed its own "Christian" organizations) as the terrain of special grace and the other, non-ecclesiastical spheres of cultural life as the terrain of common grace, the former grounded in Christ's mediatorship of redemption and the latter in his mediatorship of creation. In this, Kuyper resembled the earlier Reformed tradition's differentiation of the ecclesiastical and non-ecclesiastical realms in terms of the two kingdoms. Van Til ended up in a different place from Kuyper on this issue, but by an indirect route. In his book on common grace, Van Til disputes Kuyper's contention that basic human activities such as logic and weighing and measuring are common to believers and unbelievers such that sin has not corrupted them and regeneration does not restore them.[69] Though Van Til here was simply trying to apply Kuyper's idea of the antithesis more consistently and radically than Kuyper himself had done, it led him to eliminate entirely the idea of a "territory" of common grace in distinction from other territories of human endeavor. Both common grace and the antithesis apply to all areas and to all activities of life. Van Til's basic conviction about common grace was not, therefore, that it sustains *certain* spheres of life (e.g., the state in distinction from the church), but that it sustains *every* sphere as *earlier* grace.

By *earlier* grace, as considered above, Van Til meant that God gives common grace to all people indiscriminately for the purpose of setting the stage for the work of God's saving grace and the differentiation of people as believers and unbelievers. And this point is tied directly to the third point at which Van Til critiqued Kuyper's views, the idea of an independent purpose for the life of common grace. In connection with his critique of Kuyper on the two mediatorships, Van Til accuses Kuyper of "giving free reign to his speculative imagination" in his "idea that the development of the powers of nature by means of common grace is something independent of God's work of saving grace."[70] As discussed in Chapter 7, Kuyper did not believe that the *sole* purpose of common grace was to serve the interests of special grace and God's re-

---

reference to the older doctrine of the two mediatorships), see Lane G. Tipton, "Paul's Christological Interpretation of Creation and Presuppositional Apologetics," in *Revelation and Reason*, 95-111.

69. See Van Til, *Common Grace*, 34-44.

70. Van Til, *Common Grace*, 228-29. Here again the book that Van Til recommended on cultural engagement takes the same view; see Henry Van Til, *Calvinistic Concept*, 237.

demptive work. Instead, in the development of human cultural activity, the life of common grace has other purposes as well that bring glory to God in their own right. With this perspective, I suggested, Kuyper resembled the earlier Reformed tradition's outlook on the civil kingdom as serving purposes of truth, civility, and justice that could not be entirely reduced to the purpose of preparing a way for God's redemptive work. Van Til, refusing to distinguish the Son of God's mediatorship of creation from that of redemption and to demarcate certain areas of life as the particular realm of common grace, refused to ascribe purposes to common grace other than furthering the interests of redemption (and damnation). As earlier grace, common grace provides a forum in which the differentiation of believer from unbeliever may take place. Believers and unbelievers respond differently to the gifts of common grace, whether rain or sunshine or the preaching of the gospel, and hence what they have in common lessens over time. Whereas Kuyper envisioned special grace as *enriching* the realm of common grace and enabling common grace activities to reach a higher level of development, Van Til envisioned special grace as *eliminating* common grace until the end of history when commonness has expired altogether. Whereas Kuyper thought that believers ought to leaven the work of common grace by virtue of their special grace, Van Til thought that believers, by virtue of their special grace, ought to seek to make all people more epistemologically self-conscious in either their submission to or rejection of God and thereby to hasten the process of differentiation and of the diminishment of common grace.

I will offer some concluding reflections on Van Til and the two kingdoms doctrine, but only after a brief consideration of his relation to the Reformed natural law tradition. As observed above in regard to the two kingdoms issue, many of Van Til's convictions suggest a fundamental sympathy to the Reformed doctrine of natural law. First, he affirmed in general the existence of natural revelation, both before and after the fall into sin. In fact, he taught this idea with notable force in stating that all aspects of created reality are revelational. Connected to this idea was his view of conscience. Since all of created reality is revelational, even subjective human moral consciousness reveals God and his law. Even if Van Til's statements about conscience were not entirely lucid, his basic affirmation that God's voice is heard in the conscience and places people under accountability to God reflects historic Reformed teaching. Likewise, Van Til followed his Reformed predecessors in seeing Romans 2:14-15 as a proof-text for the reality of conscience.[71] He also

---

71. See Van Til, *Common Grace*, 87-88.

resembled many of his predecessors in writing that the good, including that which we know through the natural revelation of conscience, is good not merely because God says it is good but also because the will of God expresses the very nature of God.[72] In stating these sorts of convictions, Van Til often asserted that nature is not an autonomous or neutral entity. Here again there is similarity to the earlier tradition's teaching that the natural law is God's law and was originally bestowed in the context of the image of God and the covenant of works. In regard to Kuyper's particular emphases and development of the Reformed tradition, Van Til sounded similar strains in stressing the interconnection and mutual dependence of natural and special revelation, at times speaking of the importance of investigation of the facts of nature under the guidance of Scripture.[73]

Despite this substantial correspondence to his Reformed heritage, Van Til never affirmed a positive role for natural law, as, for example, the standard for civil law. There is probably no single explanation for why he did not. Part of the explanation surely involves his identity as a professor of apologetics and his distinctive approach to that discipline. As he sought to apply historic Reformed theology to apologetic method, he combated a conception of natural theology as a body of knowledge shared in common among believers and unbelievers. No such natural theology could serve as a foundation upon which the higher truths of Christianity could be added. The basic error of such a natural theology (and the corresponding conception of natural ethics), Van Til explained in many places, is to give natural, sinful human people an area of reality that they are able to interpret autonomously or without basic error. His principal target here was what he understood to be the basic perspective of Thomas Aquinas and the Roman Catholic tradition, though he also faulted the post-Reformation Reformed scholastic theologians for similar failings. There seems good reason to suspect that, for Van Til, the idea of natural law was poisoned by its association with the ideas of natural theology and natural ethics. Others have already argued that Van Til's understanding of the Reformed scholastic view of natural theology was skewed.[74] Of more

---

72. See Van Til, *Christian Theistic Ethics*, 20-21.

73. For an argument that Van Til's theology, though not explicitly supportive of natural law, is an important resource for a contemporary Protestant revival of natural law thought, see Thomas K. Johnson, *Natural Law Ethics: An Evangelical Proposal* (Bonn: Verlag für Kultur und Wissenschaft, 2005), 108-15.

74. Most recently, see Jeffrey K. Jue, "*Theologia Naturalis*: A Reformed Tradition," in *Revelation and Reason*, 168-89. Jue builds on the work of several scholars whose research on post-Reformation Reformed orthodoxy is cited in Chapter 5, especially that of Richard A. Muller.

direct importance for the present study, if Van Til in fact associated natural law with the idea of an autonomous, non-sin-infected realm of nature and identified it as a non-divinely-revealed ethic, then he was certainly not understanding natural law as his Reformed predecessors did.

Thus, part of Van Til's reticence about affirming positive roles for natural law in the world likely stems from construing the idea of natural law in ways different from the ways in which Reformed theology had historically construed the idea. Another reason for this reticence, I believe, is the way in which he described the *natural* in connection with his conception of the *common*. As considered above, he refused to see an independent purpose for the common but understood it *simply* as that which preceded and set the stage for the differentiation between believer and unbeliever. So also Van Til refused to see an independent purpose for the natural. The natural is merely a "limiting notion," a "playground" for this same process of differentiation. Natural revelation, he says, is "meaningless" without special revelation. However much the earlier Reformed tradition would have affirmed that the natural serves *in part* as the playground for differentiation and that Scripture is necessary for a fully accurate interpretation of natural revelation, it did not limit the natural to such a subservient purpose nor treat natural revelation on its own terms as meaningless. It ascribed great accomplishments — in scientific, political, and legal endeavors — to pagans working only with the light of nature. From Calvin to Kuyper the Reformed tradition acknowledged truth and justice accomplished through natural law without the need to relate all such accomplishments to purposes of differentiation between believers and unbelievers. Since Van Til apparently lacked this perspective, his failure to make positive affirmation of the role of natural law for civil law and other cultural endeavors seems understandable.

What might be said by way of brief conclusion regarding Van Til and the Reformed natural law and two kingdoms traditions? Van Til, in his role as an apologist, was chiefly concerned to interpret everything in terms of the antithesis between believing and unbelieving thought and thus also in terms of the differentiation of believer from unbeliever in history. From this driving concern, Van Til tended to interpret all the things that Christians and non-Christians have in common in this world, whether cultural activities or nature and natural revelation themselves, in the light of how the antithesis expresses itself and how the process of differentiation takes place. What is common is common only in being earlier to saving grace and the process of differentiation. What is natural is natural only as a limiting notion, a playground for special revelation and the same process of differentiation.

Though Van Til acknowledged a "relative" perspective and "as if" cooperation of Christians with non-Christians, therefore, these ideas seem to be simply descriptive rather than prescriptive. In other words, these ideas describe how it is that, despite the antithesis, non-Christians make many true affirmations (in a de facto manner only, without seeing these things in their broader truth context) and how Christians may put non-Christians to their service in cultural labors. But these ideas do not prescribe constructive guidance for how believers ought to engage in cultural pursuits in common with unbelievers despite differences in ultimate matters of faith. Van Til in fact pressed the antithesis with such rigor at times that his logic suggests that Christians should pursue no tasks in common with non-Christians, though obviously this was not what he intended.[75]

To put this in historical perspective, in the early church the Epistle to Diognetus and Augustine both affirmed a clear antithesis between Christians and non-Christians in regard to ultimate matters, yet also contemplated and gave positive counsel for how to pursue commonality in regard to temporal things. The early Reformed theologians also affirmed ideas about an antithesis in regard to ultimate, religious matters, and though they did not offer much concrete discussion of cultural commonality between Christians and non-Christians (living as they did in the context of Christendom), they did provide a theological groundwork, through their natural law and two kingdoms categories, for contemplating such commonality. Later figures such as Stuart Robinson and Abraham Kuyper developed the Reformed tradition by using these categories to explore the nature of life in societies marked by freedom of religion, in which the question of commonality again became a pressing concern. Van Til, as an "apostle of antithesis,"[76] gave relatively little consideration to what the relative perspective and "as if" cooperation would look like when put into practice and, even when he did, it tended to be overtaken quickly by his interest in the antithesis.

---

75. E.g., as cited above, Van Til argued that Christian children must be taught even arithmetic in Christian schools, because there is an "ultimate difference" between the Christian's and the non-Christian's affirmation that two times two equals four; see "Antithesis in Education," 7, 18. One might ask Van Til why a Christian can buy a carrot from a non-Christian who grows it without understanding agriculture from the perspective of a Christian worldview but cannot learn multiplication from a non-Christian who does not understand arithmetic from the perspective of a Christian worldview. The same logic might be pressed against Henry Van Til, who warns Christians against participating in public schools and labor unions that do not acknowledge the lordship of Christ and therefore, he says, serve the cause of antichrist. See *Calvinistic Concept*, 209.

76. As cited above, this is the terminology of Frame in *Cornelius Van Til*, 187-88.

Natural Law and the Two Kingdoms among the Van Tillians

If the preceding interpretation of Van Til is accurate, then he can be pegged as neither a strict opponent nor defender of the Reformed natural law and two kingdoms doctrines as historically articulated. But in what direction then would his students go who had more interest than he in social and cultural issues? Given the undeveloped and somewhat ambiguous nature of Van Til's handling of such issues, it is not surprising that those drawing inspiration from him have moved in various, often very different, directions. Two such Van Tillian writers whose views on matters of Christianity and culture have generated perhaps the most interest in conservative, confessional Reformed circles illustrate well these sorts of stark differences. One of them, Greg Bahnsen, a representative of the so-called "theonomic" school of ethics, advocated the application of the Mosaic civil law to contemporary legal systems and presented views much more overtly opposed to the Reformed natural law and two kingdoms doctrines than anything Van Til wrote. The other, Meredith G. Kline, took considerably more interest than Van Til in the nature of commonality in political and cultural affairs and articulated a view that, I will argue, constitutes a creative development of the Reformed natural law and two kingdoms traditions (whose existence he himself never specifically acknowledged). In this section, therefore, I first describe briefly the views of Bahnsen and then, at somewhat greater length, explore those of Kline.

Bahnsen and the Idea of Theonomic Ethics

Greg Bahnsen devoted many of his efforts to expounding and developing Van Til's apologetics,[77] but his most memorable and controversial project was defending "theonomy," an approach to ethics and social life pioneered in the generation before him by Rousas J. Rushdoony.[78] In his major work on theonomy, Bahnsen states that his "concern will be to show from God's word that the Christian is obligated to keep the whole law of God as a pattern of sanctification and that this law is to be enforced by the civil magistrate where and how the stipulations of God so designate. . . . Theonomy is crucial to

---

77. As evident, e.g., in Bahnsen, *Van Til's Apologetic.*

78. Among his works relevant for this topic, see Rousas John Rushdoony, *The Institutes of Biblical Law*, 3 vols. (Nutley, NJ: Craig, 1973).

Christian ethics, and all the details of God's law are intrinsic to theonomy. Here is the heart of the present thesis."[79] He goes on to defend the continuing obligation of the Mosaic law "in exhaustive detail,"[80] which means, most notably, that the Old Testament civil or judicial law should be the standard for the civil law of all nations at all times.

First, where does Bahnsen's thesis place him in regard to the Reformed natural law tradition? Perhaps most obviously to those who have read the previous chapters of the present book, his assertion that the Mosaic civil law continues to be the standard for the nations of the world today is directly contrary to historic Reformed teaching that natural law is the basic standard for contemporary civil law and that the Mosaic civil law as such has been abrogated. What happens to the idea of natural law for Bahnsen, then? Though he affirms general revelation, any idea of natural law in the historic Reformed sense is absent and in fact is effectively denied. In support of this claim, it may be helpful to note first that a key theme in Bahnsen's volume is that ethics (whether personal or social) must be *theonomous* rather than *autonomous,* that is, based upon God's law rather than a human beings' own self-created law.[81] This emphasis is perhaps where Van Til's influence is most readily evident, and Bahnsen in fact includes a page of quotations at the beginning of his book which includes Van Til's statement: "There is no alternative but that of theonomy and autonomy." When these terms are understood in a general way, certainly no theologian with any allegiance to historic Reformed Christianity would care to disagree. But when Bahnsen uses the term "theonomy" he means specifically the law of God as found in Scripture: "there is really no other ethical answer but that which is authoritatively revealed in God's word. One must choose theonomy *or* autonomy, but autonomy is morally crippled."[82] For classic Reformed theology, in contrast, the natural law was, without qualification, the law of God, and thus Scripture was certainly not the only place where the law of God is revealed. The idea of a natural law with positive functions in the world therefore is absent in Bahnsen's thought. Yet it is not as though the idea of natural law was unknown to him. He does on occasion mention natural law explicitly, but he describes it most clearly as *not* the law of God. He states, for example, that if the state is not governed by God's law, that is, Scripture, "then it must be one

---

79. Greg L. Bahnsen, *Theonomy in Christian Ethics* (Nutley, NJ: Craig, 1979), 34-35.

80. The title of Bahnsen, *Theonomy in Christian Ethics*, ch. 2 is "The Abiding Validity of the Law in Exhaustive Detail."

81. E.g., see his discussion and critique in Bahnsen, *Theonomy in Christian Ethics*, 4, 10, 37.

82. Bahnsen, *Theonomy in Christian Ethics*, 37.

of five alternatives. It might be *natural law,* but this is simply a projection of autonomy and satisfaction with the status quo. . . ."[83] This identification of natural law in a way so at odds with Bahnsen's own Reformed tradition seems grounded in a highly schematized and imprecise historical understanding of the "medieval scholastics" as emphasizing the "*natural* law" and of the Reformation as repudiating and countering them through their emphasis upon "God's revealed law in *Scripture.*"[84]

Bahnsen's variance from the Reformed two kingdoms doctrine is perhaps not as overt as his variance from its natural law doctrine, but it seems evident nevertheless. His general statements about Christ's kingship over the state and all things, without the older Reformed nuances as to the two different ways in which he exercises his universal kingship, provide initial evidence that Bahnsen was not thinking in two kingdoms terms. Added to this evidence is his use of "two kingdoms" kind of language in an Augustinian "two cities" sense, when he contrasts the kingdoms of God and Satan.[85] This is not necessarily any misuse of the language, but it too suggests that the Reformed two kingdoms idea was not within Bahnsen's purview. His insistence that the nature of the civil magistrate in Old Testament Israel is essentially identical to what the civil magistrate should be in all the nations of the earth today[86] and that the character of the distinction between "church and state" in Old Testament Israel should be the model for the distinction in all civil societies today[87] in some ways also reveal tension with the Reformed two kingdoms tradition, though these were matters often expressed less than coherently by the older theologians. Certainly elements of the historic two kingdoms doctrine did survive in Bahnsen's thought. This is particularly evident in his insistence that the physical sword belongs only to the state and not to the church, and that the kingdom of Christ advances by means of the word of God proclaimed in the church and not by the magistrate's sword. He adds elsewhere that "the state does not operate in the name of the Redeemer." Bahnsen's attempts to reconcile these traditional Reformed affirmations with his theonomic ethic were, however, in my judgment, often incoherent.[88]

83. Bahnsen, *Theonomy in Christian Ethics,* 399; see also 545.

84. Bahnsen, *Theonomy in Christian Ethics,* 30.

85. E.g., see Bahnsen, *Theonomy in Christian Ethics,* 2, 199, 397.

86. See Bahnsen, *Theonomy in Christian Ethics,* chapters 17-19.

87. See Bahnsen, *Theonomy in Christian Ethics,* ch. 20.

88. See Bahnsen, *Theonomy in Christian Ethics,* 414-29. For examples of two unresolved tensions here, Bahnsen on the one hand asserts that the state does not operate in the name of the Re-

In summary, Bahnsen's defense of theonomy picked up on some common Van Tillian themes such as the need to resist, in all areas of life, human attempts to be autonomous in thought and action. Yet Bahnsen's polemics against autonomy, which in various ways overlooked and rejected historic Reformed natural law and two kingdoms doctrine, certainly went beyond Van Til's own teaching. In his published writings Van Til did not look to the Old Testament Israelite polity as a direct model for contemporary civil polity[89] and in private correspondence late in life he expressed reservations about the association of his thought with that of theonomy.[90] And it is also perhaps worth noting that Bahnsen never cited or referred to Van Til in his constructive argument in *Theonomy in Christian Ethics*. All of this provokes the question whether Van Til's thought might be taken in other directions in the pursuit of a Reformed approach to culture and social life.

Kline on Covenant, Culture, and the Common

The theology of Meredith G. Kline provides such an example of how devotion to Van Til's thought could coexist with an account of culture and social life very different from that of Bahnsen. Kline was a student of Van Til at Westminster Theological Seminary and later his colleague there as professor of Old Testament. Later he held teaching posts at Gordon-Conwell Theological Seminary near Boston and Westminster Seminary California near San Diego. I argue here that Kline, though without giving indication of any better awareness of the Reformed natural law and two kingdoms traditions than Van Til or Bahnsen, presented a perspective that bears significant resemblances to the ideas that characterized these traditions, though with modification and development. I will also argue that his particular contribu-

---

deemer and on the other hand calls for Christians to seek the establishment of a "Christocracy" that operates according to biblical law holistically; Bahnsen also on the one hand claims that Christ taught Christians entering his kingdom not "to use the sword of war" and on the other hand claims that a primary responsibility of Christians is to apply biblical law to the state, which entails promoting the state's use of the sword. Bahnsen at times speaks clearly as though Christ's kingdom cannot include the sword-bearing state and at other times asserts unqualifiedly the universal rule of Christ over every area of life, including the state.

89. See the helpful discussion of this issue in T. David Gordon, "Van Til and Theonomic Ethics," in *Creator, Redeemer, Consummator: A Festschrift for Meredith G. Kline*, ed. Howard Griffith and John R. Muether (Greenville: Reformed Academic Press, 2000), 271-78.

90. See Muether, *Cornelius Van Til*, 217.

tion to the development of the Reformed natural law and two kingdoms tradition may be his more deeply rooting it in the covenant theology that has long been a distinguishing mark of Reformed theology.

Perhaps the most significant resemblance of Kline's thought to Reformed natural law and two kingdoms doctrine is how he grounded political and cultural life not in God's redemptive work but in God's preservation of the creation order. Kline clearly reflected the wing of the American Presbyterian tradition that upheld both the freedom of religion in society and the doctrine of the spirituality of the church, with its teaching that the church should refrain from engaging in social and political affairs. With this American Presbyterian tradition he blended important elements of Dutch Kuyperian theology as well, mediated especially through Van Til. Kline, therefore, drew from both streams of the Reformed tradition identified in Chapters 6 and 7 that sought to apply natural law and two kingdoms categories in the modern context of religious freedom and ecclesiastical disestablishment.

I look first at Kline's appropriation of the Reformed two kingdoms tradition through his account of culture and common grace, particularly in his *magnum opus, Kingdom Prologue*. Evident throughout this account is the Van Tillian dual emphasis upon the antithesis and common grace. As will be observed below, however, Kline developed the idea of commonality in cultural affairs to a much greater extent than Van Til did, and seems to have modified his common grace doctrine in certain respects. In regard to the antithesis, Kline posits a general Augustinian view of the contrast between the kingdom of God and the kingdom of Satan. With express reliance upon Kuyperian and Van Tillian ideas, he affirms the existence of a religious antithesis between belief and unbelief and advocates the cultivation of a uniquely biblical world and life view.[91] Yet this Augustinian antithesis between the realms of God and Satan is not the only category that he utilizes. He also identifies a realm of common grace that has a "bestial" aspect but is nevertheless "legitimate," being ordained of God for particular beneficial purposes. As distinct from the church, the common grace city cannot be identified with the redemptive kingdom of God, though neither is it identified with the kingdom of Satan.[92] Hence Kline, though not citing the earlier Reformed tradition on this point, expresses its basic two kingdoms catego-

91. Meredith G. Kline, *Kingdom Prologue: Genesis Foundations for a Covenantal Worldview* (Overland Park, KS: Two Age Press, 2000), 169-70.

92. Kline, *Kingdom Prologue*, 168-69, 172.

ries in describing the church and the common grace city as two God-ordained, legitimate realities structuring life in the present world.

Kline's thought in this area must be understood against the background of the covenant theology that was a defining and organizing feature of much traditional Reformed doctrine, especially as developed by Princeton Seminary professor Geerhardus Vos (1862-1949), who also had a significant influence on Van Til.[93] Kline made the basic Reformed distinction between a covenant of works made with Adam at creation promising eternal life on the basis of perfect obedience (but which was broken because of sin) and a covenant of grace established after the fall into sin offering eternal life through faith in a promised Messiah, Jesus Christ. In distinction from this covenant of grace, by which the church has been founded to preach its gospel of salvation, Kline also identified a covenant of common grace made with Noah after the flood in Genesis 9, a covenant not simply for people of faith but encompassing every human being. This idea of a distinct covenant of common grace had precedent in earlier Reformed theology, including Kuyper's, though Kline's work here is in some respects original.[94] His placing common grace in a covenantal context seems to be one way in which Kline sought to develop Van Til's doctrine of common grace. This common grace covenant is important for present purposes because in it Kline saw the foundation of the state and the preservation of human culture in a fallen world.

In his exposition of these matters, Kline identifies the origin of the common grace order in how God dealt with the human race after the fall into sin.

93. Most of the early professors at Westminster Theological Seminary, under whom Kline received his ministerial training, had been students and colleagues of Vos at Princeton Theological Seminary, and they in turn mediated Vos's work to Kline. For Vos's interpretation of the historical importance of the biblical covenants for Reformed theology, see Geerhardus Vos, "The Doctrine of the Covenant in Reformed Theology," *Redemptive History and Biblical Interpretation: The Shorter Writings of Geerhardus Vos,* ed. Richard B. Gaffin, Jr. (Phillipsburg, NJ: Presbyterian and Reformed, 1980), 234-67. For his own most comprehensive development of this tradition, see Geerhardus Vos, *Biblical Theology* (Grand Rapids: Eerdmans, 1948).

94. Among antecedents of Kline's view in the older Reformed tradition, see, e.g., Herman Witsius, *The Economy of the Covenants between God and Man: Comprehending a Complete Body of Divinity,* 2 vols., trans. William Crookshank (1822; reprint, Phillipsburg: P&R, 1990), 2.239 (originally published in 1677); Wilhelmus à Brakel, *The Christian's Reasonable Service,* 4 vols., trans. Bartel Elshout (Ligonier, PA: Soli Deo Gloria, 1992-95), 4.384 (originally published in 1700); A. Kuyper, *De Gemeene Gratie* (Kampen: J. H. Kok, 1945), 11-100 (originally published in 1885); and Herman Bavinck, *Reformed Dogmatics,* vol. 3, *Sin and Salvation in Christ,* trans. John Vriend (Grand Rapids: Baker, 2006), 218-19 (originally published in 1895-1901). Many Reformed theologians, however, simply understood the Noahic covenant as an administration of the one covenant of grace expressed in later administrations in the Abrahamic, Mosaic, and new covenants.

Here Kline states views somewhat different from Van Til's conception of common grace as earlier grace such that before the fall into sin all grace was common grace. For Kline, common grace is a preserving grace that comes into play only in the context of sin. Kline points initially to Genesis 4, which narrates the foundation of a civil justice system among unbelievers and their progress in various cultural endeavors. God brought this common grace order to complete expression after the flood of Noah's day, during which it had been temporarily suspended. Kline describes God's covenant with Noah in Genesis 9 as a covenant of common grace, encompassing all people of whatever religious conviction and designed especially to govern universal cultural activities.[95] Common grace entails preservation of the natural order and of important elements of the social-cultural order established at creation, such as marriage and family, the exercise of dominion, industry, and music, though with modifications suited for God's purposes in a sinful world.[96] Here again some differences with Van Til's doctrine of common grace emerge. While Van Til disputed the idea of a territory of common grace and argued that it applied equally to all areas of life, Kline, like Kuyper, seems to associate common grace especially with the activities and institutions of broader culture, in distinction from the church.

Two central and interrelated aspects of Kline's description of the life of common grace, particularly in its political, institutional forms, serve to confirm this last point. The common grace realm is "profane" (as opposed to "holy") and "common" (as opposed to being for a particular part of the human race). In both respects the common grace realm is radically different from the church, which as God's redemptive kingdom is both holy and peculiar to those professing faith in Christ. As he describes in various places, the common grace realm consists of a religiously mixed citizenry. Common grace, though existing under the shadow of the common curse pronounced in Genesis 3, brings benefits for the human race in general and permits it to be fruitful and productive to a certain degree. Its benefits, however, are very different from the redemptive benefits granted in the covenant of grace, through the church as the holy, heavenly kingdom of God, a kingdom that common grace cannot produce.[97] Christians' work in the common grace, cultural realm "is not 'kingdom (of God)' activity. Though

---

95. Kline, *Kingdom Prologue*, 164, 244-46.

96. Kline, *Kingdom Prologue*, 154-55.

97. E.g., see Kline, *Kingdom Prologue*, 153-55, 164, 245-46; and Meredith G. Kline, "Comments on an Old-New Error," *Westminster Theological Journal* 41, no. 1 (Fall 1978): 183.

it is an expression of the reign of God in their lives, it is not a building of the kingdom of God as institution or realm."[98] It is at this point that Kline explicitly parts ways with the Dooyeweerdian, neo-Calvinist development of Kuyper's thought. Whereas the neo-Calvinist approach rejects as an unwarranted dualism the distinction between holy and profane areas of life and the identification of the church alone with Christ's kingdom (which Chapter 9 associated with their rejection of the two kingdoms doctrine), Kline emphasizes the necessity of such affirmations for an accurate rendering of biblical teaching.[99]

How then does Kline describe the purpose of common grace? In distinction from the covenant of grace which brings redemption, the covenant of common grace simply holds the curse upon the world in check, thereby providing a theatre in which God's redemptive purposes are accomplished.[100] Kline uses terms such as "remedial," "temporal," and "provisional" to describe the purposes of common grace. The Noahic covenant of common grace ensures continuance of a common interim order for human beings and their culture. In distinction from the neo-Calvinists who view the cultural activities themselves as having an eschatological goal, Kline asserts that common grace and this cultural order will be terminated at the end of history when Christ returns, when only the things of the covenant of grace and the holy kingdom of Christ will be brought to eschatological consummation.[101] While Kline is clear, as noted above, that common grace serves the purposes of God's redemptive work, it is not clear that he viewed this as the *only* purpose, as did Van Til. Kline does not explicitly defend Kuyper's idea of independent purposes of common grace, but his statements seem amenable to this notion.

At the least, Kline certainly develops and enriches Van Til's notions of the "relative" perspective and "as if" cooperation of believers with unbelievers, giving them prescriptive as well as descriptive force. Kline points to the pre-Noahic believers as a model for New Testament believers in their participation "in the common political enterprise with noncovenant people" as a

---

98. Kline, *Kingdom Prologue*, 201. At this point, Kline disagreed with Vos, who took a position different from the earlier Reformed tradition in regard to the extension of the kingdom beyond the church; see Geerhardus Vos, *The Teaching of Jesus Concerning the Kingdom and the Church* (Grand Rapids: Eerdmans, 1958), 87-89.

99. Kline, *Kingdom Prologue*, 160, 169-72.

100. Kline, *Kingdom Prologue*, 155; see also 156, 199.

101. E.g., see Kline, *Kingdom Prologue*, 155, 157, 166, 245-46; and Kline, "Comments on an Old-New Error," 184.

matter of "pragmatic cooperation of all mankind in cultural endeavor," even as they kept in mind their heavenly citizenship.[102] Calling later upon Abraham and the other patriarchs and their families as examples for Christians today, Kline calls them "sojourners," "pilgrims," "strangers," and "resident aliens" in the world. Their true citizenship was in a heavenly kingdom, but they fostered common grace relationships with the occupants of the lands where they lived, relationships marked by toleration and cooperation. They prayed for the peace and prosperity of these lands, were agents of common grace benefits to their neighbors, and entered into covenants with them for economic and military purposes.[103] Even as Christians follow this model and engage in common cultural activities, however, the church itself is to limit its work to the holy ministry entrusted to it in Scripture and not take up these common cultural activities as part of its own task.[104] Through all of this runs a strong anti-postmillennial eschatology that expects no pervasive triumph of Christianity in the cultural and political life of the world.[105]

Kline therefore embraced traditional Reformed two kingdoms ideas about the different origins, natures, purposes, and functions of the church as the redemptive kingdom of Christ on the one hand and the state and other cultural institutions and activities on the other, and did so in ways designed for a post-Christendom, religiously-plural society. He pursued these ideas through adoption of the Van Tillian dual emphasis on antithesis and common grace, though he modified Van Til's ideas about common grace in certain respects and developed them particularly by placing common grace in an explicitly covenantal context and adding a prescriptive element to his notion of the relative perspective and "as if" cooperation. Commonality is something not merely to be explained but to be pursued, as a relative or temporal goal, alongside recognition of an ultimate religious antithesis.

Kline's connection to the natural law tradition is less evident than his connection to the two kingdoms tradition. Kline did not make positive appeals to natural law as such when speaking about the moral standard of the common grace cultural realm. The reason may be that Kline, like Van Til,

102. Kline, *Kingdom Prologue,* 199-200.

103. E.g., see Kline, *Kingdom Prologue,* 357-58; and Meredith G. Kline, *God, Heaven and Har Magedon: A Covenantal Tale of Cosmos and Telos* (Eugene: Wipf & Stock, 2006), 104.

104. E.g., see Kline's opposition to providing medical care on the foreign mission field for those outside of the church *as an ecclesiastical ministry,* as articulated in a minority report of his denomination's Committee on Foreign Missions: *Minutes of the Thirty-First General Assembly* (Philadelphia: Orthodox Presbyterian Church, 1964), 51-55.

105. Among explicit discussions of this, see, e.g., Kline, "Comments on an Old-New Error," 178.

opposed the idea that nature is something autonomous or neutral and associated the concept of natural law with such an error. In the end, Kline in fact embraced many aspects of Reformed natural law doctrine and developed it, as he did with the two kingdoms doctrine, in ways that rooted it more explicitly in Reformed covenant theology.

Broadly, Kline affirmed the historic Reformed belief in general revelation, namely, revelation of God and his law in the creation order.[106] In regard to the moral aspect of general revelation, Kline writes that the primary ethical and religious principles of life are inherent to human nature because of the image of God. He identifies the image of God as a likeness to the creator that entails a royal-judicial office requiring judicial discernment and decision-rendering.[107] In further development of this theme, Kline also portrays this law inherent to human nature as part of the obligation of the covenant of works at creation. As such, the creation of human beings in the image of God with its in-created law was itself a covenantal act of God. Furthermore, this inherent knowledge of the covenantal law entailed that the promise and threat of the covenant of works (eschatological life or death consequent upon obedience or disobedience) was also part of inherent, natural human knowledge.[108] As he makes such claims, arguing that there was "no original non-covenantal order of mere nature on which the covenant was superimposed," one can perceive in the background the Van Tillian opposition to the idea of nature as an autonomous realm, which Van Til associated with medieval scholasticism but also to some extent with post-Reformation Reformed scholastic theology. Though Kline was likely attempting to correct elements of his own Reformed tradition in making such statements,[109] by associating a law inherent to human nature with the image of God and the covenant of works he was in fact echoing what many of his Reformed predecessors had taught about natural law.

---

106. An interesting example of this conviction appears in some comments on Job 28 fairly early in his career; see Meredith G. Kline, "Job," in *The Wycliffe Bible Commentary,* ed. Charles F. Pfeiffer and Everett F. Harrison (Chicago: Moody, 1962), 480: "The Creator perceived wisdom in the beginning, when he was ordaining the laws of the world (vv. 25, 26). In fact, the natural creation, with its governing laws, established by God, is an expression and embodiment of wisdom (v. 27; cf. Prov 8:22-31). For wisdom is the word of his will and becomes articulate for man in God's law — natural and moral."

107. Kline, *Kingdom Prologue,* 44-45; and Meredith G. Kline, *Images of the Spirit* (Grand Rapids: Baker, 1980), 27-28.

108. Kline, *Kingdom Prologue,* 92.

109. E.g., *Westminster Confession of Faith,* 7.1 may be read to suggest the possibility that human beings could (or perhaps did) exist apart from a covenantal relationship with God.

Kline's treatment of creation, the image of God, and the covenant of works, therefore, communicates a classic Reformed doctrine of natural law, albeit without using that terminology. A number of things that he writes about human nature and life after the fall into sin also connect Kline to the earlier tradition. For example, he affirms a standard Reformed doctrine of conscience and its traditional biblical proof-texts. He ties the idea of image-bearing as an inherently ethical reality to the post-lapsarian natural knowledge of God and his law described in Romans 1:19-20, 32 and 2:14-15. In this regard, he refers to a sense of deity, conscience, and the obligation to imitate God as being written on the tables of the human heart even in the state of sin. This is an "ultimate standard," he explains, that "continues as the constant canon of human conduct."[110] While in this context Kline clearly addresses the obligation binding upon Christians, elsewhere he speaks of image-bearing and its obligation to exercise dominion over creation as central to cultural life under the modified conditions of common grace.[111] Hence, his affirmation of a lingering presence of the image of God in all people thanks to common grace implies that the basic ethical principles of life continue to be known universally as an inherent part of human nature. In regard to the universal knowledge of natural law, Kline also resembles his predecessors in the early Reformed tradition in his willingness, at least on occasion, to appeal to the righteous practice of pagans who lacked Scripture in order to make a moral or political point.[112]

An important part of the analysis of Reformed natural law in many previous chapters has involved investigation of the relation of natural law to the law of Moses. On this issue it is more difficult to locate Kline in the Reformed tradition, exacerbated perhaps by Kline's own perception of what this tradition actually taught. In large part, his view of the Mosaic law re-

110. Kline, *Kingdom Prologue*, 62-63.

111. Kline, *Kingdom Prologue*, 253.

112. E.g., see Meredith G. Kline, "*Lex Talionis* and the Human Fetus," *Journal of the Evangelical Theological Society* 20, no. 3 (Sept 1977): 200-201: "As we observed at the outset, induced abortion was so abhorrent to the Israelite mind that it was not necessary to have a specific prohibition dealing with it in the Mosaic law. The Middle Assyrian laws attest to an abhorrence that was felt for this crime even in the midst of the heathendom around Israel, lacking though it did the illumination of special revelation. For in those laws a woman guilty of abortion was condemned to be impaled on stakes. Even if she managed to lose her own life in producing the abortion, she was still to be impaled and hung up in shame as an expression of the community's repudiation of such an abomination. It is hard to imagine a more damning commentary on what is taking place in enlightened America today than that provided by this legal witness out of the conscience of benighted ancient paganism!"

flects common Reformed convictions. He rejects the idea that the Mosaic civil laws per se ought to serve as a model for contemporary civil law, but he does not deny that they may have some applicability for it. While a Reformed writer such as John Cotton said essentially the same thing, Cotton's emphasis, over against Roger Williams, was on the elements of continuity between Mosaic law and the needs of civil law today. Kline, on the contrary, clearly emphasizes the discontinuity. Over against Bahnsen and his idea of theonomy, he insists that his view of the continuing normativity of the Mosaic civil laws as a whole was "a delusive and grotesque perversion of the teaching of Scripture" and "a misreading of the Bible on a massive scale." What is perhaps puzzling in the light of previous chapters is that Kline suggests that his opponents' position may find precedent in the Westminster Confession of Faith [WCF], at least as originally composed. If the analysis of WCF 19.4 and its reference to "general equity" in Chapter 5 is accurate, then Kline's suggestion, considered narrowly, is clearly incorrect. But while Kline was wrong to associate WCF 19.4 with his opponents' view, he was not wrong to think that his own view diverged from the wording of WCF 19.4. In fact, neither Kline nor Bahnsen agreed precisely with WCF 19.4 in that neither pointed to natural law as the standard for determining the current applicability of the Mosaic civil law.

Kline's view of the continuing applicability of Mosaic civil law can only be understood in the context of his theology of common grace considered above. For Kline, Old Testament Israel, by virtue of the Mosaic covenant, was a holy and theocratic nation, but the contemporary civil state, by virtue of the Noahic covenant of common grace, is a common institution meant to govern all people no matter what their religious faith. Hence, Kline determines the present applicability of Mosaic civil laws by distinguishing which laws were "peculiarly theocratic (or typologically symbolic)" and which were not. This means, in particular, that Mosaic civil laws pertaining to the first four commandments of the Decalogue (despite their being part of the natural law written on the heart of every person) are not to be enforced in the contemporary legal setting. While the earlier Reformed tradition, then, tended to categorize Mosaic civil laws as those that are peculiarly Mosaic and those that are natural, Kline categorizes them as those that are peculiarly theocratic and those that are also appropriate for a common grace setting.[113]

Where then does Kline stand in the broader picture of the Reformed

---

113. This analysis of Kline on the Mosaic civil law is based primarily on Kline, *Kingdom Prologue*, 159; and Kline, "Comments on an Old-New Error" generally, and especially 172-75.

natural law and two kingdoms traditions? I conclude that he in large measure embraced the important categories expressed for centuries in this tradition. In doing so, he distinguished himself from the mainstream of twentieth-century Reformed thought, particularly in his grounding political and cultural life in God's work of creation and providence rather than in his work of redemption and in his insisting on a sharp distinction between holy and common realms of life. In this reflection of the older tradition, Kline displayed the influence of the American Presbyterian stream of thought that supported religious freedom in society and the spirituality of the church as well as the influence of the Kuyperian perspective that utilized common grace as an organizing category. Kline was neither limited nor constrained by these earlier expressions of the Reformed natural law and two kingdoms traditions, however. In comparison with some American Presbyterian advocates of the spirituality of the church, such as James Henley Thornwell, Kline did not forget his spirituality doctrine at convenient times when he had a pressing political concern. And in comparison with Kuyper, Kline did not lapse into confusing "Christianization" language when speaking about the common grace realm, and his insistence on the non-holy, remedial nature of the civil order kept his mode of describing it more consistent than the Dutchman's.

His most important creative contribution to the tradition, as suggested above, is probably his explicit articulation of the older ideas in terms of Reformed covenant theology. He described a natural law inherent to human nature through its creation in the image of God in the covenant of works. He also developed the idea of a covenant of common grace, through which the law inherent to human nature is preserved and a forum for the pursuit of human culture is protected. Through such concepts, Kline enriched Van Til's notion of commonality so as to give it a positive focus in conjunction with an ongoing affirmation of the antithesis between belief and unbelief. Furthermore, Kline's distinction between the cultural realm as founded in the covenant of common grace and the church as founded in the redemptive covenant of grace in a way paralleling the earlier Reformed distinction between the two kingdoms as expressed in state and church suggests a more explicit connection between the central biblical categories of covenant and kingdom than the earlier tradition provided. Whether or not one judges Kline's system to be theologically compelling, I suggest that his (somewhat unwitting) development of the Reformed natural law and two kingdoms traditions was in some respects more theoretically and practically coherent than that of the figures considered in previous chapters and is linked in much more explicit detail to the covenant theology that has so often served as an organizing substructure for the system of Reformed doctrine.

Yet Kline also left certain theological and practical matters unexplored and undeveloped. As far as I am able to determine, he did not relate his treatment of the common grace realm to some of the Trinitarian concerns of his Reformed predecessors. For example, he did not teach the doctrine of the two mediatorships of the Son of God, as did Kuyper and the Reformed orthodox (though neither did he reject this doctrine, as did his mentor Van Til). Furthermore, Kline gave little specific indication of how Christians taking up their cultural tasks in cooperation with people of other faiths are to engage in moral dialogue with them. His understanding of civil society as a common, non-holy realm and his understanding of Scripture as a series of documents entrusted to the holy, covenant community of believers suggest that Christians ought not appeal to Scripture in the civil realm in the direct, straightforward way in which they do in the church.[114] Yet neither did he offer a positive articulation of natural law as a means of moral dialogue in the civil realm. Thus, the manner in which Christians ought to engage non-Christians in their common cultural tasks remains an important area undeveloped in Kline's thought that those wishing to appropriate his work for the future of Reformed social thought would need to address.

Conclusion

In this chapter I have argued that the relation of Cornelius Van Til's theology to the historic Reformed natural law and two kingdoms traditions must be deemed rather ambiguous. Though he wrote about many issues relevant to the older natural law and two kingdoms doctrines, Van Til's focus on the discipline of apologetics (with his emphasis upon the antithesis between Christian and non-Christian thought), his relative disinterest in articulating a detailed approach to cultural and social life, and his lack of interaction with the natural law and two kingdoms doctrines as historically understood meant that he left key issues pertinent to the present study undeveloped. Van Til's apologetics did not itself dictate a specific agenda for the Christian's engagement in ordinary cultural affairs. Accordingly, it is not a surprise that his students who had more specific interest in issues of cultural and political

---

114. For his views on Scripture and the covenant community, see generally Meredith G. Kline, *The Structure of Biblical Authority* (Grand Rapids: Eerdmans, 1972).

life took his thought in very different directions, as the two notable examples examined in this chapter illustrate. For Bahnsen and the theonomists, Van Til's conception of the antithesis was extrapolated in defense of the holistic application of the Mosaic law to all areas of contemporary human life. For Kline, on the other hand, Van Til's conception of common grace was modified and expanded in defense of an approach to cultural life bearing significant similarities to the older natural law and two kingdoms traditions, set explicitly in the context of Reformed covenant theology.

The Survival and Revival of Reformed Natural Law and Two Kingdoms Doctrine

This study began by claiming that there is an important but ordinarily overlooked aspect of the history of Reformed social thought. The subsequent chapters defended this claim by arguing first that Reformed writers from the sixteenth through nineteenth centuries regularly appealed to concepts of natural law and the two kingdoms, as they grounded their social thought in the creation order as preserved after the fall into sin. Then I argued that the past century has witnessed the eclipse of these doctrines, as Reformed writers have largely ignored or explicitly rejected the ideas of natural law and two kingdoms and redirected Reformed social thought away from a foundation in the preservation of the created order toward a foundation in the redemption of the created order in Christ. This study has also observed that the Reformed theologians of the earlier centuries often applied their natural law and two kingdoms doctrines in inconsistent ways to practical social circumstances, particularly in their defense of the civil repression of religious heterodoxy. Yet a number of significant Reformed theologians from the late eighteenth to the early twentieth centuries, confronted with concrete debates about religious liberty in their pluralistic societies, utilized the older categories of natural law and the two kingdoms in defense of freedom of religion and ecclesiastical disestablishment. Nevertheless, more recent Reformed writers, while continuing to support religious liberty, have tended to look away from these older categories and to construct new paradigms for describing cultural and social life and the Christian's role within it.

Though the analysis presented in Chapters 8 through 10 indicates that the fortunes of the historic natural law and two kingdoms doctrines have been in serious decline in the Reformed social thought of the past century, a number of voices have kept these doctrines alive, either intentionally or unintentionally, through historical reminders and constructive projects. And in just the past few years several book-length treatments as well as other shorter studies have given notice of a growing interest in reviving Reformed ideas about natural law and the two kingdoms. For those intrigued by these doctrines and their prospects for enriching future discussions about Christianity and culture, this book will therefore end on a rather positive note — but with significant challenges as well.

To conclude this book, therefore, I first introduce some of the writers of the past century who have taken dissenting and contrarian views in the midst of the regnant disinterest in or even antipathy to the historic Reformed natural law and two kingdoms doctrines. Then I turn to outline some suggestions for the future study of natural law and the two kingdoms. Here I first suggest some ways in which a recovery of these doctrines could make a substantial contribution to the broader project of Christian social thought. I conclude by identifying some particular challenges that those undertaking such a project must face if they wish to provide a compelling and coherent view to the Reformed and broader Christian communities.

The Survival of Reformed Natural Law and Two Kingdoms Doctrine

As mentioned in Chapter 1, 2006 alone saw the publication of three books by Reformed authors designed to retrieve their tradition's natural law and/or two kingdoms doctrines. Stephen Grabill's study of Reformed teaching on natural law in the sixteenth and seventeenth centuries in light of the recent Reformed discomfort with this idea has broken important ground for a better understanding of this subject and for future attempts to reappropriate natural law for Reformed ethics.[1] Darryl Hart's theological defense of the concept of secularity and the separation of church and state combines historical analysis with constructive proposals largely built upon Augustine's two cities doctrine and Reformed two kingdoms teaching.[2] Finally, my own study on natural law presents a brief biblical defense of that idea in the context of the two kingdoms doctrine, primarily through the lens of Reformed covenant theology.[3] Given

---

1. Stephen J. Grabill, *Rediscovering the Natural Law in Reformed Theological Ethics* (Grand Rapids: Eerdmans, 2006).

2. Darryl Hart, *A Secular Faith: Why Christianity Favors the Separation of Church and State* (Chicago: Ivan R. Dee, 2006).

3. David VanDrunen, *A Biblical Case for Natural Law* (Grand Rapids: Acton Institute, 2006).

the character of Reformed social thought in the past century, the fact that three such books would appear within a few months of each other is rather remarkable.

But if our chronological perspective is expanded by even a few years, a number of other relevant works might be added to the list. Several of these are works of historical retrieval. Preston Graham, for example, has presented a large, appreciative study of Stuart Robinson's doctrine of the spirituality of the church, a doctrine which, as Chapter 6 above has argued, Robinson derived quite directly from historic Reformed two kingdoms teaching.[4] David McKay has attempted to clarify the teaching about Christ's kingship and hence the two kingdoms among seventeenth-century Scottish Presbyterians George Gillespie and Samuel Rutherford, along similar lines to the interpretation offered in Chapter 5 above.[5] C. Scott Pryor has contributed a study of John Calvin's understanding of natural law, drawing from him a generally positive view of contemporary appeals to natural law in the formation of civil law.[6] And James Calvin Davis also draws positive lessons about the usefulness of the Reformed natural law tradition for present social ethics, though from a more surprising source, Roger Williams, whose thought Davis places within the Reformed heritage in which he was trained.[7] Other relevant studies are primarily constructive in their focus, though they engage in some historical retrieval as well. Thomas Johnson, for instance, writing from a Reformed perspective, calls for a contemporary revival of natural law ethics among Protestants.[8] Another example is Randy Beck, who cites Augustinian two cities and Reformation two kingdoms doctrine as well as biblical material to portray Christians as citizens of two communities. He promotes active Christian involvement in the world, yet does so by defending

4. Preston D. Graham, Jr., *A Kingdom Not of This World: Stuart Robinson's Struggle to Distinguish the Sacred from the Secular during the Civil War* (Macon: Mercer University Press, 2002).

5. Most recently but more briefly, see David McKay, "From Popery to Principle: Covenanters and the Kingship of Christ," in *The Faith Once Delivered: Essays in Honor of Dr. Wayne Spear,* ed. Anthony T. Selvaggio (Phillipsburg, NJ: P&R, 2007), 136-42; at more length, see W. D. J. McKay, *An Ecclesiastical Republic: Church Government in the Writings of George Gillespie* (Carlisle: Paternoster, 1997), ch. 2. Personally McKay does not concur with Gillespie and Rutherford, or the mainstream of seventeenth-century Reformed thought, on this theological point.

6. C. Scott Pryor, "God's Bridle: John Calvin's Application of Natural Law," *Journal of Law and Religion* 22, no. 1 (2006-2007): 225-54.

7. James Calvin Davis, *The Moral Theology of Roger Williams: Christian Conviction and Public Ethics* (Louisville: Westminster John Knox, 2004).

8. Thomas K. Johnson, *Natural Law Ethics: An Evangelical Proposal* (Bonn: Verlag für Kultur und Wissenschaft, 2005).

the Western liberal political tradition against the Christian nation ideal.[9] Along similar lines, Michael Horton has offered his own defense of a common, secular civil society through appropriation of the Reformed two kingdoms doctrine and the Reformed idea of common grace.[10]

Behind these recent works, furthermore, a number of scholars contributed to keeping Reformed natural law and two kingdoms ideas alive through the twentieth century. In regard to natural law, journal articles by scholars such as John McNeill at mid-century and Paul Helm in the mid 1980s brought to light positive teaching on natural law by Calvin and other early Reformed figures.[11] Before these articles, a 1934 volume by Josef Bohatec promoted a similar perspective from a European vantage-point and, subsequently, Susan Schreiner's 1991 monograph explored it in greater detail in the context of Calvin's broader doctrine of nature and the created order.[12] One notable exponent of Reformed two kingdoms ideas in the early decades of the twentieth century was Presbyterian New Testament scholar J. Gresham Machen. In the ecclesiastical controversies of his day, Machen on a number of occasions appealed to the doctrine of the spirituality of the church and its corresponding notion of Christian liberty, both of which ideas were rooted in historic Reformed two kingdoms categories, as explored in previous chapters.[13] An essay by John Bolt in the early 1980s, in which he commends the classic Reformed idea of the two mediatorships of the Son and its relation to the Reformed *extra Calvinisticum* Christology, provides an example of a two kingdoms retrieval in the Dutch-American Reformed

9. Randy Beck, "The City of God and the Cities of Men: A Response to Jason Carter," *University of Georgia Law Review* 41, no. 1 (Fall 2006): 113-55.

10. See Michael S. Horton, "In Praise of Profanity: A Theological Defense of the Secular," in *Evangelicals and Empire,* ed. Peter Heltzel (Oxford: Oxford University Press, 2008), 252-66; and Michael Horton, *God of Promise: Introducing Covenant Theology* (Grand Rapids: Baker, 2006), ch. 6.

11. John T. McNeill, "Natural Law in the Teaching of the Reformers," *Journal of Religion* 26 (1946): 168-82; and Paul Helm, "Calvin and Natural Law," *Scottish Bulletin of Evangelical Theology* 2 (1984): 5-22. Helm has more recently expanded his work on Calvin and natural law in *John Calvin's Ideas* (Oxford: Oxford University Press, 2004), ch. 12.

12. Josef Bohatec, *Calvin und das Recht* (Feudingen: Buchdruck und Verlags-Anstalt, 1934); and Susan E. Schreiner, *The Theater of His Glory: Nature and the Natural Order in the Thought of John Calvin* (Durham: Labyrinth, 1991).

13. E.g., see J. Gresham Machen, *Selected Shorter Writings,* ed. D. G. Hart (Phillipsburg, NJ: P&R, 2004), 375, 394-95. For reflection on Machen's advocacy of these ideas, including his differences with Reformed transformationist perspectives, see Hart, "Introduction: The Forgotten Machen?" in Machen, *Selected Shorter Writings,* 13-14; and D. G. Hart, *Recovering Mother Kirk: The Case for Liturgy in the Reformed Tradition* (Grand Rapids: Baker, 2003), 65.

setting.[14] Finally, the biblical-theological work of Meredith G. Kline through the latter half of the twentieth century, as considered in the previous chapter, embraced many classic Reformed ideas about the two kingdoms especially and natural law to a lesser extent and attempted to provide richer Scriptural foundation for them — though he did so without much obvious engagement with historical sources.

The Revival of Reformed Natural Law and Two Kingdoms Doctrine

In the opening chapter, I suggested that the traditional Reformed natural law and two kingdoms doctrines have something important to contribute to broader discussions about Christianity and culture. It is now time to revisit that claim in the light of nine intervening chapters of historical analysis and the fledgling recovery of these doctrines noted immediately above. In this final section of the book, therefore, I will indicate some of the attractions of a natural law–two kingdoms paradigm in the contemporary context and then offer some reflections on the sorts of issues that future proponents on this paradigm must wrestle with in order to offer a compelling and useful proposal.

First, what are some of the attractions of a Reformed natural law–two kingdoms paradigm in the contemporary context? One thing that this paradigm has to offer is a theological account of the sharp contrast between the church as the kingdom of Christ and the kingdoms of the world. The character of the church as a loving and peaceful community in distinction from the nations of the world so often characterized by materialism and violence has been a popular theme recently among several influential schools of thought and rests upon impressive biblical evidence.[15] As observed in nu-

---

14. John Bolt, "Church and World: A Trinitarian Perspective," *Calvin Theological Journal* 18, no. 1 (April 1983): 5-31.

15. As discussed in Chapter 1, Stanley Hauerwas has been a leading exponent of this perspective; see, e.g., Stanley Hauerwas, *The Peaceable Kingdom: A Primer in Christian Ethics* (Notre Dame: University of Notre Dame Press, 1983); and Stanley Hauerwas and William H. Willimon, *Resident Aliens: Life in the Christian Colony* (Nashville: Abingdon, 1989). Among other works along a similar line cited in Chapter 1, see Richard B. Hays, *The Moral Vision of the New Testament: Community, Cross, New Creation; A Contemporary Introduction to New Testament Ethics* (New York: HarperSanFrancisco, 1996); and Craig A. Carter, *Rethinking Christ and Culture: A Post-Christendom Perspective* (Grand Rapids: Brazos, 2006).

merous previous chapters, Reformed proponents of the two kingdoms doctrine have identified stark differences between the kingdom of Christ, expressed in the church, and worldly governments, particularly in terms of the different weapons that they wield. While the state bears the physical sword to keep order by the threat of coercion, the church simply proclaims the word of God and forswears violence of any sort. In concert with many contemporary accounts of Christianity and culture, then, though over against much contemporary Reformed social thought, this paradigm refuses to see the redemptive kingdom of Christ expressed in any earthly state.

But in providing theological categories for such affirmations, the Reformed natural law–two kingdoms paradigm also gives theological rationale for affirming the genuine, God-ordained legitimacy of the state and other cultural institutions. This paradigm does not require pacifism of Christians in their civil capacities, but blesses their participation in the sword-wielding work of the state, so long as it is not confused or identified with the work of Christ's peaceful kingdom. And though the early centuries of the Reformed tradition taught the two kingdoms doctrine in connection with a belief that the civil magistrate should enforce religious purity, some significant Reformed writers of more recent centuries have applied the doctrine, in more consistent fashion, to the modern political context of religious liberty. Hence this paradigm gives reason for Christians not only to affirm the legitimacy of the sword-bearing work of the state in the abstract but also to affirm its concrete expression in the tolerant, religiously-plural societies of the modern Western world — though again without ever identifying these societies with the kingdom of Christ. From the basis of its biblical faith and sense of heavenly citizenship, this paradigm provides resources for Christians to make radical critiques of such societies (and every other earthly society), for they are ultimately temporal and vain because not associated with the enduring kingdom of Christ. But it simultaneously provides theological reason for seeing such societies (and other kinds of earthly societies) as offering many provisional, remedial benefits for the present age while Christians exist as pilgrims and resident aliens in the world. It encourages Christians to appreciate and enjoy the vast range of cultural accomplishments of the human race, whether produced by Christians or not. Hence, they can participate in modern, liberal societies, both recognizing their useful temporal purposes and refusing to have any ultimate, eschatological confidence in what they can accomplish. And this paradigm permits and encourages Christians, in this civil experience of participation with detachment, not only to have an attitude of deference to civil authority but also, through the universal moral standard of natural law, to strive for justice in the state and excellence in all of their cultural endeavors.

Whether all of this indeed constitutes an attractive paradigm to individual readers will of course rest upon each one's judgment. But in its ability to affirm multiple biblical themes simultaneously, without making any one of them trump the others, I suggest that it has a compelling and challenging character that deserves much wider consideration. It affirms the peacefulness of the church as Christ's kingdom without commending pacifism by Christians in civil life. It affirms the legitimacy of the state and other cultural institutions without looking to them for ultimate rescue from the effects of sin. It affirms the possibility of a healthy patriotism for Christians in their civil capacities without permitting the church to align itself with any particular earthly nation or political party. It affirms the antithesis between Christ's kingdom and the dominion of Satan without denying the areas of commonness between Christians and non-Christians in the world. It affirms the task of striving for justice in society and excellence in culture without insisting that the Bible must be the basis for moral discourse in the public square.

Through history, the Reformed natural law and two kingdoms categories have shown themselves receptive to modification and development. Theologians such as Stuart Robinson and Abraham Kuyper drew upon the categories while shifting their application to the novel situation of individual religious freedom and ecclesiastical disestablishment. A biblical scholar such as Meredith Kline articulated similar categories in light of a Reformed theology of the biblical covenants. As biblical and theological scholarship continues to advance and cultural and political climates change, therefore, there is reason to think that there may still be room for helpful development of these old categories to address the twenty-first-century context.

What are the particular challenges that future attempts to develop these categories may face? I close by presenting several in regard to both the two kingdoms and natural law. First, in no particular order, I mention five areas in which understandable questions or objections may be (or already have been) raised against the two kingdoms doctrine to which future constructive projects ought to develop a coherent response. One area concerns the doctrine of the two mediatorships of the Son of God. Reformed proponents of the two kingdoms idea historically grounded the origin and nature of the civil and spiritual kingdoms respectively upon the Son's distinct mediatorship of creation and of redemption. A number of Reformed writers over the past century have rejected this doctrine, however, and along with it a two kingdoms approach to social thought. Though this may seem to be an intimidating and remote topic for non-theologians wrestling with issues of Christianity and culture, those who do wish to give a theologically rich account of these issues will certainly need to wrestle with the two mediatorships idea. Can future proponents of the two kingdoms doctrine make a compelling defense of this older Reformed doctrine? Is the two kingdoms idea plausible without it? And what are the consequences of rejecting the two mediatorships for other areas of theology, such as the historic Reformed conviction that after his incarnation Christ according to his divine nature continues to exist and work even outside of his human nature (the so-called *extra Calvinisticum*)?

A second area that raises questions and potential objections is the notion of common grace and particularly the idea that the covenant with Noah in Genesis 9 represents a common grace covenant. Use of common grace as an organizing category for social thought is a relatively recent Reformed strategy and the belief that the Noahic covenant in Genesis 9 is not a part of the covenant of grace but a distinct covenant of common grace has not been the only position in the Reformed community historically. Nevertheless, these ideas were embraced by the likes of Kuyper and Kline in their constructive appropriation of older two kingdoms categories, and the latter especially has offered compelling biblical argumentation for such an approach. As past chapters have revealed, the doctrine of common grace remains a disputed topic in recent Reformed thought, and those wishing to develop further a two kingdoms theology, particularly one in conjunction with Reformed covenant theology, certainly must address this important topic.

Third, assertion of the two kingdoms doctrine raises the question as to what, if anything, has changed about the state and its authority and legitimacy with the death and resurrection of Christ. The Augustinian tendency among many Reformed two kingdoms advocates, at least more recent ones, is to find biblical support for their approach to Christianity and culture in the experience of the Old Testament patriarchs as resident aliens in Canaan and of the Israelite exiles in Babylon. This provokes the question whether post-resurrection civil governments have exactly the same standing as did the ancient Canaanite, Egyptian, and Babylonian governments. The two kingdoms doctrine may suggest that the answer is yes, and it is at this point that one important contemporary moral theologian whose thought is in many ways very congenial to a two kingdoms perspective, Oliver O'Donovan, parts ways with it.[16] Future attempts to expound the two kingdoms doctrine will surely wish to wrestle with this issue.

Fourth, the two kingdoms doctrine raises some very difficult questions regarding the holistic character of the Christian life. For example, what exactly does it mean for Christians to live non-violent lives as citizens of the kingdom of Christ and simultaneously participate in the activities of the state that rest upon the threat of coercion? How can Christians live both of these very different ways of life with integrity and without slipping into a *de facto* confinement of their Christianity to certain narrow aspects of their lives? What are the implications for a concrete moral question such as whether Christians may exercise self-defense against an intruder? Again, constructive future attempts to retrieve the two kingdoms doctrine will do well to address such questions.

Finally, a point of some perennial unclarity within the Reformed tradition also deserves some consideration. The idea that the church as the kingdom of Christ is properly concerned with *spiritual* things and not with the civil things that are the concern of the state was a standard idea from Calvin to the Reformed orthodox to the nineteenth-century Presbyterian advocates of the spirituality of the church. But as discussed especially in Chapter 6, it

---

16. In *The Desire of the Nations: Rediscovering the Roots of Political Theology* (Cambridge: Cambridge University Press, 1996), Oliver O'Donovan acknowledges something of a two kingdoms reality in parts of the Old Testament, but he emphasizes Christ's proclamation of the kingdom which announces the unity of the religious and political realms under the reign of God and challenges the two kingdoms situation (ch. 3). In Christ's resurrection, the earthly powers have been subdued and made subject to divine sovereignty; yet the sovereignty of God is not now completely manifest, and the powers are still given a certain (secular) space and authority to exercise their judicial function, though they ought to serve the church's mission (ch. 4). After Christ's ascension, therefore, the terms on which political authorities function are not the same as they were before; see here also Oliver O'Donovan, *The Ways of Judgment* (Grand Rapids: Eerdmans, 2005), 5. Society is to be transformed and its rulers disappear. Christendom ("the idea of a confessionally Christian government") is not a project of, but a response to, the church's mission, as the alien powers become attentive to the church. The Christian state may be disclosed from time to time, but it should not coerce belief or try to protect its own existence. See *Desire of the Nations*, ch. 6. In *The Ways of Judgment*, he speaks of the redemptive, transforming work of the church, gospel, and Holy Spirit on the state as the sphere of human judgment and therefore argues that there is a place for mercy in civil judgment (ch. 6). Here he also discusses the proclamation of the cross and the coming of the kingdom as a challenge to the conditions of the earthly political authority and opposes an a-political theology disinterested in social life (231-34). From the other direction, in *The Ways of Judgment* he critiques the two swords idea, originating with Gelasius, for teaching that there are certain spheres of social life that are in principle beyond the reach of governmental intervention (62).

has often not been clear exactly what it means for a thing to be "spiritual." The classic Reformed distinction between the two kingdoms in terms of body and soul and of "external" and "internal" perhaps suggests that things are spiritual in the sense of immaterial. This in turn might lend some credence to neo-Calvinist dismissal of the two kingdoms idea as an unwarranted "dualism." But identifying the spiritual with the immaterial cannot be what the older theologians meant, for it is clearly not compatible with other aspects of traditional Reformed teaching, which assigned to the church material tasks such as administering sacraments and doing diaconal works of mercy. Some theologians in the tradition seem to associate "spiritual" especially with things redemptive or heavenly-focused. In other debates it has not been clear whether a certain affair can be both spiritual and civil, and, if so, how to designate respective jurisdiction over such an affair to the church and state. Here further work is necessary in defining precisely what a "spiritual" matter is and perhaps even whether other terminology might be preferable.

Some other difficult questions and objections arise about the retrieval and development of a Reformed doctrine of natural law as the basic standard for civil law and cultural life more generally. In certain respects, the post-Christendom, post-Enlightenment, religiously-plural societies of the modern age seem an ideal context for appreciating the usefulness and appropriateness of natural law as the social norm. This context, after all, is not one in which deference to the Christian Scriptures can be taken for granted among all participants in the public square, and natural law is, according to traditional Reformed and broader Christian doctrine, a universal standard revealed to all people and binding all people through the testimony of conscience. But in other respects appeals to natural law actually made more sense in a pre-Enlightenment, pre-liberal Christendom context. Basic religious and moral presuppositions affect how one interprets human nature and moral arguments derived from it, and the inhabitants of Christendom (however many theological disagreements they may have had) certainly shared more basic presuppositions about the world and human nature than do inhabitants of modern religiously-plural societies. Furthermore, the Enlightenment emphasis upon historical consciousness and the postmodern emphasis upon contextual relativity have generated much greater skepticism than in the pre-modern world toward appeals to a universal morality derived from human nature.

In light of such concerns, probably the biggest question that faces those wishing to revive the Reformed doctrine of natural law is how, concretely,

Christians can make natural law arguments in the public square with theological integrity and some degree of persuasiveness to a religiously mixed
crowd. Natural law arguments have always been easier to dispute than to defend, and the present social context surely exacerbates the difficulty of con-
structing good natural law appeals. Thus this promises to be a major task for
future exponents of historic Reformed categories. One particular aspect of
this difficult task was raised above in the discussion of Kline's theology: if the
moral obligations of the first four commandments of the Decalogue are part
of the natural law, yet Christians believe on the basis of Scripture that these
moral obligations are not to be enforced in contemporary civil law, then how
ought Christians make arguments in the public square for religious liberty
and disestablishment of religious institutions? From a somewhat different
angle, are Christians to argue from natural law itself that some aspects of natural law should not be enforced by civil law, and, if so, how would this be
done?[17] Or do Christians have nothing but Scripture upon which to defend
publicly their views on such issues? These are challenging questions indeed.
Those who wish to reappropriate the older Reformed categories may take
heart, however, from remembering that just because a task such as making
natural law appeals is difficult does not mean that it should not be attempted
if it is the right thing to do. And they may also take heart by recognizing that
those taking the seemingly simpler route of defending public policy preferences through appeal to verses of Scripture are unlikely to be any more persuasive (and in fact likely to be much less persuasive) to the non-Christians
whose consent they are trying to win. What is more, since Scripture speaks no
more than generally and indirectly to most cultural matters, even those setting forth Scripture as *the* standard for cultural interaction must of necessity
resort to a good deal of extra-biblical reasoning themselves.

---

17. Worth consideration on this matter is the argument of Pierre Bayle in *A Philosophical
Commentary on These Words of the Gospel, Luke 14:23, "Compel Them to Come In, That My House
May Be Full",* ed. John Kilcullen and Chandran Kukathas (Indianapolis: Liberty Fund, 2005), originally published in 1686-88 and translated into English in 1708. Bayle, a French Protestant who experienced the Huguenot persecution first hand and fled his native country, offered in this work an
extensive argument for religious liberty and freedom of conscience. What is particularly interesting is how Bayle, for purposes of appealing to people of all religious convictions, attempted to argue only from reason for his contention that Christ could not have been commanding compulsion in religious matters. Though Bayle's adult commitment to orthodox Reformed theology is a
matter of some doubt and contemporary Reformed readers may not find all of his argumentation
persuasive, this work provides one significant example of a writer of Reformed heritage making a
case for religious liberty apart from biblical exegesis and with a religiously plural (albeit broadly
Christian) audience in mind.

Attempts to define a biblically faithful, theologically rich, and practically effective approach to Christian involvement in the broader culture are perennial. The Reformed natural law and two kingdoms tradition constitutes one such historical attempt that, though having its own checkered history and having fallen into hard times in recent generations, offers attractive theological resources and practical possibilities. The task will not be easy, but those accepting the challenge to reappropriate the categories and wrestle with pressing objections may hope to provide a significant contribution to the ongoing conversation within the larger Christian community.

Bibliography

Primary Sources

Althusius, Johannes, *Dicaeologicae,* translation by Jeffrey J. Veenstra in "Selections from the *Dicaeologicae,*" *Journal of Markets and Morality* 9, no. 2 (2006): 429-84.

Althusius, Johannes, *Politica (Politics Methodically Set Forth and Illustrated with Sacred and Profane Examples),* trans. and ed. Frederick S. Carney (Boston: Beacon, 1964; Indianapolis: Liberty Fund, 1995).

Augustine, *The City of God,* trans. Markus Dods (New York: The Modern Library, 1950).

Bahnsen, Greg L., *Theonomy in Christian Ethics* (Nutley, NJ: Craig, 1979).

Barth, Karl, *Church Dogmatics,* II/1, *The Doctrine of God,* ed. G. W. Bromiley and T. F. Torrance, trans. T. H. L. Parker, W. B. Johnston, Harold Knight, J. L. M. Haire (Edinburgh: T&T Clark, 1957).

Barth, Karl, *Church Dogmatics,* II/2, *The Doctrine of God,* trans. G. W. Bromiley, J. C. Campbell, Iain Wilson, J. Strathearn McNab, Harold Knight, R. A. Stewart, ed. G. W. Bromiley and T. F. Torrence (New York: T&T Clark, 1957).

Barth, Karl, *Church Dogmatics,* III/1, *The Doctrine of Creation,* trans. J. W. Edwards, O. Bussey, and H. Knight, ed. G. W. Bromiley and T. F. Torrance (New York: T&T Clark, 1958).

Barth, Karl, *Church Dogmatics,* III/4, *The Doctrine of Creation,* trans. A. T. MacKay, T. H. L. Parker, H. Knight, H. A. Kennedy, J. Marks, ed. G. W. Bromiley and T. F. Torrance (New York: T&T Clark, 1961).

Barth, Karl, *Church Dogmatics,* IV/1, *The Doctrine of Reconciliation,* trans. G. W. Bromiley, ed. G. W. Bromiley and T. F. Torrance (New York: T&T Clark, 1956).

Barth, Karl, *Church Dogmatics,* IV/2, *The Doctrine of Reconciliation,* trans. G. W. Bromiley, ed. G. W. Bromiley and T. F. Torrance (New York: T&T Clark, 1958).

Barth, Karl, *Church Dogmatics,* IV/3/1, *The Doctrine of Reconciliation,* trans. G. W. Bromiley, ed. G. W. Bromiley and T. F. Torrance (New York: T&T Clark, 1961).

Barth, Karl, *Community, State, and Church: Three Essays* (Gloucester, MA: Peter Smith, 1968) [this volume consists of three separate essays, "Gospel and Law" (1935),

"Church and State" (1938), and "The Christian Community and the Civil Community" (1946)].

Barth, Karl, *Ethics,* ed. Dietrich Braun, trans. Geoffrey W. Bromiley (New York: Seabury, 1981).

Barth, Karl, *Fides Quaerens Intellectum: Anselm's Proof for the Existence of God in the Context of His Theological Scheme* (London: SCM, 1960).

Barth, Karl, *The Knowledge of God and the Service of God According to the Teaching of the Reformation,* trans. J. L. M. Haire and Ian Henderson (London: Hodder and Stoughton, 1938).

Barth, Karl, "No!" in *Natural Theology: Comprising 'Nature and Grace' by Professor Dr. Emil Brunner and the Reply 'No!' by Dr. Karl Barth,* trans. Peter Fraenkel (London: Geoffrey Bles: Centenary, 1946), 65-128.

Bartholomew, Craig G., and Michael W. Goheen, *The Drama of Scripture: Finding Our Place in the Biblical Story* (Grand Rapids: Baker, 2004).

Bavinck, Herman, *Reformed Dogmatics,* vol. 1, *Prolegomena,* trans. John Vriend, ed. John Bolt (Grand Rapids: Baker, 2003).

Bavinck, Herman, *Reformed Dogmatics,* vol. 2, *God and Creation,* trans. John Vriend, ed. John Bolt (Grand Rapids: Baker, 2004).

Bavinck, Herman, *Reformed Dogmatics,* vol. 3, *Sin and Salvation in Christ,* trans. John Vriend, ed. John Bolt (Grand Rapids: Baker, 2006).

Bayle, Pierre, *A Philosophical Commentary on These Words of the Gospel, Luke 14:23, "Compel Them to Come In, That My House May Be Full,"* ed. John Kilcullen and Chandran Kukathas (Indianapolis: Liberty Fund, 2005).

Beza, Theodore, *Concerning the Rights of Rulers over Their Subjects and the Duty of Subjects Towards Their Rulers,* trans. Henri-Louis Gonin, ed. A. H. Murray (Cape Town: H.A.U.M., 1956).

Bonaventure, *Breviloquium,* in *The Works of Bonaventure* (Paterson: St. Anthony Guild, 1960).

Brakel, Wilhelmus à, *The Christian's Reasonable Service,* 4 vols., trans. Bartel Elshout (Ligonier, PA: Soli Deo Gloria, 1992-95).

Brunner, Emil, "Nature and Grace," in *Natural Theology: Comprising 'Nature and Grace' by Professor Dr. Emil Brunner and the reply 'No!' by Dr. Karl Barth,* trans. Peter Fraenkel (London: Geoffrey Bles: Centenary, 1946), 15-64.

Brutus, Stephanus Junius, *Vindiciae, contra tyrannos: or, concerning the legitimate power of a prince over the people, and of the people over a prince,* trans. and ed. George Garnett (Cambridge: Cambridge University Press, 1994).

Bucer, Martin, *De Regno Christi,* in *Melanchthon and Bucer,* ed. Wilhelm Pauck (Philadelphia: Westminster, 1969).

Calvin, John, "Brief Instruction," in John Calvin, *Treatises Against the Anabaptists and Against the Libertines,* trans. and ed. Benjamin Wirt Farley (Grand Rapids: Baker, 1982).

Calvin, John, *Calvin's Commentary on Seneca's De Clementia,* trans. Ford Lewis Battles and André Malan Hugo (Leiden: Brill, 1969).

Calvin, John, *Commentaries on the Catholic Epistles,* trans. John Owen, in *Calvin's Commentaries,* vol. 22 (Grand Rapids: Baker, 2003).

Calvin, John, *Commentaries on the Epistle of Paul the Apostle to the Romans,* trans. John Owen, in *Calvin's Commentaries,* vol. 19 (Grand Rapids: Baker, 2003).

Calvin, John, *Commentaries on the Epistles to Timothy, Titus and Philemon,* trans. William Pringle, in *Calvin's Commentaries,* vol. 21 (Grand Rapids: Baker, 2003).

Calvin, John, *Commentaries on the First Book of Moses Called Genesis,* trans. John King, in *Calvin's Commentaries,* vol. 1 (Grand Rapids: Baker, 2003).

Calvin, John, *Commentaries on the Twelve Minor Prophets,* vol. 3, trans. John Owen, in *Calvin's Commentaries,* vol. 14 (Grand Rapids: Baker, 2003).

Calvin, John, *Commentary on a Harmony of the Evangelists, Matthew, Mark, and Luke,* vol. 2, trans. William Pringle, in *Calvin's Commentaries,* vol. 16 (Grand Rapids: Baker, 2003).

Calvin, John, *Commentary on the Epistles of Paul the Apostle to the Corinthians,* trans. John Pringle, in *Calvin's Commentaries,* vol. 20 (Grand Rapids: Baker, 2003).

Calvin, John, *Institutes of the Christian Religion* (1536), trans. Ford Lewis Battles (Grand Rapids: Eerdmans, 1986).

Calvin, John, *Institutes of the Christian Religion,* 2 vols., trans. Henry Beveridge (Grand Rapids: Eerdmans, 1953).

Calvin, John, *Institutes of the Christian Religion,* 2 vols., ed. John T. McNeill, trans. Ford Lewis Battles (Philadelphia: Westminster, 1960).

Calvin, John, *Ioannis Calvini opera quae supersunt omnia,* ed. Guilielmus Baum, Eduardus Cunitz, and Eduardus Reuss, vols. 29-87 of *Corpus Reformatorum* (Brunswick: C. A. Schwetschke, 1863-1900).

Calvin, John, *Letters of John Calvin,* vol. 4, ed. Jules Bonnet, trans. Marcus Robert Gilchrist (New York: Burt Franklin, 1972).

Cotton, John, "An Abstract of the Laws of New-England, as They Are Now Established" (originally published, 1641), in Greg L. Bahnsen, *Theonomy in Christian Ethics* (Nutley, NJ: Craig, 1979).

Cotton, John, "The Answer of Mr. John Cotton of Boston in New-England, to the Aforesaid Arguments against Persecution for Cause of Conscience," in *The Complete Writings of Roger Williams,* vol. 3, ed. Samuel L. Caldwell (New York: Russell & Russell, 1963).

Cotton, John, *The Bloody Tenet Washed and Made White in the Blood of the Lamb,* in *The Complete Writings of Roger Williams,* vol. 3, ed. Samuel L. Caldwell (New York: Russell & Russell, 1963).

Cotton, John, *A Discourse about Civil Government in a New Plantation Whose Design Is Religion* (Cambridge: Samuel Green and Marmaduke Johnson, 1663).

Cotton, John, "How Far Moses Judicialls Bind Mass[achusetts]," reprinted in *Proceedings of the Massachusetts Historical Society,* Second Series 16 (October 1902): 282-84.

Cotton, John, "The Keys of the Kingdom of Heaven," in *John Cotton on the Churches of New England,* ed. Larzer Ziff (Cambridge: Belknap/Harvard University Press, 1968), 71-164.

Davies, Samuel, "The Mediatorial Kingdom and Glories of Jesus Christ," in *Political Sermons of the American Founding Era, 1730-1805,* ed. Ellis Sandoz (Indianapolis: LibertyPress, 1991), 181-206.

Davies, Samuel, "A Sermon Delivered at Nassau-Hall, January 14, 1761," in "Presbyterians and the American Revolution: A Documentary Account," *Journal of Presbyterian History* 52, no. 4 (Winter 1974): 325-27.

Dooyeweerd, Herman, *The Christian Idea of the State,* trans. John Kraay (Nutley, NJ: Craig, 1968).

Dooyeweerd, Herman, "Cornelius Van Til and the Transcendental Critique of Theoretical Thought," in *Jerusalem and Athens: Critical Discussions on the Philosophy and Apologetics of Cornelius Van Til,* ed. E. R. Geehan (Nutley, NJ: Presbyterian and Reformed, 1971), 74-89.

Dooyeweerd, Herman, *In the Twilight of Western Thought: Studies in the Pretended Autonomy of Philosophical Thought* (Philadelphia: Presbyterian and Reformed, 1960; Nutley, NJ: Craig, 1980).

Dooyeweerd, Herman, *A New Critique of Theoretical Thought,* 4 vols., 2d ed., trans. David H. Freeman and William S. Young (Philadelphia: Presbyterian and Reformed, 1969).

Dooyeweerd, Herman, *Roots of Western Culture: Pagan, Secular, and Christian Options,* trans. John Kraay (Toronto: Wedge, 1979).

Eusebius, *Ecclesiastical History,* trans. Roy J. Deferrari, *The Fathers of the Church,* vol. 29 (New York: Fathers of the Church, 1955).

Gillespie, George, *Aaron's Rod Blossoming; or, the Divine Ordinance of Church Government Vindicated* (London, 1646; reprinted Harrisonburg, VA: Sprinkle, 1985).

Goodman, Christopher, *How superior Powers Oght To Be Obeyd* (1558; New York: Columbia University Press, 1931).

Heppe, Heinrich, *Reformed Dogmatics,* rev. and ed. Ernst Bizer, trans. G. T. Thomson (London: Wakeman, n.d.).

Hodge, Charles, "The General Assembly," *Biblical Repertory and Princeton Review* 33 (July 1861): 511-68.

Hodge, Charles, "Presbyterianism" (originally published in 1860), in *Discussions in Church Polity* (New York: Charles Scribner's Sons, 1878), 118-33.

Hodge, Charles, "The Princeton Review on the State of the Country and of the Church," *Biblical Repertory and Princeton Review* 37 (October 1865): 627-57.

Hotman, François, *Francogallia,* ed. Ralph E. Giesey and J. H. M. Salmon, trans. J. H. M. Salmon (Cambridge: Cambridge University Press, 1972).

Justinian, *The Institutes of Justinian,* trans. Thomas Collett Sanders (Westport, CN: Greenwood Press, 1970).

Kline, Meredith G., "Comments on an Old-New Error," *Westminster Theological Journal* 41, no. 1 (Fall 1978): 172-89.

Kline, Meredith G., *God, Heaven and Har Magedon: A Covenantal Tale of Cosmos and Telos* (Eugene: Wipf & Stock, 2006).

Kline, Meredith G., *Images of the Spirit* (Grand Rapids: Baker, 1980).

Kline, Meredith G., "Job," in *The Wycliffe Bible Commentary,* ed. Charles F. Pfeiffer and Everett F. Harrison (Chicago: Moody, 1962).

Kline, Meredith G., *Kingdom Prologue: Genesis Foundations for a Covenantal Worldview* (Overland Park, KS: Two Age Press, 2000).

Bibliography

Kline, Meredith G., "*Lex Talionis* and the Human Fetus," *Journal of the Evangelical Theological Society* 20, no. 3 (Sept 1977): 193-201.

Kline, Meredith G., "Minority Report," *Minutes of the Thirty-First General Assembly* (Philadelphia: Orthodox Presbyterian Church, 1964), 51-55.

Kline, Meredith G., *The Structure of Biblical Authority* (Grand Rapids: Eerdmans, 1972).

Knox, John, *On Rebellion*, ed. Roger A. Mason (Cambridge: Cambridge University Press, 1994).

Kuyper, Abraham, *Abraham Kuyper: A Centennial Reader*, ed. James D. Bratt (Grand Rapids: Eerdmans, 1998).

Kuyper, Abraham, *De Gemeene Gratie* (Kampen: J. H. Kok, 1945).

Kuyper, Abraham, *Lectures on Calvinism* (Grand Rapids: Eerdmans, 1931).

Kuyper, Abraham, *Ons Program* (Amsterdam: J. A. Wormser, 1892).

Kuyper, Abraham, "The Ordinances of God" in *Political Order and the Plural Structure of Society*, ed. James W. Skillen and Rockne M. McCarthy (Atlanta: Scholars, 1991), 242-57.

Kuyper, Abraham, *Principles of Sacred Theology*, trans. J. Hendrik De Vries (Grand Rapids: Eerdmans, 1954).

Kuyper, Abraham, *The Problem of Poverty*, ed. James W. Skillen (Grand Rapids: Baker, 1991).

Luther, Martin, "Against the Heavenly Prophets in the Matter of Images and Sacraments," in *Luther's Works*, vol. 40, ed. Conrad Bergendoff (Philadelphia: Fortress, 1958), 73-223.

Luther, Martin, "How Christians Should Regard Moses," in *Luther's Works*, vol. 35, ed. E. Theodore Bachmann (Philadelphia: Fortress, 1960), 155-74.

Luther, Martin, "Lectures on Genesis," in *Luther's Works*, vol. 2, ed. Jaroslav Pelikan (St. Louis: Concordia, 1960).

Luther, Martin, "Lectures on Romans," in *Luther's Works*, vol. 25, ed. Hilton C. Oswald (St. Louis: Concordia, 1972).

Luther, Martin, "Temporal Authority: To What Extent It Should Be Obeyed," in *Luther's Works*, vol. 45, ed. Walther I. Brandt (Philadelphia: Muhlenberg, 1962), 81-139.

Marsilius of Padua, *The Defender of Peace*, vol. 2, *The Defensor Pacis*, trans. Alan Gewirth (New York: Columbia University Press, 1956).

Melville, James, *The Autobiography and Diary of Mr. James Melvill*, ed. Robert Pitcairn (Edinburgh: Wodrow Society, 1842).

"The National Covenant; or, the Confession of Faith," in *Westminster Confession of Faith* (Glasgow: Free Presbyterian Publications, 1990), 347-60.

Ockham, William of, *A Short Discourse on Tyrannical Government*, ed. Arthur Stephen McGrade, trans. John Kilcullen (Cambridge: Cambridge University Press, 1992).

Owen, John, "A Dissertation on Divine Justice," in *The Works of John Owen*, vol. 10, ed. William H. Goold (reprinted, Edinburgh: Banner of Truth, 1967), 483-624.

Owen, John, "Exercitations concerning the name, original, nature, use, and continuance, of a day of sacred rest," in *The Works of John Owen*, vol. 11, *An Exposition of the Epistle to the Hebrews*, ed. William H. Goold (London/Edinburgh, 1850; Philadelphia: Leighton, 1869).

Plantinga, Cornelius, Jr., *Engaging God's World: A Christian Vision of Faith, Learning, and Living* (Grand Rapids: Eerdmans, 2002).

Ponet, John, *A Short Treatise on Politique Power, and of the True Obedience Which Subjects Owe to Kings and Other Civil Governors* (Ann Arbor: University Microfilms, 1967), Early English books, 1641-1700; 252:E.154, no. 36.

The Register of the Company of Pastors of Geneva in the Time of Calvin, ed. and trans. Philip Edgcumbe Hughes (Grand Rapids: Eerdmans, 1966), 35-49.

Robinson, Stuart, "The Battle of Scottish Presbyterianism during Three Centuries for a Free Christian Commonwealth," in Preston D. Graham, Jr., *A Kingdom Not of This World: Stuart Robinson's Struggle to Distinguish the Sacred from the Secular during the Civil War* (Macon: Mercer University Press, 2002), 231-37.

Robinson, Stuart, *The Church of God as an Essential Element of the Gospel, and the Idea, Structure, and Functions Thereof* (Philadelphia: Joseph M. Wilson, 1858; reprinted Greenville: Greenville Presbyterian Theological Seminary Press, 1995).

Robinson, Stuart, "The Movement for an Orthodox Constitution of the U.S. Officially Endorsed Another Stride in the Erastian Apostasy," in Graham, *A Kingdom Not of This World*, 250-57.

Robinson, Stuart, "Our Idea," in Graham, *A Kingdom Not of This World*, 193-99.

Robinson, Stuart, "Prefatory to the *True Presbyterian*," in Graham, *A Kingdom Not of This World*, 219-22.

Robinson, Stuart, "Relation of the Temporal and Spiritual Powers Historically Considered: The Scoto-American Theory," in Graham, *A Kingdom Not of This World*, 200-218.

Robinson, Stuart, "Rev. Stuart Robinson to President Lincoln," in Graham, *A Kingdom Not of This World*, 258-76.

Robinson, Stuart, "Two Theories: The True American, as Contrasted with the New England Doctrine Touching the Relation of the Civil to the Spiritual," in Graham, *A Kingdom Not of This World*, 223-30.

Rutherford, Samuel, *The Divine Right of Church-Government and Excommunication* (London, 1646).

Rutherford, Samuel, *Lex, Rex* (1644; reprinted, Harrisonburg, VA: Sprinkle, 1982).

Scotus, Duns, *Duns Scotus on the Will and Morality*, trans. Allan B. Wolter, O.F.M. (Washington, D.C.: Catholic University of America Press, 1986).

"So-called Letter to Diognetus," in *Early Christian Fathers*, trans. and ed. Cyril C. Richardson (New York: Collier, 1970), 213-24.

Stob, Henry, *Ethical Reflections: Essays on Moral Themes* (Grand Rapids: Eerdmans, 1978).

Stob, Henry, "Natural Law Ethics: An Appraisal," *Calvin Theological Journal* 20, no. 1 (April 1985): 58-68.

Stob, Henry, "Observations on the Concept of the Antithesis," in *Perspectives on the Christian Reformed Church: Studies in Its History, Theology, and Ecumenicity*, ed. Peter De Klerk and Richard R. De Ridder (Grand Rapids: Baker, 1983), 241-58.

Stob, Henry, *Summoning Up Remembrance* (Grand Rapids: Eerdmans, 1995).

Stob, Henry, *Theological Reflections: Essays on Related Themes* (Grand Rapids: Eerdmans, 1981).

Stob, Henry, review of Herman Dooyeweerd, *Transcendental Problems of Philosophic Thought: An Inquiry into the Transcendental Conditions of Philosophy*, in *Calvin Forum* 14 (October 1948): 53-54.

"The Teaching of the Twelve Apostles, Commonly Called the Didache," in *Early Christian Fathers*, trans. and ed. Cyril C. Richardson (New York: Collier, 1970), 171-79.

Thomas Aquinas, *Summa Theologica*, trans. Fathers of the English Dominican Province, rev. ed., vols. 1-3 (1920; reprint, Allen, TX; Christian Classics, 1981).

Thomas Aquinas, *Summa Theologica*, vol. 2 (Rome: Ex Typographia Senatus, 1886).

Thornwell, James Henley, *The Collected Writings of James Henley Thornwell*, vol. 4, ed. B. M. Palmer (1875; reprinted Edinburgh: Banner of Truth, 1986).

Thornwell, James Henley, *Discourses on Truth* (New York: Robert Carter & Brothers, 1855).

Turretin, Francis, *Institutes of Elenctic Theology*, 3 vols., trans. George Musgrave Giger, ed. James T. Dennison, Jr. (Phillipsburg, NJ: P&R, 1992-1997).

Ursinus, Zacharias, "The Larger Catechism," in Lyle D. Bierma, with Charles D. Gunnoe Jr., Karin Y. Maag, and Paul W. Fields, *An Introduction to the Heidelberg Catechism: Sources, History, and Theology* (Grand Rapids: Baker Academic, 2005), 163-223.

Van Til, Cornelius, *Christian Apologetics* (Phillipsburg, NJ: P&R, 1976).

Van Til, Cornelius, *Christianity and Barthianism* (Philadelphia: Presbyterian and Reformed, 1962).

Van Til, Cornelius, *Common Grace and the Gospel* (Nutley, NJ: P&R, 1977).

Van Til, Cornelius, *In Defense of the Faith*, vol. 3, *Christian Theistic Ethics* (Phillipsburg, NJ: P&R, 1980).

Van Til, Cornelius, *The Defense of the Faith* (Philadelphia: Presbyterian and Reformed, 1955).

Van Til, Cornelius, and Louis Berkhof, *Foundations of Christian Education: Addresses to Christian Teachers*, ed. Dennis E. Johnson (Phillipsburg, NJ: P&R, 1990).

Van Til, Cornelius, *An Introduction to Systematic Theology* (Phillipsburg, NJ: P&R, 1974).

Van Til, Cornelius, "Nature and Scripture," in *The Infallible Word*, ed. N. B. Stonehouse and Paul Woolley (Grand Rapids: Eerdmans, 1946), 255-93.

Van Til, Cornelius, "Response by C. Van Til," in *Jerusalem and Athens: Critical Discussions on the Philosophy and Apologetics of Cornelius Van Til*, ed. E. R. Geehan (Nutley, NJ: Presbyterian and Reformed, 1971), 89-127.

Vermigli, Peter Martyr, commentary on Romans 13 and Judges 3:29-30 in Robert M. Kingdon, *The Political Thought of Peter Martyr Vermigli: Selected Texts and Commentary* (Geneva: Droz, 1980), 1-15, 99-101.

Witherspoon, John, "Lectures on Moral Philosophy," in *The Works of the Rev. John Witherspoon*, vol. 3, 2nd ed. (Philadelphia: William W. Woodward, 1802; reprinted Bristol: Toemmes, 2003), 367-472.

Witsius, Herman, *The Economy of the Covenants between God and Man: Comprehending a Complete Body of Divinity*, 2 vols., trans. William Crookshank (1822; reprinted, Phillipsburg: P&R, 1990).

Wolters, Albert M., *Creation Regained: Biblical Basics for a Reformational Worldview* (Grand Rapids: Eerdmans, 1985).

Wolters, Albert M., *Creation Regained: Biblical Basics for a Reformational Worldview*, 2d ed. (Grand Rapids: Eerdmans, 2005).

Zanchi, Jerome, "On the Law in General," trans. Jeffrey J. Veenstra, in *Journal of Markets and Morality* 6 (Spring 2003): 317-98; this is a translation of D. Hieronymus Zanchius, *Operum theologicorum*, tome 4, *De primi hominis lapsu, de peccato, and [sic] de legi Dei* (Genevae: Sumptibus Samuelis Crispini, 1617), Cap. X, "De lege in genere," fols. 185-221.

Secondary Sources

Adams, Marilyn McCord, "Ockham on Will, Nature, and Morality," in *The Cambridge Companion to Ockham*, ed. Paul Vincent Spade (Cambridge: Cambridge University Press, 1999), 245-72.

Adams, Marilyn McCord, "William Ockham: Voluntarist or Naturalist?" in *Studies in Medieval Philosophy*, ed. John F. Wippel (Washington, D.C.: Catholic University of America Press, 1987), 219-47.

Anderson, Marvin W., "Royal Idolatry: Peter Martyr and the Reformed Tradition," *Archiv für Reformationsgeschichte* 69 (1978): 157-201.

Armstrong, Brian G., *Calvinism and the Amyraut Heresy: Protestant Scholasticism and Humanism in Seventeenth-Century France* (Madison: University of Wisconsin Press, 1969).

Backus, Irena, "Calvin's Concept of Natural and Roman Law," *Calvin Theological Journal* 38, no. 1 (2003): 7-26.

Bacote, Vincent E., *The Spirit in Public Theology: Appropriating the Legacy of Abraham Kuyper* (Grand Rapids: Baker Academic, 2005).

Bahnsen, Greg L., *Van Til's Apologetic: Readings and Analysis* (Phillipsburg, NJ: P&R, 1998).

Ballor, Jordan J., "The Aryan Clause, the Confessing Church, and the Ecumenical Movement: Barth and Bonhoeffer on Natural Theology, 1933-1935," *Scottish Journal of Theology* 59, no. 3 (2006): 263-80.

Barbour, Reid, *John Selden: Measures of the Holy Commonwealth in Seventeenth-Century England* (Toronto: University of Toronto Press, 2003).

Bastit, Michel, *Naissance de la loi moderne* (Paris: Presses Universitaires de France, 1990).

Baylor, Michael G., *Action and Person: Conscience in Late Scholasticism and the Young Luther* (Leiden: Brill, 1977).

Beck, Randy, "The City of God and the Cities of Men: A Response to Jason Carter," *University of Georgia Law Review* 41, no. 1 (Fall 2006): 113-55.

Beer, Barrett L., "John Ponet's *Shorte Treatise of Politike Power* Reassessed," *Sixteenth Century Journal* 21, no. 3 (1990): 373-83.

Begbie, Jeremy, "Creation, Christ, and Culture in Dutch Neo-Calvinism," in *Christ in Our Place: The Humanity of God in Christ for the Reconciliation of the World*, ed. Trevor Hart and Daniel Thimell (Allison Park, PA: Pickwick, 1989), 113-32.

Bibliography

Bell, Daniel M., Jr., *Liberation Theology After the End of History: The Refusal to Cease Suffering* (New York: Routledge, 2001).

Benedict, Philip, *Christ's Churches Purely Reformed: A Social History of Calvinism* (New Haven: Yale University Press, 2002).

Berkouwer, G. C., *The Triumph of Grace in the Theology of Karl Barth* (Grand Rapids: Eerdmans, 1956).

Berman, Harold J., *Law and Revolution: The Formation of the Western Legal Tradition* (Cambridge: Harvard University Press, 1983).

Berman, Harold J., *Law and Revolution, II: The Impact of the Protestant Reformations on the Western Legal Tradition* (Cambridge: Belknap/Harvard University Press, 2003).

Biggar, Nigel, *The Hastening That Waits: Karl Barth's Ethics* (Oxford: Clarendon, 1993).

Bohatec, Josef, *Calvin und das Recht* (Feudingen: Buchdruck and Verlags-Anstalt, 1934).

Bolt, John, "Abraham Kuyper and the Search for an Evangelical Public Theology," in J. Budziszewski, *Evangelicals in the Public Square: Four Formative Voices on Political Thought and Action* (Grand Rapids: Baker Academic, 2006).

Bolt, John, *Christian and Reformed Today* (Jordan Station, Ontario: Paideia, 1984).

Bolt, John, "Church and World: A Trinitarian Perspective," *Calvin Theological Journal* 18, no. 1 (April 1983): 5-31.

Bolt, John, *A Free Church, a Holy Nation: Abraham Kuyper's American Public Theology* (Grand Rapids: Eerdmans, 2001).

Bolt, John, "Why the Covenant of Works Is a Necessary Doctrine: Revisiting the Objections to a Venerable Reformed Doctrine," in *By Faith Alone: Answering the Challenges to the Doctrine of Justification*, ed. Gary L. Johnson and Guy P. Waters (Wheaton: Crossway, 2006), 171-89.

Bornkamm, Heinrich, *Luther's Doctrine of the Two Kingdoms*, trans. Karl H. Hertz (Philadelphia: Fortress, 1966).

Bouwsma, William J., *John Calvin: A Sixteenth-Century Portrait* (New York: Oxford University Press, 1988).

Bowler, Gerry, "Marian Protestants and the Idea of Violent Resistance to Tyranny," in *Protestantism and the National Church in Sixteenth Century England*, ed. Peter Lake and Maria Dowling (New York: Croom Helm, 1987), 124-43.

Boyd, Gregory A., *The Myth of a Christian Nation* (Grand Rapids: Zondervan, 2005).

Bratt, James D., "Abraham Kuyper: Puritan, Victorian, Modern," in *Religion, Pluralism, and Public Life: Abraham Kuyper's Legacy for the Twenty-First Century*, ed. Luis E. Lugo (Grand Rapids: Eerdmans, 2000), 3-21.

Bratt, James D., *Dutch Calvinism in Modern America: A History of a Conservative Subculture* (Grand Rapids: Eerdmans, 1984).

Brett, Annabel S., *Liberty, Right and Nature: Individual Rights in Later Scholastic Thought* (Cambridge: Cambridge University Press, 1997).

Brown, Harvey Owen, "Martin Luther: A Natural Law Theorist?" in *The Medieval Tradition of Natural Law*, ed. Harold J. Johnson (Kalamazoo: Medieval Institute, 1987), 13-25.

Brown, K. M., "In Search of the Godly Magistrate in Reformation Scotland," *Journal of Ecclesiastical History* 40 (Oct 1989): 553-81.

Buckley, Thomas E., S.J., *Church and State in Revolutionary Virginia, 1776-1787* (Charlottesville: University Press of Virginia, 1977).

Buckley, Thomas E., S.J., "Church-State Settlement in Virginia: The Presbyterian Contribution," *Journal of Presbyterian History* 54, no. 1 (Spring 1976): 105-19.

Budziszewski, J., *Evangelicals in the Public Square: Four Formative Voices on Political Thought and Action* (Grand Rapids: Baker Academic, 2006).

Burns, J. H., *The True Law of Kingship: Concepts of Monarchy in Early-Modern Scotland* (Oxford: Clarendon, 1996).

Busch, Eberhard, *The Great Passion: An Introduction to Karl Barth's Theology*, trans. Geoffrey W. Bromiley (Grand Rapids: Eerdmans, 2004).

Busch, Eberhard, *Karl Barth: His Life from Letters and Autobiographical Texts* (Grand Rapids: Eerdmans, 1994).

Butler, Charles James, *Covenant Theology and the Development of Religious Liberty* (Philadelphia: Center for the Study of Federalism, 1980).

Carter, Craig A., *Rethinking Christ and Culture: A Post-Christendom Perspective* (Grand Rapids: Brazos, 2006).

Casselli, Stephan J., "The Threefold Division of the Law in the Thought of Aquinas," *Westminster Theological Journal* 61 no. 2 (Fall 1999): 175-207.

Cavanaugh, William T., *Theopolitical Imagination: Discovering the Liturgy as a Political Act in an Age of Global Consumerism* (New York: T&T Clark, 2002).

Chaplin, Jonathan, *Herman Dooyeweerd: Christian Philosopher of State and Civil Society* (forthcoming).

Chung, Paul, *Spirituality and Social Ethics in John Calvin: A Pneumatological Perspective* (Lanham: University Press of America, 2000).

Clark, R. S., "Calvin and the *Lex Naturalis*," *Stulos* 6 (May-November 1998): 1-22.

Clough, David, *Ethics in Crisis: Interpreting Barth's Ethics* (Burlington: Ashgate, 2005).

Coffey, John, *Politics, Religion and the British Revolutions: The Mind of Samuel Rutherford* (Cambridge: Cambridge University Press, 1997).

Coker, Joe L., "The Sinnott Case of 1910: The Changing Views of Southern Presbyterians on Temperance, Prohibition, and the Spirituality of the Church," *Journal of Presbyterian History* 77, no. 4 (Winter 1999): 247-262.

Coleman, Janet, *A History of Political Thought: From the Middle Ages to the Renaissance* (Oxford: Blackwell, 2000).

Cottret, Bernard, *Calvin: A Biography*, trans. M. Wallace McDonald (Grand Rapids: Eerdmans, 2000).

Couenhoven, Jesse, "Law and Gospel, or the Law of the Gospel? Karl Barth's Political Theology Compared with Luther and Calvin," *Journal of Religious Ethics* 30, no. 2 (Summer 2002): 181-205.

Courtenay, William J., "The Academic and Intellectual Worlds of Ockham," in *The Cambridge Companion to Ockham*, ed. Paul Vincent Spade (Cambridge: Cambridge University Press, 1999), 17-30.

Courtenay, William J., "Nominalism and Late Medieval Religion," in *The Pursuit of Holiness*, ed. Charles Trinkhaus and Heiko A. Oberman (Leiden: Brill, 1974), 26-59.

Cross, Richard, *Duns Scotus* (Oxford: Oxford University Press, 1999).

Bibliography

Curry, Thomas J., "Church and State in Seventeenth and Eighteenth Century America," *Journal of Law and Religion* 7, no. 2 (1989): 261-273.

Daane, James, *A Theology of Grace: An Inquiry into and Evaluation of Dr. C. Van Til's Doctrine of Common Grace* (Grand Rapids: Eerdmans, 1954).

Danner, Dan G., "Christopher Goodman and the English Protestant Tradition of Civil Disobedience," *Sixteenth Century Journal* 8, no. 3 (1977): 61-74.

Danner, Dan G., "Resistance and the Ungodly Magistrate in the Sixteenth Century: The Marian Exiles," *Journal of the American Academy of Religion* 49, no. 3 (Sept 1981): 471-81.

Davis, James Calvin, *The Moral Theology of Roger Williams: Christian Conviction and Public Ethics* (Louisville: Westminster John Knox, 2004).

Davis, William C., *Thomas Reid's Ethics: Moral Epistemology on Legal Foundations* (New York: Continuum, 2006).

Dawson, Jane E. A., "Trumpeting Resistance: Christopher Goodman and John Knox," in *John Knox and the British Reformations,* ed. Roger A. Mason (Aldershot: Ashgate, 1998), 131-53.

Dawson, Jane E. A., "The Two John Knoxes: England, Scotland and the 1558 Tracts," *Journal of Ecclesiastical History* 42 (Oct 1991): 555-76.

de Bruijn, Jan, "Calvinism and Romanticism: Abraham Kuyper as a Calvinist Politician," in *Religion, Pluralism, and Public Life: Abraham Kuyper's Legacy for the Twenty-First Century,* ed. Luis E. Lugo (Grand Rapids: Eerdmans, 2000), 45-58.

Dennison, James T., Jr., *Market Day of the Soul: The Puritan Doctrine of the Sabbath in England, 1532-1700* (Lanham: University Press of America, 1983).

Dennison, William D., "Analytic Philosophy and Van Til's Epistemology," *Westminster Theological Journal* 57, no. 1 (Spring 1995): 33-56.

Dennison, William D., "Dutch Neo-Calvinism and the Roots for Transformation: An Introductory Essay," *Journal of the Evangelical Theological Society* 42, no. 2 (June 1999): 271-91.

Dennison, William D., "Natural and Special Revelation: A Reassessment," *Kerux* 21, no. 2 (Sept 2006): 13-34.

d'Entreves, A. P., *Natural Law: An Introduction to Legal Philosophy* (London: Hutchinson, 1970).

de Witt, J. R., *Jus Divinum: The Westminster Assembly and the Divine Right of Church Government* (Kampen: Kok, 1969).

Dodaro, Robert, *Christ and the Just Society in the Thought of Augustine* (Cambridge: Cambridge University Press, 2004).

Donaldson, Gordon, *Scottish Church History* (Edinburgh: Scottish Academic Press, 1985).

Donnelly, John Patrick, *Calvinism and Scholasticism in Vermigli's Doctrine of Man and Grace* (Leiden: Brill, 1976).

Donnelly, John Patrick., S.J., "Calvinist Thomism," *Viator* 7 (1976): 441-55.

Douglas, J. D., "National Covenant," in Nigel M. de S. Cameron, *Dictionary of Scottish Church History and Theology,* ed. Nigel M. de S. Cameron (Downers Grove: InterVarsity Press, 1993), 620.

Dowey, Edward A., *The Knowledge of God in Calvin's Theology* (New York: Columbia University Press, 1952).

Draper, Jonathan A., *The Didache in Modern Research,* ed. Jonathan A. Draper (Leiden: Brill, 1996).

Eckenrode, H. J., *Separation of Church and State in Virginia: A Study in the Development of the Revolution* (1910; reprinted New York: Da Capo, 1971).

Elshtain, Jean Bethke, *Augustine and the Limits of Politics* (Notre Dame: University of Notre Dame Press, 1995).

Emerson, Everett H., *John Cotton* (New Haven: College & University Press, 1965).

Engel, Mary Potter, *John Calvin's Perspectival Anthropology* (Atlanta: Scholars Press, 1988).

Ericson, Edward E., "Abraham Kuyper: Cultural Critic," *Calvin Theological Journal* 22 (Nov 1987): 210-27.

Estelle, Bryan D., "The Covenant of Works in Moses and Paul," in *Covenant, Justification, and Pastoral Ministry,* ed. R. Scott Clark (Phillipsburg, NJ: P&R, 2007), 89-135.

Estes, James, "The Role of Godly Magistrates in the Church: Melanchthon as Luther's Interpreter and Collaborator," *Church History* 67, no. 3 (1998): 463-84.

Eusden, John D., "Natural Law and Covenant Theology in New England, 1620-1670," *Natural Law Forum* 6 (1960): 1-30.

Farmer, James Oscar, Jr., *The Metaphysical Confederacy: John Henley Thornwell and the Synthesis of Southern Values* (Macon: Mercer University Press, 1986).

Felch, Susan M., "The Rhetoric of Biblical Authority: John Knox and the Question of Women," *Sixteenth Century Journal* 26, no. 4 (1995): 805-22.

Ferguson, Sinclair B., "An Assembly of Theonomists? The Teaching of the Westminster Divines on the Law of God," in *Theonomy: A Reformed Critique,* ed. William S. Barker and W. Robert Godfrey (Grand Rapids: Zondervan, 1990), 315-49.

Fesko, J. V., and Guy M. Richard, "Natural Theology and the Westminster Confession," *The Westminster Confession into the 21st Century: Essays in Remembrance of the 350th Anniversary of the Westminster Assembly,* vol. 3, ed. J. Ligon Duncan (Fearn: Christian Focus, forthcoming).

Field, Lester L., Jr., *Liberty, Dominion, and the Two Swords: On the Origins of Western Political Theology (180-398)* (Notre Dame: University of Notre Dame Press, 1998).

Finnis, John, *Aquinas: Moral, Political, and Legal Theory* (Oxford: Oxford University Press, 1998).

Foote, William Henry, *Sketches of Virginia: Historical and Biographical* (1850; reprinted Richmond: John Knox, 1966).

Ford, James Thomas, "Wolfgang Musculus on the Office of the Christian Magistrate," *Archiv für Reformationsgeschichte* 91 (2000): 149-67.

Ford, John D., "*Lex, rex iusto posita:* Samuel Rutherford on the Origins of Government," in *Scots and Britons: Scottish Political Thought and the Union of 1603,* ed. Roger A. Mason (Cambridge: Cambridge University Press, 1994), 262-90.

Fox-Genovese, Elizabeth, and Eugene D. Genovese, "The Divine Sanction of Social Order: Religious Foundations of the Southern Slaveholders' World View," *Journal of the American Academy of Religion* 55, no. 2 (Summer 1987): 211-33.

Bibliography

Foxgrover, David L., "John Calvin's Understanding of Conscience" (Ph.D. diss., Claremont Graduate School, 1978).

Frame, John M., *Cornelius Van Til: An Analysis of His Thought* (Phillipsburg, NJ: P&R, 1995).

Franklin, Julian H., *Constitutionalism and Resistance in the Sixteenth Century: Three Treatises by Hotman, Beza, & Mornay* (New York: Pegasus, 1969).

Freppert, Lucan, O.F.M., *The Basis of Morality According to William Ockham* (Chicago: Franciscan Herald Press, 1988).

Fuchs, Josef, S.J., *Natural Law: A Theological Investigation,* trans. Helmut Reckter, S.J., and John A. Dowling (New York: Sheed and Ward, 1965).

Gamble, Richard C., "The Christian and the Tyrant: Beza and Knox on Political Resistance Theory," *Westminster Theological Journal* 46, no. 1 (Spring 1984): 125-39.

Ganoczy, Alexandre, *The Young Calvin,* trans. David Foxgrover and Wade Provo (Philadelphia: Westminster, 1987).

Garnett, George, "Editor's introduction," in Stephanus Junius Brutus, the Celt, *Vindiciae, contra tyrannos: or, concerning the legitimate power of a prince over the people, and of the people over a prince,* ed. and trans. George Garnett (Cambridge: Cambridge University Press, 1994).

Giesey, Ralph E., and J. H. M. Salmon, "Introduction," in François Hotman, *Francogallia,* ed. Ralph E. Giesey and J. H. M. Salmon, trans. J. H. M. Salmon (Cambridge: Cambridge University Press, 1972).

Gill, Theodore A., "Barth and Mozart," *Theology Today* 43, no. 3 (Oct 1986): 403-11.

Gordis, Lisa M., *Opening Scripture: Bible Reading and Interpretive Authority in Puritan New England* (Chicago: University of Chicago Press, 2003).

Gordon, T. David, "Van Til and Theonomic Ethics," in *Creator, Redeemer, Consummator: A Festschrift for Meredith G. Kline,* ed. Howard Griffith and John R. Muether (Greenville: Reformed Academic Press, 2000), 271-78.

Goris, Harm, "Thomism in Zanchi's Doctrine of God," in *Protestant Scholasticism: Essays in Reassessment,* ed. Carl Trueman and R. Scott Clark (Carlisle: Paternoster, 1999), 121-40.

Gorski, Philip S., *The Disciplinary Revolution: Calvinism and the Rise of the State in Early Modern Europe* (Chicago: University of Chicago Press, 2003).

Grabill, Stephen J., "Introduction," *Journal of Markets and Morality* 6 (Spring 2003): 309-16.

Grabill, Stephen J., "Natural Law and the Noetic Effects of Sin: The Faculty of Reason in Francis Turretin's Theological Anthropology," *Westminster Theological Journal* 67 (Fall 2005): 261-79.

Grabill, Stephen J., *Rediscovering the Natural Law in Reformed Theological Ethics* (Grand Rapids: Eerdmans, 2006).

Graham, Preston D., Jr., *A Kingdom Not of This World: Stuart Robinson's Struggle to Distinguish the Sacred from the Secular during the Civil War* (Macon: Mercer University Press, 2002).

Graham, W. Fred, *The Constructive Revolutionary: John Calvin and His Socio-Economic Impact* (Richmond: John Knox Press, 1971).

447

Greaves, Richard L., *Theology and Revolution in the Scottish Reformation: Studies in the Thought of John Knox* (Grand Rapids: Christian University Press, 1980).

Griffin, Keith L., *Revolution and Religion: American Revolutionary War and the Reformed Clergy* (New York: Paragon House, 1994).

Gummere, Richard M., "Samuel Davies: Classical Champion of Religious Freedom," *Journal of Presbyterian History* 40, no. 2 (June 1962): 67-74.

Gunnoe, Charles Dewey, Jr., "Thomas Erastus in Heidelberg: A Renaissance Physician during the Second Reformation, 1558-1580" (Ph.D. dissertation, University of Virginia, 1998).

Gustafson, James M., *Ethics from a Theocentric Perspective*, vol. 1, *Theology and Ethics* (Chicago: University of Chicago Press, 1981).

Haakonssen, Knud, *Natural Law and Moral Philosophy: From Grotius to the Scottish Enlightenment* (Cambridge: Cambridge University Press, 1996).

Haas, Guenther H., *The Concept of Equity in Calvin's Ethics* (Waterloo: Wilfrid Laurier University Press, 1997).

Haas, Guenther, "Kuyper's Legacy for Christian Ethics," *Calvin Theological Journal* 33 (Nov 1998): 320-49.

Haddorff, David, "Karl Barth's Theological Politics," in *Community, State, and Church: Three Essays* (Eugene: Wipf and Stock, 2004), 1-69.

Hall, Pamela M., *Narrative and the Natural Law: An Interpretation of Thomistic Ethics* (Notre Dame: University of Notre Dame Press, 1994).

Hall, Timothy L., *Separating Church and State: Roger Williams and Religious Liberty* (Urbana: University of Illinois Press, 1998).

Hamburger, Philip, *Separation of Church and State* (Cambridge: Harvard University Press, 2002).

Hancock, Ralph C., *Calvin and the Foundation of Modern Politics* (Ithaca: Cornell University Press, 1989).

Hart, D. G., "American Presbyterianism: Exceptional," *Journal of Presbyterian History* 84, no. 1 (Spring/Summer 2006): 12-16.

Hart, D. G., "Introduction: The Forgotten Machen?" in J. Gresham Machen, *Selected Shorter Writings*, ed. D. G. Hart (Phillipsburg, NJ: P&R, 2004), 1-20.

Hart, D. G., *Recovering Mother Kirk: The Case for Liturgy in the Reformed Tradition* (Grand Rapids: Baker Academic, 2003).

Hart, D. G., *A Secular Faith: Why Christianity Favors the Separation of Church and State* (Chicago: Ivan R. Dee, 2006).

Hart, Hendrik, "Notes on Dooyeweerd, Reason, and Order," in *Contemporary Reflections on the Philosophy of Herman Dooyeweerd*, ed. D. F. M. Strauss and Michelle Botting (Lewiston, NY: Edwin Mellen, 2000), 125-46.

Hart, John W., *Karl Barth vs. Emil Brunner: The Formation and Dissolution of a Theological Alliance, 1916-1936* (New York: Peter Lang, 2001).

Hart, Trevor, "Revelation," in *The Cambridge Companion to Karl Barth*, ed. John Webster (Cambridge: Cambridge University Press, 2000), 37-56.

Haskins, George Lee, *Law and Authority in Early Massachusetts: A Study in Tradition and Design* (New York: Macmillan, 1960).

Hauerwas, Stanley, *The Peaceable Kingdom: A Primer in Christian Ethics* (Notre Dame: University of Notre Dame Press, 1983).

Hauerwas, Stanley, and William H. Willimon, *Resident Aliens: Life in the Christian Colony* (Nashville: Abingdon, 1989).

Hawkins, Peter S., "Polemical Counterpoint in *De Civitate Dei*," *Augustinian Studies* 6 (1975): 97-106.

Hays, Richard B., *The Moral Vision of the New Testament: Community, Cross, New Creation; A Contemporary Introduction to New Testament Ethics* (New York: HarperSanFrancisco, 1996).

Heimert, Alan, *Religion and the American Mind: From the Great Awakening to the Revolution* (Cambridge: Harvard University Press, 1966).

Helm, Paul, "Calvin and Natural Law," *Scottish Bulletin of Evangelical Theology* 2 (1984): 5-22.

Helm, Paul, *Calvin and the Calvinists* (Edinburgh: Banner of Truth, 1982).

Helm, Paul, *John Calvin's Ideas* (Oxford: Oxford University Press, 2004).

Helm, Paul, "Thomas Reid, Common Sense and Calvinism," in *Rationality in the Calvinian Tradition*, ed. Hendrik Hart, Johan Van der Hoeven, and Nicholas Wolterstorff (Lanham: University Press of America, 1983), 71-89.

Helseth, Paul Kjoss, "Moral Character and Moral Certainty: The Subjective State of the Soul and J. G. Machen's Critique of Theological Liberalism" (Ph.D. dissertation, Marquette University, 1997).

Heslam, Peter S., *Creating a Christian Worldview: Abraham Kuyper on Calvinism* (Grand Rapids: Eerdmans, 1998).

Hesselink, I. John, *Calvin's Concept of the Law* (Allison Park, PA: Pickwick Publications, 1992).

Hildebrandt, Esther, "The Magdeburg Bekenntnis as Possible Link Between German and English Resistance Theories in the Sixteenth Century," *Archiv für Reformationsgeschichte* 71 (1980): 227-53.

Hockman, Dan M., "Hellish and Malicious Incendiaries: Commissary William Dawson and Dissent in Colonial Virginia, 1743-1752," *Anglican and Episcopal History* 59, no. 2 (1990): 150-80.

Hoekema, Anthony A., *The Bible and the Future* (Grand Rapids: Eerdmans, 1979).

Holifield, E. Brooks, *The Gentlemen Theologians: American Theology in Southern Culture, 1795-1860* (Durham: Duke University Press, 1978).

Hollerich, Michael J., "John Milbank, Augustine, and the 'Secular,'" in *History, Apocalypse, and the Secular Imagination: New Essays on Augustine's* City of God, ed. Mark Vessey, Karla Pollmann, and Alan D. Fitzgerald, O.S.A. (Bowling Green: Philosophy Documentation Center, 1999), 312-26.

Holwerda, David E., "Eschatology and History: A Look at Calvin's Eschatological Vision," in *Exploring the Heritage of John Calvin*, ed. David E. Holwerda (Grand Rapids: Baker, 1976), 110-39.

Hood, Fred J., *Reformed America: The Middle and Southern States, 1783-1837* (University, AL: University of Alabama Press, 1980).

Hood, Fred J., "Revolution and Religious Liberty: The Conservation of the Theocratic Concept in Virginia," *Church History* 40, no. 2 (June 1971): 170-81.

Hopfl, Harro, *The Christian Polity of John Calvin* (Cambridge: Cambridge University Press, 1982).

Horton, Michael S., "Calvin and the Law-Gospel Hermeneutic," *Pro Ecclesia* 6 (Winter 1997): 27-42.

Horton, Michael S., "Covenant, Election and Incarnation: Evaluating Barth's Actualist Christology" (forthcoming).

Horton, Michael S., *God of Promise: Introducing Covenant Theology* (Grand Rapids: Baker, 2006).

Horton, Michael S., "In Praise of the Profane: A Theological Defense of the Secular," in *Evangelicals and Empire*, ed. Peter Heltzel (Oxford: Oxford University Press, forthcoming).

Howe, Daniel Walker, *Making the American Self: Jonathan Edwards to Abraham Lincoln* (Cambridge: Harvard University Press, 1997).

Huber, Wolfgang, "The Barmen Theological Declaration and the Two Kingdom Doctrine. Historico-Systematic Reflections," in *Lutheran Churches — Salt or Mirror of Society? Case Studies on the Theory and Practice of the Two Kingdoms Doctrine*, ed. Ulrich Duchrow (Geneva: Lutheran World Federation, 1977), 28-48.

Hudson, Winthrop S., *John Ponet (1516?-1556): Advocate of Limited Monarchy* (Chicago: University of Chicago Press, 1942).

Hueglin, Thomas O., "Covenant and Federalism in the Politics of Althusius," in *The Covenant Connection: From Federal Theology to Modern Federalism*, ed. Daniel J. Elazar and John Kincaid (Lanham: Lexington, 2000).

Hugo, André Malan, "Introduction," in *Calvin's Commentary on Seneca's De Clementia* (Leiden: Brill, 1969).

Hunsinger, George, *Disruptive Grace: Studies in the Theology of Karl Barth* (Grand Rapids: Eerdmans, 2000).

Hunsinger, George, *How to Read Karl Barth: The Shape of His Theology* (Oxford: Oxford University Press, 1991).

Isaac, Rhys, *The Transformation of Virginia: 1740-1790* (New York: W. W. Norton & Company, 1982).

James, Charles F., *Documentary History of the Struggle for Religious Liberty in Virginia* (1900; reprinted New York: Da Capo, 1971).

James, Frank A., III, "Peter Martyr Vermigli: At the Crossroads of Late Medieval Scholasticism, Christian Humanism and Resurgent Augustinianism," in *Protestant Scholasticism: Essays in Reassessment*, ed. Carl Trueman and R. Scott Clark (Carlisle: Paternoster, 1999), 62-78.

Jefford, Clayton, *The Didache in Context: Essays on Its Text, History, and Transmission*, ed. Clayton Jefford (Leiden: Brill, 1995).

Johnson, Thomas K., *Natural Law Ethics: An Evangelical Proposal* (Bonn: Verlag für Kultur und Wissenschaft, 2005).

Jongsma, Sally, "Football Is Coming," *The Voice* 52, no. 4 (Summer 2007): 10.

Jue, Jeffrey K., "*Theologia Naturalis*: A Reformed Tradition," in *Revelation and Reason: New Essays in Reformed Apologetics*, ed. K. Scott Oliphint and Lane G. Tipton (Phillipsburg, NJ: P&R, 2007), 168-89.

Kalsbeek, L., *Contours of a Christian Philosophy: An Introduction to Herman Dooyeweerd's Thought,* ed. Bernard and Josina Zylstra (Toronto: Wedge, 1975).

Kasteel, P., *Abraham Kuyper* (Kok: Kampen, 1938).

Kelley, Donald R., *François Hotman: A Revolutionary's Ordeal* (Princeton: Princeton University Press, 1973).

Kendall, R. T., *Calvin and English Calvinism to 1649* (Oxford: Oxford University Press, 1979).

Kilcullen, John, "The Political Writings," in *The Cambridge Companion to Ockham,* ed. Paul Vincent Spade (Cambridge: Cambridge University Press, 1999), 302-25.

King, Peter, "Ockham's Ethical Theory," in *The Cambridge Companion to Ockham,* ed. Paul Vincent Spade (Cambridge: Cambridge University Press, 1999), 227-44.

Kingdon, Robert M., *Adultery and Divorce in Calvin's Geneva* (Cambridge: Harvard University Press, 1995).

Kingdon, R. M., "Calvin and the Government of Geneva," in *Calvinus Ecclesiae Genevensis Custos,* ed. Wilhelm Neuser (Frankfurt am Main: Peter Lang, 1984), 49-67.

Kingdon, Robert M., "Introduction," in *The Political Thought of Peter Martyr Vermigli: Selected Texts and Commentary* (Geneva: Droz, 1980), i-xxiii.

Kirby, Torrance, "Peter Martyr Vermigli and Pope Boniface VIII: The Difference Between Civil and Ecclesiastical Power," in *Peter Martyr Vermigli and the European Reformations: Semper Reformanda,* ed. Frank A. James III (Leiden: Brill, 2004), 291-304.

Kirk, James, *Patterns of Reform: Continuity and Change in the Reformation Kirk* (Edinburgh: T&T Clark, 1989).

Klapwijk, Jacob, "Antithesis and Common Grace," in *Bringing into Captivity Every Thought: Capita Selecta in the History of Christian Evaluations of Non-Christian Philosophy,* ed. Jacob Klapwijk, Sander Griffioen, and Gerben Groenewoud (Lanham: University Press of America, 1991), 170-79.

Klauber, Martin I., *Between Reformed Scholasticism and Pan-Protestantism: Jean-Alphonse Turretin (1671-1737) and Enlightened Orthodoxy at the Academy of Geneva* (Selinsgrove, PA: Susquehanna University Press, 1994).

Klempa, William, "John Calvin on Natural Law," in *John Calvin and the Church: A Prism of Reform,* ed. Timothy George (Louisville: Westminster/John Knox, 1990), 72-95.

Kramnick, Isaac, and R. Laurence Moore, *The Godless Constitution: A Moral Defense of the Secular State* (New York: W. W. Norton, 2005).

Kraynak, Robert P., *Christian Faith and Modern Democracy: God and Politics in the Fallen World* (Notre Dame: University of Notre Dame Press, 2001).

Kuiper, Herman, *Calvin on Common Grace* (Grand Rapids: Smitter, 1928).

Kuklick, Bruce, *Churchmen and Philosophers: From Jonathan Edwards to John Dewey* (New Haven: Yale University Press, 1985).

Kyle, Richard, "John Knox and the Purification of Religion: The Intellectual Aspects of His Crusade against Idolatry," *Archiv für Reformationsgeschichte 77* (1986): 265-80.

Lachman, D. C., "Solemn League and Covenant" in Nigel M. de S. Cameron, *Dictionary of Scottish Church History and Theology,* ed. Nigel M. de S. Cameron (Downers Grove: InterVarsity Press, 1993), 786-87.

Lambert, Frank, *The Founding Fathers and the Place of Religion in America* (Princeton: Princeton University Press, 2003).

Lamont, Stewart, *The Swordbearer: John Knox and the European Reformation* (London: Hodder & Stoughton, 1991).

Lang, August, "The Reformation and Natural Law," trans. J. Gresham Machen, in *Calvin and the Reformation: Four Studies* (New York: Fleming H. Revell, 1909), 56-98.

Langemeijer, G. E., "An Assessment of Herman Dooyeweerd," in L. Kalsbeek, *Contours of a Christian Philosophy: An Introduction to Herman Dooyeweerd's Thought,* ed. Bernard and Josina Zylstra (Toronto: Wedge, 1975), 10-13.

Langston, Douglas C., *Conscience and Other Virtues: From Bonaventure to MacIntyre* (University Park: Pennsylvania State University Press, 2001).

Lazareth, William, *Christians in Society: Luther, the Bible, and Social Ethics* (Minneapolis: Fortress, 2001).

Leith, John H., "James Henley Thornwell and the Shaping of the Reformed Tradition in the South," in *Probing the Reformed Tradition: Historical Studies in Honor of Edward A. Dowey, Jr.,* ed. Elsie Anne McKee and Brian G. Armstrong (Louisville: Westminster John Knox, 1989), 424-47.

Linder, Robert D., "John Calvin, Pierre Viret and the State," in *Calvin and the State,* ed. Peter de Klerk (Grand Rapids: Calvin Studies Society, 1993), 171-88.

Lisska, Anthony J., *Aquinas's Theory of Natural Law: An Analytic Reconstruction* (Oxford: Clarendon, 1996).

Lloyd, H. A., "Calvin and the Duty of Guardians to Resist," *Journal of Ecclesiastical History* 32, no. 1 (Jan 1981): 65-67.

Lohse, Bernhard, *Martin Luther's Theology: Its Historical and Systematic Development,* trans. and ed. Roy A. Harrisville (Minneapolis: Fortress, 1999).

Long, D. Stephen, *Divine Economy: Theology and the Market* (New York: Routledge, 2000).

Lovin, Robin W., *Christian Faith and Public Choices: The Social Ethics of Barth, Brunner, and Bonhoeffer* (Philadelphia: Fortress, 1984).

Lyall, Francis, *Of Presbyters and Kings: Church and State in the Law of Scotland* (Aberdeen: Aberdeen University Press, 1980).

MacDonald, Alan R., "Ecclesiastical Representation in Parliament in Post-Reformation Scotland: The Two Kingdoms Theory in Practice," *Journal of Ecclesiastical History* 50 (Jan 1999): 38-61.

Machen, J. Gresham, *Selected Shorter Writings,* ed. D. G. Hart (Phillipsburg, NJ: P&R, 2004).

MacIntyre, Alasdair, *After Virtue,* 2d ed. (1981; Notre Dame: University of Notre Dame Press, 1984).

Maclear, J. F., "Samuel Rutherford: The Law and the King," in *Calvinism and the Political Order,* ed. George L. Hunt (Philadelphia: Westminster, 1965), 65-87.

Maddex, Jack P., "From Theocracy to Spirituality: The Southern Presbyterian Reversal on Church and State," *Journal of Presbyterian History* 54 (Winter 1976): 438-57.

Manetsch, Scott M., *Theodore Beza and the Quest for Peace in France, 1572-1598* (Leiden: Brill, 2000).

Mangina, Joseph, *Karl Barth: Theologian of Christian Witness* (Louisville: Westminster John Knox, 2004).

Markus, Robert A., *Christianity and the Secular* (Notre Dame: University of Notre Dame Press, 2006).

Markus, R. A., *Saeculum: History and Society in the Theology of St. Augustine* (1970; Cambridge: Cambridge University Press, 1988).

Marquardt, Friedrich Wilhelm, *Theologie und Sozialismus: Das Beispiel Karl Barths* (Munich: Kaiser, 1972).

Marsden, George M., *Fundamentalism and American Culture: The Shaping of Twentieth-Century Evangelicalism: 1870-1925* (New York: Oxford University Press, 1980).

Marshall, John L., "Natural Law and the Covenant: The Place of the Covenantal Framework of Samuel Rutherford's *Lex, Rex*" (Ph.D. dissertation, Westminster Theological Seminary, 1995).

Marshall, Rosalind Kay, *John Knox* (Edinburgh: Birlinn, 2000).

Mason, Roger A., "Covenant and Commonweal: The Language of Politics in Reformation Scotland," in *Church, Politics and Society: Scotland 1408-1929,* ed. Norman MacDougall (Edinburgh: John Donald, 1983), 97-126.

Mason, Roger A., *Kingship and the Commonweal: Political Thought in Renaissance and Reformation Scotland* (East Lothian: Tuckwell, 1998).

Mason, Roger, "Rex Stoicus: George Buchanan, James VI and the Scottish Polity," in *New Perspectives on the Politics and Culture of Early Modern Scotland,* ed. John Dwyer et al. (Edinburgh: John Donald, 1982), 9-33.

Mason, Roger A., and Martin S. Smith, "Introduction," in *A Dialogue on the Law of Kingship among the Scots: A Critical Edition and Translation of George Buchanan's De Iure Regni apud Scotos Dialogus,* ed. Roger A. Mason and Martin S. Smith (Burlington, VT: Ashgate, 2004), xv-lxxi.

Masselink, William, *General Revelation and Common Grace: A Defense of the Historic Reformed Faith Over Against the Theology and Philosophy of the So-called "Reconstructionist" Movement* (Grand Rapids: Eerdmans, 1953).

Matheny, Paul D., *Dogmatics and Ethics: The Theological Realism and Ethics of Karl Barth's* Church Dogmatics (New York: Peter Lang, 1990).

McCormack, Bruce L., *Karl Barth's Critically Realistic Dialectical Theology: Its Genesis and Development 1909-1936* (Oxford: Clarendon, 1995).

McGrade, A. S., "Natural Law and Moral Omnipotence," in *The Cambridge Companion to Ockham,* ed. Paul Vincent Spade (Cambridge: Cambridge University Press, 1999), 273-301.

McGrade, Arthur Stephen, "Ockham and the Birth of Individual Rights," in *Authority and Power: Studies on Medieval Laws and Government Presented to Walter Ullmann on His Seventieth Birthday,* ed. Brian Tierney and Peter Linehan (Cambridge: Cambridge University Press, 1980), 149-65.

McGrade, Arthur Stephen, *The Political Thought of William of Ockham: Personal and Institutional Principles* (Cambridge: Cambridge University Press, 1974).

McGrath, Alistair, *A Life of John Calvin: A Study in the Shaping of Western Culture* (Oxford: Blackwell, 1990).

McKay, David, "From Popery to Principle: Covenanters and the Kingship of Christ," in *The Faith Once Delivered: Essays in Honor of Dr. Wayne Spear,* ed. Anthony T. Selvaggio (Phillipsburg, NJ: P&R, 2007), 135-69.

McKay, W. D. J., *An Ecclesiastical Republic: Church Government in the Writings of George Gillespie* (Carlisle: Paternoster, 1997).

McNeill, John T., "Natural Law in the Teaching of the Reformers," *Journal of Religion* 26 (July 1946): 168-82.

McNeill, John T., "Natural Law in the Thought of Luther," *Church History* 10 (Sept 1941): 211-27.

Meilaender, Gilbert, "Wrong from Wright," *First Things,* no. 170 (Feb 2007): 9-11.

Menninga, Clarence, "Critical Reflections on Abraham Kuyper's *Evolutie* Address," *Calvin Theological Journal* 33 (Nov 1998): 435-43.

Milbank, John, "Socialism of the Gift, Socialism by Grace," *New Blackfriars* 77 (1996): 532-48.

Milbank, John, *Theology and Social Theory: Beyond Secular Reason* (Oxford: Blackwell, 1990).

Mohle, Hannes, "Scotus's Theory of Natural Law," in *The Cambridge Companion to Duns Scotus,* ed. Thomas Williams (Cambridge: Cambridge University Press, 2003), 312-31.

Moon, Byung-Ho, *Christ the Mediator of the Law: Calvin's Christological Understanding of the Law as the Rule of Living and Life-Giving* (Waynesboro, GA: Paternoster, 2006).

Moore, Edwin Nisbet, *Our Covenant Heritage: The Covenanters' Struggle for Unity in Truth as Revealed in the Memoir of James Nisbet and Sermons of John Nevay* (Fearn, Ross-shire: Christian Focus, 2000).

Moore, James, "The Two Systems of Francis Hutcheson: On the Origins of the Scottish Enlightenment," in *Studies in the Philosophy of the Scottish Enlightenment,* ed. M. A. Stewart (Oxford: Clarendon, 1990), 37-59.

Morrison, Jeffry H., *John Witherspoon and the Founding of the American Republic* (Notre Dame: University of Notre Dame Press, 2005).

Mouw, Richard J., "Some Reflections on Sphere Sovereignty," in *Religion, Pluralism, and Public Life: Abraham Kuyper's Legacy for the Twenty-First Century,* ed. Luis E. Lugo (Grand Rapids: Eerdmans, 2000), 87-109.

Mouw, Richard J., *When the Kings Come Marching In: Isaiah and the New Jerusalem* (Grand Rapids: Eerdmans, 1983).

Muether, John R., *Cornelius Van Til: Reformed Apologist* (Phillipsburg, NJ: P&R, 2008).

Mulder, Philip N., "Converting the New Light: Presbyterian Evangelicalism in Hanover, Virginia," *Journal of Presbyterian History* 75, no. 3 (Fall 1997): 141-51.

Muller, Richard A., *After Calvin: Studies in the Development of a Theological Tradition* (Oxford: Oxford University Press, 2003).

Muller, Richard A., "*Fides* and *Cognitio* in Relation to the Problem of Intellect and Will in the Theology of John Calvin," *Calvin Theological Journal* 25 (Nov 1990): 207-24.

Muller, Richard A., "A Note on 'Christocentrism' and the Imprudent Use of Such Terminology," *Westminster Theological Journal* 68 (Fall 2006): 253-60.

Muller, Richard A., *Post-Reformation Reformed Dogmatics: The Rise and Development of Reformed Orthodoxy, ca. 1520 to ca. 1725*, 4 vols. (Grand Rapids: Baker, 2003).

Muller, Richard A., *The Unaccommodated Calvin: Studies in the Foundation of a Theological Tradition* (New York: Oxford University Press, 2000).

Naphy, William G., *Calvin and the Consolidation of the Genevan Reformation* (Manchester: Manchester University Press, 1994).

Nelson, Daniel Mark, *The Priority of Prudence: Virtue and Natural Law in Thomas Aquinas and the Implications of Modern Ethics* (University Park: Pennsylvania State University Press, 1992).

Neuhaus, Richard John, *The Naked Public Square: Religion and Democracy in America*, 2d ed. (Grand Rapids: Eerdmans, 1986).

Niebuhr, H. Richard, *Christ and Culture* (New York: Harper & Brothers, 1951).

Niederwimmer, Kurt, *The Didache* (Minneapolis: Fortress, 1998).

Noll, Mark A., *America's God: From Jonathan Edwards to Abraham Lincoln* (New York: Oxford University Press, 2002).

Noll, Mark A., "Introduction," in *The Princeton Theology 1812-1921: Scripture, Science, and Theological Method from Archibald Alexander to Benjamin Breckinridge Warfield*, ed. Mark A. Noll (Grand Rapids: Baker, 2001), 11-48.

Oakley, Francis, "Medieval Theories of Natural Law: William of Ockham and the Significance of the Voluntarist Tradition," *Natural Law Forum* 6 (1961): 65-83.

Oakley, Francis, *The Political Thought of Pierre d'Ailly: The Voluntarist Tradition* (New Haven: Yale University Press, 1964).

Oberman, Heiko Augustinus, *The Dawn of the Reformation: Essays in Late Medieval and Early Reformation Thought* (Edinburgh: T&T Clark, 1986).

Oberman, Heiko, *The Harvest of Medieval Theology: Gabriel Biel and Late Medieval Nominalism* (1963; reprinted Grand Rapids: Baker, 2000).

O'Donovan, Oliver, "Augustine's *City of God* XIX and Western Political Thought," *Dionysius* 11 (Dec 1987): 89-110.

O'Donovan, Oliver, *The Desire of the Nations: Rediscovering the Roots of Political Theology* (Cambridge: Cambridge University Press, 1996).

O'Donovan, Oliver, *The Ways of Judgment* (Grand Rapids: Eerdmans, 2005).

Oliphint, Scott, "The Consistency of Van Til's Methodology," *Westminster Theological Journal* 52 (Spring 1990): 27-49.

Oliphint, K. Scott, "Cornelius Van Til and the Reformation of Christian Apologetics," in *Revelation and Reason: New Essays in Reformed Apologetics*, ed. K. Scott Oliphint and Lane G. Tipton (Phillipsburg, NJ: P&R, 2007), 279-303.

Oliphint, Scott, "Jerusalem and Athens Revisited," *Westminster Theological Journal* 49 (Spring 1987): 65-90.

Olson, Jeannine E., "Calvin and Social-ethical Issues," in *The Cambridge Companion to John Calvin*, ed. Donald K. McKim (Cambridge: Cambridge University Press, 2004), 153-72.

Olthuis, Jim, "Of Webs and Whirlwinds; Me, Myself and I," in *Contemporary Reflections* on the Philosophy of Herman Dooyeweerd, ed. D. F. M. Strauss and Michelle Botting (Lewiston, NY: Edwin Mellen, 2000), 31-48.

Oosterhaven, M. Eugene, The Spirit of the Reformed Tradition (Grand Rapids: Eerdmans, 1971).

Palmer, Timothy P., "Calvin the Transformationist and the Kingship of Christ," Pro Rege 35, no. 3 (March 2007): 32-39.

Parker, T. H. L., Calvin: An Introduction to His Thought (Louisville: Westminster John Knox, 1995).

Parker, T. H. L., The Doctrine of the Knowledge of God: A Study in the Theology of John Calvin (Edinburgh: Oliver and Boyd, 1952).

Pattison, Bonnie L., Poverty in the Theology of John Calvin (Eugene: Pickwick, 2006).

Pennington, Kenneth, The Prince and the Law, 1200-1600: Sovereignty and Rights in the Western Legal Tradition (Berkeley: University of California Press, 1993).

Pilcher, George William, Samuel Davies: Apostle of Dissent in Colonial Virginia (Knoxville: University of Tennessee Press, 1971).

Platt, John, Reformed Thought and Scholasticism: The Arguments for the Existence of God in Dutch Theology, 1575-1650 (Leiden: Brill, 1982).

Polishook, Irwin H., Roger Williams, John Cotton and Religious Freedom: A Controversy in New and Old England (Englewood Cliffs: Prentice-Hall, 1967).

Porter, Jean, Natural and Divine Law: Reclaiming the Tradition for Christian Ethics (Grand Rapids: Eerdmans, 1999).

Powell, H. Jefferson, "The Earthly Peace of the Liberal Republic," in Christian Perspectives on Legal Thought, ed. Michael W. McConnell, Robert F. Cochran, Jr., and Angela C. Carmella (New Haven: Yale University Press, 2001), 73-92.

Praamsma, Louis, Let Christ Be King: Reflections on the Life and Times of Abraham Kuyper (Jordan Station: Paideia, 1985).

Pryor, C. Scott, "God's Bridle: John Calvin's Application of Natural Law," Journal of Law and Religion 22, no. 1 (2006-2007): 225-54.

Raunio, Antti, "Divine and Natural Law in Luther and Melanchthon," in Lutheran Reformation and the Law, ed. Virpi Mäkinen (Leiden: Brill, 2006), 21-61.

Raunio, Antti, "Natural Law and Faith: The Forgotten Foundations of Ethics in Luther's Theology," in Union with Christ: The New Finnish Interpretation of Luther, ed. Carl E. Braaten and Robert W. Jenson (Grand Rapids: Eerdmans, 1998), 96-124.

Rehnman, Sebastian, "Alleged Rationalism: Francis Turretin on Reason," Calvin Theological Journal 37 (2002): 255-69.

Reid, W. Stanford, "John Knox's Theology of Political Government," Sixteenth Century Journal 19, no. 4 (1988): 529-40.

Reid, W. Stanford, "John Knox: The First of the Monarchomachs?" (Philadelphia: Center for the Study of Federalism, 1981).

Reid, W. Stanford, Trumpeter of God: A Biography of John Knox (New York: Scribner, 1974).

Rhonheimer, Martin, Natural Law and Practical Reason: A Thomist View of Moral Autonomy, trans. Gerald Malsbury (New York: Fordham University Press, 2000).

Richards, Jeffrey H., "Samuel Davies and the Transatlantic Campaign for Slave Literacy in Virginia," *The Virginia Magazine of History and Biography* 111, no. 4 (2003): 333-78.

Richards, Peter Judson, "'The Law Written in Their Hearts'?: Rutherford and Locke on Nature, Government and Resistance," *Journal of Law and Religion* 18, no. 1 (2002): 151-89.

Roberts, Frank C., "Response," in *Calvin and the State*, ed. Peter De Klerk (Grand Rapids: Calvin Studies Society, 1993), 103-8.

Rommen, Heinrich A., *The Natural Law: A Study in Legal and Social History and Philosophy*, trans. Thomas R. Hanley (St. Louis: Herder, 1949).

Rosenmeier, Jesper, "John Cotton on Usury," *William and Mary Quarterly* 47 (Oct 1990): 548-65.

Runia, Klaas, "The Kingdom of God in the Bible, in History, and Today," *European Journal of Theology* 1, no. 1 (1992): 37-47.

Ruokanen, Miika, *Theology of Social Life in Augustine's* De civitate Dei (Göttingen: Vandenhoeck & Ruprecht, 1993).

Rushdoony, Rousas John, *The Institutes of Biblical Law*, 3 vols. (Nutley, NJ: Craig, 1973).

Schilder, K., *Heaven: What Is It?* trans. Marian M. Schoolland (Grand Rapids: Eerdmans, 1950).

Schreiner, Susan E., "Calvin's Use of Natural Law," in *A Preserving Grace: Protestants, Catholics, and Natural Law*, ed. Michael Cromartie (Washington, D.C.: Ethics and Public Policy Center; Grand Rapids: Eerdmans, 1997), 51-76.

Schreiner, Susan E., *The Theater of His Glory: Nature and the Natural Order in the Thought of John Calvin* (Durham: Labyrinth, 1991).

Shea, William M., *The Lion and the Lamb: Evangelicals and Catholics in America* (New York: Oxford University Press, 2004).

Shogimen, Takashi, "From Disobedience to Toleration: William of Ockham and the Medieval Discourse on Fraternal Correction," *Journal of Ecclesiastical History* 52, no. 4 (Oct 2001): 599-622.

Simon, Yves, *The Tradition of Natural Law: A Philosopher's Reflections* (1965; reprinted New York: Fordham University Press, 1992).

Skillen, James, "From Covenant of Grace to Equitable Public Pluralism: The Dutch Calvinist Contribution," *Calvin Theological Journal* 31 (1996): 67-96.

Skinner, Quentin, *The Foundations of Modern Political Thought*, vol. 2, *The Age of Reformation* (Cambridge: Cambridge University Press, 1978).

Sloan, Douglas, *The Scottish Enlightenment and the American College Ideal* (New York: Teachers College Press, 1971).

Smith, James K. A., *Introducing Radical Orthodoxy: Mapping a Post-secular Theology* (Grand Rapids: Baker, 2004).

Smith, Morton H., *Studies in Southern Presbyterian Theology* (1962; reprinted Phillipsburg, NJ: P&R, 1987).

Smolin, David M., "A House Divided? Anabaptist and Lutheran Perspectives on the Sword," in *Christian Perspectives on Legal Thought*, ed. Michael W. McConnell, Robert F. Cochran, Jr., and Angela C. Carmella (New Haven: Yale University Press, 2001), 370-85.

Smylie, James H., "We, the Presbyterian People: On Celebrating the Constitution of the U.S.A.," *American Presbyterians* 65, no. 4 (Winter 1987): 245-46.

Spade, Paul Vincent, "Introduction," in *The Cambridge Companion to Ockham,* ed. Paul Vincent Spade (Cambridge: Cambridge University Press, 1999), 1-16.

Spade, Paul Vincent, "Ockham's Nominalist Metaphysics: Some Main Themes," in *The Cambridge Companion to Ockham,* ed. Paul Vincent Spade (Cambridge: Cambridge University Press, 1999), 100-117.

Spencer, Stephen R., "Francis Turretin's Concept of the Covenant of Nature," in *Later Calvinism: International Perspectives,* ed. W. Fred Graham (Kirksville, MO: Sixteenth Century Journal Publishers, 1994), 71-91.

Spykman, Gordon J., "Sphere-Sovereignty in Calvin and the Calvinist Tradition," in *Exploring the Heritage of John Calvin,* ed. David E. Holwerda (Grand Rapids: Baker, 1976), 163-208.

Stackhouse, Max L., *Creeds, Society, and Human Rights* (Grand Rapids: Eerdmans, 1984).

Staloff, Darren, *The Making of an American Thinking Class: Intellectuals and Intelligentsia in Puritan Massachusetts* (New York: Oxford University Press, 1998).

Stassen, Glen H., D. M. Yeager, and John Howard Yoder, *Authentic Transformation: A New Vision of Christ and Culture* (Nashville: Abingdon, 1996).

Stassen, Glen H., and David P. Gushee, *Kingdom Ethics: Following Jesus in Contemporary Context* (Downers Grove: InterVarsity, 2003).

Steinmetz, David C., *Calvin in Context* (New York: Oxford University Press, 1995).

Steinmetz, David C., *Luther in Context,* 2nd ed. (Grand Rapids: Baker, 2002).

Stevenson, William R., "Calvin and Political Issues," in *The Cambridge Companion to John Calvin,* ed. Donald K. McKim (Cambridge: Cambridge University Press, 2004), 173-87.

Stewart, John W., and James H. Moorhead, ed., *Charles Hodge Revisited: A Critical Appraisal of His Life and Work* (Grand Rapids: Eerdmans, 2002).

Stout, Harry S., *The New England Soul: Preaching and Religious Culture in Colonial New England* (New York: Oxford University Press, 1986).

Strange, Alan D., "2001 Preface to Charles Hodge's *The Church and Its Polity,*" *Mid-America Journal of Theology* 13 (2002): 25-37.

Sweetman, Brendan, *Why Politics Needs Religion: The Place of Religious Arguments in the Public Square* (Downers Grove: InterVarsity, 2006).

TeSelle, Eugene, *Living in Two Cities: Augustinian Trajectories in Political Thought* (Scranton: University of Scranton Press, 1998).

Thompson, Ernst Trice, *Presbyterians in the South,* vol. 1: *1607-1861* (Richmond: John Knox, 1963).

Thompson, Ernst Trice, *Presbyterians in the South,* vol. 2: *1861-1890* (Richmond: John Knox, 1973).

Thompson, Ernst Trice, *The Spirituality of the Church: A Distinctive Doctrine of the Presbyterian Church in the United States* (Richmond: John Knox, 1961).

Thompson, Robert Ellis, *The American Church History Series,* vol. 6, *A History of the Presbyterian Church in the United States* (New York: Charles Scribner's Sons, 1900).

Thompson, W. D. J. Cargill, *The Political Thought of Martin Luther* (Sussex: Harvester Press, 1984).

Tierney, Brian, *The Crisis of Church & State: 1050-1300* (Englewood Cliffs, NJ: Prentice-Hall, 1964).

Tierney, Brian, *The Idea of Natural Rights: Studies on Natural Rights, Natural Law and Church Law 1150-1625* (Atlanta: Scholars Press, 1997).

Tipton, Lane G., "Paul's Christological Interpretation of Creation and Presuppositional Apologetics," in *Revelation and Reason: New Essays in Reformed Apologetics*, ed. K. Scott Oliphint and Lane G. Tipton (Phillipsburg, NJ: P&R, 2007), 95-111.

Todd, Margo, *The Culture of Protestantism in Early Modern Scotland* (New Haven: Yale University Press, 2002).

Torrance, James, "Interpreting the Word by the Light of Christ or the Light of Nature? Calvin, Calvinism, and Barth," in *Calviniana: Ideas and Influence of Jean Calvin*, ed. Robert V. Schnucker (Kirksville, MO: Sixteenth Century Journal Publishers, 1988), 255-68.

Torrance, T. F., "Kingdom and Church in the Thought of Martin Butzer," *Journal of Ecclesiastical History* 6 (April 1955): 48-59.

Trevor-Roper, H. R., *George Buchanan and the Ancient Scottish Constitution* (London: Longmans, 1966).

Trinterud, Leonard J., *The Forming of an American Tradition: A Re-examination of Colonial Presbyterianism* (Philadelphia: Westminster, 1949).

Troeltsch, Ernst, *The Social Teaching of the Christian Churches*, 2 vols., trans. Olive Wyon (New York: Macmillan, 1931).

Troxel, A. Craig, "Charles Hodge on Church Boards: A Case Study in Ecclesiology," *Westminster Theological Journal* 58 (1996): 183-207.

Troxel, A. Craig, and Peter J. Wallace, "Men in Combat over the Civil Law: 'General Equity' in WCF 19.4," *Westminster Theological Journal* 64 (Fall 2002): 307-18.

Trueman, Carl R., "John Owen's *Dissertation on Divine Justice:* An Exercise in Christocentric Scholasticism," *Calvin Theological Journal* 33 (1998): 87-103.

Trueman, Carl, and R. Scott Clark, eds. *Protestant Scholasticism: Essays in Reassessment* (Carlisle: Paternoster, 1999).

Updike, John, "Foreword," in Karl Barth, *Wolfgang Amadeus Mozart*, trans. Clarence K. Pott (Grand Rapids: Eerdmans, 1986).

van Asselt, Willem J., and Eef Dekker, eds., *Reformation and Scholasticism: An Ecumenical Enterprise* (Grand Rapids: Baker, 2001).

Vanden Berg, Frank, *Abraham Kuyper* (Grand Rapids: Eerdmans, 1950).

van der Kooi, C., "A Theology of Culture. A Critical Appraisal of Kuyper's Doctrine of Common Grace," in *Kuyper Reconsidered: Aspects of His Life and Work*, ed. Cornelis van der Kooi and Jan de Bruijn (Amsterdam: VU Uitgeverij, 1999).

Vander Stelt, John C., *Philosophy and Scripture: A Study in Old Princeton and Westminster Theology* (Marlton, NJ: Mack, 1978).

van der Vyver, Johan D., *Seven Lectures on Human Rights* (Cape Town: Juta, 1976).

van de Sandt, Huub, and David Flusser, eds., *The Didache: Its Jewish Sources and Its Place in Early Judaism and Christianity* (Minneapolis: Fortress, 2002).

VanDrunen, David, *A Biblical Case for Natural Law* (Grand Rapids: Acton Institute, 2006).

VanDrunen, David, *Law and Custom: The Thought of Thomas Aquinas and the Future of the Common Law* (New York: Peter Lang, 2003).

VanDrunen, David, "Natural Law and the Works Principle under Adam and Moses," in *The Law Is Not of Faith: Essays on Works and Grace in the Mosaic Covenant*, ed. Bryan D. Estelle, J. V. Fesko, and David VanDrunen (Phillipsburg, NJ: P&R, 2009), 283-314.

Van Dyke, Harry, *Groen Van Prinsterer's Lectures on Unbelief and Revolution* (Jordan Station, Ontario: Wedge, 1989).

Van Dyke, Harry, "How Abraham Kuyper became a Christian Democrat," *Calvin Theological Journal* 33 (Nov 1998): 420-35.

van Oort, Johannes, *Jerusalem and Babylon: A Study into Augustine's* City of God *and the Sources of His Doctrine of the Two Cities* (Leiden: Brill, 1991).

Van Til, Henry R., *The Calvinistic Concept of Culture* (1959; Grand Rapids: Baker, 2001).

van't Spijker, Willem, "Bucer's Influence on Calvin: Church and Community," in *Martin Bucer: Reforming Church and Community*, ed. D. F. Wright (Cambridge: Cambridge University Press, 1994), 32-44.

van't Spijker, Willem, "The Kingdom of Christ according to Bucer and Calvin," in *Calvin and the State*, ed. Peter De Klerk (Grand Rapids: Calvin Studies Society, 1993), 109-32.

van Vliet, Jan, "From Condition to State: Critical Reflections on Cornelius Van Til's Doctrine of Common Grace," *Westminster Theological Journal* 61, no. 1 (Sept 1999): 73-100.

Varner, William, *The Way of the Didache: The First Christian Handbook* (Lanham: University Press of America, 2007).

von Balthasar, Hans Urs, *The Theology of Karl Barth: Exposition and Interpretation*, trans. Edward T. Oakes, S.J. (San Francisco: Ignatius, 1992).

Vorster, J. M., *Ethical Perspectives on Human Rights* (Potchefstroom: Potchefstroom Theological Publications, 2004).

Vos, Geerhardus, *Biblical Theology* (Grand Rapids: Eerdmans, 1948).

Vos, Geerhardus, "The Doctrine of the Covenant in Reformed Theology," *Redemptive History and Biblical Interpretation: The Shorter Writings of Geerhardus Vos*, ed. Richard B. Gaffin, Jr. (Phillipsburg, NJ: Presbyterian and Reformed, 1980), 234-67.

Wallace, Ronald S., *Calvin, Geneva and the Reformation: A Study of Calvin as Social Reformer, Churchman, Pastor and Theologian* (Grand Rapids: Baker, 1988).

Walzer, Michael, *The Revolution of the Saints: A Study in the Origins of Radical Politics* (Cambridge: Harvard University Press, 1965; London: Weidenfeld and Nicolson, 1966).

Ward, Graham, *Christ and Culture* (Oxford: Blackwell, 2005).

Ward, Graham, "Radical Orthodoxy and/as Cultural Politics," in *Radical Orthodoxy? — A Catholic Enquiry*, ed. Laurence Paul Hemming (Burlington, VT: Ashgate, 2000), 97-111.

Weaver, Richard M., *Ideas Have Consequences* (Chicago: University of Chicago Press, 1948).

Weber, Max, *The Protestant Ethic and the Spirit of Capitalism* (1904-1905; London: Allen and Unwin, 1978).

Webb, Stephen H., *American Providence: A Nation with a Mission* (New York: Continuum, 2004).

Webster, John, *Barth* (New York: Continuum, 2000).

Webster, John, *Barth's Ethics of Reconciliation* (Cambridge: Cambridge University Press, 1995).

Webster, John, *Barth's Moral Theology: Human Action in Barth's Thought* (Grand Rapids: Eerdmans, 1998).

Weeks, Louis B., *Kentucky Presbyterians* (Atlanta: John Knox, 1983).

Weigel, George, "The Church's Political Hopes for the World; or, Diognetus Revisited," in *The Two Cities of God: The Church's Responsibility for the Earthly City,* ed. Carl E. Braaten and Robert W. Jenson (Grand Rapids: Eerdmans, 1997), 59-77.

Weigel, George, *The Cube and the Cathedral: Europe, America, and Politics Without God* (New York: Basic Books, 2005).

Weir, David A., *Early New England: A Covenanted Society* (Grand Rapids: Eerdmans, 2005).

Weir, David Alexander, "*Foedus Naturale:* The Origins of Federal Theology in Sixteenth Century Reformation Thought" (Ph.D. thesis, University of Saint Andrews, 1984).

Werpehowski, William, "Karl Barth and Politics," in *The Cambridge Companion to Karl Barth,* ed. John Webster (Cambridge: Cambridge University Press, 2000), 228-42.

Westburg, Daniel, "The Reformed Tradition and Natural Law," in *A Preserving Grace: Protestants, Catholics, and Natural Law,* ed. Michael Cromartie (Grand Rapids: Eerdmans, 1997), 103-17.

Whitford, David M., "*Cura Religionis* or Two Kingdoms: The Late Luther on Religion and the State in the Lectures on Genesis," *Church History* 73, no. 1 (2004): 41-62.

Wilken, Robert L., "Augustine's City of God Today," in *The Two Cities of God: The Church's Responsibility for the Earthly City,* ed. Carl E. Braaten and Robert W. Jenson (Grand Rapids: Eerdmans, 1997), 28-41.

Williamson, Arthur H., "British Israel and Roman Britain: The Jews and Scottish Models of Polity from George Buchanan to Samuel Rutherford," in *Jewish Christians and Christian Jews: From the Renaissance to the Enlightenment,* ed. Richard H. Popkin and Gordon M. Weiner (Dordrecht: Kluwer, 1994), 97-117.

Willis, E. David, *Calvin's Catholic Christology: The Function of the So-Called Extra Calvinisticum in Calvin's Theology* (Leiden: Brill, 1966).

Witte, John, Jr., "The Development of Herman Dooyeweerd's Concept of Rights," *The South African Law Journal* 110 (Nov 1993): 543-62.

Witte, John, Jr., "Facts and Fictions About the History of Separation of Church and State," *Journal of Church and State* 48 (Winter 2006): 15-45.

Witte, John, Jr., *God's Joust, God's Justice: Law and Religion in the Western Tradition* (Grand Rapids : Eerdmans, 2006).

Witte, John, Jr., *Law and Protestantism: The Legal Teachings of the Lutheran Reformation* (Cambridge: Cambridge University Press, 2002).

Witte, John, Jr., "Moderate Religious Liberty in the Theology of John Calvin," *Calvin Theological Journal* 31 (Nov 1996): 359-403.

Witte, John, Jr., *The Reformation of Rights: Law, Religion, and Human Rights in Early Modern Calvinism* (Cambridge: Cambridge University Press, 2007).

Witte, John, Jr., and Robert M. Kingdon, *Sex, Marriage, and Family in John Calvin's Geneva*, vol. 1, *Courtship, Engagement, and Marriage* (Grand Rapids: Eerdmans, 2005).

Wolf, Ernst, "The Law of Nature in Thomas Aquinas and Luther," in *Faith & Action: Basic Problems in Christian Ethics: A Selection of Contemporary Discussions*, ed. H.-H. Schrey (Edinburgh: Oliver & Boyd, 1970), 236-68.

Wollman, David H., "The Biblical Justification for Resistance to Authority in Ponet's and Goodman's Polemics," *Sixteenth Century Journal* 13, no. 4 (Winter 1982): 29-41.

Wolter, Allan B., O.F.M., *Duns Scotus on the Will and Morality* (Washington, D.C.: Catholic University of America Press, 1986).

Wolters, Albert M., "The Intellectual Milieu of Herman Dooyeweerd," in *The Legacy of Herman Dooyeweerd: Reflections on Critical Philosophy in the Christian Tradition*, ed. C. T. McIntire (Lanham: University Press of America, 1985), 2-15.

Wolterstorff, Nicholas, "Christian Political Reflection: Diognetian or Augustinian," *Princeton Seminary Bulletin* 20, no. 2 (1999): 150-68.

Wolterstorff, Nicholas, *Thomas Reid and the Story of Epistemology* (Cambridge: Cambridge University Press, 2001).

Wood, Rega, *Ockham on the Virtues* (West Lafayette: Purdue University Press, 1997).

Wright, N. T., *Paul: In Fresh Perspective* (Minneapolis: Fortress, 2005).

Yardeni, Myriam, "French Calvinist Political Thought, 1534-1715," in *International Calvinism, 1541-1715*, ed. Menna Prestwich (Oxford: Clarendon, 1985), 315-37.

Yoder, John Howard, *Karl Barth and the Problem of War* (Nashville: Abingdon, 1970).

Yoder, John Howard, *The Politics of Jesus: Vicit Agnus Noster* (Grand Rapids: Eerdmans, 1972).

Young, Davis A., *John Calvin and the Natural World* (Lanham: University Press of America, 2007).

Young, William, "Historic Calvinism and Neo-Calvinism," *Westminster Theological Journal* 36 (Fall 1973): 48-63, and continued in *Westminster Theological Journal* 36 (Winter 1974): 156-73.

Zachman, Randall C., *The Assurance of Faith: Conscience in the Theology of Martin Luther and John Calvin* (Minneapolis: Fortress, 1993).

Ziff, Larzer, *The Career of John Cotton: Puritanism and the American Experience* (Princeton: Princeton University Press, 1962).

Zuidema, S. U., "Common Grace and Christian Action in Abraham Kuyper," in *Communication and Confrontation* (Toronto: Wedge, 1972), 52-105.

Index

Adopting Act of 1729, 235

Althusius, Johannes, 18, 151-52; on natural law, 155-73 *passim;* on the two kingdoms, 173-206 *passim*

Antithesis, 5, 429; in Augustine, 22-31; in Calvin, 71, 91; in Dooyeweerd, 353-55; in Kline, 412-16; in Kuyper, 291-95, 303, 310; in Luther, 59; in neo-Calvinism, 374, 378; in Reformed orthodoxy, 210; in Van Til, 394-99, 406-7

Aquinas, Thomas. *See* Thomas Aquinas

Aristotle, 141

Augustine (Two Cities), 22-32, 71, 86, 91, 158, 207, 210, 228, 266, 303, 307, 371, 374, 378, 388-89, 407, 410

Bahnsen, Greg, 215, 389, 408-11, 419, 422

Barth, Karl, 19, 114, 309, 314-31, 348-49, 354; on natural law, 331-39, 343-47; on the two kingdoms, 331-33, 339-47

Bartholomew, Craig, 368-69, 381-84

Bavinck, Herman, 274, 288-89, 378

Beck, Randy, 425-26

Begbie, Jeremy, 308-9, 313

Benedict, Philip, 83

Berkeley, George, 268

Beza, Theodore, 119-43 *passim,* 198, 363

Biel, Gabriel, 157

Bigger, Nigel, 335

Bohatec, Josef, 426

Bolt, John, 75-76, 426-27

Boniface VIII, 34-36, 91-92

Brett, Annabel, 53

Brunner, Emil, 317, 323, 325, 333-34, 338, 354, 361

Bucer, Martin, 115-16

Buchanan, George, 120, 143-45

Calvin, John, 18, 67-69, 354, 364; on civil disobedience, 121-22; on natural law, 93-115, 117-18, 133-35, 170, 231; on the two kingdoms, 69-93, 110-18, 173-74, 177, 182, 186-87, 190, 192-93, 206-7, 255, 306, 342-43, 374-75

Calvin vs. the Calvinists, 68-69, 149-51, 153-55

Christian liberty, 73-74, 173, 190-92, 218, 253, 258-60, 262-63, 426

Common grace: in Barth, 325-26, 347; in Dooyeweerd and neo-Calvinism, 354-84 *passim;* in future study, 430; in Kline, 412-20; in Kuyper, 277-78, 294-313; in Van Til, 394-407

Common sense realism. *See* Scottish common sense realism

Conscience: in Barth, 335-36; in Calvin, 100-102; in Cotton, 223-24; in Duns Scotus, 49; among eighteenth-century Virginia Presbyterians, 242; in Hodge and Thornwell, 259; in Kline, 418; in

Kuyper, 281, 287, 289; in Luther, 65; in Reformed orthodoxy, 156, 159-60, 190-92; in Reformed resistance theory, 133, 140, 147; in Thomas Aquinas, 44; in Van Til, 389-90, 404-5; in Witherspoon, 270-71; in Wolters, 380

Cotton, John, 19, 213-16; on natural law, 229-34, 275; on the two kingdoms, 216-29, 275

Covenant of works: in Barth, 344-45; in Dooyeweerd and neo-Calvinism, 349, 361, 367, 376, 381, 384; in Kline, 413, 417, 420; in Kuyper, 289; in Reformed orthodoxy, 162-64, 271; in Van Til, 405

Cunningham, William, 260

Davies, Samuel, 236-40

Davis, John Calvin, 425

Decalogue: in Calvin, 88, 100-101, 104, 109, 118; in Duns Scotus, 50-51; in Kline, 419; in Kuyper, 287; in Luther, 63; in Reformed orthodoxy, 160-61, 165, 201; in Reformed resistance theory, 134, 147; in Thomas Aquinas, 46

Didache, 23

Dodaro, Robert, 31

Dooyeweerd, Herman, 4, 7, 19, 348-59, 369, 378, 385-86, 415; on natural law, 359, 362-68; on the two kingdoms, 359-62

du Plessis-Mornay, Philippe, 124

Duns Scotus, 42, 48-51, 108, 157-59

Edward VI, 115-16

Epistle to Diognetus, 23-24, 303, 307, 407

Equity, 108-10, 135-36, 169-71, 230-31, 233, 271, 419

Erastianism, 116, 179-80, 219

Eternal law, 43-44, 65, 104-5, 157-58

Eusebius, 25-26

Foxgrover, David L., 100-101

Gardiner Spring Resolutions, 263-64

Gelasius I, 33-34, 91-93, 207, 267

Geneva: social life in, 82-86

Gillespie, George, 153, 173-206 *passim,* 303, 425

Goheen, Michael, 368-69, 381-84

Goodman, Christopher, 119-43 *passim*

Grabill, Stephen, 15, 424

Graham, Preston, 425

Gustafson, James, 17

Hall, Timothy, 217

Hamburger, Philip, 246-47

Hankins, George, 230

Hanover Presbytery, 234-37, 240-45

Hart, Darryl, 424

Hauerwas, Stanley, 8

Helm, Paul, 426

Heppe, Heinrich, 179

Hodge, Charles, 214, 256-66, 275

Horton, Michael, 426

Hotman, François, 119-43 *passim*

Hopfl, Harro, 102

Hume, David, 268

Hunsinger, George, 321, 345-46

Hutcheson, Francis, 269

Image of God, 99, 105, 161-62, 417, 420

Jeanne d'Albret, 115

John Major, 97

Johnson, Thomas, 425

Junius, Franciscus, 219

Jure divino Presbyterianism, 214, 247-52, 257-60, 262, 266

Kalsbeek, L., 358

Kingdon, Robert, 84

Klapwijk, Jacob, 360-61

Kline, Meredith G., 387-89, 411-22, 427, 429, 430, 433

Knox, John, 119-43 *passim*

Kramnick, Isaac, 246-47

Kuyper, Abraham, 4, 19, 274, 276-78, 369, 378, 397, 401-4, 407, 429, 430; on natural law, 278-89, 339, 346-47; on the two kingdoms, 289-314, 346-49, 360-61, 366-67

Lambert, Frank, 246 47
Languet, Hubert, 124
Lohse, Bernhard, 55
Luther, Martin, 354; on natural law, 62-65, 106, 108, 110, 114-15; on the two kingdoms, 55-62, 71, 91-93, 114-15, 207, 341-42

McCormack, Bruce, 317
McGrade, A. S., 41, 53
Machen, J. Gresham, 426
McKay, David, 425
Mackemie, Francis, 235
McLaren, Brian, 9
McNeill, John, 426
Markus, R. A., 28-30
Marsilius of Padua, 37-38, 41n.58
Mediatorships of Christ: in Barth, 343-47; in Calvin, 75-76; in Cotton, 218, 220, 226; in Davies, 238-39; in Dooyeweerd and neo-Calvinism, 348, 360-61, 374, 378, 384; in future study, 426-30; in Kline, 421; in Kuyper, 301-15 *passim;* in Reformed orthodoxy, 176-83; in Robinson, 250-55; in Van Til, 397, 401-2
Melanchthon, Philipp, 354, 363
Melville, Andrew, 174, 253
Milbank, John, 9, 30
Moore, R. Laurence, 246-47
Mosaic law: in Bahnsen, 408-11; in Calvin, 108-10, 118; in Cotton, 226, 229-33; in Kline, 418-19; in Luther, 63-64; in Reformed orthodoxy, 165-71; in Reformed resistance theory, 147; in Kuyper, 283-84, 288; in Thomas Aquinas, 46-47; in Van Til, 411; in Witherspoon, 271; in Wolters, 380
Mozart, Wolfgang Amadeus: Barth on, 326-28
Musculus, Wolfgang, 116-17

National Covenant, 197-201, 206
Neo-Calvinism, 3-5, 12, 19-20, 314-15, 349-50, 368-70, 384-85, 415, 432
Niebuhr, H. Richard, 371

Noll, Mark, 215
Nominalism, 42, 47-48, 54, 96-97, 102-3, 117, 339

Ockham. *See* William of Ockham
O'Donovan, Oliver, 430-31
Owen, John, 152-53

Perkins, William, 216
Plantinga, Cornelius, 368-69, 373-77
Ponet, John, 119-43 *passim*
Power (ordained and absolute), 50, 54
Presbyterianism. *See* Jure divino Presbyterianism
Pryor, C. Scott, 425
Przywara, Erich, 339

Radical Orthodoxy, 9-10
Realism, 42, 47, 96, 98, 156-57. *See also* Scottish common sense realism
Regulative principle of worship, 191-92
Reid, Thomas, 268
Robinson, Stuart, 19, 212-14, 234, 247-56, 266-68, 274-75, 307, 407, 425, 429
Roman law, 97, 141, 168
Rosenmeier, Jesper, 230
Rushdoony, R. J., 408
Rutherford, Samuel, 18, 120, 145-46, 151-52, 173-206 *passim*, 218, 303, 425

Schleiermacher, Friedrich, 17
Scottish common sense realism, 268-74
Second Book of Discipline, 175, 183-95 *passim*, 213
Schreiner, Susan, 426
Sibbes, Richard, 216
Skinner, Quentin, 128
Solemn League and Covenant, 197-201
Sphere sovereignty, 296-98, 307-8, 355-58, 378
Spirituality of the church, 214, 247-56, 260-67, 412, 425-26, 431-32
Spring, Gardiner. *See* Gardiner Spring Resolutions
Stewart, Dugald, 269
Stob, Henry, 368-73

Synderesis, 44, 49, 65

Thomas Aquinas, 42-47, 98-99, 101-10, 134n.62, 157-58, 339, 363, 405
Thomism, 117, 363, 373
Thornwell, John Henley, 19, 214, 256-74
Tierney, Brian, 53
Troeltsch, Ernst, 48
Turretin, Francis, 18, 151-52; on natural law, 155-73 *passim*, 231; on the two kingdoms, 173-206 *passim*, 217-18
Turretin, J. A., 338
Two Cities. *See* Augustine
Two Swords, 32-36, 91-93

Van Til, Cornelius, 7, 20, 352, 386-408, 411, 421-22
Vermigli, Peter Martyr, 116-17, 122
Via antiqua, 96
Via moderna, 96
Vindiciae contra Tyrannos, 119-43 *passim*, 198

Vollenhoven, D. H. Th., 370, 378
Voluntarism, 42, 47-48, 96, 102-4, 156-59
Vos, Geerhardus, 413

Westminster Confession of Faith and Catechisms, 151-92 *passim*, 235, 245-46, 260, 264-65, 419
William of Ockham, 36-42, 48, 51-54, 96, 108, 157, 184, 267, 354
Williams, Roger, 216, 220, 223-28, 231-33, 425
Winthrop, John, 214, 230
Witherspoon, John, 268-74
Witte, John, 84, 91, 93, 362
Wolters, Albert, 368-69, 377-81
Worldview, 291-94, 303, 312, 350-84 *passim*, 393-94
Wright, N. T., 7

Zachman, Randall, 100
Zanchi, Jerome, 117-18, 152, 166
Zuidema, S. U., 309-10